Cross-Disciplinary Advances in Human Computer Interaction:
User Modeling, Social Computing, and Adaptive Interfaces

Panayiotis Zaphiris
City University of London, UK

Chee Siang Ang
City University of London, UK

INFORMATION SCIENCE REFERENCE

Hershey • New York

Director of Editorial Content:	Kristin Klinger
Director of Production:	Jennifer Neidig
Managing Editor:	Jamie Snavely
Assistant Managing Editor:	Carole Coulson
Typesetter:	Chris Hrobak
Cover Design:	Lisa Tosheff
Printed at:	Yurchak Printing Inc.

Published in the United States of America by
Information Science Reference (an imprint of IGI Global)
701 E. Chocolate Avenue, Suite 200
Hershey PA 17033
Tel: 717-533-8845
Fax: 717-533-8661
E-mail: cust@igi-global.com
Web site: http://www.igi-global.com

and in the United Kingdom by
Information Science Reference (an imprint of IGI Global)
3 Henrietta Street
Covent Garden
London WC2E 8LU
Tel: 44 20 7240 0856
Fax: 44 20 7379 0609
Web site: http://www.eurospanbookstore.com

Library of Congress Cataloging-in-Publication Data

Cross-disciplinary advances in human computer interaction : user modeling, social computing, and adaptive interfaces / Panayiotis Zaphiris, Chee Siang Ang, editors.

 p. cm.
Includes bibliographical references and index.

 Summary: "This book develops new models and methodologies for describing user behavior, analyzing their needs and expectations and thus successfully designing user friendly systems"--Provided by publisher.

ISBN 978-1-60566-142-1 (hardcover) -- ISBN 978-1-60566-143-8 (ebook) 1. Human-computer interaction. I. Zaphiris, Panayiotis. II. Ang, Chee Siang.
 QA76.9.H85C82 2009
 004.01'9--dc22
                          2008033937

British Cataloguing in Publication Data
A Cataloguing in Publication record for this book is available from the British Library.

All work contributed to this book set is original material. The views expressed in this book are those of the authors, but not necessarily of the publisher.

Editorial Advisory Board

Table of Contents

Detailed Table of Contents

Chapter I

Emotional Digitalization as Technology of the Post-Modern:

Claus Hohmann, Autostadt, Germany

This chapter introduces emotional digitalization as a phenomenon of future information systems. It argues that emotional digitalization is a progress that will lessen the gap between technology and humanity as well as between computer and man. The author develops and verifies his assumption besides theoretical references arising from his experiences with the information technology within the BrandLand Autostadt.

Chapter II

Bridging User Requirements and Cultural Objects:

Elias A. Hadzilias, IÉSEG School of Management, France
Andrea Carugati, Åarhus School of Business, Denmark & IÉSEG School of Management, France

This chapter aims at defining a framework for the design of e-government services on cultural heritage. Starting from an analysis of three cases on digitization of different types of cultural objects the author highlights the problems existing in the creation of e-services on cultural heritage. These cases show the existence of four key issues in the development of this kind of information systems: digitization, requirements engineering, standardization, and interoperability. The proposed framework addresses these issues focusing on the user requirements and the cultural object representation. Dynamic content exchange requires the use of a prescriptive framework for the development of cultural heritage Web sites. This chapter provides such a framework using observation from concrete applications and knowledge of information systems development methodologies.

Chapter III

From Beliefs to Success:

Samantha Bax, Murdoch University, Australia

Tanya McGill, Murdoch University, Australia

The technology acceptance model (TAM) is a popular model for the prediction of information systems acceptance behaviors, defining a causal linkage between beliefs, attitudes, intentions, and the usage of information technologies. Since its inception, numerous studies have utilized the TAM, providing empirical support for the model in both traditional and Internet-based computing settings. This chapter describes a research study that utilizes an adaptation of the TAM to predict successful Web page development, as an introduction of the TAM to a new domain, and the testing of a new dependent variable within the model. The study found some evidence to support the use of the TAM as a starting point for the prediction of Web development success, finding causal linkages between the belief constructs and the attitude constructs, and the intent construct and the successful development of Web pages. However, additional research is required to further study the expanded model introduced within this chapter.

Chapter IV

George E. Heilman, Winston-Salem State University, USA

Jorge Brusa, Texas A&M International University, USA

This study assesses the psychometric properties of a Spanish translation of Doll and Torkzadeh's End-User Computing Satisfaction (EUCS) survey instrument. The results show that the EUCS Spanish version is a valid and reliable measure of computing satisfaction among computer users in Mexico and adds support to the usefulness of the instrument in countries other than the United States and in languages other than English.

Chapter V

Understanding the Impact of Culture on Mobile Phone Usage on Public Places:

Ishraga Khattab, Sudan Academy for Banking and Financial Science, Sudan

Steve Love, Brunel University, UK

Over the last several years, the ubiquitous use of mobile phones by people from different cultures has grown enormously. For example, mobile phones are used to perform both private and business conversations. In many cases, mobile phone conversations take place in public places. In this chapter, the authors attempt to understand if cultural differences influence the way people use their mobile phones in public places. The material considered here draws on the existing literature of mobile phones, and quantitative and qualitative work carried out in the UK (as a mature mobile phone market) and the Sudan (that is part of Africa and the Middle East culture with its emerging mobile phone market). The results presented in the chapter indicate that people in the Sudan are less likely to use their mobile phones on public transport or whilst walking down the street, in comparison to their UK counterparts. In addition, the Sudanese are more willing to switch off their mobile phones in places of worship, classes, and meetings. Implications are drawn from the study for the design of mobile phones for different cultures.

Chapter VI
Discourses on User Participation – Findings
from Open Source Software Development Context 90
Netta Iivari, University of Oulu, Finland

This chapter critically examines discursive construction of user participation in academic literatures and in practice, in IT artifact development. First three academic discourses constructing user participation are discussed. Then the discursive construction of user participation is explored in OSS development literature. Afterwards, results from several empirical, interpretive case studies are outlined. Some of them have been carried out in the IT artifact product development organizations, others in the OSS development context. Clear similarities can be identified in the discourses constructing user participation in these divergent IT artifact development contexts. The academic discourses on user participation clearly also legitimate certain ways of constructing user participation in practice. The OSS development literature bears resemblance mainly with the Human Computer Interaction (HCI) discourse on user participation. Therefore, it is argued that especially the HCI community should carefully reflect on what kinds of discourses on user participation it advocates and deems as legitimate.

Chapter VII
Exploring "Events"as an Information Systems Research Methodology 108
Anita Greenhill, The University of Manchester, UK
Gordon Fletcher, University of Salford, UK

This chapter builds upon existing research and commentary from a variety of disciplinary sources including Information Systems, Organizational and Management Studies, and the social sciences that focus upon the meaning, significance and impact of "events" in the information technology, organizational, and social context. The aim is to define how the examination of the event is an appropriate, viable and useful Information Systems methodology. The line of argument pursued is that by focusing on the "event" the researcher is able to more clearly observe and capture the complexity, multiplicity, and the mundane of the everyday lived experience. An inherent danger of existing traditional "event" focused studies and "virtual" ethnographic approaches are the micromanagement of the research process. Using the notion of "event" has the potential to reduce methodological dilemmas such as this without effacing context (Peterson 1998, 19). Similarly, this chapter addresses the over-emphasis upon managerialist, structured, and time-fixated praxis that is currently symptomatic of Information Systems research. All of these concerns are pivotal points of critique found within event-oriented literature regarding organizations (Peterson 1998; Gergen & Thatchenkery 2004).

Chapter VIII
Different Levels of Information Systems Designers'
Forms of Thought and Potential for Human-Centered Design 122
Hannakaisa Isomäki, University of Lapland, Finland

This chapter describes a study clarifying information systems (IS) designers' conceptions of human users of IS by drawing on in-depth interviews with 20 designers. The designers' lived experiences in their work build up a continuum of levels of thought from more limited conceptions to more comprehensive ones reflecting variations of the designers' situated knowledge related to human-centered design. The resulting forms of thought indicate three different but associated levels in conceptualizing users. The separatist form of thought provides designers predominantly with technical perspectives and a capability for objectifying things. The functional form of thought focuses on external task information and task productivity, nevertheless, with the help of positive emotions. The holistic form of thought provides designers with competence of human-centered information systems development (ISD). Furthermore, the author hopes that understanding the IS designers' tendencies to conceptualize human users facilitates the mutual communication between users and designers.

Chapter IX

    Barbara Jones, MBS University of Manchester, UK
    Angelo Failla, IBM Fondazione Milan (Director), Italy
    Bob Miller, MBS University of Manchester, UK

Phenomena in two widely differing organizations suggest that parallel evolution is occurring in different contexts conditioned by the wider context of Information and Communication Technologies (ICT) development and other trends of Post-Modernity. Constant renewal of the self-image and self-knowledge of the organization becomes part of the day-to-day knowledge-in-use of front-line practitioners and driven by the client-centered approach this process feeds back into the dynamics of the wider organization. Post-modernity is understood as the abandonment of the model of society as moving towards a rational division of labor meeting the natural needs of rational man. This model assumed the fixity of social spheres and economic sectors based on the centrality of different principles or technologies, which in retrospect can be seen as resulting from spatial and temporal co-ordination and transaction costs. The Network Enterprise is a model of business conducted by shifting alliances of partners developing innovative products and processes in close collaboration with their leading clients. Organizations now abandon the concept of a central product and instead define themselves as providers of solutions. The authors draw on the experience of two "solution-providers", one for-profit and one not-for-profit. The concept of a solution or transition creates a greater role for the front-line practitioner in identifying and mobilizing the resources available. The need for practitioners to consider every individual case drawing on their individual knowledge of the accessible competencies and capacities of the organization means that choices among the possible solutions to the client's problems can lead to unpredictable effects on the dynamics of the wider organization. The necessarily personal use of heuristics magnifies the inescapable element of drift inherent in the network enterprise. This may be a source of innovation, but the value of this innovation will depend on the ability of the wider organization to develop new standards and solution bundles.

Interpretive flexibility is a term used to describe the diverse perspectives on what a technology is and can or can not do during the process of technological development. In this chapter, the authors look at how interpretive flexibility manifests through the diverse perceptions of stakeholders involved in the diffusion and adoption of the NHS Care Records Service (NCRS). Our analysis shows that while the policy makers acting upon the application of details related to the implementation of the system, the potential users are far behind the innovation decision process namely at the knowledge or persuasion stages. The authors use data from a local heath authority from a county close to London. The research explores compares and evaluates contrasting views on the systems implementation at local as well as national level. The authors believe that our analysis is useful for NCRS implementation strategies in particular and technology diffusion in big organizations in general.

Chapter XI

This chapter reviews the literature on networks and more specifically on the development of community telecommunication networks. It strives to understand the collaboration needed for innovative projects such as intelligent networks. Guided by a change management framework, collaboration within a community network is explored in terms of the formation and performance phases of its development. The context, content, and process of each phase is analyzed, as well as the interaction of the two phases. User involvement and technology appropriation are discussed. Collaboration challenges are identified and linked to the sustainability of the community network. Policy makers are presented with a model that gives some insight into planning and managing a community network over time.

Chapter XII

In this chapter, wireless technology use is addressed with a focus on the factors that underlie wireless interaction. A de-construction of the information processing theories of user/ technology interaction is presented. While commercial and useful applications of wireless devices are numerous, wireless inter-action is emerging as a means of social interaction, an extension of the user's personal image, and as an object of amusement and play. The technology/ user interaction theories that have driven the discussions of computer assisted communication media are information richness, communicative action, and social influence modeling. This chapter will extend this theoretical view of wireless devices by using flow theory to address elements of fun, control, and focus. These technology/user interaction theories are then used with respect to wireless devices to propose areas for future research.

This chapter suggests a critical realistic framework, which aims at modeling sociotechnical change linked to end-users' IT appropriation: the "archetypal approach". The basic situations it includes (the "socio-technical archetypes"), and the possible appropriative trajectories that combine them, together with three propositions linked to the model, are developed. They are illustrated by means of a case study describing the implementation of an e-learning system within a French university. The chapter then presents an instrumentation of the theoretical framework, based on a quantitative longitudinal approach: the Process Patterns Recognition (PPR) method. This one draws mainly on Doty, Glick, and Huber (1993, 1994) who propose to evaluate the distance between organizational archetypes and empirical configurations by means of Euclidean distance calculus. The adaptation consists in evaluating the distance between appropriative trajectories (embodied by series of theoretically specified vectors) and empirical processes linked to the implementation of computerized tools in organizations. The PPR method is then applied to the same organizational setting as the one related to the case study. It validates the relevance of this type of a research strategy, which makes it possible to model sociotechnical dynamics related to end-users' IT appropriations.

Today's media are vast in both form and influence; however, few cultural studies scholars address the video gaming industry's role in domestic maintenance and global imposition of U.S. hegemonic ideologies. In this study, video games are analyzed by cover art, content and origin of production. Whether it is earning more "powers" in games such as Star Wars, or earning points to purchase more powerful artillery in Grand Theft Auto, capitalist ideology is reinforced in subtle, entertaining fashion. This study shows that oppressive hegemonic representations of gender and race are not only present, but permeate the majority of top-selling video games. Finally, the study traces the origins of best-selling games, to reveal a virtual U.S. monopoly in the content of this formative medium.

This chapter argues that Information Ethics (IE) can provide a successful approach for coping with the challenges posed by our increasingly globalized reality. After a brief review of some of the most fundamental transformations brought about by the phenomenon of globalization, the chapter distinguishes between two ways of understanding Global Information Ethics, as an ethics of global communication or as a global-information ethics. It is then argued that cross-cultural, successful interactions among micro and macro agents call for a high level of successful communication, that the latter requires a shared ontology friendly towards the implementation of moral actions, and that this is provided by IE. There follows a brief account of IE and of the ontic trust, the hypothetical pact between all agents and patients presupposed by IE.

Chapter XVI

In this chapter, it will be examined whether information ethics is culture-relative. If it is, different approaches to information ethics are required in different cultures and societies. This would have major implications for the current, predominantly Western approach to information ethics. If it is not, there must be concepts and principles of information ethics that have universal validity. What would they be? The descriptive evidence is for the cultural relativity of information ethics will be studied by examining cultural differences between ethical attitudes towards privacy, freedom of information and intellectual property rights in Western and nonwestern cultures. It will then be analyzed what the implications of these findings are for the metaethical question of whether moral claims must be justified differently in different cultures. Finally, it will be evaluated what the implications are for the practice of information ethics in a cross-cultural context.

Chapter XVII

A study of the concept of offence can shed some light on global ethical issues. While offence is frequently not taken very seriously, the contention here is that it should be. A better understanding of why offence is taken and why some instances of giving offence are reprehensible and others are not can assist our understanding of what is necessary in a global ethics. The argument here focuses on the morality of giving offence rather than on what kinds of offence, if any, should be subject to legal restrictions. The recent case of the Danish cartoons illustrates the importance of the notion of offence. Unless offence is taken seriously, that case has no interesting moral dimension. It is simply an instance of someone exercising their legitimate right to freedom of expression and others unjustifiably objecting. The Danish publisher was right to do what he did and the offended Muslims were wrong to object. If however, offence is taken seriously then the question of who was right and who was wrong becomes more problematic, and the issue can be seen as a real clash of values. In liberal democratic states, freedom of expression is highly valued, but this is not universal. Perhaps it should be, but when considering ethics in a global context we are not starting with a clean slate. The realities of the world are where we start. In some parts of the world the general notion of freedom of expression is not even entertained. It simply is not an issue to be taken into account. Social cohesion and religious beliefs are all important. The society rather than the individual comes first. Once that is realized the offence that was taken is more comprehensible. From the perspective of the offended, there is a good reason for taking offence; there has been a violation of an important religious value for no apparent reason other than denigration of the Muslim faith. While the situation was undoubtedly more complicated and some took advantage of the cartoons for their own ends, that fact is that it was relatively easy for them to do this, partly because of a lack of understanding of the importance of freedom of speech in most Western countries and the feeling that their religion was not being respected.

This chapter shows how standard, widely-used technology – when used innovatively – can bring many benefits to many stakeholders with reasonable costs and changes in business processes. As a theoretical background, the authors use the transaction cost approach. Reserving, canceling, and reallocating dentist care time spots are all transactions. The authors also present and analyze the function of an SMS message-based dental service appointment reservation system that has been implemented in Lahti, Finland. The analysis contains a description of the system's function, as well as some assessment of the success from the service provider and customer point of view.

Both academics and practitioners have invested considerably in the information systems evaluation arena, yet rewards remain elusive. The aim of this chapter is to provide rich insights into some particular political and social aspects of evaluation processes. An ethnographic study of a large, international financial institution is used to compare the experience of observed practice with the rhetoric of company policy, and also to contrast these observations with the process of IS evaluation as portrayed within the literature. Our study shows that despite increasing acknowledgement within the IS evaluation literature of the limitations and flaws of the positivist approach, typified by quantitative, "objective" assessments, this shift in focus towards understanding social and organizational issues has had little impact on organizational practice. In addition, our observations within the research site reveal that the veneer of rationality offered by formalized evaluation processes merely obscures issues of power and politics that are enmeshed within these processes.

This chapter frames the requirements definition phase of systems design as a problem of knowledge transfer and learning between two communities of practice: IS designers and system users. The theoretical basis for the proposed approach is Wenger's framework for social learning, which involves three dimensions: alignment, imagination, and engagement. The chapter treats the requirements definition task in systems design as a set of activities involving mutual learning and knowledge transfer between two communities of practice (CoP) along these three dimensions. In taking this approach, the chapter maps the results of past research on the systems design process onto this CoP framework and illustrates that the proposed framework encompasses the same activities used by traditional methods of requirements definition. However, this approach focuses attention on the learning that must take place between the two CoPs and thereby helps resolve some of the inherent shortcomings of prior efforts and approaches. The framework provides both a more encompassing conceptual lens for research on improving the requirements definition task and practical guidance for managers who are charged with a systems design project.

Chapter XXI

Tanya Bondarouk, University of Twente, The Netherlands
Maarten van Riemsdijk, University of Twente, The Netherlands

This chapter reflects on a SAP_HR system introduced in a Dutch university. The project planning seemed to be reasonably straightforward: the system's introduction was intended to take place gradually, including pilots in various departments and appropriate feedback. The end-users (HR professionals) faced the challenge of reassigning job tasks, building a new HR community in the organization, and increased responsibilities for daily HR tasks during the SAP_HR installation. In this chapter, the authors conceptualize the implementation process associated with SAP_HR as an experiential learning one (Kolb, 1984), and analyze qualitative data collected using discourse analysis during a six-month case study. The results confirmed the atuhors' assumption of the importance of experience-based learning in the implementation of Information Technologies (IT). The authors saw that a lack of communication plus misunderstandings between the different parties involved in the project led to mistakes in working with the system at the beginning, sometimes leading to financial problems for the university and, as a result, in attempts to slow the implementation project. However, with encouragement from the "top" to improve learning, working with the system became easier for the whole group involved and for the individual users. After eighteen months, the implementation was still experiencing delays and difficulties, but the users had begun to deal with it in a stable way. Although Kolb's theory is widely acknowledged by academics as a fundamental concept that contributes towards our understanding of human behavior, the authors propose another use – to consider this theory in association with an IT implementation strategy to identify the mechanism of IT adoption in an organization.

Chapter XXII

Pietro Murano, University of Salford, UK
Patrik O'Brian Holt, The Robert Gordon University, Scotland

Experimental work on anthropomorphic feedback in user interfaces has shown inconsistent results and researchers offer differing opinions as to the potential usefulness of this style of user interaction. A review of the literature shows that experimental work can be improved and enhanced by taking onto account issues that characterize human-human communications. Results from three experiments are reported that exhibit the previously observed inconsistencies but this is arguably a function of task context. An alternative explanation is that the results are a reflection of the cognitive nature of tasks. Overall, the results point the way to further and future results in terms of refining procedures but also in terms of theoretical focus.

Chapter XXIII

This study explores decision premises of technochange management by comparing business maxims as said by top managers to their consequences. The idea of decision premises is re-introduced as a simple representation of complex dynamics of human values. Decision premises were explored through the cross-questioning in interviews and applying of linguistic techniques. The consequences were identified using the evidence of documents, observable practices, as well as usage and configuration of software. Once decision premises are formed, they are applied over any individual situation and particularly upheld in conflict situations. The system of decision premises is typically hierarchical, self-causal as well as self-contradictory. By virtue of being several but not many, the decision premises reinforce the dynamics of many outcomes stemming from a few causes, also known as "the 80-20 rule". The impact of decision premises on IT management is discussed in regard to the issues of cost-saving, business ownership of software development and irregularities of IT management. The premises of economic and efficient technochange can have drawbacks, such as delays in in-house software development, short-sided business capability decisions and work fragmentation for the front-line employees. The study describes "primitive" but practical ways of complexity management.

Chapter XXIV

This chapter considers the question of how we may trust automatically generated program code. The code walkthroughs and inspections of software engineering mimic the ways that mathematicians go about assuring themselves that a mathematical proof is true. Mathematicians have difficulty accepting a computer-generated proof because they cannot go through the social processes of trusting its construction. Similarly, those involved in accepting a proof of a computer system or computer generated code, cannot go through their traditional processes of trust. The process of software verification is bound up in software quality assurance procedures, which are themselves subject to commercial pressures. Quality standards, including military standards, have procedures for human trust designed into them. An action research case study of an avionics system within a military aircraft company illustrates these points, where the Software Quality Assurance (SQA) procedures were incommensurable with the use of automatically generated code.

Preface

The computer is becoming a medium through which more and more people search for information, communicate, and have fun. The complexity of this collection of information has attracted the interest of the Human-Computer Interaction (HCI) research community. Researchers have focused their attention in developing new models and methodologies for describing user behavior, analyze their needs and expectations, and thus successfully design user friendly systems.

The application of HCI can have an effect of organizational and social dimensions. For example, the area of computer supported collaborative work (CSCW) explores the effect the introduction of technology can have an effect on the organizational structure and the way of work of companies and organizations. Similarly the study of how we use technology to communicate with each other is gaining strong interest in the HCI research community.

The expansion of the Internet has resulted in an increase in the usefulness of Computer Mediated Communication (CMC) and the popularity of online communities. It is estimated that 25% of internet users have participated in chat rooms or online discussions (Madden & Rainie, 2003).

December (1997) defines CMC as "the process by which people create, exchange, and perceive information using networked telecommunications systems (or non-networked computers) that facilitate encoding, transmitting, and decoding messages". He emphasizes that studies of CMC view this process from different interdisciplinary theoretical perspectives (social, cognitive/psychological, linguistic, cultural, technical, political) and often draw from fields such diverse as human communication, rhetoric and composition, media studies, human-computer interaction, journalism, telecommunications, computer science, technical communication, and information studies.

The cyberspace is the new frontier in social relationships, and people are using the Internet to make friends, colleagues, lovers, as well as enemies (Suler, 2004). As Korzeny pointed out, even as early as 1978, online communities are formed around interests and not physical proximity (Korzeny, 1978). In general, what brings people together in an online community is common interests such as hobbies, ethnicity, education, and beliefs. As Wallace (1999) points out, meeting in online communities eliminates prejudging based on someone's appearance, and thus people with similar attitudes and ideas are attracted to each other.

Another application area in which HCI plays an important role is the computer-augmented environments, or commonly known as augmented reality or mixed reality. It refers to the combination of real-world and computer-generated data visualization. In other words it is an environment which consists of both real world and virtual reality. For instance, a surgeon might be wearing goggles with computer generated medical data projected on it. The goggles are said to augment the information the surgeon can see in the real world through computer visualization. Therefore, it is not difficult to see the connection of augmented reality with ubiquitous computing and wearable computers.

Since its inception, augmented reality has had an impact on various application domains. The most common use is probably the support of complex tasks in which users need to perform a series of complicated actions while having access to large amount of information at the same time, such as surgery, assembly and navigation. Apart from these, augmented reality is also used for learning and training, such as flight and driving simulations.

Augmented reality implementation usually requires additional devices for input and output in order to integrate computer generated data into real world:

- A Cave Automatic Virtual Environment multi-user, room-sized, high-resolution, 3D video and audio immersive environment in which the virtual reality environment is projected onto the walls. The user wearing a location sensor can move within the display boundaries, and the image will move with and surrounds the user.
- A head-up display (HUD) is transparent display that presents data without obstructing the user's view. It is usually implemented on vehicles in which important information is projected directly in the driver's viewing field. Thus the user does not need to shift attention between what is going on in the real world and the instrumental panel.
- A head-mounted display is a display device, worn on the head or as part of a helmet that has a small display optic in front of one or both eyes.

Some of these devices have become commercially available and increasingly affordable. The challenge of HCI lies in the design of information visualization which is not obtrusive to the users' tasks.

A lot of effort has been put in coupling learning and technology to design effective and enjoyable learning. Various areas, namely e-learning, computer-based learning, serious games, and so forth have emerged, hoping to utilize the interactive power of computers to enhance teaching and learning experience. A myriad of design strategies have been proposed, implemented and evaluated, these include the early use of computer in presentation, drill and practice (the behaviorist paradigm), tutorials (cognitivist paradigm), games, story telling, simulations (constructivist paradigm), and so forth. As we progress from behaviorist to constructivist, we notice an explosion of user interface complexity. For instance, drill and practice programs usually consist on a couple of buttons (next, previous buttons, buttons for multiple choice, etc.) while simulations could involve sophisticated visualization (outputs) and various user interface elements for manipulating parameters (input). Recently, computer-based learning has moved from single user offline environments to online network spaces in which a massive number of users can interact with each other and form a virtual learner community. This social constructivist learning paradigm requires not only traditional usability treatment, but also sociability design in which the system includes not only the learning tools, but other sociability elements such as rules and division of labors.

Information visualization is an area in HCI which can be related to many other areas such as augmented reality just described before. Most modern computer applications deal with visual outputs. Graphical user interface has almost entirely replaced command-based interaction in many domains. Information visualization can be defined as "the use of computer supported, interaction, visual representations of abstract data to amplify cognition" (Shneiderman, 1992). To amplify cognition means that visualization shifts cognitive loads to the perceptual system, thus expanding working memory and information storage.

Visualization provides a more perceptually intuitive way of viewing raw data, thus allowing users to identify relevant patterns which would not have been identified in raw data.

Therefore, it has a huge impact on many applications domains, ranging from engineering, education, various fields in science, and so forth.

In HCI, the most obvious application is the use of visualization in the design of graphical user interface that allows more intuitive interaction between human and computers. Various innovative interaction styles have been developed such as WIMP (window, icon, menu, pointing device) which is so familiar in today's software. Three-dimensional graphics are also emerging although currently they are mostly used in computer games and computer-aided design. One recent example of 3D graphical interface is the new windows navigation and management known as Windows Flip 3D in Windows Vista which allows the user to easily identify and switch to another open window by displaying 3D snapshot thumbnail preview of all windows in stack.

Today, information visualization is not only about creating graphical displays of complex information structures. It contributes to a broader range of social and collaborative activities. Recently, visualization techniques have been applied on social data to support social interaction, particularly in CMC. This area is known as social visualization by (Donath, Karahalios, & Viégas, 1999). Other technique such as social network analysis has also become increasingly important in visualization social data.

Other areas where HCI plays an important role include: Intelligent and agent systems; Interaction design; Interaction through wireless communication networks; Interfaces for distributed environments; Multimedia design; Non–verbal interfaces; Speech and natural language interfaces; Support for creativity; Tangible user interfaces; User interface development environments and User support systems.

HCI issues like usability evaluation, presents an additional interesting complexity. Due to the variety in design of systems, and the variety of user-goals while interacting with them, the task of choosing and properly using the appropriate evaluation method becomes a challenge. New approaches and methodologies for analysis, design and evaluation of such systems have been developed, and this book presents some of those.

This book also points out that beyond the technical aspects, we need to systematically take into account human interaction and activity, and the completely renewed social and cultural environments that such digital environments and interfaces are calling for and technologies are now capable of delivering.

The book brings together 10 chapters that cover in depth some of the recent HCI issues of interest to academia and industry.

REFERENCES

December, J. (1997). Notes on defining of computer-mediated communication. *Computer-Mediated Communication Magazine, 3*(1).

Donath, J., Karahalios, K., & Viégas, F. (1999, 8 May 2008). *Visualizing conversation.* Paper presented at the Proceedings of the 32nd Annual Hawaii International Conference.

Korzenny, F. (1978). A theory of electronic propinquity: Mediated communication in organizations. *Communication Research, 5*, 3-23.

Madden, M., & Rainie, L. (2003). *Pew Internet & American Life Project Surveys.* Pew Internet & American Life Project, Washington, DC.

Shneiderman, B. (1992). *Designing the user interface: Strategies for effective human-computer interaction.* 2nd edition.Reading: Addison-Wesley.

Suler, J. (2004). *The Final Showdown Between In-Person and Cyberspace Relationships.* Retrieved November 3, 2004 from http://www1.rider.edu/~suler/psycyber/showdown.html

Wallace, P. (1999). *The Psychology of the Internet.* Cambridge: Cambridge University Press.

Chapter I
Emotional Digitalization as Technology of the Post-Modern:
A Reflexive Examination from the View of The Industry

Claus Hohmann
Autostadt, Germany

ABSTRACT

This chapter introduces emotional digitalization as a phenomenon of future information systems. It argues that emotional digitalization is a progress that will lessen the gap between technology and humanity as well as between computer and man. The author develops and verifies his assumption besides theoretical references arising from his experiences with the information technology within the BrandLand Autostadt.

INTRODUCTION

"The inmost force / which binds the world, and guides its course"is no longer only a philosophical thought or religious voice, as in Goethe's "Faust", verse 382-383. But they are also not just bits and bytes, cable and monitors. The connection of these elemental substructures of modern civilization first shows where the path must go. The functional elements of our daily life must subordinate themselves to our principles of thought

and aesthetics. And they must also appeal to the people in an aesthetic, as well as communicative and sense. The modern, as a synonym for freedom and democracy, could thereby obtain a new dimension – to become an ethical entity. The technology of the third millennium must also define the new standards.

As the post-modern breaks down the barriers between art and pleasure, it breaks through the wall between technology and emotion. The aesthetic sensation from looking at, for example, a corporate homepage, accessible to all, suggests a fundamental change in the meaning which will be attributed to the presentation of technology today, when in direct comparison with the functional-rationalistic views of modern, purely informational Web sites. The Autostadt, Volkswagen's new communication platform for marketing and culture, is on several levels a culmination of different developments, which operate under the term "postmodern" and therefore contribute to theoretical discussion.

This radical change of the basic conditions of our life has put us on a path, which will be indicated by a catchy, yet, imprecise, phrase: "postmodernity". The rationalization of the modern is being counteracted by the pluralization of our culture and humanization of technology, which was demanded, but not achieved, by the modern (Giddens, 1995). With Anthony Giddens, whose critique is applied here, we regard "posthistory" as "a succession of immanent changes", in order to face the prevalent conceptual dilemma (Giddens, 1995). One focuses the view to information technologies and sees that the humanization has an effect, particularly on aesthetics. And here alongside the desired effects lies a formidable danger: does IT go in the same ambivalent direction as the classic technologies, will it give the manipulators of this world a leg up?

THE WORLD TODAY AND TOMORROW

The core problems of the industrial society (saturated markets, over-indebtedness, mass unemployment, etc.) demanded drastic mental reorientation and have, at the same time, uncovered innovation potentials. Spirituality and mental dimensions begin to replace the abstraction - the dream becomes a legend. The new technologies of the third millennium must also surrender to these new demands. With help from the most current technologies, we learn to tell stories. Contrary to the findings of Lyotard from the end of the great narrations of history[1], one could also speak about a fragmentation, which transfers this narration from people to technology, especially the digital technologies. With a new neologism, one speaks of the necessity of a "homuter society", which is in a position to propitiate the people with (information) technologies (Haefner, 1984). Haefner uses this term freely in order to verbalize his skepticism of the possibilities of future developments, which was obtained during the cold war. However, we could also read it with a conscious hope.

Thus, a great possibility of the future lies in the developing of technologies, stimulating creativity and inspiring thoughts: the aesthetic layout of, for example, an intranet and the constantly used user interfaces eases the employee's accessing of the media, prevents fatigue from using information and inspires emotions in the exposure to IT in everyday work. The effect is to state a higher degree of identification to the corporation, a more emotional, eventually better relationship to the employer and – ultimately and ideally considered – an increased labor efficiency accompanied by increased happiness. In this manner, IT of the post-modern can manage the reconciliation of the contradictions between technology and art, which are unimaginably present in the modern.

The IT of the present has the function of supporting the thoughts and actions of the individual and not to automate their work in order to eventually replace them. Comparably, the focus should be put on the installation of technologies that will save time. IT must be used to support work processes, in order to optimize the concrete procedures and reduce the time requirements. Networked, Web -based systems with access points for all employees could be a first step. Important here are the user interfaces, which are adjusted to the work processes, aesthetically configured, self-explanatory, intuitive and can be understood spontaneously, and thereby helping save time and increase room for further assignments.

The same exposed meaning, which electrification and mechanization had for the modern, could be digitization and computerization in the postmodern. The unreality, which challenges our terminology and understanding in increased measure, seems to be a display of something new in relation to the more palpable technological advances of the modern. We see, in this transition of information technology, a movement for a new understanding of our time, which can be labelled as "postmodern", which is in this sense, in the shadows of abstract, fragmentary, simultaneously emotional media. Thereby, no clearly differentiated epochs or outlined theories should be suggested – it should continue to deal with a change in our perception and "Lebenswelt". In doing so, we understand post-modern as the "conscious of a socio-historical transition" [2] and not as a "meta-historical category" of each epoch. [3]

One of the basic requirements of this transition is the change from a technology that replaces the people, to a technology that supports the people – because they "understand" it. Thereby, it is imperative to restore various elements of IT, from management decisions and business processes down to connections with trade and commerce, to an original understanding of "experience". The anchor of the complicated, indiscernible world in tangible lives can show in this manner how post-modernity can be made visible. The metaphor can be helpful to establish the meaning behind the experience.

POSTMODERNITY AND IT

The implementation and deployment of aesthetics in the technological area is a characteristic of the realization that IT is anchored fast in our world, and no longer accepted as a modern achievement of an exceptional position outside our consciously experienced everyday life. This insight allows changed societal requirements to be inferred, but what about the above meaning is postmodern?

Important is our understanding after the liberation from a conditioned past in a (self-) conscious act. As the technologies of modernity stand out due to their distinctiveness and are clearly contrasted with the people and their emotional world, in which they coldly, precisely, and rationalistically fulfill their duties, the IT of postmodernity goes down a different path.

With the integration of aesthetics and emotion, the digitization completes the circle and appears as a new quality. This is only successful because IT has already begun to reflexively examine and question itself and its success, and not in the least can be measured as a clearly calculated result of other factors. A basic requirement therefore, is the development of technology that supports activities with which people are discontent as a result of the holistic pursuit of new goals – with the focus on the people. IT must be there for the people, not the other way around, and it must be aware of this. It must be noticeable, but not necessarily visible.

When the technologies in our new world function imperceptibly and no longer distort the view of the contents from the surface, new space for aesthetics and emotion is created. Technological progress can and must give the people more time, space and capacity for creativity and to unleash their imagination to make the fundamental, structural change perceptible and understandable [4]. In sociological terms, postmodernity seems to accompany the departure from middle-class feudalism. Information technology, which has been more or less privatized by the personal computer (PC), can also lead to further democratization and contribute to free communication – but it can also lead to chaos by making corporations unmanageable.

Thus, in the end, the various technology images of "two cultures", which are Lebenswelt- and system-orientated, according to Charles Percy Snow, should be brought into unison. [5] But in order to accomplish this, technology will be considered as a social phenomenon – with the help of metaphor and symbolization: [6] the symbols must orient themselves on the life-world, in that they become a part of the life-world. Just as modernity, with its dichotomies and ambivalences, can be said to be a failure in dialect, it is conceivable that the discussion in the post-modern, founded in the definition of difference [7], will reveal endeavors leading to the harmony between the various positions. Contrary to Lyotard's assertion, unanswerable contradictions, which lie in the open availability of information, could strengthen the democratizing tendencies of information technologies. [8]

WITH THE EYES OF INDUSTRY

With the beginning of the new millennium, the world changes its vision. The blind trust of technology has a conscious practice of giving way to its possibilities. For example, Volkswagen's corporate platform for culture and marketing – the Autostadt - allows this change, which is currently being experienced by industry and society, to be precisely identified. With this example, we want to discuss the topic of postmodernity from the view of information technology, in order stimulate further thoughts from the industry. Progress is nowadays something completely different, as it questions itself. Reflexivity and self-criticism take the place of the unconscious self-awareness of modern advances. Technology along with the information technology of modernity has undertaken a rapid development, which leaves the people and their imagination helplessly behind. In the physical sense, it is completely impossible to grasp IT, and an attempt at understanding it requires shifting the focus from a purely technical, modern-rational meaning to the interpersonal: addressing emotions via aesthetics, design and a process-logical functioning.

In practical industrial terms, the example of a "gated community", such as the Autostadt, is used here to illustrate this transformation and discuss

post-modernity in the digital light of information technology, [9] in order to stimulate further ideas. The Volkswagen Group's Autostadt presents itself as a holistic concept, which includes all details in a complex structure: "There are no details in the execution". [10] The mass tourism and amusement parks shape the leisure time culture of modernity, but the Autostadt vastly transcends this. It integrates, specifically with the involvement of IT – the science of the world of industry with the goal of getting through to the people.

The privatization of technology has extended continually since the 1980s, the influence and impact of IT to all areas of life, but especially to the areas of personal computers and music and television technologies, but also to all other levels of everyday life. With the Autostadt, the attempt is made to take on these societal changes and harmoniously unite them. In the Autostadt, the ubiquity of IT starts with the central purpose of the corporation, namely the delivery of new cars from the Volkswagen Group to its customers. The delivery process is completely supported by digitization. From the ordering to the handing over of the new Volkswagen to the customer, IT technologies are deployed to support the process. Already in the sales dialog, the employee, by making use of online applications, is enabled to have a virtually intimate discussion, having a positive impact.

Also presentations, such as the CarTower Discovery (Visitors are able to visit the Car Towers from inside), the SunFuelLab (a plant computer, which generates personally assigned biofuels) or the NavigationsSpiel (a virtual Labyrinth), are entirely digitally controlled. However, even internal support processes such as the lighting controls in the buildings and at events, the watering of the on-site parks and the digital menus in the restaurants are based on IT-technologies and displayed systematically. In all of these areas, IT supports the employees, as it is deployed in order to assist them in effectively accomplishing their work and saving time.

Naturally, this all comes with limits: the Autostadt has not realized certain global interactivity, and their video arts suggest only a portion of the "Iconic Turn" of these years [11], but even with the example of the Autostadt, it's clear that the practical IT supports a form of the philosophy of imagery. The Autostadt is thereby also active in the area of bringing to life aesthetic contents in the framework of its marketing scene, and in this lies a threshold experience.

Entities such as the Autostadt must have come into existence, and not as a storm of individual thoughts, but rather as a logical consequence of the mentioned societal changes. The Autostadt is then an answer to the liberation of the postmodern individual, unique to the VW Group, and thereby not a blueprint that can be taken as a model for others. In doing so, what can the technology accomplish?

The industry serves here as an aesthetic-philosophical realization, and in the case of the Autostadt, the first deliberate BrandLand. The societal developments have encouraged, if not called for, the opening of more subtle theme parks. Others have just been, opened: Daimler-Chrysler, the BMW-World and Dr. Oetker, just to name a few from the nearby surroundings. With the help of IT, the economy of aesthetics and art can be greatly improved.

The interfaces of the IT, acting as the window to foreign worlds, allow a new "cultural relocation" in the sense of "immobile mobility", [12] which places the people back in the focus. This liberation of the realm of reality expands, in a virtual manner, the consciously experienced world of the individuals, which would be impossible without IT. The people learn, experience, and fulfill desires (and generate new desires) and expand their horizons via purposefully installed, yet unconsciously experienced, IT. The IT gives the phenomenology of perception [13] a new, different touch. Multi-perspective observation possibilities allow a concrete regard to objects and forms of interactivity. In this way, IT allows us to consider

something from all sides, without forcing us to change our, or its, location.

The Autostadt is also a symbol for a trend. Corporations today present themselves differently. But what exactly is the Autostadt?

THE AUTOSTADT PROJECT

At a crucial interface, residing between the company and society, and with the old factory in the background in order to illustrate the coexistence of industry and BrandLand, the Autostadt is presented as a landscaped park with integrated, individually configured brand pavilions, where nature and technology are connected in an aesthetic manner, so that the relevance of the corporate values are consciously absorbed by the people, via the polyvalently applied presentations. The fundamental concept does not view art as a decorative end in itself, but rather as "a link between designed environments and the visitor experiencing them". [14]

The borders between art and presentation are blurred in this regard. Culture, understood as a variable system of seeking truth and orientation relating to a variety of artistic forms of expression, education, and living, is finally the added value, which allows the Autostadt to obtain visitors. Thereby, it shows itself as an innovative cultural platform in a new understanding of the marketing of experiences and events. [15]

In this context, great significance is given to the development of innovative technologies, as the visible, evident use of digitization would inevitably undermine the functioning of the entire concept of the Autostadt based upon art and aesthetics. The organizational level of the Autostadt has therefore been deliberately made invisible and move to underground tunnel systems and cable ducts. This form of understatement certainly gives the nearly ambitious technology a poetic touch. And just one step further are the Web-based information systems of the Autostadt with aesthetic aspects taking priority over self-portrayal. User-friendly IT gives the individuals freedom. Obvious complexity, by contrast, puts them in chains.

The glass auto-towers with their transparent aesthetics give the sublimity back to the technology and astonish the observer, yet their architecture, infused with aesthetics, prevents fright from their size, which large technologies commonly provoke. And in the park, the straight line, as the enemy of everything living, is already conceptually forbidden. Intuition and emotionality operate in the place of regularization and rationalization. The Autostadt triggers as the identification location of a momentum, that which is required of good advertisements (Jung & Von Matt, 2003). In doing so, it takes in the danger of a novel logo-centric aberrance, as the brand, for which the logo is emblematic, outshines the product (Klein, 2001). What happens here is the becoming of a metaphor. The BrandLand, with its architecture, becomes a metaphor for the contents, the values of a corporate group, and simultaneously for the manner in which the underlying IT will be deployed in the post-modern.

The implementation of these requirements in the framework of the superior philosophy of a customer-oriented, personal technology seems to be a success. With examples such as the CCC (Customer Care Center) and the IAS (Integrated Autostadt System), the changed awareness with regard to the integration of technology in the personal and organisational relationships allows itself to be realized. It becomes clear, that the path to a new, more emotional technology is possible and necessary. The Autostadt takes the first important steps on this long path. Beginning with the installation of networking and dataflow, which are not visible anywhere on the grounds of the park, to the artistic arrangement of the exhibits, which utilize the technical possibilities of imagery, sound and movement without seeming intrusive,

and even with the Internet presence, which gives preference to aesthetics over self-presentation – technology gains acceptance and meaning in the service to ideas and content.

THE DIGITAL HEART: INVISIBLE NETWORKS

Embedded in a concept of future-oriented service, this is where the heart of the Autostadt beats. The "digital heart" is thereby probably only a paradox. Technology no longer presents itself, but rather it puts itself in the service of the people and subordinates to them. Digital technology, originally considered to be cold and sober, should become communicative and people-oriented, only to appear on the surface when necessary. This new "warmth" of the digital world can be transferred from the visitor to the relationship to the Volkswagen Group and serves as a branding strategy based upon emotions. This is related to the paradigm shift in which technology is expected, regardless of its importance, to adapt to the people and act in the background like a good butler or referee.

The beautifully maintained park should have a convincing effect on the guests, positively touching the senses. Together with the architecture, it subliminally conveys an important message of the corporation; perfection. Thereby, it should convey a constant ability to renew itself. This breaking-out of the limits of style has the goal of higher quality and better service: the guest should feel well taken care of, safe and understood. But in order to ensure that this "emotional work" produces the "right" emotions, the IT systems are trusted with the responsible task of ensuring that the customer is served flawlessly. As the computer, with its algorithmic, binary-coded thinking, simplifies the concept of rationality, IT in the post-modern society can once again combine information with emotion and come across with a humanized approach (Glaser, 1994).

"The chip-revolution", expands Glaser, "with its algorithmic, binary-coded thinking, made the concept of rationality radically one-sided" – with the danger of dehumanization, but yet the post-modern society still combines information and emotion (Glaser, 1994).

With the example of the Autostadt, it is recognizable that steps for a realization of the post-modern are just passable in the area of IT. Whereas the post-modern is concerned comparatively little with reality, the people-conscious deployment of IT shows that the path to a new, more emotional technology is possible and necessary. Endeavors, such as the Autostadt, take the first steps on this long path. To a far greater extent than in previous decades, today one's wishes, demands and requirements constitute the parameters of successful process engineering.

The human aspect, particularly in such a service-oriented environment, assumes absolute priority. Thus, the Autostadt is not to be understood as a demonstration of technology; butt rather as putting itself in the service of, and subsequently subordinating itself to, the people and the demonstration. In other words: without IT, much of the Autostadt would not have been realizable, and thereby cannot be dismissed, but still presents itself in a gentle understatement. Due to this fact, it is explainable why the CTO (Chief Technology Officer) of the Autostadt is not an IT-specialist, but rather pursues psychodynamic, sociological and organizations-logical aspects in the exposure of IT in the Autostadt and thus sees his emphases in this area.

IT AND POST-MODERNITY IN THE AUTOSTADT

The Autostadt is, as the communication platform of the Volkswagen Group, the actual location of direct dialog between the producer and the consumer, the meeting point for the VW Group and its brands. The values of Volkswagen and the delivery of its automobiles will be "staged" here. The "stylistic device" of the Autostadt is infused with emotions and the urbanistic overall concept is based on the paradigm "structure and event". Every square meter is staged, and nature and technology meet in a dialog, which is significantly supported by IT.

The IT in the Autostadt constantly produces new, surprising, emotion-awakening effects. For this reason, it is correct to assume that the actual core process of the Autostadt is the "process of generating feelings", which should then be subsequently visualized. Based on its philosophy, the Autostadt pioneers new and surprising trails in the world of IT. A paradigm shift takes place, which can rightly be referred to as "emotional digitization".

The concurrence of park, buildings, exhibits, staff and events results in a unity of the main components of emotional stimulants at the Autostadt. The conveyance of perfection is an attribute, for which most individuals strive. In this sense, the charisma of the park positively influences the senses and subliminally conveys an important message of the corporate group. The buildings are also in accordance, as they also portray a measure of perfection. They are constructed entirely modern and stylistic. The visitor discovers methods of construction which are seldom, if ever, to be seen in normal surroundings. Beside the perfection, a new effect develops: the progress, orientation to new pathways, and the ability to continuous reinvent itself.

With images, metaphors and sequences, the corresponding philosophies of the brands will be conveyed in the individual pavilions, giving further impulses to the above characteristics. In addition, in the events, the impossible will often be made possible with style. Further stylistic devices are also present in the perfection and progress. The Autostadt would like to inform the customer of new trends, acting as the trendsetter for the corresponding impulses.

For example, the POIs (Points of Information) are central components of the information landscape, but in the Autostadt, the POIs are elements of the "Lebenswelt". The highly complex network computer with its front-end software allows itself to be intuitively understood and operated. The guests are not only using systems; they are experiencing technology. The POIs approach the visitor, they adapt to the user's size and position. Direct contact with the touchscreen can be seen as a metaphor for human interaction with the invisible network of information technology. As "emotional engineering", this connection can be understood as a link between the complexities of IT, human gestures, and aesthetics. The physically present technologies undergo an emotional exchange with the intellectual techniques to allow the visitor interactive comprehension.

We strive for understatement – that is how we see postmodern IT, which is what makes it possible to "produce" emotions in this context in the first place. Digital technology must be communicative and people-oriented. The complex system structure clearly shows the workload involved in making IT "invisible". How is it possible to control something that is nearly invisible? Or to state it more clearly, how is the Autostadt itself capable of identifying possible malfunctions at the earliest point in time? Solutions have also been found for this. With the bidirectionally media control center "Creston", the presentations and the technology are systematically controlled: systems monitoring systems – technology becomes self-referential.

All employees of the Autostadt have access, via PC workstations or central lounges for the Web -based intranet, to all information, e-mail and the Internet. The technology would better be described as "experienced" rather than "used". This all proves that the possibilities of digitization can be used and exploited to prepare the visitor for what they will experience. The invisible, unobtrusive digital elements can help to make sure that people will not be forgotten, even in a technological environment. Even the demand of

philosophy for avant-garde art "within scientific-technical modernization rationality" can only be fulfilled where technology creates space (and scope) for art and aesthetics.

THE FUTURE OF IT

Has postmodernity found its end in the attempt to unify its differences? Have we at least reached a new level of the postmodern, with our humanization-oriented technology? And we continue to ask: where will information technology go from here? We no longer pull levers, we push a virtual button on a touchscreen and in the real world a reaction follows; a lamp goes on, a door closes, and a lawn sprinkler starts watering. The same fascinating moments offered by technology in its early mechanical stages are now being provided by virtual technology. Is modernity simply repeating itself on a higher, more abstract level, or is the beginning of something new?

In the interactive worlds of virtual media, something like a metaphor crystallizes itself out of reality: Due to IT, we experience and learn things, which would normally be far out of reach. And what comes along are the new medias demand and encourage a strengthened inclusion of aesthetics in our daily life, and as each is more unobtrusive, its effect becomes stronger. Thus, the success of IT lies in its inclusion in our daily life, which must take place without obstruction and recognition.

The Internet presence of the Autostadt connects a demand of aesthetics to the POIs. The design quality, in which both Web -based systems will communicate informative content and interactive elements, has already been awarded prizes from, amongst others, New York and Cannes. In an intranet, which is (regarding its public sister) conceptionally and aesthetically behind in nothing, the employees can inform themselves about all-important concerns of the corporation. Standards will also be set here – almost unnoticeable to the public.

The formative characteristic of this aesthetic demand is not the eye-catching distinctive feature, but rather the opposite: the enjoyable appearance, the pleasing control of the view and the (visual) self-explanatory function and order, which lie behind the contents. These aesthetics in the simulation of contents is effectively "unmodern" in a cultural sense, as a principal departure from rationalization. The people experience IT, they use it subconsciously; IT, as a medium, will be internalized and no longer understood and perceived as a "machine", a tool, or means to an end. IT will become a medium for emotions and information. The visualized aesthetics of virtual worlds serve in the same way as the aesthetic architecture in the Autostadt.

One could also see the Autostadt as a metaphor, but it was not planned this way. It is a frame of reference for the characteristics and symbols of the postmodern world (not only for the area of IT). Everything – the automobile, as well as the art – will be presented in a different, atypical context. The character systems interlock virtually, and what results is a BrandLand as a liminal space, an area of the threshold, a location of change and the intervention – the barely apprehensible space between the world, which causes a threshold experience of the senses. A location, where we can foretell the future, without being able to see it.

What remains? The IT has taken a significant step: it has become a production factor; it has retreated to the background of business processes, because an IT-networked implementation is the prerequisite for "the social dimension of processes". The workforce can no longer continue to work autistically: interdisciplinary qualities such as commercial knowledge and organization talent are vital, at least in strategically decisive positions. The supporting IT does not serve as only the acceleration of post-modern phenomena such as globality and mobility, but it also serves – and far more readily available – as the bridge between the aestheticizing and emotionalizing of our every day world!

But it won't stop here. It is conceivable that IT in future mechanical engineering will not exist as a purpose in its own right, but will produce tools (systems) for the generation of products, to transfer knowledge. This forces everyday aspects back in the place of revolution, and finally integrates IT permanently into our post-modern world. In spite of all the risks of abuse and autonomy that accompany IT – the possibilities are there.

REFERENCES

Albrecht, H. (1993). Technik – Gesellschaft – Zukunft. In: H. Albrecht & C. Schönbeck (Eds.), *Technik und Gesellschaft* (=Technik und Kultur, Bd. 10) (pp.451-474) Düsseldorf; Germany: VDI-Verlag.

Bauman, Z. (1992). *Moderne und Ambivalenz. Das Ende der Eindeutigkeit.* Hamburg, Germany: Junius Verlag GmbH.

Bauman, Z. (1999). *Unbehagen in der Postmoderne.* Hamburger Edition, Hamburg, Germany.

Bhabha, H. (Ed.) (1990). *Nation and Narration.* London: Routledge, an imprint of Taylor & Francis Books.

Bhabha, H. (Ed.) (2000). *Die Verortung der Kultur.* Tübingen, Germany: Stauffenburg Verlag.

Derrida, J. (1972). *Die Schrift und die Differenz.* Frankfurt/Main, Germany: Suhrkamp Verlag.

Eco, U. (1986). *Nachschrift zum Namen der Rose.* München, Germany: dtv.

Flusser, V. (1993). *Digitaler Schein.* In: Ders. *Lob der Oberflächlichkeit. Für eine Phänomenologie der Medien.* (= Schriften Bd.1) p.272-285. Mannheim, Germany: Bollmann.

Funke-Kloesters, B. (2004). *Autostadt GmbH: Marketing und Kultur.* unveröffentlichter Text, Wolfsburg, Germany.

Giddens, A. (1995 &1990). *Konsequenzen der Moderne*. Frankfurt/Main, Oxford: Suhrkamp.

Glaser, H. (1994). *Industriekultur und Alltagsleben*. Vom Biedermeier zur Postmoderne. Frankfurt/Main, Germany: S.-Fischer-Verlag.

Haefner, K. (1984). *Mensch und Computer im Jahre 2000*. Ökonomie und Politik für eine humane computerisierte Gesellschaft. Basel, Boston, Stuttgart: Birkhäuser Verlag AG.

Jung, H., & Von Matt, J.-R. (2002). *Momentum*. Die Kraft, die Werbung heute braucht. Berlin, Germany: Lardon Verlag.

Klein, N. (2001). *No Logo!* Der Kampf der Global Players um Marktmacht. Ein Spiel mit vielen Verlierern und wenigen Gewinnern. München, Germany: Goldmann Verlag.

Kreuzer, H. (Ed.) (1987). *Die zwei Kulturen: Literarische und naturwissenschaftliche Intelligenz*. C.P. Snows These in der Diskussion. München, Germany: d-tv / Klett-Cotta Verlag.

Lyotard, J. (1986). *Das Postmoderne Wissen*. Wien, Österreich: Passagen Verlag.

Lyotard, J. (1989). *Der Widerstreit. München*. Germany: Fink Wilhelm Verlag.

Maar, C. / Burda, H. (2004). *Iconic Turn. Köln*. Germany: Dumont Literatur und Kunst Verlag.

Merleau-Ponty, M. (1966). *Phänomenologie der Wahrnehmung*. Berlin, Germany: Gruyter Verlag.

Schütz, A. & Luckmann, T. (1984). *Strukturen der Lebenswelt*. Bd.2, p.197. Frankfurt/Main, Germany: Utb Verlag.

Snow, C. (1967). *Die zwei Kulturen: Literarische und naturwissenschaftliche Intelligenz*. Stuttgart, Germany: Klett Verlag.

Valery, P. (1924). Eupalinos ou l'Architecte. In: Architectures, *Edité par Gallimard*, Paris.

Zima, P. (1997),. Moderne – Postmoderne. Gesellschaft, Philosophie, Literatur. p.18.Tübungen, Germany: Utb Verlag.

ENDNOTES

[1] Cp. Jean-Francois Lyotard: Der Widerstreit. München 1989. p.225-226: "Don't 'we' explain ourselves anymore – and let it be with bitterness or rejoicing – the great explanation from the end of the great explanations? Is it sufficient that the thinking of the end of history thinks according, so that it remains modern? Or is post-modernity the business of an old man who searches through the trash can of usefulness for left-overs […] and therefore […] wins his promise of change!"

[2] Peter V. Zima: Moderne – Postmoderne. Gesellschaft, Philosophie, Literatur. Tübingen, Basel 1997. p.18 – For Zima, "post-modernity" is embossed by the crisis of the modern value system. – The term "Lebenswelt" encompasses the entire spectrum of an individual's or society's life, experiences and understanding.

[3] Umberto Eco: Nachschrift zum "Namen der Rose". München 1986. p.77: "One could say that every epoch has had its post-modernity, as one had said that every epoch has had its Mannerism (and perhaps, I ask myself, is post-modern the modern name for Mannerism as a meta-historical category)."

[4] Cp. Helmuth Albrecht: Technik – Gesellschaft – Zukunft: In: Helmuth Albrecht / Charlotte Schönbeck (Ed.): Technik und Gesellschaft (=Technik und Kultur Bd.10). Düsseldorf 1993. p.451-474. here p.452: "Airplane and automobile, radio and television, and especially the modern electronic based upon computers have effectively changed our world and society in the short time of only three generations."

5   Cp. to C.P. Snow and the debate of his thesis, especially Helmut Kreuzer: Literarische und Szientifische Intelligenz. In: the same (Ed.): Literarische und naturwissenschaftliche Intelligenz. Dialog über die "zwei Kulturen". Stuttgart 1969. p.128-142. – Cp. also Charles Percy Snow: Die zwei Kulturen: literarische und naturwissenschaftliche Intelligenz. Stuttgart 1967.

6   Cp. Alfred Schütz / Thomas Luckmann: Strukturen der Lebenswelt. Bd.2. Frankfurt/ Main 1984. p.197: "The symbolic meanings are also – fixed to certain objects bearing significance – memories of experiences in atypical realities, which are brought from other states to the normal state of the everyday life."

7   Cp. Zygmunt Bauman: Unbehagen in der Postmoderne. Hamburg 1999. p.63. – Cp. also Zygmunt Bauman: Moderne und Ambivalenz. Das Ende der Eindeutigkeit. Hamburg 1992. p.128: "Freedom, equality, brotherliness was the battle call of modernity. *Freedom, difference, tolerance* is the ceasefire formula of post-modernity. And when tolerance evolves into *solidarity,* the ceasefire could actually evolve into peace." – Ccp. also Jacques Derrida: Die Struktur, das Zeichen und das Spiel im Diskurs der Wissenschaften vom Menschen. In: the same: Die Schrift und die Differenz. Frankfurt/Main 1972. p.422-442.

8   Cp. Jean-Francois Lyotard: Das postmoderne Wissen. Wien 1986. p.152: "There is no scientific secret."

9   Vilém Flusser: Digitaler Schein. In: the same: Lob der Oberflächlichkeit. Für eine Phänomenologie der Medien (= Schriften Bd.1). Hrsg. v. Stefan Bollmann und Edith Flusser. Bensheim und Düsseldorf 1993. p.272-285.

10   Paul Valery: Eupalinos ou l'Architecte. In: Architectures. Paris 1924. p.87: "Il n'y a point de détails dans l'exécution."

11   Cp. for example Bazon Brock: "Quid tum". Was folgt aus dem Iconic Turn. In: Christa Maar / Hubert Burda (Ed.): Iconic Turn. Köln 2004. p.323-332.

12   Cp. Homi K. Bhabha (Ed.): Die Verortung der Kultur. Tübingen 2000. p.1: "Beginnings and ends are arguably the primary myths of the middle ages; but in *fin de siècle*, we find the moment of change, where time and space meet and complex configurations of difference and identity, of past and future, inside and outside, inclusion and exclusion procreate."

13   Maurice Merleau-Ponty: Phänomenologie der Wahrnehmung. Berlin 1966.

14   Cp. for the following: Brigitte Funke-Kloesters: Autostadt GmbH: Marketing und Kultur. Wolfsburg 2003. [unv.] p.12.

15   Ibid. p.12.

Chapter II
Bridging User Requirements and Cultural Objects:
A Process–Oriented Framework for Cultural E–Services

Elias A. Hadzilias
IÉSEG School of Management, France

Andrea Carugati
Åarhus School of Business, Denmark & IÉSEG School of Management, France

ABSTRACT

This chapter aims at defining a framework for the design of e-government services on cultural heritage. Starting from an analysis of three cases on digitisation of different types of cultural objects the authors highlight the problems existing in the creation of e-services on cultural heritage. These cases show the existence of four key issues in the development of this kind of information systems: digitisation, requirements engineering, standardization, and interoperability. The proposed framework addresses these issues focusing on the user requirements and the cultural object representation. Dynamic content exchange requires the use of a prescriptive framework for the development of cultural heritage Web sites. This chapter provides such a framework using observation from concrete applications and knowledge of information systems development methodologies.

INTRODUCTION

The Lisbon strategy for eEurope (EU Report, 2008) and the following eEurope 2002, eEurope 2005, eEurope+ and i2010 strategies, drafted as results of the activities of the European Council aim at making the European Union the most competitive and dynamic knowledge-based economy with improved economy and social cohesion by 2010. In concrete terms this means broadband and high-level Internet based services for the entire population of the European Union. The means envisioned to achieve this goal are largely based on increasing both demand and offer of e-services respectively from the public/users and the providers. The problem has been framed as a "chicken and egg" problem and the solution has therefore been to address both ends: increase government-side services and create a friendly legislation for the implementation and sale of broadband connections (EU Report, 2008). This chapter focuses on the demand side, that is, on the development of the public electronic services.

On the demand side, electronic government initiatives involve providing services in e-Government, e-Learning, e-Health, and e-Business (EU Report, 2008). While the efforts of e-Government are focusing on providing services to citizens in order to achieve higher efficiencies through automation (tax filing, certification, electronic voting, information provision, etc) one other important area of investment regards the facilitation of access to cultural resources. The regional and local cultural heritage (to be defined in a broad sense, from museums to regional gastronomy and folklore) is one of Europe's greatest economic assets, and ICT (Information and Communication Technologies) and other advanced technologies can dramatically increase the possibility of its exploitation. Until now the government initiatives for the divulgation of electronic material on the local cultural heritage have been varied in nature and include the creation of portals for information on cultural events which is the most common model of exploitation today, the digitisation of artwork for archives, the creation of virtual tri-dimensional museum visits with tri-dimensional **digitisation** of art works, and the rendering of archaeological visits in digital formats (Carugati, Hadzilias, & Demoulin, 2005).

Nevertheless the potential of using electronic services for cultural heritage applications is far from being fully exploited and many initiatives have remained at the stage of pilot projects. Of these pilot projects few are completed and most contain only one or very few examples of art digitisation. Until now, experiences of use of **ICT** in cultural heritage sectors too often fail in providing valuable economic results due to a number of problems, and have generated disappointment among the potential players and beneficiaries. The main problems have been:

- In general, at regional and local level there is shortage of experience and expertise about the use of ICT in cultural heritage areas. Therefore, local and regional administrators have to rely on ICT vendors and consultants, and these in general are mainly able to suggest general purpose solutions, non-optimised for the specific sector, since even large IT (Information Technology) consulting companies have limited expertise in the cultural heritage area.

- If we consider the "conventional" cultural heritage, e.g. museums and galleries, this sector lacks expertise and experience in marketing and business promotion on electronic media, which makes it difficult to develop credible business models and plans, and to attract investments.

- There are analogous problems also in the cultural tourism sector. There are hundreds of projects and initiatives related to cultural tourism in Europe, but they often have been designed on "supply oriented" thinking, without systematic investigation into what the customer, the "cultural tourist", is looking for. The issue of user diversity should be considered in the system development process as pointed out by Klawe and Shneiderman (2005) since it is a critical success factor to steer user preferences. This is valid not only for business purposes but also and foremost at community level (Carroll, 2001). Finally, as e-Government services are Web-based, they are available to different users. Even though the expectations in terms of services might differ, Nielsen (2005) states that **usability** factors influence for both professionals and other categories the success of the service.

- More generally, the problem of mutual understanding between the cultural sector, service industry and **ICT** experts, due to their different ways of thinking, makes it difficult to achieve a fruitful cooperation in areas ranging between education and multimedia production, where the availability of content from the cultural heritage could open very promising development perspectives. In order to be able to develop innovative and marketable products and services with a real cultural added value, the personal direct involvement of experts from the cultural area is absolutely required.

Despite the above-mentioned issues, in Europe as well as elsewhere there are a number of interesting examples and initiatives, on various scales, of successful economic promotion of the cultural heritage (some of these mentioned above). Unfortunately, they have often only a local or regional visibility, and their positive (and negative) experiences cannot be fully exploited and shared by other projects.

To resolve these issues, the paper proposes an integrated framework for developing e-Government services on cultural heritage. The framework emerges from the study of multiple cultural heritage electronic initiatives and the in depth investigation of three case studies. This framework is represented using the **modelling** method **ARIS** (ARchitecture of integrated Information Systems), where all necessary steps, inputs, outputs, rules, and roles are described in a hierarchical manner.

The chapter is organised in the following way: first the research methodology is explained, secondly we present the case studies and analyse them to highlight key issues, then we describe the ARIS modelling technique, and we continue presenting the development framework focusing on user segmentation and interoperability. Finally we conclude with a discussion of the proposed framework highlighting the need for a systemic approach to the activities.

RESEARCH METHODOLOGY

The research was carried out following the constructive paradigm of the case study approach (Yin, 2002). In this context the research used a practice-based lens to identify processes and problems in the development of e-Government services on cultural heritage. The process comprised of three steps:

1   Identify representative cases of e-Government cultural services
2   Identify the different functionalities for the expected users and the problems incurred in these specific cases of information systems development.
3   Propose a way to consider these problems given the constraint of limited resources.

As a first step we carried out an extensive survey to record most electronic initiatives in the culture domain. The survey identified 142 initiatives which should cover the bulk of such services for the 8 languages spoken by the authors (English, Italian, Greek, French, Danish, Swedish, German, Spanish). The languages cover the vast majority of projects in this domain. Among these initiatives we have selected three that are the most representative because they fit specific criteria that we set out in our research: 1) they continue to exist after the end of the pilot project; 2) they are complete in terms of the cultural content they were supposed to cover; 3) they provide additional functionalities with respect to similar services; 4) they use more advanced technologies;

5) the informative material about the case was comprehensive.

As a second step we analyse the three cases in a structured manner looking at a) functionalities provided to the users; b) functionalities provided to other institutions; and c) the development process. These three elements are compared and integrated to indicate key leverage points of these initiatives. In this step we include usability testing for the two initiatives available online (the Piero della Francesca Project and the Incunabula manuscripts in the Herzog August library) in order to see if the users find the functions of the Web site friendly and value-adding. For doing this, we carry out the testing with five users representing different categories (Nielsen & Landauer, 1993). The layout of the testing follows the indication of Molich (1999, p. 109) with a testing room and an observation room. According to the testing protocol, the users were given different tasks to carry out and were required to speak over their actions.

In the third step we employ the **ARIS** modelling method to describe a high-level design framework for implementing e-Government services for cultural heritage. The framework expands on treating the key points identified in step two.

The proposed solution is therefore the result of deductive reasoning and is prescriptive in nature.

CASE STUDIES

According to the selection process we consider the following case studies: the Electronic Beowulf Project at the British Library (UK), the Piero della Francesca Project in Arezzo (Italy), and the digitisation of the incunabula manuscripts in the Herzog August Library in Cologne (Germany).

Beowulf: The Pioneer Project

The Electronic Beowulf Project represents a pioneering effort in the digitisation of cultural heritage. Beowulf is both the first English literary masterpiece and one of the earliest European epics written in the vernacular, or native language, instead of literary Latin. The story survives in one fragile manuscript copied by two scribes near the end of the 10th or the first quarter of the 11th century. Until quite recently, most scholars thought that this surprisingly complex and poignant poem was written in the 8th century or earlier, but Kiernan (1981) stirred up controversy asserting that the work was composed in the 11th century, and that the manuscript itself may have even been the author's working copy. The manuscript has been damaged over time and the original surviving today is in very poor conditions (adapted from http://www.library.unr.edu/subjects/guides/beowulf.html - accessed on 3-6-2008).

The Electronic Beowulf Project was carried out in the period 1993-1999 in order to digitise the original Beowulf manuscript, of which the original is now in the British Library, and has been made accessible to everyone in electronic format.

Development Process

Since the Beowulf represents one of the first attempts to digitise a cultural heritage object many difficulties were encountered in different aspects of the project, as the work in preparing the digital edition was very complex in the period considered. Technical difficulties concerned scanning technologies, storing media, and managing the transfer across large distances of large quantities of data or moving 24-bit colour images across different technical platforms. In some cases it was necessary to devise innovative technical solutions to achieve the desired end result. The following is a quote from Prof. Kiernan's Web site highlighting the technical difficulties encountered in 1993:

The equipment we are using to capture the images is the Roche/Kontron ProgRes 3012 digital camera, which can scan any text, from a letter or a word to an entire page, at 2000 x 3000 pixels in 24-bit colour. The resulting images at this maximum resolution are enormous, about 21-25 MB, and tax the capabilities of the biggest machines. Three or four images - three or four letters or words if that is what we are scanning - will fill up an 88 MB hard disk, and we have found that no single image of this size can be processed in real time without at least 64 MB of RAM. In our first experiments in June with the camera and its dedicated hardware, we transmitted a half-dozen images by phone line from the Conservation Studio of the British Library to the Wenner Gren Imaging Laboratory at the University of Kentucky, where identical hardware was set up to receive the data. Most of these images are now available on the Internet through anonymous ftp or Mosaic (http://www.uky.edu/~kiernan/eBeowulf/main. htm- accessed on 3-6-2008).

Besides the technical challenges there were also issues in the coordination and collaboration of the human resources due to the variety of disciplines necessary to carry out this task. The domain experts comprised scholars, curators, conservators, photographers and technical experts (Prescott, 1997) who had to agree on how the activities had to be carried out in order to record the maximum information without damaging the precious document.

In the case of Beowulf the development was mainly oriented towards the utilization of information technology for capturing cultural content. This activity was not only done to preserve the artefact but also to enhance the comprehension of the text. From the multiple sources about this project we can see that, given these requirements, the main activity was to create digital images of the text with different scanning techniques (B&W, 24 bit color, ultraviolet, high level fiber optic light). This was performed once in order to minimise damage and retain the maximum information digitised because of the extensive erasure and correction in the original manuscript.

The development process followed was a pure waterfall approach (Boehm, 1988), in the situation the requirements had to be set at the offset of the project and the digitisation was done only once per page. Afterwards the content was used to populate a database.

Functionalities for Users

The Electronic Beowulf Project is available to users on CD format that can be purchased from the British Library. The interface provides access to the digital content of a database that contains both pictures and transcribed text. The CD contains multiple transcriptions of the Beowulf from different accredited authors. Different search criteria are available to query Line (Edition), Folio (Edition), FolioLine (Transcript), Fitt (Edition or Transcript), Scribe (Edition or Transcript). Images can be zoomed to a very high detail in order to be studied by paleographers and calligraphers (see figure 1). Alternatively the layout of the screen can show both the original manuscript and the

Figure 1. Zoom function

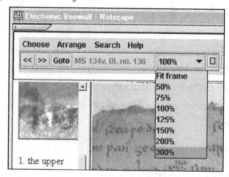

Figure 2. Texts comparison

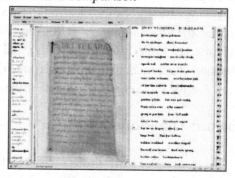

Figure 3. Scanning under multiple light sources

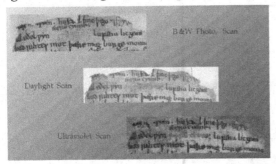

transcription which is intended to be used by researchers interested in the content of the poem (see figure 2).

The electronic version enables readers to place the original manuscript's leaves side by side, to examine the color and texture of the vellum leaves by magnifying the images and to explore the work of the early scribes (see figure 3). Building on this material the CD features multiple versions of restoration of which the most recent one was made possible by the different scanning techniques.

Functionalities for Institutions

This project was part of the strategy of the British Library to create the capability to increase access to its collections by use of imaging and network technology. As such the Beowulf project was not directly geared towards providing content, services, or functionalities to other institutions and remains a stand alone product.

One of the collaboration that emerged from this project was the inclusion of the Thorkelin's transcript of the Beowulf catalogued in the Royal Library of Copenhagen.

Piero della Francesca: From Restorers to Children

The project of Piero della Francesca regards the digitisation of the series of frescos "Leggenda della Vera Croce" situated in the Bacci chapel in the Basilica of St. Francis of Arezzo (Italy). The project was started in the mid 80's to repair the severe damages that the frescos suffered in the early 80's. The project was lead by the cultural and artistic heritage authority of Arezzo (Soprinten- denza per i Beni Architettonici, Artistici e Storici di Arezzo). The causes of the damage were not clear and therefore the Soprintendenza decided to begin a series of deep and comprehensive sci- entific and historic researches to determine the reasons of the fresco detrimental conditions. The aim was the preservation of the masterpiece for future generations and in order to achieve this it was necessary to find the right technique to restore the painted plaster as well as the building structure itself.

As the project evolved and the restoration work finished, the initial goal was complemented by the creation of a permanent documentation center for future study and diffusion of information. This center focuses on the study and conservation of the mural paintings of Piero della Francesca and another aim is to construct, with the use of computer technology, an organic database for the Project and an interactive multimedia system to be hooked up to the international electronic network and available for public consultation (http://www. pierodellafrancesca.it accessed on 3-6-2008).

The project is considered one of the most advanced and demanding efforts of the entire scientific restoration field in Italy and abroad.

Development Process

Originally this project was carried out to provide professional restorers with new tools for restoring the artworks of Piero della Francesca. For this reason the initial requirements were set by the restorers and as a result the quality and detail of the digitised material is very high. For example they integrated text, vectorial information (CAD draw- ing) and raster information (images) which, from a data processing point of view are of a completely different nature and very complicated. Figure 4

Figure 4. Activities in the project of Piero della Francesca

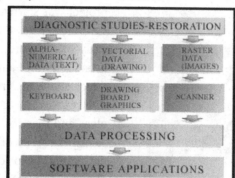

Figure 5. Data capturing and sample images in the project of Piero della Francesca

shows the process followed by the project team from preliminary study, to material collection and data processing, and finally the development of software applications.

The four basic activities in this project: data capture, CAD drawing, and raster images (overlaid) are presented in Figure 5.

As in the Beowulf case, the development approach followed the waterfall model. Restorers, together with state institutions, and private and public research institutes, carried out a long preliminary research to set out the requirements. Leading scholars and expert technicians used state of the art information technology to develop the applications that were used to successfully define the restoration approaches to solve the fresco complex problems.

After the end of the restoration work the development continued with the creation of a Web site that used the same collected material from the professional applications but provided function-

alities that were interesting for the wider public. In this second cycle of development a new set of requirements was created to address the goal of creating the permanent documentation center.

Functionalities for Users

For the restorers, the developed applications provided functionalities to store and search thousands of documents: illustrations of the church choir were compiled in a basic cartographic model and in a variety of thematic mappings with reference to historical studies, visual surveys, diagnostic studies, and scientific analyses and complemented by about 1000 historical/chronological records. The catalogued images could be called up individually from a special menu where they were arranged according to distinct categories. This technology was particularly effective in the phases of correlation, control, and updating of the various studies conducted. The images could also be called up from a relational database which allowed the efficient consultation of records.

Furthermore the software allowed keeping record of the restoration in process (work site diary, graphs and charts of the work performed, technical specifications etc.) as well as adding new cultural content.

To help restorers in their work the applications operate in the complete respect of the iconographic and technical value of the artist's work providing a documentation of the various painting techniques employed by the artist: from the transfer of the preparatory design through the use of stenciled cartoons, etched lines and coloured threads, to the application of colour to the fresh plaster (a fresco), partially dried plaster (a mezzo fresco), and finally to the dried plaster with special temperas and organic blending agents. A further example of the system's capabilities is that it provides a chronological reconstruction of the artist's production. Connected to this, the system allows to study the relationship between the saline deposits and the presence of fixatives added during earlier restorations or, alternatively, to view the deposits in relation to the various painting techniques used by the artist.

To satisfy the need for rapid consultation in the service of monitoring the state of conserva-tion and the progress of the restoration, system designers developed a thematic glossary with a unified terminology of key words for research and access to the data organized first in separate technical files and then electronically translated to permit interactive consultation.

Finally, the applications were on-line with the work site, in order to manage the traditional paper documentation kept by the project director and the restoration technicians and allowing them to have immediate access to and use of the data stored in the system.

In the public Web site, one of the services provided is the classic function of archive. The archive allows searching for historical events by date or by keyword and presents the results combining digital images with metadata. The result of one search is presented in figure 6.

Other interesting functionalities provided are games based on the thematic mappings. The Web site proposes two games: one that consists of adding colours to a black-and-white painting and the other where parts of the paintings have been divided (electronically) into pieces that the player is supposed to reassemble like a puzzle. These two games have an underlying pedagogic reason and would not be possible without the existence of the digitised material specifically

Figure 6. Public archive from the Web site http://www.pierodellafrancesca.it

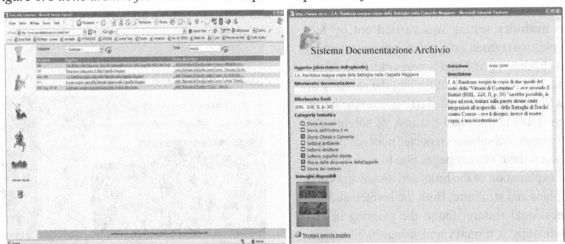

Figure 7. Puzzle game

Figure 8. Painting game

created and mapped for the restorers. The Web technologies deployed for this purpose were active images and java applets. An example of the two games is presented in figures 7 and 8.

Usability Testing

The **usability** testing was carried out by five people: two laymen, one professional restorer and two children aged 7 and 8 years old. The adults were assigned the task of finding the painting of "La Madonna del Parto" starting from the home page. The children had the task of solving the two games. All subjects reported poor navigation between the different pages due to non-existent text explanation of the links and unconventional graphics and structure. Both the laymen and the professional restorer found the painting in approximately 3 minutes and using 30/32 mouse

clicks (against 1 minute and 8 clicks that would take for an experienced user of the system). The information presented pleased the professional but not the laymen that reported it as too complex and dull. All three cases showed a critical design error when the user had to pass from the classic Web site view to the database of the art works, because we had to intervene in order to guide the users on how to continue their search.

In consideration of their age, the children were not asked to navigate through the Web site and were presented directly with the games. The children did not understand what they had to do and also complained that there was no evaluation of their performance. Using the words of the children these games were reported to be: boring and meaningless.

Despite the interesting use of the digitised material for a wider audience, the outcomes were not value-adding neither for the laymen nor for the children.

Functionalities for Institutions

The system provides two levels of access to the project material. At the first level the information is available on the Web site that is hosted by the sponsor of the project (Banca Etruria) and at the second level, which is more complete and contains the full record of the restoration project, the system is available at the offices of the cultural and artistic heritage authority of Arezzo. This

Figure 9. System functionalities

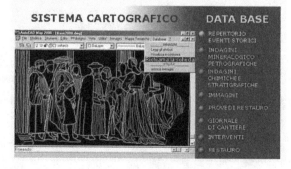

local system can be accessed only under official authorisation. Data can be processed through a cartographic system based on photogrammetric surveys of the painted walls. The relational database is structured in a series of indexes. Files are divided into didactic, diagnostic, and intervention sections. The local system is addressed to institutions that seek in depth knowledge not only of the artworks but also of the restoration process, the mineralogical analysis and the chemical analysis performed. Figure 9 shows on the left side the local cartographic system and on the right frame the functionalities for professionals. The green dot indicates the access to the public archive via the Web.

Distributed Digital Incunabula Library: an Architecture for Sharing

The "Distributed Digital Incunabula Library" (http://inkunabeln.ub.uni-koeln.de accessed on 3-6-2008) is a project aimed at the digitisation of all German incunabula. Incunabula, Latin for cradle, are books printed between 1454 and 1500. Worldwide, approximately 550.000 incunabula have been preserved. The Distributed Digital Incunabula Library project was organised as a joined effort of the "Koelner Universitaets und Stadtbibliothek" and the "Herzog August Bibliothek Wolfenbüttel" libraries. The two libraries involved, hold together approximately 5.800 copies Incunabula. Out of these, 350.000 pages (approximately 2.000 – 3.000 titles) were selected for this project, of which 40 % were digitised in the first ten months of the two year effort. When completed, the 350.000 pages could represent as much as six percent of the titles of Incunabula preserved world wide (Loebbecke & Thaller, 2005).

As a mean of achieving global integration while simultaneously keeping institutional independence, this project proposed as reference architecture a new tool called "Digital Autonomous Cultural Objects (DACOs)". DACOs are characterised by a common behavioural code that provides for informing about cultural objects on request. The code involves the object wrapping itself in mark-up language. It also provides a persistent addressing scheme allowing for control of the individual institution holding the good as well as a mapping scheme. Thus, even if the technology (e.g., HTML, XML, SGML, VRML objects, Flash movies, SVG constructions) can be chosen by the individual institution, the structure of basic elements integrated into a DACO is predetermined.

Figure 10. Development process and system landscape of Incunabula Library

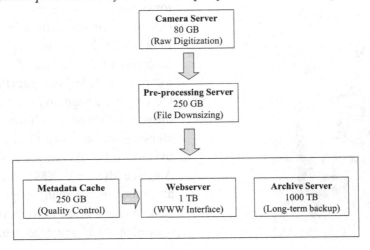

Development Process

In order to deal with the vast amount information to be digitised, a standard development process was followed, which is depicted in figure 10.

At the first stage of the development was the raw **digitisation** of the single pages, which was conducted using a Nikon DXM 1200 and a camera server that stored the images with total capacity of 80 GB. A book cradle for photos in an angle of 45 degrees (see figure 11) allowed treating the Incunabula carefully while simultaneously saving time and money. The pages were scanned in a 24-bit colour scheme using a resolution of 3800x3072 pixel leading to a data file size of 34 MB/page. With such a digitisation procedure more than 80% of Incunabula were digitised leading to about 12 TB raw data volume.

At the second step, the digitised data was transferred through a local area network to a pre-processing server with 250 GB storage capacity. This server was responsible for the transformation of the output files to the size that is efficient for Web site access and for the different users.

Finally, the files were forwarded to the Web server environment and the digitised files were available on the Internet, after passing a quality control at the Metadata Cache and being transformed to DACOs. These versions of the original files were not more than 10% of the original data size, so that they can be accessed quickly from the Internet. During this phase, the data supervision and the production of the copy-referred development data took place. The archive server offers a storage area for disaster recovery purposes.

The entire architecture was based on cost-efficient Linux servers highly performing for the hierarchical storage organisation.

Obviously, beyond tackling the technical challenges, cost played a major role in pushing such a **digitisation** effort forward. The most important cost factors were:

- Content and subject classification based on the already existing Incunabula Short Title Catalogue (ISTC)
- Workflow/data importation
- Raw digitisation
- Storage capacity
- Development and maintenance of the WWW server.

Considering all cost components in this project, the costs for one page amount roughly 0.75 € (plus metadata and work environment) (Loebbecke & Thaller, 2005).

Functionalities for Users

The users are able to run queries in the Incunabula resources in two levels: text-based and image-based. In the former, there are query criteria for locating the page or pages under consideration containing all metadata and the digitised images. In the latter, there is an image archive with three sublevels of Incunabula description: the Incunabula Short Title Catalogue (ISTC) classification, the original image and the transcription of the image. Furthermore, additional tools are provided allowing for browsing through the manuscripts like in traditional libraries, as shown in figure 12. A native 'dynamic' XML database administers all codicological manuscript descriptions. For some codices those descriptions amount to the equivalent of fifty printed pages.

Figure 11. Book cradle for 45 degrees photos

Figure 12. Query results (http://inkunabeln.ub.uni-koeln.de/ visited on 3/6/2008)

There are four different viewing levels of the scanned images suitable for the categories of users who will study the cultural object. Figure 12 shows the query result with the overview level (notice the eye, the glasses, the loop, and the microscope icons above the scanned image). Figure 13 shows higher level of detail.

Another e-service offered, is that the users can download several tools which measure the performance of typical types of codicological / palaeographic work (e.g. measurement of single characters). As far as available without copyright restrictions, the main scientific literature to work with the codices is also made available in digital form.

Using DACOs, one URL (Uniform Resource Locator) of the library dissolves into about 600,000 URLs of individual references to a specific cultural heritage object that can be referenced directly from any other cultural heritage resource (see for example the code *ig00227000* above the scanned page in figure 12). This is due to the various views of the metadata and different levels of resolution.

Figure 13. Multiple levels of details for the users

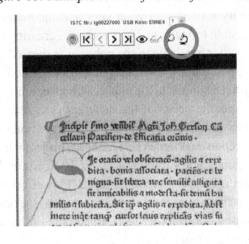

Usability testing

Given the content of this site we had to carry out a careful selection of the five users. Finally, we selected three librarians and two history researchers. Even though the test subjects did not research specifically the Incunabula, they were selected for their knowledge in the research and management of historical documents. They were assigned two tasks: to find the document "Mensa philosophica" and the complete production of Gerson. The users completed the first task in less than 2 minutes and with 10/14 mouse clicks (compared to an experienced user that requires 7 mouse clicks). They completed the second task restarting from the main page with 7 mouse clicks in less than 1 minute. The users reported the site to be easy to navigate, even though it was in German language. However, they evidenced two major failures in the database operation: that the field tables were not linked and that the navigation functions in the index instead of visualising the records alphabetically, were providing erratic results.

Functionalities for Institutions

The highest added value of this project lies in the inter-institutional cultural content sharing. Cultural heritage brokers, connected to servers recognizing DACOs, integrate many DACOs from different institutions into specialised interfaces, thus serving the interests of laymen and researchers. The communication between the servers takes place via the DACO protocol consisting of several XML-codes transmitted via Hyper Text Transfer Protocol (HTTP). When addressed by a broker, the DACO server describes itself through providing a list of supported "access venues" (e.g., titles, authors, years, etc). The access venues can be used by the broker to develop a search mask.

Case Analysis

After examining thoroughly the three case studies of e-services in the cultural sector and with the knowledge of the other existing initiatives, we observed that the greatest challenge lies on the management of four dimensions: digitisation, requirements engineering, standardisation and interoperability.

The survey we carried out shows that several European countries are making efforts to comply with the Lisbon strategy and are moving, albeit at different paces, towards the digitisation of their cultural heritages. However, given the sheer size of the material, the variety of the applications developed and approaches taken by the different governments it appears clear that the seamless integration of the cultural heritages of multiple countries is a very complex task and it is addressed in multiple ways. The three cases showed that **digitisation** is the starting point of these efforts aiming at the preservation of the cultural content and its availability to a large spectrum of users. All three cases show a very similar approach to the digitisation problem using various scanning technologies to create digital fax-simile of cultural objects.

The second dimension concerns the **requirements engineering**. In the three cases observed the requirements were set initially by the most demanding groups namely the professionals working with cultural objects in their daily working life. Researchers were in contact with the technical developers in order to discuss and define the initial set of requirements. This helped to set very high quality standard for what later became material available to laymen. The process of creating the Web sites available to the public was carried out following a top-down approach that provided the digitised content to the public without examining the specific needs of the different categories of users. A notable exception is the functionality offered in the Piero della Francesca project where the pedagogic games addressed the needs of the specific target group of children. This effort followed however the same push strategy as the other two and our usability tests proved the limitation of this approach.

Table 1. Overview of the findings

	Beowulf (1993)	Piero della Francesca (1991)	Incunabula (2001)
Digitisation	Flat documents partly damaged with different light sources. Major issue: technology.	Three and two dimensional objects: data capture, CAD drawing, and raster images.	Flat documents in different resolutions. Major issue: cost.
Requirements engineering	Top-down approach from professionals' perspective	Top-down approach from professionals' perspective.	Top-down approach from professionals' perspective with special focus on interoperability.
Standardisation	Ad-hoc approach. Standards applied to the image format.	Ad-hoc approach using standard rules for relational database and graphic file formats.	Use of XML standard. DACO typology candidate for becoming a European standard.
Interoperability	Not addressed. Available on CD-ROM.	The archive is partially available online but the content is not accessible from other Web sites.	Content shared with other institutions thanks to specially designed XML objects (DACO).

As far as **standardisation** is concerned there seems to be a trend towards finding a common way to represent cultural objects. In the early cases the standardisation regarded the format of the digitised images (e.g. jpg, tiff, bmp formats). The incunabula project shows instead a more structured approach to the standardisation problem using the DACOs where not only the images but also the metadata follow a specific standard.

Finally we have also observed an evolution towards higher **interoperability** of cultural information systems. The early example of the Beowulf was designed as a stand-alone project and it is only available to users on CD-ROM to be bought from the British Library. The Piero della Francesca project started as an independent solution for professionals, but it was later made available on the Web with some of the original functionalities activated. The Incunabula project was – from the offset – born as a Web-based information system to execute queries on the pages of digital Incunabula. This last effort is directly geared to making the material and the tools available to other cultural Web sites. In order to increase the interoperability of existing or future applications there should be distributed, localised development of content that can be integrated as it is created.

The summary of the case analysis is shown in the following Table 1.

In an era where content exchange is becoming the norm and access to cultural content is mandate by law (i2010 strategy) it becomes paramount for the different governments to develop their content respecting a framework that will allow different Web sites to freely exchange content. The framework will have to address the four dimensions just described and embed them into a process of information system development. The development of such a framework will be the focus of the next part of the chapter beginning with the description of the **modelling** technique used that is ARIS.

ARIS: THE MODELLING TECHNIQUE

In order to model our framework we selected a modelling technique that was at the same time suitable to easily convey a message and at the same time did not impose methods or techniques on the system modelled. Among the possible techniques (e.g. Data Flow Diagram, ERD, UML, etc) we have selected **ARIS** for its flexibility well knowing that experts easily translate it into any other modelling tool (Scheer, Kruppke, Jost, & Kindermann 2006). More specifically, we used the Extended Event-driven Process Chain (eEPC) diagrams of the ARIS method.

An eEPC diagram contains functions (rounded rectangles), events (hexagons), organisational units (ellipses) and inputs/outputs (rectangles). A function is triggered by one or more events and produces one or more events upon completion. An organisational unit depicts the agent who performs the function and the Input/Output boxes reflect the transformation process of the function. Event and function symbols form an alternating chain linked via control flows - dashed arrows. If more than one event is involved, they must be combined using rules - one of the AND ($\wedge$), OR ($\vee$) or XOR operators, enclosed in a circle. For example, the following construct represents an AND triggering condition involving events Event1 and Event2.

DESCRIPTION OF THE PROPOSED FRAMEWORK

Based on the analysis of the cases, the exhaustive survey of the cultural heritage initiatives, our theoretical and practical knowledge on information systems development, we propose a framework for the development of e-services for cultural heritage based on 4 ideas: 1) e-services for cultural heritage are, in essence, information systems. As such, existing methodologies can be adopted and adapted for their development. 2) ARIS is a proven **modelling** approach for the development activities of information systems. 3) The impact of Web sites for cultural heritage increases with the enhancement of content inte-

gration from multiple sites: a one-stop cultural heritage site can be imagined as the ideal goal and therefore compatibility of the finished local products is paramount. 4) Multiple types of public have to be served by these sites; satisfying each group is important to serve the goal of increasing demand for services in the i2010 strategy. According to these four ideas and the four dimensions identified in the analysis we develop a framework which contains the following five phases: collection of user requirements, digitisation of cultural content, system interoperability design, cultural content organisation and e-Government cultural portal development. These phases are expressed as activities in the ARIS model of Figure 15.

The organisational units that we have identified are:

- Users. This organisational unit includes art specialists (like the restorers in the Piero della Francesca case), historians, researchers, and the public in general. In the following figure 15, it is shown that the "users" support the collection of user requirements, the organisation of cultural content and the development of e-service. The participation of users in these activities ensures the user-centered evaluation that the usability testing proved essential to avoid critical errors.
- Technical project team. This organisational unit includes the project manager, the system architects, the system analysts, the database designers, and the developers including the Web designers. In the following figure 15, it

Figure 14. eEPC example

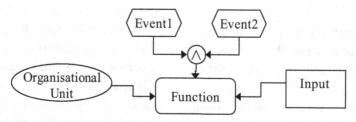

is shown that the "technical project team" supports the collection of users' requirements, the digitisation of cultural content, the design of system interoperability, and the development of e-service. The participation of the technical project team in these activities ensures that the users' needs can

be supported by the technology and the resources available.

- The cultural organisation. It includes all the experts in the specific art works that are part of the cultural heritage e-service (curators, conservation scientists, archivists, museum technicians). This organisational

Figure 15. ARIS eEPC model of the proposed framework

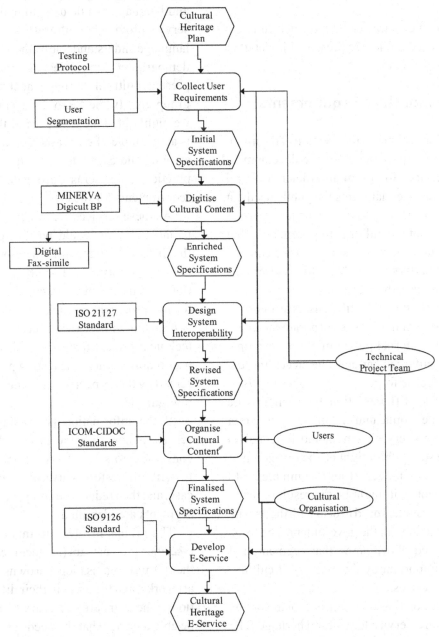

unit is discrete from the users because they provide information about the art works and are not necessarily using the service. The participation of the cultural organisation in these activities ensures that the art work will be treated in the proper way, that the needs of other cultural organisations in terms of exchange of the digitised materials are upheld, and that the metadata is correct and complete.

The specific characteristics of each function of the proposed model are presented in detail in the following sections.

Collection of User Requirements

This function is aimed at the creation of the initial specification requirements for the development of the e-service. To design an efficient cultural heritage e-service that meets the public needs, it is first of all necessary to define the target group users and understand the requirements that have to be addressed. The survey of the cultural heritage initiatives highlighted different groups of users. One classification (see Dipartimento dei Beni Culturali, Italy) identified users as internal, private (customer market), or corporate (business market). The internal public might for example be the law enforcement agencies accessing the artwork database for research on fakes or stolen material. The differentiation between private and corporate is quite unusual in a governmental service since every citizen should be equal in front of the state. This might be the indication of a trend to adopt models from e-commerce into e-Government or it might be the result of using technology providers used to deal with the private sector instead of with the government. The three cases analysed above show that segmentation is deemed important by the creators of cultural heritage e-services.

The input of this function is a plan for the creation of an e-service for cultural heritage. The plan may originate from a specific need like in the case of Piero della Francesca, from a research interest like in the Beowulf case, or from a long term plan for the distribution of content like in the incunabula project.

"User segmentation" Input shown in Figure 15, guides how the requirements will be created. The users can be classified according to their profession, location, affiliation, age, and interests (Sen, Padmanabhan, & Tuzhilin, 1998). Region and language can be used to make sure that the service provided is culturally acceptable and the language understandable by the audience. Among demographical variables, age may be useful to present cultural heritage accurately at every group age. In the Piero della Francesca project we highlighted the existence of the games. This is an example of customisation of the content to a young audience. Occupation or community of practice of the user is a strong determinant of the requirements for the e-service.

As these services are rather new it is difficult to fathom what would be the requirements of the different groups. It is therefore important to develop prototypes for the requirements definition. The user-centered evaluation following the testing protocols of Nielsen (1993) and Molich (1999) should be carried out to assure that the technical project team has well interpreted the user requirements. The testing protocol is represented by the respective "Testing protocol" Input in Figure 15.

If the information is missing because the service is new than the cases indicate that it is convenient to serve the most demanding group first, like the restorers in the Piero della Francesca case, and then reduce the complexity as other user segments are identified.

The groups involved in this activity are the e-service project team (the technical developers), the cultural organisation that owns or manages the art works, and the users in their different declinations. The users are necessary because they will be able to state what the needs are. Users should be representative of the categories identified in the segmentation exercise. The technical team is necessary because of the preparation for the technical work ahead. They have to make sure that the requirements can be technically satisfied. Finally the cultural organisation is also necessary because they know how the art works can be handled and what are the aspects of their digitisation that are most valuable to cover. As an example, the case of the Beowulf showed that it was necessary to do the scanning under ultraviolet light and only specialists could point that out.

Despite a careful segmentation the actual collection of the requirements can result in a quite challenging process. Most constituencies, especially laymen, will in fact be unaware of what they want since innovative e-services are still very limited. While the mental model of a museum or an archaeological visit is shared among people of different countries there might be requirements that no user can state simply because one cannot ask what is not known. For the elicitation of requirements from the final users it would then seem appropriate to engage with the different constituencies in an iterative process using prototypes of interfaces. This prototype-based requirement elicitation should be done autonomously from the setting of the requirements for the content digitisation where the use of an agreed upon standard is required.

The output of this function is the initial requirements document. For the technical project team, it will contain the functional specification of the e-service to be developed. For the cultural organisation, it will contain the specification for the preparation of the art works and the specifications for the descriptions to be prepared.

Digitisation of Cultural Content

This is the function of digitisation of cultural content. The reasons for digitisation, or more precisely for the digital conversion of non-digital cultural source material, are varied and may well overlap. The decision to digitise has the following objectives:

- To increase access: this is the most obvious and primary reason, where a high demand from users is estimated and the administration has the desire to improve public access to a specific collection.
- To improve services to an expanding user's group by providing enhanced access to the institution's resources with respect to education and lifelong learning.
- To reduce the handling and use of fragile or heavily used original material and create a backup copy for endangered material such as brittle books or documents.
- To give the administration opportunities for the development of its technical infrastructure and staff skill capacity.
- To develop collaborative resources, sharing partnerships with other administrations to create virtual collections and increase worldwide access of a country's heritage.
- To seek partnerships with other administrations to capitalise on the economic advantages of a shared approach.
- To take advantage of financial opportunities, for example the likelihood of securing funding to implement a program, or of a particular project being able to generate significant income.

According to which of these needs are deemed more important the requirements document is taken from the previous function and transformed into two outputs: the digital fax-simile and an enriched systems specification document revised after the digitisation. The technical project team and the cultural organisation collaborate in this activity which – as seen in all three cases above – is very demanding.

The control is provided by the MINERVA guidelines. MINERVA, MInisterial NEtwoRk for Valorising Activities in digitisation (http://www.

minervaeurope.org/), is a resource for guidelines concerning the digitisation of cultural content. MINERVA was created by a network of European Union (EU) Member States' Ministries to discuss, correlate and harmonise activities carried out in digitisation of cultural and scientific content for creating an agreed European common platform, recommendations and guidelines about digitisation, metadata, long-term accessibility and preservation. Due to the high level of commitment assured by the involvement of EU governments, it aims at coordinating national programs, and its approach is strongly based on the principle of embeddedness in national digitisation activities. The use of the MINERVA guidelines insures therefore the contacts with other European countries, international organisations, associations, networks, international and national projects involved in this sector.

The output of this activity is the digitised content. This content can exist independently from the creation of the e-service that uses it (like a repository) or will be used in the development activity. The other output is the revised version of the enriched specifications document in accordance to the problems and opportunities that the digitisation phase might bring to the surface.

System Interoperability Design

This activity is aimed at assuring the compatibility of the content generated across e-services. This activity takes as input the enriched systems specifications produced during digitisation and adjusts them for **interoperability**.

For this activity, we propose as input the adoption of the ISO 21127 standard (http://www.iso.org/). ISO 21127 is a domain ontology for cultural heritage information. As such, it is designed to be explanatory and extensible rather than prescriptive and restrictive. Currently, no specific formalism for semantic models has been widely accepted as standard, which is proven by the existence of the DACO used in the Incunabula case. However the semantic deviations between the various available models are minimal. We prefer at this stage

to recommend the use of ISO 21127 instead of the DACO as control since the DACOs are not recognised as a standard yet.

The ISO 21127 standard has been formulated as an object-oriented semantic model, which can easily be converted into other object-oriented models. This presentation format will be both natural and expressive for domain experts, and easily converted to other machine readable formats such as RDF (Resource Description Framework) and XML. Considerable effort has gone into achieving these goals; all cross-references and inheritance of properties, for example, are explicitly resolved. This has led to a certain degree of redundancy, but makes the document more readily comprehensible and facilitates its use as a reference document.

The standard is intended to cover all concepts relevant to cultural heritage information, but most particularly those needed for wide area data exchange between museums, libraries, and archives. Due to the diversity of the subject matter and the nature of cultural heritage collections, this goal can be achieved only by extensions to the standard. However, thanks to its object-oriented nature, the ontology offers a backbone of powerful general concepts, which have a wide application.

The primary purpose of ISO 21127 is to offer a conceptual basis for the mediation of information between cultural heritage organisations such as museums, libraries and archives. The standard aims at providing a common reference point against which divergent and incompatible sources of information can be compared and, ultimately, harmonised.

The organisational units involved are the cultural organisation and the technical project team. The reason why this cooperation is required is that this function is both technical – it will shape the technical development of the e-service – but is also highly connected to the conservation practices. Only the experts in the management of the cultural content can in fact specify how and what parts of the content would need to be shared.

The output of this function is the revised systems specification document complemented with the information about interoperability.

Cultural Content Organisation

In this function the content is organised. In particular the cultural organisation (the organisational unit) takes care of creating the descriptive data about the digitised material: the metadata. The description is based on the specification document and takes into consideration the interoperability needs specified in the previous functions.

The specific functions that we have identified in our survey of existing e-services are the following:

- Primary data registration and description of cultural objects. This data refers to basic identification information, classification, physical shape, condition, geographical location, construction date, application, properties and relation with other objects.
- Collection of the administrative information concerning the relevant collection and monument management. This information is the prerequisite for the management and documentation of monuments or objects which are part of a museum collection.
- Documentation information of digital products and processes. To this category belong the meta-data that concern the processes of digitisation, identification, quality and thematic content of the digitised material.
- Preservation information of the cultural content. This information refers to metadata for the long-term preservation of the digitised material.
- Publishing data of the cultural content. The digitised material is published in the Internet and is also stored in optical technology media (CD-ROMs, DVDs). The data included in this category aims at the educational use of the cultural digitised material and the effective creation of multilingual versions.

Considering these activities, and the revised specification document we recommend, as input, the use of the ICOM/CIDOC standards (see references 1, 2, and 3). The ICOM/CIDOC standards are the result of a joint effort across museums, archaeological sites, and other cultural initiatives to create internationally accepted guidelines for museum object information. Since the ICOM/CIDOC standards have been agreed by the cultural organisations their use should be straightforward.

The output of this function is the finalised requirements document containing functional, structural, and process specifications.

E-Service Development

Once the requirements have been collected, the material digitised, and the standards set, then the time for the actual e-service development arrives. We envision the e-service to be, as a starting point, of the kind presented in the Incunabula project: a complete, widely accessible, shared content of precious cultural material.

The e-service development can be regarded as a problem of information system development. In the particular case of cultural heritage e-services there are particular conditions that make them different in relation to the needs of traditional Web sites treated in the literature (Baskerville & Pries-Heje, 2004). The needs for quick adaptability and flexibility (ibid) do not apply in most cultural heritage cases where the data is stable and the user interfaces are also quite stable in time. The presentation of the artworks is also quite stable in time and it has achieved a quite agreed upon format. Furthermore the digitisation might involve very fragile artworks, besides being very complex and time consuming, and therefore it cannot be envisaged that the basic data coming from digitisation can be recreated multiple times.

The development should therefore not focus on rapid and continuous development but rather comply with the more traditional system development lifecycle focusing on long term usage: efficiency, reliability, low cost maintenance, and robust functionalities (Truex, Baskerville, & Klein, 1999). However, given that most e-services will be Web-based, some of the characteristics of Web sites can be used advantageously in cultural heritage services. The interface must be particularly cured as visitors are varied in age and education therefore particular attention to usability must be taken. Furthermore standards must be strictly respected as presented above since data might and should be used in multiple sites or in multiple ways in the same site. Being prepared to provide multiple views of the same digitised material will be a critical factor for the success of cultural heritage e-services over time because the development of views and interfaces will demand much less work compared to the digitisation of content. Finally, particular attention should be posed to scalability of e-services given the staggering quantity of material potentially available for display.

Our case and our survey show that for most e-services the first user group to be served are professionals. Serving professionals – with high requirements on the quality of the digitisation and on the metadata – is very good starting point because, for the reasons connect to the material explained above, it is easier to simplify a high-quality digitisation rather then re-digitise to add information.

We envision therefore at least a double loop development where - in a first instance – the cultural organisations and the professionals are served. Once professional e-services are created then a second loop of development can be carried out where other services are added for the wider public. The first loop uses as organisational unit the technical team, the cultural organisation and the professional users. The second loop uses the technical team and representatives of the public as organisational units in the first function.

The Input proposed for this activity is the ISO 9126 standard which is concerned primarily with the definition of quality characteristics to be used in the evaluation of software products. Using this standard as Input, should assure the quality of the e-service.

The resulting event of this activity is one or multiple cultural heritage e-services.

REFLECTION ON THE FRAMEWORK AND ISD METHODOLOGIES

The framework resembles at first sight a variation of the waterfall methodology for information system development. This impression is undoubtedly strengthened by the fact that the e-services for cultural heritage are indeed information systems. However the framework proposed in figure 15 does not propose a waterfall-like development, but rather shows the event-driven functions involved with their organisational units, inputs and outputs. The framework proposes the sequence of the project activities, in order to be comprehensive for the interested parties and also possible to be transformed to a Gantt chart. Therefore, project management is supported with a specific time dimension.

The order in which the functions are actually carried out during the project of e-service development should be decided contextually by the actors involved. Our research has pointed out the importance of user involvement where users are not only professionals but also and foremost laymen. Appealing to the wider laymen category will in fact ensure the long term interest in the e-service. Therefore the use of a process that contains iterations based on user testing is highly recommended.

CONCLUSION

The study of the existing initiatives of e-Government on cultural heritage shows that the different member states are pursuing the Lisbon strategy for i2010, but in different ways and at different paces. While some countries are more advanced than others, even for the leading ones it is difficult to speak about concerted action to create a one-stop site for cultural heritage being this at subject level (archaeology, graphical art, sculptures etc), local level, national level, or international level. While cooperation obviously exists among museums, ministries, universities and other institutions, this cooperation only very recently begins to be addressed seriously. While cultural organisations, research institutions and standard organisations have begun to create usable standards, one of the main issues that we have observed in an initial survey is the lack of a methodology that systematically integrates and adopts these standards.

The in depth examination of three case studies of e-services has pointed out four dimensions that are important to address when developing these services: **digitisation, requirements engineering, standardisation** and **interoperability**.

These dimensions have been linked to the existing standards to create a development framework which addresses both practical issues and future needs.

In our view the problem of advancement in the cataloguing and divulgation of electronic material does not reside in technology but in organisational traditions and cultures that, knowingly or unknowingly, might be retarding the process and in the recognition that electronic cataloguing and presentation of artwork is not locally limited (e.g. at museum or site). Politicians and administrators need to understand that to achieve the goals of i2010, cultural heritage needs to move from the physical place to the electronic space. We believe that this chapter provides a solid framework to achieve this goal. The proposed framework is easy to understand: based on ARIS; clear in its content and in the definition of what is needed, who is needed, what rules apply and what are the goals for each function. It provides, to the willing and open-minded team, the right guid-

ance – without being restrictive – towards the development of e-services for cultural heritage that are not only effective upon completion for a specific location but that will stay effective in the future and without borders if the standards for interoperability are respected.

This framework should be further examined in an action research environment where not only the framework should be put into use but the organisational conditions that characterise this type of projects could be studied, as well. This will allow us not only to validate the framework but also to study the condition under which the "cultural heritage e-service plan" (the primary input of the framework) is actually made.

REFERENCES

Abramson, M. A., & Means, G. E. (2001). E-Government 2001. *IBM Center for the Business of Government Series*, Rowman and Littlefield, Lanham.

Aquarelle (1999). *Sharing Cultural Heritage through Multimedia Telematics*. DGIII, ESPRIT Project 01/01/1996 - 31/12/1998.

Baskerville, R., & Pries-Heje, J. (2004). Short cycle time systems development. *Information Systems Journal, 14*(3), 237-265.

Carroll, J. M. (2001). Community computing as human – Computer interaction. *Behaviour & Information Technology, 20*(5), 307-314.

Coursey, D., & Killingsworth, J. (2000). Managing Government Web Services in Florida: Issues and Lessons. In D. Garson (Ed.), *Handbook of Public Information Systems*. New York: Marcel Dekker.

EU Report (2008). *Preparing Europe's digital future i2010 Mid-Term ReviewCOM*, 199, SEC(2008) 470 Volumes 1, 2, 3, April, ISBN 978-92-823-2434-9, European Communities.

Fountain, J. (2001). *Building the Virtual State:*

Information Technology and Institutional Change. Brookings Institution, Washington.

Fountain, J. (2003). Electronic Government and Electronic Civics. In B. Wellman(Ed.), *Encyclopedia of Community.* Great Barrington, Berkshire, 436– 441.

Ho, A.T.-K. (2002). Reinventing Local Governments and the E-Government Initiative. *Public Administration Review, 62*(4), 434–445.

Kiernan, K. S. (1981). *Beowulf and the Beowulf Manuscript.* Rutgers University Press, New Brunswick.

Klawe, M., & Shneiderman, B. (2005). Crisis and Opportunity in Computer Science. *Communications of the ACM,* November, *48*(11), 27-28.

Loebbecke, C., & Thaller, M. (2005). Preserving Europe's Cultural Heritage in the Digital World. *Proceedings of the European Conference on Information Systems (ECIS),* Regensburg, Germany, May.

Molich, R. (1999). *Bruger-venlige edb-systemer.* (in Danish) Teknisk Forlag, Copenhagen.

Moon, M.J. (2002). The Evolution of E-Government among Municipalities: Reality or Rhetoric? *Public Administration Review, 62*(4), 424–433.

Nielsen, J., & Landauer, T. K. (1993). A mathematical model of the finding of usability problems. *Proceedings of ACM INTERCHI'93 Conference,* Amsterdam, The Netherlands, 24-29 April, 206-213.

Nielsen, J. (2005). B-to-b users want sites with b-to-c service, ease. *B to B, 90*(7), 48.

Prescott A. (1997). The Electronic Beowulf and Digital Restoration, *Literary and Linguistic Computing, 12,* 185-195.

Scheer, A.-W., Kruppke, H., Jost, W., & Kindermann, H. (2006). *Agility by ARIS Business Process Management: Yearbook Business Pro-*

cess Excellence 2006/2007, X, 281 p. 125, ISBN: 978-3-540-33527-6.

Sen, S., Padmanabhan, B., & Tuzhilin, A. (1998). The Identification and Satisfaction of Consumer Analysis-Driven Information Needs of Marketers on the WWW. *European Journal of Marketing, 32* (7/8), 688-702.

Shi, Y., & Scavo, C. (2000). Citizen Participation and Direct Democracy through Computer Networking. In D. Garson (Ed.), *Handbook of Public Information Systems.* New York: Marcel Dekker.

Thomas, J. C., & Streib, G. (2003). The New Face of Government: Citizen-Initiated Contacts in the Era of E-Government. *Journal of Public Administration Research and Theory, 13*(1), 83–101.

Truex, D. P., Baskerville, R., & Klein, H. K. (1999). Growing Systems in Emergent Organisations. *Communications of the ACM, 42*(8), 117-123.

Yin, R. K. (2002). *Case Study Research, Design and Methods.* 3rd ed. Newbury Park, Sage.

West, D. M. (2004). E-Government and the Transformation of Service Delivery and Citizen Attitudes. *Public Administration Review, 64*(1), 15–27.

Web Sites Referenced (all Web Sites visited on 3/6/08)

Aquarelle Project, http://vcg.isti.cnr.it/projects/miscellanea/aquarelle/3Dvisual.presentation.html

Direzione Generale per i Beni Archeologici – Italy: Virtual visit of the Villa Adriana http://www.archeologia.beniculturali.it/pages/atlantearcheo/1_VAD/pano/Atla_Pano_VAD_08.html

The Louvre Museum, Paris, France: http://www.louvre.fr/

National Museum, Stockholm, Sweden: http://www.nationalmuseum.se/

Project Piero della Francesca: http://www.piero-dellafrancesca.it

Uffizi Gallery, Florence, Italy: http://www.uffizi.firenze.it

Ministries and Departments of Culture Visited (Web Sites Visited on 3/6/08)

Denmark: Kulturministeriet: http://www.kultur-ministeriet.dk/sw16739.asp (press release about the law on conservation of cultural heritage through digitisation in Denmark)

France: Ministère de la Culture et de la Communication : http://www.culture.fr/ (specific site dedicated to cultural activities)

Greece: Hellenic Ministry of Culture: http://www.culture.gr/

Ireland: The Department of Arts, Sport and Tourism: http://www.arts-sport-tourism.gov.ie/

Italy: Ministero per i Beni e le Attività Culturali: http://www.beniculturali.it/

Spain: Ministerio de Educación y Ciencia: http://wwwn.mec.es/index.html

United Kingdom: Department for Culture, Media, and Sport: http://www.culture.gov.uk/

References for the Cultural Content Section (Web Sites Visited on 3/6/08)

CIDOC, Paris, 1995, ISBN 92-9012-125-4. http://cidoc.mediahost.org/publication(en)(E1).xml#icom

DIG35 Metadata Specification Version 1.1, Digital Imaging Group http://www.i3a.org/

Digital Preservation Coalition Handbook http://www.dpconline.org/graphics/handbook/

Draft International Core Data Standard for Archaeological Sites and Monuments, ICOM/

Encoded Archival Description (EAD) Version 2002, Society of American Archivists and the Library of Congress. http://www.loc.gov/ead/

IEEE Final 1484.12.1-2002 LOM Draft Standard for Learning Object Metadata http://ltsc.ieee.org/wg12/20020612-Final-LOM-Draft.html

International guidelines for museum object information: the CIDOC information categories, ICOM/CIDOC, Paris, 1995. ISBN 92-9012-124-6.

International Core Data Standard for Ethnology/Ethnography, ICOM/CIDOC, Paris, 1996, ISBN 960-214-012-7. http://cidoc.mediahost.org/publication(en)(E1).xml

Metadata Standards for Museum Cataloguing http://www.chin.gc.ca/English/Standards/metadata_description.html

A Metadata Framework to Support the Preservation of Digital Objects, OCLC/RLG Working Group on Preservation metadata. http://www.oclc.org/research/projects/pmwg/pm_framework.pdf

MIDAS: A manual and Data Standard for Monument Inventories. http://www.english-heritage.org.uk/upload/pdf/MIDAS3rdReprint.pdf

MPEG7 multimedia content description, ISO/IEC TR 15938-8:2002 http://www.iec.ch/cgi-bin/get-corr.pl/isoiec15938-8-cor1%7Bed1.0%7Den.pdf?file=isoiec15938-8-cor1%7Bed1.0%7Den.pdf

OpenGIS Reference Model (Kurt Buehler, ed.), Open GIS Consortium Inc., Ref. No. OGC 03-040 Ver. 0.1.2 http://www.opengeospatial.org/standards

Sharable Content Object Reference Model (SCORM), http://www.adlnet.gov/scorm/index.aspx

SPECTRUM: The UK Museum Documentation Standard, 2nd edition, Museum Documentation Association, Cambridge, United Kingdom http://

www.mda.org.uk/spectrum.htm

Text Encoding Initiative (TEI) http://www.tei-c.org/

Translation Memory eXchange format (TMX), OSCAR Recommendation, Localisation Industry Standards Association, 2004. http://www.lisa.

Chapter III
From Beliefs to Success:
Utilizing an Expanded TAM to Predict Web Page Development Success

Samantha Bax
Murdoch University, Australia

Tanya McGill
Murdoch University, Australia

ABSTRACT

The technology acceptance model (TAM) is a popular model for the prediction of information systems acceptance behaviors, defining a causal linkage between beliefs, attitudes, intentions, and the usage of information technologies. Since its inception, numerous studies have utilized the TAM, providing empirical support for the model in both traditional and Internet-based computing settings. This chapter describes a research study that utilizes an adaptation of the TAM to predict successful Web page development, as an introduction of the TAM to a new domain, and the testing of a new dependent variable within the model. The study found some evidence to support the use of the TAM as a starting point for the prediction of Web development success, finding causal linkages between the belief constructs and the attitude constructs, and the intent construct and the successful development of Web pages. However, additional research is required to further study the expanded model introduced within this chapter.

INTRODUCTION

The TAM is a well-established model for the prediction of information systems usage. However, despite a number of studies being conducted with the Internet as a research domain (e.g. Chen, Gillenson, & Sherrell, 2002; Childers, Carr, Peck, & Carson, 2001; Halawi & McCarthy, 2007; Heinrichs, Lim, & S., 2007; Klopping & McKinney, 2004; Lim, Lim, & Heinrichs, 2005; Magal & Mirchandani, 2001; Saade, Nebebe, & Tan, 2007), very few of these studies consider more than the usage of Internet technologies. We propose that this research should be extended to the domain of Web page development, as this activity forms a critical component of the Internet and its usage. Furthermore, Web page development is increasingly becoming a large part of the information technology activities of organizations (Taylor, Mc-William, Forsythe, & Wade, 2002), and concerns have been raised about the increasing numbers of individuals who create Web pages without sufficient skills to do so (Gellerson & Gaedke, 1999). However, very little research has focused on the success of these applications or factors which may influence their success. The study described in this paper uses an adaptation of the TAM to investigate the relationships between an individual's beliefs, attitudes, intentions and their subsequent success, as an attempt to ascertain whether these factors can be used to predict the success of Web application development.

The Technology Acceptance Model

Davis's (1989) TAM is grounded in the theoretical underpinnings of the theory of reasoned action (TRA)(Fishbein & Ajzen, 1975). The TRA asserts that an individual's actual behavior is linked to their beliefs, attitudes, and intentions to perform that behavior; such that an individual's beliefs toward a particular action, influences their attitudes (or "general feeling[s] of favorableness or unfavorableness" (Fishbein & Ajzen, 1975, p. 216)) toward that action. These attitudes then influence their intention to perform that action, which finally affects their undertaking of that particular action (Fishbein & Ajzen, 1975).

The TAM refines the TRA in order to model the user acceptance of information systems (Davis, Bagozzi, & Warshaw, 1989). This model has since been declared as "one of the most influential

Figure 1. The technology acceptance model (TAM) (adapted from Davis, Bagozzi, and Warshaw (1989))

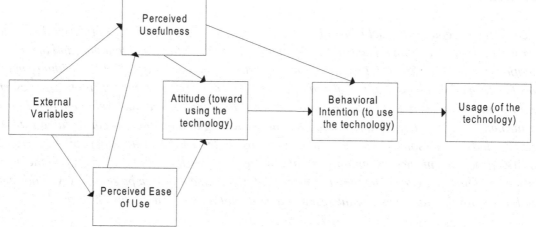

research models in studying the determinants of IT usage" (Chau, 2001, p. 26). It has also been important in the theorizing of the causal linkages between external factors, internal beliefs, attitudes and behavioral intentions (Davis, Bagozzi, & Warshaw, 1989). The TAM is presented in Figure 1.

Guided by previous research in the field identifying determinants of information technology acceptance (e.g. DeSanctis, 1983; Robey, 1979; Schultz & Slevin, 1975; Swanson, 1987), the TAM utilizes the two variables of perceived usefulness and perceived ease of use as determinants of an individual's attitude toward using a particular technology. These two variables form the belief constructs within the TAM (Davis, Bagozzi, & Warshaw, 1989). Perceived usefulness has been defined as "the degree to which a person believes that using a particular system would enhance his or her job performance"(Davis, 1989, p. 320); whilst perceived ease of use is defined as "the degree to which a person believes that using a particular system would be free of effort" (Davis, 1989, p. 320). These two factors are theorized to be the fundamental variables in the prediction of information technology acceptance (Davis, Bagozzi, & Warshaw, 1989).

The attitude construct within the TAM pertains to an individual's attitude toward using a particular information technology, whilst the intention construct refers to the individual's intention to use the technology in question, and the behavioral construct concerns the actual usage of the information system (Davis, Bagozzi, & Warshaw, 1989). Therefore, the TAM states that an individual's acceptance of an information technology is dependent on their beliefs about the usefulness and ease of use of the technology; which in turn influences their attitudes toward using, and then intentions to use that technology. The intention to use is then causally linked to the individual's actual usage of a particular information technology.

Studies Involving the TAM

Numerous studies of the predicted relationships within the TAM have been conducted in traditional as well as Internet computing environments. These studies have obtained valid and reliable empirical support for the model in both computing settings (e.g. Adams, Nelson, & Todd, 1992; Chen, Gillenson, & Sherrell, 2002; Childers, Carr, Peck, & Carson, 2001; Gardner & Amoroso, 2004; Halawi & McCarthy, 2007; Heinrichs, Lim, & S., 2007; Klopping & McKinney, 2004; Lederer, Maupin, Sena, & Zhuang, 2000; Magal & Mirchandani, 2001; Moon & Kim, 2001; Saade, Nebebe, & Tan, 2007; Seyal, Rahman, & Rahim, 2002; Teo, Lim, & Lai, 1999; Venkatesh & Davis, 1994, 1996) . However, despite the large number of studies, few have utilized a dependent variable other than that of system usage.

As described previously, the TAM has been "specifically tailored for modeling [the] user acceptance of information systems" (Davis, Bagozzi, & Warshaw, 1989 p. 985), a measure of an information system's success (Mason, 1978). However, Mason (1978) has identified a number of other measures of information system success, including: user satisfaction, organizational impact, system quality and information quality. Each of these constructs have been studied (e.g. DeLone & McLean, 1992; Guimaraes & Igbaria, 1997; Igbaria, Guimaraes, & Davis, 1995; Igbaria & Tan, 1997; McGill, Hobbs, & Klobas, 2003), however, there has been little research on how these constructs might relate to the user acceptance modeled in TAM. In addition, the investigation of the relationship between behavior and objective outcome measures such as performance and quality within the TAM, is an issue which has been noted as requiring further study (Simon, Grover, Teng, & Whitcomb, 1996)

Furthermore, despite studies being conducted utilizing the Internet (e.g.Chen, Gillenson, & Sherrell, 2002; Childers, Carr, Peck, & Carson, 2001; Halawi & McCarthy, 2007; Heinrichs, Lim,

& S., 2007; Klopping & McKinney, 2004; Lim, Lim, & Heinrichs, 2005; Magal & Mirchandani, 2001; Saade, Nebebe, & Tan, 2007), few of these do more than consider the usage of the technology (Lim, Lim, & Heinrichs, 2005). We propose that studies should also be conducted on the development of Web pages, a critical component of the Internet, which determines a great deal of its usage. Furthermore, Web page development is playing an increasing role in organizational application development activities (Goupil, 2000; Nelson & Todd, 1999; Taylor, McWilliam, Forsythe, & Wade, 2002). However, of particular concern is that Web development activity is predominantly undertaken on an ad hoc basis (Gellerson & Gaedke, 1999; Russo & Graham, 1998; Wiegers, 1999), with most current Web development procedures relying purely on the expertise of the individual developer (Gellerson & Gaedke, 1999), which may be inadequate for the tasks at hand.

Taylor et al (2002 p. 390) warns that: "without appropriate Web site design techniques…there is the real risk that overly complicated and messy Web sites will be developed" leading to the failure of these information systems. However, little is yet known about what influences people to learn the skills necessary in order to create quality Web pages. Nor is much known about what factors affect an individual's success at Web page creation. The TAM is suggested as a starting point for these investigations into Web page development and Web page development success.

THE RESEARCH MODEL

Studies involving the TAM have consistently demonstrated that perceived usefulness is associated with the use of technologies (e.g. Adams, Nelson, & Todd, 1992; Venkatesh & Davis, 1994, , 1996). The level of usage of technologies has also been proposed to influence the success of an information system (DeLone & McLean, 1992). There have also been several proposed

extensions to the TAM that include performance or information systems success as the dependent variable (e.g. Dishaw & Strong, 1999; Lucas & Spitler, 1999). This study proposes and tests an extended TAM that incorporates the construct of Web development success to test the applicability of the TAM in the prediction of successful Web page development.

The model developed for this study is grounded in the theories that underlie the TAM. Similar to the TAM, our model identifies a causal linkage between an individual's beliefs, attitudes, intentions and behaviors. However, the current research model considers beliefs and attitudes toward using computer and Internet technologies as independent constructs. In line with the TAM (see Figure 1), this study also introduces several demographic and related variables as antecedents to both computer-usage and Internet-usage related beliefs. This is in accordance with Davis's (1993) recommendation that external variables should be investigated as determinants of information technology beliefs. The variables chosen for this study include: age, gender, computer experience, Internet experience, computer training and Internet training.

The self-efficacy construct, as a measure of "an individual's perceptions of his or her ability to use computers in the accomplishment of a task" (Compeau & Higgins, 1995, p. 191) is included as a belief construct, in the research model. This construct was first mentioned in relation to the TAM as one of two basic mechanisms through which attitudinal and behavioral intentions are influenced (Davis, Bagozzi, & Warshaw, 1989). Since then, many studies have included the self-efficacy construct in their investigations of the TAM, in both traditional and Internet environments (Chau, 2001; Compeau & Higgins, 1995; Fenech, 1998; Igbaria & Iivari, 1995; Torkzadeh & Van Dyke, 2002; Venkatesh & Davis, 1996). From a consideration of these studies, it is apparent that an individual's self-efficacy (or self-confidence in their skills), is an important determinant of their attitudes toward using technology, and thus, a determinant of their actual behavior. Both computer self-efficacy and Internet self-efficacy are therefore included within the research model.

Perceived computer usefulness and perceived Internet usefulness are incorporated within the model directly from the TAM. These constructs as well as the computer and Internet self-efficacy constructs represent the beliefs of an individual which are considered to influence their attitudes toward using both information technologies. Research on the role of perceived ease of use in the TAM has been mixed. Whilst there is consensus about its influence on perceived usefulness, a number of studies have found that perceived ease of use has little direct effect on information technology acceptance (e.g. Subramanian, 1994; Venkatesh & Davis, 1996). "One interpretation is that as systems become easier to use and users become more technologically savvy, the variation in the perceived ease of use dimension is reduced" (Klopping & McKinney, 2004, p.42-43). Ma and Liu (2004) undertook a meta-analysis of research on the TAM and have concluded that the relationship between ease of use and acceptance is weak, and as such does not pass the fail-safe test. Therefore, the ease of use construct was not included in the research model.

The intent construct of the research model refers to an individual's intention to learn Web development skills. As such, it represents an individual's intention to succeed at Web page development. The behavior construct of this model is Web development success, or an individual's success at developing Web pages. This construct is considered to consist of aspects of the system quality, as well as the information quality of developed Web pages, and thus should form an sufficient measure of Web page development success. The research model is presented as Figure 2.

RESEARCH QUESTIONS AND HYPOTHESES

The following research questions and hypotheses follow from the model presented in Figure 2 and the theories which underlie it.

RQ1: How do an individual's background characteristics affect their beliefs toward a particular information technology?

Figure 2. The research model

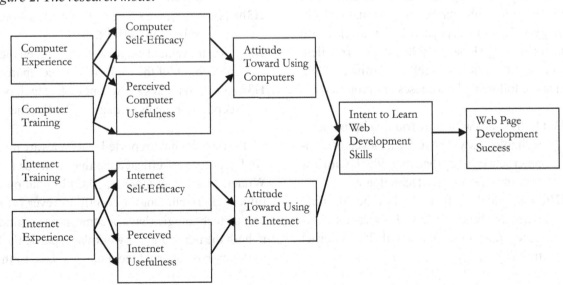

There is evidence to suggest that greater experience with a particular information technology is related to a more positive set of beliefs in relation to that technology (e.g. Al-Jabri & Al-Khaldi, 1997; Igbaria & Iivari, 1995; Liaw, 2002; Orr, Allen, & Poindexter, 2001). The following hypotheses are thus proposed:

H1a: Individuals with more experience with computers will have higher levels of computer self-efficacy than individuals with less computer experience

H1b: Individuals with more experience with the Internet will have higher levels of Internet self-efficacy than individuals with less Internet experience

H1c: Individuals with more experience with computers will have higher levels of perceived computer usefulness than individuals with less computer experience

H1d: Individuals with more experience with the Internet will have higher levels of perceived Internet usefulness than individuals with less Internet experience.

Evidence also suggests that individuals with more training with a particular information technology will have more positive beliefs in relation to that technology (Igbaria, 1990, , 1993; Orr, Allen, & Poindexter, 2001; Rozzell & Gardner, 1999). Thus the following hypotheses are proposed:

H2a: Individuals with more training in computer technologies will have higher levels of computer self-efficacy than individuals with less training in computer technologies

H2b: Individuals with more Internet training will have higher levels of Internet self-efficacy than individuals with less Internet training

H2c: Individuals with more training in computer technologies will have higher levels of perceived computer usefulness than individuals with less computer training

H2d: Individuals with more Internet training will have higher levels of perceived Internet usefulness than individuals with less Internet training

Whilst age and gender are not proposed to influence Web page development success, two sets of null hypotheses have been proposed to enable the confirmation of these proposals. These are presented within the following section.

Studies in the past have noted a distinction between older and younger individuals in regards to their beliefs toward information technologies, suggesting that younger individuals have more positive beliefs in relation to computer technologies than their older counterparts (Harrison & Rainer, 1992; Igbaria, 1993). However, due to the pervasiveness of computers and also that of Internet technologies, this age distinction has become less evident (e.g. Parish & Necessary, 1996). Therefore the following hypotheses are proposed:

H3a: An individual's age will not affect their level of computer self-efficacy

H3b: An individual's age will not affect their level of Internet self-efficacy

H3c: An individual's age will not affect their perception of the usefulness of computers

H3d: An individual's age will not affect their perception of the usefulness of the Internet.

Past studies have reported that males are more confident (or self-efficacious) than females (e.g. Wilder, Mackie, & Cooper, 1985) in relation to information technology. Recently however, information technologies have become more common in both the home and the workplace, particularly in the case of Internet technologies. Due to this factor, the gender distinction has largely disappeared (e.g. Parish & Necessary, 1996). Thus, the following hypotheses are proposed:

H4a: An individual's gender will not affect their level of computer self-efficacy

H4b: An individual's gender will not affect their level of Internet self-efficacy

H4c: An individual's gender will not affect their perception of the usefulness of computers

H4d: An individual's gender will not affect their perception of the usefulness of the Internet.

RQ2: How do an individual's information technology related beliefs affect their attitudes toward using a particular information technology?

The following set of hypotheses is drawn directly from the theories that underlie the TAM. The relationships link an individual's beliefs directly to their attitudes toward using a particular technology:

H5a: Individuals with higher levels of computer self-efficacy will have more positive attitudes toward using computers.

H5b: Individuals with higher levels of Internet self-efficacy will have more positive attitudes toward using the Internet.

H5c: Individuals with higher levels of perceived usefulness of computers will have more positive attitudes toward using computers.

H5d: Individuals with higher levels of perceived usefulness of the Internet will have more positive attitudes toward using the Internet.

RQ3: How do an individual's attitudes toward using a particular information technology affect their intent to learn to perform successfully with that particular information technology?

The following two hypotheses are adapted from the theories underlying the TAM, whereby an individual's intention to perform a particular behavior is governed by his or her attitude toward that behavior (Fishbein & Ajzen, 1975). In this case the behaviour in question is the usage of computer and Internet technologies and the following hypotheses are proposed:

H6a: Individuals with more positive attitudes toward using computers will exhibit higher levels of intent to learn Web development skills.

H6b: Individuals with more positive attitudes toward using the Internet will exhibit higher levels of intent to learn Web development skills.

RQ4: How does an individual's intention to learn to perform successfully with a particular information technology affect their successful performance with that particular information technology?

The following hypothesis is adapted from the theories underpinning the TAM, whereby an individual's intention to perform a particular behavior, is related to his or her actual completion of that behavior (Ajzen 1985; Fishbein & Ajzen 1975). Ajzen has stated that in the majority of cases, individuals are observed to act consistently with their intentions in a variety of situations (1985). Thus the following hypothesis is proposed:

H7a: Individuals, who have higher levels of intent to learn Web development skills, will exhibit higher levels of Web development success.

THE RESEARCH DESIGN

Research Procedure

The study was conducted with students taking part in an introductory Internet and Web development course. The students in this course, possessed a wide range of backgrounds in terms of computer and Internet usage; as well as Web development. The research data was collected primarily by means of a questionnaire administered during the first lecture of the course. The questionnaire collected information relating to the background characteristics of participants, as well as information relating to their beliefs and attitudes toward using both computers and the Internet. Additional data was collected by the evaluation of Web pages developed by the participants, and also of students' attendance at the course tutorials.

The research sample and environment was essentially one of convenience. However, its major strength is in the availability of a consistent measure of Web development success that could be used to compare all individuals within the research sample. Such a consistent measure would not ordinarily be available in the more generalizable setting of the workplace. Thus, the use of the chosen research sample and environment brings a high level of internal validity to the research undertaken.

It was stressed that participation in the research project was voluntary and that the study formed no part of their assessment. The questionnaire was distributed to 280 students and 193 responses were received (a response rate of 68.9%). Of those who responded, 143 students were noted as attending the course's tutorials, and 154 of the original sample were noted as having undertaken the final Web page development assignment.

Operationalization of Constructs

In order to ensure construct validity within this study, every effort was made to utilize well-vali-dated measures that were shown to be reliable within previous studies. See Appendix 1 for a copy of the questionnaire items.

Computer and Internet experience were measured as the number of years that an individual had been using the relevant technology. An individual's level of training with both computers and the Internet was measured using self-report measures, which comprised of 7-point scales where (1) indicated no training and (7) indicated an extensive amount of training. Training for each of the technologies was measured with separate scales for both formal training and self-administered training. These measures were then summed for a measure of the individual's total training in each technology.

The computer related belief and attitude constructs were measured using three subscales of Loyd and Gressard's (1984) Computer Attitude Scale (CAS). Computer self-efficacy was measured using the computer confidence subscale, consisting of items 11-20 of the CAS (with a Cronbach's alpha of 0.96). Perceived computer usefulness was measured using the usefulness subscale, consisting of items 31-40 of the CAS (with a Cronbach's alpha of 0.93). Attitude toward using computers was measured using the computer liking subscale, consisting of items 21-30 of the CAS (with a Cronbach's alpha of 0.95).

The belief and attitude constructs relating to the Internet were measured using three subscales of Liaw's (2002) Web Attitude Scale (WAS). Internet self-efficacy was measured using the Web self-efficacy subscale, consisting of items 1-4 of the WAS (with a Cronbach's alpha of 0.93). Perceived Internet usefulness was measured using the Web usefulness subscale, consisting of items 9-12 of the WAS (with a Cronbach's alpha of 0.85). Attitude toward using the Internet was measured using the Web liking subscale, consisting of items 5-8 of the WAS (with a Cronbach's alpha of 0.83). All of the six subscales used to measure computer and Internet beliefs and attitudes were shown to be reliable with Cronbach alphas of above 0.70 as suggested by Nunally (1978).

Intent to learn Web development skills was measured by utilizing an individual's voluntary tutorial attendance (out of a possible 12), as recorded by the tutors during class time. This score forms a surrogate measure for an individual's intent to successfully create Web pages. The skills required to create quality Web pages were predominantly taught during these classes. Thus if a student intends to perform successfully in the development of Web pages, it is likely that he or she will attend more tutorials in order to better learn these skills.

Web page development success was measured using the participants' mark on the final Web page development assignment. The assignment consisted of the creation of a set of linked Web pages in basic XHTML. Marks were allocated for content (e.g. meeting requirements, clarity of information provided), design features (e.g. use of color, text and images) These factors mirror those of Klopping and McKinney who suggest that "information is sufficiently detailed…information is obvious, accurate, and easy to find…is current, readable, and understandable" as the objectives of a successful Web site (2004, pp. 44). Further, factors relating to the coding of the Web page (e.g. layout, commenting and the ability to pass basic code validators) were also considered. Therefore these factors were chosen as measures relating to the system and/or information quality of the Web pages, and thus, forming an operational measure of Web page development success.

RESULTS AND DISCUSSION

The summarized results of the descriptive analysis of the research variables and constructs are presented in Table 1, and discussed in the following section.

The final research sample consisted of 193 individuals of whom 138 (71.5%) were male, and 55 (28.5%) were female. The ages of the participants ranged from 17 years of age to 52 years of age, with the average age being 22 years of age. The participants' experience with computers ranged from several months to a number of years, with the average amount of experience being 8.5 years. Experience with the Internet ranged from no experience at all, to 11 years of Internet use. The average amount of Internet experience was 4.5 years. In terms of computer training, on average relatively high levels (above mid-level) of training were reported, with an average of 8.38 out of a possible 14. Internet training was also reported to be above mid-level, averaging 7.52 out of a possible 14.

The participants expressed generally positive beliefs toward using both computers and the Internet. Computer self-efficacy was scored highly, with the mean of all scores being 38.1 out of 50, and computers were also perceived to be very useful, with an average score of 40.6 out of 50. A similar pattern was noted in terms of Internet technologies. Internet self-efficacy scores resulted in a mean of 17.3 out of 20, whilst perceived usefulness of the Internet was on average 17.1 out of 20.

The research participants also expressed attitudes toward using computers and the Internet that were positive. On average the attitude toward using computers score was 35.4 out of 50, whilst the average attitude toward using the Internet score was 15.8 out of 20.

The measure of intent to learn Web development skills averaged 7.82 out of a possible 12 (i.e. on average participants attended between seven and eight of the twelve tutorials). The Web development success score was on average 38.1 out of a possible 100.

Hypothesis Testing

Path analysis using Ordinary Least Squares hierarchical multiple regression was performed to test the proposed hypotheses. The results are shown in Table 2, and discussed in the following section.

Table 1. Summary of descriptive statistics for external variables and model constructs

	Number	Mean	Standard Deviation	Minimum	Maximum
Background Variables					
Computing Experience (yrs)	184	8.55	4.60	0.58	30.00
Internet Experience (yrs)	187	4.50	2.08	0.00	11.00
Computer Training (/14)	193	8.37	2.39	3.00	14.00
Internet Training (/14)	192	7.52	2.53	2.00	14.00
Age (yrs)	192	22.39	6.94	17.00	52.00
Belief Constructs					
Computer Self-Efficacy	193	38.11	8.70	12.00	50.00
Perceived Computer Usefulness	190	40.61	8.31	4.00	50.00
Internet Self-Efficacy	188	17.30	3.08	5.00	20.00
Perceived Internet Usefulness	188	17.05	2.82	5.00	20.00
Attitude Constructs					
Attitude toward using Computers	191	35.35	9.47	9.00	50.00
Attitude toward using the Internet	188	15.82	3.31	4.00	20.00
Intent Construct					
Intent to Learn Web Development Skills (/12)	143	7.82	4.07	0.00	12.00
Success Construct					
Web Development Success Score (/100)	154	38.12	31.14	0.00	86.00

Computer experience was significantly related to computer self-efficacy (β=0.160, p=0.016), confirming hypothesis H1a. Similarly, Internet experience was found to be significantly related to Internet self-efficacy (β=0.280, p=0.000), providing support for hypothesis H1b. However, computer experience was not found to be significantly related to perceived computer usefulness, and thus, hypothesis H1c was not supported. Hypothesis H1d was supported with Internet experience found to be significantly related to perceived Internet usefulness (β=0.311, p=0.000).

The non-significant result between computer experience and perceived computer usefulness contradicts the findings of previous studies, (e.g. Al-Jabri & Al-Khaldi, 1997; Igbaria & Iivari, 1995; Liaw, 2002; Orr, Allen, & Poindexter, 2001), which found that increased experience with a technol-

ogy was associated with more positive beliefs toward using it. This contradictory result may be related to the operationalization of experience as length of time of use, without consideration of the frequency or duration of computer usage. Consideration of the frequency and duration of usage may have allowed for a better measure of the experience variable. Further research is required to study these alternative measures of experience in terms of their relationships to an individual's information technology related beliefs.

A significant relationship was found between computer-related training and computer self-efficacy (β=0.424, p=0.000), as predicted by hypothesis H2a. Similarly, Internet-related training was found to be significantly related to Internet self-efficacy (β=0.171, p=0.026), in accordance with hypothesis H2b. However, computer-related

Table 2. Summary of path analysis results (Note: Gender was coded as male = 1 and female = 2)

PATH			
From	**To**	**Coefficient**	**Probability**
Computer Experience	Computer Self-Efficacy	0.160	0.016
Computer Training	Computer Self-Efficacy	0.424	0.000
Age	Computer Self-Efficacy	0.075	0.236
Gender	Computer Self-Efficacy	-0.305	0.000
R²	0.385		
Computer Experience	Perceived Computer Usefulness	0.095	0.233
Computer Training	Perceived Computer Usefulness	0.112	0.163
Age	Perceived Computer Usefulness	0.049	0.521
Gender	Perceived Computer Usefulness	-0.297	0.000
R²	0.129		
Internet Experience	Internet Self-Efficacy	0.280	0.000
Internet Training	Internet Self-Efficacy	0.171	0.026
Age	Internet Self-Efficacy	-0.045	0.537
Gender	Internet Self-Efficacy	-0.024	0.734
R²	0.148		
Internet Experience	Perceived Internet Usefulness	0.311	0.000
Internet Training	Perceived Internet Usefulness	0.066	0.393
Age	Perceived Internet Usefulness	0.017	0.819
Gender	Perceived Internet Usefulness	-0.133	0.061
R²	0.132		
Computer Self-Efficacy	Attitude toward using Computers	0.578	0.000
Perceived Computer Usefulness	Attitude toward using Computers	0.319	0.000
R²	**0.654**		
Internet Self-Efficacy	Attitude toward using the Internet	0.346	0.000
Perceived Internet Usefulness	Attitude toward using the Internet	0.465	0.000
R²	**0.620**		
Attitude toward using Computers	Intent to Learn Web Development Skills	-0.362	0.011
Attitude toward using the Internet	Intent to Learn Web Development Skills	0.195	0.176
R²	**0.113**		
Intent to Learn Web Development Skills	Web Development Success	0.440	0.000
R²	**0.314**		

training was not significantly related to perceived computer usefulness; and neither was Internet-related training related to perceived Internet usefulness. Thus, hypotheses H2c and H2d were not supported. This result does not conform to other previous studies (Igbaria, 1990, , 1993; Orr, Allen, & Poindexter, 2001; Rozzell & Gardner, 1999), which found that increased levels of training are associated with more positive beliefs. These inconsistent results suggest that although training may increase an individual's self confidence in their skills, training alone does not contribute to an individual perceiving a technology to be more or less useful than any other technology. It may also be possible that computer-related technologies are currently so pervasive that that they are considered to be useful by the general population, regardless of the amount of experience or training that an individual may have. However, further research should attempt to better understand these relationships.

An individual's age was not found to be significantly related to any of the belief constructs within the research model, providing support for hypotheses H3a-d. Significant relationships were found between gender and computer self-efficacy (β=-0.305, p=0.000) and also gender and perceived computer usefulness (β=-0.297, p=0.000), indicating that females are still less confident and less convinced of the usefulness of computers than males are (Sun & Zhang, 2006b), contradicting hypotheses H4a and H4c. However, no significant relationship was noted between gender and Internet self-efficacy, or gender and perceived Internet usefulness, in accordance with hypotheses H4b and H4d. This finding indicates that in terms of pervasive Internet technologies, gender differences in self-confidence and perceptions of the usefulness of these particular computer systems have largely dissipated.

Computer self-efficacy was found to be significantly related to attitudes toward using computers (β=0.578, p=0.000), as predicted by hypothesis H5a. A significant relationship was also found

between perceived computer usefulness and attitudes toward using computers (β=0.319, p=0.000), providing support for hypothesis H5b. Similarly, significant relationships were found between Internet self-efficacy and attitudes toward using the Internet (β=0.346, p=0.000) and between perceived Internet usefulness and attitudes toward using the Internet (β=0.465, p=0.000) consistent with hypotheses H5c and H5d. All of these findings are consistent with the theories that underlie the TAM.

A significant, but negative relationship was found between attitudes toward using computers and the intent construct (β=-0.362, p=0.011); however, this relationship is in the opposite direction to that predicted, and thus hypothesis H6a is not supported. This finding suggests (in consideration of the theories underlying the TAM) that an individual with more negative attitudes toward using computers will intend to learn Web development skills to a greater degree than an individual with more positive attitudes toward using computer technologies. This relationship may exist because individuals who feel unfavorably toward using computers may not feel that they have the necessary skills to easily pass a Web development course, and thus attend more tutorials to gain the necessary skills to perform well within this environment.

No significant relationship was identified between attitudes toward using the Internet and the intent construct. Thus, no support was found for hypothesis H6b. This contradicts the relationship predicted by the theories underlying the TAM, and implies that regardless of whether an individual feels favorably or unfavorably toward using the Internet, there is no association between that attitude and his or her intention to succeed within a Web development environment. This could be explained if there is a distinction between attitudes toward using the Internet as a source of information and entertainment and attitudes toward using it for Web page development activities. Attitudes toward Web development might therefore be a more useful construct than attitudes toward using the Internet within this context. Another explanation for this finding, might be that because the Internet is such a pervasive technology, individuals already have gained some Web development skills prior to enrolling in the Web development course, and thus may not consider that they need to attend the tutorials to learn Web development skills. Therefore, regardless of their attitude, an individual may not believe that he or she needs to attend the course's tutorials, as they believe that they already have the skills they need to be successful. Furthermore, additional factors (and in particular affectual constructs) may in fact play a role in the determination of the intent construct. This is an area which has received very little attention in the past (Sun & Zhang, 2008).

A final explanation for the lack of support for the relationships hypothesized in H6a and H6b may come from the operationalization of the intent construct. In hindsight, it can be questioned whether tutorial attendance is a good indication of the intent to learn Web development skills. Participants had access to online teaching materials and may have exhibited intent to learn outside the traditional classroom environment.

Intent to learn Web development skills was found to be significantly related to Web development success (β= 0.440, p= 0.000). This suggests that the greater the intention to learn Web development skills (i.e.: the more tutorials that an individual attends) the more successful that individual will be in developing Web pages. This provides support for hypothesis H7a, and also provides support for the theories underlying the TAM. However, given the concern expressed about the operationalization of the intent construct, this result must be treated with a degree of caution. The relationships discussed in the preceding section are illustrated as a path diagram, presented in Figure 3.

The Research Model

The following section analyses the predictive power of each of the constructs within the research model, as indicated by the R^2 reported in Table 2.

The external variables proposed as influencing the belief constructs within the research model were found to explain a moderate amount of the variance in computer self-efficacy, with an R^2

Figure 3. Path diagram of the research model showing strengths of individual paths

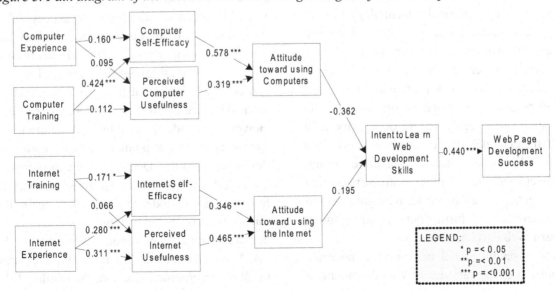

value of 38.5% (i.e.: 38.5% of the variability in self-efficacy was explained by the external variables present within the research model). However, the variables only explained a small proportion of the variability of the constructs of perceived computer usefulness (12.9%), Internet self-efficacy (14.8%) and perceived Internet usefulness (13.2%). This suggests that additional variables not included within the current model also directly influence the belief constructs.

The research model was found to explain a high proportion of the variance in computer and Internet attitudes with R^2 values of 65.4% and 62.0% respectively. However, the model only explained a small proportion of the variance in the intent construct (intention to learn Web development skills), resulting in an R^2 value of 11.3%. This result may be indicative of the weak operationalization of the intent construct as discussed within the previous section, and thus, further research is required to test the relationship between attitude, intent and success.

However, recent research, have reported the construct of perceived enjoyment as having a significant and direct influence on behavioral intention (Atkitson & Kydd, 1997; Sun & Zhang, 2006a; Sun & Zhang, 2008; Van der Heijden, 2004). Perceived enjoyment is said to refer to an individual's perception of receiving pleasure from the act of using a particular technology (Sun & Zhang, 2006a; Sun & Zhang, 2008), and thus can be deemed an attitude. The enjoyment construct can be easily perceived as acting through computer and Internet technologies, particularly in the case of Web page development activities, which could be considered a highly hedonistic activity, as it is often a personal activity, and one that is often self-fullfilling in its own action. Therefore, extending the current research model with the perceived enjoyment construct should be investigated within future research as a further determinant of intent to learn Web development skills.

The research model explained a moderate proportion of the variance in Web development

success, with a R^2 value of 31.4%. This result suggests that there are additional constructs that may also directly influence Web development success. These constructs may include: cognitive ability (Simon, Grover, Teng, & Whitcomb, 1996) and prior Web development experience. There is also the possibility that mechanisms other than that of beliefs and attitudes may exist through which success is influenced. Whilst the TAM suggests that the influence of external variables on behavior is mediated through beliefs, studies have shown that user characteristics have a direct influence on performance (e.g. Hubona & Cheney, 1994). Future research should test an expanded research model that considers additional constructs and explores these possible direct effects. A student-learning model such as Biggs' (2003) 3P model of teaching learning might also be useful in explaining the outcomes.

CONCLUSION

The study described in this paper uses an adaptation of the TAM to investigate whether an individual's beliefs, attitudes and intentions can be used to predict the success of their Web application development. An evaluation of the proposed model has provided mixed evidence about the role of beliefs and attitudes in the success of an individual's Web page development activities. Beliefs about computers and the Internet determined attitudes toward using computers and the Internet, respectively; and intent to learn Web development skills predicted Web development success. However, attitudes toward using computers and the Internet did not predict intent to learn web development skills. Despite some contradictory findings, the research model provides support for the theories that underlie it. As a first step in the introduction of Web development success as the dependent variable of a model derived from the TAM; as well as the introduction of the TAM into the Web development domain, the results of the study provide a starting point for future research, which should explore the generalisability of this model to real world development.

REFERENCES

Adams, D. A., Nelson, R. R., & Todd, P. A. (1992). Perceived usefulness, ease of use, and usage of information technology: A replication. *MIS Quarterly, 16*(2), 227-247.

Al-Jabri, I. M., & Al-Khaldi, M. A. (1997). Effects of user characteristics on computer attitudes among undergraduate business students. *Journal of End User Computing, 9*(2), 16-22.

Atkitson, M. A., & Kydd, C. (1997). Individual characteristics associated with Wold Wide Web use: an empirical study of playfulness and motivation. *The DATA BASE for Advances in Information Systems, 28*(2), 53-62.

Biggs, J. (2003). *Teaching for Quality Learning at University: What the Student Does* (2nd ed.). Philadelphia, Pa: Society for Research into Higher Education & Open University Press.

Chau, P. Y. K. (2001). Influence of computer attitude and self-efficacy on IT usage behavior. *Journal of End User Computing, 13*(1), 26-33.

Chen, L., Gillenson, M., & Sherrell, D. (2002). Enticing online consumers: An extended technology acceptance perspective. *Information & Management, 39*(1), 705-719.

Childers, T., Carr, C., Peck, J., & Carson, S. (2001). Hedonic and Utilitarian motivations for online retail shopping behaviour. *Journal of Retailing, 77*(4), 35-48.

Compeau, D. R., & Higgins, C. A. (1995). Computer self-efficacy: Development of a measure and initial test. *MIS Quarterly, 19*(2), 189-211.

Davis, F. D. (1989). Perceived usefulness, perceived ease of use, and user accceptance of information technology. *MIS Quarterly, 13*(3), 319-340.

Davis, F. D. (1993). User acceptance of information technology: System characteristics, user perceptions and behavioral impacts. *International Journal of Man Machine Studies, 38*, 475-487.

Davis, F. D., Bagozzi, R. P., & Warshaw, P., R. (1989). User acceptance of computer technology: A comparison of two theoretical models. *Management Science, 35*(8), 982-1003.

DeLone, W. H., & McLean, E. R. (1992). Information systems success: The quest for the dependent variable. *Information Systems Research, 3*(1), 60-95.

DeSanctis, G. (1983). Expectancy theory as an explanation of voluntary use of a decision support system. *Psychological Reports, 52*(247-260).

Dishaw, M. T., & Strong, D. M. (1999). Extending the technology acceptance model with task-technology fit constructs. *Information & Management, 36*(1), 9-21.

Fenech, T. (1998). Using perceived ease of use and perceived usefulness to predict acceptance of the world wide web. *Computer Networks and ISDN Systems, 30*, 629-630.

Fishbein, M., & Ajzen, I. (1975). *Belief, Attitude, Intention, and Behavior: An introduction to theory and research*. Reading, Massachusetts: Addison-Wesley Publishing Company.

Gardner, C., & Amoroso, D. L. (2004). *Development of an instrument to measure the acceptance of Internet technology by consumers*. Paper presented at the Proceedings of the 37th Hawaii International Conference on System Sciences.

Gellerson, H., & Gaedke, M. (1999). Object orientated web application development. *IEEE Internet Computing, 3*(1), 60-68.

Goupil, D. (2000). End-user application development: Relief for IT. *Computing Channels*(June), 2-4.

Guimaraes, T., & Igbaria, M. (1997). Assessing user computing effectiveness: An integrated model. *Journal of End User Computing, 9*(2), 3-14.

Halawi, L., & McCarthy, R. (2007). Measuring faculty perceptions of Blackboard using the Technology Acceptance Model. *Issues in Information Systems, 8*(2), 160-165.

Harrison, A. W., & Rainer, R. K. (1992). The influence of individual differences on skill in end-user computing. *Journal of Management Information Systems, 9*(1), 93-111.

Heinrichs, J. H., Lim, K. S., & S., L. J. (2007). Determining factors of academic library Web site usage. *Journal of the American Society for Information Science and Technology, 58*(14), 2325-2334.

Hubona, G. S., & Cheney, P. H. (1994). System effectiveness of knowledge-based technology: The relationship of user performance and attitudinal factors. *Proceedings of the Twenty-Seventh Hawaii International Conference on System Sciences, 4*, 532-541.

Igbaria, M. (1990). End-User Computing Effectiveness: A Structural Equation Model. *OMEGA International Journal of Management Science, 18*(6), 637-652.

Igbaria, M. (1993). User Acceptance of Microcomputer Technology: An Empirical Test. *OMEGA International Journal of Management Science, 21*(1), 73-90.

Igbaria, M., Guimaraes, T., & Davis, G. B. (1995). Testing the determinants of microcomputer usage via a structural equation model. *Journal of Management Information Systems, 11*(4), 87-114.

Igbaria, M., & Iivari, J. (1995). The effects of self-efficacy on computer usage. *OMEGA International Journal of Management Science, 23*(6), 587-605.

Igbaria, M., & Tan, M. (1997). The Consequences of Information Technology Acceptance on Subsequent Individual Performance. *Information and Management, 32*, 113-121.

Klopping, I. M., & McKinney, E. (2004). Extending the Technology Acceptance Model and the Task-Technology Fit model to consumer E-commerce. *Information Technology, Learning, and Performance Journal, 22*(1), 35-48.

Lederer, A. L., Maupin, D. J., Sena, M. P., & Zhuang, Y. (2000). The technology acceptance model and the world wide web. *Decision Support Systems, 29*, 269-282.

Liaw, S.-S. (2002). An Internet survey for perceptions of computers and the world wide web: Relationship, prediction, and difference. *Computers in Human Behavior, 18*, 17-35.

Lim, K. S., Lim, J. S., & Heinrichs, J. H. (2005). Structural model comparison of the determining factors for E-purchase. *Seoul Journal of Business, 11*(2), 119-143.

Loyd, B. H., & Gressard, C. (1984). Reliability and factorial validity of computer attitude scales. *Education and Psychological Measurement, 44*, 501-505.

Lucas, H. C., & Spitler, V. K. (1999). Technology use and performance: A field study of broker workstations. *Decision Sciences, 30*(2), 291-311.

Ma, Q., & Liu, L. (2004). The technology acceptance model: A meta-analysis of empirical findings. *Journal of Organizational and End User Computing, 16*(1), 60-72.

Magal, S. R., & Mirchandani, D. A. (2001). *Validatiion of the technology acceptance model for Internet tools*. Paper presented at the Proceedings of the Americas Conference on Information Systems.

Mason, R. O. (1978). Measuring information output: A communication systems approach. *Information and Management, 1*(5), 219-234.

McGill, T., Hobbs, V., & Klobas, J. (2003). User developed applications and information systems success: A test of DeLone and McLean's model. *Information Resources Management Journal, 16*(1), 24-45.

Moon, J.-W., & Kim, Y.-G. (2001). Extending the TAM for a world-wide-web context. *Information and Management, 38*, 217-230.

Nelson, R. R., & Todd, P. (1999). Strategies for managing EUC on the web. *Journal of End User Computing, 11*(1), 24-31.

Nunally, J. C. (1978). Psychometric Theory. New York: McGraw-Hill.

Orr, C., Allen, D., & Poindexter, S. (2001). The effect of individual differences on computer attitudes. *Journal of End User Computing, 13*(2), 26-39.

Parish, T. S., & Necessary, J. R. (1996). An examination of cognitive dissonance and computer attitudes. *Educational Technology, Research and Development, 116*(4), 565-566.

Robey, D. (1979). User attitudes and management information system use. *Academy of Management Journal, 22*, 527-538.

Rozzell, E. J., & Gardner, W. L. I. (1999). Computer-related success and failure: A longitudinal field study of the factors influencing computer-related performance. *Computers in Human Behavior, 15*, 1-10.

Russo, N., & Graham, B. (1998). *A first step in developing a web application design methodology: Understanding the environment.* Paper presented at the Sixth International Conference on Information Systems Methodology, Salford University, Manchester, U.K.

Saade, R. G., Nebebe, F., & Tan, W. (2007). Viability of the "Technology Acceptance Model" in Multimedia Learning Environments: A comparative study. *Interdisciplinary Journal of Knowledge and Learning Objects, 3*, 175-184.

Schultz, R. L., & Slevin, D. P. (1975). *Implementing Operations Research/Management Science.* New York: American Elsevier.

Seyal, A. H., Rahman, M. N. A., & Rahim, M. M. (2002). Determinants of academic use of the Internet: A structural equation model. *Behavior and Information Technology, 21*(1), 71-86.

Simon, S. J., Grover, V., Teng, J. T. C., & Whitcomb, K. (1996). The relationship of information systems training methods and cognitive ability to end user satisfaction, comprehension, and skill transfer: A longitudinal field experiment. *Information Systems Research, 7*(4), 466-490.

Subramanian, G. H. (1994). A replication of perceived usefulness and perceived ease of use measurement. *Decision Sciences, 25*(5,6), 863-874.

Sun, H., & Zhang, P. (2006a). Causal relationships between perceived enjoyment and perceived ease of use: An alternative approach. *Journal of the Association for Information Systems, 7*(9), 618-645.

Sun, H., & Zhang, P. (2006b). The role of moderating factors in user technology acceptance. *International Journal of Human-Computer Studies, 64,* 53-78.

Sun, H., & Zhang, P. (2008). An exploration of affect factors and their role in user technology acceptance: Mediation and causality. *Journal of the American Society for Information Science and Technology, 59*(8), 1-12.

Swanson, E. B. (1987). Information channel disposition and use. *Decision Sciences, 18*, 131-145.

Taylor, M. J., McWilliam, J., Forsythe, H., & Wade, S. (2002). Methodologies and Web site development: A survey of practice. *Information and Software Technology, 44*(6), 381-391.

Teo, S. H. T., Lim, V. K. G., & Lai, R. Y. C. (1999). Intrinsic and extrinsic motivation in Internet usage. *OMEGA International Journal of Management Science, 27*, 25-37.

Torkzadeh, G., & Van Dyke, T. P. (2002). Effects of Training on Internet Self-Efficacy and Computer User Attitudes. *Computers in Human Behavior, 18*(5), 479-494.

Van der Heijden, H. (2004). User acceptance of hedonic information systems. *MIS Quarterly, 28*(4), 695-704.

Venkatesh, V., & Davis, F. D. (1994). Modeling the determinants of perceived ease of use. *15th International Conference on Information Systems,* 213-227.

Venkatesh, V., & Davis, F. D. (1996). A model of the antecedents of perceived ease of use. *Decision Sciences, 27*(3), 451-481.

Wiegers, K. (1999). Software process improvement in web time. *IEEE Software, 16*(4), 78-86.

Wilder, G., Mackie, D., & Cooper, J. (1985). Gender and computers: Two surveys of computer-related attitudes. *Sex Roles, 13*(3/4), 215-228.

APPENDIX

Questionnaire items

1. Gender   Male   Female

2. Age: ___

3. How long have you been using computers?   Years___   Months___

4. How long have you been using the Internet/World Wide Web?

          Years___   Months___

	None						Extensive

5. How would you describe your level of formal computer   1 2   3 4 5 6 7
training (i.e. training from school/TAFE/university etc.)?

          None   Extensive

6. How would you describe your level of self-administered   1 2 3 4 5 6 7
computer training (i.e. training yourself from a book/CD-
ROM/computer program/trial and error etc.)?

          None   Extensive

7. How would you describe your level of formal Internet/   1 2 3 4 5 6 7
World Wide Web training (i.e. training from school/TAFE/
university etc.)?

          None   Extensive

8. How would you describe your level of self-administered   1 2 3 4 5 6 7
Internet/World Wide Web training (i.e. training yourself from
a book/CD-ROM/computer program/trial and error etc.)?

Please indicate the degree to which you agree with the following statements by circling the most appropriate option.

These questions relate to how you feel about computers:

          strongly   strongly
          disagree   agree

1. Computers scare me   1 2 3 4 5

2.	Working with a computer would make me very nervous	1 2 3 4 5
3.	I feel threatened when others talk about computers	1 2 3 4 5
4.	I feel aggressive and hostile toward computers	1 2 3 4 5
5.	It would bother me to take computer courses	1 2 3 4 5
6.	Computers make me feel uncomfortable	1 2 3 4 5
7.	I would not feel at ease in a computer class	1 2 3 4 5
8.	I get a sinking feeling when I think of trying to use a computer	1 2 3 4 5
9.	I would not feel comfortable working with a computer	1 2 3 4 5
10.	Computers make me feel uneasy and confused	1 2 3 4 5
11.	I am good with computers	1 2 3 4 5
12.	Generally I would feel OK about trying a new problem on the computer	1 2 3 4 5
13.	I think I would do advanced computer work	1 2 3 4 5
14.	I am sure I could do work with computers	1 2 3 4 5
15.	I am the type to do well with computers	1 2 3 4 5
16.	I am sure I could learn a computer language	1 2 3 4 5
17.	I think using a computer would be very easy for me	1 2 3 4 5
18.	I could get good grades in computer courses	1 2 3 4 5
19.	I think I could handle a computer course	1 2 3 4 5
20.	I have a lot of self-confidence when it comes to working with computers	1 2 3 4 5
21.	I would like working with computers	1 2 3 4 5

22. The challenge of solving problems with computers appeals to me   1 2 3 4 5

23. I think working with computers would be enjoyable and stimulating   1 2 3 4 5

24. Figuring out computer problems appeals to me   1 2 3 4 5

25. When there is a problem with a computer application that I can't immediately solve, I would stick with it until I have the answer   1 2 3 4 5

26. I understand how some people can stand so much time working with computers and seem to enjoy it   1 2 3 4 5

27. Once I start to work with the computer, I would find it hard to stop   1 2 3 4 5

28. I will do as much work with computers as possible   1 2 3 4 5

29. If a problem is left unresolved in a computer class, I would continue to think about it afterward   1 2 3 4 5

30. I enjoy talking with others about computers   1 2 3 4 5

31. I will use computers many ways in my life   1 2 3 4 5

32. Learning about computers is not a waste of time   1 2 3 4 5

33. Learning about computers is worthwhile   1 2 3 4 5

34. I'll need a firm mastery of computers for my future work   1 2 3 4 5

35. I expect to have much use for computers in my daily life   1 2 3 4 5

36. I can think of many ways that I will use computers in my career   1 2 3 4 5

37. Knowing how to work with computers will increase my job possibilities   1 2 3 4 5

38. Anything that a computer can be used for, I will not be able to do as well in some other way   1 2 3 4 5

39. It is important to me to do well in computer classes   1 2 3 4 5

40. Working with computers will be important to me in my life's work   1 2 3 4 5

These questions relate to how you feel about the Internet/World Wide Web:

		strongly disagree			strongly agree	
41.	I feel confident using the Internet/World Wide Web (WWW)	1	2	3	4	5
42.	I feel confident using E-mail	1	2	3	4	5
43.	I feel confident using WWW browsers (e.g. Internet Explorer, Netscape Communicator)	1	2	3	4	5
44.	I feel confident using search engines (e.g. Yahoo, Excite, Lycos)	1	2	3	4	5
45.	I like to use E-mail to communicate with others	1	2	3	4	5
46.	I enjoy talking with others about the Internet	1	2	3	4	5
47.	I like to work with the Internet/WWW	1	2	3	4	5
48.	I like to use the Internet from home	1	2	3	4	5
49.	I believe using the Internet/WWW is worthwhile	1	2	3	4	5
50.	The Internet/WWW helps me to find information	1	2	3	4	5
51.	I believe the Internet makes communication easier	1	2	3	4	5
52.	The multimedia environment of WWW (e.g. text, image) is helpful to understand online information	1	2	3	4	5
53.	I believe the Internet/WWW has potential as a learning tool	1	2	3	4	5
54.	I believe that the Internet/WWW is able to offer online learning activities	1	2	3	4	5
55.	I believe that learning how to use the Internet/WWW is worthwhile	1	2	3	4	5
56.	Learning Internet/WWW skills can enhance my academic performance	1	2	3	4	5

Chapter IV
Assessing a Spanish Translation of the End–User Computing Satisfaction Instrument

George E. Heilman
Winston-Salem State University, USA

Jorge Brusa
Texas A&M International University, USA

ABSTRACT

This study assesses the psychometric properties of a Spanish translation of Doll and Torkzadeh's End-User Computing Satisfaction (EUCS) survey instrument. The results show that the EUCS Spanish version is a valid and reliable measure of computing satisfaction among computer users in Mexico and adds support to the usefulness of the instrument in countries other than the United States and in languages other than English.

INTRODUCTION

The evaluation of user perceptions about **system "success"** has been a topic of interest among information system (IS) researchers for a number of years. Examples can be found in Zmud's (1979) extensive review of studies about the impact of user differences on **system success** measures such as performance, usage and satisfaction, and in Ives and Olsen's (1984) review of research on the effect of user involvement on IS **success** variables such as system quality, system usage and information satisfaction. While these early reviews focused on the independent variables affecting **success**,

Delone and McLean (1992) were more concerned with the nature of **success** as a dependent variable. They reviewed 180 formative IS articles with the intent of categorizing the manner in which **success** had been operationalized and identified six **success** taxa: system quality, information quality, individual impact, organizational impact, use, and user satisfaction. They found user satisfaction to be the most widely used measure of IS **success**, and suggested that satisfaction is the preferred measure when system use is mandatory.

An important instrument that is frequently used to assess user satisfaction is the **End-User Computing Satisfaction (EUCS) survey** developed by Doll and Torkzadeh (1988). The **EUCS survey** consists of a single second-order factor (**End-User Computing Satisfaction**) composed of 5 first-order factors (Content, Accuracy, Format, Ease of Use, and Timeliness) measured by 12 questions. Doll and Torkzadeh (1988) validated their survey instrument using a multi-step process and found that the instrument could be used across a variety of applications, hardware platforms, development modes and job positions.

Extensive testing by numerous researchers in a variety of settings has established the **EUCS instrument**'s **reliability**, content **validity**, construct **validity**, internal **validity**, statistical conclusion **validity**, and multigroup invariance. Examples include studies for Web sites (Abdinnour-Helm et al., 2005; Zviran et al., 2006), voice and e-mail applications (Adams et al., 1992), assessment of users' overall satisfaction (Aladwani, 2002), decision support, database and transaction processing systems (Doll et al., 2004), enterprise systems (Deng et al., 2008; Somers et al., 2003), interactive telephone voice mail systems (Dowing, 1999), mainframe and PC applications (Hendrickson et al., 1994), computer simulation (McHaney & Cronan, 1998, 2001; McHaney et al., 1999), CASE tools (Kim & McHaney, 2000), on-line banking (Pikkarainen et al., 2006; Hwang et al., 2006), and computer-related training methods (Simon et al., 1996).

The **EUCS survey** also has been used successfully in different cultural and linguistic contexts including studies in Finland (Pikkarainen et al., 2006), Great Britain (Al-Gahtani & King, 1999), India (Deng et al., 2008), Israel (Igbaria & Zviran, 1996), Kuwait (Aladwani, 2002), New Zealand (Igbaria et al., 1998), Singapore (Igbaria & Tan, 1997), Taiwan (Deng et al., 2008; Igbaria, 1992; Igbaria & Zviran, 1996; McHaney et al., 2002) and Western Europe (Deng et al., 2008). Studies which have used versions of **EUCS** in languages other than English include translations in Arabic (Deng et al., 2008), Chinese (McHaney et al., 2002), Finnish (Pikkarainen et al., 2006) and Hebrew (Igbaria, 1992; Igbaria & Zviran, 1996). Interestingly, the use of a standard IS research instruments like the **EUCS** remains largely unexplored in Latin America. The primary goal of this investigation is to address this gap in the IS literature and examine the robustness of the **EUCS** survey when applied to Latin American subjects.

More precisely, this study will examine the **validity** and **reliability** of a **Spanish translation** of the **End-User Computing Satisfaction survey instrument** administered to **Mexican** respondents. Since most end-user computing research is conducted in the U.S., there is a belief that these results can be generalized to other countries (Shayo et al., 1999). However, the belief that instruments like **EUCS** can be generalized across countries many be ill advised since cultural characteristics, socio-work roles and IT sophistication levels might influence the satisfaction process and produce results different from those observed in America using English surveys (Hofstede, 1980; Shayo et al., 1999). Therefore, before instruments like the **EUCS** can be applied confidently in new cultural, country or linguistic contexts, it is recommended that its universality be established through an investigation of the instrument's **validity**, psychometric stability, and robustness (Davis, 1989; 1994; McHaney et al., 2002; Shayo et al., 1999; Somers et al., 2003).

According to Bourdeau et al., (1982) and Davis et al. (1989), testing of established instruments in different environments helps to identify a common framework of measures that can integrate various streams of research, cumulate knowledge, and assure comparability across studies. Without a solid **validation** of the instruments used in the collection of data, the scientific basis of quantitative research is threatened because the conclusions and inferences reached with these instruments could be wrong or misleading (Boudreau et al., 2001). Recognizing the importance of the **validation** process and the gap in the IS literature, this study examines the **validity** and **reliability** of a **Spanish translation** of the **EUCS survey instrument** administered to **Mexican** respondents

We hypothesize that the **Spanish translation** of the **End-User Computing Satisfaction instrument** will validly and reliably measure user computing satisfaction. To test the hypothesis we asked computer users living and working in northern **Mexico** to complete the translated **EUCS**. The survey contains 12 questions focused specifically on the users' level of satisfaction with the computer systems they use at work. A confirmatory factor analysis is used to determine if the collected data supports the hypothesis regarding the **validity** and **reliability** of the survey instrument. The results of this investigation indicate that the **Spanish translation** of the **EUCS** is a valid and reliable survey instrument when applied to **Spanish** speaking computer users in northern **Mexico**, and researchers can use the survey instrument confidently in this environment.

THE SURVEY INSTRUMENT

Doll and Torkzadeh (1988) originally proposed that the 12-item **EUCS instrument** represented a five factor structure (Content, Accuracy, Format, Ease of Use, and Timeliness). Subsequent research, however, indicates these are actually five sub-factors under a single second-order **EUCS** factor as shown in Figure 1 (Chin & Newsted, 1995; Doll et al. 1994). The Content sub-factor is measured by four questions, while the Accuracy, Format, Ease of Use and Timeliness sub-factors are measured by two questions each.

The **EUCS questionnaire** was translated to **Spanish** by an individual fluent in both **Spanish** and English and reviewed by two additional

Figure 1. Structural model of the end-user computing satisfaction measure

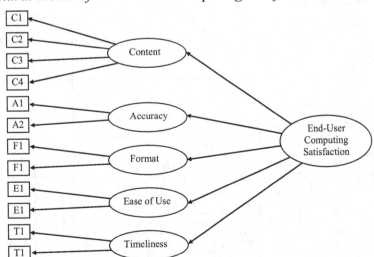

individuals fluent in both English and **Spanish**. The original English version of the **EUCS** questions and their **Spanish translation**s are shown in Appendix A.

Responses to the questions are measured by a five point Likert-type scale where 1 = "almost never," 2 = "some of the time," 3 = "about half the time," 4 = "most of the time," and 5 = "almost always." In the **Spanish** version of the survey, 1 = "casi nunca," 2 = "algunas veces," 3 = "la mitad de las veces," 4 = "muchas veces," and 5 = "casi siempre."

THE SAMPLE

1200 copies of the translated **questionnaire** were distributed among employees at a variety of randomly selected private and public organizations in northern **Mexico**. No incentives were given to the organizations or the employees to complete the **survey**. A total of 302 **surveys** (25.1%) were returned.

Of the 302 returned **surveys**, 237 (78.5%) contained complete information and were usable 130 respondents (54.9%) were male and 107 (45.1%) were female. In terms of the organizations with

which the respondents were affiliated, 129 (54.4%) worked in private companies, 16 (6.8%) worked in public companies, 2 (0.8%) worked in local government, 85 (35.9%) worked in universities, 2 (0.8%) worked in high schools and 3 (1.3%) did not specify. 143 respondents (60.4%) were between the ages of 20 and 30, 74 (31.2%) were between 31 and 40, 18 (7.6%) were between 41 and 50, and 2 (0.8%) were over the age of 50.

CONSTRUCT VALIDATION

A confirmatory factor analysis was performed with Lisrel 8 to determine if the data collected from the **Mexican** respondents support the hypothesized factor structure of the **End-User Computing Satisfaction construct** shown in Figure 1. Table 1 shows the correlation matrix of the 12 **questionnaire** items used in the analysis. For purposes of scaling and statistical identification, the factor loading of one indicator in each sub-factor is set to 1 and the variance of the second-order **End-User Computing Satisfaction** factor is set to 1 (Byrne, 1998).

The following sections provide a textual description of the analysis results. Figure 2

Table 1. EUCS correlation matrix

	C1	C2	C3	C4	A1	A2	F1	F2	E1	E2	T1	T2
C1	1.000											
C2	0.721	1.000										
C3	0.705	.753	1.000									
C4	0.646	0.738	0.717	1.000								
A1	0.753	0.747	0.671	0.651	1.000							
A2	0.643	0.782	0.739	0.732	0.713	1.000						
F1	0.755	0.723	0.749	0.690	0.690	0.672	1.000					
F2	0.703	0.799	0.756	0.723	0.693	0.779	0.741	1.000				
E1	0.638	0.766	0.705	0.666	0.668	0.651	0.678	0.748	1.000			
E2	0.674	0.767	0.746	0.712	0.672	0.680	0.755	0.773	0.874	1.000		
T1	0.653	0.694	.680	0.686	0.716	0.709	0.651	0.674	0.682	0.666	1.000	
T2	00.671	0.737	0.718	0.793	0.724	0.752	0.686	0.701	0.716	0.743	0.770	1.000

presents a diagrammatic summary of the results showing factor loadings with significance levels in parentheses.

Reliability

Reliability refers to the degree to which scores are free from measurement errors. It is a necessary but not sufficient condition for instrument **validity**. One method commonly used to assess internal-consistency **reliability** is coefficient alpha, which is based on the notion of splitting a measure into as many parts as the number of items. Alpha, then, is the average of all possible split-half **reliability** coefficients for the measure (Pedazur & Schmelkin, 1991). Coefficient alphas greater than .70 indicate reliable **constructs** (Fornell & Larker, 1981). The alphas for the **EUCS** sub-factors are: Content = .91, Accuracy = .83, Format = .85, Timeliness = .87, and Ease of Use = .93. Coefficient alpha for the overall instrument is .97, which is well above the recommended threshold and compares favorably with the .92 reported by Doll and Torkzadeh (1988) in their initial study. The conclusion is that the second-order **EUCS construct** and its five first-order sub-factors are reliable.

Convergent Validity

Convergent **validity** refers to the convergence among different methods designed to measure the same **construct** (Pedhazur & Schmelkin, 1991). One technique for evaluating convergent **validity** views each item in a **construct** as a different approach to measuring the **construct**. If t-tests for the loadings of all the indicators measuring a single **construct** are statistically significant, all indicators are effectively measuring the same **construct** and the **construct** exhibits convergent **validity** (Anderson & Gerbing, 1988).

Table 2 shows the indicator loadings for each **construct** along with their corresponding t-values. Indicant loadings that were fixed during model

Table 2. Analysis of convergent validity

Construct \ Indicant	1	2	3	4
Content	0.915 (16.81)	0.961 (18.52)	0.941 (17.76)	1.000 *
Accuracy	0.967 (16.62)	1.000 *		
Format	0.958 (17.91)	1.000 *		
Timeliness	0.939 (18.24)	1.000 *		
Ease of Use	0.962 (25.07)	1.000 *		

analysis have a loading of 1. T-values greater than 3.29 are significant at the .001 level. The loadings for all freed indicants are significant at the .001 level. The conclusion is that **EUCS** sub-factors exhibit convergent **validity**.

Discriminant Validity

Discriminant **validity** implies that one **construct** can be empirically differentiated from other **constructs** that may be similar (Kerlinger, 1986). Discrimination may be demonstrated with a chi-square difference test among all possible pairs of **constructs**, in this case the five sub-factors - Content, Accuracy, Format, Timeliness, Ease of Use - that make up **End-User Computing Satisfaction** (Ahire et al.,1996).

Two confirmatory factor analyses (CFAs) are run for each selected pair of sub-factors. In the first CFA, correlation is allowed between the sub-factors. In the second CFA the correlation between the pair is fixed to 1.00, creating a difference with 1 degree of freedom between the models. If the chi-squares from the two tests are statistically significantly different, the **constructs** exhibit discriminant **validity**.

The chi-square critical values for 1 degree of freedom are 3.84 at the .05 significance level, 6.63 at the .01 significance level, and 7.88 at the .005

Table 3. Analysis of discrminant validity

	Accuracy	Format	Timeliness	Ease of Use
Content	5.80 (p<.05)	5.55 (p<.05)	6.74 (p<.01)	6.01 (p<.05)
Accuracy		6.00 (p<.05)	7.06 (p<.01)	11.24 (p<.005)
Format			9.54 (p<.005)	5.36 (p<.05)
Timeliness				7.53 (p<.01)

significance level. Table 3 presents the results of the difference tests, showing the differences in chi-squared values between pairs and their corresponding p-values. All differences were significant at the .05 level or lower. The conclusion is that **EUCS** sub-factors exhibit discriminant **validity**.

Structural Analysis

Table 4 presents the goodness of fit indices for the **EUCS** structural model along with guidelines for evaluating the fit values (Browne & Cudeck, 1993; Hair et al., 1992; Pedhazur & Schmelkin, 1991; Sharma, 1996). Though always reported, the chi-square test is not considered to be practically meaningful and is typically discounted in favor of other methods for evaluating fit of the model to the data (Bearden et al., 1982). All indices except chi-square yield acceptable values. The

conclusion is that the model provides a good fit for the data.

Since the model fit is acceptable, the loadings of the sub-factors on the second-order factor can be evaluated. As shown in Table 5, all sub-factor loadings are significant at the .001 level. These findings indicate that our model, summarized in Figure 2, is a valid representation of the **EUCS construct**, and supports prior research characterizing **EUCS** as a second-order factor with five first-order sub-factors.

CONCLUSION

The purpose of this study is to extend the generalizability of the **EUCS instrument** by assessing the psychometric properties of a **Spanish translation** of the **EUCS survey** administered to subjects living and working in **Mexico**. An assessment of the **survey instrument**'s **reliability** using

Table 4. Analysis of model fit

Goodness of Fit Indicator	Value	Recommended Value	Conclusion
chi-square (49 d.f.)	153.99 (p < .01)	p > .05	Poor
Normed chi-square (chi-square/d.f.)	3.14	< 5	Good
GFI	.91	> .90	Good
AGFI	.85	> .80	Good
NFI	.95	> .90	Good
NNFI	.95	> .90	Good
CFI	.97	> .90	Good
RMR	.027	< .20	Good

Table 5. Analysis of structural loadings on EUCS

	Content	Accuracy	Format	Timeliness	Ease of Use
EUCS	.897 (17.62)	.850 (16.20)	.874 (16.94)	.850 (16.19)	.852 (16.27)

Figure 2. Structural model of the end-user computing satisfaction measure

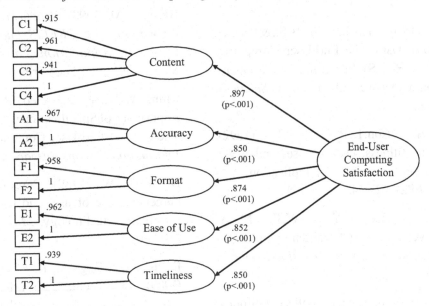

coefficient alpha supports the conclusion that the second-order **EUCS construct** and each of its five first-order sub-factors are reliable. An assessment of t-tests on indicant loadings supports the conclusion is that **EUCS** sub-factors exhibit convergent **validity**. An assessment of chi-square difference tests among **construct** sub-factors supports the conclusion that the **EUCS** sub-factors exhibit discriminant **validity**. An assessment of the fit indices supports the conclusion that the proposed **EUCS** model provides a good fit to the **Mexican** data. And finally, the significant loadings of the five sub-factors - Content, Accuracy, Format, Ease of Use, and Timeliness - on the **EUCS** variable provides support for a model with second-order model **construct (EUCS)** composed of five first-order sub-factors.

The findings indicate that the **Spanish translation** of the **EUCS survey** is a valid and reliable **instrument** that can be used confidently by researchers in investigations involving **Spanish** speaking computer users in northern **Mexico**. These results add support to the greater generalizability of the **EUCS instrument** and its robustness as a valid measure of computing satisfaction and surrogate for **system success** in a variety of cultural and linguistic settings.

The results, however, do not imply that **End-User Computing Satisfaction** will be valid in all cultural and linguistic contexts. Even this particular translation may not be valid in all **Spanish** speaking countries. For example, the Microsoft Word language function lists 20 variations for **Spanish translation**s. Our translation conforms to Microsoft's "**Mexican**" **Spanish** and was administered only in northern **Mexico**. Generalizability of **EUCS** will be enhanced by expanding this study's **validation** testing throughout **Mexico** and into other **Spanish** speaking countries.

REFERENCES

Abdinnour-Helm, S. F., Chaparro, B. S., & Farmer, S. A. (2005). Using the End-User Computing Satisfaction (EUCS) Instrument to Measure Satisfaction with a Web Site. *Decision Sciences, 26*(2), 349-364.

Adams, D. A., Nelson, R. R., & Todd, P. A. (1992). Perceived usefulness, ease of use, and usage of information technology: A replication. *MIS Quarterly, 16*(2), 227-247.

Ahire, S. L., Golhar D. Y., &. Waller, M. A. (1996). Development and Validation of TQM Implementation Constructs. *Decision Sciences, 27*(1), 23-56.

Al-Gahtani, S. S., & King, M. (1999). Attitudes, satisfaction and usage: factors contributing to each in the acceptance of information technology. *Behaviour & Information Technology, 18*(4), 77-297.

Aladwani, A. M. (2002). Organizational actions, computer attitudes, and end-user satisfaction in public organizations: an empirical study. *Journal of End User Computing, 14*(1), 42-49.

Anderson, J. C., & Gerbing, D. W. (1988). Structural Equation Modeling in Practice: A Review and Recommended two-step Approach. *Psychological Bulletin, 103*, 411-423.

Bearden, W. O., Sharma, S., & Teel, J. E. (1982). Sample Size Effects of Chi-Square and Other Statistics Used in Evaluating Causal Models. *Journal of Marketing Research, 19*, 425-430.

Boudreau, M., Gefen, D., & Straub, D.W. (2001). Validation in Information Systems Research: A State-of-the-Art Assessment. *MIS Quarterly, 25*(1), 1-16.

Browne, M. W., & Cudeck, R. (1993). Alternate Ways of Assessing Model Fit. In K.A. Bollen & J.S. Long (Ed.) *Testing Structural Equation Models* (pp. 139-154). Newbury Park, CA: Sage Publications,

Byrne, B. M. (1998). *Structural Equation Modeling with LISREL, PRELIS, and SIMPLIS: Basic Concepts, Applications, and Programming.* Mahwa, NJ: Lawrence Erlbaum Associates.

Chin, W. W., &. Newsted, R. N. (1995). The Importance of Specification in Causal Modeling: The Case of End-User Computing Satisfaction. *Information Systems Research, 6*(1), 73-81.

Davis, F. W. (1989). Perceived usefulness, perceived ease of use, and user acceptance of information technology. *MIS Quarterly, 13*(3), 319-340.

Davis, F. D., Bagozzi, R. P., & Warshaw, P. R. (1989). User acceptance of information technology: A comparison of two theoretical models. *Management Science, 35*(8), 982-1003.

Delone, W. H., & McLean, E. R. (1992). Information Success: The Quest for the Dependent Variable. *Information Systems Research, 3*(1), 60-95.

Deng, X., Doll, W. J., Al-Gahtani, S. S., Larsen, T. J., Pearson, J. M., & Raghunathan, T. S. (2008). A cross-cultural analysis of the End-User Computing Satisfaction instrument: A multi-group invariance analysis. *Information & Management, 45*(4), 211-220.

Doll, W. J., Deng, X., Raghunathan, T. S., Torkzadeh, G., & Xia, W. (2004). The Meaning and Measurement of User Satisfaction: A Multigroup Invariance Analysis of the End-User Computing Satisfaction Instrument. *Journal of Management Information Systems, 21*(1), 228-262.

Doll, W. J., & Torkzadeh, G. (1988). The Measurement of End-User Computing Satisfaction. *MIS Quarterly, 12*(2), 259-274.

Doll, W. J., Xia, W., & Torkzadeh, G. (1994). A Confirmatory Factor Analysis of the End-User Computing Satisfaction Instrument. *MIS Quarterly, 18*(4), 453-461.

Dowing, C. E. (1999). System usage behaviour as a proxy for user satisfaction: An empirical investigation. *Information & Management, 35,* 203-216.

Fornell, C., & Larker, D. F. (1981). Evaluating Structural Equation Models with Unobserved Variables and Measurement Error. *Journal of Marketing Research, 18,* 39-51.

Hair, J. F. Jr., Anderson, R. E., Tatham, R. L., & Black, W. C. (1992). *Multivariate Data Analysis with Readings, Third Edition.* New York, NY: Macmillan Publishing Company, 426-496.

Hendrickson, A. R., Glorfeld, L. W., & Cronan, T. P. (1994). On the Repeated Test-Retest Reliability of the End-User Computing Satisfaction Instrument: A Comment. *Decision Sciences, 25*(4), 665-667.

Hofstede, G. (1980). Motivation, leadership and organization: Do American theories apply abroad. *Organizational Dynamics, 9*(1), 42-63.

Hwang, H., Chen, R., & Lee, J. Measuring customer satisfaction with internet banking: an exploratory study. *International Journal of Electronic Finance, 1*(3), 321-335.

Igbaria, M., (1992). An examination of microcomputer usage in Taiwan. *Information & Management, 22*(1), 9-28.

Igbaria, M., & Tan, M. (1997). The consequences of information technology acceptance on subsequent individual performance. *Information & Management, 35*(1), 113-121.

Igbaria, M., Zinatelli, N., & Cavaye, A. L. M. (1998). Analysis of information Technology Success in Small Firms in New Zealand. *International Journal of Information Management, 18*(2), 103-119.

Igbaria, M., & Zviran, M. (1996). Comparison of end-user Computing characteristics in the U.S., Israel and Taiwan. *Information & Management, 30*(1), 1-13.

Ives, B., & Olson, M.H. (1984). User Involvement and MIS Success: A Review of Research. *Management Science, 30*(5). 586-603.

Kerlinger, F. N. (1986). *Foundations of Behavioral Research, Third Edition.* Fort Worth, TX: Harcourt Brace Jovanovich College Publishers.

Kim, S., & McHaney, R. (2000). Validation of the End-User Computing Satisfaction Instrument in Case Tool Environments. *Journal of Computer Information Systems, 41*(1), 49-55.

McHaney, R., & Cronan, T. P. (1998). Computer simulation success: on the use of the End-User Computing Satisfaction instrument. *Decision Sciences, 29*(2), 525-536.

McHaney, R., & Cronan, T. P. (2001). A Comparison of Surrogate Success Measures in On-Going Representational Decision Support Systems: An Extension of Simulation Technology. *Journal of End User Computing, 13*(2), 15-25.

McHaney, R., Hightower, R., & Pearson, J. (2002). A validation of the End-User Computing Satisfaction instrument in Taiwan. *Information & Management, 39*(6), 503-511.

McHaney, R., Hightower, R., & White, D. (1999). EUCS test-retest reliability in representational model decision support systems. *Information & Management, 36*(2), 109-119.

Pedhazur, E. J., & Schmelkin, L. P. (1991). *Measurement, Design, and Analysis: An Integrated Approach.* Hillside, NJ: Lawrence Erlbaum Associates.

Pikkarainen, K., Pikkarainen, T., Karjaluoto, H., & Pahnila, S. (2006). The measurement of End-User Computing Satisfaction of online-banking services: empirical evidence from Finland. *The International Journal of Bank Marketing, 24*(3), 158-172.

Sharma, S. (1996). *Applied Multivariate Techniques*. New York, NY: John Wiley and Sons.

Shayo, C., Guthrie, R., & Igbaria, M. (1999). Exploring the Measurement of End User Computing Success. *Journal of End User Computing, 11*(1), 2-26.

Simon, S. J., Grover, V., Teng, J. T. C., & Whitcomb, K. (1996). The relationship of information training methods and cognitive ability to end-user satisfaction, comprehension, and skill transfer: A longitudinal field study. *Information Systems Research, 7*(2), 466-490.

Somers, T. M., Nelson, K., & Karimi, J. (2003). Confirmatory Factor Analysis of the End-User Computing Satisfaction Instrument: Replication within an ERP Domain. *Decision Sciences, 34*(3), 595-621.

Zmud, R.W. (1979). Individual Differences and MIS Success: A Review of the Empirical Literature. *Management Science, 25*(10), 966-979.

Zviran, M., Glezer, C., & Avni, I. (2006). User Satisfaction from commercial web sites: The effect of design and use. *Information & Management, 43*(2), 157-178.

APPENDIX A: EUCS QUESTIONS

Content

C1: Does the System provide the precise information you need?

¿El sistema provee la información que usted necesita?

C2: Does the information content meet your needs?

¿Es la información provista por el sistema lo que usted necesita?

C3: Does the system provide reports that seem to be just about exactly what you need?

¿Los reportes del sistema son lo que usted necesita?

C4: Does the system provide sufficient information?

¿Piensa usted que el sistema provee suficiente información?

Accuracy

A1: Is the system accurate?

¿Es el sistema preciso?

A2: Are you satisfied with the accuracy of the system?

¿Esta usted satisfecho con la precisión del sistema?

Format

F1: Do you think the output is presented in a useful format?

¿Es el resultado del sistema presentado en una forma útil?

F2: Is the information clear?

¿Es la información del sistema clara?

Ease of Use

E1: Is the system user friendly?

¿Para los usuarios, es el sistema fácil de usar?

E2: Is the system easy to use?

¿Es el sistema fácil de usar?

Timeliness

T1: Do you get the information you need in time?

¿Recibe la información que necesita en tiempo?

T2: Does the system provide up-to-date information?

¿Provee el sistema información actualizada?

Chapter V
Understanding the Impact of Culture on Mobile Phone Usage on Public Places:
A Comparison between the UK and Sudan

Ishraga Khattab
Sudan Academy for Banking and Financial Science, Sudan

Steve Love
Brunel University, UK

ABSTRACT

Over the last several years, the ubiquitous use of mobile phones by people from different cultures has grown enormously. For example, mobile phones are used to perform both private and business conversations. In many cases, mobile phone conversations take place in public places. In this chapter, the authors attempt to understand if cultural differences influence the way people use their mobile phones in public places. The material considered here draws on the existing literature of mobile phones, and quantitative and qualitative work carried out in the UK (as a mature mobile phone market) and the Sudan (that is part of Africa and the Middle East culture with its emerging mobile phone market). The results presented in the chapter indicate that people in the Sudan are less likely to use their mobile phones on public transport or whilst walking down the street, in comparison to their UK counterparts. In addition, the Sudanese are more willing to switch off their mobile phones in places of worship, classes, and meetings. Implications are drawn from the study for the design of mobile phones for different cultures.

INTRODUCTION

Despite the unlimited benefits of the Internet in its ability to facilitate social interaction, learning environment and business opportunities, people in the developing countries do not have the same access to the Internet in comparison to the developed world. In turn, people in the developing world are eliminated from the chance of forming and participating on online communities. The Internet penetration rates vary vastly from one continent or even country to the other. For example, in Europe, 312,722,892 users have Internet access (38.7% of the population), whereas in Africa, only 3.6% of the population have Internet access (ITU, 2004). According to Internetworldstats (2006) the total number of 32,765,700 African Internet users is smaller than those who use the Internet in the UK (37,600,000). Most African Internet users are centred in the capitals and urban areas, as in rural areas, the existence of PCs and Internet connection is scarce (Donner, 2005).

There are many reasons for the lack of access to the Internet in Africa. For example, the affordability of computer equipment. Oyeyinka and Adeya (2004) conducted a cross-country examination in Nigeria and Kenya and found that Internet use was constrained by structural as well as cost factors. In their study, they found that the cost of owning a PC compels users (especially academics) to access the Internet in cyber cafes and other public places.

Therefore, the poor connectivity of the Internet, the high cost entailed to afford the required equipment, and the cost of maintaining a monthly Internet connection have unintentionally excluded some users from communicating through the Internet. However, on the other hand, people in these parts of the developing world have made use of another available medium of communication that is the mobile phone. According to Donner (2005) the mobile phone plays an important role in Africa to manoeuvre social interaction, facilitate learning as well as creating business opportunities.

Mobile phones in the developing world especially in Africa, in addition to its expected uses, enabled its users to communicate in an analogous way as communication on online communities. For example, Agar (2003) observed how people used the mobile phone to offer support for each other during the volcanic eruption in Eastern Congo. Donner (2005) reported that in Rwanda the mobile phone is used to link rural health clinics involved with the treatment of HIV patients. The support provided through the mobile phone can be similar to that received in online communities.

Interestingly, similar to online 'community of practice', Idowu, Ogunbodede & Idowu (2003) found that Nigerian doctors use mobile phones to communicate with each other across different parts of a large hospital to share knowledge, and to respond to emergencies when offsite.

The mobile phone has also been used for e-learning in Africa (Masters, 2005; Mutula, 2002; Stone, Lynch & Poole, 2003). These researchers found that the mobile's portability, simplicity, and affordability make it a natural fit for education programmes in places where PCs and Internet connectivity may be limited.

Some (Bray, 2005; Sesay, 2005) noted that mobile providers can have a positive impact on calming conflict situations in post-conflict nations like Rwanda, Afghanistan and East Timor. Others look to the everyday, arguing that mobile phones contribute to stronger social capital in Africa (Goodman, 2005). Donner (2005) found that the mobile phone is used to facilitate new business connections for small businesses. The New York Times (2005) reported on an illiterate woman living on the Congo River, who asked her customers to call her on her mobile phone if they wanted to buy fresh fish. *"She does not have electricity, she can not put the fish in the freezer"*, Mr. Nkuli of Vodacom said, *"So she keeps them in the river, tethered live on a string, until she is called on her mobile phone. Then she retrieves them and prepares them for sale".*

The importance of the mobile phone as almost the solitary tool in the developing world to maintain social support, share knowledge and its role in e-learning, e-business and politics, is undeniable. Kelly, Minge and Gray (2002) went further, as they found that the mobile phone can actually narrow the digital gap between the developing and the developed world more than the Internet.

Therefore, it can be said that the pervasive use of the mobile phone has yielded new forms of mobile phone interaction that take place in public places. It is common now to notice 'private mobile conversations' occurring in public places. The use of mobile phones in public places has offered users the chance to create their own private spaces regardless of where they are in physical spaces (Fortunati et al., 2000). Geser (2002) argues that public places are 'privatised' by the private lives of mobile users. Plant (2002) observed that mobile phones have created "simultaneity of place": a physical space and a virtual space of conversational interaction. The extensive use of mobile phones in public places has made mobile phone users develop new attitudes while they are on the phone. For example, turning away from people when talking on the phone. Bystanders have also developed a matching behaviour to show their uninterest in the mobile conversation performed in close proximity to them. For example, Love and Perry (2004) reported on bystanders' attitudes when a mobile phone conversation takes place, in this study bystanders were found to pretend not to be listening to the mobile phone conversation by adopting various actions such as gazing away or walking around the room.

In addition, Ling (2004) highlights how mobile phone use in public places has raised questions of what is appropriate or inappropriate behaviour in such places. In this study, he found that people perceived mobile phone use in places such as restaurants as unacceptable, partly because the restaurants norms do not cater for loud voices. Mobile phone users tend to talk louder than usual so that people nearby feel intruded upon, embar-

rassed, and have a sense of being coerced into the role of eavesdropper on a private conversation.

Research has also shown that mobile phones can occupy concurrent social spaces, spaces with behavioural norms that sometimes conflict, such as the space of the mobile phone user, and the virtual space where the conversation takes place (Palen, Salzman & Youngs, 2000). This feeling of conflict has led researchers in this area to propose that the use of mobile technology in public places is creating a new mixture of public and private space that has yet to be accommodated by users of mobile technology and bystanders in terms of what is acceptable or unacceptable behaviour.

This phenomenon has been analysed predominantly by using concepts drawn from Goffman's analysis of social interaction in public places (Goffman, 1963). In this work, Goffman suggested that people have specific 'public faces' and personas for different public social locations. The idea behind this is that individuals have rules that determine their behaviour in public places, or what Burns (1992) refers to as the "observance of social propriety". For example, Murtagh (2001) presented findings from an observational study of the non-verbal aspects of mobile phone use in a train carriage. Murtagh found that changing the direction of one's gaze, turning one's head and upper body away from the other people sitting next to one in the carriage were common features of mobile phone behaviour on trains. These behavioural responses were seen as being indicative of the subtle complexities involved when using mobile phones in public locations. This study suggests that mobile phone users are actively engaged in trying to distance themselves from their current physical location in order to enter a virtual environment with the person with whom they are having a mobile phone conversation.

Licoppe and Heurtin (2002) investigated the effect of mobile phone use in ongoing face-to-face interaction and found that the incoming mobile phone call causes a risk to the in progress physical interaction and consequently to the social setting.

This is due to the fact that the person receiving the call starts instantly to partition himself/ herself from those were engaged with him/her in a face-to-face interaction. In addition, Ling (2004) found that the user of the mobile phone in a public place usually tries to move to a less crowded spot of the public area to continue his or her call. The receiver of the mobile phone call enters an immediately created virtual space and engages in a greeting dialogue with a remote partner, whereas the physical partner who was participating in the face-to-face interaction just interrupted by the call has to accommodate the withdrawal of the mobile phone user into his/her virtual space.

In relation to this, Love and Perry (2004) used role play experiments to investigate the behaviour and attitudes of bystanders to a mobile phone conversation by a third party. They found that participants had strong views on embarrassment, discomfort and rudeness. They also reported that during the mobile phone call participants adopted various body language techniques such as folding their arms, walking around the room or gazing at something in front of them (e.g. newspaper). Although their non-verbal body postures implied that they were not listening to the ongoing mobile phone dialogue, they were all able to report accurately on the content of the conversation when asked later by the experimenters.

This unavoidable situation forces the bystander to eavesdrop on these ongoing conversations. Love (2001) pointed out that bystanders' personality may have an effect on how they feel when mobile phone conversations are carried out within close proximity to them. Love argued that bystanders with an introvert personality trait felt that they were drawn short-term into the mobile phone users' personal space and were uncomfortable about this.

However, to date, most of the research reported in this area has tended to focus on what is termed the developed world. Mobile phones are also transforming people's lives in the developing world as well. In Africa, the unreliable and inef-

ficient landline telecommunication infrastructure has made the mobile phone the solitary available communication tool for many people (BBC, 2004). However, as mobile phone use in Africa continues to grow, there is a need for mobile phone companies who are entering this market to consider the possible impact of cross-cultural differences in people's attitude towards mobile phone and service applications.

WHAT IS CULTURE?

Culture is a complicated paradigm that is difficult to accurately define. According to some researchers culture must be interpreted (van Peursson, in Evers and Day, 1997). Hofstede (1980) conceptualized culture as 'programming of the mind' suggesting that certain reactions were more likely in certain cultures than in others, based on differences between the basic values of the members of different cultures (Smith et al., 2004). Culture can also be seen as a collection of attributes people acquire from their childhood training. These attributes are associated with their environment, surroundings that influence the responses of people in that culture to new ideas, practices and use new technology (such as mobile phones). Given that culture may affect the way people behave and interact in general, Ciborowski (1979) identified a close link between knowledge and culture. In the context of mobile phone communication, it may be argued that culture influences knowledge or the individual's general experience therefore affecting, in this instance, their attitude towards mobile phone usage patterns.

Another explanation of culture has been offered by Hofstede (1980). He produced a cultural model that focuses on determining the patterns of thinking, feeling and acting that form a cultures "mental programming". This model has been adopted for the study reported in this paper as researchers in the area of cross-cultural differences and technology use consider it a valid and useful measure of systematic categorization (e.g. Mooij, 2003 and Honald, 1999). In addition, it is also considered to be directly related to the relationship between product design and user behaviour (Mooij, 2002). An explanation of Hofstede cultural dimensions is presented below:

- **Power distance**: The extent to which less powerful members expect and agree to unequal power distribution within a culture. The two aspects of this dimension are high and low power distance.
- **Uncertainty avoidance**: Discusses the way people cope with uncertainty and risk. The two faces of this dimension are high uncertainty avoidance and low uncertainty avoidance.
- **Masculinity vs. femininity:** Refers to gender roles, in contrast to physical characteristics, and is usually regarded by the levels of assertiveness or tenderness in the user. The two aspects of to this dimension are masculinity and femininity.
- **Individualism vs. collectivism:** Deals with the role of the individual and the group, and is defined by the level of ties between an individual in a society. The two aspects of this dimension are individualism and collectivism.
- **Time orientation:** Deals with the extent to which people relate to the past, present and future. The two aspects of this dimension are short-term orientation and long-term orientation.

Cross-Cultural Studies

Given that culture may affect the way people behave and interact in general, Ciborowski (1979) identified a close link between knowledge and culture. In this context, a number of cross-cultural studies have investigated differences in attitudes towards new technology. Smith, et al., (2001) carried out a study using Hofstede's model. They

adapted the Taguchi method – a partial factorial experimental design in order to investigate differences between British and Chinese users' satisfaction and preferences for websites. They found significant differences between British and Chinese users in their preference of detailed e-finance product information. For example, Chinese users tend to adopt a more holistic approach to viewing web content as compared to British users.

In another study, Honald (1999) found that German mobile phone users preferred clearly-written and inclusive rich user manuals, whereas Chinese mobile phone users focused on the quality of the pictorial information.

Evers and Day (1997) found that there are clear cultural differences between users acceptance of interfaces for different cultural groups. In their study, they found differences between Chinese and Indonesian users. Indonesians were found to like soft colours, black and white displays, and pop-up menus more than Chinese users. Also, Indonesian users seemed to prefer alternative input and output modes (e.g. sounds, touch screens, data gloves and multimedia) in comparison to the Chinese, who preferred the use of many different colours for the interface design.

Riviere and Licoppe (2005) noted distinct differences between the French and Japanese users in relation to uses of SMS. They found that the Japanese use SMS with a large number of contacts within the inner and outer circles, whereas French users limit their SMS to close correspondents. Japanese SMS users also considered text messages to be an effective medium to manage relationships within their inner circle and used them to save time and attention. French SMS users are more sensitive to the expected behaviour in public and private places. For example, they choose to use SMS to distance themselves and their remote partners from bystanders.

Rose, Evaristo and Straub (2003) studied the effect of culture on the attitude of e-commerce users towards web download time. The study is based on Hall's (1976) cultural model. According to Hall (1976), perceptions of time in different cultures are either monochronic or polychronic. Monochronic cultures tend to work on one issue at a time, and therefore delays in one task will have a delaying impact on the other tasks. People in monochronic cultures tend to be task-oriented; they value speed and normally do not change plans at the last minute (Bluedorn, Kaufman and Lane, 1992). Examples of monochronic cultures are the European /North American.

On the other hand, Hall (1976) found that people in polychronic cultures tend to change plans and focus on relationships rather than on tasks. Tella (2000) gave an example of how polychronic people perform their tasks in parallel; he suggested that polychronic people find it acceptable to answer their phone whilst having a videoconference with foreign partners, or even talk to a student while leaving the foreign partner on the line to wait. Polychronic cultures tend to perform more than one task at once; they can carry out other tasks while waiting for the first task to process. A person could simply turn his/ her attention from a main task to another that can be performed in parallel segments. Since polychronic cultures tend to perform more than one task at once, this attitude has made them more accommodating for delays in web download time. Example of polychronic cultures are Latin American and Middle Eastern countries (Hall, 1976).

In their study, Rose, Evaristo and Straub (2003) chose the US and Finnish cultures as representatives of monochronic cultures, and Egypt and Peru as representatives of polychromic cultures. Results showed that participants from polychronic cultures were significantly less concerned with download delays than participants in monochronic cultures. Also, perceived wait times varied significantly between the two types of culture. The result of this study suggested that the reason polychronic people were more willing to accept longer download time in e-commerce was not just related to their multi-tasking characteristic, but it

can also be related to their 'cultural training' that prepared them to endure longer waits, even in the absence of parallel tasks to occupy their time.

In addition, people in monochronic cultures would appear to prefer a reduction in some functionalities and features in order to reduce time delay in comparison to their polychronic counterparts. Rose, Evaristo and Straub (2003) indicated that this finding may suggest that polychronic cultures can cater for more services than would have been assumed, based on monochronic interests.

Choi, Lee and Kim (2005) studied the role of cultural differences in the design of a mobile data service in Finland, Korea and Japan. They drew out critical attributes that users in the three cultures required. The results of the study indicated that users' preferences for design attributes of a mobile data service differ from one culture to another. Four cultural dimensions developed by Hofstede (1980) and Hall (1976) were adopted to analyse the data: uncertainty avoidance, individualism vs. collectivism, that are part of the Hofstede (1980) framework, and context and time perception that are part of the Hall (1976) analysis. According to Hofstede (1980) Japanese and Koreans are part of the high uncertainty avoidance cultures, whereas Finnish belong to a low uncertainty avoidance culture. The results indicated that Korean and Japanese participants were found to be more averse to unclear situations. They preferred an efficient layout or space usage, a large amount of information within a screen, clear menu labelling, and secondary information about content. These features were found to help Japanese and Korean users to visualise the overall structure of menu items without moving to the next page. Marcus and Gould (2000) echoed the same results when they studied the effect of culture on website design and found that a large amount of information within the screen and clear menu labelling and secondary information about site contents decrease ambiguous situations and ultimately satisfy users' specific cultural needs.

In contrast, Finnish users had a negative attitude towards secondary information about content. According to Hofstede (1980), they are part of the low uncertainty group and are more willing to take risk and thus explore their required data without the need to have much information about the content.

Hofstede (1980) classified the Japanese and Finnish as part of the individualistic society. Choi, Lee and Kim (2005) found that Japanese and Finnish participants were more positive about having a limited variety of options for content but were not too keen on having too much information on the actual content as this interferes with their individualism. Finnish and Japanese participants perceived the variety of options available on content as a means to enhance their interaction experience. For example, knowing about popular mobile phone ring tones can be handy but not essential information for both Finnish and Japanese users.

In contrast, Korean participants preferred to have a wide variety of content, especially ranked content as ranked content provides detailed information about topics covered on the website such as movies, songs, books, etc.. For example, knowing more information about the name of the movie, how many people watched the movie, and the ranking of the movie helped Korean participants make their decisions in relation to buying movies. Accessing information that has already been browsed and ranked by others helps web surfers from a collectivistic society to feel more connected to other groups, and this attitude corresponds with their collectivistic nature as defined by Hofstede (1980).

Based on Hall's (1976) analysis, Koreans and Japanese belong to high context cultures, and according to Hall, in such cultures people prefer implicit messages and the use of metaphors, they also tend to prefer visual elements and symbols. In contrast, low context cultures (such as Finland) prefer explicit information in clear and simple messages. Results obtained from Choi, Lee and

Kim (2005) indicated that Japanese and Korean participants preferred to have an iconic menu style, a variety of font colours, and a selection of font sizes. In contrast, Finnish participants were found not to be interested in font colours and iconic menus, they preferred the mono-colour and text–based screen layouts.

The fourth dimension used to interpret the result of this study was time perception. Hall (1976) found that there is monochronic time perception and polychronic time perception, and according to him, Japan and Korea are parts of the monochronic time culture whereas Finland is part of the polychronic culture.

The results from Choi, Lee and Kim (2005) indicated that Korean, Japanese Finnish participants all showed monochronic traits. For example, participants from all the three countries chose to perform only one task at a time when using mobile data services, for example, downloading ring tones, downloading games, reserving movie tickets, and reading sports news.

In another study, Siala, O'Keefe and Hone (2004) studied the relationship between participants' religion and their attitudes towards websites that represent their faith. Muslim, Christian and non-religious participants took part on this study. The results indicated that Muslim participants were more trusting of a Muslim site compared to a Christian one. Muslims were also found to be more trusting of a Muslim site than the other two sites, whereas Christians preferred the non-religious one to the Christian site.

Despite the importance and the relevance of cultural factors and their impact on the use of global products and services (such as mobile phones), little research has compared the effect of cultural differences on issues such as social usability of mobile phones in the developing and the developed world. Han and Hong (2003) developed a relationship model to identify differences and similarities in the design features related to affective satisfaction of Korean, Hong Kong Chinese, and US users. They defined affective satisfaction as the user's subjective feelings towards the product shape and the actual impression they had after using the product. Han and Hong (2003) found that a mobile phone design that is accepted in Korea may not affectively satisfy US or Hong Kong Chinese users. Therefore they suggested that mobile phone designers need to tailor mobile phone design features to suit the nationality of the target user group. In support of this, Sun (2003) argues that variation in cultural states will cause different attitudes or ways of using mobile phones.

If mobile phone users have different usage patterns, the question that the study in this paper addresses is can we assume that people from different countries use mobile phones in the same way? Thus the question arises are there any roles for cultural differences in the way people use their mobile phones in public places? Therefore, the attitude of the British (a mature mobile phone user market) and the Sudanese (an emerging mobile phone user market) were examined in relation to their attitudes towards the use of mobile phones in public places.

METHODLOGY

Participants

Eighty eight participants took part in the study. 43 British (22 male, 21 female) and 45 Sudanese (20 male and 25 female) ranging in age from 15 to 63 years old, with the average age of 30 years. All participants were mobile phone users. The range of mobile phone use for the Sudanese participants was from 2-5 years whereas the British participants had used mobile phones for 4-12 years.

Data Collection

Data was collected in this study using a questionnaire and an interview. The development of the questionnaire went through several stages. Firstly,

the generation of the questionnaire was collated by employing an exhaustive review of the literature generally on mobile phones, human computer interaction and cultural issues in mobile phone use. Secondly, an in-depth session was conducted with participants from both countries (the UK and the Sudan) to develop the questionnaire. Initially a total of 9 Likert type questions were developed. The scale was then tested for content validity, which can be defined as the extent to which a test actually measures what it is supposed to measure (Rust and Golombok, 1989). This was undertaken using what is known as the judgemental approach, with three mobile HCI experts.

As a result of this process, the questionnaire was subsequently revised to consist of 6 Likert-type questions. The 6 Likert statements focused on attitudes towards the use of mobile phones in public places. An example of the Likert statement used in this study is given below:

Mobile phones should not be switched off during meetings :

☐ Strongly agree ☐ Agree ☐ Neutral
☐ Disagree ☐ Strongly disagree

The attitude scale had a combination of positive and negative statements in order to control for any possible acquiescence effect from participants when they were completing the attitude questionnaire. This is a phenomenon whereby participants in a study may unwittingly try to respond positively to every question in order to help the investigator with their study. This type of questionnaire format is one of the most common methods used to elicit attitudes from users in HCI research (Love, 2005).

In addition to the questionnaire, a semi structured interview was carried out. The interview questions included open ended and closed questions and were designed to gather information on the use of mobile phones in public places, the practice of the missed call, and other features such as the use of mobile phone Caller ID. The main points that were covered in the interview were:

1. Attitude towards the use of mobile phones in public places.
2. The use of the missed calls types in the two cultures. For example, the type of missed calls used and the social messages sent through the missed call and how recipients differentiate between these types of missed call.

Examples of questions covered in the interview were:

How do you feel about using mobile phone on public transport?

How do you feel about using mobile phone on places of worships?

How do you feel about using mobile phone in restaurants?

Procedure

Participants were chosen from an opportunistic sample in both the UK and Sudan and asked to complete the questionnaire and return them to the researcher once they had completed them.

The questionnaires took approximately 15 minutes to complete. At this point, an arrangement was made to interview a subset of the participants who had been selected randomly and volunteered to answer the interview questions. Participants were informed from the outset that the results of the study would be anonymous and they would be able to obtain the results of the study from the researcher on request.

RESULTS

An independent sample T test was carried out to compare attitudes towards using mobile phones in

public places in the UK and the Sudan. There was a significant difference found in the attitudes for using mobile phones in public transport between the British and the Sudanese. (t=5.99, p<0.001). The British were more willing to use it on public transport than the Sudanese.

Another significant difference was noted between the two countries towards using mobile phones whilst walking on the street. Again the British were more favourable towards this than the Sudanese (t=3.884, p<0.001). The Sudanese were found to be more willing to switch off their mobile phones in places of worships, meetings and in schools during classes. Please see Table 1 for a summary of the main results.

In terms of differences between the attitude of the British and the Sudanese males an Un-related T test revealed that the British males are more willing to use mobile phones on public transport and when walking on the street than the Sudanese males. (t=-2.912, t=.869, p<.001). Please see table 2 for a full summary of the results.

Comparing the attitudes of the British and the Sudanese females towards the use of mobile phones in public places. an Un-related t-test revealed the British females are more relaxed using mobile phones in public transport than the Sudanese females(t=2.348,p<.001). Please see table 3 for a full summary of the results.

Interview Results

The interview results corresponded with the questionnaire data indicating that there is a difference between the British and the Sudanese attitudes' towards the use of mobile phone in public places. Sudanese were found to be less willing to use mobile phone in public places than their British counterparts. In the interview Sudanese participants revealed various reasons for their uncomfortable attitude towards the use of mobile phones in public places. For example, some of the participants felt that the use of mobile phone in public transport is unacceptable because it can

Table 1. Attitudes towards the use of mobile phones in public places in the UK and the Sudan

	COUNTRY	N	Mean	Std. Deviation	Std. Error Mean	t	df	P Value Sig 2 tailed	
I would be comfortable using my mobile phone in restaurants	British	42	2.83	1.146	.177	1.325	70.241	.189	
	Sudan	45	2.56	.755	.113				
I would not be comfortable using my mobile phone on public transport	British	42	3.29	1.175	.181	5.925	69.046	.000	***
	Sudan	45	2.02	.753	.112				
I would be comfortable using my mobile phone whilst walking down the street	British	42	3.69	1.070	.165	3.884	82.171	.000	***
	Sudan	45	2.84	.952	.142				
Mobile phones should be switched off in places of worship	British	42	4.45	.861	.133	3.094	51.314	.003	**
	Sudan	45	4.89	.318	.047				
Mobile phones should not be switched off during meetings	British	42	3.88	.968	.149	2.316	69.411	.023	*
	Sudan	45	4.29	.626	.093				
Mobile phones should be switched off in schools during classes	British	42	4.00	1.307	.202	2.552	61.278	.013	*
	Sudan	45	4.58	.690	.103				

*P<0.05
**P<0.01
***P<0.001

be disturbing to other people in close proximity to the mobile phone user. As one of the Sudanese interviewees commented:

Using a mobile phone in public places, especially on public transport where you are closely surrounded by people is not something that you can do comfortably. It is viewed as improper and unacceptable as it disturbs others.

Another Sudanese interviewee added

The use of mobile phones on public transport may be considered as a sign of disrespect to others. In particular to older passengers, who you have to respect and act quietly around them.

An added justification that was revealed by Sudanese participants for not feeling comfortable using mobile phone in public places was related to their tight rules in keeping private issues private as one of the interviewee commented:

The use of mobile phones in public places to discuss private matters can put you in an awkward situation; because most of the people surrounding you will hear your conversation and this attitude in itself is not acceptable in our community. People are not expected to discuss private issues so publicly.

On the other hand, British participants were found to be more comfortable using mobile phones

Table 2. Attitude difference between the Sudanese males in using mobile phones in public places and the British males

	Gender	N	Mean	Std. Deviation	Std. Error Mean	t	df	P value sig 2 tailed	
Mobile phones should be switched off in places of worship	Sudanese Male	20	4.90	.308	.069				
	British Male	23	4.43	.992	.207	2.134	26.761	.042	
Mobile phones should be switched off during meetings	Sudanese Male	20	4.20	.523	.117				
	British Male	23	3.83	1.154	.241	1.397	31.583	.172	***
Mobile phones not to be switched on in schools during classes	Sudanese Male	20	4.50	.827	.185				
	British Male	23	4.17	1.403	.293	.942	36.374	.352	
I would be happy using mobile phones in restaurants	Sudanese Male	20	2.50	.688	.154				
	British Male	23	2.70	1.105	.230	-.706	37.389	.485	*
I would not be comfortable using a mobile phone on public transport	Sudanese Male	20	2.25	.786	.176				
	British Male	23	3.13	1.180	.246	-2.912	38.570	.006	**
I would be comfortable using a mobile phone whilst walking on the street	Sudanese Male	20	3.15	.813	.182				
	British Male	23	4.04	.825	.172	.869	40.330	.001	**

*P<0.05
**P<0.01
***P<0.001

in public places as one of the interviewees commented:

I have no problems using my mobile phone in public places and especially on public transport, as I can make use of time while sitting there doing nothing.

Another British interviewee added:

I use my mobile phone in public places all the time and it does not bother me at all that people are listening to my mobile phone conversations. I do not know them and it is unlikely they are going to know more details about the topic I am discussing.

The results of this study also indicated that Sudanese females were less willing to use mobile phones in public places than British females. Sudanese females felt that the use of mobile phones in public places, especially on public transport, could attract unwanted attention to them in a society that expects females to keep a low profile. This was echoed in one of the Sudanese female interviewee's comments:

I do not like using my mobile phone in public places at all as it only magnetizes others' attention towards me. If you are on the mobile phone in a public place people start gazing at you unappreciatively.

Table 3. Attitude differences between females in the UK and the Sudan

	Gender	N	Mean	Std. Deviation	Std. Error Mean	t	df	P value sig 2 tailed	
Mobile phones should be switched off in places of worship	Sudanese Female	25	2.60	.816	.163				
	British Female	19	3.00	1.202	.276	-1.248	30.068	.222	
Mobile phones should be switched off during meetings	Sudanese Female	25	1.84	.688	.138				
	British Female	19	3.47	1.172	.269	-5.408	27.256	.000	***
Mobile phones should not be switched in schools during classes	Sudanese Female	25	2.60	1.000	.200				
	British Female	19	3.26	1.195	.274	-1.955	34.863	.059	
I would be happy to use my mobile phone in a restaurant	Sudanese Female	25	4.88	.332	.066				
	British Female	19	4.47	.697	.160	2.348	24.196	.027	*
I would not be comfortable using a mobile phone on public transport	Sudanese Female	25	4.36	.700	.140				
	British Female	19	3.95	.705	.162	1.929	38.758	.061	
I would be comfortable using a mobile phone whilst walking on the street	Sudanese Female	25	4.64	.569	.114				
	British Female	19	3.79	1.182	.271	2.892	24.322	.008	**

*P<0.05
**P<0.01
***P<0.001

Another Sudanese females interviewee added:

Usually I do not use my mobile phone in public places, I prefer to keep a low profile. For me this attitude is a sign of respect for my self and others.

British females appeared to have different view, most of the interviewees were found to feel more comfortable using their mobile phones in public places. As one of the British interviewees commented:

I prefer to use my mobile phone in public places, it keeps me busy and in a way safe, for example

when I want to get my car from the car park when it is dark, I always make sure that I am talking to one of my friends on the mobile phone just in case something happens.

Missed Call Use

An interesting finding that emerged from this study was the missed call practice and uses of missed call. A missed call can be defined here as a caller ending a mobile phone call to a third party before they answer the call.

From the results, it seemed that both British and Sudanese used the missed call to request a call back. However, the British are more likely to use this type of missed call if the recipient has free talking time to call back, as one of the interviewees said:

I request a call back from my mum or friend if I know that she has free minutes to call me back.

The Sudanese were found to be more interested in using the missed call as an emotional gift than the British. According to the Sudanese, in this case, it can contain different sets of emotions or messages that can be transmitted and shared with the recipient. For example, it can mean "hi", or "thinking of you" "how are you today?" etc. The Sudanese seem to enjoy the emotional gift and trying to unfold its meaning, as one of the interviewees commented:

Missed call as emotional gift is understandable; although it is just a ring, it means a lot. I usually get them from my friends who are distant and we do not meet every day, so we make sure we are fine, also I use it with my extended family as well.

Missed call as an emotional gift makes me happy and it is a nice way to stay in touch especially if you do not have credit. When I get one of them, I usually reply back by a phone call, SMS or even a missed call, depending on my credit.

In contrast, British mobile phone users were found to prefer using phone calls or SMS to socialise and convey their social messages rather than sending a missed call. This was expressed by one of the interviewees as follows:

A missed call is just a ring even if it is used as an emotional gift. How would I know that the caller wanted to send me an emotional gift? Maybe it was done accidentally. Perhaps the caller pressed my number by mistake when he actually wanted to delete my name from his contact list.

In this study, the value of the missed call as an emotional gift was also compared to the SMS in its ability to recall past thoughts. Again, the British were found to prefer the SMS as an emotional gift and they appreciate its ability in recalling past thoughts. One of the reasons for this appreciation is related to the explicit merit of the SMS and the fact that the SMS is more tangible and significant in comparison to the missed call as one of the interviewees commented:

SMS are more definite, actual words are put into it. The message you receive has value and meanings and it brings up a memory trigger.

Another element that was regarded as an added value to the SMS is the wider spectrum of emotions and messages that can be transmitted. As one of the interviewees commented:

No, I can't compare them because the missed call as an emotional gift can't convey any form of emotional reflection, unlike SMS which has some sort of context for you to interpret.

SMS as an emotional gift are more affectionate as you are putting your emotions in words, whereas the missed call is just a ring, it's not the same. Additionally, with the missed call as an emotional gift, you need to arrange with receivers in advance what sort of message you are intending to send".

One of the reasons British participants expressed their unwillingness to use the missed call as an emotional gift is they feel that as an emotional gift it does not embrace tangible objects or visual contexts that can be shared with friends. According to the British participants, the ring of the missed call is a mystery announcement that is only known to the recipients, therefore they cannot share the emotional thoughts associated with the ring that the sender intended. As one of the interviewees commented:

Usually, when I get a nice SMS I tend to share it with my friends. How will I share a ring with them even if it is from a loved one?.

On the other hand, although the Sudanese were found to acknowledge the significance of the SMS as an emotional gift in recalling past thoughts they also appreciated the ability of the missed call as an emotional gift in doing so. One of the Sudanese interviewees expressed her appreciation of the emotional gift conveyed in a missed call in the following way:

Hearing the short ring tone and seeing the caller's name helps me to understand the nature of the missed call and when I realise it is an emotional gift, that is really exciting and amazing. It enables you to evoke feelings and emotions.

Some interviewees went a step further as they appreciated the value of both the SMS and missed call. They actually considered the missed call as a unique feature to convey messages in a cost effective way.

I grade them the same, both mean you are remembered by the caller and every time I see the caller's number on my log call I enjoy the pleasant feeling, plus the missed call is free.

In addition, Sudanese participants seem to use the missed call as a creative form of conveying a special emotion, especially if it used in the context of romance. As one of the interviewees commented:

Missed calls as an emotional gift can be extra special if you get them from a known person like your fiancé, for example, because it brings a special shared feeling that has an inspired way of communication.

The mobile phone ring tone is another aspect that the Sudanese seem to identify between the SMS and the missed call as an emotional gift. The shortness of the missed call ring tone is considered to have a negative impact on the merit of the missed call because the sound of the missed call is short in comparison to the SMS ring tones.

In addition, the fact that the ring tone is very short, and that mobile phone ring tones,

in general, tend to start quiet and then escalate louder as it goes on, have increased the chances of not hearing the emotional gift when it is received. Consequently, it may lose its purpose and impact in relation to the specific intention with which it has sent. As several of the interviewees commented:

Missed calls generally are a short and quick ring that is cut quickly, but with emotional gift it is made even shorter.

On one occasion, my friend sent me an emotional gift missed call to make sure that 'I arrived home safely'. As I did not hear the ring tone, I did not receive the gift on time, in a way it lost its significance.

The practice of the missed call provides a clear proof of how users from different cultures can develop their own style of using technologies. Both sets of participants agreed that the meaning of the missed call can be easily misunderstood because of the confusion related to the code developed between users, and also the need to have mutual agreement on the meaning of the missed call in advance.

DISSCUSION

The results from the study were interpreted in the light of Hofstede's (1980) cultural dimensions to try and gain some insight into the way culture may influence the use of mobile phones in public places.

It appears from the results that the British generally are more comfortable using mobile phones in public places than their Sudanese participants, who are more reluctant to use mobile phones in contexts such as public transport and whilst walking along the street.

The collectivistic culture to which the Sudan belongs to (using Hofstede's criteria) indicates an inclination toward a tightly-knit social framework (Hofstede, 1980). The priority is for the groups' needs rather than the individual wishes. Therefore, perhaps the use of mobile phones in public places for private talks can be seen as a self-centred act and quite impertinent for the group needs. The group expect the individual to be considerate to the established social etiquette. The mobile phone user in public transport is expected to adhere to the social protocol and to respect other people's privacy.

Another reason for the British comfortable attitude to mobile phone use in public places may be due to bystanders' non-verbal communication attitude. This concept is highlighted by Goffman (1963) where he refers to it as "civil inattention", the ways in which people acknowledge the existence of others without paying them extra attention; he regarded this as a gesture of respect required from strangers. Lasen (2002) found that "civil inattention" is clearly present in UK culture; the British tend to avoid open and straightforward looking at other people and keeping away from paying direct attention to others, especially on public transport, such as the Underground. He suggested that this attitude may encourage British mobile phone users to talk more freely outdoors without being concerned about others watching them.

In contrast, in the Sudan, it was noted that 'civil inattention' is not clearly evident. Sudanese people tend to look at each other directly. Lasen (2002) suggested that a lack of proper gaze in certain cultures where 'civil inattention' does not rule may be viewed as a lack of respect or ignorance. This lack of civil inattention perhaps justifies the reason behind the Sudanese unwillingness to use mobile phones in public places, as they are influenced by a bystander's non-verbal communication attitude. Perhaps one can say that the more civil inattention paid to others, the more free and relaxed they might feel towards using their mobile phones, and vice versa.

Another justification for not using mobile phones in public places might be due to the high score that the Sudan attained on Hofstede's uncertainly avoidance dimension. According to Hofstede, cultures with high uncertainty avoidance tend to be expressive; people talk with their hands, raise their voices, and show emotions.

These characteristics can play a role in decreasing the need to carry out private conversations in public places, because people in these cultures know that they tend to talk loudly and expressively, which attracts bystanders' attention. Plus, there is a high risk of being known to people round about you.

Another important point is that as Sudanese people in general talk loudly and in an expressive way, this tends to increase the level of external noise for mobile phone users. Therefore, people talking on mobile phones need to raise their voices more to win over competitive speakers. This loud talking may attract bystanders' attention and invite eavesdroppers, which can cause a feeling of embarrassment on the part of the mobile phone user. In addition, mobile phone users may feel bystanders might disrespect them if they discuss their private matters publicly.

Additionally, the Sudanese attitude might be related to the high score obtained on Hofstede's power distance dimension where a tight set of rules is established and people are expected to follow and respect these rules. For example, the social protocol for behaviour in public places is well recognised in the Sudan and people are expected to behave in a certain way and not to speak loudly in front of others (especially older people). Private issues should be kept private and dealt with in a private manner and in private settings. It is considered improper to breach these norms. Although in the UK a social protocol for behaviour in public places also exists, the maturity of the UK mobile phone market may have relaxed or altered people's expectations and acceptance of mobile phone behaviour in public places. Palen et al., (2000) found that a person's attitude towards public cell phone use changes (becomes more accepting) as his/her mobile phone use increases. In addition, Palen (2002) predicted that as adoption of mobile phones increases, people will be less disturbed about proper use, but will still prefer to have 'cell free' zones.

Another justification for the British willingness to use mobile phones in public places might be related to their individualistic nature and their appreciation of personal time according to Hofstede's typology. Therefore, the British generally value time greatly and this reflects on their willingness to use mobile phones in public places. For example, they use the mobile phones on public transport to make use of the "time" available. In contrast, the Sudanese perceive 'time' in a more relaxed way and this perhaps decreases the urge to make use of time to carry out private talk in a public domain.

In terms of specific gender differences, Sudanese females were found to be more uncomfortable about using mobile phones in public places in comparison to British females. This attitude fits in with the 'Masculine attribute of the Sudan culture suggested by Hofstede (1980), where women are expected to care for others. The UK, in contrast, is judged by Hofstede to be more Feminine-oriented where the caring for others is the responsibility of men and women..

Although the Sudanese females practise all their rights in terms of education, work, leisure, and the like, they are looked after and cared for by the whole society. As a result of this caring perception towards females in the Sudanese culture, their attitudes and behaviours are more controlled and guarded and they are expected to follow social protocols more than men. For example, Sudanese females are expected to keep a low profile and deflect attention from themselves by talking quietly and preferably avoid talking in public spaces.

On the other hand, according to the results of this study, British females are more comfortable using mobile phones in public places. In contrast to the Sudanese females, British females can use mobile phones in public places as "symbolic body-guards" (Lasen, 2002); mobile phones are used as a technique to defend your private space within areas that are heavily populated with unknown strangers (Cooper, 2000; Haddon, 2000). As Goffman (1963) has remarked, women especially do not like to show themselves alone in public places because this may indicate that they are not in a relationship, a condition which (1) provides a bad impression of their social status, and (2) leaves them in a vulnerable situation which can be acted upon by unknown males. To deal with these situations the mobile phone is quite useful, as it works as a safety net and indicates that this person has social networks and is not isolated (Plant, 2002).

The other significant result reported in this study is that the Sudanese are more likely to switch off their mobile phones in places of worship. Measuring these results against the Hofstede typology, the Sudanese score high on the uncertainty avoidance scale; religion is valued and greatly respected. People's attitude towards switching off mobile phones in places of worship in the Sudan is therefore expected. It is also related to the high scores Sudan has on power distance, as roles are set and religious men are very much valued and respected in the society, so both Muslims and Christians in the Sudan tend to be aware of the importance of switching off their mobile phones in places of worship. This result could also be related to the reduced number of people in the UK attending places of worship.

The Sudanese also appear more willing to switch off their mobile phones during meetings than the UK participants. This attitude may be related to their high score in the power distance dimension where people are expected to respect the structure, rules and the norms of the setting where they are currently present.

As for the British disinclination to switch off their mobile phones during meetings it might be related to the individualistic feature of the British society, where time is valued and there is a push for making good use of it. It may also be related to the maturity of British mobile phone adoption where mobile phones have blurred the borders between business and social rules. In relation to this, Churchill (2001) found that the mobile phones in the UK are used to form and maintain both work and leisure relationships.

Results obtained from the study also indicated that there were differences in attitude towards missed call use between UK and Sudanese participants. In the UK, mobile phone users prefer not to use the missed call to communicate but yet use the missed call to request a call back (especially among young users). The British also used the missed call after sending SMS to draw the recipient's attention, or as a reminder for a prior arrangement. However, they were not in favour of using the missed call as an emotional gift, unlike the Sudanese, who used the missed call to send social and emotional messages such as "I'm thinking of you", or just to say "Hi". In addition, the Sudanese use the missed call to request a call back from friends and family and they used the missed call for other applications such as before sending SMS to check the status of the recipient's mobile phone and as a reminder for prior arrangements.

CONCLUSION

The increase use of mobile phones by people from different cultural backgrounds has become an integral part of our world phenomena, yet to date the impact of cultural differences on the way people use their mobile phones and its implications on mobile phone design has failed to be investigated comprehensively. As this chapter illustrates, mobile phone users with cultural differences were found to use their mobile phones in different ways and their attitudes may have been influenced by their cultural norms. Although one can argue that cultural norms can be reshaped by technology, results obtained from this study indicate that cultural heritage would appear to influence users' mobile phone behaviour.

The increasing popularity of different types of missed calls in different cultures highlights the need for an effective way of understanding and interpreting the meaning of a missed call. Both sets of participants agreed that the meaning of the missed call can be easily misunderstood because of the confusion related to the code developed between users, and also the need to have mutual agreement on the meaning of the missed call in advance. Until now, the missed call as a form of communication has not been considered in mobile phone design, and developers of mobile phones need to determine the technological choices required to develop mobile phones that meet cultural needs.

Overall, therefore, the results obtained from this study suggest that mobile phone designers need to develop a richer understanding of culture in order to develop mobile phones that satisfy cultural specific needs and thus support mobile phone users' in their current and potential future communication activities. This is an issue we intend to explore in the next phase of our research.

REFERENCES

Agar, J. (2003). *Constant Touch: A Global History of the Mobile Phone*. UK: Icon Books

Bray, J. (2005) *International companies and post-conflict reconstruction* (Social Development Papers No.79). Washington DC: The World Bank

BBC News (2004). Africans rush for mobile phones. BBC News. Published May 5, 2004. http://news.bbc.co.uk/1/hi/world/africa/3686463.stm

Bluedorn, A. C., Kaufman, C. J., & Lane, P. M. (1992). How Many Things Do You Like to Do at Once? An Introduction to Monochronic and Polychronic Time. *The Academy of Management Executive*, 17-26.

Burns, T. (1992), *Erving Goffman*. London: Routledge

Churchill, E. (2001). *Getting About a Bit: Mobile Technologies & Mobile Conversations in the UK*. FXPL.International Technical report, FXPAL. TR.01-009.

Ciborowski, T. J. (1979). Cross-Cultural aspects of Cognitive Functioning: Culture and Knowledge. In A. J. Marsella, R. G. Tharp, and T. J. Ciborowski (Eds), *Perspectives on Cross-Cultural Psychology*. New York, NY: Academic Press Inc.

Choi, B., Lee, I., Kim, J., & Jeon, Y. (2005). A Qualitative Cross-National Study of Cultural Influences on Mobile Data Service Design. In *Proceedings of CHI 2005*, (Portland, Oregon, USA), pp.. 661-670.

Cooper, G. (2000). *The Mutable Mobile: Social Theory in the Wireless World*. Paper presented at the 'Wireless World' workshop, University of Surrey, April 7th.

Donner, J. (2005c). *The Rules of Beeping: Exchanging Messages using Missed Calls on Mobile Phones in Sub-Saharan Africa*. Paper presented at the 55th Annual Conference of the International Communication Association: Questioning the Dialogue, New York.

Evers, V., & Day, D. (1997). The Role of Culture in Interface Acceptance. In Mende S. Howard, J. Hammond and G.Lindgaard, *Proceedings of the Human Computer Interaction INTERACT'97 Conference* (pp. 260 – 267). Sydney: Chapman and Hall.

Fortunati, L. (2000). *The Mobile Phone: New Social Categories and Relations*. Paper presented at the seminar 'Sosiale Konsekvenser av

Mobiltelefoni', organised by Telenor, 16th June, 2000, Oslo.

Geser, H. (2005). Towards a Sociological Theory of the Mobile Phone. In Zerdick, A., Picot, A, Scrape. K., Burgleman, J-C, Silverstone, R., Feldmann, V., Wernick, C. and Wolff, C. (Eds.). *E-Merging Media: Communication and the Media Economy of the Future*. Springer, Berling. (pp.235-60). Also available at http://socio.ch/mobile/t_geserl.pdf

Goffman E. (1963). *Behaviour in Public Places. Notes on the Social Organization of Gatherings*. New York: Free Press.

Haddon, L. (2000). *The Social Consequences of Mobile Telephony: Framing Questions*. Paper presented at the seminar 'Sosiale Konsekvenser av Mobiltelefoni', organised by Telenor, 16th June, 2000, Oslo.

Hall, E. T. (1976). *Beyond Culture*. Garden City, NY: Anchor Doubleday Press

Han, S. H., & Hong, S. W. (2003, October). A systematic approach for coupling user satisfaction with product design. *Ergonomics*, *46*(13/14), 1441-1461.

Hofstede, G. (1980). *Culture's Consequences: International Differences in Work-Related Values*. Beverly Hills, California: SAGE Publications.

Honold, P. (1999, May). Learning How to Use a Cellular Phone: Comparison Between German and Chinese Users. *Jour Soc. Tech. Comm.*, *46*(2), 196-205.

Idowu, B., & Ogunbodede, E. (2003). Information and communication technology in Nigeria. *Journal of Information Technology Impact, 3(2)*, 69-76

Internetworldstats (2006, December). www. Internetworldstats.com/stats.htm [accessed January 2007]

ITU- International Telecommunications Union (2004). Social and Mobile Communications for a more Mobile World. *Background Paper ITU/MIC Workshop on shaping the Future Mobile Information Society*, International Telecommunications Union, 2004.

Kelly, T., Minges, M., & Gray, V. (2002). *World Telecommunication Development report: reinventing Telecoms, Executive summary*. Available at http://ww.itu.int

Lasen, A. (2002b). *A comparative Study of Mobile Phone Use in London, Madrid and Paris*.

Licoppe, C., & Heurtin, J-P, (2002). France: Preserving the Image. In J. Katz and R. Aakhus (eds) *Perpetual Contact: Mobile Communication, Private Talk, Public Performance*. Cambridge: Cambridge University Press. (pp. 99-108).

Ling, R. (2004). *The mobile connection: The cell phone's impact on society*. San Francisco: Morgan Kaufmann.

Love, S. (2005) Understanding Mobile Human-Computer interaction. Elesvier Blueworth Heinemann, London.

Love, S., & Perry, M. (2004). Dealing with mobile conversations in public places: some implications for the design of socially intrusive technologies. Proceedings of CHI 2004, Vienna, 24-29 April, ACM 1-58113-703-6/04/2004.

Love, S. (2001). Space invaders: Do mobile phone conversations invade people's personal space? In Human factors in telecommunication. In K. Nordby (Ed.), *Bergen, Human Factors in Telecommunications*.

Oyelaran-Oyeyinka, B., & Nyaki Adeya, C. (2004). Internet Access in Africa: Empirical Evidence from Kenya and Nigeria. *Telematics and Informatics, 21*(1), 67-81.

Palen, L. (2002). *Mobile Telephony in a Connected Life*. Communications of the ACM, *45*(3), 78-82.

Palen, L., Salzman, M., & Youngs, E. (2000). Going Wireless:Behaviour and Practice of New Mobile Phone Users. *Proceedings of the Conference on Computer Supported Cooperative Work (CSCW'00)*, 201-210.

Plant, S. (2002). *On the Mobile: The Effects of Mobile Telephones on Social and Individual Life*. Motorola, London. Available at http://motorola.com/mot/doc/0/267_MotDoc.pdf

Marcus, A., & Gould, E. W. (2000). Crosscurrents: Cultural dimensions and global Web user-interface design. *Interactions, 7*(4), 32-46.

Mooij, M. (2003). *Consumer Behavior and Culture. Consequences for Global Marketing and Advertising*. Thousand Oaks, CA: Sage Publications Inc.*Eurobarometer 55 and The Young Europeans* (2001) Brussels: European Commission Directorate.

Mooij, M. (2002). Convergence and divergence in consumer behavior: implications for international retailing. *Journal of Retailing, 78*, 61-69.

Murtagh G. M. (2001). Seeing the rules preliminary observations of action, interaction and mobile phone use. In B. Brown, N. Green, & R. Harper, (Eds), *Wireless World. Social and Interactional Aspects of the Mobile Age*. London: Springer-Verlag. (pp. 81-91).

Riviere, C. A., & Licoppe, C. (2005). From voice to text: Continuity and change in the use of mobile phones in France and Japan (pp 103-126). In R. Harper (Eds.), *The Inside Text: Social Perspectives on SMS in the Mobile Age*. London: Springer-Verlag.

Rose, G. M., Evaristo, R., & Straub, D. (2003). Culture and Consumer Responses to Web Download Time: A Four-Continent Study of Mono-and Polychronism. *IEEE Transactions on Engineering Management, 50*(1), 31-44.

Rust, J., & Golombok, S. (1989). *Modern pychometrics: The science of psychological assessment*. New York: Routledge.

Siala, H., O'Keefe, R., & Hone, K. (2004). The Impact of Religious Affiliation on Trust in the Context of Electronic Commerce. *Interacting with Computers, 16*(2004) 7-27.

Smith A., Dunckley, L., French, T., Minocha, S., & Chang, Y. (2004). A Process Model for Developing Usable Cross-Cultural Websites. *Interacting with Computers, 16*, 63–91.

Smith, A., French, T., Chang, Y., & McNeill, M. (2001). E-Culture: A comparative study of eFinance web site usability for Chinese and British users. Designing for global markets. Conference (6th. 2001). In D. Day & L. Duckley (Eds.), *Proceedings of the third international workshop on internationalisation of products and systems*. Buckinghamshire: The Open University. (pp. 87-100).

Sun, H. (2003). *Exploring Cultural Usability: A Localization Study of Mobile Text Messaging Use*. Paper presented at the CHI 2003, Ft. Lauderdale, FL.

Tella, S., & Mononen-Aaltonen, M. (2000). *Towards Network-Based Education:*

A Multidimensional Model for Principles of Planning and Evaluation.

The New York Times (2005). *Cellphones catapult rural Africa into the 21st Century*. Accessed 25th August 2005.

Chapter VI
Discourses on User Participation:
Findings from Open Source Software Development Context

Netta Iivari
University of Oulu, Finland

ABSTRACT

Users should participate in information technology (IT) artifact development, but it has proven to be challenging. This applies also in the open source software (OSS) development. This chapter critically examines discursive construction of user participation in academic literatures and in practice, in IT artifact development. First three academic discourses constructing user participation are discussed. Then the discursive construction of user participation is explored in OSS development literature. Afterwards, results from several empirical, interpretive case studies are outlined. Some of them have been carried out in the IT artifact product development organizations, others in the OSS development context. Clear similarities can be identified in the discourses constructing user participation in these divergent IT artifact development contexts. The academic discourses on user participation clearly also legitimate certain ways of constructing user participation in practice. The OSS development literature bears resemblance mainly with the Human Computer Interaction (HCI) discourse on user participation. Therefore, it is argued that especially the HCI community should carefully reflect on what kinds of discourses on user participation it advocates and deems as legitimate.

INTRODUCTION

This paper critically examines discursive construction of user participation in academia and in practice - in information technology (IT) artifact[1] development. User participation refers to users' participative activities including 'both formal and informal, direct and indirect, and active and passive activities, performed alone or with others" (Barki & Hartwick, 1994, pp. 61). Specific attention is paid to open source software (OSS) development context, which has been acknowledged as a relevant development context both in Information Systems (IS) and Human Computer Interaction (HCI) research (Andreasen et al. 2006, Cetin et al 2007, Fitzgerald 2006, Niederman et al 2006, Nichols & Twidale, 2003; Zhao & Deek 2006). Characteristic to OSS development is that the source code needs to be "available for anyone who wants to use or modify it", even though due to differences in the licensing agreements, there actually is a "continuum of openness" (Niederman et al 2006: 131).

OSS development context has also been considered a challenging context from the viewpoint of user participation. User population of OSS is becoming larger, including a growing number of non-technical, non computer professional users, who are not interested in OSS development, but only in the resulting solution (Cetin et al 2007, Franke & von Hippel 2003, Frishberg et al. 2002, Nichols & Twidale 2006, Niederman et al. 2006, Scacchi 2002, Viorres et al. 2007, Ye & Kishida 2003). From the point of view of these users, usability of OSS tends to he poor, and the development process anything but 'user centered' (Andreasen et al. 2006, Benson et al 2004, Bødker et al 2007, Cetin et al 2007, Feller & Fitzgerald 2000, Nichols & Twidale 2006, Twidale & Nichols 2005, Zhao & Deek 2005, Zhao & Deek 2006).

This paper adopts a critical poststructuralist approach informed by Foucaultian tradition for the analysis of discourses on user participation in IT artifact development. This approach has been

discussed more thoroughly in Iivari (2006). This paper relies on that description. This paper critically examines discourses on user participation. Regarding the construction of user participation in research, it has been argued that user participation is a very vague concept and there is a variety of views of what user participation is, and how it should be accomplished (e.g. Asaro, 2000; Barki & Hartwick, 1994). The influential role of academic communities in imposing meanings and 'truths' to the social world has been recognized (Cooper & Bowers, 1995; Bloomfield & Vurdubakis, 1997; Finken, 2003; Weedon, 1987). Some studies (Cooper & Bowers, 1995; Finken, 2003) have already examined HCI and participatory design (PD) traditions in the Foucaultian spirit as discourses constructing their objects of study (e.g. the users and the user interface, UI) in particular ways and at the same time legitimizing their existence. This paper continues their work, but adds new insights by reviewing more recent literature and by incorporating an OSS development perspective in the analysis.

Regarding user participation in practice, existing literature has warned that user participation may be used only as a buzzword or a weapon for achieving surprising or even paradoxical ends (Beath & Orlikowski, 1994, Catarci et al., 2002; Hirschheim & Newman, 1991; Howcroft & Wilson, 2003; Kirsch & Beath, 1996; Nielsen, 1999; O'Connor 1995, Robey & Markus, 1984; Symon, 1998). Some studies on discourses (e.g. Alvarez, 2002; Bloomfield & Vurdubakis, 1997; Nielsen, 1999; Sarkkinen & Karsten, 2005) have already analyzed discourses in IT artifact development, criticizing them for mainly reinforcing management agendas and goals. However, there is a clear lack of both empirical studies and studies on discourses on user participation in the challenging OSS development context. Therefore, this paper takes a step towards filling this gap by utilizing a poststructuralist approach informed by Foucauldian tradition. This approach has also gained increasing attention in IS research during recent years, and empirical studies on discourses relying on Foucaultian tradition have proliferated (e.g. Doolin, 1999; Iivari 2006, Sayer & Harvey, 1997; Wynn et al. 2003), even though none of them address discourses on user participation in the challenging OSS development context.

The paper is organized as follows. The next section introduces the poststructuralist approach utilized in this paper. The third section identifies academic discourses on user participation in IS and HCI literatures. In addition, OSS development literature is reviewed from the viewpoint of user participation. The fourth section presents discourses on user participation identified in empirical case studies in the IT artifact product development context. In addition, results from interpretive case studies in OSS development context (see Iivari 2008a, Iivari 2008b, Iivari, Hedberg & Kirves 2008) are compared to the results. The discourses identified from the empirical material are also related to the wider discursive field in which the academic IS and HCI communities participate and contribute. The final section discloses the central observations of the paper, discusses their implications and outlines paths for future work.

POSTSTRUCTURALIST APPROACH

This paper relies on a critical poststructuralist approach informed by Foucaultian tradition in the analysis of discourses on user participation (see Iivari 2006). Within this approach language, subjectivity and power are central notions. Language is in a critical position: it is assumed that language doesn't represent reality, but produces it. It is maintained that all prevalent definitions are constructed in language. (Weedon, 1987; Weedon, 2004.) Discourses are 'certain ways of speaking' that 'systematically form the objects of which they speak' (Foucault, 1972: 49). Discourses compete with each other and struggle over meanings in language. There is a quest to

disseminate the preferred understandings of the world. (Fairclough & Wodak, 1997; Foucault, 1972, Weedon, 1987.)

Discourses are both socially constituted and socially constitutive. Discourses construct our identities and our objects of knowledge. (Fairclough & Wodak, 1997; Weedon, 2004.) Subjectivity is assumed to be fragile, contradictory and constantly constituted in discourses (Weedon, 1987: 33, Weedon, 2004). Discourses offer individuals subject positions that must be occupied if participating in the discourses (Foucault, 1972; Foucault, 1980). People are continuously persuaded as subjects in the discourses that constitute individuals as 'subjects of a certain kind'. However, people do not only adopt the discourses and the subject positions offered to them, but the discourses can also be questioned and challenged. (Weedon, 1987; Weedon, 2004.) Nevertheless, some discourses are more available and influential than others. On the other hand, one needs to acknowledge also that access to the discourses might be limited and not all individuals have the right to participate in a discourse. (Foucault, 1972; Weedon, 1987.)

Based on this discussion, guidelines for the analysis of discourses on user participation are outlined. First, it is important to analyze the formation of objects. One needs to analyze the statements that constitute the objects (e.g. users and their participation) in discourses. One needs to focus on 'certain ways of speaking' that exclude other ways. Foucault maintains that 'everything is never said' and 'few things are said of the totality'. Therefore, one needs to concentrate on statements that have emerged excluding others. Second, one needs to analyze the subject positions individuals must occupy to take part in a discourse – both as speakers and as listeners (i.e. subject positions offered to and adopted by the researchers and practitioners advocating user participation or participating as users). Discourses invite people as subjects into the discourses. However, it is also important to acknowledge that access might be limited and only a limited amount of individuals may be allowed to adopt the subject position and consequently participate in the discourse. (Foucault, 1972; Foucault, 1980.)

DISCOURSES ON USER PARTICIPATION - IN RESEARCH

In IT Artifact Development in General

It is widely accepted that users should participate in the development of IT artifacts, but there is a multiplicity of ways to understand and interpret user participation. Next, few HCI and IS discourses on user participation identified in the existing literature are outlined. First, a **practical HCI discourse** constructing *user* participation has been identified (Iivari 2006). This discourse has been identified from very practical HCI textbooks and articles addressing issues such as how to 'design quality HCI' and 'make your organization user-centric'. The speaker is positioned as a consultant and a change agent offering advice on this quest. This discourse constitutes user participation of indirect nature. There are to be 'user surrogates' (called HCI specialists from now on), 'representing the users in development' (Aucella, 1997; Bias & Reitmeyer, 1995; Cooper 1999, Fellenz, 1997; Nielsen 1993, Tudor, 1998; Vredenburg, 1999). However, this has proven to be very challenging - the position of the HCI specialists is articulated as problematic (Aucella, 1997; Bias & Reitmeyer, 1995; Mayhew, 1999a; Mayhew, 1999b; Rosenbaum et al., 2000).

Another position assigned to HCI specialists is that of a user surrogate involving the developers, by manipulating and seducing them to 'buy into HCI work'. The developers are postulated as a very important target group (Aucella, 1997; Bloomer & Croft, 1997; Boivie et al., 2003; Cooper, 1999; Grudin, 1991b; Fellenz, 1997; Mayhew, 1999a; Mayhew, 1999b; Muller & Carey, 2002; Nielsen, 1993; Seffah & Andreevskaia, 2003; Tudor, 1998;

Vredenburg, 1999), who should be involved in HCI work (Aucella, 1997; Billingsley, 1995; Bloomer & Croft, 1997; Fellenz, 1997; Tudor, 1998). They should be involved early in order that the activities affect the design (Aucella, 1997; Grudin, 1991a; Grudin, 1991b). Altogether, project teams should 'buy into usability' (Aucella, 1997) and the teams should perceive HCI specialists as team members and allies (Bias & Reitmeyer, 1995; Fellenz, 1997; Mayhew, 1999a; Mayhew, 1999b; Muller & Carey, 2002; Rosenbaum et al., 2000).

Furthermore, HCI specialists are positioned as change agents that address many different target groups – management, documentation, training, marketing, different kinds of change and improvement efforts – in their organization. Management's commitment is postulated as an important criterion for success (Beyer & Holtzblatt, 1998; Bias & Reitmeyer, 1995; Billingsley, 1995; Boivie et al., 2003; Cooper, 1999; Grudin, 1991b; Fellenz, 1997; Mayhew, 1999b; Nielsen, 1993). A high-level champion allows HCI work to have authority, autonomy and access to development (Beyer & Holtzblatt, 1998; Billingsley, 1995; Boivie et al., 2003; Nielsen, 1993). Furthermore, HCI specialists should be perceived as allies of different kinds of improvement initiatives in organizations (Bloomer & Croft, 1997; Mayhew, 1999a). In addition, marketing, training and documentation should be addressed and cooperation initiated. In all, HCI specialists should be able to tailor their message and present their results in languages that each target group understands. (Beyer & Holtzblatt, 1998; Billingsley, 1995; Bloomer & Croft, 1997; Cooper, 1999; Grudin, 1991b; Mayhew, 1999a; Mayhew, 1999b; Rosenbaum et al., 2000; Seffah & Andreevskaia, 2003.)

Altogether, HCI specialists are supposed to seduce and manipulate a multitude of stakeholder groups to 'buy into usability'. The literature argues that HCI work should be 'sold' into organizations (Mayhew, 1999a; Mayhew, 1999b). One should also be able to show the benefits achieved (Cooper, 1999; Mayhew, 1999a; Mayhew, 1999b;

Rosenbaum et al., 2000). The business perspective is highlighted (Beyer & Holtzblatt, 1998; Bloomer & Croft, 1997; Cooper, 1999; Fellenz, 1997; Mayhew, 1999a; Mayhew, 1999b; Rosenbaum et al., 2000) - HCI work should make sense from the business perspective and be related to key business goals (Beyer & Holtzblatt, 1998; Bloomer & Croft, 1997; Cooper, 1999; Fellenz, 1997). Consideration of costs and benefits is recommended, since cost-benefit tradeoffs may play a major role in the adoption of HCI work. (Mayhew, 1999b; Nielsen, 1993; Vredenburg et al., 2002.) Resources should be well planned and budgeted (Aucella, 1997; Mayhew, 1999b; Nielsen, 1993) to assure that HCI work doesn't increase development costs and time (Bloomer & Croft, 1997; Nielsen, 1993).

Altogether, a competitive advantage and competitiveness in the marketplace achievable through HCI work are emphasized. 'Selling HCI work into organizations' by highlighting the business point of view and cost benefit analyses, and by using the language that sales, marketing and management understand, is advocated. Within this discourse an ideology of managerialism is evident; management goals are constructed as the main motivator for HCI work. The discourse emphasizes profit maximization, work intensification and successful implementation achievable through HCI work (c.f. Asaro, 2000; Hirschheim & Klein, 1989; Spinuzzi, 2002).

Second, a **reflective PD discourse** constructing user participation has been identified (Iivari 2006). There is literature in proximity to HCI, but clearly separating itself from 'mainstream HCI'. This literature separates itself from non-reflective, objectivist HCI and positions itself within the PD tradition, even though acknowledging there might be a need for some kind of 'facilitators' (HCI specialists, researcher designers) between users and developers. This literature argues for more cooperative work and for more reflection related to design practice. The literature maintains that design should be seen as cooperative work, in

which people with different competencies appreciate each other and jointly create new work practices. Design needs to be seen as a creative and communicative process involving 'mutual reciprocal learning' and 'design by doing'. HCI specialists need to support everyone's participation and make everyone comfortable in participating. (Anderson & Crocca, 1993; Blomberg & Henderson, 1990; Buur & Bagger, 1999; Bødker & Buur, 2002; Bødker & Iversen, 2002; Bødker et al., 2000; Gadner, 1999; Kyng, 1994; Kyng, 1998; Löwgren, 1995.) Furthermore, emphasis should be on reflection and improvisation. It is argued that PD should not consist of applying decontextualized methods. Instead, professionalism, reflection and creativity are important. (Anderson & Crocca, 1993; Bansler & Bødker, 1993; Beyer & Holtzblatt, 1998; Bødker & Buur, 2002; Bødker & Iversen, 2002; Clement & Van den Besselaar, 1993; Löwgren, 1995; Löwgren & Stolterman, 1999.)

The speakers within this discourse have adopted the subject position of a reflective researcher designer. This discourse legitimizes its existence by differentiating itself from objectivist, non-reflective HCI (and IS). In this discourse users are positioned as skillful partners in the design process. The HCI specialists, if needed at all - are positioned as reflective facilitators of cooperation and reflection among users and developers. This discourse has a clear background in the tradition labeled as the PD tradition (see Greenbaum & Kyng, 1991; Schuler & Namioka, 1993).

Third, a **critical IS discourse** constructing user participation has also been identified (Iivari 2006). This relies on the Scandinavian trade unionist tradition that has been postulated as a very critical and management-hostile tradition in IT artifact development. This tradition focused on workplace democracy and trade union involvement in the development of IT artifacts. The tradition had a strong Marxist flavor and relied on the notion of conflict between capital and labor. (Asaro, 2000; Bjerknes & Bratteteig,

1995; Bansler, 1989; Bansler & Kraft, 1994; Clement & Van den Besselaar, 1993; Iivari & Hirschheim, 1996; Kraft & Bansler, 1994; Kyng, 1998; Spinuzzi, 2002.) The goal of user participation was democratic empowerment of the users, which maintains that workers should be able to participate in decision-making in their workplace (Clement 1994). In current literature, critical perspective is still evident is some studies. Studies criticizing user participation only as a buzzword or a weapon (Beath & Orlikowski, 1994; Hirschheim & Newman, 1991; Howcroft & Wilson, 2003; Kirsch & Beath, 1996; Nielsen, 1999; Symon, 1998) can be interpreted to employ a critical stance. Many studies also highlight the influence of politics and conflicts in IT artifact development (Alvarez, 2002; Bansler & Bødker, 1993; Beck, 2002; Bjerknes & Bratteteig, 1995; Gärtner & Wagner, 1996; Howcroft & Wilson, 2003; Kirsch & Beath, 1996; Nielsen, 1999; Sarkkinen & Karsten, 2005; Symon, 1998), some of them having adopted a clearly management-hostile position (Bjerknes & Bratteteig, 1995; Gärtner & Wagner, 1996; Howcroft & Wilson, 2003).

Within this discourse the speaker is positioned as a warrior, partisan or emancipator (Hirschheim & Klein, 1989) fighting on the side of the oppressed against the oppressors. HCI specialists are offered no position within this discourse, since users need to be active agents in the design process. They are not to be 'represented'. Altogether, this discourse clearly relies on a critical tradition; conflict between capital and labor and emancipation of the workers are emphasized (cf. Asaro, 2000; Hirschheim & Klein, 1989; Spinuzzi 2002) In this literature the target of criticism is IS literature (as well as apolitical PD); traditional systems development methodologies, 'prescriptive IS literature' (Hirschheim & Klein, 1989; Kirsch & Beath, 1996) as well as capitalist approaches and methods claiming to involve or empower users/workers popular especially in North America (Asaro, 2000; Bansler & Craft,

1994; Beck, 2002; Beath & Orlikowski, 1994; Hirschheim & Newman, 1991; Kraft & Bansler, 1994; Kyng, 1998; Spinuzzi, 2002). They are accused of being apolitical, neglecting the role of conflict and only serving management goals (Asaro, 2000; Bansler & Bødker, 1993; Beck, 2002; Beath & Orlikowski, 1994; Bjerknes & Bratteteig, 1995; Hirschheim & Newman, 1991; Howcroft & Wilson, 2003; Finken, 2003; Kirsch & Beath, 1996; Spinuzzi, 2002).

In OSS Development in Particular

User participation has been emphasized as an important element of OSS development (Feller & Fitzgerald 2000, Nichols & Twidale 2006, Zhao & Deek 2005). However, it has also been noticed that in OSS development the distinction between user and developer is blurred (Zhao & Deek 2005). In OSS development context all users are potential developers. However, the project leader and the core members have the most influence on the OSS, while active developers carry out the main part of the development work, peripheral developers occasionally contribute, bug fixers and bug reporters contribute only by fixing or discovering and reporting bugs, readers only read the source code to try to understand the system, and finally, passive users only use the system (Ye & Kishida 2003). In OSS development context, the developers typically produce the OSS for themselves to serve their particular needs without considering the passive users at all. However, also for that same reason, OSS development has also been argued of utilizing a truly user-driven approach (Nichols & Twidale 2006, Zhao & Deek 2006).

User participation has been argued to be an important element in OSS development. Typically there are means such as discussion forums, mailing lists and bug reporting and feature request systems for user-developer cooperation in OSS projects, through which users can deliver input and feedback and developers provide user support

(Lakhani & von Hippel 2003, Scacchi 2002, Ye & Kishida 2003). Especially bug reporting has been suggested as a way through which users can participate in OSS development (Andreasen et al. 2006, Benson et al 2004, Bødker et al. 2007, Cetin et al. 2007, Nichols & Twidale 2003, Zhao & Deek 2005, Zhao & Deek 2006). However, it ahs also been reported that the non-technical users may be uninterested, intimidated or unable to use these means (Cetin et al. 2007, Nichols & Twidale 2003, Nichols & Twidale 2006, Scacchi 2002, Twidale & Nichols 2005, Zhao & Deek 2005, Zhao & Deek 2006).

The OSS community is now acknowledging that from the point of view of non technical users, the development process should be characterized as anything but user-centered (Andreasen, Nielsen, Schrøder & Stage 2006, Benson et al 2004, Feller & Fitzgerald 2000, Nichols & Twidale 2003, Nichols & Twidale 2006, Twidale & Nichols 2005, Viorres et al. 2007, Zhao & Deek 2005, Zhao & Deek 2006). HCI oriented OSS research emphasizes the need of HCI specialists to contribute to the development. Related to that, problematic is that the HCI specialists do not typically participate in the OSS development and the OSS developers do not normally have the HCI knowledge and skills needed (Benson et al 2004, Bødker, et al. 2007, Cetin et al. 2007, Frishberg et al 2002, Nichols & Twidale 2003, Nichols & Twidale 2006, Twidale & Nichols 2005, Zhao & Deek 2005, Zhao & Deek 2006).

OSS development is argued to be a new, challenging context for the HCI community to enter into, and the HCI specialists have to work as evangelists with engineers, who are typically not familiar with HCI and are accustomed to working according to a decentralized and engineering-driven approach (Benson et al 2004). The HCI specialists should be able to convince the developers and be accepted by them, but this might be challenging. There typically are very few, if any, HCI specialists working in OSS projects

and they tend to be isolated and neglected by the developers (Cetin et al 2007, Nichols & Twidale 2003, Twidale & Nichols 2005). In addition, it might be difficult to introduce HCI methods and processes to OSS development, since they can be seen as being in contrast with the open source philosophy (Benson et al 2004, Bødker, et al. 2007, Cetin et al. 2007, Zhao & Deek 2005).

However, it is argued that there is a great potential for HCI work to contribute to OSS development. Especially different kinds of usability evaluations are suggested for OSS development context – particularly empirical usability testing related to which there is typically a large user base available (Andreasen et al. 2006, Nichols & Twidale 2003, Nichols & Twidale 2006, Zhao & Deek 2005, Zhao & Deek 2006). Another solution suggested is the use of HCI guidelines that outline the best practices of HCI. Especially large corporations that nowadays participate in OSS development can provide both professional HCI resources and guidelines (Andreasen et al. 2006, Benson et al 2004, Cetin et al. 2007, Nichols & Twidale 2003, Viorres et al. 2007). However, related to company involvement, an important topic of future research is the integration of OSS with the commercial world, in which there is a desire for profit maximization, while in OSS the emphasis is on 'collectivist, public-good community values' (Fitzgerald 2006: 596). There is a potential for tension between 'value for money' and 'acceptable community values', the companies typically being not thought highly by the OSS communities (Fitzgerald 2006: 596).

Related to the discourses constructing user participation, the existing OSS development literature bears resemblance mainly with the **practical HCI discourse**. The HCI specialists are offered a subject position of a user surrogate representing (if not fighting for) the users in development. The HCI specialists are also offered the subject position of a user surrogate involving the developers by manipulating and seducing them to 'buy into

HCI work'. However, there is no mention of the HCI specialists as change agents addressing other stakeholder groups in OSS development, making them to 'buy into HCI work'. Competitive advantage and competitiveness in the marketplace achievable through HCI work are not emphasized. Altogether, the ideology of managerialism is lacking, which is quite natural in OSS development context, which opposes the world of commercial IT artifact development.

Regarding the **reflective PD discourse,** on the other hand, the results do not support the notion that 'participative design' – especially reflective PD - has been realized in OSS development context. User participation as 'users developing the OSS' and as 'users reporting bugs of the OSS' were brought up, but it was also emphasized that the non technical, non computer professional users do not take part in the OSS development or bug reporting. Therefore, there was no mention of the OSS development practice as cooperative work, in which people with different competencies appreciate each other and jointly create new work practices for users. No HCI specialists or researcher-designers were mentioned as needed as facilitators to support everyone's participation and make everyone comfortable in participating.

Finally, the **critical IS discourse,** relying on an ideal of democratic empowerment of the skilled workers and on the view of them as active agents in the design process, which is political and full of conflicts that need to be acknowledged, is contrasted with the OSS development literature. Interestingly, even though the OSS development bears some resemblance with the critical tradition, since it opposes the world of commercial IT artifact development, the OSS literature constructing user participation does not mention critical tradition at all (see also Iivari 2008b). Even though the management goals are not constructed as the main motivators of user participation, the democratic empowerment of the users is not highlighted either.

DISCOURSES ON USER PARTICIPATION - IN PRACTICE

In IT Artifact Product Development Context

Discourses constructing user participation in practice have also been identified (Iivari 2006). They are summarized next. First, a discourse constructing **HCI work as a tradition** has been identified in IT artifact product development organizations (Iivari 2006). IT artifact product development organizations emphasize that 'taking the users into account' is important and has been acknowledged a long time ago in their organization. Especially management highlights this, i.e. it seems that they wish to be positioned as friendly allies appreciating HCI work.

Second, a discourse constructing **HCI work as an image factor and a selling argument** has been identified (Iivari 2006). Within this discourse, meanings influenced by a clearly business-oriented viewpoint are assigned to HCI work. HCI work is deemed useful – it can be used to address and manipulate the customer. User participation is constructed as useful in overcoming resistance and in ensuring acceptance (cf. Nandhakumar & Jones 1997) – the customers as well as the users need to be convinced that the 'company knows better', i.e. to company knows what kind of solution is best for the customer. Within this discourse the capitalist management orientation is evident: profit maximization and a competitive advantage achievable through user participation (cf. Asaro, 2000; Spinuzzi, 2002) are highlighted. From the managerial point of view, this seems to be a tempting discourse on HCI work positioning the speaker as a 'business and profit oriented utlizer of HCI work'. From the HCI specialists' viewpoint, this can be seen as a discourse which to utilize as a change agent while 'selling HCI work into the development organization' (cf. Bloomer & Croft, 1997; Mayhew, 1999a; Rosenbaum et al., 2000).

The third discourse identified (Iivari 2006), on the other hand, condemns HCI work as a waste of time and money. Within this discourse HCI work is seen as inefficient and time-consuming. Typically, the adopters of this discourse are the personnel responsible for the IT artifact development – the developers and their managers – who position themselves as sceptics in relation to HCI work until proven otherwise. The arguments of the practical HCI discourse, highlighting the importance of developers' and managers' 'buy in' (cf. Aucella, 1997; Bloomer & Croft, 1997; Fellenz, 1997; Mayhew, 1999a; Rosenbaum et al., 2000), can also be read as an implicit fear of the existence of this discourse.

However, in so far as HCI work is viewed as useful, it can still be constructed by relying on different kinds of discourses (Iivari 2006). One possibility is to adopt a discourse that constructs **HCI work as a controllable, measurable quality improvement effort** that should and could be treated like other large-scale quality improvement efforts in organizations. This discourse postulates HCI work as improving the design process (cf. Nandhakumar & Jones, 1997) – as improving the quality of the process and the product. It is also assumed that the developers need to be controlled and monitored to achieve this. Another possibility is to adopt a discourse constructing **HCI work as persuading, marketing, manipulating** (Iivari 2006). This discourse on HCI work is distinctive in its view of HCI work as a phenomenon that should be sold to the IT artifact development preferably by 'sneaking in'. This discourse, as well as the previous one, position usability specialists as the ones 'empowering the developers', but these discourses attach clearly divergent meanings to this 'empowering'. In the former discourse HCI work is constructed as 'controlling and monitoring', while in the latter discourse HCI work means 'sneaking in'. This can be accomplished e.g. through the HCI specialists employing influential positions. Within this discourse HCI specialists act as change agents who address many different target groups

and tailor their message to languages that each target audience understands (cf. Bloomer & Croft, 1997; Mayhew, 1999a; Rosenbaum et al., 2000). However, developers are postulated as the most important target group (cf. Aucella, 1997; Bloomer & Croft, 1997; Fellenz, 1997; Mayhew, 1999a) who should buy in to HCI and perceive HCI specialists as allies (cf. Aucella, 1997; Fellenz, 1997; Mayhew, 1999a; Rosenbaum et al., 2000).

In OSS Development Context

Next results from two interpretive case studies carried out in the OSS development context are discussed in relation to the discourses identified above. The first study analyzes a usability oriented OSS project from the viewpoint of user participation and usability: how are these issues dealt with in the project (Iivari 2008a). The second study, furthermore, examines usability and user participation in company OSS development context (Iivari et al. 2008), i.e. in an IT artifact development company taking part in the OSS development, utilizing OSS as part of their products and further developing both open source and closed source parts of their solution.

In both studies, resemblance with the discourse constructing HCI work as a tradition can be identified. In the OSS project, a usability discussion forum has been established and the OSS developers have invited users to take part in the discussions to improve usability and the UI of the solution. This discussion forum also has been a rather active one with around 1600 messages posted to it. The OSS developers have also strongly emphasized the importance of HCI specialists, even though there have not been HCI specialists in their project. (Iivari 2008a.) Despite that, the developers can be seen as implying that their OSS project strongly emphasizes 'taking the users into account' and has acknowledged this already a while ago. In this case the OSS developers emphasize this, not the managers. This is quite natural, since typically there are no managerial relationships in OSS projects. However, in OSS projects, the core team of OSS developers ultimately have the power to make the decisions related to what to include in the solution. These OSS developers are in that position in the project, and interestingly they have positioned themselves as friendly allies appreciating HCI work in a similar way as have the managers in the IT artifact product development context.

In the study in the company OSS development context, on the other hand, it is reported that the company has a strong background in usability and UI development. Their importance is also emphasized in this case a lot. Both the managers, developers and HCI specialists maintain that usability is 'the most essential thing' to be ensured in the development and its importance has even increased during the recent years. (Iivari et al. 2008.) Since the data has been gathered from an IT artifact product development organization, it is not surprising to encounter this type of discourse also in this case.

In the discourse constructing **HCI work as an image factor and a selling argument**, meanings influenced by a clearly business-oriented viewpoint are assigned to HCI work. This type of discourse can not be identified from the OS project. In traditional OSS projects, there are no customers in the sense someone purchasing and paying for the solution. However, in the company OSS development context the solutions are developed for consumer markets. In this context this type of discourse is observable: it is emphasized that usability needs to be achieved since: ""[Usability is] while developing UI, one of the most essential things" (…) "[The firm] makes devices for people. Why would anybody buy a product that was difficult to use, compared to competitors? So market is the reason [for usability]" (…) "[Usability is] extremely important: competitive edge, brand, image."" (Iivari et al. 2008: 362). Furthermore, the UI (and its quality) is even constituted as a competitive edge for the company, emphasizing further the business aspects of HCI work.

On the other hand, the third *discourse* condemning **HCI work as a waste of time and money** is not observable in the OSS development context. In the OSS project there have not been any HCI specialists involved yet. Therefore, the OSS developers might not yet have detailed knowledge of what is included in HCI work. In the company OSS development context, on the other hand, tight deadlines are mentioned to hinder HCI work, but the use of OSS as part of the products is seen as a solution allowing more time to the HCI work. The developers and managers do not question the importance or usefulness of the HCI work in this case either.

Finally, as mentioned, as far as HCI work is deemed as useful, it can still be constructed by relying on different kinds of discourses. The discourse constructing **HCI work as persuading, marketing, manipulating** was not evident in the OSS development context. This discourse assumes that HCI work should be sold to the IT artifact development by 'sneaking in'; HCI specialists influencing other people those not even noticing the influence. This is a discourse the HCI specialists might adopt, since it clearly represents their point of view. In the OSS project there are no HCI specialists who could have adopted the discourse. In the company OSS development context, on the other hand, the HCI specialists as well as the developers maintain that the HCI work is needed, but not through 'sneaking in'. Actually, in both cases the HCI specialists are wished for 'commenting the solutions' and for 'helping the developers'. However, related to this issue, neither the discourse constructing **HCI work as a controllable, measurable quality improvement effort** is identifiable in the cases. The HCI specialists are to help and give comments, but they not expected to have power over the developers. Altogether, it is assumed that the HCI specialists are needed for representing the user, for carrying out the UI design, for commenting the solutions and for helping the developers to produce quality solutions.

CONCLUDING DISCUSSION

Summary of the Results

This paper has examined discursive construction of user participation in academic literatures and in practice, in IT artifact development. First three academic discourses constructing user participation were presented. Then the discursive construction of user participation was explored in OSS development literature. It was argued that the existing OSS development literature bears resemblance mainly with the practical HCI discourse. Neither the reflective PD discourse nor the critical IS discourse were identifiable from the OSS development literature related to user participation. User participation was constituted only as 'users developing the OSS' and as 'users reporting bugs of the OSS'. HCI specialists were assumed to represent the (non technical, non computer professional) users in the development. In addition, even though the OSS development bears some resemblance with the critical tradition, since it opposes the world of commercial IT artifact development, the OSS literature constructing user participation did not rely on critical tradition. Even though the management goals were not constructed as the main motivators of user participation, the democratic empowerment of the users was not highlighted either.

Afterwards, results from several empirical, interpretive case studies were outlined. Some of them have been carried out in the IT artifact product development organizations, others in the OSS development context. In the OSS development context, results from a study on an OSS project and on a company OSS development unit were outlined. Clear similarities were identified in the discourses constructing user participation in these divergent IT artifact development contexts. In the OSS development context, resemblance with the discourse constructing HCI work as a tradition was clearly identifiable. The discourse constructing HCI work as an image factor and

a selling argument was also identifiable in the company OSS development context. However, the discourse condemning HCI work as a waste of time and money was not observable in the OSS development context. In both cases HCI work seemed to be highly appreciated. However, even though HCI work was deemed as useful, the discourse constructing HCI work as persuading, marketing, manipulating or the discourse constructing HCI work as a controllable, measurable quality improvement effort were not evident in the OSS development context. Altogether, it was assumed in the cases in the OSS development context that the HCI specialists are needed for representing the user, for carrying out the UI design, for commenting the solutions and for helping the developers to produce quality solutions. However, decision making power was not assumed to be given to the HCI specialists. This finding is in line with the previous results (see Iivari 2006) showing that the discourses the HCI specialists utilize are typically submissive, and the HCI specialists do not seem to employ very influential position in the IT artifact development.

Critical Remarks

It was argued that the discourses identified from the empirical settings can be related to wider discursive fields in which both the HCI and IS communities participate and contribute. As mentioned, existing literature has made us aware that user participation might be used only as a buzzword and a slogan (Catarci et al., 2002; Hirschheim & Newman, 1991; Kirsch & Beath, 1996; Nielsen, 1999; O'Connor 1995). The discourse assigning HCI work a central position in the OSS context might be viewed as relating to the same phenomenon. The data indicates that this important position has not always been fully realized yet, even though being talked about in enthusiastic manner. In addition, the second discourse that constructs HCI work as useful, since it can be used as an image factor and a selling argument, warns us that within this discourse the management goals may be the main (sole?) motivator for HCI work. HCI work is useful for the company in making more profit and in improving the image of the company, even in the company OSS development case.

Altogether, this type of capitalist orientation related to HCI work identified in the company OSS development context might be viewed as a 'realization of Scandinavians' (trade unionists) worst fears' (Spinuzzi, 2002) totally neglecting the original aim of user participation, i.e. democratic empowerment of the oppressed workers. Related to this, it is maintained that 'empowerment' and 'involvement' can be used only as rhetorical tools that try to conceal that IT artifacts are always developed to serve management goals. 'Involvement' may actually mean exclusion and marginalization rather than empowerment of the ones who are oppressed. (Howcroft & Wilson 2003, O'Connor 1995.) Particularly when user participation is only indirect, as is the case when the HCI specialists represent the users in the development; it is a question mark whether and how users could be 'emancipated' or empowered in the democratic sense. However, in the OSS development context, generally, the technically capable users are empowered in the democratic sense, but the non technical users are clearly in a weak position (Iivari 2008b).

Relevance to Practice

This type of critical studies can be argued to lack relevance to practice, which seems to be a very important goal in both IS and HCI research. However, as a defense for this type of studies, one might argue that relevance can be achieved in many ways. For example, researchers can act as the conscience of society (Lee, 1999), and they can reshape the practitioners' thinking and actions in the longer perspective (Lyytinen, 1999) – also these issues have been interpreted to be relevant to

practice. Therefore, critical examinations of user participation in IT artifact development should be considered useful in the sense of highlighting the risk of user participation becoming only a buzzword and a slogan whose acceptance and utilization is totally dependant on short-term financial motivators. Related to this, the influential role of academic communities is also emphasized (Cooper & Bowers, 1995; Finken, 2003; Foucault, 1972; Weedon, 1987). It is recommended that especially the HCI community should carefully reflect on what kinds of discourses on user participation it advocates and deems as legitimate. The HCI literature seems to have some influence also on the OSS development literature.

Furthermore, this paper emphasizes the importance of non technical user participation in the OSS development context. It has been emphasized that the technically capable users can contribute in the OSS development, but the non technical users are neglected. One possibility in trying to improve the situation is to try to make the HCI specialists to take part in the OSS projects to represent the users, to carry out the UI design, to comment the solutions and to help the developers to produce quality solutions. However, also the PD tradition offers interesting insights on non technical user participation. This tradition maintains that design should be seen as cooperative work, in which people with different competencies appreciate each other and jointly create new work practices. Design should to be seen as a creative and communicative process involving 'mutual reciprocal learning' and 'design by doing'. HCI specialists are needed to support everyone's participation and make everyone comfortable in participating. The users should be invited as equal partners into the design process. Also this type of an approach could be experimented with in the OSS development context, even though the distributed nature of OSS development clearly imposes some challenges to it.

Paths for Future Work

Regarding paths for future work, especially studies that critically analyze literature on user participation from the viewpoint of the ethical assumptions they advocate are recommended. One should continue this work by examining more comprehensively the divergent literatures offering advice on user participation in different kinds of IT artifact development contexts. On a more practical level, empirical studies on non technical user participation as well as HCI specialist participation in the different kinds of OSS development contexts (traditional, company OSS) are also recommended. Contextual factors affecting (helping and hindering) non technical user and HCI specialist participation should be examined. Finally, studies that critically examine power, politics, marginality and exclusion (c.f. Beck 2002) in the divergent IT artifact development context are warmly recommended.

REFERENCES

Alvarez, R. (2002). Confessions of an information worker: a critical analysis of information requirements discourse. *Information and Organization* 12(2), 85-107.

Anderson, W. & Crocca, W. (1993). Engineering practice and codevelopment of product prototypes. *Communications of the ACM* 36(4), 49-56.

Andreasen, M., Nielsen, H., Schröder, S. & Stage, J. (2006). Usability in Open Source Software Development: Opinions and Practice. *Information Technology and Control* 25(3A), 303-312.

Asaro, P. (2000). Transforming Society by Transforming Technology: the science and politics of participatory design. *Accounting, Management and Information Technologies* 10, 257-290.

Aucella. A. (1997). Ensuring Success with Usability Engineering. Interactions 4(3), 19-22.

Bansler, J. (1989). Systems development research in Scandinavia: Three theoretical schools. *Scandinavian Journal of Information Systems* 1, 3-20.

Bansler, J. & Bødker, K. (1993). A Reappraisal of Structured Analysis. *ACM Transactions on Information Systems* 11(2), 165-193.

Bansler, J. & Kraft, P. (1994). Privilege and invisibility in the new work order: A reply to Kyng. *Scandinavian Journal of Information Systems* 6(1), 97-106.

Barki, H. & Hartwick, J. (1994). Measuring User Participation, User Involvement, and User Attitude. *MIS Quarterly* 18(1), 59-81.

Beath, C. & Orlikowski, W. (1994). The Contradictory Structure of Systems Development Methodologies: Deconstructing the IS-User Relationship in Information Engineering. *Information Systems Research* 5(4), 350-377.

Beck, E. (2002). P for Political. Participation is not enough. *Scandinavian Journal of Information Systems* 14(1), 77-92.

Benson, C., Müller-Prove, M., Mzourek, J.(2004). Professional usability in open source projects: GNOME, OpenOffice.org, NetBeans. In *Proc. Extended Abstracts of the Conference on Human Factors in Computer Systems* (pp. 1083-1084). New York, ACM Press.

Beyer, H. & Holtzblatt, K. (1998). *Contextual Design: Defining Customer-Centered Systems.* San Francisco: Morgan Kaufmann Publishers.

Bias, R. & Reitmeyer, P. (1995). Usability Support Inside and Out. *Interactions* 2(2), 29-32.

Billingsley, P. (1995). Starting from Scratch: Building a Usability Program at Union Pacific Railroad. *Interactions* 2(4), 27-30.

Bjerknes, G. & Bratteteig, T. (1995). User Participation and Democracy. A Discussion of Scandinavian Research on System Development. *Scandinavian Journal of Information Systems* 7(1), 73-98.

Blomberg, J. & Henderson, A. (1990). Reflections on Participatory Design: Lessons from the Trillium Experience. In *Proc. Conference on Human Factors in Computer Systems* (pp. 353-359). New York: ACM Press.

Bloomer, S. & Croft, R. (1997). Pitching Usability to Your Organization. *Interactions* 4(6), 18-26.

Bloomfield, B. & Vurdubakis, T. (1997). Visions of Organization and Organizations of Vision: The Representational Practices of Information Systems Development. *Accounting, Organizations and Society* 22(7), 639-668.

Boivie, I., Åborg, C., Persson, J. & Löfberg, M. (2003). Why usability gets lost or usability in in-house software development. *Interacting with Computers* 15, 623-639.

Buur, J. & Bagger, K. (1999). Replacing Usability Testing with User Dialogue. *Communications of the ACM* 42(5), 63-66.

Bødker, M., Nielsen, L. & Orngreen, R. (2007). Enabling User-Centered Design Processes in Open Source Communities. In *Proc. Human Computer Interaction International, Part I: Usability and Internationalization*. LNCS 4559 (pp. 10-18). Berlin: Springer.

Bødker, S. & Buur, J. (2002). The Design Collaboratorium – a Place for Usability Design. *ACM Transactions on Computer-Human Interaction* 9(2), 152-169.

Bødker, S. & Iversen, O. (2002). Staging a Professional Participatory Design Practice. Moving PD Beyond the Initial Fascination of User Involvement. In *Proc. 2nd Nordic conference on Human-computer interaction* (pp. 11 – 18). New York: ACM Press.

Bødker, S., Nielsen, C. & Petersen, M. G. (2000). Creativity, cooperation and interactive design. In *Proc. 3rd conference on Designing interactive systems* (pp. 252-261). New York: ACM Press.

Catarci, T., Matarazzo, G. & Raiss, G. (2002). Driving usability into the public administration: the Italian experience. *International Journal of Human-Computer Studies* 57, 121-138.

Cetin, G., Verzulli, D. & Frings, S. (2007). An Analysis of Involvement of HCI Experts in Distributed Software Development: Practical Issues. In *Proc. Human Computer Interaction International: Online Communities and Social Computing*. LNCS 4564 (pp. 32-40). Berlin: Springer.

Clement, A. (1994). Computing at Work: Empowering Action By 'Low-level Users'. *Communications of the ACM* 37(1), 52-63.

Clement, A. & Van den Besselaar, P. (1993). A Retrospective Look at PD Projects. *Communications of the ACM* 36(4), 29-37.

Clifford, J. & Marcus, G. (Eds.) (1986). *Writing culture: the poetics and politics of ethnography.* Berkeley: University of California Press.

Cooper, A. (1999). *The inmates are running the asylum: Why high-tech products drive us crazy and how to restore the sanity.* Indianapolis: Sams.

Cooper, C. & Bowers, J. (1995). Representing the users: Notes on the disciplinary rhetoric of human-computer interaction. In P. Thomas (Ed.): *The Social and Interactional Dimensions of Human-Computer Interfaces* (pp. 48-66). Cambridge: Cambridge University Press.

Doolin, B. (1999). Information Systems, Power, and Organizational Relations: A Case Study. In *Proc. 20th International Conference on Information Systems* (pp. 286-290). Atlanta: AIS.

Fairclough, N. & Wodak, R. (1997). Critical Discourse Analysis. In T. van Dijk (Ed.): *Discourse as Social Interaction. Discourse Studies: A Multidisciplinary Introduction*. Vol. 2 (pp. 258-284). London: SAGE Publications.

Fellenz, C. (1997). Introducing Usability into Smaller Organizations. *Interactions* 4(5), 29-33.

Feller, J. & Fitzgerald, B. (2000). A Framework Analysis of the Open Source Development Paradigm. In *Proc. 21ˢᵗ International Conference on Information Systems* (pp. 58-69). Atlanta: AIS.

Finken, S. (2003). Discursive conditions of knowledge production within cooperative design. *Scandinavian Journal of Information Systems* 15, 57-72.

Fitzgerald, B. (2006). The Transformation of Open Source Software. *MIS Quarterly* 30(3), 587-598.

Foucault, M. (1972). *The Archaeology of Knowledge and the Discourse on Language.* New York: Pantheon Books.

Foucault, M. (1980). *The History of Sexuality. Volume 1: An Introduction.* Translated by Robert Hurley. New York: Vintage Books.

Franke, N. & von Hippel, E. (2003). Satisfying heterogeneous user needs via innovation toolkits: the case of Apache security software. *Research Policy* 32, 1199-1215.

Frishberg, N., Dirks, A. M., Benson, C., Nickel, S. & Smith, S. (2002). Getting to know you: open source development meets usability. In *Proc. Extended Abstracts of the Conference on Human Factors in Computer Systems* (pp. 932-933). New York, ACM Press

Greenbaum, J. & Kyng, M. (Eds.) (1991). *Design at Work. Cooperative Design of Computer Systems.* New Jersey: Lawrence Erlbaum Associates.

Grudin, J. (1991a). Interactive Systems: Bridging the Gaps between Developers and Users. *IEEE Computer* 24(4), 59-69.

Grudin, J. (1991b). Systematic Sources of Suboptimal Interface Design in Large Product Development Organizations. *Human-Computer Interaction* 6, 147-196.

Gärtner, J. & Wagner, I. (1996). Mapping Actors and Agendas: Political Frameworks of Systems Design and Participation. *Human-Computer Interaction* 11, 187-214.

Hirschheim, R. & Klein, H. (1989). Four Paradigms of Information Systems Development. *Communications of the ACM* 32(10), 1199-1216.

Hirschheim, R. & Newman, M. (1991). Symbolism and Information Systems Development: Myth Metaphor and Magic. *Information Systems Research* 2(1), 29-62.

Howcroft, D. & Wilson, M. (2003). Paradoxes of participatory practices: the Janus role of the systems developer. *Information and Organization* 13, 1-24.

Iivari, J. & Hirschheim, R. (1996). Analyzing Information Systems Development: a Comparison and Analysis of Eight IS Development Approaches. *Information Systems* 21(7), 551-575.

Iivari, N. (2006). Exploring the 'Rhetoric on Representing the User' - Discourses on User Involvement in Academia and in Software Product Development Industry. *International Journal of Technology and Human Interaction* 2(4), 53-80

Iivari, N. (2008a). Usability in open source software development – an interpretive case study. In *Proc. 16th European Conference on Information Systems,* June 9.-11.2008, Galway, Ireland.

Iivari, N. (forthcoming). Empowering the Users? A Critical Textual Analysis of the Role of Users in Open Source Software Development. *AI & Society.*

Iivari, N., Hedberg, H. & Kirves, T. (2008). Usability in Company Open Source Software Context. Initial Findings from an Empirical Case Study. In *Proc. 4ᵗʰ International Conference on Open Source Systems* (co-located with the World Computer Congress), September 7.-10. 2008, Milan, Italy.

Kirsch, L. & Beath, C. (1996). The enactments and consequences of token, shared, and compliant participation in information systems development. *Accounting, Management, & Information Technologies* 6(4), 221-254.

Kraft, P. & Bansler, J. (1994). The Collective Resource Approach: The Scandinavian experience. *Scandinavian Journal of Information Systems* 6(1), 71-84.

Kyng, M. (1994). Scandinavian Design: Users in Product Development. In *Proc. Conference on Human Factors in Computer Systems* (pp. 3-9). New York: ACM Press.

Kyng, M. (1998). Users and computers: A contextual approach to design of computer artifacts. *Scandinavian Journal of Information Systems* 10(1&2), 7-44.

Lakhani, K. & von Hippel, E. (2003). How Open Source Software Works: "Free" User-to-User Assistance. *Research Policy* 32(6), 923-943.

Lee, A. (1999). Rigor and relevance in MIS research: beyond the approach of positivism alone. *MIS Quarterly* 23(1), 29-33.

Lyytinen, K. (1999). Empirical research in information systems: on the relevance of practice in thinking of IS research. *MIS Quarterly* 23(1), 25-28.

Löwgren, J. (1995). Applying Design Methodology to Software Development. In *Proc. 1st conference on Designing interactive systems* **(pp.** 87-95). New York: ACM Press.

Löwgren, J. & Stolterman, E. (1999). Design Methodology and Design Practice. *Interactions* 6(1), 13-20.

Mayhew, D. (1999a). Strategic Development of Usability Engineering Function. *Interactions* 6(5), 27-34.

Mayhew, D. (1999b). *The usability engineering lifecycle: a practitioner's handbook for user interface design*. San Francisco: Morgan Kaufmann Publishers, Inc.

Muller, M. J. & Carey, K. (2002). Design as a Minority Discipline in a Software Company: Toward Requirements for a Community of Practice. In *Proc. Conference on Human Factors in Computer Systems* (pp. 383-390). New York: ACM Press.

Nandhakumar, J. & Jones, M. (1997). Designing in the Dark: the Changing User-Developer Relationship in Information Systems Development. In *Proc. 18th International Conference on Information Systems* (pp. 75-86). Atlanta: AIS.

Nichols, D. & Twidale, M. (2003). The Usability of Open Source Software. *First Monday* 8(1), 21 pp.

Nichols, D. & Twidale, M. (2006). Usability Processes in Open Source Projects. Software *Process Improvement and Practice* 11, 149-162.

Niederman, F., Davis, A. Greiner, M., Wynn, D. & York, P. (2006). A Research Agenda for Studying Open Source I: A Multilevel Framework. *Communication of the Association for Information Systems* 18, 129-149.

Nielsen, J. (1993). *Usability engineering*. Boston: Academic Press.

Nielsen, S. (1999). Talking about Change: An Analysis of Participative Discourse Amongst IT Operations Personnel. In *Proc. 10th Australasian Conference on Information Systems* (pp. 691-702). December 1.-3.1999, Wellington, New Zealand.

O'Connor, E. (1995). Paradoxes of Participation: textual analysis and organizational change. *Organization Studies* 16(5), 769-803.

Orlikowski, W. & Iacano, C. (2001). Research Commentary: Desperately Seeking the "IT" in IT Research – A Call to Theorizing the IT Artifact. *Information Systems Research* 12(2), 121-134.

Robey, D. & Markus, M. (1984). Rituals in Information System Design. *MIS Quarterly* March 1984, 5-15.

Rosenbaum, S., Rohn, J. A. & Humburg, J. (2000). A Toolkit for Strategic Usability: Results from Workshops, Panels, and Surveys. In *Proc. Conference on Human Factors in Computer Systems* (pp. 337-344). New York: ACM Press.

Sarkkinen, J. & Karsten, H. (2005). Verbal and visual representations in task redesign: how different viewpoints enter into information systems design discussions. *Information Systems Journal* 15(3), 181-211.

Sayer, K. & Harvey, L. (1997). Empowerment in Business Process Reengineering: an Ethnographic Study of Implementation Discourse. In *Proc. 18th International Conference on Information Systems* (pp. 427 – 440). Atlanta: AIS.

Scacchi, W. (2002). Understanding the requirements for developing open source software systems. *IEE Proceedings – Software* 149(1), 24-39.

Schuler, D. & Namioka, A. (Eds.) (1993). *Participatory Design: Principles and Practices.* New Jersey: Lawrence Erlbaum Associates.

Seffah, A. & Andreevskaia, A. (2003). Empowering Software Engineers in Human-Centered Design. In *Proc. 25th International Conference on Software Engineering,* (pp. 653-658). Washington: IEEE

Spinuzzi, C. (2002). A Scandinavian Challenge, a US Response: Methodological Assumptions in Scandinavian and US Prototyping Approaches. In *Proc. 20th Annual International Conference on Computer Documentation* (pp. 208-215). New York: ACM Press.

Symon, G. (1998). The Work of IT System Developers in Context: An Organizational Case Study. *Human-Computer Interaction* 13(1), 37-71.

Tudor, L. (1998). Human Factors: Does Your Management Hear You? *Interaction* 5(1), 16-24.

Twidale, M. & Nichols, D. (2005). Exploring Usability Discussions in Open Source Development.

In *Proc. 38th Hawaii International Conference on System Sciences.* Washington: IEEE.

Viorres, N., Xenofon, P., Stavrakis, M., Vlanhogiannis, E., Koutsabasis, P. & Darzentas J. (2007). Major HCI Challenges for Open Source Software Adoption and Development. In *Proc. Human Computer Interaction International: Online Communities and Social Computing.* LNCS 4564 (pp. 455-464). Berlin: Springer.

Vredenburg, K (1999). Increasing Ease of Use – Emphasizing organizational transformations, process integration, and method optimisation. *Communications of the ACM* 42(5), 67-71.

Vredenburg, K., Mao, J, Smith, P. W. & Casey, T. (2002): A survey of user-centered design practice. In *Proc. Conference on Human Factors in Computer Systems* (pp. 471-478). New York: ACM Press.

Weedon, C. (1987). *Feminist Practice and Poststructuralist Theory.* Oxford: Basil Blackwell Ltd.

Weedon, C. (2004). *Identity and Culture: Narratives of Difference and Belonging.* New York: Open University Press.

Wynn, E. H., Whitley, E. A., Myers, M. D. and DeGross, J. I. (Eds.) (2002): *Global and organizational discourse about information technology.* Boston: Kluwer.

Ye, Y. & Kishida, K. (2003). Toward an Understanding of the Motivation of Open Source Software Developers. In *Proc. 25th International Conference on Software Engineering* (pp. 419-429). Washington: IEEE.

Zhao, L. & Deek, F. (2005). Improving Open Source Software Usability. In *Proc. 11th Americas Conference on Information Systems* (pp. 923-928). August 11.-14.2005, Omaha, USA.

Zhao, L. & Deek, F. (2006). Exploratory inspection: a learning model for improving open source software usability. In *Proc. Extended Abstracts of the Conference on Human Factors in Computer Systems* (pp. 1589-1594). New York: ACM Press.

ENDNOTE

[1]   Defined as "bundles of material and cultural properties packaged in some socially recognizable form such as hardware and/or software" (Orlikowski & Iacano, 2001, pp. 121)

Chapter VII
Exploring "Events" as an Information Systems Research Methodology

Anita Greenhill
The University of Manchester, UK

Gordon Fletcher
University of Salford, UK

ABSTRACT

In this article we build upon existing research and commentary from a variety of disciplinary sources, including information systems, organisational and management studies, and the social sciences that focus upon the meaning, significance and impact of "events" in the information technology, organisational and social context. Our aim is to define how the examination of the event is an appropriate, viable and useful information systems methodology. The line of argument we pursue is that by focusing on the "event" the researcher is able to more clearly observe and capture the complexity, multiplicity and mundaneity of everyday lived experience. An inherent danger of existing traditional "event" focused studies and "virtual" ethnographic approaches is the micromanagement of the research process. Using the notion of "event" has the potential to reduce methodological dilemmas such as this without effacing context (Peterson, 1998, p. 19). Similarly, in this chapter we address the overemphasis upon managerialist, structured and time-fixated praxis that is currently symptomatic of information systems research. All of these concerns are pivotal points of critique found within event-oriented literature regarding organisations (Gergen & Thatchenkery, 2004; Peterson, 1998).

INTRODUCTION

An examination of event-related theory within interpretative disciplines directs our focus toward the more specific realm of the "event scene." The notion of the "event scene" originated in the action based (and antiacademy) imperatives of the situationists and emerged in an academic sense as critical situational analysis. Event scenes are a focus for contemporary critical theory where they are utilised as a means of representing theoried inquiry in order to loosen the restrictions that historical and temporally bound analysis imposes upon most interpretative approaches. The use of event scenes as the framework for critiquing established conceptual assumptions is exemplified by their use in *CTheory*. In this journal's version and articulation of the event-scene poetry, commentary, multivocal narrative and other techniques are legitimated as academic forms. These various forms of multidimensional and multivocal expression are drawn upon to enrich the understandings of the "event" to extricate its meaning and to provide a sense of the moment from which the point of analysis stems.

The objective of this paper is to advocate how information systems research can (or should) utilise an event scene oriented methodology. The paper is organised as follows: we begin by presenting the theoretical background and definitions of "event scenes" and the "event." We do this as a means of illustrating how events capture multidimensional and multivocal forms of expression. The significance of this method is that it is a nonlineal and less time focused approach that has the potential to challenge the managerialist, structured and time-fixated praxis that is currently dominating information systems research and development. In the next section we illustrate why and how event oriented methods advocate including elements of illogical asemiosis of experience that eschews the application of management process and articulates arhythmic patterns of life, including political and cultural

experience. We then argue there is a need to utilise consumption based approaches in information systems research away from traditional production-based systems understandings. Finally and most importantly, utilising an event-based focus in information systems can challenge existing constructs that perpetuate mainstream regimes of power by widening the boundary of what we understand as "the system."

WHAT ARE EVENTS AND EVENT SCENES?

The whole life of those societies in which modern conditions of production prevail presents itself as an immense accumulation of spectacles. All that once was directly lived has become mere representation. (Debord, 1994, Thesis 1)

In this paper we present a sample of literature concerning event-oriented approaches, especially those inspired by the situationists, in order to consider the more specific representational issues found in the specific praxis of the "event scene." We build upon Peterson's (1998) literature review that offers a taxonomy of organisational events to develop a critical debate regarding the relationships of events to organisations. The event scene is the direct descendant to the situationism's act of détournement, in which significant and insignificant elements of observations are isolated and inserted into new and unexpected contexts. Détournement is most readily explained with examples such as found art and the work of artists such as Tracey Emin that includes her Curriculum Vita (CV) presented as a framed piece and more recently an abusive text message sent to a fan. A majority of Emin's work places the mundane in a formal environment in unexpected ways, forcing the viewer to (hopefully) reconsider their position and view the subject of the works in new ways. As a necessarily obtuse explanation of this tactic, Debord and Wolman (1956) describe détournement as being "less effective the more it approaches a rational reply" to the cultural situation it critiques. The situationist's invocation for obscurity is a political resistance to the likelihood of mainstream recuperation — of being made irrelevant by becoming commodified. Event scenes are a mechanism utilised by contemporary critical theory in order to loosen the restrictions of historical and temporally bound analysis that are a consequence of most interpretive methods.

Our emphasis is primarily interpretative and contrasts with the growing use of *Complex Event Processing* (Mohamed, 2006; Niblett & Graham 2005). This theorisation of the event has developed from a computer science and processual perspective. While the founding rationale for this approach could arguably be seen as similar to our own, its implementation and general focus of attention differs significantly.

The general theoretical orientation of this work is drawn from the situationism of Debord's (1994) *Society of the Spectacle* (Albright, 2003), de Certeau (1988), Lefebvre (1992) and a cautious reading of Baudrillard's work (1988, 1998) regarding simulation and hyperreality. We acknowledge that this selection is a somewhat distorted representation of a situationist work. Debord and Baudrillard, for example, have been claimed as being at odds with one another intellectually at various points in their careers, as well as with the general development of situationism (Albright, 2003). Debord's (1994) identification of the spectacle informs the meaning of the event scene used in this paper and assists in justifying our position that it is a legitimate approach to researching contemporary cultural and organisational phenomena. Baudrillard's (1993) argument regarding the balance between the mundaneity of everyday life and moments of tension also positions the observation of event-driven culture.

In the face of the threats of a total weightlessness, an unbearable lightness of being, a universal promiscuity and a linearity of processes liable *to plunge us into the void, the sudden whirlpools that we dub catastrophes are really the thing that saves us from catastrophe. Anomalies and aberrations of this kind recreate zones of gravity and density that counter dispersion.* (Baudrillard, 1993, p. 69)

In contemporary culture, even for the Frankfurt School of Critical Studies two generations ago, "diversion, distraction, and amusement had become the norm." (Hoover & Stokes, 1998). Attention to the minuscule of everyday life is both the norm of everyday life as well as being the representational tactic employed within the event scene (Peterson, 1998, p. 20).

The focal point of the event could be claimed as a complex potlatch; it is no coincidence that *Potlatch* was a key journal that inspired origianl situationist thought. The event is the mundane, the integrative blending of moments that constitute everyday life, the nonlinearity of experience, the illogic of expectations, the indeterminate acceleration and deceleration of personal temporality and the moments of the unexpected or unforeseen (Albright, 2003; Debord, 1994; Gergen & Thatchenkery, 2004; Peterson, 1998, p. 24; Plant, 1997, p. 236). The researcher is politically obliged within this framework to represent the event (any event) as an event scene — the excised moment of observation and experience captured and individually emphasised by them (Peterson, 1998, p. 20). Representing human experiences in the context of the "immediate" supports our claim that research methods that are less dependent upon historical and temporal references have the potential to reveal alternative and important understandings of information systems development and use.

EVENTS AND COLLECTIVE MEANING

Collectively considered together, "events" are the combination of situations and occurrences that have persistent significance to a social group as shared meaning-making and identity-making constructions (Urry, 2002). The examination and interpretation of events and their representation as event scenes is not a new research enterprise. Its foundations lie in classical historical analysis, including the documentation of significant moments of humanities' progress through time (see Burke's 1978 mainstream détournement). As Burke (1978) acknowledges through his own somewhat unconventional view of history, an event offers different meaning to different social groups that reflect divergent genealogies of events. Within information systems research, attention to structure and process produces a lack of sensitivity to the everyday and constant interplay of events. Plant (1997, p. 12) also provides an indefinite definitional basis for the spectacle when she identifies it as the "materialisation of ideology." In the broadest sociological sense, contemporary events include reality television programmes, sports fixtures and annual festivals. All of these have been made the focus of theoried examination through a variety of methodological lenses. In an information systems context events exist in a variety of forms, including version change, system failure (in its many well-documented permutations), new personnel and new cohorts of "users" (such as the annual induction of higher education students to virtual learning environments). Events in this way are imprecisely situated within a historical, temporal, political and locational morass. The logic of information systems *events* is more clearly defined and understood by their shifting interrelationship to one another rather than their position on a Gantt chart, in a timeline, physical location or particular management regime.

It is those events that are shared and recalled (although not necessarily in any linear or logical fashion) as significant referents that engender cultural dynamism and contribute to the perpetuation of social structures. It has been argued by Urry (2002) that events such as wars, inventions, rituals, ceremonies, births and deaths are the core

elements in the construction of shared meaning and are vital for the establishment of individual as well as social identity. The documentation of past events — or, alternatively, written histories — are significant cultural artefacts that retain collective consciousness in a tangible and objectified manner. Similarly, the documentation of future events in procedures and system designs embed historical, temporal, political and locational bias and assumptions that are effaced (or at least obscured) by the internal "logic" of documentation practice and the "structure" of a system's design. These realisations are implied as central concerns for the situationists with their criticism of contemporary art and visual representation (Plant, 1997). Situationist thought, which by implication informs the event-driven perspective more generally, understands that the indirect experience of the event encapsulates a hidden but mediating representation that contributes to the obfuscation of the influences that the holders of "real" power have in contemporary society (Albright, 2003). The mechanism by which events or other units of enquiry are represented and labeled through a seemingly neutral "methodology" is consequently recognised as a powerful (and empowering) aspect of the research process. The embedded political relations found in research-based representations of events also contributes to a wider agenda that preserves the existing structures of mainstream power, whether this be political, gendered, ethnic or economic. De Certeau (1988, p. xvii) expresses this concern as the marginality of the majority.

Marginality is today no longer limited to minority, but is rather massive and pervasive; this cultural activity of the non-producers of culture, an activity that is unsigned, unreadable and unsymbolized, remains the only one possible for all those who nevertheless buy and pay for the showy products through which a productivist economy articulates itself.

The event that was the attack on New York in September 2001 and its later evolution into the media-driven event scenes of "9/11" a year later is one indication that the representation of events is a powerful political tool. The difficulty with representational strategies is that they can be used equally by situationists and critics of contemporary culture as well as by the holders of existing power (Albright, 2003; Plant, 1997). Realisation that the political motivations of situationism had itself been recuperated by the mainstream as "witty" ads and ironic play was a pivotal cause in the fracturing and dissolution of the movement. The *Sex Pistols* are one example of this tension. As their manager manipulated mainstream sensibilities to commercial success, the band's own initial political and social commentary became increasingly questionable. We advocate, in the largely conservative environment of organisational studies, a critical re-examination of what methodology "does" but do not *ad hoc* reject all existing methodological paradigms (Gergen & Thatchenkery, 2004, p. 235). The issue being critiqued here is the current practice within information system's research for continuous, but empty, justification and reiteration of "its" methods. Modernist desire for self-legitimation obscures recognition of the continuous sequence of interrelated events that *is* the information system in order to emphasise the research activity itself and to legitimate its utility (Gergen & Thatchenkery, 2004, p. 240). More significantly, debate concerning methodological appropriateness, if we apply the concerns of situationism, obscures examination of the real power holders who benefit from the events that are represented.

A VIEW OF THE EVERYDAY

To dérive was to notice the way in which certain areas, streets, or buildings resonate with states of mind, inclinations, and desires, and to seek out reasons for movement other than those for which an environment was designed. (Plant, 1997)

At first glance the effort to dérive (to become a *derivite*, to drift) appears to be the opposite political action called for by the desire to represent, recognise, and respond to the complacency of mundaneity. However, the act of dérive is better viewed as the political and methodological act of looking beyond the veil of hegemonic expectations in order to see the actuality of use in places and with things. In an information systems context this could be (merely) seen as looking beyond the managerialist and structuralist views of a system (Peterson, 1998). The contemporary seminal example of the act of dérive are the unfocused, random and personal actions of the "Web surfer" (Andersen, 1998; Hartmann, 2003). Observation and participation within a system is contextual within a continuous sequence of interrelated events that captures what is actually done on a day to day basis rather than what is expected of individuals.

The role of the everyday within information systems research is, however, only marginally articulated or acknowledged in the majority of seminal information systems literature. Such a paucity of material is despite the significant impact that information systems themselves have upon daily life, both in a workplace context and increasingly in the domestic environment. However, the discussion of everyday life and its critical debates are well covered elsewhere (in other disciplinary contexts) by writers such as de Certeau (1988) and Lefebvre (1992). Both of these authors had also recognised association with situationist thought. De Certeau (1988, p. xviii) in discussing the personal interrelationships of everyday life claims that

statistical investigation remains virtually ignorant of these trajectories, since it is satisfied with classifying, calculating and putting into tables the "lexical" units which compose them but to which they cannot be reduced, and with doing this in reference to its own categories and taxonomies.

These claims can be rightly construed as a critique of quantitative and positivist praxis. The implication in a critique of this type is that these approaches produce their own internal logic that obscures external influences of power upon those people and "things" being tabulated, and who are ultimately affected. De Certeau (1988) argues for the significance of the interrelatedness of everyday life when he claims that "the analysis of the images broadcast by television and of the time spent watching television should be complemented by a study of what the cultural consumer 'makes' or 'does' during this time and with these images." Basden (2005), in examining the works of Dooyeweerd, also claims that

though we cannot theorize scientifically about everyday life, we can understand it philosophically as an integration of the aspects of our experience. In the everyday, all aspects play their proper place to a greater or lesser extent. This is why, for example, it has an important social aspect and a religious (pistic) aspect, as well as a sensory aspect. But it also means that everyday living is not devoid of analytical activity (which is akin to theoretical thinking), though this takes the form of an analytical subject-object relationship rather than a theoretical Gegenstand-relation. This provides a useful foundation for analysing the richness of everyday life, everyday engaged attitudes and tacit knowledge.

The situationist view of the everyday is not, however, celebratory. Situationist association of everyday life with people's oppression and disempowerment largely prohibits this perspective, at least directly. De Certeau's general observations regarding everyday life also reflect this political hesitation.

...our society is characterized by a cancerous growth of vision, measuring everything by its ability to show or be shown and transmuting communication into a visual journey. It is a sort of epic of the eye and of the impulse to read. The economy itself, transformed into a "semiocracy", encourages a hypertrophic development of reading. Thus for the binary set production consumption, one would substitute its more general equivalent: writing reading. Reading (an image or a text), moreover, seems to constitute the maximal development of the passivity assumed to characterize the consumer, who is conceived of as a voyeur in a show-biz society. (de Certeau, 1988, p. xxi)

As the indivisible stage of experience, everyday life is the venue for the construction and articulation of events (Peterson, 1998, p. 20). Understanding information systems in this context places them in the realm of everyday life, where they cease to exist in any systematic or singular sense. Information systems (whatever these may be) as an experience of everyday life become (perhaps merely) a surfeit of received information so that "today, the population is subjected to a continuous bombardment of damned stupidities that are not in the least dependent on the mass media" (Debord, 2002, p. 130). Debord (2002, p. 130) sustains this critique by claiming that "information theory straightaway ignores the chief power of language which lies on its poetic level; to compete and supercede." Information does not have inherent power solely as a consequence of the scale of individual collections (with the Internet being the uber example) but in conjunction with the manner that information is read and reinterpreted; in short, how it is presented and represented.

THE MULTIPLICITY OF EXPERIENCE

The event-based approach is a rejection of the linearity of practice that is assumed within predominant "systems" based approaches. Methods that seek to understand "the system" commence with a series of assumptions that include the belief in an *a priori* presence of a system "merely" because the concentrated accumulation and representations of information is labeled as such. Belief in the systemic nature of everyday life is an agreement of coherence and semiosis that is not borne out by experience. An event-oriented method, in contrast, integrates and recognises the illogical asemiosis of experience that eschews the application of management process and articulates arhythmic patterns of life (Peterson, 1998). For example, organisational studies of university management would attend to the application of documented policy, the process of committee based decision making and the general hierarchy of authority within a university. An event-oriented approach applied to the same environment may focus on the "hidden" flows of e-mails between colleagues, the use of "chair's action" for decision making and the day to day solving of problems that contradict documented policy.

Critical and contemporary social studies no longer unwittingly accept the dominant historical accounts of events as the only "truth." Nor do these perspectives blindly accept the unseen influences of power in the constitution of social phenomena or even identity. Writers such as Baudrillard (1998), Bergson (1910) and Game (1996) have all challenged the linearity of history and have gone so far as to argue for, at least in some cases, the death of history. In this rethinking of history the temporally cemented event — fixed, reified and glorified — is challenged. Raising doubt regarding the "certainty" of specifically identified events is particularly true in relation to the role that history plays as the central parameter of cultural understanding. The exploration of notions of time and space and their philosophical relationships is a central focus in contemporary studies of the social. Time, Bergson argues, has philosophically become spatialised (1910). That is, when time is spatialised it is understood as being able to be touched, seen as having discrete elements or presence and, most significantly, it can be presumed to be represented in this way (Game, 1996). As Game states "the common

conception of time is that it is abstract, linear, and homogenous; homogenous empty time" (Game, 1996, p. 95). It is Bergson's notion of multiplicity, however, that positions — even anchors — the construction of event scenes and the representation of everyday life experiences. The method of multiplicity, outlined by Bergson, employs dislocation by taking any object and disassociating its different moments, or its different ways of meaning (Game, 1996, p. 92). Bergson's multiplicity mirrors the political strategy and research method of détournement (the disentanglement of cultural products to present new and oppositional meanings). Pulling apart the normality of everyday life plays with the meanings (and understandings) of the single instance and multiple events (their interlocking relationships) (Debord & Wolman, 1956). Bergson is critical of the approach and idea that "the present contains nothing more than the past, and what is found in the effect was already the cause" (Bergson, 1910, p. 15). The influences of historical materialism is readily identified within both qualitative ethnographic works and quantitative longitudinal studies (two methodological approaches that currently find favour within information systems research). Historical materialism presumes that what has preceded is the key relationship and source of understanding. However, for the contemporary moment it is an under theorised enquiry.

CAPTURING THE EVENT WITHIN THE RESEARCH PROCESS

The diverse approaches to systems thinking utilised in the field of information systems necessitates critical engagement with the question of the research position as the actual site of analysis and point of observation of the event. Systems theory methodologies require a boundary to be placed at the site of analysis (Heylighen, 1998). Encapsulating the subject under examination reduces the endless combinations and interactions of complex systems — the wide range of events — that can be observed. It is at the nexus between advocacy for the need for boundaries and alternatively their permeability that debates regarding the meaning and purpose of information systems research exists. General systems theory applies boundaries in order to present a minimalised but holistic position of analysis (Heylighen, 1998). The bounded conceptualisation of a system exists within the broader continuum of system theory approaches and has been utilised across the information systems field, which ranges from the "hard system/cybernetic" approaches to "soft systems" (see Checkland & Howell, 1998 for a history of systems thinking in information systems development).

Systems operating within organisations are usually considered open in that there is recognition of the dynamic interaction of the system with the surrounding environment (Robbins & Barnwell, 1994). The system's boundary serves to enclose internal operational elements from those external to the system and environmental conditions which may impact upon the system as a whole. However, the system's boundary is permeable (Greenhill, 2002). Within the system, information is processually transformed from input to the output stage. Systems developers expect and plan for information taken into a system to be altered in predictable *systematic* ways up to the final point of output, of release from the system. Bundled with this initial assumption, the meanings and purposes associated with specific information are also fixed. Baskerville and Pries-Heje's (1998) study on the management of knowledge capability and maturity in a small to medium size software development organisation is a pertinent example of the expectations of the systems developers in developing and maintaining fixed meanings within systems. The company Baskerville and Pries-Heje studied experienced difficulties developing organisational and Web-based systems. Assessment of the company's situation was carried out primarily in managerial

terms, rather than as a sequence of events, as the employees themselves claim.

I realise that all documents needed to support this, namely customer contract, project presentation, budget and requirements specification, were nowhere, and there were a thousand different meanings within Proventum about how they should look... Today we have as many different contracts as we have employees, because we don't have a template to work from. (Jan in Baskerville and Pries-Heje, 1998, p. 183)

We need to be better at exploiting the knowledge from previous projects, much better, so we don't make the same things again and again and again. (Henrik in Baskerville and Pries-Heje, 1998, p. 183)

Many systems designs rely on the fact that there can be no unsystematic, nonprocessual or unexpected alterations to the *meaning* of information (no unforeseen events). The experience of the system is not regarded as a varied combination of interconnected events but a continuous timeline of neatly packaged and logical actions. In the case of this often cited example, information was seen in management terms to remain static and continuously available to enable its exploitation in the future. However, from an event-based perspective the purpose and use of the information within a planned system does not necessitate or provide any singular or fixed accumulation of meanings. In place of uniform certainty is an array of interrelated meanings that the user may variously interpret from a system and its usage. It is only the genealogy and association crafted through organisational culture that produces mutually shared understanding of the system. As Wittgenstein observed, there can be no "private language." Understanding and mutual comprehensibility is a joint-action (Gergen & Thatchenkery, 2004).

The interpretive position offered by Orlikowski & Gash (1994) and Feldman & March (1981) are two examples of the influence of situationism on information systems research. The assertion that information *always* holds multiple meanings challenges any methodological assumption surrounding the construction and representation of meaning that presumes a linear monodimensional process (Baudrillard, 1994). An event-oriented perspective enables the identification of many taken-for-granted positions to be found in current methodological frameworks through the act of détournement, and reveals rather than obscures the political environment around which information is manipulated (Baskerville, Travis, & Truex, 1992). The foundational model for information systems was developed within a modernist context and utilises static and linear understanding to the meaning of information. It is only now that we, as participants within a postmodern cultural condition, are able to critique and question the appropriateness of static models of systems models usage.

Generally, analysis of systems operations and information systems utilise the modernist tradition, which emphasises and restricts understanding through the processes of production (see Alter, 1996; Hirscheim, Klein & Lyytinen, 1995). The information system is represented and understood as a Fordist information "factory." For example, the system Baskerville and Pries-Heje (1998) explore is a knowledge management system that requires the system output – knowledge – to be managed. The input into the system is garnered from knowledge obtained from new and existing employees on the software programming team. More specifically, new knowledge, meanings and hence inputs that the individuals have in relation to database technology, Internet technology and Web technology are inserted into the system (Baskerville & Pries-Heje, 1998). The management of this knowledge within the monolithic managerial perspective requires information at the input stage to remain deterministically static

in order to be both predictable and reusable. The application of this knowledge *may* be required at a later date (as systemic output). Therefore, it must be controlled in terms similar to those of a factory process. The system is valued purely in terms of this restrictive and narrow, but tangible, output. Processual approaches restrict the understanding of a system to an examination of data, its utilisation and manipulation. The goal or objective of the system is reached by asking whether the end product or output is effective and achieves the desired outcomes. Outcomes are generally assessed from a managerial perspective, simultaneously reducing the day-to-day user to a component of the system. Mechanistic positions reflect much of the contemporary information systems thinking (see Alter, 1996; Achterberg, van Es & Heng, 1991; Hirscheim, Klein & Lyytinen, 1995; Morgan & Smircich, 1980). Incorporating the event into systems analysis challenges production driven theorisations by shifting analysis away from production and the privilege of the manager. Consideration of events and the role of less privileged users reduces the dominance of hierarchical and managerial views of the system. Ultimately, the political aim of this perspective is to reposition those who contribute to events *in* the system as owners of that system.

METHODS FOR REVEALING AND REPRESENTING THE EVENT

Much of the methodological challenge that is taken up by event based analysis has been described ad hoc under the rubric – "the postmodern turn" (Brown, 1990, p. 196). Although this "turn" is yet to be fully articulated within the studies of organisations, commentaries such as that of Gergen and Thatchenkery (2004) do justify the turn for further critical work. Although postmodernism has been posited as antithetical to the modernist project, the relationship is not simply a structuralist dichotomy (Lagopoulos, 1993). Foster (1983,

p. xi) suggests that the task of postmodernism is to extend the project of modernism by opening "its closed systems to the heterogeneity of texts." The politically confining aspects of modernist methodology are alternately accentuated, ignored or rejected in the various "postmodern" approaches (Huyssen, 1992; Jencks, 1992,). Klotz (1988), in his attempt at reaching a definition of architectural postmodernism — itself a potentially modernist task — provides the basic framework for critical social research. He cites ten defining characteristics of the postmodern experience, ranging from geographic specificity and poetic cultural constructions to a need for relativism. Recognition of these cultural conditions irrevocably alters the justification of modernist methodology. The recognisable traits of postmodernism all emphasise the irrevocably altered nature of social relations in advanced mainstream capitalism, including what we claim is a surfeit of events. Among other qualities found in Klotz's (1988) definition of postmodernism are the use of fiction in conjunction with function, the ironic "use" of history, the plurality of style, and a movement away from the perceived inevitability of technological progress. Capturing this complex social environment is more readily done through the gaze of the dérive — looking at the world of everyday life from the outside — and engaging in détournement — tearing down the supposed stability of systems.

The urban form, the visual, a celebration of the mundane, the embodiment of readable messages within material culture items and, obliquely, the increasing importance of entertainment in daily life are all elements of a critical methodology that attempts to understand contemporary social life. The movement away from modernist method and its quantifying concerns has been paralleled with an interest in the study of the popular and — to its extreme manifestation — kitsch (Jameson, 1983). What had been previously dismissed as not worthy of study or as being simply ugly have acquired undiscovered qualities, bringing them into the framework of theoried examination. The academic study of the products in the everyday life of mainstream capitalism, such as tourist's souvenirs and the car, is compatible with the attitudes of the dérive.

Examining the mundane "things" of everyday life and their relationship to other "things" also emphasises a shift in focus from production-based analysis to more consumption-orientated approaches. This is a view which is confirmed by Shields (1992, p. 2), who believes that "in general, the modernist separation of economy and culture has left little room for serious engagement with consumption practices." Consumption-based methods provide a degree of flexibility and encompass a significant part of an individual's social life. Being "out" in the public sphere is to be consuming, not just foodstuffs and fuels, but more intangible items, including events and information. The practice of consuming in advanced capitalist social life has become synonymous with social participation (Derrida, 1978). People's ability to remain social participants is determined by their consumption practices. In this sense consuming events and gazing upon objects are important aspects of everyday life, and by implication the research methodologies concerned with human experience. Consumption encompasses a significant proportion of social life when the supposedly "ordinary" can be viewed both as spectacle and as the parody of spectacle — the unspectacular event.

Within the context of everyday life the consumption of events is sublimated into the realm of the ordinary slipping from political consciousness to reinforce existing power structures. The situationists provide two methodological tactics that support their underlying theoretical and political standpoint: dérive and détournement. A third methodological tactic was identified by the situationists as the position and action that must be resisted, that of recuperation (being subsumed into the mainstream). Much of the obscurity, complexity and incoherence of the original situationist works was incorporated as a defense mechanism against this counter-tactic. Criticism of later works with a situationist heritage could also be understood through the realisation of this tactic and proactive resistance. Writings such as Baudrillard's (1998) "postmodernism" and Derrida's (1978) "poststructuralism" are two immediately obvious examples.

There is a tendency to isolate an individual tactic of situationism and celebrate its relevance. Of the three methods this response is most commonly found with the dérive and the Web (Andersen, 1998; Hartmann, 2003). However, this methodological isolation is a disservice to the original intent of the situationists. The *Internationale Situationiste* (1958) claim for détournement, as "the integration of past or present artistic production into a superior construction of a milieu," continues to have relevance in relation to information systems as an inter-related combination of events that are not constrained by the arbitrary boundary of a documented system. Setting the information system free of unfounded delineation requires the act of the dérive. To drift and discern the location of these relevant but distanciated events requires the attitude that mirrors Baudelaire's *flaneur* who is not constrained by the conventions that the recuperated information system seeks to sustain and perpetuate upon its hierarchically labeled and systemically controlled users.

Existing examples of event-oriented critiques of information systems are not readily found as printed documents. However, the increasing domestication of information technology acts as an enabling mechanism that brings event-based critique to the Web. These are generally visual and visualisation projects. The *Digital Landfill* project (*www.potatoland.org/landfill*) takes images and texts from randomly selected Web sites and détournes them into a single image that seems to be "almost" meaningful. Similarly, the home page of *spaceless.com* generates a random selection of images gathered from everyday life that *appears* to be a coherent collection. The semiotic obscurity of the resultant combination of images resists recuperation while standing as a critique of the vast asemiotic information system that is the Web. A more focused use of situationist tactics to develop a critique of an e-commerce system was the ongoing dispute between *etoy.com* and *etoys.com* (Stallabrass, 2003). *Etoy.com* became the vehicle from which "toy war" was launched. This "war" parodied the techniques of online business to détourne the meaning of e-commerce. The final result of this political engagement was the corporate failure and bankruptcy of *etoys.com*.

However, some Internet art projects reach beyond détournement and this is explained by Debord and Wolman's definition of the tactic. "The distortions introduced in the détourned elements must be as simplified as possible, since the main impact of a détournement is directly related to the conscious or semiconscious recollection of the original contexts of the elements" (Debord & Wolman, 1956). This tactic is consequently not an anarchic free for all, but rather a considered and theoried technique that specifically endeavours to produce a political response to the observed world and *status quo*.

THE DEATH OF HISTORY (OR THE DEATH OF CRITICAL INFORMATION SYSTEMS RESEARCH)

This chapter has presented the definitions of event scenes and the theoretical background regarding events. We provide an overview of existing research and commentary that focus upon the meaning, significance and impact of "events" in the information technology, organisational and social contexts. Peterson's (1998) literature review provides initial guidance in revealing the possibilities for a taxonomy of organisational events. In this way, we have developed the foundations for a critical debate regarding the relationships of events to organisations.

The argument presented here has demonstrated how the "event" as a method can capture multi-dimensional and multivocal forms of expression. We have shown how the examination of the event can form the basis for an appropriate, viable and useful information systems methodology. By focusing on the "event" the researcher or system designer can observe and capture the complexity, multiplicity and mundaneity of everyday lived experience. By utilising an "event" focus in IS research, we argue for the potential to reconstitute the mundane, the integrative blend of moments that constitute everyday life, the nonlinearity of experience, the illogic of expectations, the indeterminate acceleration and deceleration of personal temporality and the moments of the unexpected or unforeseen (Albright, 2003; Debord, 1994; Gergen & Thatchenkery, 2004; Peterson, 1998; Plant, 1997).

We have argued that utilising the event-oriented method, including elements of illogical asemiosis of experience, eschews the application of management process and articulates arhythmic patterns of life. The significance of the event-based approach to information systems development and research is that a nonlineal method challenges managerialist, structured and time-fixated praxis that currently dominate information systems research and development. The implication of our critique is that these existing popular approaches produce their own internal logic that obscures the influences of power on people and "things" located and ordered within the system. The influences of historical materialism can readily be identified in the preference for current research approaches. Historical materialism presumes that what has preceded is the key relationship and source of understanding — the event, in contrast, is currently an under theorised enquiry. Such theoretical foundation means that systems developers expect and plan for information taken into a system to be altered in predictable *systematic* ways up to the final point of output, where they are released from the control of the system. However, from an event-based perspective, the purpose and use of the information within a planned system does not necessitate or provide any singular or fixed accumulation of meanings. Consideration of events and the role of less privileged users reduces the dominance of hierarchical and managerial views of the system. Ultimately, the political aim of an event-oriented perspective is to make those *in the system* the owners of that system.

Finally, what is being presented in the event and the event-scene is not a metamethod for information systems research but an attempt to incorporate the complexities of everyday life and the subtleties of political meaning into the sterility of systemic systems thinking. Event-oriented perspectives in information systems offer the opportunity to engage in détournement for the purpose of both understanding existing environments and contributing to the development of future systems' "architecture." The active engagement in re-engineering echoes the situationist's own town planning and architectural experiments (Sadler, 1998). Rebuilding the component parts found in the détournement produces new, unexpected and politically challenging approaches to the mundaneity of everyday life. Information systems research, in contrast, has been recuperated from its inception. Its methods, philosophy and advocacy continuously return to questions of business efficiency, process improvement and time management. As information systems become increasingly domesticated, the continuous and automatic reiteration of these perspectives without debate or critique will merely serve to perpetuate existing mainstream regimes of power.

REFERENCES

Achterberg, J., van Es, G., & Heng, M. (1991). Information systems research in the postmodern period. In H. Nissen, H. Klein, & R. Hirschheim (Eds.), *Information systems research: Contemporary approaches and emergent traditions* (pp. 281-292). Amsterdam: Elsevier Science.

Albright, D. (2003, Winter). Tales of the city: Applying situationist social practice to the analysis of the urban drama. *Criticism*.

Alter, S. (1996). *Information systems: A management perspective*. Menlo Park, CA: The Benjamin/Cummings Publishing Company.

Andersen, K. (1998). A virtual derive. Retrieved September 17, 2006, from http://www.aac.bartlett. ucl.ac.uk/ve/Work9798/kristina/derive.html

Basden, A. (2005). The lifeworld: Dooyeweerd's approach to everyday experience. Retrieved September 17, 2006, from http://www.isi.salford. ac.uk/dooy/everyday.html#chcs

Baskerville, R., & Pries-Heje, J. (1998). Information technology diffusion: Building positive barriers. *European Journal of Information Systems, 7*, 17-28.

Baskerville, R., Travis, J., & Truex, D. (1992). Systems without method: The impact of new technologies on information systems development projects. In K. Kendall, K. Lyytinen, & J. DeGross. (Eds.), *The impact of computer supported technologies on information systems development* (pp. A-8). Amsterdam: Elsevier Science.

Baudrillard, J. (1988). The year 2000 has already happened. In A. Kroker & M. Kroker (Eds.), *Body invaders: Sexuality and the postmodern condition*. Basingstroke: Macmillian Press.

Baudrillard, J. (1998). *The transparency of evil* (J. Benedict, Trans.). London: Verso.

Bergson, H. (1910). *Time and free will: An essay on the immediate data of consciousness* (F. Pogson, Trans.). London: George Allen and Unwin.

Brown, R. (1990). Rhetoric, textuality and the postmodern turn in sociological theory. *Sociological Theory, 8*(2), 188-197.

Burke, J. (1978). *Connections*. London: Macmillian Press.

Checkland, P., & Howell, S. (1998). *Information, systems and information systems: Making sense of the field*. Chichester: Wiley.

De Certeau. (1988). *The practice of everyday life*. Berkeley.

Debord, G. (1994). *Society of the spectacle*. (D. Nicholson-Smith, Trans.). New York: Zone Books.

Debord, G. (2002). Editorial notes: Priority communication. In T. McDonough (Ed.), *Guy Debord and the situationist international: Text and documents*. Cambridge, MA: The MIT Press.

Debord, G., & Wolman, G. (1956, May). A user's guide to détournement. *Les Lèvres Nues, 8*. Retrieved September 17, 2006, from http://www. bopsecrets.org/SI/detourn.htm

Derrida, J. (1978). *Writing and difference*. (A. Bass, Trans.). London: Routledge & Kegan Paul.

Feldman, M., & March, J. (1981). Information in organizations as signal and symbol. *Administrative Science Quarterly, 26*, 171-186.

Foster, H. (1983). Postmodernism: A preface. In H. Foster (Ed.), *Postmodern culture*. London: Pluto Press.

Game, A. (1996). *Passionate sociology*. London: Sage Publications.

Gergen, K., & Thatchenkery, T. (2004, June). Organization science as social construction: Postmodern potentials. *The Journal of Applied Behaviorial Science, 40*(2), 228-249.

Greenhill, A. (2002, August 9-11). Critiquing reality: The mind/body split in computer mediated environments. In R. Ramsower, J. Windsor, & J. DeGross (Eds.), *Proceedings of the 8th Americas Conference on Information Systems*.

Hartmann, M. (2003, May 19-23). Situationist roaming online. In *Proceedings of Melbourne-*

DAC 2003, The 5th International Digital Arts and Culture Conference.

Heylighen, F. (1998). Basic concepts of the systems approach. *Principia Cybernetica Web*. Retrieved September 17, 2006, from http://pespmc1.vub.ac.be/SYSAPPR.html

Hirschheim, R., Klein, H., & Lyytinen, K. (1995). *Information systems development and data modelling: Conceptual and philosophical foundations*. Cambridge: Cambridge University Press.

Hoover, M., & Stokes, L. (1998, Fall). Pop music and the limits of cultural critique: Gang of four shrinkwraps entertainment. *Popular Music and Society.*

Huyssen, A. (1992). Mapping the postmodern. In H. Haferkamp & N. Smelser (Eds.), *Social change and modernity*. Berkeley: University of California Press.

Internationale Situationiste (1958, June) Definitions. No. 1. Retrieved October 12, 2006, from http://www.cddc.vt.edu/sionline/si/definitions/html

Jameson, F. (1983). Postmodernism and consumer society. In H. Foster (Ed.), *Postmodern culture*. London: Pluto Press.

Jencks, C. (1992). Preface: Post-modernism - the third force. In C. Jencks (Ed.), *The post-modern reader*. London: Academy Editions.

Klotz, H. (1988). *The history of postmodern architecture*. (R. Donnell, Trans.). Cambridge, MA: The MIT Press.

Lagopoulos, A. (1993). Postmodernism, geography, and the social semiotics of space. *Environment and Planning D: Society and Space, 11*, 255-278.

Lefebvre, H. (1992). *The production of space*. Oxford: Blackwell.

Mohamed, A. (2006, January 24). Managing complexity is the main event. *Computer Weekly*, 20.

Morgan, G., & Smircich, L. (1980). The case for qualitative research. *Academy of Management Review, 5*(4), 491-500.

Niblett, P., & Graham, S. (2005, December). Events and service-oriented architecture: The OASIS Web services notification specifications. *IBM Systems Journal, 44*(4), 869-887.

Orlikowski, W., & Gash, D. (1994). Technological frames: Making sense of information technology in organizations. *Transactions on Information Systems, 12*(2), 174-207.

Peterson, M. (1998, January-February). Embedded organizational events: The units of process in organization science. *Organization Science, 9*(1), 16-33.

Plant, S. (1997). *The most radical gesture: The situationist international in a postmodern age*. London: Routledge.

Robbins, S., & Barnwell, N. (1994). *Organisation theory in Australia*. New York: Prentice Hall.

Sadler, S. (1998). *The situationist city*. Cambridge, MA: The MIT Press.

Shields, R. (1992). Spaces for the subject of consumption. In R. Shields (Ed.), *Lifestyle shopping: The subject of consumption*. London: Routledge.

Stallabrass, J. (2003). *Internet art: The online clash of culture and commerce*. London: Tate Publishing.

Urry, J. (2002). The global complexities of September 11th. *Theory, Culture & Society, 19*(4), 57-69.

This work was previously published in International Journal of Technology and Human Interaction, Vol. 3, Issue 1, edited by B. Stahl , pp. 1-16, copyright 2007 by IGI Publishing, formerly known as Idea Group Publishing (an imprint of IGI Global).

Chapter VIII
Different Levels of Information Systems Designers' Forms of Thought and Potential for Human–Centered Design

Hannakaisa Isomäki
University of Lapland, Finland

ABSTRACT

This chapter describes a study clarifying information systems (IS) designers' conceptions of human users of IS by drawing on in-depth interviews with 20 designers. The designers' lived experiences in their work build up a continuum of levels of thought from more limited conceptions to more comprehensive ones reflecting variations of the designers' situated knowledge related to human-centred design. The resulting forms of thought indicate three different but associated levels in conceptualising users. The separatist form of thought provides designers predominantly with technical perspectives and a capability for objectifying things. The functional form of thought focuses on external task information and task productivity, nevertheless, with the help of positive emotions. The holistic form of thought provides designers with competence of human-centred information systems development (ISD). Furthermore, the author hopes that understanding the IS designers' tendencies to conceptualise human users facilitates the mutual communication between users and designers.

INTRODUCTION

As information systems (IS) increasingly pervade all aspects of everyday life, of utmost importance is how applications of IS are adjusted to human action. In particular, in current information systems development (ISD) it is essential to take into account human characteristics and behaviour; that is, to humanise IS (Sterling, 1974). In the same vein, Checkland (1981) argues that ISD should be seen as a form of enquiry within which IS designers' understandings regulate an operationalisation of their intellectual framework into a set of guidelines for investigation that require particular methods and techniques for building the system. Regarding the humanisation of IS, a notion concerning the nature of the human being is a crucial element of the intellectual framework. As a consequence, within this kind of enquiry, the way humans are taken into account in ISD is dependent on the operationalisation of the IS designers' conceptualisations of users. With respect to human-centeredness, attention should be paid to the fundamental qualities of people without any explicit or implicit domination of the other elements of IS, such as data, formal models and technical appliances, or managerial belief systems that treat humans instrumentally. This is necessary in order to conceptualise humans in their own right, and thus avoid the reduction of humans to something that exists only in relation to particular instrumental needs and purposes (cf. Buber, 1993).

Of essential importance is the nature of IS designers' insights into human characteristics and behaviour that are essential with respect to the IS-user relationship. The most crucial insight regarding human-centred design is to be able to conceptualise users as active subjects comprised of physical, cognitive, emotional, social and cultural qualities, an insight which is the prerequisite for design that promotes subsequent user acceptance and satisfaction. Yet conspicuously absent from contemporary IS literature are empirical studies investigating IS designers' conceptions of the human users, which have been studied more intensively two decades ago when the systems designers' inadequate view of the user has been stated to be one reason for the behavioural problems often experienced while implementing IS (Bostrom & Heinen, 1977; Dagwell & Weber, 1983). Also, the lack of knowledge of human needs and motivation on the part of the systems designers has been claimed to cause IS implementation failures (Hawgood, Land & Mumford, 1978). Further, Hedberg and Mumford (1975) have defined the nature of the view of human being held by systems designers as an essential factor in the IS design process. The systems designers' view of the user is also included in some studies as one of the targets of value choices during the ISD process (Kumar & Bjørn-Andersen, 1990; Kumar & Welke, 1984) and is therefore defined as a value rather than an insight in these studies. Dagwell and Weber (1983), in their replication study, rely on Hedberg-Mumford's definition of the concept but also refer to Kling (1980). "we know very little about the perceptions that computer specialists have of the users they serve and the ways in which they translate these perceptions into concrete designs (p. 47)." Bostrom & Heinen (1977), in turn, define systems designers' assumptions of people as one of the system designers' implicit theories or frames of reference. These previous works do not take an explicit stance toward the definition of the concept "conception," and do not align the nature of conceptions in detail. For instance, from where do conceptions derive their origins, and what is the nature of those conceptions? In a more recent study, Orlikowski and Gash (1994) discuss their definition of the IS designers' views. They elaborate the concept "*frame of reference*" by comparing it to the concept "*schema*" (Neisser, 1976, pp. 9-11), "*shared cognitive structures*" or "*cognitive maps*" (Eden, 1992, pp. 261-262), "*frames*" (Goffman, 1974, pp. 10-11), "*interpretative frames*" (Bartunek & Moch, 1987, p. 484), "*thought worlds*" (Dougherty,

1992, p. 179), "*interpretative schemes*" (Giddens, 1984, pp. 29-30), "scripts" (Gioia, 1986, p. 50), "*paradigms*" (Kuhn, 1970, p. 43), and "*mental models*" (Argyris & Schön, 1978). They end up by defining their own meaning for the concept frames as a general concept of shared cognitive structures, not especially regarding humans.

This chapter describes a study which aims to clarify IS designers' conceptions of users of IS by drawing on in-depth interviews with 20 IS designers. The analytical choices carried out in this study regard IS designers' conceptions of users as experiences inherent in their lifeworlds, particularly during the different phases of ISD. The lived experiences build up conceptions that form a structure of meaning, which incorporates a continuum of levels from more limited understandings to more comprehensive notions; that is, different levels of thought reflecting variations of the designers' situated, practical knowledge. In this way the development of IS is understood as knowledge work. It is an intellectual and personal process which takes its form according to the conceptions of the performers of the process. IS designers are then applying the ISD methodologies according to their own observations and thinking (Avison & Fitzgerald, 1994; Hirschheim et al, 1995; Mathiassen, 1998). Then the most important tool for ISD, and a key resource in contemporary IT companies, is the IS designers' thought and insight (Nonaka & Takeuchi, 1995; Quinn, 1992). Particularly with respect to the humanisation of IS, designers' conceptualisations of the human users are seen as knowledge that reflects the designers' competence in humanising IS. In this way, IS designers' conceptions may be seen as intellectual capital that mirrors the know-how, practices, and accumulated expertise of practitioners within a particular profession (Kogut & Zander, 1992).

In what follows, first, the assumptions informing this study are presented by introducing the interpretative approach referred to as phenomenography. Second, the resulted forms of thought are presented and discussed. The IS designers' conceptualisations presenting their mental schemes of the human user result in three forms of thought, revealing both context-centred and human-centred understandings of what humans are. These three levels of understanding indicate that IS designers tend to conceptualise uses in terms of technology, business and work, and that seldom are users taken into account according to their human qualities. Finally, the different levels of conceptualisation are discussed in relation to human-centred ISD.

DIFFERENT LEVELS OF UNDERSTANDING

This study merges with the principles of phenomenography, which is a qualitatively oriented method of empirical research for investigating the different ways in which people experience aspects of reality (Marton, 1981; Marton & Booth, 1997). Essentially, phenomenography is about individual meaning construction, which results in a conception. The primary focus is on the structure of the meaning of conceptions, which are seen in the light of the phenomenological notion according to which person and world are inextricably related through a person's lived experience of the world (e.g., Husserl, 1995; Merleau-Ponty, 1962). Our intentionality is seen as qualitatively varying foci on the horizon of our life worlds. While experiencing the world, individuals form conceptions, including qualitative dissimilarities, which are inherent in the intertwined referential and structural aspects of an experience. Different levels are due to the way the structural aspect and the referential aspect merge with each other. Then an experience is specified by the analytical distinctions of a structural aspect and a referential aspect (Figure 1). The structural aspect denotes how a particular phenomenon is both discerned from its environment and how the phenomenon's parts relate to each other as well as to the whole

Figure 1. The analytical distinctions of an experience (Marton & Booth, 1997)

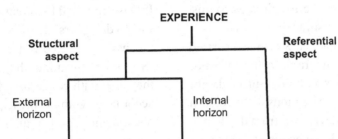

phenomenon. That which surrounds the phenomenon experienced, including its contours, is its external horizon. The parts and their relationships, together with the contours of the phenomenon, are its internal horizon. The referential aspect signifies the meaning of the conception. These two aspects are dialectically intertwined and occur simultaneously within an experience. Thus, people create conceptions with respect to the structural aspect's external and internal horizons of a phenomenon that are dialectically merged with the referential aspect of that particular phenomenon.

On the one hand, conceptions differ in terms of content, and on the other hand, they differ in terms of the extent of the form that a certain phenomenon is experienced, as a part of that phenomenon, or more as a whole. When detached parts of a phenomenon are the focus of thought instead of relating the parts meaningfully to the whole phenomenon, the meaning of the phenomenon is understood in a way that refers to a more narrow view. Respectively, when the focus of thought is more comprehensive regarding the whole meaning of a phenomenon instead of on separate parts of it or even the surroundings of the phenomenon, the more explanatory conceptions are. Further, the more explanatory power conceptions have, the better they support competent action with respect to the phenomenon in question (Sandberg, 2000). Based on these differences, conceptions form a structure of meaning, which incorporates a continuum of levels from more limited understandings to more comprehensive notions. The qualitative variation in the ways that IS designers conceptualise users reflects their different conceptions of users, and simultaneously forms different levels in the designers' understandings, reflecting variations of their situated, practical knowledge as forms of thought. These forms of thought, in turn, suggest different levels of competence in humanising IS, because the subjective conceptualisations of IS designers refer to their intention of action (Säljö, 1994).

The interview method is accomplished with respect to phenomenographic principles. To promote multiple interpretations within individual designers, first, opening questions with varying perspectives into the different phases of ISD, such as planning, design, implementation, use and maintenance, was incorporated in the interview framework. Second, to sustain the connection between the designers' reflection and the actual work within ISD phases while the in-depth interviews aimed at achieving mutual and authentic understanding that proceeded from the interviewees' expressions. The interviews were taped at the designers' workplaces to maintain the work practice orientation and to facilitate the expression of the connection between the respondents' immediate experiences and the subsequent conception. Second, the respondents represent a variety of geographical location, age, gender, educational background and work experience. They came from various different application areas of

IS practice, such as e-commerce, tele and media communications, groupware, health care systems, office automation and insurance systems.

The analysis of the interview data was carried out against the phenomenographical theory. Since phenomenography does not offer grounds for defining the content of conceptions within data, a coding paradigm was developed from the data in order to facilitate the identification and categorisation of meanings in the data (Glaser & Strauss, 1967; Tesch, 1990; Strauss & Corbin, 1990). The development of the coding paradigm was based on the phenomenographical principle regarding the intentionality of conceptions. Conceptions are context-dependent and every experience is described in content-loaded terminology (Säljö, 1994,). That is, the descriptions are carried out in terms of the nature of the situational experiences in question. Consequently, the meanings are to be found in accordance with the underlying assumptions concerning the intentional nature of ISD. In addition, since it is assumed in phenomenography that the meanings of the respondents' mental acts exist in the data and are constitutive of the data (Walsh, 1994), the way meanings are understood in this study should also be in accordance with the types of intentionality existing in the data. Thus, the coding paradigm was finalised by bracketing away any preconceived ideas of what the IS designers' views might be like (Francis, 1993), and letting the analysis be informed by the underlying assumptions of intentionality in ISD.

First, the data includes utterances that describe various actions and objectives concerning ISD. These expressions indicate intentionality as defined by Hirschheim et al. (1995, p. 16). They state that "IS development is intentional, to the extent it reflects a planned change. It is based on developers' intentions to change object systems towards desirable ends", and go on to say that (1995, p. 17) "intentions in systems development are expressed by objectives. These are related to general value-orientations and represent what 'one ought to do' or 'what is good'." From this it can be

concluded, in the first place, that intentionality in ISD is expressed by intentional action. That is to say, IS designers' descriptions of the actions and means they are involved with when developing an IS reveal the meanings they give to the phenomena they deal with concerning ISD. This notion is in accordance with the principle of contextuality in phenomenography, which denotes that people's conceptualisations are not detachable, either from their context or the content of the task at hand. This stance also reinforces the interpretative nature of phenomenographical analysis in that the researcher must see the designers' action as inherently meaningful (cf. Schwandt, 2000). In the second place, as Hirschheim et al. (1995) point out, intentions are expressed by objectives of ISD. Consequently, it is an appropriate way to define that the way the IS designers understand the human user of an IS is revealed through descriptions in which the respondents' focus of reflection is on the objectives of ISD. That is to say, in addition to the actions and means the designers refer to, the IS designers' intentions to change object systems toward desirable ends reveal the meanings they give to the phenomena they deal with concerning ISD. These desirable ends or objectives represent the things that are regarded most important in ISD. In this way, the IS designers' descriptions of action, means and objectives also implicitly indicate value orientations included in the process of ISD. Therefore, the described actions and objectives represent the things that are regarded important, and thus reveal the referential aspect in terms of intentionality as an implied value orientation. This means that the initial referential aspects of conceptions may be found in utterances in which the designers refer to their way and means of building systems and the objectives of their actions.

Second, the data includes descriptions in which the respondents' thoughts are attached to human objects. These descriptions of people indicated human features and also value orientations toward people. Often these descriptions also included expressions which indicated emotionally toned reactions. These kinds of expressions within the data indicate intentionality that is in accordance with Uljens (1991), who states that the process of qualitative individuation of a mental act has been done when an object and a psychological mode, referred to as an attitude, is shown. In other words, how a particular object of thought is experienced denotes the respondents' attitudes toward the phenomenon that is being reflected on. In brief, the inherent meaning of an utterance may be seen as the correlation between the what- and how-aspects in that they are not detachable from each other, but are interrelated in a particular logical way, indicating what a particular phenomenon is, in what it is revealed, and what kind of values and attitudes are related to it. As described above, the search for the meanings in the data, data analysis, was initiated by establishing a coding paradigm, which suggests that the meanings in the data are found in utterances in which the designers refer to their actions, means, and objectives concerning ISD, as well as to human characteristics.

The subsequent analysis procedures followed the idea, firstly, of iterating between the meaning (referential aspect) of single statements, their surrounding statements, and the data as a whole, and second, iterating between the features that reveal different levels in these meanings (structural aspect). The analysis appreciates the phenomenological notion of "Lebenswelt" in that the continuum of levels from more limited forms of thought to more comprehensive understandings reflects associative connections within the designers' conceptions rather than direct, law-like logical relations between them (cf. Husserl, 1995). The analysis revealed the designers' conceptions as different levels of understanding, which appear as the separatist, functional, and holistic forms of thought. These forms of thought reveal three different levels of understandings incorporating both context-centred and human-centred notions. In the descriptions associated with the context-centred conceptions, the designers' focus of reflection is on

technology, work, and business. The human-centred conceptions deal with knowledge, emotions, and the designers' selves. The following description delineates the specific contents of the conceptions as parts of the three forms of thought by highlighting some exemplary conceptions.

THE SEPARATIST FORM OF THOUGHT

The most partial way in which the IS designers conceptualise humans is through the separatist form of thought. It demonstrates how IS designers see humans within the affordances and constraints of contemporary IS and their development as separated from fluid and coherent interactions. Within this form of thought, the user is positioned outside the IS designers' awareness through objectivist conceptualisations. An objectivist pattern is evident in the context-centred separatist conceptions, which reflect understandings according to which reality exists independent of humans and can thus be understood independent of humans (cf. Lakoff, 1987; Orlikowski & Baroudi, 1991). In this case, when discussing human-centred issues of ISD, the designers' focus of reflection is directed to technology, job titles, and market mechanisms. For example, within the conception of *"the human being displaced by technology"* IS designers refer to humans in terms of technology:

R: What are these requirements and wishes like? Could you tell me more about them?

D16: Well, because it is a question of – let's say — a feedback channel that our company offers as a product to its clients, it means that if the client purchases, for instance, a datanet-based customer network, they have datanet and router accesses through which they operate between their networks and use the whole telecommunication network. Then there are a lot of this kind of usability issues, response times and load percentages, or in a way, how it (telecommunication network) sort of behaves, what happens there.

In the above interview extract, the designer considers the customers' needs as a piece of software — "a feedback channel" — and the main point that emerges is how this item of software works with the functions of a telecommunications network. The designer's train of thought becomes focussed on technology instead of human-centred issues and needs, such as how the software is built in regard to the humans that will be using it. In the same vein, within the conception of *"the human being as a market"* the designers make use of expressions which show their intention is to build products that are profitable and, therefore, easy to sell. Yet they do not base their intentions upon human features, such as spontaneous and mood-related online behaviour that could be a prerequisite for selling their products (e.g., Hoffman & Novak, 1996; Bellman et al, 1999):

D5: It is more reasonable to develop a mass product which has a lot of users. The point here is that then it can be copied and sold.

In contrast to notions that emphasise understanding human consumption behaviour, the IS designers adhere to the idea that humans are simply a featureless mass of consumers who form a market for IT products. Because the above conception does not incorporate any human characteristics, but refers to a mass market, it is thereby making a clear distinction between the market and the features of the people assumed to form that market. For this reason, the conception appears as objectivist. This conception also implies a predisposition according to which the current development of IS as an industry is that of a rational institution which produces mass culture by reducing humans to members of a mass (cf. Slater, 1997). Furthermore, humans become separated attitudinally from IS and their development due to a presumed lack of technological knowledge,

and thus are forced to encounter disparaging attitudes. The separatist human-centred conception of *"the technology-illiterate human bein'"* produces accounts according to which the most distinct characteristic of humans is that they are ignorant of technology, specifically computers, software and ISD methodologies. In particular, this illiteracy is seen as a contrast to the literacy of the IS designers:

R: Have you ever wondered why people behave in that way — that they cannot say what they want from the system?

D17: I think that it's because they don't know how these [IS] are defined. If one doesn't know these methods, one can't do it. That is the biggest reason, not that they aren't willing to say what they want but they don't have the know-how.

Beath and Orlikowski (1994) report similar findings in their analysis of a relatively new representative of the ISD methodologies' rationalist tradition, information engineering (IE). According to the analysis, the IE text creates and sustains both implicitly and explicitly a dichotomy between users and IS designers by characterising the users as technologically ignorant in regard to the use of technology. When operationalised, these characterisations are likely to generate nonviable and unsatisfactory interactions between users and IS designers. It seems also that the designers do not consider the weaknesses in users' knowledge and thought as an issue that deserves to be taken into account in design. However, when humans are included in the design considerations, the weaknesses in people's thinking should be understood as natural flaws in human cognitive behaviour that can be appropriately guided, or even prevented by adequate design (Kirs, Pflughoeft, & Kroeck, 2001; Norman, 1989; Robillard, 1999). The idea then is that designers should have awareness of and be able to recognise these erroneous tendencies in users in order to carry out IS planning and design with the express aim of preventing people from committing faulty actions during computer use, rather than conceptualising users as technologically ignorant.

Moreover, negative emotions and physical stress symptoms have the effect of separating humans from IS. The conception of *"the computer anguished human being"* reveals views acknowledging that IS cause negative emotional arousal in users. These reactions are manifested as negative attitudes, resistance, fear and discomfort in situations where people are confronted by plans for the future use of computers or in situations in which individuals are using computers:

R: How in your mind do people learn to use software?

D6: ... I have also met users who have so much fear of the user interface that they don't dare to explore or try anything, they just do what is familiar and safe.

These conceptualisations are consistent with statements concerning the widespread existence of technophobia (Brosnan, 1998a). Besides being an obviously unpleasant and undesired experience, negative emotions, such as anxiety and fear, make people's behaviour withdrawn and elusive by narrowing their action (Fredrickson & Branigan, 2001), as well as decreasing the quality of their performance (Brosnan, 1998b).

In brief, within the separatist form of thought, the human being becomes separated from viable interactions with both the IS designers themselves and IS. This is due to a tendency to an objectivist conceptualisation, which blurs the designers' thought to such an extent that people are no longer recognised as humans. The overall narrative style of this form of thought is reminiscent of the style of a nomothetic science reflecting technical, strategic views aiming at controlling the IS-related social system with the technical system (cf. Deetz, 1996). Further, people become separated from the development of IS due to disparaging attitudes inherent in designers' assumptions that users are technologically ignorant. Moreover, this form of thought brings to the fore human characteristics, such as negative emotions, which are seen as an obstacle to a viable IS-user relationship.

THE FUNCTIONAL FORM OF THOUGHT

The functional form of thought consists of conceptualisations in which humans are seen to act in an insubstantial manner, adapting to the external functions of technology, work tasks and the way the IS designers themselves use computers. Within this adaptive response, positive emotions are required in order to create and sustain viable interactions with IS. In this way, the IS-user relationship is seen as functional: the action of people is seen as determined by their external environment, and the role of human emotion is to facilitate this process. The different conceptions that build up this form of thought reveal a behaviourist understanding of the human being.

For instance, the conception of *"the invisible human being"* denotes humans as using IS in an insubstantial manner. Typical of this conception is the belief that there is a user who uses an IS. Yet the user is not characterised further but is assumed just to use the system:

R: If you think of a situation where you are creating an application, who do you think you're making it to?

D16: Hm.....

R: Do you think of certain types of people or how does it show that you are making it for people?

D16: I don't think of particular types of people but I think that the human being is in some sense always a part of the system. If it is a system that has a user interface so there must be somebody who uses it. Even if it is a system that runs by timer initiation, there must be a user interface, too, for setting the timer parameters in the system, so there must be somebody to use it, too. To my mind there is always someone using the systems, they (systems) are not fully automated.

A functioning relation between people and IS is thus acknowledged, but this does not include any features originating from the mental, social or cultural human modes of being. In other words, humans and their behaviour are understood as purely physical-organic responses to technology, as established in the tenets of Skinnerian behaviourism (Skinner, 1938, 1991). Similarly, the IS designers' conception of *"the human being behind the process of work"* denotes humans in conformity with behaviourist thinking. Within this conception individuals are seen in terms of their work tasks or organisational work processes. Characteristic of these conceptualisations is that the people performing the tasks are not portrayed further, but are assumed merely to use IS according to the external task flows:

R: How would you define users' needs?

D8: They consist of the utilising organisation's needs at all levels, beginning with what the people need in order to continually do their work tasks, and ending with the things that the organisation expects from the system, what can be abstracted from the process and be used to develop and control action.

Here, human action is seen as a series of direct responses to external work tasks issued to people. Zuboff's (1988) well-known distinction between "automating work" and "informating work" highlights the difference between implied behaviourist and nonbehaviourist assumptions concerning human action in computerised work (pp. 9-10). Automating work refers to deploying

technology in ways that increase the self-acting and self-regulating capacities of technical systems, which are expected to minimise human intervention. Because human intervention is minimised and machines perform the work tasks, interactions between individuals and computers become determined by the structure and sequence of computerised workflows to which, in turn, humans are supposed to respond. Zuboff's term of automating work, thus, implies a behaviourist assumption of humans and their behaviour.

Quite the opposite is suggested by the term informating work, which adds to the automating view of work in that information technology can be used to automate, but at the same time, it has the ability to translate the automated activities into a form that renders work processes, objects, events and behaviours visible, knowable and sharable for people (Zuboff, 1988). That is to say, within the interaction of humans and computers, people actively observe, interpret and share the information which is mediated to them by IS. They do not just respond like marionettes to the information offered by IS, but actively construct their own conceptions of the computer-mediated tasks they are given and act according to their own interpretations of the particular situation. Thus, in order to accomplish fluid and coherent interaction designs between humans and computers in regard to particular tasks, the users' mental models, especially those concerning the tasks submitted to them, should also be designed (Norman, 1989; Preece, 1994).

Also typical of the functionalist form of thought is that the role of human emotion is to facilitate people's adaptation to technology. Within the conception of *"The techno-enthusiast human being"* the designers depict positive emotions, such as enthusiasm, as essential features in humans:

R: Do you think there are common features in those people for whom you have built systems?

D17: Well, at least during very recent years, it has been enthusiasm.

In particular, positive emotional reactions in people are seen to be induced by technology. Positive feelings are especially seen as a prerequisite for the successful use of IS. These conceptualisations reveal a functional understanding of positive emotions. Whereas negative emotions are associated with specific tendencies, such as an urge to escape or to avoid disquieting things, positive emotions seem to spark changes in cognitive activity in addition to producing behavioural tendencies (Fredrickson & Branigan, 2001). Therefore, the IS designers' accounts of positive emotions as a prerequisite for the use of computers imply an understanding of the role of human emotional features in promoting successful functioning.

To sum up, within the functional form of thought humans and their behaviour are understood from a behaviourist stance, which renders human substance only as physical and organic by nature, denoting that the movements of people can be explained by the laws of mechanics (Wilenius, 1978). However, this form of thought adds to the previous separatist way of thinking in so far as humans are actually depicted as performing tasks with computers, whereas in the separatist form of thought the conceptualisations either totally omit human features or humans are seen as unable to use computers. In addition, the human emotional feature that is recognised in this form of thought appears as positive — even though functional — in nature. This way of thinking acknowledges humans as users, and therefore is more developed than the previous separatist form of thought.

THE HOLISTIC FORM OF THOUGHT

The most developed form of thought by which the IS designers conceptualise humans as users of IS is the one characterised as holistic. Its holistic qual-

ity is revealed in several ways. First, unlike the preceding forms of thought, the designers recognise a number of human characteristics. Second, these observed human features are often seen to coexist or intertwine with each other. Third, these conceptualisations suggest that the relationship between users and designers, as well as the IS-user relation, is a reciprocal process, including characteristics typical of human behaviour.

To begin with, the conception of *"the human being reflected in technology"* reveals the specific goal of constructing computer interfaces with human-like features: the interaction between people and computers is then envisaged as enriched with dialogues conveying both the rational and emotional meanings of the information in question (e.g., Nakazawa, Mukai, Watanuki & Miyoshi, 2001). Respectively, the depictions of various human features in technology reveal understandings suggesting human features built into technology render the interaction between users and IS as resembling the interplay of cognitive, emotional and social aspects that occur between humans:

R: What kind of user interface do you think that people would want to use?

D4: I strongly believe that 3D interfaces are coming. They could offer kind of human-like facial features as agents, which would bring a human sense to the systems. The third dimension could also be utilised so that interfaces become tangible and accessible.

Further, the context-centred conception of *"the human being as an organisational learner,"* which highlights people as organisations which learn about their own work processes, refers indirectly to learning, which stresses both cognitive and social human features. Collective cognitive features are referred to as an organisation's ability to form new insights into its work processes and to guide the deployment of IS effectively (Robey, Boudreau & Rose, 2000). A social dimension is also implied when it is assumed that people learn as an organisation:

D8: Needs are prone to change rapidly, especially after the implementation of the system, because they teach an organisation a lot about itself, and an organisation's self-knowledge increases and usually needs change in a more clever direction. Then there very quickly happens a sort of 'learning leap', which is often experienced as if the system is not valid at all although it is a question of the organisation's increased knowledge of its own activity.

Within the conception of *"the knowledge sharing human being"* the designers open up their view of learning by specifying mutual understanding between users and designers as essential. *"It is important to be able to explain things so that we understand each other."* The capability of taking another's perspectives into account form the core of this conception, which highlights knowledge sharing as a particularly important instance within the processes of organisational learning. Knowledge sharing is the link between individual and group learning, and signifies the expansion of individuals' cognitive maps into shared understandings (Crossan, Lane & White, 1999). In particular, the ability to take the perspective of others into account is an indispensable prerequisite for knowledge sharing (Boland & Tenkasi, 1995). Buber (1993) ascertains that, in order to be able to take others' perspectives into account fully, one has to treat others as equal human beings and respect the current circumstances of others. In these kinds of relationships positive emothional features, such as care and joy, need to be acknowledged and combined with cognitive and social abilities (Fredrickson & Branigan, 2001)

Moreover, the conception of *"the emotionally coping human being"* refers to an ability to regulate in a successful way both negative and positive subjective feelings in computerised situations.

In this way, the designers see emotional coping in the light of positive outcomes (cf. Folkman & Moskowitz, 2000, pp.648-649):

D8: ... a skilful user always has such peace of mind and attitude. She or he kind of has a better tolerance for stress, and an ability to cope with contradictions in a better way than others. For some reason this kind of attitude leads to a particular resourcefulness and an ability to utilise the system in a more natural way, compared to a person who has some negative emotional features, fear or hostility towards the system, and who then ends up having difficulties with the system due to her/his heavy attitude.

A cognitive aspect is seen as inherent in emotional coping in that it requires that individuals' recognise their different emotional experiences. However, in addition to these internal cognitive-affective features, emotion regulation refers to the external social and cultural factors that redirect, control, and shape emotional arousal in such a way that an individual is able to act adaptively in emotionally activating situations (Pulkkinen, 1996). While ISD is often seen as a stressful process which requires an ability to endure changing emotional experiences, such as interest and frustration (Newman & Noble, 1990) in recurrent situations of failure and subsequent success (Robey & Newman, 1996), it is understandable that the designers regard people who are able to regulate their emotions successfully as skilful.

Briefly, the holistic form of thought is comprised of conceptualisations that regard humans as cognitive, emotional, social and cultural creatures. The conceptions belonging to this form of thought embody similar basic human modes of being, as shown above. However, the aforementioned basic modes of being emerge in these conceptions as different behavioural affordances. The cognitive mode of being is seen as intellect, reasoning, learning, reflection, understanding and awareness of something. Similarly, the emotional mode of being is conceptualised as empathy, stress, tranquillity, commitment, contentment and a feeling of mastery. Further, the social mode of being is referred to as a need for communication, group learning, interpersonal power and connection, as well as knowledge sharing. These behavioural affordances are seen as incorporated in technology, appearing between humans, or within the interaction of humans and IS.

THE FORMS OF THOUGHT IN ISD

The IS designers' forms of thought revealed in the results of this study are regarded as important tools for ISD, and are seen to have implications for the ways that humans are taken into account as users within the different situations of ISD. These different situations refer to the phases of ISD such as planning, design, implementation, use and maintenance. The phases are cyclical and intertwining (e.g., Beynon-Davies, Carne, Mackay, & Tudhope, 1999). Planning refers to initiation and requirements analysis actions, including client contacts and definition of user requirements. During this phase the greatest degree of interaction occurs between users and designers (Newman & Noble, 1990). In order to accomplish requirements analysis, the designers should understand many human issues in addition to technical ones (Holtzblatt & Beyer, 1995). Design denotes procedures where requirements are refined and turned into specifications and finally software. Then technical reliability and maintainability of the system, user interface's applicability for the intended purpose of the system, as well as the aesthetical appearance of the system, are designed (Smith, 1997). Winograd (1995) emphasises that, in addition to technical requirements, the properties of a user interface should meet with the social, cognitive and aesthetic needs of people. Especially within new ubiquitous technological environments, the design of IS-user relationship should focus, in addition to social and cultural features, on individuals' perceptual, cognitive and emotional space (Stephanidis, 2001).

How would the designers then perform according to their forms of thought? The strength of the designers utilising a separatist form of thought would be technical knowledge, especially the ability to fluently conceptualise issues of design in accordance with objective definitions, a skill that is needed in creating formal specifications. However, the validity of objectifying design issues is dependent on the focus of such definitions. From a human-centred perspective, valid definitions would require being theoretically sensitive to human activity and deriving second-order conceptions from that activity (see Walsham, 1995), rather than creating objectivist conceptualisations, which overlook humans and their behaviour. An obvious disutility would be a tendency to treat users as technologically ignorant, which implies incompetence in social relationships with users.

The designers embracing the functional form of thought possess technical knowledge, and value such knowledge in users. They tend to focus on formal job descriptions, external work tasks and individuals' task productivity. A deficit from a human-centred perspective would be the tendency to overlook human issues and to focus instead on the functional purposes of IS; that is, external task information regarding an organizations' process improvements. Often such conceptualisations are regarded to yield Tayloristic designs, which underestimate the social context. However, they possess competence in functional and technical systems design. Their strength would be increased social competence to fulfil the demand for mutual understanding, which is regarded of utmost importance in ISD (cf. Heng, Traut, & Fischer, 1999).

The designers building upon the holistic form of thought emphasise clients' satisfaction, which ensures sustainable customer relationships and regard mutual understanding during ISD as essential between users and designers. Their strength would be increased social competence fulfil the demand for mutual understanding, which is regarded of utmost importance in ISD (e.g., Klein & Hirschheim, 1993; Lyytinen & Ngwenyama, 1992). It seems also likely that they have competence in IS planning which aims at the improvement of organisational processes and are identified as functional, such as sales and purchasing processes, and emphasise mutual understanding. Also, they understand how to maintain customership instead of just visioning economic gains or focusing on people's task productivity. Besides possessing technical competence, these holistic designers would be able to consolidate definitions of formal and external work tasks into human issues. A particularly significant capability would be to understand the process of organisational learning, which is essential in order to adjust the evolving requirements during the process of ISD. Moreover, they value balanced emotional behaviour, and thus intuitively grasp the possible dangers of relying on superfluous emotional behaviour.

With respect to the humanisation of IS, a holistic conception is required in ISD. It is then assumed that the human being is actualised in intertwined physical, cognitive, emotional, social and cultural qualities, and that these qualities are fundamentally different. Without the simultaneous existence of all of the qualities, it is not possible to consider a creature as a human. Yet the qualities cannot be reduced from one quality to another, but rather need to be understood as a whole (Rauhala, 1983). Considering the human being as an actor, as a user of an IS, the whole of a human being is understood as an active subject adjoining to IS. Then the IS-user relationship consists of human action involving explicit and tacit affordances that emerge dynamically in the interaction between humans and IS. In other words, the static characteristics of humans and technology take on a new form within their intertwining activity, which is shaped according to the affordances that, on the one hand, the human substance embodies, and which, on the

other hand, the properties of IS support or ignore. Consequently, understanding humans and their behaviour as users of IS requires insight into these emerging human experiences appearing within the affordances and constraints of contemporary IS and their development. Especially at present when the IS are no longer merely tools for personal and professional instrumental productivity, but also (re)constituting and mediating different social structures and practices (e.g., Orlikowski, 1992; Orlikowski, 2000), IS acts as social spaces that are important growing social and cultural reference points for users and, thus also for IS designers. Design that takes into account the consequences of the form and functions of IS to usersl social qualities, such as self-identity, is indeed and necessity if contemporary IS development aims at high-quality and usable systems (Greenhill & Isomäki, 2005).

In summary, the resulting forms of thought indicate three different but associated levels of intellectual competence in conceptualising humans as users of IS. The separatist form of thought provides designers predominantly with technical perspectives and a capability for objectifying things. However, it is worth noticing that the validity of objectifying design issues is dependent on the focus of such definitions. From a human-centred perspective, valid definitions would require being theoretically sensitive to human activity and deriving abstracted conceptions from that activity rather than creating objectivist conceptualisations, which overlook humans and their behaviour. The functional form of thought focuses on external task information and task productivity, nevertheless, with the help of positive emotions. The holistic form of thought provides designers with competence of human-centred ISD, even though all the aspects of the richness of the human condition are not revealed. It seems the designers are intellectually more oriented toward designing IS for objectified, streamlined organisational processes consisting of external work tasks, and that this orientation challenges the human-centred orientations.

REFERENCES

Avison, D.E., & Fitzgerald, G. (1994). Information systems development. In W. Currie & R. Galliers (Eds.), *Rethinking management information systems: An interdisciplinary perspective* (pp. 250-278). Oxford: Oxford University Press.

Beath, C.M., & Orlikowski, W. (1994). The contradictory structure of systems development methodologies: Deconstructing the IS-user relationship in information engineering. *Information Systems Research, 5*(4), 350-377.

Bellman, S., Lohse, G.L., & Jordan, E.J. (1999). Predictors of online buying behavior. *Communications of the ACM, 42*(12), 32-38.

Beynon-Davies, P., Carne, C., Mackay, H., & Tudhope, D. (1999). Rapid application development (RAD): An empirical review. *European Journal of Information Systems, 8*, 211-223.

Boland, R.J., & Tenkasi, R.V. (1995). Perspective making and perspective taking in communities of knowing. *Organization Science, 6*(4), 350-372.

Bostrom, R.P., & Heinen, J.S. (1977). MIS problems and failures: A socio-technical perspective. Part I: The causes. *MIS Quarterly, 1*(3), 17-32.

Brosnan, M. (1998a). *Technophobia. The psychological impact of information technology.* London: Routledge.

Brosnan, M. (1998b). The impact of computer anxiety and self-efficacy upon performance. *Journal of Computer Assisted Learning, 14*, 223-234.

Buber, M. (1993). *Sinä ja minä* [I and Thou]. Juva: WSOY.

Checkland, P. (1981). *Systems thinking, systems practice.* Chichester: Wiley.

Cotterman, W.W., & Kumar, K. (1989). User cube: A taxonomy of end users. *Communications of the ACM, 32*(11), 1313-1320.

Crossan, M.M., Lane, H.W., & White, R.E. (1999). An organizational learning framework: From intuition to institution. *Academy of Management Review, 24*(3), 522-537.

Dagwell, R., & Weber, R. (1983). System designers' user models: A comparative study and methodological critique. *Communications of the ACM, 26*(11), 987-997.

Deetz, S. (1996). Describing differences in approaches to organization science: Rethinking Burrell and Morgan and their legacy. *Organization Science, 7*(2), 191-207.

Folkman, S., & Moskowitz, J.T. (2000). Positive affect and the other side of coping. *American Psychologist, 55*(6), 647-654.

Francis, H. (1993). Advancing phenomenography: Questions of method. *Nordisk Pedagogik, 13*, 68-75.

Fredrickson, B.L., & Branigan, C. (2001). Positive emotions. In T. Mayne & G. Bonanno (Eds.), *Emotions: Current issues and future directions* (pp. 123-151). New York: Guilford Press.

Glaser, B.G., & Strauss, A.L. (1967). *The discovery of grounded theory. Strategies for qualitative research.* London: Weidenfeld and Nicolson.

Greenhill, A., & Isomäki, H. (2005). Incorporating self into Web information system design. In A. Pirhonen, H. Isomäki, C. Roast, & P. Saariluoma (Eds.), *Future interaction design* (pp. 52-66). London: Springer-Verlag.

Hawgood, L., Land, F., & Mumford, E. (1978). A participative approach to forward planning and systems change. In G. Bracchi, & P.C. Lockermann (Eds.), *Information systems methodology. Proceedings of the 2nd Conference of the European Cooperation in Informatics* (pp. 39-61), Venice, Italy. Springer-Verlag.

Hedberg, B., & Mumford, E. (1975). The design of computer systems: Man's vision of man as an integral part of the system design process. In E. Mumford, & H. Sackman (Eds.), *Human choice and computers* (pp. 31-59). Amsterdam: North Holland.

Heng, M.S.H., Traut, E.M., & Fischer, S.J. (1999). Organisational champions of IT innovation. *Accounting, Management and Information Technology, 9*(3), 193-222.

Hirschheim, R., & Klein, H.K. (1989). Four paradigms of information systems development. *Communications of the ACM, 32*(10), 1199-1216.

Hirschheim, R., Klein, H.K., & Lyytinen, K. (1995). *Information systems development and data modeling. Conceptual and philosophical foundations.* Cambridge University Press.

Hoffman, D.L., & Novak, T.P. (1996). Marketing in hypermedia computer-mediated environments: conceptual foundations. *Journal of Marketing, 60*(3), 50-68.

Holtzblatt, K., & Beyer, H.R. (1995). Requirements gathering: The human factor. Communications of the ACM 38(5), 31-32.

Husserl, E. (1995). Fenomenologian idea. Viisi luentoa [The phenomenological idea. Five lectures] (Himanka, Hämäläinen & Sivenius, Trans.). Helsinki: Loki-kirjat.

Kirs, P.J., Pflughoeft, K., & Kroeck, G. (2001). A process model cognitive biasing effects in information systems development and usage. *Information & Management, 38*, 153-165.

Klein, H.K., & Hirschheim, R.A. (1993). The application of neo-humanist principles in information systems development. In D.E. Avison, T.E. Kendall, & J.J. DeGross (Eds.), *Human, organizational, and social dimensions of information systems development* (pp. 263-280). Amsterdam: Elsevier.

Kling, R. (1977). The Organizational Context of User-Centered Software Designs. MIS Quarterly 1(4), 41-52.

Kogut, B., & Zander, U. (1992). Knowledge of the firm, combinative capabilities and the replication of technology. *Organization Science, 3*(5), 383-397.

Kumar, K., & Bjørn-Andersen, N. (1990). A cross-cultural comparison of IS designer values. *Communications of the ACM, 33*(5), 528-538.

Kumar, K., & Welke, J. (1984). Implementation failure and system developer values: Assumptions, truisms and empirical evidence. In *Proceedings of the 5th International Conference on Information Systems* (pp. 1-12), Tucson, AZ.

Lakoff, G. (1987). *Women, fire and dangerous things.* University of Chicago Press.

Marton, F. (1981). Phenomenography: Describing conceptions of the world around us. *Instructional Science, 10*, 177-200.

Marton, F., & Booth, S. (1997). *Learning and awareness.* Mahwah, NJ: Lawrence Erlbaum.

Mathiassen, L. 1998. Reflective systems development. *Scandinavian Journal of Information Systems, 10*(1/2), 67-118.

Merleau-Ponty, M. (1962). *Phenomenology of perception.* London: Routledge.

Nakazawa, M., Mukai, T., Watanuki, K., & Miyoshi, H. (2001). Anthropomorphic agent and multimodal interface for nonverbal communication. In N. Avouris, & N. Fakotakis (Eds.), *Advances in human-computer interaction I. Proceedings of the PC HCI 2001* (pp. 360-365), Athens, Greece.

Newman, M., & Noble, F. (1990). User involvement as an interaction process: A case study. *Information Systems Research, 1*(1), 89-110.

Nonaka, I., & Takeuchi, H. (1995). *The knowledge-creating company: How Japanese companies create the dynamics of innovation.* Oxford University Press.

Norman, D.A. (1989). *Miten avata mahdottomia ovia? Tuotesuunnittelun salakarit* [The psychology of everyday things]. Jyväskylä: Gummerus.

Orlikowski, W.J. (1992). The duality of technology: Rethinking the concept of technology in organizations. *Organization Science, 3*(3), 398-427.

Orlikowski W.J. (2000). Using technology and constituting structures: A practice lens for studying technology in organizations. *Organization Science, 11*(4), 404-428.

Orlikowski, W.J., & Baroudi, J.J. (1991). Studying information technology in organizations: Research approaches and assumptions. *Information Systems Research, 2*(1), 1-28.

Orlikowski, W.J., & Gash, D.C. (1994). Technological frames: Making sense of information technology in organizations. *ACM Transactions on Information Systems, 12*(2), 174-207.

Preece, J. (1994). *Human-computer interaction.* Harlow, UK: Addison-Wesley.

Pulkkinen, L. (1996). Female and male personality styles: A typological and developmental analysis. *Journal of Personality and Social Psychology, 70*(6), 1288-1306.

Quinn, J.B. (1992). The intelligent enterprise: A new paradigm. *Academy of Management Executive, 6*(4), 48-63.

Rauhala, L. (1983). *Ihmiskäsitys ihmistyössä* [The conception of the human being in human work]. Helsinki: Gaudeamus.

Robey, D., Boudreau, M.C., & Rose, G.M. (2000). Information technology and organizational learning: A review and assessment of research. *Accounting, Management & Information Technology, 10*(1), 125-155.

Robey, D., & Newman, M. (1996). Sequential patterns in information systems development: An application of a social process model. *ACM Transactions of information systems, 14*(1), 30-63.

Robillard, P.N. (1999). The role of knowledge in software development. *Communications of the ACM, 42*(1), 87-92.

Säljö, R. (1994). Minding action. Conceiving the world vs. participating in cultural practices. *Nordisk Pedagogik, 14*, 71-80.

Sandberg, J., (2000). Understanding human competence at work: An interprettive approach, *Academy of Management Journal 43*(1), 9-25.

Schwandt, T., (2000). Three epistemological stances for qualitative inquiry. Interpretivism, hermeneutics, and social constructionism. In Denzin, N.K. &Y.S. Lincoln (Eds.) The handbook of qualitative research (2nd ed.). Thousand Oaks, CA: Sage, 189-213.

Skinner, B.F. (1991). The behavior of organisms: An experimental analysis. Acton, MA: Copley. Originally published in 1938.

Slater, D. (1997). *Consumer culture and modernity.* Malden, MA: Blackwell.

Smith, A. (1997). *Human computer factors: A study of users and information systems.* London: McGraw-Hill.

Stephanidis, C. (2001). Human-computer interaction in the age of the disappearing computer. In N. Avouris, & N. Fakotakis (Eds.), *Advances in human-computer interaction I. Proceedings of the PC HCI 2001* (pp. 15-22), Athens, Greece.

Sterling, T.D. (1974). Guidelines for humanizing computerized information systems: A report from Stanley House. *Communications of the ACM, 17*(11), 609-613.

Strauss, A., & Corbin, J. (1990). *Basics of qualitative research: Grounded theory procedures and techniques.* Newbury Park, CA: Sage Publications.

Tesch, R. (1990). *Qualitative research: Analysis types and software tools.* New York: Falmer Press.

Uljens, M. (1991). Phenomenography: A qualitative approach in educational research. In L. Syrjälä, & J. Merenheimo (Eds.), *Kasvatustutkimuksen laadullisia lähestymistapoja.* Oulun yliopiston kasvatustieteiden tiedekunnan opetusmonisteita ja selosteita 39 (pp. 80–107).

Walsh, E. (1994). Phenomenographic analysis of interview transcripts. In J.A. Bowden, & E. Walsh (Eds.), *Phenomenographic research: Variations in method* (pp. 17-30). The Warburton Symposium. Melbourne: The Royal Melbourne Institute of Technology.

Walsham, G. (1995). Interpretive case studies in IS research: Nature and method. *European Journal of Information Systems, 4*(2), 74-81.

Wilenius, R. (1978). *Ihminen, luonto ja tekniikka* [The human being, nature and technology]. Jyväskylä: Gummerus.

Winograd, T. (1995). From programming environments to environments for designing. *Communications of ACM, 38*(6), 65-74.

Zuboff, S. (1988). *In the age of the smart machine: The future of work and power.* New York: Basic Books.

This work was previously published in International Journal of Technology and Human Interaction, Vol. 3, Issue 1, edited by B. Stahl , pp. 30-48, copyright 2007 by IGI Publishing, formerly known as Idea Group Publishing (an imprint of IGI Global).

Chapter IX
Tacit Knowledge in Rapidly Evolving Organisational Environments

Barbara Jones
MBS University of Manchester, UK

Angelo Failla
IBM Fondazione Milan (Director), Italy

Bob Miller
MBS University of Manchester, UK

ABSTRACT

Constant renewal of the self-image and self-knowledge of the organisation becomes part of the day-to-day knowledge-in-use of front-line practitioners. The Network Enterprise is a model of business conducted by shifting alliances of partners developing innovative products and processes in close collaboration with their clients. Organisations abandon the concept of a central product, redefining themselves as providers of solutions. We draw on the experience of two 'solution-providers', one for-profit and one not-for-profit. The concept of a solution or transition requires practitioners to consider each individual case drawing on personal knowledge of the organisation's accessible competencies and capacities. Choices among the possible solutions to the client's problems can have unpredictable effects on the dynamics of the wider organisation. The necessarily personal use of heuristics magnifies the inescapable element of 'drift' inherent in the network enterprise. The dynamics generated by this will require the wider organisation to develop new standards and solution bundles.

INTRODUCTION

Phenomena in two widely differing organisations suggest that parallel evolution is occurring in different contexts conditioned by the wider context of information and communication technologies (ICT) development and other trends of Post-modernity. Constant renewal of the self-image and self-knowledge of the organisation becomes part of the day-to-day knowledge-in-use of front-line practitioners and driven by the client-centred approach this process feeds back into the dynamics of the wider organisation. Post-modernity is understood as the abandonment of the model of society as moving toward a rational division of labour meeting the natural needs of rational man. This model assumed the fixity of social spheres and economic sectors based on the centrality of different principles or technologies, which in retrospect can be seen as resulting from spatial and temporal coordination and transaction costs. The network enterprise is a model of business conducted by shifting alliances of partners developing innovative products and processes in close collaboration with their leading clients. Organisations now abandon the concept of a central product and instead define themselves as providers of solutions. We draw on the experience of two "solution-providers," one for-profit and one not-for-profit. The concept of a solution or transition creates a greater role for the front-line practitioner in identifying and mobilising the resources available. The need for practitioners to consider every individual case drawing on their individual knowledge of the accessible competencies and capacities of the organisation means that choices among the possible solutions to the client's problems can lead to unpredictable effects on the dynamics of the wider organisation. The necessarily personal use of heuristics magnifies the inescapable element of drift inherent in the network enterprise. This may be a source of innovation, but the value of this innovation will depend on the ability of the wider organisation to develop new standards and solution bundles.

TACIT KNOWLEDGE IN RAPIDLY EVOLVING ORGANISATIONAL ENVIRONMENTS

This chapter examines how new technologies, which enable the emergence of new organisational forms, lead to the development of new kinds of tacit knowledge. In fact, we find that in addition to product and process innovation, innovation in the form of organisations is a major source of the emergence of "tacit knowledge" as a topic of discussion and research. All use of skill and knowledge in practice presupposes a background of tacit knowledge, what Michael Polanyi calls the "tacit component." This tacit component remains invisible so long as its acquisition is an integral part of the socialisation of the individual, their education and professional training, and their assimilation into the culture of a particular firm or organisation. The emergence of "tacit knowledge" as a problem discussed and debated in economic and management literature is a function of the increasing pace and importance of innovation and of the perceived need to plan and foster innovation in every sphere of activity. The result is that new materials, new technologies and processes, and new forms of organisation and communication are developed and widely implemented long before it is possible to foresee their full implications and possibilities. The ways in which practitioners actually use and combine these innovations is itself a permanent source of new innovation. Much of the new knowledge developed in this way is inherently "tacit," developed without any necessary realisation that what one is doing is new, unusual, or innovative. Even where this realisation is present, the exact nature of the innovation involved is often unclear because the practitioners involved do not have information on what they are doing differently from others.

We will examine two variants of the organisational model of the "Network Enterprise" in combination with the business model of the "solutions provider." Both of these phenomena depend on highly developed systems of ICT-mediated communication, information-sharing, and applications. The model of the "Network Enterprise" can be seen as a situation where both the negative and the positive effects of "Drift," as perceived by Claudio Ciborra, can be discerned. The development of a sophisticated system of internal communication within an organisation can become an end in itself if it is not part of a radical turn of the organisation toward the rapid assimilation and dissemination of innovation generated on the interface with the organisation's environment. The model of the solutions provider is, among other things, an expression of the felt need to be as close as possible to the final user in order to have access to the tacit knowledge generated by the real use of new products and processes and the problems that arise with them. When successful, this model gives rise to the question of the extent and direction of the dissemination of the information acquired. This relates to the ownership of the restandardised package that may be evolved on the basis of feedback from lead users. Solutions providers want to provide each client with a customised product specific to their situation, but they can only effectively do so by selecting from a palette of solution components that have been developed and tested with a wide range of clients. The "Network Enterprise" may partly be a response to the fact that disputes over ownership of information are more easily solved in trade-offs between commercial organisations than in turf wars between departments and sections of a single organisation. This problem will increasingly re-emerge within public-private partnerships that are converging on the "Network Enterprise" model.

It is argued here that phenomena appearing in two widely differing organisations suggest that parallel evolution is occurring in different contexts conditioned by the wider context of ICT development and other trends associated with the concept of Post-modernity. The outcome of these developments is that constant updating of the self-image and self-knowledge of the organisation becomes part of the day-to-day knowledge-in-use of front-line practitioners. The client-centred approach of these practitioners means that their variable use of the resources of the organisation, mediated by the extent of their knowledge of what is available, in turn feeds back into the evolution of the wider organisation.

Post-modernity is taken to be the abandonment of the model of society as moving toward a rational division of labour aimed at meeting the natural needs of rational man. This model was associated with an assumption of the fixity of a number of social spheres and economic sectors that were based on the centrality of different principles or technologies. In retrospect, these phenomena can be seen as products of the clustering of various subsidiary functions around central functions as a result of problems of spatial and temporal coordination and transaction costs. Associated with this were product-centred enterprise and the assumption that organisational change primarily arose from technological advance within different sectors.

ICTs had the initial effect of bringing into prominence the concept of the Value-Chain. This means that different technological platforms in the process from raw materials to finished goods and services can be linked on the basis of profitability and criticality, while lower transaction costs and despatialisation allow outsourcing of staple inputs. This paradigm has spread from for-profit to not-for-profit sectors because of its benefits in cost-reduction and responsiveness to final outcomes. A further twist in this process takes place when organisations abandon all concept of a central product and instead define themselves as providers of solutions. We draw on the experience of two "solution-providers," one for-profit and one not-for-profit. The subordination of all of the products and services offered to the concept of a solution or transition leads to a greater role for the front-line practitioner in deciding what inputs are required and how to source them. This can only take place within a context of ICT-mediated communication and in a context of standard-setting and information sharing.

The new organisational model that has developed to describe this phenomenon is that of the Networked Enterprise, as described by Manuel Castells. Castells has also worked out the most highly developed conceptualisation of the New Economy, principally in Castells 2001 (pp. 64-115, the chapter *e-Business and the New Economy*), drawing on the concepts developed earlier in Castells 1996 (pp.151-200, the chapter *The Network Enterprise*). He sees the New Economy as characterised by the appearance of a new kind of economic meta-entity, the Network Enterprise, which is characterised by the networked communication between shifting groups of partners in development projects and in the ongoing production, marketing and improvement of products. The constitution of these partnerships is shifting from project to project, depending on their specific requirements, so that it is the pool of partners who engage in these ongoing collaborations which constitute the network enterprise. In this sense, the network enterprise is a disembodied version of the cluster (see Dosi, Teece, & Chytry, 1998; Swann, Prevezer, & Stout, 1998) or the industrial district (Marshall, 1949, pp. 225-226) and also shows parallels to the business group (e.g., Shiba & Shimotani, 1997).

Because of the variety of inputs contributing to the development of products, the client-facing partner is the holder of the brand that guarantees the quality of the inputs to the final user. Castells sees the extension of the network communication through to the client (in wholesale and business-to-business) or the consumers (in retail) as essential to the feedback of forward information into the network. Another essential element is the possibility of sourcing inputs firm-internally, locally (cluster-internally), or globally. Castells identifies a key element in the growth of global networks to be the creation in the developing nations of Asia of start-up, spin-off and buy-out firms by persons who have previously worked for multinationals or in the global centres such as Silicon Valley. In a process analogous to the dismantling of the major Japanese firms some decades ago, networks are created based on information sharing and high levels of supervision of quality of inputs into the collaborative process. Castells considers that this process of clustering was also already underway in other economies decades ago, and that it was not initially caused by the Internet (some networks were experimenting with their own information-sharing technologies before the appearance of the Internet) but that the Internet has enabled the process to become global.

The model of the network enterprise is complementary to the assumptions of the resource-based and knowledge-based theories of the firm (see Loasby, 1976; Nelson, 1991; Nelson & Winter 1982; Penrose, 1995). Within the context of IT-mediated transaction cost reductions and information-sharing cost reductions, there is a pattern of incentives which leads firms to concentrate on their core product or process and to divest themselves of activities which can be done better by others. This would lead every enterprise to be based around the core of knowledge which they develop in the constant improvement of their core products or processes, while the activities they outsource can become the core activity of other businesses and therefore become subject to competitive pressure to innovate from which they were previously protected (see Baumol, 2002; Nelson, 1990). Bhagwati (1984), opened the question of the differential dynamics of innovation when the manufacturing and services components of industries are separated by outsourcing.). One result of this is that there is a premium on communication with the final consumers in order to integrate feedback from users into ongoing innovative processes. Where the final product is a bundle of products and services as provided by solution providers, the effective Network Enterprise must enable the throughput and distribution of user feedback to the appropriate participants in the network, since only they will be able to use this feedback in the most effective way in improving their contribution to the joint product. The groupware systems of the network enterprise must be able to facilitate this process. The collaboration of the participants in the network enterprise must be enabled by the systems in place, although there are inevitably conflicts and trade-offs between the partners and some strategic decisions to attempt to shift positions in the value and supply chain.

The necessarily personal use of tacit knowledge is a factor in the inescapable element of drift which arises in this context. The need for practitioners to consider every individual case, drawing on their individual knowledge of the accessible competencies and capacities of the organisation or of its network of external partners, means that a succession of choices between the possible solutions to the client's problems has unpredictable outcomes for the dynamics of the wider organisation. However, we should remember the implications of the word drift, and its contrast with the aspect of outsourcing and corporate breakup. For Ciborra, drift is not necessarily merely a passive submission to disintegrative influences from the environment (Ciborra, 1996, 2002; Ciborra & Hanseth, 2000). Ciborra later merged his earlier concept of "Drift" into that of the "Dérive" (Ciborra, 2002). The freedom of action of the front-line practitioners is the converse of the unifying effect of in-house information systems. In the paradigm of "drift" the attempts of management to provide ICT-mediated horizontal communication within the organisation as a substitute for vertical directives can lead to "drift" if these horizontal channels do not mediate the necessary motivations. One answer to this is to shift the locus of motivation to the client-centred practitioner. They are then the channel by which the needs of the client exert an influence on the

use of resources. This at least is the paradigm of successful openness to drift, although Ciborra also discusses failures, which in many cases arise from failure to take up or fully exploit the opportunities provided by in-house information systems. The organisations discussed here both face the challenge of simultaneously managing the successful opening to drift generated by in-house IT systems with the parallel need to open these same systems to continuous communication about ongoing transactions with their partners within the "network enterprise." In both cases, this is partly driven by a need to restandardise the results of ad hoc collaborations initially driven by client requirements in order to diffuse best practice for further instances of similar problems which may become more prevalent.

TACIT KNOWLEDGE AS UNDERSTOOD IN MANAGEMENT AND ORGANISATION THEORY

Within management theory, tacit knowledge has been discussed in contrast with explicit knowledge. In this context, explicit knowledge is usually underdefined. If we look at an organization top-down, we can expect to find a wide array of legal, technical, commercial and insurance-related documentation of the ownership, property, machinery, goods, and contractual relationships of the organisation, and descriptions of its processes and the roles of individuals in those processes. So ostensibly the organization has a body of explicit knowledge that describes what it does and how it does it. If we look at explicit knowledge bottom-up, we could find that a starter in the organization is immediately confronted with a highly signed environment, with a wide range of traffic and safety signage, departmental and personal nameplates, and maps and diagrams of work procedures and flows. We need to ask, how do these masses of texts and signs become knowledge? Obviously this can only happen by being read, and by being read and understood, and by being read and understood as relevant to a particular context.

Explicit knowledge is thus always specific to the ability and habituation of the user to acquire and absorb information from the media used. This generally requires literacy in one specific language, and even when signage is designed without script, it still assumes a basic familiarity with some conventions of signage itself.

Explicit knowledge may be fully explicit both in terms of being codified and expressed in a common language, and may actually be talked about on a day-to-day basis, and yet may come to be posited in fact on a number of assumptions and presuppositions, the taken-for-grantedness of which is lost sight of by the participants. This is one of the forms of so-called "tacit" knowledge analyzed by Boisot, namely that of an in-group idiolect used by a group which does not question its own assumptions unless forced to do so by organizational change or cooperation with another organization. This phenomenon may also turn out to be simultaneously an instance of the second of Boisot's categories, that of knowledge which can be made explicit, but only at a non-negligible cost. Boisot emphasizes that knowledge is "sticky," because knowledge cannot be communicated without some remainder or a plus of knowledge sticking to the originators of the knowledge (Boisot, 1998, pp. 56-57).

The third of Boisot's categories is that which he considers to be Michael Polanyi's own use of the term. In our view, unfortunately, he considers this to be knowledge which is irretrievably "tacit," in the sense of necessarily implicit. In his system there is a hard core of knowledge which cannot be made explicit. This is a serious limitation of Polanyi's insight. When Polanyi says that "we can know more than we can tell" (1966, p. 4), it does not simply mean that there are things we, personally, tacitly know but cannot express. How people ride bicycles, swim, walk, or eat are things some people can perfectly well explain, and

anyone can begin to learn about. Polanyi would agree that what we tacitly know is infinite, and thus inexhaustible. In fact, this is also true of what we explicitly know and all the inferences which we could draw from it. However, the more immediate point of Polanyi"s statement was that there are two ways of "knowing" and what we tacitly "know" can be paralleled and communicated by explicit knowledge and explicit knowing without this ever replacing the mode of tacit knowing.

We will explain the full details of Polanyi's concept later, but for now the important point is that tacit knowledge and explicit knowledge are not divisions of a single container of knowledge, so that when one grows the other shrinks. They are two modes of knowledge. Knowledge is information, and both tacit knowledge and explicit knowledge can be replicated. Explicit knowledge can be replicated in a variety of media, but tacit knowledge can only be replicated in human beings through the processes known as apprenticeship in the widest sense. The recovery of explicit knowledge from its material embodiment in printed or digital symbols is itself a process requiring tacit knowledge of systems of language, literacy, propositional thinking and symbolism. There are also systems of apprenticeship in these skills. In many cases it will also require a pre-existing body of lower-level tacit knowledge about the specific context, which is why apprenticeship tends to follow uniform pathways of approach.

TACIT KNOWLEDGE WITHIN NEW CONTEXTS OF MARKET RESPONSIVENESS

Automation was a leading factor in creating an assumption that productivity improvement was a management-led top-down process. In recent decades the importance of the transfer of tacit knowledge by the movement of workers has been highlighted by the literature on clusters, which has drawn on Marshall's older work on industrial districts. Silicon Valley and Central Italy have been seen as examples of areas within which new technical knowledge has been rapidly diffused and has served as a basis for competition to be concentrated on product design, boosting the competitive advantage of the cluster as a whole. Interest in clusters as sources of competitive advantage has combined with wider policy trends toward privatization and the use of market forces to lead many large corporations to introduce market principles into their internal arrangements. These processes parallel the way in which large Japanese corporations have outsourced some of their inputs to firms with which they maintain cross-shareholding and developmental information sharing. This means that the dichotomy between Western and "Eastern" (actually largely Japanese) approaches to the value of tacit and explicit knowledge (in whatever sense) has been softened by a convergence toward more complex relationships between and within large organizations and supplying contractors. Nonaka and Takeuchi (1998) investigated this East-West dichotomy in the appreciation of tacit knowledge. (For a case study and an introduction to the wider literature, see Lincoln & Ahmadjian, 2001).

An example of the drive to introduce market principles into both the working of a government service and its relationships with its users is the UK government Connexions service. The aim of the service is to facilitate the transition from school to work for all 13-19 year olds in England, with equivalent services in the other parts of the UK to converge on this model in time. All personal, family, sexual, legal, drugs, disability, housing, educational, and training problems are to be dealt with by a one-stop service oriented to the individual, with cooperation between all kinds of professionals, and a reduction of the stigma arising from the need for help in more sensitive areas, as the service is universal.

Parallel investigations of the use of competency and personal development systems within the Connexions service and within IBM gave rise to interesting and surprising parallels (Failla & Mazzotti, 2004; Jones & Miller, 2004). Despite the obvious differences between a profit-oriented corporate business serving principally other corporate clients and a government-provided service aimed primarily at individuals, a number of similarities were observed in the processes that arise when the individual units of large organisation may take differing steps to adjust their responsiveness to client demands. Knowing the location and relevance of clusters of expertise within the wider organisation becomes an important aspect of the tacit knowledge of each section, while the old methods of spreading best practice become problematic, because the different units may be applying their practice in significantly different contexts.

THE UK CONNEXIONS SERVICE CONTEXT

The Connexions service has been organised around the concept of the Connexions advisor. This is a new professional profile intended to unify the roles of careers advisor, family support workers, and young people's support workers. The new-style Connexions advisors are each to be seen as possible "one-stop-shops." This means that a young person may in the first instance establish contact with any advisor, whether through a school, through a Web site or hotline, or through outreach projects, and this advisor will then begin to set in motion whatever processes are necessary to address the young person's problems. While individuals with particular profiles of problems may be attached to an advisor who is a specialist in these problems, most should be able to maintain a relationship with the first advisor with whom they come into contact.

The Connexions service presents itself as a product brand that appeals to potential users as a service to which they are entitled and which they should take up. This general trend in presentation of all government services is more extreme in the Connexions service because of the age of the target group and the corresponding assumption that they are more likely to use the Internet, mobile phones, and texting than older groups. They are seen as being subjected to a wider range of alternative claims on their attention, which the Connexions service must challenge on the common ground of consumerist culture and media styles.

The Connexions partnerships are thus an example of a general trend in UK public services sector delivery and a precursor of wider developments in the same direction. The main components of the service are:

1. An online one-stop advice shop.
2. A universal service offer for all members of the target group; in this case, all young people aged 13-19, and
3. A range of deeper services, some available on demand, others taking over statutory roles when required, which deal with all of the problems of the target group in moving toward the goals set by policy.

The objective is that all young persons, despite any disability, personal problems, family problems, or problems in relating to institutions, should make a successful transition from full-time education into the labour market, either directly or through further and higher education.

The aim of the one-stop shop approach is to include as many as possible of the special services which young people may require within the blanket service, and thus reduce all stigma arising from labelling. Since the career service is a universal institution, the use of which does not stigmatise its users, it was regarded as the most appropriate service to provide the wider context within which the specialist advice, help, and guidance is provided.

This change is not merely cosmetic, but gives rise to a fundamental redefinition of the occupational roles of all those involved. Those

previously in the career's service were always oriented toward pastoral guidance for those who found entry into the adult world problematic, but now the normal and the problematic cases are regarded as a continuum. Conversely, those advisers previously occupied with help, support and guidance for individuals with specific problems are finding that they are operating within a framework with a definite goal, the successful transition of all individuals from education into the labour market by age 20.

In this context there has been some concern about the cut-off point of age 20 and what may happen to the more vulnerable individuals after the Connexions service ceases to be responsible for them. A general criticism of target- and goal-based systems is that they distort priorities and produce a manipulation of targeted outcomes that may not be effective in the long-term. In the case of the UK Public Employment Services, this led in some cases to the placement of individuals in employment that was predicted to be short-term. While there are arguments for keeping individuals in touch with the labour market, even if only on a short-term basis, overall this kind of system has been seen as responding to perverse incentives and wasting resources that should be devoted to preparing the individuals for more secure employment. The 19-20 age cut-off is seen as a potential danger due to the possible production of equivalent perverse incentives to rush individuals into nonpermanent placements in work or training in the run-up to the end of the service's responsibility for them.

The Connexions service currently operates through nine regions in England. Within these regions are 47 areas where 151 partnerships are operating. Human Resources management is located at the area level, and each area can employ between 500 and 1000 personal advisors. The Connexions partnerships are of two kinds, Direct Delivery and Subcontracting. The latter breaks down into two subgroups, the "Basket of Services" model and the "Thematic Support" model.

In Direct Delivery areas, a single organisation takes the contract for the delivery of all Connexions services. In these areas, the local Connexions partnerships are divisions of the area partnership. The management services of the partnership and the face-to-face delivery of the services to clients are all carried out by the Direct Delivery organisation.

In Subcontracting Areas, the face-to-face services to clients are carried out by subcontractors working for the area Connexions partnership. The way in which this is organised can take two forms.

1. In the areas operating the "Basket of Services" model, the local Connexions partnerships contract to provide the Connexions service for a local district within which they are responsible for all services to clients. Some of these contractors are local organisations that developed out of government service providers. Others are purely commercial organisations that submit multiple tenders for services in a number of different areas and localities. The Connexions partnership for the area is responsible for ensuring that these subcontractors deliver the services and for providing them with a number of management services, including human resources.

2. In the areas operating the "Thematic Support" model, subcontractors do not provide area-based services, but rather specialist services such as career guidance, drugs advice, or specialist workers for the hard-to-reach clients. The area-based Connexions partnership remains the provider of general services for the whole area.

These different business models cut across distinctions of urban and rural settings and also do not correlate to the number of partnerships within an area.

Connexions Direct presents itself as a Web site that offers advice through Web chat, texting and telephone communication on an 800 number. Advisors will also ring out to users who text or e-mail their telephone number. Connexions Direct began operating before the Connexions partnerships were fully established. The relationship between Connexions Direct and local Connexions partnerships is very uneven nationally and determined by the perceived strengths and weaknesses of the different agencies in different places. Connexions Direct is not the only Connexions Web site. Local Area Connexions Partnerships have developed their own Web sites, which they use to communicate directly with their local target audience and to provide services to their users. These Web sites are very varied in their visual design and approach.

Many Connexions advisors are located in schools where they exercise a variety of functions. Schools have a Connexions budget which is allocated locally in consultation to provide a mixture of full-time and part-time, generalist, specialist, and outreach services. Schools have complained that career advice for the entire school population has begun to suffer as a result of the skewing of both budget provision and the actual take-up of Connexions resources toward problem children and special needs (e.g., Ward, 2005). It seems unlikely, however, that any future restoration of a dedicated or "ring-fenced" schools career advice service would result in the abandonment of the wider Connexions advisor approach.

The National Occupational Standards (NOS) for Connexions are derived from the Functional Map for the service. The functions which the organisation is statutorily required to carry out have been mapped and the occupational profile is a direct iteration of this mapping. More precisely, there is a mapping of the common and shared functions which are common to all professions providing support services for children, young people, and their families. The professionals were consulted on the mapping of these functions, but within a context which ultimately derives individual functions from the organisational imperatives. The National Occupational Standards work from the key purpose of the organisation through a number of key roles, which are themselves broken into units and elements. within each element there are performance criteria, a knowledge requirement and a range indicator.

The Connexions service has been given the responsibility of developing a common language and a secure database for the sharing of data on the cases of children and young people between the various agencies involved. However, part of the problem of developing systems for competency mapping and performance mapping of the individual advisors and units within the Connexions service is that much of the data concerning problems and outcomes of individual cases are client-confidential. Such data are therefore not directly available to the personnel departments for detailed assessment.

Part of the role of the Connexions advisor is to be aware of the resources available to help them in carrying out their tasks. This implies that keeping up with a wide variety of legislative, scientific, procedural, and market knowledge is an essential part of the occupation. This knowledge will be disseminated within Connexions by a variety of bulletins, seminars, and Web sites, but the onus is on the individual advisor to take advantage of this information and know how to find and interpret it.

However, the Connexions advisor will also need to be aware of what skills and knowledge they can call upon from colleagues in their area. This is not a simple matter. Connexions advisors work through a variety of modalities. Some are full-time, some part-time, and some work part-time for a number of different Connexions services or partner organisations, making up a full-time job. Most are employees, but many are freelance. A single large school may contain three or four Connexions advisors employed on different systems and with different remits. Schools and other qualifying bodies such as youth clubs may have a budget for Connexions advisors, the level and use of which is renegotiated each year. Colleagues may be working together who belong to statutory organisations, charities, commercial contractors, municipal offshoots working under commercial contract, or bodies in the process of privatisation.

THE IBM CONTEXT

IBM has evolved from a business machine manufacturer to a computer manufacturer, and then to a computer system developer, and now identifies itself as a computer system consultant. Its business consists in finding and implementing solutions to clients' needs using new technologies on the interface of communication, data management, and process management. In 1994, it began implementation of the Customer Relationship Management system (CRM; see Ciborra & Failla, 2000; Ciborra & Hanseth, 1998). This means that development of an answer to a business opportunity becomes the responsibility of a single individual, the Opportunity Owner, who takes responsibility for carrying out the whole project. They will then have the responsibility of using the entire IBM information warehouse to find the necessary collaborators to process the development. As part of a general trend toward supplying consultancy rather than hardware or software, this means they will be seeking individuals with knowledge and skills in the areas of processes and products similar to those of the particular client in order to develop a complete business solution for the client organisation. This change has influenced the skills mapping and the professional template used within IBM, as it has become necessary to coordinate skills within the organisation with the processes of clients rather than with the contours of IBM-internal production and development processes.

In 2003, IBM's $36 billion turnover was composed of 45% services, 34% hardware, 16% software, 4% financial services, and 1% other services. The expansion of the services share of turnover is expected to continue.

The framework for skills management in IBM comprises IBM Foundational Competencies, which are common to all employees, Basic/soft skills, of which 16 are used and divided into three groups, Business, Leadership, and Relationship skills, and Professional Core skills, which are each specific to a particular profession or job roll and of which there are more than 25,000. IBM currently has some 319,000 employees globally, distributing 167,000 in the Americas region, 100,000 in the Europe, Middle East, and Africa region, and 49,000 in the Asia Pacific region.

The competency profiles of individual employees and working groups are databased and provide a pool of information that can be used as a resource to draw up a pool of potential collaborators in any new undertaking. However, it is recognised that even this level of mapping of competencies does not provide an immediate match for the relevance of experience in one area for application in another. Therefore, the Opportunity Managers and Opportunity Owners are encouraged to make their own investigations of exactly what competencies and knowledges are present in other parts of the organisation. One facility to encourage this is the Intranet Customer Room, where experience with particular clients is pooled between different Opportunity Owners. It has been realized that central production of a compendium of these things would merely create a rapidly dating resource, which could become an obstacle to the development of new and possibly creative encounters between different units and individuals. Instead, there is a database of solutions, which is not to be used simply as a document of what has been done in the past, but rather should lead to communication between units to compare experience and to discuss the relevance of past solutions to new problems.

The outcome of these steps is that Opportunity Managers and Opportunity Owners should not be reliant on higher management to delegate tasks within a development project or to pass on historical knowledge about similar cases. It is part of the work of the Opportunity Managers and Opportunity Owners themselves to find the right people and to exchange information about the client or about other comparable development processes. This is in part because a global organisation of the size of IBM could not rely on purely informal exchanges to produce sufficient information flow simply because of the large number of units and employees. But it is also a recognition of the value of the tacit knowledge which is built up through both success and failure and which cannot be captured by any compendium.

TACIT KNOWLEDGE AS A NAVIGATIONAL TOOL WITHIN COMPLEX CHANGING ORGANISATIONS

The two case studies, originally undertaken in order to investigate the value of competency mapping tools for the organisations concerned, gave rise to a realisation that there was a new kind of tacit knowledge arising within large organisations of ostensibly quite different types. This appears to be arising from the combination of increasing internal organisational complexity and the perceived need for small units and individual professionals to work in a client-centred way within the constraints of a number of differing outcome requirements. As a first approximation, the two organisations investigated appear to display the following common characteristics:

1. The practitioners operate within a context of tension between the wider goals of the organisation and the immediate needs of the clients they are directly in contact with. In a general sense, this may always have been the case, but managing the tension between these potentially conflicting goals is increasingly filtering down to become a direct responsibility of the front-line practitioner.

2. The drive to provide the client with a one-stop shop or a single contact for a product development puts the practitioner under the obligation to constantly review the degree to which they can manage the interaction within their existing skills and whether the resolution to any problem is to extend their skills or draw on the skills of others.

3. The professional needs to have and constantly update a map of the availability of skills and competencies within the organisation. A complete explicit map of the availability of skills is of relatively little use here, because (A) both the level and the location of available skills is under constant evolution and (B) any such compendium necessarily abstracts from the specifics of the use of skills, which is precisely what is relevant to their application to a new problem.

This is the organisational context within which we will return to the ideas of Michael Polanyi, and begin to develop an approach to the interaction between tacit knowledge and explicit knowledge in the way in which practitioners make use of the massive bodies of documented or databased explicit knowledge about their own organisation and the skills and competencies of its members. (The following exposition draws mainly on Polanyi, 1958, but Polanyi, 1966, 1969 and Polanyi & Prosch, 1975 have been consulted). A more developed presentation of our investigation of Polanyi will be found in Jones and Miller (2006).

IMPLICATIONS OF THE CONTINUAL INTERACTION OF EXPLICIT AND TACIT KNOWLEDGE

Michael Polanyi was fully aware that there is a continual interaction of tacit and explicit knowledge. The clearest expression of this is his discussion of the process of learning to interpret pulmonary X-ray images. The medical student progresses from seeing nothing but a few shadowy ribs to being able to intuit the implications of subtle spidery patterns for the health of the lungs. This is not done by a process of dumb induction, simply comparing the images with real lungs and implicitly developing a mapping of characteristics from one medium to the other. It is mediated by language, so that every development of explicit knowledge through verbal instruction is linked with the display of actual cases, while the student is also only able to follow the verbal instruction because the examples give substance to what is initially incomprehensible jargon (Polanyi, 1958).

Tacit knowledge is not a special stock of knowledge alongside explicit or implicit knowledge. It is knowledge in activation in a particular context and under the imperative of achieving particular goals. It is this which makes tacit knowledge "ineffable" or inexpressible; not any hidden quality of the knowledge itself, but the fact that it only comes alive and makes sense in an active context of goal-directed action. To make this entire context explicit would be an infinite task. But tacit knowledge is not simply implicit knowledge either. Large parts of tacit knowledge may have originated in explicit knowledge and may be reproducible as explicit knowledge, but in use this knowledge becomes tacit by being backgrounded, while the individual focuses on the goals they wish to achieve. The attunement of the individual to the achievement of these goals within the given context is inseparable from the person's commitment to that particular context as one of their contexts, and it is this attunement that can only be acquired through action.

Polanyi begins from the fact that the greatest part of our knowledge is subservient to our goals and actions. It is in the background, but is not called on in the form of statements. Most of what we do, we do on the basis of routines which are familiar and within which we follow established patterns and familiar heuristics of interpretation of what is taking place. We cannot focus on the knowledge necessary to accomplish these actions without detracting from the performance itself, "putting ourselves off." When we have to concentrate on a skilled action we are mostly focusing on what could go wrong rather than on the positive components which are necessary but which can be taken for granted.

This is tacit knowing, but what is tacit knowledge? If we looked at our knowledge from the point of view of logical implication, our knowledge could be said to be infinite. Linguistics tells us we can generate an infinite number of sentences. Does that mean that we "know" how to do this? Knowledge of classes of things can likewise generate infinite propositional statements. In Polanyi's way of thinking there is no ultimate distinction between "knowing that" and "knowing how." Knowing how to carry out a skilled performance of any action includes having the capacity to generate a potentially infinite stock of judgements about the progress of the action and the possible risks and causes of failure. "These two aspects of knowing have a similar structure and neither is ever present without the other. This is particularly clear in the art of diagnosing, which intimately combines skillful testing with expert observation." (Polanyi, 1966, p. 7).

For Polanyi, the process of "From-to" knowing is always part of a process of achieving something. Polanyi considers that there are two stages in the tacitness of knowledge. When we are engaged in any action we focus on the aim and we background all of the conditions of success of the action, unless a problem arises. But we also focus through the object of our action on the ultimate aim for which the action is undertaken. Whether the

action is proceeding adequately is not generally determined by a fixed idea of what the physical form of the outcome should be, but on whether it is an adequate basis for the next stage of a continuous chain of actions. In modern society we have become accustomed to see action through the paradigm of the manufacture of a series of almost-identical and interchangeable objects. This is a misleading paradigm for the teleology of most human action, which is not driven by a blueprint but by adequacy to a goal. This final goal is itself subject to shifting conceptions of what success would consist of and how to achieve it. Connexions and IBM are examples of the move away from the old paradigm.

Polanyi uses the word "commitment" to signify the fact that in order to meaningfully doubt any particular thing, we must make prior commitments to the validity of a wide range of other things. We can never question and investigate the vast range of assumptions on which our life is based. There is a further stage of commitment, which is indwelling. Indwelling means accepting a particular context as a context which defines us and which will continue to be involved with us. As we develop our goals and aims, and the habits and heuristics which we need to achieve them, we become embedded in and determined by the contexts we choose. We can only develop our powers and aptitudes in adjustment to particular contexts, which are not neutral environments. Because they are human creations, they embody human teleologies, and in becoming part of them we absorb the aims and goals of our context. The process of achieving goals is also a process of formation in which the understanding of how to achieve goals can lead to a process of redefining goals and of what would count as achieving them.

We have a fund of knowledge about objects and processes that is embedded in our commitment to values, contexts, and goals. Personal knowledge is thus a process of continual development and discovery, which is also a continual process of adjustment of the individual to their contexts.

The tools we use, both physical and mental, become extensions of our body. In the case of tools, we adjust our propriosensory settings so that we process the information received as being "out there" as we do with sight and hearing input. In the case of heuristics we also make the reality of their postulates part of our world, like assuming the solidity of floors and chairs, and we experience an equivalent shock when they are invalidated. This is another part of commitment, which arises because we cannot constantly check all parameters and values. We must take some things for granted in order to be able to apply ourselves to action.

The information from tools used as probes (the blind person's stick, the rower's oar, the carpenter's screwdriver, the punter's pole, a bent wire used to investigate an inaccessible recess) are not experienced as events in or on the user's hand and fingers, but as data about what is really there in the appropriate part of space. This is not surprising, as we also locate our own hand not solely by information from the hand but from the entire arm and body. We learn to interpret the messages from our nerves as being "about" our hands and fingers only by patterns of correlation between visual and kinetic information of grasping and manipulating objects. We learn to interpret a particular pattern of pressures on our fingertips as being "about" something six inches away or a pattern of pressures on the palms of our hands as being "about" something six feet away. We have simply become accustomed to associate this pattern with the feel of the screw encountering hard, soft, or rotten wood, or the pole encountering stone, clay, or soft mud.

Polanyi considers that our heuristics work in the same way. We have expectations about the likely future actions of rocks, chairs, trees, and animals. We each have a differently tuned set of these expectations based on our experience of these things. This affects both the expectations we have and the way in which we classify things into classes, giving rise to different expectations.

The heuristics of higher level skills are similar. Such heuristics are an extension of the self into the world. We can experience the same feelings of shock and harm when our most familiar heuristics do not "work" as when we sit on a chair and find that it collapses. Our reasonable and normally reliable map of the world and our place and potential for action within it are suddenly upset. Heuristics are thus the limit case of how body and mind work together to produce and experience tacit knowledge.

There are currently two schools of psychological research that prominently use the word *heuristics*, the *Heuristics and Biases* approach, developed by Kahnemann, Slovic, and Tversky and a wide range of other collaborators over the last thirty years, and the *Simple Heuristics* approach recently begun by Gerd Gigerenzer. (The major collections of articles of the *Heuristics and Biases* group are Kahnemann, Slovic & Tversky, 1982 and Gilovich, Griffin & Kahnemann, 2002. This approach was presented to a wider audience by Piatelli-Palmarini, 1994). For a critique of their assumptions, see Gigerenzer (2000, pp. 237-266). The *Simple Heuristics* approach is exemplified by Gigerenzer, Todd, and the ABC Research Group (1999), and by Gigerenzer (2000). See also the extensive peer reviews and replies of Todd and Gigerenzer (2000).

However, although the problems discussed by these schools are relevant to many aspects of Polanyi's theory, Polanyi's use of the term predates the appearance of either of these approaches and is to be explained by two contemporary influences. One of these is the use of the term *heuristic* in the development of problem solving techniques in thermodynamics, relativity, and quantum theory in the first half of the 20th century, during which time Polanyi was an active member of this community, as attested by Popper (1968, p. 443, without mention of Polanyi). The other is Polanyi's lifelong dialogue with his close friend George Pólya, who used the term in his classical and influential studies of mathematical problem solving. See Pólya (1945), and the introduction by Ian Stewart in the 1990 reprint, and also Pólya (1954, 1959). Polanyi (1958, pp. 124-131) reviews Pólya's work and explicitly relates it to his own understanding of heuristics.

It is perhaps useful to report that the technical subject of discovery in problem solving is called *heuristic*, and that when we (and the other authors mentioned) talk about *heuristics,* we are talking about a plurality of discrete methods and procedures. When Polanyi describes heuristics, he is talking about methods and procedures that *can* be generalised, but within his overall perspective of the contextual nature of learning, the mental pathways by which heuristics are formed by individuals may be strongly linked with particular contexts, so that their effective activation may be context-dependent. Context-dependency will be stronger when heuristics are developed tacitly, as may be the case when practitioners develop their own rules of thumb in uncharted and under-described contexts (the classic investigation of context-dependent learning is Lave, 1988).

The process of acquiring and using mathematical and other scientific forms of heuristics can be taught explicitly, as in the works of George Pólya. Case-based work in areas such as medicine, social work, advice, and guidance can likewise be taught as a series of procedures to be followed to ensure that all relevant considerations are considered; possible causes of problems, possible outcomes, possible interventions, and possible action to be undertaken by the client. Business consultancy, systems analysis, and organisational restructuring can also be taught and learnt explicitly. But in action all of this knowledge must become part of the "tacit component" of the action of the practitioner. Until recently, the processes of professional education and induction were seen as adequate to ensure that practitioners acquired a stock of heuristics that would evolve during their working lifetime as contexts changed. We suggest that the emergence of interest in "tacit knowledge" is a symptom of the acceleration of change in ways that threaten the relevance of inherited "bundles" of explicit knowledge and action schemes. The practitioners in the contexts we have investigated are subject in common to a number of trends which both tend to invalidate old tacit knowledge and to put a premium on the development of new tacit knowledge. In these particular contexts, the form of tacit knowledge most under pressure is that of heuristics, the ingrained habits of problem solving pathways and envisioning possible outcomes.

In these contexts, practitioners are working under pressures which threaten to undermine the "tacit component" of their older heuristics. At the same time the new heuristics they develop in the course of their work make them privileged holders of new "tacit knowledge," that their organisation would in principle like to diffuse, but which is difficult to extract from its "sticky" relationship to the contexts from which it arises. First, the practitioners are constantly presented with new problems and new constellations of problems by their clients, any of which may turn out to be indicative of wider trends that will impact the organisation as a whole in the future. Secondly, they are required to navigate the contours of their "Network Enterprise" to find the necessary collaborators within their own organisation, within long-term external partners, or within spin-off or outsourced organisations. Thirdly, as part of this, they are working with information-sharing systems designed and developed under different circumstances and which may undergo rapid change under organisational or technological pressures. Fourthly, they are working within "one-stop-shop" client-centred "solutions" or "transitions" model, which also gives rise to the pressure to contribute to the restandardisation of solution bundles from the bespoke elements evolved working with particular clients, and to attempt to ensure that the resources thus bundled are used as a solution of first resort in future analogous cases.

The unintended consequence of these pressures will be that practitioners are likely to develop heuristics, habitual pathways of problem-solving, which are tacit in several ways. They may have developed unconsciously, through conditioning by the environment rather than by conscious thought. Equally, they may never be discussed with other practitioners, and they may be stimulus-dependent and only activated by the particular contexts in which they arose. While they *may* embody practices that are useful to the organisation, it is also possible that because they have evolved tacitly, they are actually only *satisficing* rather than *optimising* solutions. This is a significant component of the negative aspect of the phenomenon which Ciborra describes as "Drift." When an in-house information system is introduced, it will give rise to habits developed as individuals attempt to work with it, which do not necessarily use the full potential of the system, but which may be difficult to eradicate, giving rise to inertia and resistance to further change.

A more positive side of "Drift" may be discerned when it is possible to orient the information systems of the organisation to produce openness to the new needs evolving within the client base. This is certainly the intention behind the systems introduced in both of the contexts examined. Both organisations envisage themselves as frameworks for the evolution of standards and the development of information systems within which innovation will arise by the direct confrontation of practitioners, working in varied and shifting coalitions, with the newly-arising problems of key client groups. These innovative practices will give rise to restandardisation of best practice, and to more efficient delivery of new solutions to clients who present with similar new problems. The implicit model underlying this and similar "internal market" initiatives is to abandon the drive to management-driven top-down uniformity, and instead create a dynamic "fitness landscape" within which new methods of working and of working together can develop and demonstrate their potential. See the organisation-theory oriented discussion of the "fitness landscape" in Marion (1999, pp. 235-271), drawing on Kauffman (1993, 1995). The serendipitous appearance of effective innovations can then be rapidly diffused within the wider organisation, facilitated by the mechanisms for rapid standard-setting and rebundling of standard components.

In this context "tacit knowledge" is a double-edged sword. On the one hand, the development of client-facing tacit knowledge can give an edge in developing new solutions to new problems. On the other hand, the diffusion of new tacit knowledge is difficult because of the inherent stickiness of the tacit knowledge involved. Part of this follows from the context-dependent nature of the habits and heuristics that are developed. This difficulty increases when the composition of work teams is itself variable and ad hoc. Tacit knowledge and skills will be developed within particular divisions of labour, and may not be easy to transfer to differently organised groups, or to groups that are themselves unstable and subject to shifting patterns of collaboration. Nelson and Winter argued that the routine is the effective unit of economic evolution, and that economically effective tacit knowledge was not embodied by individuals, but by teams which were able to carry out routines. They also argue that innovation is itself a routine, that creating new routines is itself a routine, and that the replication of teams that can carry out routines is itself a routine (Nelson & Winter, 1982). The "Network Enterprise" must struggle to retain these capabilities, while simultaneously attempting to take advantage of the opportunities of more fluid partnerships and collaborations between in-house and external collaborators. This is reflected in the emphasis placed on team leadership, but the need to reproduce patterns of tacit knowledge within teams and routines may cut across the flexibility won by adopting the internal market model.

HEURISTICS IN THE MANAGEMENT OF CLIENT-CENTRED PROCESSES

To unite our themes of the appearance of similar phenomena in two ostensibly widely different forms of organisation, and of the interaction of tacit and explicit knowledge, the heuristic is the actual form of operation of the "knowledge" which is notionally embodied in the organisational mapping of an institution. Information systems only come alive when used by individual practitioners to develop their plan of action in meeting the needs of particular clients. There is already an analogy in the parallel by which the needs of a client may only be gradually disclosed so that a plan of action for meeting their needs may develop new branches or may be completely recentred by the emergence of new, more pressing needs.

Against this target, the practitioner has to put together a team of collaborators from a pool of colleagues and units which they know to be experienced or to be in the process of developing experience in particular fields of work. They also have to gauge the pressure of work that these individuals or units may be experiencing. The inherent technical knowledge of collaborators also has to be weighed against their experience in dealing with the particular problems of the particular kind of client. This in turn can involve knowing that one kind of client can often turn out to be a different kind of client as the process develops. In a context of compartmentalised provision, there was always the last resort of referral to another professional or service. Manufacturers can always say, well, we don't make *them*. The system consultant and the one-stop shop practitioner no longer have these options.

The Connexions service has the remit to ensure the school-to-work transition of all 13-19 year olds in England. It will refer its clients to appropriate medical and legal professionals and services, housing, or educational authorities, but these referrals are never final. The service always remains responsible for monitoring the outcome of these referrals and ensuring their success. The service as a whole is thus the site of first and last resort for all of the problems of its cohorts. Within this context, the total responsibility of the organisation as a whole is delegated to the individual advisor. They become responsible for mobilising all of the resources internal and external on which the service can call. They cannot do this by constantly referring to encyclopaedic reference books and directories. It is inevitable that one of the most important tasks of the advisor is to maintain a mental map of the most common pathways on which their clients will be travelling.

IBM has no legal responsibility to accept all business opportunities that arise. In fact, one of the responsibilities of the Opportunities Manager within the CRM is to decide whether a particular opportunity flagged by a representative is worth pursuing. However, new opportunities presenting new problems may also present valuable data on the way in which business system needs are evolving. Having moved on from hardware to software and then to consultancy, IBM cannot dictate what kind of problems it will provide consultancy on without risking being left behind by newly emerging trends. Of course, IBM has experience in managing the risk involved in open-ended development projects, and problematic client requests will be looked at by the relevant specialists. Nevertheless, becoming a consultant inevitably means opening the organisation to the pull of external dynamics. IBM has put itself into a position where it will have to navigate these without the internal structure that was once provided by the existence of given product lines and by final higher decisions about new product development.

Claudio Ciborra argued that this drift could be positive and creative if it is experienced against a background of a platform such as is provided by the standards and systems, which allow feedback on what is happening to be used creatively in the wider organisation (Ciborra, 2002; Ciborra & Associates, 2000). This means that the element of drift which arises when management step back from prescribing the specifics of collaboration within the organisation and institutes information systems which allow lateral collaboration and communication assumes a positive aspect when there are simultaneously channels which allow the process to be driven by client needs. Our examples may be seen as a paradigm of a new type of organisation that, within overall imperatives and standards, opens itself to drift generated by the expressed and elicited needs of its clients. Interestingly, this parallel seems to hold both for real paying clients, such as those of IBM, and for users who are given the status of clients as part of a strategy to make take-up of services part of a consumer culture and to banish the stigma of dependency. Within these organisations, the need to bring together a range of professional advice and knowledge to provide a unitary response to the client's needs leads to the growing importance of the tacit knowledge of each individual on the interface with the client about the structure of the organisation and its component units and collaborators. The need to provide solutions to problems that arise in the course of the client relationship means that every such worker builds up a picture of the possible collaborations and referrals they can make. Precisely because the organisation is constantly evolving in response to new needs, the tacit knowledge generated by contact and collaboration in client-centred work becomes indispensable. It cannot be replaced by centrally disseminated data, but it is possible to create structures which facilitate channels of lateral communication.

This chapter started from the observation that the procedures adopted by two organisations, one for-profit and the other not-for-profit, seemed to be converging on a new model which devolves to the client-facing front-line practitioner the task of assembling an ad hoc team of collaborators to deal with the particular mix of problems elicited from that client. This means that the tacit knowledge of the practitioner must encompass the possibilities and limitations of the possible collaborations available to meet the client's needs in a rapidly evolving environment of organisational change. In order to situate this observation, we have drawn on the model of the Network Enterprise (Castells, 1996) and the concept of Drift (Ciborra). We have presented relevant aspects of the business model of IBM and Connexions (UK) to illustrate the kind of environment practitioners are navigating in. We have adopted and presented the understanding of tacit knowledge of Michael Polanyi, as first introduced into economic theory by Nelson and Winter, as the appropriate model to understand the necessarily personal and situated nature of the knowledge and associated heuristics which develop from working in such open, shifting, and evolving environments. We conclude that the model of the Network Enterprise and the "solutions" approach to product and process development necessarily creates a constantly evolving body of practitioner tacit knowledge, which information systems must be designed to facilitate and foster and which cannot usefully be made explicit because of its inherently situated and dynamic context. This leads to the conclusion that tacit knowledge should be accepted as a necessary product of continuous innovation and change.

REFERENCES

Baumol, W. (2002). *The free-market innovation machine*. Princeton, NJ: Princeton University Press.

Bhagwati, J. (1984, June). Splintering and disembodiment of services and developing nations. In J. Bhagwati (Ed.), *The world economy*. (Reprinted from *Writings on International Economics*, pp. 433-446, Oxford: Oxford University Press. (& Delhi 1998: Oxford University Press).

Boisot, M. (1998). *Knowledge assets*. Oxford: Oxford University Press.

Castells, M. (1996-1998). *The information age: Economy, society and culture.* 3 volumes. Oxford: Blackwell.

Castells, M. (2001). *The Internet galaxy.* Oxford: Blackwell.

Ciborra, C. (Ed.). (1996). Introduction. *Groupware and teamwork, invisible aid or technical hindrance?* (pp. 1-19). Chichester: Wiley.

Ciborra, C. (2002). *The labyrinths of information.* Oxford: Oxford University Press.

Ciborra, C., & Failla, A. (2000). Infrastructure as a process: The case of CRM in IBM. In C. Ciborra, & Associates, *From control to drift* (pp. 105-124). Oxford: Oxford University Press.

Ciborra, C., & Hanseth, O. (1998). From tool to gestell. *Information Technology and* People, *11*(4), 305-327. (Reprinted as Ch. 4, pp. 56-82, by C. Ciborra, 2002).

Ciborra, C., & Hanseth, O. (2000). Introduction. In Ciborra & Associates, *From control to drift* (pp. 1-15) Oxford: Oxford University Press.

Dosi, G., Teece, D., & Chytry, J. (Eds.) (1997). *Technology, organization, and competitiveness.* Oxford: Oxford University Press.

Failla, A. (1996). Technologies for co-ordination in a software factory. In C. Ciborra (Ed.), *Groupware and teamwork, invisible aid or technical hindrance?* (pp. 61-88). Chichester: Wiley.

Failla, A., & Mazzotti, S. (2004). *Competent. Project Validation phase of Scenario 1 Human Resources Developer: Valorising the Company Asset Base.* Fondazione IBM Italia Milano.

Gigerenzer, G. (2000). *Adaptive thinking.* Oxford: Oxford University Press.

Gigerenzer, G., Todd, P., & the ABC Research Group (1999). *Simple heuristics that make us smart.* Oxford: Oxford University Press.

Gilovich, T., Griffin, D., & Kahnemann, D. (2002). *Heuristics and biases.* Cambridge, MA: Cambridge University Press.

Jones, B., & Miller, A. (2004). *Competent. The connexions partnerships: Pilot site scenario 3: UK public employment services.* Manchester School of Management European Work & Employment Research Centre.

Jones, B., & Miller, B. (2006). *Innovation diffusion in the new economy: Tthe tacit dimension.* London: Routledge.

Kahnemann, D., Slovic, P., & Tversky, A. (Eds.). (1982). *Judgement under uncertainty: Heuristics and biases.* Cambridge, MA: Cambridge University Press.

Kaufmann, S. (1993). *The origins of order.* New York: Oxford University Press.

Kauffman, S. (1995). *At home in the universe.* New York: Oxford University Press.

Lave, J. (1988). *Cognition in practice.* Cambridge, MA: Cambridge University Press.

Lincoln, J., & Ahmadjian, C. (2001). Shukko (employee transfers) and tacit knowledge exchange in Japanese supply networks. In I. Nonaka & T. Nishiguchi (Eds.), *Knowledge emergence* (pp. 247-269). Oxford: Oxford University Press.

Loasby, B. (1976). *Choice, complexity, and ignorance.* Cambridge, MA: Cambridge University Press.

Marion, R. (1999). *The edge of organization.* Thousand Oaks: Sage.

Marshall, A. (1949). *Principles of economics* (8th ed). London: Macmillan. 1st ed. 1890, 8th. ed. 1920; pp. 271-272, pp. 225-226 in the 1949 reprint

Nelson, R. (1990). Capitalism as an engine of progress. *Research Policy* (pp. 193-214). (Reprinted The sources of economic growth (1996)

pp. 52-83, by R. Nelson, Cambridge. MA/London: Harvard University Press).

Nelson, R. (1991). Why do firms differ, and how does in matter? *SMJ, 4*, 61-74. (Reprinted from pp.100-119, by R. Nelson, 1996).

Nelson, R. (1996). *The sources of economic growth*. Cambridge, MA/London: Harvard University Press.

Nelson, R., & Winter, S. (1982). *An evolutionary theory of economic change*. Cambridge, MA: Harvard University Press.

Nonaka, I., & Takeuchi, H. (1998). *The knowledge-creating company*. New York: Oxford University Press.

Penrose, E. (1995). *The theory of the growth of the firm* (3rd ed.). Oxford: Oxford University Press.

Piatelli-Palmarini, M. (1994). *Inevitable illusions*. New York: Wiley.

Polanyi, M. (1958). *Personal knowledge*. Chicago: University of Chicago Press/London: Routledge & Kegan Paul.

Polanyi, M. (1966). *The tacit dimension*. Chicago: University of Chicago Press.

Polanyi, M. (1969). *Knowing and being*. In M. Grene (Ed.). London: Routledge & Kegan Paul.

Polanyi, M., & Prosch, H. (1975). *Meaning*. Chicago: University of Chicago Press.

Pólya, G. (1959). Heuristic reasoning in the theory of numbers. *American Mathematical Monthly, 66*, 375-384. (Reprinted Mathematics and plausible reasoning (1968) pp. 193-202, by G. Pólya, (vol. II) Princeton : Princeton University Press).

Pólya, G. (1968, 1954). *Mathematics and plausible reasoning* (2nd ed.). 2 vol. Princeton, NJ: Princeton University Press.

Pólya, G. (1990, 1945). *How to solve it*. London: Penguin.

Popper, K. (1968, 1959). *The logic of scientific discovery* (3rd ed.). London: Hutchinson.

Shiba, T., & Shimotani, M. (Eds.). (1997). *Beyond the firm. Business groups in international and historical perspective*. Oxford: Oxford University Press.

Swann, P., Prevezer, M., & Stout, D. (Eds.). (1998). *The dynamics of industrial clustering, international comparisons in computing and biotechnology*. Oxford: Oxford University Press.

Todd, P., & Gigerenzer, G (2000). Précis of simple heuristics that make us smart. *Behavioural and Brain Sciences, 23*, 737-780.

Ward, L. (2005, February 2). Careers and guidance service may be replaced. *The Guardian*. http://education.guardian.co.uk/schools/story/0,,1403768,00.html

This work was previously published in International Journal of Technology and Human Interaction, Vol. 3, Issue 1, edited by B. Stahl, pp. 49-71, copyright 2007 by IGI Publishing, formerly known as Idea Group Publishing (an imprint of IGI Global).

Chapter X
Interpretive Flexibility Along the Innovation Decision Process of the UK NHS Care Records Service (NCRS):
Insights from a Local Implementation Case Study

Anastasia Papazafeiropoulou
Brunel University, UK

Reshma Gandecha
Brunel University, UK

ABSTRACT

Interpretive flexibility is a term used to describe the diverse perspectives on what a technology is and can or can not do during the process of technological development. In this chapter, we look at how interpretive flexibility manifests through the diverse perceptions of stakeholders involved in the diffusion and adoption of the NHS Care Records Service (NCRS). Our analysis shows that while the policy makers acting upon the application of details related to the implementation of the system, the potential users are far behind the innovation decision process, namely at the knowledge or persuasion stages. We use data from a local heath authority from a county close to London. The research explores, compares, and evaluates contrasting views on the systems implementation at the local as well as national level. We believe that our analysis is useful for NCRS implementation strategies, in particular, and technology diffusion in large organisations, in general.

INTRODUCTION

With medical errors becoming a cruel reality in the provision of healthcare worldwide, the role of information technology in preventing those errors becomes predominant. It is recognised that more people die every year due to medical errors than from vehicle accidents, breast cancer, or AIDS (Kohn, et al. 2000). The American Hospital Association CDER (2004) relates the vast majority of medication errors to lack of appropriate information and processes such as:

- Incomplete patient information
- Unavailable drug information
- Miscommunication of drug orders due to poor handwriting, similarly named drugs, misuse of zeroes and decimal points, confusion of metric and other dosing units, and inappropriate abbreviations
- Lack of appropriate labelling
- Environmental factors, such as lighting, heat, noise, and interruptions that can distract health professionals from their medical tasks.

One way to reduce medical errors is to make efficient, accurate, reliable medical decisions, based on reliable and up-to-date information or patient records. Integrated patient records can reduce medical errors by using information technology (Booth, 2002). Medical errors can be reduced with the provision of order entry systems with computerized prescriptions and using bar-coding for medications, blood, devices, and patients. In order to avoid the medical errors, medical centres are investing in computerized patient records, bringing patients and clinicians within the ambit of an integrated health care system that provides real-time patient records. Nelson (1998) cites the American Medical Association (AMA) as stating that 30% of all patient visits are completed without access to the patient's chart. Access anytime anywhere to patient information,

by the concerned and authorized persons, is the key concept of computerized patient records. Medical errors are reduced when all hospitals implement proven medication safety practices using computerized medication lists and health care providers can readily see patient medications and avoid duplications of tests.

In this article, we are looking at the diffusion and adoption of the NHS (National Health Service) Care Records Service (NCRS) in the United Kingdom, which has the potential to support healthcare professionals by offering an integrated electronic patience record system that would potentially reduce medical errors. It is worth mentioning that the medical care in the United Kingdom is a social service and not fee-paid as in other countries such as the United States. This has great implications for the modernisation of the health care system, which is of high political importance and one of the main priorities in the United Kingdom's government agenda. This service is one of the four key deliverables set out in the NHS IT procurement strategy "Delivering 21st Century IT Support for the NHS," published in June 2002. NCRS is a portfolio of services covering the generation, movement, and access to health records, which includes electronic prescribing in hospitals and workflow capacities to manage patients' care pathways through the NHS. Its benefits include convenience, integration of care, improving outcomes using evidence, supporting analysis, and improving efficiency (NHSIA, 1998). With estimates that 25% of nurse and doctor time is taken up collecting data, and the potential increase in speed and efficiency of communication, the benefits appear very straightforward with the promise of "seamless care" (NHSIA, 1998).

The proposed system will work by assisting all healthcare professionals and other prospective users. Whenever they log on to the system, they will be presented with a personal home page permitting them to combine a number of screens. Then, they will be in a position to look for a patient by a 10-digit NHS number or a known detail such as name, date of birth, age, sex, phone number, or their general practitioner's (GP) name. Also, patients will be in a position to view their own records and ultimately become involved in planning their treatment by the use of the "My health space" feature on the NHS Direct web site. The "data spine" is planned to go live in three phases:

1. The first core service, including some patient records, is expected to be up and running by December 2004.
2. By the end of 2006, it is expected to be equipped to cover the entire population.
3. The final version is expected to be accomplished by 2010.

NCRS is one of the National Program for Information Technology (NPFIT) targets and, as with many healthcare IT projects, its evaluation will be difficult, provided that government led IT projects in the NHS have a history of notable project failures. The complexity of such huge investments, currently £7.6 billion, calls for a clear understanding of the environments in which healthcare networks exist.

The research focus here is the diffusion of the NCRS from the policy makers at a highest decision making level to the users of the system. We examine how diffusion receivers (users, such as doctors or nurses) perceive the NCRS implementation in comparison to policy makers. We argue that there is a gap between the demand and the supply side of the diffusion process, which reveals a broad barrier in the NCRS implementation. We use primary and secondary data to capture the perceptions of both diffusers and diffusion receivers in order to get a better understanding of the NCRS diffusion process. The primary data was collected through interviews with the managerial and technical staff as well as future users of the NCRS within a specific county in the United Kingdom. These were supported by

extensive literature review, and use of archival records such as NHS policy documents and county specific information through local press and staff newsletters.

Our aim is, by drawing a clear picture of the NCRS diffusion process, to identify existing barriers and perception gaps in order to offer recommendations towards a more efficient implementation strategy. With the allocation of £2.3 billion to fund this project (NHS, 2002), there is renewed optimism and genuine interest to bridge the gap between strategy and realisation to implementation of NCRS (Firth, 2003).

The article is structured as follows. Section two gives an overview of the diffusion of innovations theory, highlighting its critiques while proposing the use of ideas from the social construction of technology theory to support our framework. The next section describes the methodology used for the collection of the case study data, while sections four and five include the analysis of the data. Finally, in section six, we draw some general conclusions about the future on the diffusion of NCRS.

DIFFUSION OF INNOVATIONS THEORY AND ITS CRITIQUES

Diffusion of innovations is a complex longitudinal process, which in the case of individual adopters is mainly concerned with the process of decision making towards the adoption or rejection of the innovation. In the case of innovation adoption by organisations, once the decision to adopt has been made, implementation does not always follow directly (Rogers, 1995). The complexity of the diffusion process is becoming higher, as a number of individuals with different interests and agendas are part of this process.

Rogers broadly defines diffusion as "the process by which an innovation is communicated through certain channels over time among the members of a social system" (Rogers, 1995, p.10). The messages spread by diffusion are seen as new ideas or inputs to the system. The four main elements of diffusion are thus innovation, communication, time and social systems. In this model, innovation is defined as any object, idea, or practice that is perceived as new. The technological, cultural, and economic characteristics of innovation will determine how quickly it is adopted throughout the social system. Diffusion involves time in several different ways, firstly through the innovation-decision process. This is the mental process spanning the five steps involved in innovation-decision: knowledge, persuasion, decision, implementation, and confirmation of the decision to reject or adopt the innovation. Second, innovativeness refers to the amount of time individuals take to adopt an innovation relative to others in the social system. Third, the rate of adoption refers to the relative speed with which members of a social system will adopt a new idea. Rogers sees the social system as interrelated units that participate in problem solving in order to bring about a common goal. The diffusion of innovations can be impeded or facilitated by the communication and social structures of the system.

According to Rogers, the innovation-decision process, in which a decision-making unit passes from first knowledge of an innovation to the decision to adopt or reject it, plays a crucial role for the diffusion of an innovation. In this process, five steps are defined:

- Knowledge occurs when a potential adopter learns about the existence of the innovation and gains some understanding of how it functions.
- Persuasion occurs when a potential adopter forms a favourable or unfavourable attitude towards an innovation.
- Decision occurs when a potential adopter undertakes activities, which lead to the adoption or rejection of an innovation.
- Implementation occurs when an innovation is actually put to use.
- Confirmation occurs when an adopter seeks reinforcement of an innovation-decision that has already been made, but the adopter may reverse this previous decision if exposed to conflicting messages about the innovation.

The first and very important step of the innovation-decision process is that of knowledge. There are three particular types of knowledge: awareness knowledge, how-to-knowledge, and principles-knowledge. The first of these types, awareness-knowledge, is information that an

Figure 1. The five stages of the innovation decision process

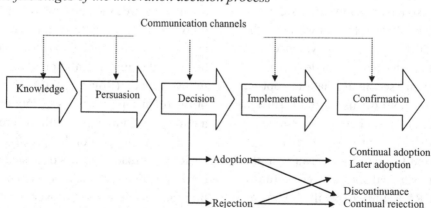

innovation exist. Awareness-knowledge then triggers the potential adopter to seek information of how to use the innovation. When an inadequate level of how-to-knowledge is obtained, then rejection and discontinuance are likely to result. Principles-knowledge consists of information regarding the functioning principles of the innovation. The innovation decision process is presented in Figure 1.

Diffusion of innovations theory is sought to explain reasons behind individual or collective adoption of an innovation, but has been criticised as not taking in to consideration the particularities of complex information technologies (Lyytinen and Damsgaard, 2001). Thus, it has been judged (e.g., Kautz and Pries-Heje, 1996; Elliot and Loebbecke, 2000; Allen, 2000, Papazafeiropoulou, 2002) as poorly equipped to understand how different groups interact in the production and provision of innovation as well as lacking attention to reinvention and consequences of innovation. The use of other social theories such as stakeholder theory, social shaping of technology, and economics of innovation theories have been proposed as supportive to DOI for the understanding of the diffusion and adoption of complex information systems phenomena. In the case of healthcare provision, actor network theory has been explicitly used to compliment innovation diffusion theory for the examination of the factors affecting IT adoption by rural GPs in Australia (Wenn, et al., 2002).

In this article, we take a similar approach in criticising DOI theory and we are mostly concerned about the theory's lack of understanding of the different views, opinions, and agendas involved in the innovation diffusion process. These are included in the communication channels, but their description in Roger's work is very general and mostly related with the influence certain individuals have on others towards the adoption or the rejection of an innovation. In his work, it is assumed that there is an objective understating of the stage were the technology

under investigation is positioned at a certain point in time. Nevertheless, we are interested to examine how different groups involved in the diffusion process have different views about the same technology, its features, and maturity level. Drawing insights from the Social Construction of Technology theory (SCOT) (Pinch and Bijker, 1984), we see how the *relevant social groups* view the implementation of the technological artifact (in our case, the NCRS) along the innovation diffusion process. We argue that the notion of *interpretive flexibility* is relevant here as our data shows that different groups have different opinions about where NCRS lays within the stages of the diffusion process at the same point in time. We believe that the possibilities of a *closure* (resolve of conflicts and reach of an agreement) can be increased when policy makers get a more realistic picture of what the potential uses know about the system under development.

METHODOLOGY

A number of interviews were scheduled and carried out during the collection of data for this research, which started in April 2002, and a representative number of interviews have been carried out with stakeholders in the county. The name of the county is not revealed according to the interviewees wish, showing the sensitivity as well as the significance of the subject under investigation. A pilot study was conducted initially comprising a few unstructured interviews with the previous IT chair of the local implementation group in the county. This work addressed the structural technological changes that had taken place at the national and local level of the primary care organizations and trusts.

The core objective of this study has been to find out the perception about the implementation process among the policy makers and the potential users of information that will be generated from the implementation of NHS Patent Record

Service (NCRS). The collapse of the previous local implementation plans in August 2002 was an incentive to study the issues under investigation further. Therefore, this paper is part of the work carried out over a 25-month period between August 2002 and September 2004.

A number of meetings were attended and interviews conducted such as:

- Extensive interviews with a chief pharmacist at the NHS information authority, chief information officer, programme lead of the county's local medical council clinician.
- Participation in local implementation group meetings in May- June 2004.
- Participation in NPfit Programme board meeting in October 2004.

The approach that was taken for the interviews was to include views from both the policy makers and administrators as well clinicians in order to examine the diversity of opinions. More specifically, we contacted staff who support the implementation of NCRS, but do not usually work in a surgery or at emergency scenes, for example, board directors and senior managers, members of the NPfit programme board as well as doctors, pharmacists, and nurses. Conversations were taking place, when circumstances permitted, with staff as they were attending the project board meetings, which are part of their day to day work. Interviews were recorded and transcribed later, whereas notes were taken during meetings and periods of observation.

Additionally, this study draws upon various internal documentation sources, including meeting minutes, procedure manuals, project plans, corporate and technology strategies, and project reports. The documentation also included copies of service plans, annual meetings, various internal communication e-mails, newspaper articles, and radio programmers about the NPfit and the department of health. The NPfit has "official"

and "unofficial" Web sites and the researchers were given access to the latter, where sensitive internal information of the delivery targets to achieve NCRS was outlined.

This work adopts a "broadly interpretive" stance (Walsham, 1993), reflecting our efforts to identify multiple actors' interpretations of a specific three-year period of information systems implementation and related organizational change of achieving the NHS Care Records in the county. The narrative is reconstructed from public inquiry reports and people's memories, and further informed by observations of the current electronic record systems in operation during the fieldwork efforts. This article presents the case study narrative. It will trace the main events and initiatives that took place from the collapse of the Local Implementation Strategy (LIS) plans in March 2002 to a National Programme Initiative (NPfit) announced in March 2003 into the plans for implementation of the national electronic spine by December 2004.

THE NCRS IMPLEMENTATION PLAN IN THE COUNTY

The county's strategic health authority consists of 21 organizations of which 13 are primary care trusts and 8 are acute hospital trusts. The implementation phase of the computerization of NHS records for the patients in the county has been reported as part of an ongoing study. The need for NCRS implementation was recognized and the local Strategic Health Authority (SHA) was established to cater to this part of the country located in the northeast of London. The county is near London and many of its settlements function as towns or villages where London workers raise their families. Therefore, the fulfillment of healthcare needs of the county also caters indirectly to the health of economic labour for the city of London.

The county invested £11 million in 2003 to put workstations on clinicians' desks and to provide faster networks. The local implementation body is working closely with a consultant company to ensure that the county is at the forefront of the IT revolution, which will transform the way patients are diagnosed, treated, and cared for. Accenture (a private consulting company) has been announced as the Local Service Provider and BT has been awarded a 10-year contract to provide the infrastructure, which will enable the setting up and running of the electronic NHS Care Records Service. This means, for the first time, information about patients will be available to all clinicians involved in their treatment and care and not locked away in a filing drawer.

For materializing the implementation plan of the NCRS in the county, the local Strategic Health Authority (SHA) was established in order to make sure there is progress and improvement across the NHS providing the link with the government's department of health. It has been formed to ensure that there is a clear strategy for the county in terms of the role it needs to play in the changing trends in National Health Care strategy and programme. The body has been formed to manage the performance of the NCRS in the county where each NHS trust and primary care trust is accountable to the strategic health authority. The body ensures that the county has the buildings, equipment, workforce, and organisations to deliver the NHS Plan and to see whether all NHS organisations are working within the government's plan to the same overall targets for improvement and to agreed national standards. It provides the link between national policy and local action, which relies on the Strategic Health Authority. As part of the national programme for information technology, the county will form part of a cluster of five strategic health authorities in eastern England that will work with one as yet to be chosen IT provider. The county has been seen as being in a very strong position to move ahead swiftly with NHS implementation programme.

The national plan for NCRS implementation that the county has to follow in order to be compliant with the NHS targets (as they are listed in the introduction section of this paper) will be developed in several stages. These stages are:

- **Stage 1 (to be delivered by the 31st of Dec 2004):** The system will include e-mail, browsing, ability to view radiology and possible medical records, and other non-interactive elements.
- **Stage 2 (to go live by on the 31st of Dec 2006):** The system will become interactive, including GP booking, e-booking, e-referral, and the ability to transfer radiology pictures.
- **Stage 3 (to be delivered by the 31st of Dec 2008):** The non-interactive electronic patient record will be achieved and GPs would be able to log on and get test results and so forth from these medical records

Thirty-one suppliers will be selected after a bidding process and the plan includes what is called "penalty clause" in which, if the suppliers do not deliver, there will be penalties, while the NHS will be able to sue suppliers. Each local implementation has to deliver what is called an output-based specification, which will have basic information about the users' needs. These documents will be on restricted circulation and a lot of the work will be done on a tendering basis and therefore, will be confidential. The suppliers have been short-listed through consortia and the selected suppliers that will be given the output-based specification through national applications and local service provider applications. According to a chief pharmacist for the NHS information authority, the structure of this delivery plan is in constant state with the national targets being the first priorities.

CASE STUDY ANALYSIS: PERCEPTIONS OF THE NCRS IN THE COUNTY

We asked the key managers at the county under investigation about their opinion on how realistic the plan is and how far the county has been in implementing it at local level. According to the chief information officer, the current legacy systems in the county do not support the core business function and so they are a cost overhead, without actually applying any value. These systems do not have electronic prescribing, auto communications, care pathways, or supervision support. They are a stretch on the administration systems, with some clinical coding but very little else. Therefore, these systems will be scrapped once the National Programme is implemented. He was very enthusiastic about the successful implementation of NCRS claiming that:

The National Programme will be a single system, pulling across the whole of the North East and Eastern cluster forming two fifths of the NHS. Accenture [the consults involved in the project] will be providing the patient record service and will be bound by the confidentiality agreements regarding sensitive patient data. There is a strong information governance regime that's layered onto the whole National Programme. Patients will be allowed to secure elements of their data record that they cannot do at the moment. The whole new way of delivery of project in the NHS is by "new way" which is how it was done in the private sector. This way is to get suppliers to do it for you.

When asked about the previous failure of the NHS to implement such a system (the NHS Information Authority's Electronic Record Development and Implementation Program (ERDIP)), he said that one of the key reasons why ERDIP never took off the ground was because it was a bunch of small research programmes that were delivering very little value; "they were just a waste of time." He said that the NCRS's success

is a matter of the local systems being connected to the national spine.

Concerning the benefits that the system can offer to the clinicians, he said:

The National Programme aims to put the clinicians in a more informed environment. At the moment, they are in an information desert where they are surrounded by information. NHS will provide them with a system for using and managing information, especially that of the patients. It will make sure that the information from the diagnostic services is provided in a format that will make clinical decisions in real-time. There will be a lot less paperwork because everything will be done automatically. There will be huge sharing of information, so there will be no nurses' notes, and no dietetic notes, and no medical and surgical notes; there will just be patients' notes. They will have all of that in a structured format that is easy to handle and easy to gain access to. You don't have to be close to the patient to get access to it; you can be wherever you are. The information will be, and the systems will have an ergonomic that is focused on clinician as well as focused on the patient, which is a technical challenge in its own right, but it's not a difficult one.

Similarly, to the chief information officer, the programme leader in the south west area of the county was rather enthusiastic about the implementation plan. He said that the legacy systems will be removed and the clinicians working in a hospital or GP surgery will connect to the national spine, while they will have access to the NHS network. According to him: "Clinicians will have access, within normal security arrangements, access to anybody's record, at anytime wherever they are." He also show confidence to the consulting company involved in the project (Accenture), saying that they are internationally recognized and have done work in the same areas many times.

The optimism showed by the top managerial staff was, nevertheless, not supported by the future users such as doctors, nurses, and pharmacists. More specifically, according to a clinician at the local medial council: "All we know is that the National system will provide a wonder solution. The existing system will no longer be used and the new system will take over."

We received the same reaction from all clinical staff we interviewed: while they mentioned some clinical workshops being held as motivations to use the new system, they did not seem to have enough information about them. They knew that there was someone from their department involved with the national programme for IT in the county, so he would refer us to him for further information. Additionally, the newsletter distributed among clinicians was advertising awareness workshops, which only started taking place at the time of the interviews in the summer of 2004 (ESHA, 2004).

The differences in perceptions between policy makers and users that is apparent in this case study is further manifested at the national level as demonstrated through secondary resources and it is not surprising that the IT plan has been criticized for lacking support from clinical staff. A survey conducted in 2003 by the Association of ICT Professionals in Health and Social Care (Assist) found considerable scepticism about the programme. Only 49% of those surveyed thought that real benefits would be delivered to their organizations. Scepticism also abounded concerning workload, resources, timescales, and the ability to deliver on the part of the companies that win the big contracts. Another survey recently conducted found that most doctors have not yet been informed about the national programme, despite the fact that leaders have warned that the programme will fail without the full involvement of the doctors. Some doctors are likely to be won over by improved access to tests and services, but others may be alienated by the push toward team working and protocol-delivered care (Whitfield, 2003).

DISCUSSION

Similar to prior examples of promising innovations such as electronic commerce (Papazafeiropoulou, 2002), the NCRS implementation has not been as efficient as expected. Being an authority innovation-decision (Rogers, 1995), where the choice of its adoption or rejection has been made by relatively few individuals in a system that possess power, status, and technical expertise, a number of barriers hiding the realisation of the government's strategy (NHS, 2002) have been reported.

In the case of the UK NHS, the diffusion of new technologies such as the NCRS takes a political disposition, as this is part of the national healthcare programme. The NHS consists of 28 autonomous Strategic Health Authorities and related agencies that need to cooperate towards the adoption of the new technology. With the IT project undertaken by the NHS, technology is moving into the political arena. "For the first time, big IT projects are critical to the success or failure of the government," said Liberal Democrat IT spokesman Richard Allan. "When things go wrong in the Passport Agency, for example, it might be annoying for a lot of people, but it is not make or break for the government. The National Programme is a sink or swim issue," (Arnott, 2003). In other words, the "desire" of the policy makers, acting as changes agents, to diffuse the system with success becomes a matter of professional survival for them. This "urge" for success does not always bring the desired results. For example, the NHS Information Authority is currently working out the details of patient confidentiality and addressing the issue in ways that may be problematic. In this process, the patient is to specify what confidential information is to be made available to pre-specified institutions or clinicians, or certain individuals. The information will be sealed and can only be accessed by specific institutions or individuals. Two problems associated with this approach are that patients may not be able to predict who might need to see their data. In addition, health professionals may find it time-consuming to maintain a cross-referenced database for each patient. Additionally, the British Medical Association protested that the encryption technology chosen would also allow the Government Communications Headquarters to access electronically transmitted data—an apparent intrusion into the doctor-patient privacy and privilege.

According to the data collected during our case study, the relevant social groups have very diverse opinions about the maturity of the NCRS along the innovation diffusion process (Figure 1). Although the decision to adopt the new system has been made and the government has put plans in place for implementing the system, potential users seem to lack essential knowledge about the new service and its functionality. Looking at the innovation decision process, which includes the stages of knowledge, persuasion, decision, implementation, and confirmation, the potential users of NCRS appear to be at the first stages of the innovation-decision process, such as the stages of knowledge and persuasion. Policy makers on the other side are making plans for the system implementation, which is one of the latest stages of the process. The representation of the *relevant social groups*, as only policy makers and potential users, is clearly very simplistic and is there to symbolise the diversity of views (*interpretive flexibility*) on the innovation decision process. The innovation-decisions, pertaining to the implementation of the NCRS, have been made by the policy makers within the system who have decision making power. Innovation diffusion may be succeed or fail, depending on the degree of success that the policy makers have persuading clinicians and other diffusion receivers that the innovation is for the good of the greatest number of actors in the system. The *closure* can only then be achieved when all relevant social groups position themselves at the same stages within the innovation decision process. This is depicted in Figure 2, where we have extended the innovation decision process as presented in Figure 1 to include the different perceptions of the relevant social groups.

The lack of knowledge from the users' perspective points to the known problem—user representation. Nevertheless, in the case of large systems

Figure 2. The perception gaps along the innovation decision process of NCRS

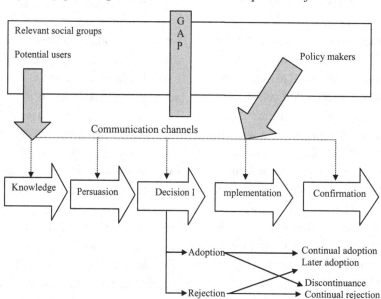

such as NCRS, the desirable involvement of users is not always an easy task. Pouloudi and Whitley (2000) note that representing the stakeholders in the UK NHS is problematic. Actors, who have been assumed to be the most easily defined, also are not always clearly represented because vital information is easily overlooked during the filtering of apparently unrelated information. Additionally, although the patients are important stakeholders, they are less involved than any others in the discussions about healthcare delivery. The doctors as stakeholders typically claim to speak for the patients; other stakeholders suspect that the doctors need an issue such as this, in order to maintain control over their own roles and the subordinate position of their patients.

The difficulties in stakeholders' representation are further deteriorating with uncertainty and instability, coming from structural changes within the NHS. The NHS has made many changes between 1980 and 1991, and each time it paused to redefine aims and re-examine boundaries. The IT systems will doubtless affect the workings of the NHS in a radical way, and in the current environment of uncertainty, the change will probably not be wholeheartedly welcomed. In addition, the tension between centralisation and decentralisation will fuel further structural change, given the centralisation of functions in IT. The state of the organisation is still fluctuating; relationships are still being hammered out, new institutions are appearing on the scene, and centralisation becomes tempting.

CONCLUSION

It is essential that responsibility for successful health care systems implementation rests with the chief executive and not delegated down the management line. Chief Executive Officers (CEOs), Chief Information Officers (CIOs), NHS Information Authority staff, and Program Leads may be ignorant of ICTs or of dealing with complex information projects. They also manage heavy workloads and may not enthusiastically embrace difficult and time-consuming projects. CEOs and CIOs are also de-motivated by fear. Managers are expected to pursue innovative solutions to health care, but at the same time, audits loom and over-expenditures as well as missed goals are scrutinised (Fairey, 2003). And finally, the clinicians who are the users of the system are only beginning to be aware of the national spine and the new computerised IT system. The findings in this case study confirm the fears raised in the Computer Weekly that this gap between the perception of the programme by ministers and IT managers on the front line could add to the problems inherent in managing such a large programme.

This research sought to demonstrate the importance of realising the lack of common understating along the innovation decision process of the NCRS. We showed that innovation of diffusions theory can not be applied without taking into consideration diverse viewpoints, concerning the innovation under investigation. There is no objective reality when it comes to the interpretation of the maturity and applicability of a technology, especially when a very large number of stakeholders are involved. The use of socio-technical theories and approaches such as social construction of technology theory can be useful in giving a more realistic and holistic view of the technology adoption reality. We believe that this research can help policy makers to realise their own position, from one hand, but also get a more realistic view of the users' perspectives, on the other. This way the users' needs can be better addressed and the seamless systems implementation and quicker closure can be a reality. Researchers in the technology adoption field can also benefit by this study, after realising the need to emphasis the socio-technical approaches to innovation diffusion studies. Future research will include the detailed identification of all relevant social groups and their perceptions with the view to get a better understanding of the NCRS diffusion process. The framework will also be used in the implementation of technologies in the healthcare domain in different geographical settings and cultural settings.

REFERENCES

Allen, J. P. (2000). Information systems as technological innovation. *Information Technology and People, 13*(3), 210-221.

Arnott, S. (2003). NHS reform makes IT a political issue, *Computing*. Retrieved January 4, 2004 from http://www.computing.co.uk/Analysis/1137926

Booth, N. (2002). *Making the right choices- using computer consultation*. Retrieved January 4, 2004 from http://www.ncl.ac.uk

CDER. (2004). *FDA/Centre for Drug Evaluation and Research, medication errors*. Retrieved November 11, 2004 from http://www.fda.gov/cder/drug/MedErrors/default.htm

Elliot, S. & Loebbecke, C. (2000). Interactive, inter-organisational innovations in electronic commerce. *Information Technology and People, 13*(1), 46-66.

ESHA (2004, July). *Strategic health authority internal NPfit staff bulletin*. (2).

Fairey, M. (2003). Barriers to the success of delivering 21st century IT support for the NHS. *British Journal of Healthcare Computing & Information Management, 20*(2), 28-31.

Firth, P. (2003). Preparing for healthcare and social care integration: Some current barriers to ICT based sharing of information. *The British Journal of Healthcare Computing & Management, 20*(5), 21-24.

Kautz, K. and Pries-Heje, J. (1996). *Diffusion and adoption of information technolog.*, London: Chapman & Hall.

Kohn, L. T., Corrigan, J.M., & Donaldson, M.S. (Eds). (2000). *To err is human: Building a safer health system*. Chicago: Institute of Medicine.

Lyytinen, K. J., & Damsgaard, J. (2001, April). *What's wrong with the diffusion of innovation theory*. Paper presented at the Diffusing software product and process innovations, Banff, Canada.

Nelson R. (1998). Computerized patient records improve practice efficiency and patient care. *Health Care Data Systems, 52*(4), 86,88.

NHS. (2002). *The NHS explained the NHS IM/T 21st century strategy*. Retrieved January 29, 2003 from http://www.nhs.uk/thenhsexplained/how_the_nhs_works.aspNHS

NHSIA. (1998). *An information strategy for the modern NHS 1998-2005, a national strategy for local implementation*. Retrieved January 29, 2003 from http://www.nhsia.nhs.uk/def/pages/info-4health/contents.asp

Papazafeiropoulou, A. (2002). *A stakeholder approach to electronic commerce diffusion*. Unpublished doctoral dissertation, Brunel University, London.

Pinch, T.J. and Bijker, W.E. (1984). The social construction of facts and artefacts: Or how the sociology of science and the sociology of technology might benefit each other. *Social Studies of Science, 14*(1), 399-441.

Pouloudi, A., & Whitley, E.A. (2000). Representing human and non-human stakeholders: On speaking with authority. *Organisational and Social Perspectives on Information Technology. Department of Information systems London School of Economics and Political Science Working Paper Series 88*. Retrieved January 4, 2004 from http://is.lse.ac.uk/wp/pdf/WP88.PDF

Rogers, E. M. (1995). *Diffusion of innovations* (4th ed.). New York: Free Press.

Walsham, G. (1993). *Interpreting information systems in organisations.* Chichester: Wiley.

Wenn, A., Tatnall, A., Sellitto, C., Darbyshire, P. & Burgess, S. (2002). *A socio-technical investigation of factors affecting IT adoption by rural GPs.* Paper presented at IT in Regional Areas, ITiRA conference, Rockhampton, Australia.

Whitfield, L. (2003). NHS staff buy-in is essential for project success. *Computing.* Retrieved January 4, 2004 from http://www.computing. co.uk/News/1143868

This work was previously published in International Journal of Technology and Human Interaction, Vol. 3, Issue 2 , edited by B. Stahl, pp. 1-12 , copyright 2007 by IGI Publishing, formerly known as Idea Group Publishing (an imprint of IGI Global).

Chapter XI
Collaboration Challenges in Community Telecommunication Networks

Sylvie Albert
Laurentian University, Canada

Rolland LeBrasseur[1]
Laurentian University, Canada

ABSTRACT

This article reviews the literature on networks and, more specifically, on the development of community telecommunication networks. It strives to understand the collaboration needed for innovative projects such as intelligent networks. Guided by a change management framework, collaboration within a community network is explored in terms of the formation and performance phases of its development. The context, content, and process of each phase is analyzed, as well as the interaction of the two phases. User involvement and technology appropriation are discussed. Collaboration challenges are identified and linked to the sustainability of the community network. Policy makers are presented with a model that gives some insight into planning and managing a community network over time.

INTRODUCTION

Collaboration in networks and managing performance across organizations has gained the attention of researchers (Huxham & Vangen, 2000). Our comprehension of collaborative networks[2] has progressed substantially over a couple of decades (Oliver & Ebers, 1998), but it lacks integration (Ebers, 2002).

Collaborative networks cover a range of purposes such as innovation requiring heavy investment in R&D, international ventures, and the delivery of public services like health and education. This chapter is focused on telecommunication networks that operate within a physical and shared community space. The more ambitious community networks aim to become "intelligent" communities with broad participation and significant impact on the local social and economic development. To understand them as a dynamic phenomenon, a framework is needed that can accommodate and organize the conceptual pillars of organizational environment, structure, culture, leadership, and management. Pettigrew (1992, 1987) offers such a framework, and Ebers (2002) and LeBrasseur et al. (2002) demonstrate its effective application.

Organizations in all sectors have become more interested in inter-organizational collaboration to encourage synergy, innovation, and economic development. Although there are many pockets of successful collaborative efforts, there is a continuing need to identify the challenges and opportunities inherent to community networks. With this focus, this chapter is divided into four main sections. First, collaborative networks are defined and described, and community telecommunication networks and their potential for supporting intelligent communities are analyzed. Second, key collaboration challenges that impact on the development of a community network are introduced. Third, the literature is reviewed and organized according to the context, content, and process involved in these community networks during their two phases of development–formation and performance. The collaboration challenges present in each phase of development are explored, including challenges that the users experience. Fourth, the chapter concludes with policy implications for network planners.

TELECOMMUNICATION NETWORKS AS AN EXAMPLE OF COLLABORATION

Collaboration is the pooling of resources (e.g., information, money, labour), by two or more stakeholders or partners[3], to solve a set of problems, which neither can solve individually (Gray, 1985). It involves an interactive process whereby

organizations, using shared rules, norms, and structures, act or decide on issues related to a problem domain (Wood & Wood, 1991). The intentional goal-oriented collaborative arrangement that emerges is that of a network (Poyhonen & Smedlund, 2004).

Networking represents a particular form of organizing or governing exchange relationships among organizations and is an alternative to markets and hierarchies (Ebers, 2002, p. 23). Network partners maintain their autonomy and retain residual property rights over their resources that have been pooled to achieve mutually agreed outcomes (Bailey & McNally-Koney, 1996; Brown et al., 1998; Gray & Hay, 1986; Huxham & Vangen, 2000; Oliver & Ebers, 1998). The principal coordination mechanisms for allocating resources are negotiation and concurrence. Informal social systems, rather than bureaucratic ones, coordinate complex products or services and reduce uncertainty (Jarillo, 1988; Jones et al., 1997).

Networks have gained in importance over the last two decades. For the private sector, globalization and the speed of change have encouraged collaborative efforts. For government, downloading[4] since the 1990s has forced new ways to view management of programs and services for resource maximization (Bradford, 2003; Bailey et al., 1996). Municipalities and regions have also demonstrated an increased interest in collaboration efforts and network development to attract new opportunities and maintain their competitive advantage. Collaborative networks typically increase the scale and visibility of program efforts, increase support for projects, and leverage capital to enhance feasibility, speed, and effectiveness (O'Toole, 1997). Synergy is achieved through improved resource management and intensive exchanges on specific projects.

To achieve synergistic gains and programming enhancements from sharing resources, risks, and rewards, stakeholders need to shift their focus toward collaborative rather than competitive advantage (Lowndes & Skelcher, 1998). Too often in the past, public sector organizations built independent silos and their private sector counterparts viewed potential partners as competitors rather than collaborators. Public policies dealing with ambitious or complex issues, like community sustainability, are likely to require networked structures that allow for the pooling and mobilization of resources from both private and public sectors within a government policy initiative (O'Toole, 1997).

Community telecommunication networks reflect the trend in western society away from bureaucratic government to network governance (Sorensen, 2002): the latter delivers more services efficiently with less risk and uncertainty (Considine & Lewis, 2003; Jones et al., 1997). Stakeholders and collaborators include municipalities, health, education, social services organizations, and private sector organizations. These networks are part of a wider agenda to increase the country's capability for the knowledge-based economy.

There are several kinds of community networks (Gurstein, 2000; Pigg 2001), ranging from those serving a restricted membership (usually called private networks) to those serving a broader segment of the community or region. A private network may, for example, link several schools and/or municipal sites, and members would include the students, administration, and staff of these organizations. In contrast, a community network is built on a platform that gives broad access to community citizens, businesses, and agencies; it encourages many stakeholders to become a user and service provider. These stakeholders may come together simply to upgrade an aging infrastructure, especially when market forces cannot be relied upon to meet community needs or to co-build economic foundations. Leading communities strive to build partnerships and synergy to overcome barriers to access, job creation, and innovation (Agres et al.,1998; Eger, 2001; Tan, 1999; Industry Canada, 2002a, 2002b). Community networks facilitate information dissemination, discussion, and joint activity by connecting neighbours, creating new opportuni-

ties, and empowering residents, institutions, and regions (Carroll & Rosson, 2001; Igbaria et al., 1999; Canadian National Broadband Task Force, 2001).

A community network has four basic components: a telecommunication infrastructure with broadband capability, applications or content, devices (such as computers, cellular telephones, i-pods, and blackberries), and users. The development of a community telecommunication network typically occurs through a governing board representing the needs of users, which is supported by a small management structure (e.g., executive committee and network manager). The network relies on information and communication technologies (ICTs) and allows the community to import and export knowledge, encourage innovation, and overcome distance. The opportunities for economic and social development are contingent on attracting many users and creating a culture of "digital" use. The network must fulfill user needs and be attentive to their requirements, which may include a fair price, access to computers and the Internet, and training and education.

Infrastructure investment in the telecommunication network aims for the widest possible coverage of the community and region, with the constraint of reasonable cost. Investment also tries to ensure that users have access devices; some users have modest means, and schools and other organizations may have budget constraints. On the human resources front, technical training of local staff may be required to install the infrastructure and devices, and provide support to users. Organizations may need to re-design processes in order to meet the changing needs of their supplier and distribution partners, and to offer services online to end-users. The transformation effort may also require promotion campaigns to attract both individual and organizational users. These many resource challenges imposed on the community require a collaborative effort to pool resources and find innovative solutions.

A community network has users at the individual, organizational, and community levels of human activity and endeavours. Individuals or end-users use the network to communicate with friends, play games, access information, obtain training, and occasionally innovate. Organizations are often stakeholders and use the network for a wide variety of purposes (Waits, 2000), including providing information and services, and selling online. They are intermediate users (Williams et al., 2005) and are the drivers of the development of the network. These organizations are the channels through which collective innovation is exercised and community change takes place (de la Mothe, 2004; Rycroft, 2003). At the community level, these individuals and organizations create aggregate demand and use of the network, and determine the sustainability of the network. The challenge is to create a culture of "digital" use that is integrated into the broader culture that is shared by community members.

During the development of the network, user involvement can be traced through participation in articulating a "digital" vision for the community, in the purchase of access devices and services that will connect users to the network (e.g., telephone, cable, wireless, computers, and Internet), and in the utilization of applications being made available through these access devices. Users may also be involved in creating employment by innovating on the network configuration, and in helping to create a culture of use by providing additional attractive applications.

Good governance requires legitimacy with an appropriate range of stakeholders, and involves building cohesion and commitment. Relationships are voluntary, and network survival depends upon the collective will and commitment of the stakeholders. The intentionally-planned network takes on a collaborative structure composed of local residents, non-governmental organizations, private sector businesses, and government. The stakeholders create a product that reflects the concerns, priorities, and aspirations of the local population. If the infrastructure, devices, and applications meet the needs of the users, a culture of "digital" use emerges as an organic extension of existing community ways and practices. Without broad participation, the network is likely to reflect narrow interests and weaken the community's social sub-system, which in turn will limit the economic success of the network.

A sustainable community telecommunication network makes consistent and positive contributions to the economic and social development of the community (ITU, 2003), thereby enhancing the community's capital base. In large measure, these positive outcomes depend upon the collaboration of partners. They also reinforce the efforts invested in collaboration. Networking allows individuals, professionals, and entrepreneurs to access information and knowledge, learn about a wide range of issues, recognize opportunities, and achieve innovative products and services (Suire, 2004; Martin & Matlay, 2003; Corbett, 2002; Ardichvili & Cardozo, 2000; Kickul & Gundry, 2000). Whether a community network realizes its potential depends upon how well it is developed.

The above discussion portrays the formal structure of a community network as a fluid organization composed of volunteers with the purpose of facilitating the community's transition and participation in the information society. However tempting, this viewpoint is non-critical in nature; it ignores the community context and processes by which the network emerges (Pigg, 2001; Day 2002).

COLLABORATION CHALLENGES FOR COMMUNITY NETWORKS

Communities around the world have demonstrated that transformation is possible using network technology. For example, Sunderland (UK) reduced unemployment from 30% to 4% by moving from a shipbuilding and coal industrial base to a knowledge and technology economy. Similarly, Spokane Washington (USA), once a railroad town reliant on natural resources, dramatically improved the fortunes of its downtown by installing the highest density of broadband in the country. In Tianjin (China), a major push on broadband connectivity was accompanied by rapid user growth, from 20,000 to 2,700,000 in two years. Their stories make ample reference to the intensive collaboration of many actors, but the patterns of influence are not well articulated.[5] Bell (2001) compared six urban communities noted for their telecommunication achievements and identified two effective patterns of collaboration: (1) a comprehensive and formal plan, and (2) a coherent pattern of individual initiatives. Similarly, Williams et al. (2005) reviewed numerous ICT initiatives, both small and large, and emphasized the overlapping nature of the planning, implementation, and use stages of development. These patterns are explored under the phases of network development section of this chapter.

Individuals and organizations involved in the creation of a community network face four collaboration challenges:

1. Defining and agreeing on the transformation effort (includes vision, transformation, and planning)
2. Assembling and mobilizing resources (includes interdependence, tasks, and structure)

3. Assembling and mobilizing trust (includes prior experience, communication, and distribution of power among collaborators)
4. Balancing leadership and collaborative management (includes the broadening requirements of the network, user appropriation, and power).

These challenges are tied to the coherence and adaptability of the network, and specifically to the dynamic relationship between the formation and performance phases of its development. Collaboration is inter-woven in each of these challenges. Network sustainability is achieved by collaboration efforts that evolve during the network's development.

PHASES OF DEVELOPMENT OF A COMMUNITY NETWORK

We propose that network development takes place in two phases that are iterative in nature. Phase 1, the formation of the community network, is marked by the emergence of a leader and/or a board of directors, to respond to environmental pressures. These pressures may occur as a result of globalization and the need to remain competitive in the face of other communities or regions. It may occur as a result of downsizing or social development pressures (e.g., lack of medical

Table 1. Influencing factors at the formation phase

Context	Content	Process
• Economy • Social/cultural • Political • Urbanization • Funding • Technology • Globalization & competition • Cost Benefit/ Synergy	• Vision • Power • Board Membership • Concept of Sustainability • User representation	• Values • Expectations • Goals • Planning • Leadership (transformational, visionary)

practitioners, youth out-migration). The broad goals of the network are developed, including a representation of the future user. Phase 2, network performance, involves the concrete objectives and steps that the board takes to achieve the community goals that were agreed upon and the measures taken to attract and retain users. User involvement can and should take place in both phases of development.

Smaller communities need collaborators to solve a wide variety of challenges including infrastructure availability. Larger communities tend to have more resources and thus need collaboration to resolve economic and social pressures rather than infrastructure issues. In this second phase, the network can develop a culture and structure that gives meaning and coherence to a variety of projects. Some communities are more liberal and hands-off, allowing the private sector and citizens to develop content and opportunity. Others intentionally plan a vision of community transformation based on an improved telecommunication infrastructure. Phase 1 depends highly on leadership dynamics whereas Phase 2 is closer to managerial dynamics but with a distinctive collaborative flavor. These two phases are interdependent over time in that formation sets the stage for performance, and performance impacts on the board and leadership dynamics. Positive outcomes at the performance phase consolidate the dynamics of the formation phase; negative outcomes challenge the board and leadership and initiate a re-formation phase. This iterative process was demonstrated in the feedback loop identified by Arino and de la Torre (1998) and Thomas (1993).

Because networks are fluid in nature (pooling from existing resources, changing membership, and varied timelines) and focused on both results and relationships, two interactive phases are considered sufficient. The two phases are supported by case studies of strategic alliances (Doz, 1996) that found that successful partners actively exchanged information, re-evaluated the project (in terms of efficiency, equity and adaptability), and consequently readjusted the initial conditions of their cooperation. They are also consistent with the ICT social learning findings of Williams et al. (2005).

Formation Phase

The push and pull factors in the environment impact on the community members and prompt them to consider uniting their forces to address the issue or opportunity that has been identified. Under the leadership of a visionary, and through ample interpersonal communication, a group is assembled that represents the initial membership of a potential network. If a consensus on vision and goals is attained, the group becomes the founding board of a network and plans for the performance phase. The principal outcome is a collaborative base on which to build the network. Table 1 provides an overview of the critical factors present in the formation phase.

Context of Formation

The outer context or environment includes factors such as economic, political, culture, demographics, funding opportunities, pressures from government agencies, and technology innovation trends (Agres et al.,1998; Bailey & McNally-Koney, 1996; Igbaria et al., 1999; Keenan & Trotter, 1999; and Tan, 1999). Global competitiveness and turbulence are the underlying catalysts for creating networks for organizations, communities, and governments (Poyhonen & Smedlund, 2004; Scheel, 2002).

Interdependencies exist because organizations possess or control vital resources (material, human, political, structural, or symbolic) and thus are the source of environmental pressures for one another (Wood & Wood, 1991). Organizations seek to reduce these pressures and manage the interdependencies by gaining control over crucial resource supplies. The network form, as opposed to markets and hierarchies (e.g., vertical integration), provides a neutral space within which organizations can meet to explore solutions and synergies.

International bodies such as the World Bank (1999), the United Nations (1998), and OECD (1997) have adopted the paradigm of the information society as a guide to many of their development policies. According to Castells (1996, 1997, 1998), ICTs have produced a network society in which mobilizing knowledge and information have become more important than mobilizing physical resources. He argued that both organizations and individuals can benefit from electronic networks; they support the development and dissemination of knowledge and information, and facilitate innovation. Castells warns that these changes are accompanied by growing wealth disparities, social fragmentation, and dislocation. Governments are addressing these concerns, in part, by financially supporting the creation of community networks with broad accessibility. Locally, these new opportunities are often communicated through the chamber of commerce and other economic development agencies to mobilize or inspire stakeholders into action.

Communities come in all sizes and density, and all are influenced by the urbanization trend. Rural settings are witnessing the exodus of their youth and an erosion of their economic base as cities attract both talent and investment, including initiatives in telecommunications (OECD, 2004). Recent studies of Canadian rural communities concluded that ICTs can act as enablers of community building and development processes (New Economy Development Group Inc., 2001; Canadian Advisory Committee on Rural Issues, 2004). Given that the Internet is content-rich, offers online education, facilitates social networking, and offers a platform for the creation of new enterprises and the expansion of existing ones, the viability of the digital community network becomes crucial for the future of small communities.

When governments create generous programs to create community networks (e.g., Brown et al., 1998), communities are pressured to apply for capital funds even when they may not have the organizational and resource capacity to sustain the network. Smaller communities have relatively fewer and less diverse resources and a push-style policy may be the only way to spur action. Another example of a push factor is when a major telecom firm seeks a community partner for a demonstration project, or when the private sector chooses to make an investment to upgrade its infrastructure. The telecom supplies the ICTs, but the community stakeholders still need to demonstrate and plan on how the technology can be applied to personal and organizational purposes. Often, infrastructure is built and languishes until there are other pressures in the environment of the community, such as closure of a major employer or the arrival of a strong champion. At other times, communities struggle with the lack of open access that inhibits economic development and competition. Pushing for open access can discourage the involvement of incumbent carriers, at least at the onset. The key here is to evaluate how context issues can stimulate communities into action toward their transformation.

Content of Formation

Stakeholders need to find the community vision attractive and see a benefit for themselves and for their organization. When the problem is broad in scope and complex, such as economic development, it requires a larger variety of stakeholders with legitimate interest to devise solutions and bring sufficient resources to bear. Stakeholders must have the right and the capacity to participate, and include organizations with legitimate power as well as those who will be affected by the network.

Collaborative action necessarily involves interdependence between individuals and organizations (Ouchi, 1980) and can yield both intangible (e.g., image of citizenship) and tangible benefits (e.g., cost reductions and additional revenues). Interdependence is strongly linked to the vision of the network and the factors motivating stakeholders. It allows for an exchange among stakeholders that is built on trust, and an understanding of mutual benefit or advantage. According to Olk and Young (1997), the more ties an organization has to others in a network, the less likely is it to act opportunistically. Blois (1990) argued that collaborators should engage in bargaining on who will accept responsibility for certain elements of the transaction costs. They must come to the table understanding their role and develop a level of interdependence and mutual benefit in order to sustain the network effort.

The economic and social exchanges that take place are mediated by mutual trust. Ring (2002) distinguishes between "fragile" and "resilient" trust. The former is typical of opportunistic settings such as markets and involves the formal processes of negotiation, transaction, and administration. In contrast, the latter is the foundation of successful networks and is based on the informal processes of sense-making, understanding, and commitment. However, prescribing resilient trust does not ensure that is takes place. Ring proposed that it will emerge when the participants have a shared history of experience and when reputations for reliability are well established. On the other hand, Doz (1996) has documented the role of trusted intermediaries in helping other participants to shift gradually from fragile to resilient trust. We conclude that if a community has rich social relations, it can establish resilient trust early, but that parachuting in partners and stakeholders makes fragile trust more likely. However, if trusted intermediaries become involved, they can build the level of trust within the network.

There is a need for legitimate authority, credibility, and multiple memberships (Bailey & McNally-Koney, 1996; Gray & Hay, 1986) if a sustained transformation is to occur. Jones et al. (1997) have argued that networks need to restrict membership access and choose its members according to their reputation and status. Important stakeholders may choose to join a network or a project because of the presence of other members. A smaller number of leaders may allow the network to realize quick wins, reduce coordination costs, and improve interaction frequency. One could argue that success will breed success—trust will increase, motivation will increase, and faster output can be generated. This view is less applicable to community networks where innovation, legitimacy, and broad reach is critical and leads to a large membership and numerous exchanges. Therefore, a smaller, more restricted network may be mobilized quickly and act efficiently, but be less effective in producing varied output. The larger network may slow the pace of change, but may be important enough to attract accomplished leaders. Structure issues become important in managing a larger group of stakeholders and are discussed in the performance phase of the network.

Another content issue is sustainability. Stakeholders want to know, "How much will it cost," but few ask "How will the network become sustainable in the long-run?" Sustainability is a function of revenues (stemming from the use of the infrastructure and its applications), and the costs of the network (human resources, equipment, and materials). There are opportunities for synergistic gains when partners chose to purchase as a group, or share the operating costs. At the formation phase, the concept of sustainability is hazy, but becomes clearer as projects develop during the performance phase. Nevertheless, the board must carefully address the sustainability issue early to ensure that it becomes incorporated into their common frame of reference.

In the formation stage, the planning includes an explicit model of future users, their communication needs, and their likely use of the telecommunication network. Williams et al. (2005, p. 112, Figure 5.2) identify ways for direct involvement of users, such as user panels, market research, and trials. They also identify sources of indirect evidence about users through information on demand and markets for similar products, and competitive offerings. With the additional input of board members who understand their community, a representation of the users is developed. This user-centered approach is helpful in guiding the design of the system and identifying training and promotion requirements. However, Williams et al., emphasize its limitations and the design fallacy that it breeds: "the presumption that the primary solution to meeting user needs is to build ever more extensive knowledge about the specific context and purposes of an increasing number and variety of users in the technology design" (p.102). The idea of perfect user representation ignores the reality that users are active agents and appropriate the technology later, primarily in the performance phase of network development.

Communities would be wise to involve users in all facets of their formation stage, but users are often thought of as passive participants that can be surveyed for the eventual purchase of devices or services at the performance stage. Yet, users have concerns over ownership, access and distribution of information, privacy, security, and copyrights (Agres et al., 1998), and most of these issues need consideration early on. However, the design fallacy mentioned above emphasizes the limitations of comprehensive user involvement in the formation phase.

Process of Formation

Leaders and champions can enhance or constrain the development of a community network (Industry Canada, 2002; Jones et al., 1997; Huxham & Vangen, 2000). Leaders tap into the collective awareness of the community stakeholders and mobilize the initial change efforts by supplying a vision and practical steps to realize it (Bailey & McNally-Koney, 1996; Roberts & Bradley, 1991). Sustaining collaboration depends on the emergence of a common view of the community

and shared organizational values. Leaders and champions play a role in consolidating and expanding the collaborative initiatives, but a wider involvement is needed to foster innovation. It is important to have a community cross-section of members as well as individuals with sufficient power to rally other stakeholders. The parties must freely participate, knowing and agreeing on who is involved and in what capacity (Glatter, 2004; Roberts & Bradley, 1991); prior experience and trust facilitate the membership drive.

Network goals are created, implemented, evaluated, and modified through purposeful social construction among network stakeholders and partners (Van de Ven & Poole, 1995; Ring & Van de Ven, 1994). Network effectiveness may be defined as the harmonization, pursuit, and attainment of the goals sought by the various stakeholders and partners. With diverse stakeholders, it becomes difficult to satisfy all parties equally; therefore, managing expectations and potential conflicts help to maintain the social cohesion of the network. Members will likely persist so long as they can positively identify with the intermediate and long term outcomes, whether they are social or economic in nature.

According to Hardy and Phillips (1998), when individuals come to share a vision of the issues and the solutions, they become stakeholders and begin to create a collective identity with mutually agreed upon directions and boundaries that, in time, may become a permanent network. The catalyst is a transformational leader who encourages collaboration as a means to create synergy for innovation, growth, or to protect against future turbulence. Engaging the stakeholders in a planning exercise can address their many concerns; tasks and roles can be organized and assigned within the network to fit their expectations. Because work is complex and elaborate in networks, planning and coordinating task-specialized activities is required (Roberts & Bradley, 1991). However, planning follows the visioning that the leader has enacted.

Challenges in the Formation Phase

Defining and Agreeing on the Transformation Effort

It is argued that a multi-sectoral and multi-organizational network is needed for a transformation to an intelligent community. The wide variety of stakeholders impact the style of leadership and structure needed for joint initiatives. The leader (or leaders in the case of shared roles) shares a vision of a desirable future and initiates a flexible structure that can accommodate differences in orientation (profit versus not for profit), time horizons (short versus long term), and civic engagement (self versus community focus). Given the diversity of stakeholders, the visioning must be consistent and persuasive, but large enough in scope so that stakeholders can personalize the vision to suit their personal and organizational interests. Key activities include:

- Utilizing context issues to create a sense of urgency and sell the concept of the community network
- Identifying solutions to problems and synergistic opportunities
- Preparing a plan for producing meaningful and motivating outcomes

Agreeing on the vision depends on the availability and abilities of the local leader. Individuals with strong communication skills, an established reputation of trustworthiness, an ability to deliver on promises made, and conceptual skills to craft a vision are in short supply. While large communities have a greater pool of candidates, small communities may have to draw more on external talent and work hard on establishing trustworthiness.

Assembling and Mobilizing Resources

The community network depends upon its board to acquire the physical, financial, and organizational resources that make a broadband network functional. Collaboration among stakeholders and partners facilitates the pooling of their resources. Choosing board members should flow from resource requirements and the likelihood that the stakeholders recruited or volunteering are favorably disposed to sharing with other organizations. Community citizenship of board members channels the resources to create and enhance the network. Key activities include:

- Assembling the representatives of a variety of public and private sector organizations to form the board, including both small and large stakeholders;
- Mobilizing the resources controlled by board members and reaching out to obtain vital resources from the environment.

Too many resources may harm the development of the network if the board lacks the capability to make good use of them. Waste would damage the network's reputation and make future resource acquisitions more difficult. Likewise, too few resources can harm the network because the scope of activities would be narrow and appeal to only a small segment of the community's population. A narrow focus would appear self-serving and lack broad legitimacy.

Assembling and Mobilizing Trust

For the board to be effective in creating and enhancing the network's resource base, its members must trust each other so that extensive sharing becomes possible. When stakeholders engage in joint efforts and initiatives, they are putting the community first and themselves second, making them vulnerable to exploitation by less citizen-minded organizations. When trust exists on the board, stakeholders can tolerate some exposure. Therefore building and maintaining trust in a realistic manner is essential to the network's resource base and projects. Key activities include:

- Assembling the board membership on the basis of reputation, prior experience, and diversity of stakeholders;
- Creating a shared vision that reflects the underlying values of community spirit;
- Distinguishing between fragile and resilient trust, and building the latter.

Building and maintaining resilient trust is at the core of the inter-dependent culture that emerges in the network. When a transformational vision is complemented with solid resources and trust, the community network has met the challenges of the formation phase of its development and is ready to shift into the performance phase.

Performance Phase of Development

The performance phase of network development is centred on concrete projects that require the pooling of resources by its members. The resources may be tangible (finances, staff secondment, office space, and equipment) and intangible (time, information, influence, and reputation) in nature. Pooling is facilitated by both the culture and structure of the network in which horizontal interactions, exchanges among equals, are based on trust. These resources are organized and controlled to attain the project objectives, and the management style is collaborative and accountable to the membership of the network. Pursuing these objectives gives collaborators opportunities to learn how they can make the network function

effectively. In the short term, the level of attainment of the project's objectives dominates; small wins and their public recognition are important to confirm the value of the network (Bouwen & Taillieu, 2004). Effective project management is needed. In the long term, the board focuses on the level of attainment of the broad goals of the network. To ensure that the projects and the general management of the network are aligned with the original vision and goals, effective leadership is required. Table 2 provides an overview of the critical factors in the performance phase.

CONTEXT OF PERFORMANCE

The interdependence of members within a community network is reflected in both its structure (O'Toole, 1997) and culture. Structure requires careful attention because a poor structure—one that gives too much power to one partner or that does not embody the values of stakeholders—will affect the performance and longevity of the collaboration.

Poyhonen and Smedlund (2004) and Nooteboom (1999) identified three network structures: vertical, horizontal, and diagonal. The latter consists of firms and organizations from several different lines of business. A diagonal structure is appropriate for community networks because it includes as many collaborators as possible to create synergy and innovation within and between sectors; transformational, as opposed to incremental

Table 2. Influencing factors at the performance phase

Context	Content	Process
- Structure - Roles - Trust - Power of stakeholders - Interdependence & Culture	- Goals - Achievement/output - Innovation	- Team management - User appropriation - Communication

change, is facilitated. The success of collaborative networks is contingent on managing the ambiguity, complexity, and dynamics of the structure. It becomes more important in the performance phase because it must sustain an action plan and organize resources to carry it out. However, a telecommunication network is developed to resolve dynamic context issues and can only do so within a process of continuous improvement. A rigid structure that minimizes innovation diminishes the network's sustainability. Though difficult to assess, the effectiveness of the structure can be judged by its internal coherence and fit with the culture of the network. This puzzle, identified by Bailey & McNally-Koney (1996), needs a solution that retains the fluidity of communications and decision-making, while providing for a framework for productivity and sustainability.

Collaboration is associated with incremental innovation when partners share on several levels: a larger purpose, explicit and voluntary membership, an interactive process, and temporal property (Roberts & Bradley, 1991). Hardy and Phillips (1998) pointed out that more powerful stakeholders may force collaboration on weaker players to control them. Consequently, there is a lessening of the level of interdependence and common vision. Weaker stakeholders are bound to minimize their participation and find excuses to exit the network when they are being coerced. Though asymmetrical power is a likely reality, leaders that seek innovation must put less emphasis on control and more on incentives and opportunities.

Creating a culture of collaboration gives coherence to the stream of actions that builds the community network. Collaboration is described as a relational system of individuals within groups in which individuals share mutual aspirations and a common conceptual framework (Bailey & McNally-Koney, 1996). Individuals are guided by their sense of fairness and their motives toward others (caring and concern, and commitment to work together over time). Through communica-

tion and shared experiences, they create a system of shared assumptions and values, and accepted approaches and solutions to problems, including collective sanctions, to safeguard exchanges and reinforce acceptable behaviors (Jones et al., 1997). Sanctions may include exclusion from certain benefits (present or future) and opportunities (participation in projects), and as a last measure forced exit (temporary or permanent) from the network.

Collaborators often choose to stay in a poorly performing network based on the strength of their social ties. However, if they conclude that they can meet all of their needs outside of the network, they may view the network as superfluous (Brown et al., 1998). Linkages or interdependence must be solid and intentional (Bailey & McNally-Koney, 1996) and may be a strong indicator of sustainability (Olk & Young, 1997). Conversely, Brown et al. (1998) identified that greater resource interdependence makes successful partnerships more difficult to achieve. In order to find common ground and encourage persistence, the reasons for enhancing an interdependence need to be emphasized, and stakeholders must want to belong and believe in the vision.

Content of Performance (Specific Projects)

The content of performance includes a wide variety of projects that meet the goals of the network, including the needs of stakeholders and users. Among them are projects to launch or upgrade an infrastructure, acquire devices to deliver applications, develop content for the network, and promote the network to potential users. The outcomes include cost savings to deliver services, revenues from users, and additional capability for the social and economic development of the community.

Waits (2000) described collaborative networks in terms of their pursuits:

- **Co-inform:** Actions to identify members and impacts, promote a heightened awareness of the issues, and improve communication among the members;
- **Co-learn:** Educational and training programs sponsored by the network;
- **Co-market:** Collective activities that promote member products or services abroad or domestically;
- **Co-purchase:** Activities to strengthen buyer supplier linkages or to jointly buy expensive equipment;
- **Co-produce:** Alliances to make a product together or conduct R&D together;
- **Co-build economic foundations:** Activities to build stronger educational, financial, and governmental institutions that enable them to compete better.

Some of these pursuits appear easier to realize and only require fragile trust (co-inform and co-learn). They are more likely to give quick "small wins." Others may be challenging and require resilient trust (co-market, co-purchase, and co-produce); their success will take more time but are more highly valued. Co-building economic foundations appeals less to self-interest and more to a communal interest, and depends on a broad vision that will lead to a series of concrete actions and sustained effort. Waits' objectives are compatible with each other, but have different time horizons and commitments. The strength of the formation phase influences the commitment of stakeholders in the development phase. In particular, a strong collaborative climate encourages them to be patient and willing to invest additional time and resources to achieve long term goals.

PROCESS OF PERFORMANCE

Leaders require managerial sophistication to recognize appropriate circumstances and tools for collaboration (Glatter, 2004). In networks,

collaboration depends upon an ongoing communicative process (Lawrence et al., 1999). Roles and responsibilities are negotiated in a context where no legitimate authority is necessarily recognized (Glatter, 2004; Lawrence et al., 1999; Lowndes & Skelcher, 1998). Like in partnerships, there is concern for trust, politics, emotions, and results. Furthermore, leaders require an understanding of user appropriation of the digital network to effectively channel the collaborative efforts.

Du Gay et al. (1997) describe the appropriation of technology as an active process in which users make choices around the selection and local deployment of the technological components, and create meaning and sense of the technology. Appropriation has both a technical and cultural side. In this spirit, Williams et al. (2005) have argued that user appropriation has two distinct but inter-related processes: innofusion (users adjust and innovate to improve the usefulness of the technology) and domestication (users adapt the use of the technology to integrate it meaningfully in their activities). When both processes are fully engaged, the community may be said to have a "digital" culture that sustains the network.

The pace of change within the network must be properly managed. Effective use of communication will allow collaborators to react and contribute. Because of large boards and membership and turnover in representation, some collaborators may not know everyone or their status. Indeed, some may be confused over the degree of autonomy they have in making decisions for their organization (Huxham & Vangen, 2000). Changes in government mandates and organizational priorities create uncertainty as collaborators plan and structure the network. Communication and recognition of accomplishments become important to keep everyone focused.

The board's effectiveness in tackling problems within their community as well as within their respective organizations will directly influence the achievement of the intelligent community objectives. Leaders need to guide the board and create bridges with important outside players. They must align the requirements of their own organization with the vision of the intelligent community initiative for success; they must create a high performance team environment (Albert, 2005; Wheelan, 1999; Smith, 1994). This standard is not easily achievable, especially for a volunteer board with diverse membership and affiliation.

Challenges in the Performance Phase

Continuing Challenges from the Formation Phase

The consensus on the community vision that was created in the formation phase needs to be reinforced. The leader can remind stakeholders of the urgency to capture opportunities, but must incorporate measures for sustaining collective efforts. Key transformation activities include:

- Expanding planning and monitoring projects and measures of performance;
- Marketing the network concept to mobilize and gain the support of the wider community and further engage the stakeholders.

In terms of resources, the community network continues to depend upon its board to acquire resources to develop, acquire, and develop applications to attract numerous users. Key activities include:

- Modifying board membership to improve the resource base of the network as projects change over time;
- Engaging both small and large partners for innovation to create new resources;
- Creating a small management structure for the performance phase of the network.

As for trust, the performance phase requires continuing sharing of resources in the face of uncertain outcomes. Key activities include:

- Applying different trust standards as the situation warrants;
- Encouraging the broad sharing of resources instead of specialized contributions.

Resilient trust can block new stakeholders and partners from joining the network; they may have key resources but be deemed untrustworthy. In such a case, the network requires the flexibility to resort to fragile trust with its emphasis on formal agreements and contracts. The reverse situation can also damage the network, when fragile trust dominates relationships. While formal contracts increase accountability of the parties, they are narrow in scope and participation is contingent on self-interests being satisfied. Community considerations remain secondary. In time and through active leadership, these new members may buy into community citizenship through association and success.

Balancing Leadership and Collaborative Management

Both the formation and performance phases of development have their champion. The leader dominates the formation (and re-formation) phase through visioning, planning, and attracting and retaining stakeholders with key resources and disposed to collaborate. The manager guides and maintains the performance phase, and ensures that both tangible and intangible benefits are created for the stakeholders and the community.

The "collaborative" manager is needed to reinforce the user appropriation by supporting the innofusion and domestication in which users engage. By encouraging the involvement of intermediaries (e.g., Chamber of Commerce, owner of a cybercafé, entrepreneur who wants to keep control), the network manager allows the network to evolve along lines that reflect the different groups and segments in the community's population (Williams et al., 2005).

Formal planning becomes less important, as a pattern of coherent projects becomes established. At the same time, these intermediaries (or small groups of individuals in large networks) interact to keep the board informed and reinforce their individual efforts. By working together, they ensure that the vision of the network creates a coherent set of initiatives and projects, and opportunities and issues relevant to the board meetings are identified. Key activities include:

- Encouraging innovation and proper planning to achieve the transformation effort;
- Reaching out to intermediaries to broaden user involvement;
- Ensuring that the vision that binds the board members remains true to the community values as the network develops and expands;
- Confronting head-on the need to modify the board composition to respond to internal or external factors;
- Managing projects with a blend of fragile and resilient trust, the former with binding contracts and the latter with negotiation and concurrence;
- Choosing projects that are likely to succeed and that are valued by the stakeholders;
- Building and maintaining redundant communication systems, both formal and informal, to reflect the culture of inter-dependence that binds the stakeholders of the network.

The network can be damaged by a dominant leader or manager who insists on being involved at all times and on controlling the process, whether at the board or project level. This situation emerges when there is a failure to share multiple roles and to act as a team. The lack of experienced persons may push one individual to assume both the leadership and managerial role; this solution ensures positive momentum, but may block future sharing of roles as the incumbent becomes entrenched. Similarly, the abundance of strong and experienced personalities facilitates the sharing of roles, but

may slow down momentum as too many persons insist on prominence. Developing a team spirit among members of the board and management should be encouraged as early as possible in the network's development (Albert, 2005).

Collaboration Challenges for Users

At the formation stage, the infrastructure and applications are planned and guided by a vision. Stakeholder requirements are addressed in the planning of the network through the methods of user representation. At the performance stage, when the network is functional, the users actualize the network in both expected and emerging ways. A community network is validated by the applications it makes available to its users, and the extent to which the users actually use them. Furthermore, the design features of the telecommunication network influence the collaboration opportunities that the network creates. When the network design enhances collaboration, it has succeeded in creating effective socio-technical patterns (Huysman & Wulf, 2005; Evans & Brooks, 2005).

Challenges for Individual Users

IT and a community network challenge the individual because they put into question existing ideas and routines, and add knowledge and skill requirements. Being open to change means making efforts to understand and use the network. The younger generation makes more use of the internet than the established older generation for social contact and is likely to push for internet connection in the home (Bernier & Laflamme, 2005; Crowley, 2002). The older adults are more likely to be introduced to ICT changes in the workplace. Age aside, the Internet facilitates the local-global link through which knowledge and expertise from around the world can be channelled to community members (Stevenson, 2002). Creative individuals can interact to exchange expertise and create innovations (e.g., open source development), and are motivated by reputation and recognition built into the Web site (Fischer et al., 2004). To generate ideas, group support systems that ensure anonymity appear more effective (Pissarra & Jesuino, 2005). In general, the individual must learn to assess the trustworthiness of the Internet information sources (Franklin, 1999; May, 2002) and assume risks when making transactions online. Similarly, participating in virtual communities and discussion forums challenges the individual to change roles from spectator to contributor (Ginsberg, 2001) and activist.

Challenges for Organizational Users

Organizations that are stakeholders in the community network need to share their "network" vision with their board members, managers, employees, and organizational partners within their supply chains and customer/client networks. Key individuals likely were involved in the network formation stage to ensure that the design of the systems would support expected transactions and activities. At the performance stage, each organization is challenged to mobilize its ICTs, skill base and network use, and do so in dialogue and coordination with their organizational networks. Internally, this means empowering employees and lower levels of management through information systems and decision-making authority. Externally, this refers to the network of relations and the integration of the organizational and community networks. Failure to have extensive collaboration diminishes the benefits that the community network can deliver to stakeholders. Knowledge sharing (Van den Hooff et al., 2004) and knowledge management (Ackerman & Haverton, 2004) are useful frameworks for channelling this collaboration. In addition, involvement can include intra-preneurship (Von Oetinger, 2005) and joint ventures supported by collaborative groupware (McKnight & Bontis, 2002). The organization can also reach out to innovators and entrepreneurs in

the community, who view the network as their business platform, and initiate partnerships. The above array of activities pushes leaders and senior managers to adopt an organizational model that incorporates trust.

Challenges for the Community

As the community network is fully implemented, the stewardship vision (Block, 1993) incipient in the formation phase must be reinforced by extending inclusiveness to all segments of the local population, imagining a broad culture of use, and providing for economic development with a digital component. Community leaders should have concrete programs to diminish access barriers such as network connectivity at a reasonable cost (or at no cost for public terminals) and to training and education. Adoption of the network will vary across socio-economic dimensions, and programs are needed that are adapted to specific groups such as youth, seniors, and the non-profit and small business sectors. Developing and implementing these programs can take place with community stakeholders in collaborative projects. An innovation culture (Martins & Terblanche, 2003), linked to the network, can be encouraged.

A culture of "digital" use is emerging in many communities; the Internet and its many activities are being integrated into everyday routines of social communication, work, and play (Bernier & Laflamme, 2005; Crowley, 2002; Wellman et al., 2001). In contrast, civic participation has had less success. The evidence indicates that internet use reinforces civic participation and makes it more sophisticated, but does not increase the levels of activity (Shah, 2002; Uslaner, 2004; Warkentin & Mingst, 2000; Wellman et al., 2001). Pigg (2001) has argued that networks can be designed to enhance civic participation, but so far, these designs have failed to incorporate the nature of participation. The designs typically focus on customer services and support instead of sharing of information, ideas, and knowledge to influence civic decisions. With a customer focus, the civic authorities may increase the satisfaction of its citizenry, whereas a participation focus obliges the authorities to share decision-making powers and accept more uncertainty in the process and outcomes.

CONCLUSION

A community network faces four inter-related collaboration challenges during its development that are tied to transformation, resources, trust, and management. When these challenges are met, the network will have a solid culture and structure of interdependence, and the flexibility to change over time. The network will maintain a positive momentum that is constructive and manageable, and lead to medium and long-term sustainability. When these challenges are not met adequately, the pace of change will be either too slow or too fast, or blocked at some point in time. Sustainability of the network will be compromised unless the underlying issues are addressed.

These four challenges are anchored in the proposed network development model where formation and performance phases, and adaptation through reformation are critical for the sustainability of the community network. Policy makers and change agents among the stakeholders of community networks are well advised to shape their interventions with the aim of establishing and maintaining positive momentum, while paying continued attention to issues of visioning, resources, trust, leadership, and management. They would do well to expand their views of technology development to include user appropriation and the challenges that users face. They must accept the uncertainty that is inevitable with user involvement to support the goal of network sustainability.

REFERENCES

Ackerman, M., & Haverton, C. (2004). Sharing expertise: The next step for knowledge management. In M. Huysman & V. Wulf (Eds.) *Social capital and information technology* (Chapter 11). Cambridge, USA and London, England: The MIT Press.

Agres, C., Edberg, D., & Igbaria, M. (1998). Transformation to virtual societies: Forces and issues. *The Information Society, 14*(2), 71-82.

Albert, S. (2005). Smart community networks: Self-directed team effectiveness in action. *Team Performance Management, 1*(5), 144-156.

Ardichvili, A., & Cardozo, R. N. (2000). A model of the entrepreneurial opportunity recognition process. *Journal of Entreprising Culture, 8*(2), 103-119.

Arino, A., & de la Torre, J. (1998). Learning from failure: Towards an evolutionary model of collaborative ventures. *Organizational Science, 9*(3), 306-325.

Bailey, Darlyne, & McNally-Koney, K. (1996). Interorganizational community-based collaboratives: A strategic response to shape the social work agenda. *Social Work, 41*(6), 602-610.

Bell, R. (2001). *Benchmarking the intelligent community—a comparison study of regional communities.* The Intelligent Community Forum of World Teleport Association.

Bernier, C., & Laflamme, S. (2005). Uses of the Internet according to type and age: A double differentiation. [Usages d'Internet selon le genre et l'age: Une double differenciation] *The Canadian Review of Sociology and Anthropology/La Revue Canadienne De Sociologie Et d'Anthropologie, 42*(3), 301-323.

Block, P. (1993). *Stewardship—Choosing service over self-interest.* San Francisco: Berrett-Koehler Publishers.

Blois, K. (1990). Research notes and communications—transaction costs and networks. *Strategic Management Journal, 11*, 493-496.

Bouwen, R., & Taillieu, T. (2004). Multi-party collaboration as social learning for interdependence: Developing relational knowing for sustainable natural resource management. *Journal of Community & Applied Social Psychology, 14*, 137-153.

Bradford, R. (2003). Public-private partnerships? Shifting paradigms of economic governance in Ontario. *Canadian Journal of Political Sciences, 36*(5), 1005-1033.

Brown, M., O'Toole, L., & Brudney, J. (1998). Implementing information technology in government: An empirical assessment of the role of local partnerships. *Journal of Public Administration Research and Theory, 8*(4), 499-525.

Canadian National Broadband Taskforce. (2001). *Report of the national broadband taskforce: The new national dream: Networking the nation for broadband access.* Ottawa, Canada: Industry Canada.

Canadian Rural Partnership. (2004, October). *Report of the advisory committee on rural issues.* Paper presented at the Third National Rural Conference, Red Deer, Canada.

Carroll, J. M., & Rosson, M. (2001). Better home shopping or new democracy? Evaluating community network outcomes. *3*(1), 372-377.

Castells, M. (1996). *The rise of network society, vol. 1 of the information age: Economy, society and culture.* Oxford: Blackwell.

Castells, M. (1997). *The power of identity, vol. 2 of the information age: Economy, society and culture.* Oxford: Blackwell.

Castells, M. (1998). *End of millennium, vol. 3 of the information age: Economy, society and culture.* Oxford: Blackwell.

Caves, R. (2001). E-commerce and information technology: Information technologies, economic development, and smart communities: Is there a relationship? *Economic Development Review, 17*(3), 6-13.

Considine, M., & Lewis, J. (2003). Networks and interactivity: Making sense of front-line governance in the United Kingdom, the Netherlands and Australia. *Journal of European Public Policy, 10*(1), 46-58.

Corbett, A. (2002). Recognizing high-tech opportunities: A learning and cognitive approach. *Frontiers of Entrepreneurship Research* (pp. 49-60).Wellesley, MA: Babson College.

Crowley, D. (2002). Where are we now? Contours of the internet in Canada. *Canadian Journal of Communication, 27*(4), 469-508.

Day, C. (2002). *The information society—a sceptical view.* Malden, MA: Blackwell Publishers.

De la Mothe, J. (2004). The institutional governance of technology, society, and innovation. *Technology in Society, 26*, 523-536.

Doz,Y. (1996). The evolution of cooperation in strategic alliances: Initial conditions or learning processes? *Strategic Management Journal, 17*, 55-83.

Du Gay, P., Hall, S., Janes, L., Mackay, H., & Negus, K. (1997). *Doing cultural studies: The story of the Sony, Walkman,* London and New Delhi: Sage.

Ebers, M. (2002). *The formation of inter-organizational networks.* Oxford: Oxford University Press.

Eger, J. (2001, November). *The world foundation for smart communities.* Retrieved January 28, 2003 from www.smartcommunities.org

Evans, J., & Brooks, L. (2005). Understanding collaboration using new technologies: A structural perspective. *Information Society, 21*(3), 215-220.

Fischer, G., Scharff, E., & Ye, Y. (2004). In M. Huysman & V. Wulf (Eds.). *Social capital and information technology* (Chapter 14). Cambridge, MA and London: The MIT Press.

Franklin, U. (1999). *The real world of technology.* Toronto: House of Anansi Press.

Ginsburg, M. (2001, November). *Realizing a framework to create, support, and understand virtual communities.* Maastricht, Holland: Infonomics.

Glatter, R. (2004). Collaboration, collaboration, collaboration: The origins and implications of a policy. *MiE, 17*(5), 16-20.

Gray, B. (1985). Conditions facilitating interorganizational collaboration. *Human Relations, 38*(10), 911-936.

Gray, B., & Hay, T. (1986). Political limits to interorganizational consensus and change. *The Journal of Applied Behavioral Science, 22*(2), 95-112.

Gurstein, M. (2000). *Community informatics: Enabling communities with information and communications technologies* (Introduction, pp. 1-29). Hershey, PA: Idea Group Publishing.

Hardy, C., & Phillips, N. (1998). Strategies of engagement: Lessons from the critical examination of collaboration and conflict in interorganizational domain. *Organizational Science, 2,* 217-230.

Hock, D. (2000). Birth of the chaordic age, *Executive Excellence, 17*(6), 6-7.

Huxham, C., & Vangen, S. (2000). Ambiguity, complexity and dynamics in the membership of collaboration. *Human Relations, 53*(6), 771-805.

Huysman, M., & Wulf, V. (2004). *Social capital and information technology.* Cambridge, MA and London: The MIT Press.

Huysman, M., & Wulf, V. (2005). The role of information technology in building and sustaining the relational base of communities. *The Information Society, 21*(2), 81-89.

Igbaria, M., Shayo, C., & Olfman, L. (1999). *On becoming virtual: The driving forces and arrangements* (pp. 27-41). New Orleans, LA: ACM.

Industry Canada. (2002a, April 4). *Fostering innovation and use.* Retrieved July 30, 2002 from http://broadband.gc.ca/Broadband-document/english/chapter5.htm

Industry Canada. (2002b, April 4). *Smart communities broadband.* Retrieved July 12, 2002 from http://smartcommunities.ic.gc.ca/index_e.asp

ITU (International Telecommunications Union). (2003). *World summit on the information society* (pp. 1-9). Retrieved from www.itu.int

Jarillo, C. (1988). On strategic networks. *Strategic Management Journal, 9*(1), 31-41.

Jones, C., Herterly, W., & Borgatti, S. (1997). A general theory of network governance: Exchange conditions and social mechanisms. *Academy of Management Review, 22*(4), 911-945.

Keenan, T., & Trotter, D. (1999). The changing role of community networks in providing citizen access to the Internet. Internet Research. *Electronic Networking Applications and Policy, 9*(2), 100-108.

Kickul, J., & Gundry, L. (2000). Pursuing technological innovation: The role of entrepreneurial posture and opportunity recognition among internet firms. In *Frontiers of Entrepreneurship Research,* MA: Babson College.

Lawrence, T., Phillips, N., & Hardy, C. (1999). Watching whale watching. *The Journal of Applied Behavioral Science, 35*(4), 479-502.

LeBrasseur, R., Whissell, R., & Ojha, A. (2002). Organizational learning, transformational leadership and implementation of continuous quality improvement in Canadian hospitals. *Australian Journal of Management, 27*(2), 141-162.

Lowndes, V., & Skelcher, C. (1998). The dynamics of multi-organizational partnerships: An analysis of changing modes of governance. *Public Administration, 76*, 313-333.

Martin, L., & Matlay, H. (2003). Innovative use of the Internet in established small firms: The impact of knowledge management and organizational learning in accessing new opportunities. *Qualitative Market Research, 6*(1), 18-26.

Martins, E. & Terblanche, F. (2003). Building organisational culture that stimulates creativity and innovation. *European Journal of Innovation Management, 6*(1), 64-74.

May, C. (2002). *The information society—A sceptical view.* Cambridge, UK: Polity Press.

McKnight, B. & Bontis, N. (2002). E-improvisation: Collaborative groupware technology expands the reach and effectiveness of organizational improvisation. *Knowledge and Process Management, 9*(4), 219-227.

New Economy Development Group Inc. (2001). *Sustainability project on sustainable communities.* Paper presented at the Canadian Rural Partnership. Rural Research and Analysis, Government of Canada.

Nooteboom, B. (1999). Innovation and inter-firm linkages: New implications for policy. *Research Policy, 28*(8), 793.

OECD. (1997). Organisation for economic co-operation and development. *Towards a global information society.* Paris: OECD.

OECD. (2004). Organization for economic co-operation and development. *Information and communication technologies and rural development.* Paris, France: OECD Publication Service.

Oliver, A., & Ebers, M. (1998). Networking network studies: An analysis of conceptual configurations in the study of inter-organizational relationships, *Organization Studies, 19*, 549-83.

Olk, P., & Young, C. (1997). Why members stay in or leave an R&D consortium: Performance and conditions of membership as determinants of continuity. *Strategic Management Journal, 18*(11), 855-877.

O'Toole, L. (1997). Treating networks seriously: Practical and research-based agendas in public administration. *Public Administration Review, 57*(1), 45-52.

Ouchi, W. (1980). Markets, bureaucracies, and clans. *Administrative Science Quarterly, 1*, 129-141.

Pettigrew, A. (1992). The character and significance of strategy process research. *Strategic Management Journal, 13*, 5-16.

Pettigrew, A. (1987). Context and action in the transformation of the firm. *Journal of Management Studies, 24*(6), 649-670.

Pigg, K. (2001). Applications of community informatics for building community and enhancing civic society. *Information, Communication & Society, 4*(4), 507-527.

Pissarra, J., & Jesuino, J. (2005). Idea generation through computer-mediated communication: The effects of anonymity. *Journal of Management Psychology, 20*(3/4), 275-291.

Poyhonen, A., & Smedlund, A. (2004). Assessing intellectual capital creation in regional clusters. *Journal of Intellectual Capital, 5*(3), 351-365.

Ring, P. (2002). Processes facilitating reliance on trust in inter-organizational networks. In M. Ebers (Ed.), *The formation of inter-organizational networks* (pp. 113-45). Oxford, England: Oxford University Press

Ring, P., & Van de Ven, A. (1994). Developmental processes of cooperative interorganizational relationships. *Academy of Management Review, 19*, 90-118.

Roberts, N., & Bradley, R. (1991). Stakeholder collaboration and innovation: A study of public policy initiation at the state level. *Journal of Applied Behavioral Science, 27*(2), 209-227.

Rycroft, R. (2003). Technology-based globalization indicators: The creativity of innovation network data. *Technology in Society, 25*(3), 299-317.

Scheel, C. (2002). Knowledge clusters of technological innovation systems. *Journal of Knowledge Management, 6*(4), 356-367.

Shah, D. (2002). Nonrecursive models of internet use and community engagement: Questioning whether time spent online erodes social capital. *Journalism & Mass Communication Quarterly, 79*(4), 964-987.

Snow, C. & Thomas, J. (1993). Building networks: Broker roles and behaviours. In P. Lorange, B. Chakravarthy, J. Roos, & A. Van de Ven (Eds.), *Implementing strategic processes: Change, learning and co-operation* (pp. 217-38). Oxford: Blackwell.

Sorensen, E. (2002). Democratic theory and network governance. *Administrative Theory & Praxis, 24*(4), 693-720.

Stevenson, T. (2002). Communities of tomorrow. *Futures, 34*(8), 735-744.

Suire, R. (2004). Des réseaux de l'entrepreneur aux ressorts du créatif Quelles stratégies pour les territoires? *Revue Internationale PME, 17*(2), 123-143.

Tan, M. (1999). Creating the digital economy: Strategies and perspectives from Singapore. *International Journal of Electronic Commerce, 3*(3), 105-22.

United Nations. (1998). *Knowledge societies: Information technology for sustainable development*. Report prepared by R. Mansell & U. Wehn. Oxford: United Nations Commission on Science and Technology for Development/Oxford University Press.

Uslaner, E. M. (2004). Trust, civic engagement, and the Internet. *Political Communication, 21*(2), 223-242.

Van de Ven, A. & Poole, M. (1995). Explaining development and change in organizations. *Academy of Management Review, 20*(3), 510-540.

Van den Hooff, B., de Ridder, J. & Aukema, E. (2004). Exploring the eagerness to share knowledge: The role of social capital and ICT in knowledge sharing. In M. Huysman, & V. Wulf (Eds.), *Social capital and information technology* (Chapter 7). Cambridge, USA and London, England: The MIT Press.

Von Oetinger, B. (2005). From idea to innovation: Making creativity real. *The Journal of Business Strategy, 25*(5), 35-41.

Waits, M. (2000). The added value of the industry cluster approach to economic analysis, strategy development, and service delivery. *Economic Development Quarterly, 14*(1), 35-50.

Warkentin, C., & Mingst, K. (2000). International institutions, the state, and global civil society in the age of the World Wide Web. *Global Governance, 6*(2), 237-257.

Wellman, B., Haase, A. Q., Witte, J., & Hampton, K. (2001). Does the internet increase, decrease, or supplement social capital? Social networks, participation, and community commitment. *American Behavioral Scientist, 45*(3), 436-455.

Wheelan, S. (1999). *Creating effective teams: A guide for members and leaders* (p. 154). Thousand Oaks, CA: Sage Publications.

Williams, R., Stewart, J., & Slack, R. (2005). *Social learning in technological innovation—Experimenting with information communication technologies*. Cheltenham, UK and Northampton, USA: Edward Elgar.

Wood, D., & Wood, G. (1991). Toward a comprehensive theory of collaboration. *Journal of Applied Behavioral Science, 27*(2), 139-162.

World Bank (1999). *World development report 1998/99: Knowledge for development.* New York: Oxford University Press.

Zollo, M., Reuer, J., & Singh, J. (2002). Interorganizational routines and performance in strategic alliances. *Organizational Science, 13*(6), 701-713.

ENDNOTES

[1] The authors acknowledge the helpful comments of the reviewers. By addressing their concerns and suggestions, this chapter found a better balance between organizational and involvement issues.

[2] Multi-organizational collaboration, partnerships, and networks are considered interchangeable terms and refer to a variety of organizations collaborating for a common purpose. "Collaborative network" is proposed as an inclusive alternative.

[3] A stakeholder is defined as an organization that contributes programs and services to the network. A partner is one that makes a financial contribution to the overall project.

[4] The term downloading has become a popular expression in Canada as a result of higher levels of government shifting responsibility for programs to lower levels of government. Municipalities have inherited a number of costs and responsibilities previously held by the province and the province has inherited responsibilities previously held by the federal government.

[5] These communities have been highlighted at the annual conference of ICF (Intelligent Communities Forum).

This work was previously published in International Journal of Technology and Human Interaction, Vol. 3, Issue 2, edited by B. Stahl , pp. 13-33, copyright 2007 by IGI Publishing, formerly known as Idea Group Publishing (an imprint of IGI Global).

Chapter XII
A De–Construction of Wireless Device Usage

Mary R. Lind
North Carolina A&T State University, USA

ABSTRACT

In this article, wireless technology use is addressed with a focus on the factors that underlie wireless interaction. A de-construction of the information processing theories of user/technology interaction is presented. While commercial and useful applications of wireless devices are numerous, wireless interaction is emerging as a means of social interaction—an extension of the user's personal image—and as an object of amusement and play. The technology/user interaction theories that have driven the discussions of computer assisted communication media are information richness, communicative action, and social influence modeling. This article will extend this theoretical view of wireless devices by using flow theory to address elements of fun, control, and focus. Then, these technology/user interaction theories are used with respect to wireless devices to propose areas for future research.

INTRODUCTION

Within the United States, wireless devices have become ubiquitous communication devices. Yet, in Europe and the Far East, these devices are not only widely used as communication devices, but as vehicles of commerce and of entertainment. It is widely known that the GSM telecommunications standard is not fully implemented in the United States, inhibiting the development of wireless applications by firms to support their mobile customers. Yet, there seems to be more to this than telecommunication standards. This chapter will examine social behavioral issues that affect wireless usage and propose a model to better understand this usage.

Wireless devices, serving as transmitters of information at a reasonable cost from point to point without being tethered to a wired line, are profoundly impacting how we communicate and perform work (Rudy, 1996). Little research exists on how to design wireless technologies to better support wireless communications and applications (Te'eni et al., 2001). Research on information technology design finds that the technology should be fit to the user's task needs (Senn, 1998, Swanson, 1988). Since wireless devices provide a tool for convergence of voice, text, audio, photos, videos, and data (Yager, 2003), it is critical that the design of these wireless devices fits the multiple modes of data exchange and usage supported by the wireless devices.

Models to explain information technology design and adoption are rooted in the assumptions of the usefulness and usability afforded by the technology (Davis, 1989, Swanson, 1988), where the context for these technology design and adoption models is the workplace. As information technologies have become pervasive throughout the culture (Gaver, 2005), these technologies, while still an instrument to perform work more efficiently, have become a means of social networking, diversion, and entertainment for the homo luden (Huizinga, 1950). Yet along with this play aspect, the homo luden also gains control of his/her personal space. These aspects of mobile information technologies, usefulness, usability, play, and control will be explored in this chapter to determine how these dimensions of mobile information technology interaction can enable flow (Csikszentmihalyi, 1975) and enable homo ludens (Huizinga, 1950) to seamlessly process information for work and for play. Huizinga (1950) notes that play influences the culture of the players as well as Gaver (2005) observes that pervasive, "ambient" technologies also shape the culture in which the technologies are used. In this chapter, the discussion focuses on the use of these wireless technologies that have become artifacts representative of work, social, and play activities in our everyday cultural contexts, and how these same cultural contexts, in turn, are shaped by the wireless artifacts, and through this interaction, the enactment of additional uses for the wireless devices.

THEORETICAL FOUNDATION FOR WIRELESS MEDIA USAGE

Two theoretical approaches will be examined. First, the view of wireless devices as communication media based in information richness theory is presented, followed by the theoretical view of wireless devices using the social networking theory perspective. Secondly, wireless media will be addressed as objects of play and of control. Finally, a model is developed showing the bidirectional impact of wireless devices as artifacts that influence culture and the resulting culture that in turn impacts perceptions of the wireless artifacts.

Media Richness Theory

The rational choice model contends that users select the most effective medium for data exchange. Media richness theory (Daft & Lengel, 1984; Lind & Zmud, 1991) proposed that managers will use richer media in ambiguous contexts and the leaner media for more structured tasks. For example, face-to-face media that permit the transmission of nonverbal clues and immediate feedback will be used in contexts that are unclear and need to be sorted through in order to reduce the ambiguity of the context. In information richness theory (Daft & Macintosh, 1981; Daft & Weick, 1984; Daft & Lengel, 1984), it was proposed that communication channels vary in their ability to convey information and meaning. This theory suggests a continuum where the richest channels are those that provide for more face-to-face interaction and feedback, allowing for the communication of nuances, often unspoken, in adding meaning to communication. The leanest channels are those written or printed. Since research into information richness theory has met with conflicting results, especially in the area of e-mail studies, other theories and theory extensions have been explored. Neither voice mail nor e-mail allow for face-to-face interaction, but voice mail records the actual voice of the speaker while e-mail provides much quicker feedback than printed media. Thus, the underlying media richness theory is the assumption that individuals seek to be efficient communicators and make rational decisions, selecting a communication medium that fits the nature of the information being communicated.

Other theories have addressed the use of media as a social construct (El-Shinnawy & Markus, 1997). Using the social influence model of technology use, Fulk, Schmitz, and Steinfield (1990) proposed that perceptions of communication media, such as richness, are socially constructed. They found that individuals were more influenced in communication channel use and perceptions by their co-workers than by their supervisors. Also, they found that keyboard skill and computer experience were important predictors of perceptions of electronic mail richness. The communication medium became viewed as an artifact that reflects the social circumstances of the communicating partners that in turn impacts the social context for their social network, thus becoming an influence on the culture of that social group.

Ngwenyama and Lee (1997) proposed a critical social theory perspective for communication channel richness using the work of Weick (1969) and Habermas (1984), they posit that the richness of a communication channel is determined by how the person using that channel enacts the channel. Thus, critical social theory advocates the notion that the interpretation of the information conveyed through a channel is in the mind of the receiver. Some may filter complex, rich information and seek to simplify it to fit their simplistic view of

the organization. While others may embrace complex, rich information and revel in trying to interpret the many dimensions of often ambiguous but rich information. It cannot be assumed that greater usage means a richer channel. It may just mean that the channel is more accessible or easier to use for short messages than the telephone or face-to-face media. Thus, critical social theory shows that the enactment of the communication artifact is determined by that individual's context and the individual's perception of that context and as the use of the communication artifact becomes widespread then the culture will develop shared perceptions of its attributes, which can then have a broad impact on the culture.

Communicative Action Theory

The object of most communication is to convey information so that the communicating partners reach a mutual understanding, regarding the topic at hand. Habermas (1984), in his theory of communicative action, addresses the concept of communicative rationality, where a mutual understanding is reached through processes that signal commonalities in culture that promote understanding. Thus, the goal of communication is to reach a common understanding between the communicating parties. However, according to Habermas, different cultural groups may interpret different signals for enacting this mutual understanding. Hence, channel richness for one such group may differ from another group. Thus, communication action theory recognizes that the media are enacted differently in different cultural contexts, but the rational goal is to achieve a common understanding using the medium for communication.

Communication Channel Enactment

Addressing this issue of enacted meaning, Carlson and Zmud (1992) proposed communication channel extension theory and showed that one's past communication experiences, both in terms of the communication channels and the person with whom one is communicating via the channel, will in turn shape one's perception of a communication channel. Thus, different levels of experience with a computer mediated channel in an organizational context will shape one's perceptions, and use of such computer mediated channels, just as one's past experiences in engaging in face-to-face communication will influence face-to-face communication. This view of channel enactment then shows the circular impact of the channel on the communication content, within a cultural context where the perceptions of the communication partners influence future expectations of that channel.

Flow Theory

A different explanation has been proposed with little relationship to richness theory—flow theory (Trevino & Webster, 1992; Ghani & Deshpande, 1994). In flow theory, the channel is enacted as an article of amusement. Flow theory (Csikszentmihalyi, 1975; Miller, 1973) suggests that a flow state is a playful, exploratory experience where flow is a continuous variable from none to intense. Thus, some communication channels, particularly the computer mediated ones, may enact such playful behavior. Trevino and Webster (1992) proposed that, through flow, the individual has a sense of control of the interaction and thus finds it more interesting. This seems particularly true as the communication medium becomes a tool of commerce and work activity. Thus, control of the interaction engages the attention of the person using that medium. Csikszentmihalyi (1990, p. 4) developed the theory of optimal flow as, "the state in which people are so intensely involved in an activity that nothing else seems to matter; the experience itself is so enjoyable that people will do it even at great cost, for the sheer sake of doing it." Here, the context, rather than individual differences, is used to explain human

motivation (Maehr, 1989; Weiner, 1990), and the focus is on the total concentration on an activity and the enjoyment resulting from that activity (Ghani, 1991; Malone & Lepper, 1987). Wireless devices serve as artifacts of communication and entertainment for many. When not talking on the wireless device, people are observed looking at the screen for text messages, browsing the Web, playing games, and so forth. These artifacts of our culture have become a source of time absorption for many, as they wait for the next meeting or walk to their destinations.

Further, Csikszentmihalyi (1990, p. 25) characterized flow theory as, "A phenomenological model of consciousness based on information theory." Consciousness deals with the flow ordering of information regarding intended actions and goals (Parr and Montgomery, 1998). One of the dimensions of flow is the challenge of the experience (Ghani and Deshpande, 1994). Csikszentmihalyi (1990, p. 3) said, "The best moments usually occur when a person's body or mind is stretched to its limits in a voluntary effort to accomplish something difficult or worthwhile." Ghani and Deshpande (1994) state that a second dimension of flow is control by the users. Csikszentmihalyi (1994, p. 3) states, "We have all experienced times when, instead of being buffeted by anonymous forces, we do feel in control of our actions (on such occasions) we feel a sense of exhilaration, a deep sense of enjoyment." Turkle (1984) discussed how a computer user may work because of the fun of the interaction, not necessarily to achieve a specific goal. In flow, Csikszentmihalyi (1990) discussed how a person loses their sense of time. So flow enables a person to process information best when the effort expended by the individual is within that individual's control and when the challenge of the experience meets the skills of the person. The interaction with the wireless artifact must match the skill level of the user. The communication and Web browsing aspect of these wireless artifacts are compatible with already learned skills, using wireless artifacts for other activities, such as entertainment or games, requires skills interaction that match those the user will have to insure concentration on the activity. In any case, the control of the wireless artifact is in the hands of the user where this accessibility encourages increased usage.

Psychic-entropy is a counter force to flow in which there is disorder in consciousness. This occurs whenever, "Information...conflicts with extreme intentions or distracts us–from carrying them out." (Csikszentmihalyi, 1990, p. 36) Anxiety, fear, jealousy, or rage describes disordered experiences. Entropy drains our psychic energy, fragmenting attention. Attention is the process for collecting, storing, and retrieving information. Flow is an experience in which attention is freely invested in the accomplishment of goals allowing the self to develop, increasing complexity (Csikszentmihalyi, 1990). The control afforded by the wireless artifact helps to counter the force of psychic-entropy, giving the user more control over their environment (communication, schedules, messaging), where adjustments can be made in schedules easily, without the user being tethered to land based devices. Parr and Montgomery (1998, p. 27) state "Flow experiences have been characterized as the following, merging of action and awareness; centering of attention on a limited stimulus field; letting go of self-consciousness (transcendence of ego); a feeling of competence and control; having unambiguous goals and receiving immediate, specific feedback; and being intrinsically motivated." Thus, this aspect of flow looks for balance between one's goals and one's skills in achieving those goals. Flow is more closely associated with positive emotions, greater concentration, and a greater sense of control. A person must see that there is something worthwhile to do and that he/she has the ability to do it (Csikszentmihalyi, 1990). As one increases his/her skill level, she/he is motivated to seek out increasingly challenging activities (Mandigo & Thompson, 1998). Csikszentmihalyi (1990) indicates that the flow state is so enjoyable

that the participant will want to continue with the activity for the sake of participation.

The communication, enabled by the wireless artifacts, creates a sense of flow for the wireless communities. These communities can achieve collaborative action (Crane, 1972) using the wirelessly connected communities. The wireless communities are not bounded by space and can connect easily to take action so that the communities are empowered by the collective strength and ability to influence actions in their space. So another aspect of flow enabled by the wireless artifacts is control over collective action.

Flow is about optimizing the happiness that occurs from the everyday immersion in life's activities, "It is by being fully involved with every detail of our lives whether good or bad, that we find happiness, not by trying to look for it directly." (Csikszentmihalyi, 1990, p. 2) A key component to the flow experience is participation or active involvement in something. It comes when an individual is participating in an activity that makes a difference in the person's life. "The concept of flow—the state in which people are so involved in an activity that nothing else seems to matter; the experience itself is so enjoyable that people will do it even at great cost, for the sheer sake of doing it." (Csikszentmihalyi, 1990, p. 4) This connectedness to communities can become an absorbing aspect of the wireless artifact. Yet paradoxically, the wireless artifact absorption can be with music, games, or Internet browsing afforded by the wireless artifact, which is largely a nonsocial activity. However, games are increasingly played via online networks, creating online gaming communities.

Much of the experience of finding flow is about order and goals. "When goals are clear, feedback relevant, and challenges and skills are in balance, attention becomes ordered and fully invested." (Csikszentmihalyi, 1990, p. 31) Here, a defining factor within a flow experience is the ability to recognize and accept clear boundaries in terms of the goals and acceptable behavior. This means that a flow activity must be ordered to some extent by conforming to cultural or social boundaries. "Athletes, mystics, and artists do very different things when they reach flow, yet their descriptions of the experience are remarkably similar." (Csikszentmihalyi, 1997b, p. 29) Although one person's experience with flow may be solitary and pertain simply to their specific circumstances, chances are that the flow is experienced as a member of a social network.

Therefore, within any given flow experience and particularly with usage of the wireless artifact, it is important to pinpoint the organizational frameworks or structural boundaries to which the participants adhere. It is within this willing submission to structural boundaries that highlights an important dimension for understanding the flow experience. What needs do these boundaries fulfill? And if the flow experience is a group activity, how is this mutual submission to ordered rules enhancing the flow experience and leading paradoxically to a freer, happier existence? Submission to overarching rules is found often within games, sports, social networks, and organizations. Membership in these groups brings meaning to its members, whereby meaning is imbued in the artifacts that provide the linkages for these groups. It is through these wireless artifacts, and the resulting linkages within the communities, that trust in the social network develops. While the wireless devices enable multiple modes of communication between and within the communities, their interactions can be shared using common codes and symbols in text messaging and in gaming communities.

Csikszentmihalyi lays out three main qualities of a flow experience. These are: first, when there is a clear set of goals; second, when immediate feedback is provided; and third when all of a person's skills are being used to overcome challenges. (Csikszentmihalyi, 1997b, p. 29-30)

Because of the total demand on psychic energy, a person in flow is completely focused. There is no space in consciousness for distracting thoughts, irrelevant feelings. Self-consciousness disappears, yet one feels stronger than usual. The sense of time is distorted: hours seem to pass by in minutes. When a person's entire being is stretched in the full functioning of body and mind, whatever one does becomes worth doing for its own sake; living becomes its own justification. In the harmonious focusing of physical and psychic energy, life finally comes into its own. (Csikszentmihalyi, 1997b, p. 31-32)

Figure 1. Wireless artifact

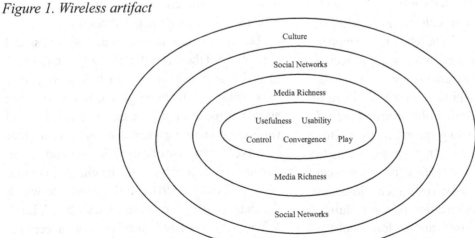

It seems that, during the flow experience, the participant is able to forget about any larger problem and completely focus for the span of time while they are completing their activity. Absorption with games, online chats, blogging, and so forth, all provide clear rules and immediate feedback. In the context where the user's skills match the demands of the interface, the result can be total immersion.

From this discussion of the development of the theory for communications technology interaction and specifically wireless devices based in media richness theory and social network theory, the concept of flow was introduced, providing a multilayer perspective on wireless artifacts. So, in addition to the convergence achieved via the communication media, the media also engage the user by providing means for play and for control over, not only the play and communications activities enabled by the wireless device, but work activities as well. An assumption built into these wireless devices is that they are both useful and useable. The theoretical layers of wireless devices discussed in this section are shown in Figure 1.

Culture and Phratria—Wireless Artifact Interaction

Shiller (1979, p. 29) defines culture as a way of life in which our life's activities shape our culture. As technologies are adopted within society, these technologies shape our culture. For example, Tomlinson (1991) states, "The relationship implied in this is the constant mediation of one aspect of culture experienced by another: what we make of a television programme or a novel or a newspaper article is constantly influenced and shaped by whatever else is going on in our lives. But, equally, our lives are lived as representations to ourselves in terms of the representations present in our culture." Thus, the wireless technologies as artifacts enable communication, play, scheduling tasks, information search, and so forth, but the artifact itself shapes the culture and the expecta-

tions of those in the culture using these wireless devices. Huizinga (1950, p. 12) observed that play affects culture, "It would be rash to explain all the associations which the anthropologist calls "phratria"—for example, clans, brotherhoods, and so forth—simply as play-communities. Nevertheless, it has been shown again and again how difficult it is to draw the line between, on the one hand, permanent social groupings—particularly in archaic cultures with their extremely important, solemn, indeed sacred customs—and the sphere of play on the other." As discussed, these wireless artifacts enable social groupings. In some contexts, these phratria are for work purposes, but in many contexts, these groupings are social and for pleasure. Thus, the play is evidenced in the form of the type of phratia as well as the type of diversion, such as games or Internet browsing enabled by wireless devices.

Thus, flow applications are those that accomplish a repetitive activity, but do it in a way that makes doing the activity enjoyable, almost effortless with security. Flow applications blend in with our daily lives, causing little disruption. As the widely accepted technology acceptance model (TAM) has shown (Davis, 1989), the user must perceive both usefulness and ease of use, while the flow model adds the dimensions of enjoyment and control. Table 1 shows the items for assessing usefulness and ease of use. Added to the TAM dimensions are the proposed flow dimensions of enjoyment and control.

Davis (1989) showed that task usefulness and ease of use of the technology are key components of technology acceptance. In flow theory, it is advocated that technology enables a carefree approach to doing a task that is effortless and fun, while enabling greater control. Two other factors affecting use of a specific communication channel are accessibility of the channel (Zmud, Lind, & Young, 1991) and the degree to which the channel affords rapid feedback (Zmud, Lind, & Young, 1991). Few things are more accessible than a wireless device that can be carried in a

Figure 2. Model of wireless usage

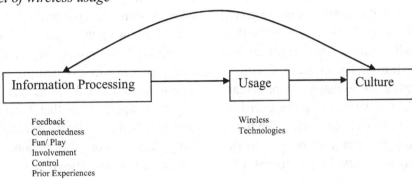

Table 1. Technology acceptance model and flow

Usefulness
Using technology x enabled me to accomplish tasks more quickly.
Using technology x improved my task performance.
Using technology x increased my task productivity.
Using technology x enhanced my effectiveness while performing the task.
Using technology x made it easier to do my task.
Technology x is useful in my task.
Ease of Use
Learning to use technology x is easy for me.
I find it easy to get technology x to do what I want to do.
My interaction with technology x is clear and understandable.
I find technology x flexible to interact with.
It is easy for me to become skillful at using technology x.
I find technology x easy to use.
Proposed Flow Dimenstion
Using technology x was a fun experience for me.
While using technology x I felt in control.
Using technology x gave me more control over my work activities.
Using technology x was a challenge that used my skills.
Using technology x was a pleasant adventure.

person's pocket and these devices enable rapid feedback. So, the richness dimension of feedback, identified by Zmud et al. (1991), is an inherent factor discussed by Csikszentmihalyi (1997a) in flow theory.

FURTHER RESEARCH NEEDED

To move beyond using the devices as voice communication devices, applications that enable the dimension of flow are needed. These are applications for the user that enable them to carry out routine activities easily and with a great degree of control and applications that enable the connectedness with phatria. These applications will enable rich transaction exchanges within the phatria, whether the exchange is for social networking, collaborative action, gaming, or for mobile commerce. Applications enable the flow immersion, giving the user control over work activities and play activities. These applications should provide seamless intergration as the user moves from the work space to the play space to the social network space.

From a broad communication perspective, it has been shown that there are systematic differences in communication by gender. Women have a tendency to work harder at maintaining conversation in face to face situations (Fishman, 1983; Meyers et al., 1997). It has been shown that women value connection and cooperation more than men (Meyers et al., 1997), suggesting that this tendency to maintain the conversation level is evidence of insecurity. Both Allen and Griffeth (1977) and Gefen and Straub (1997) have examined the relationship between gender and information processing. Allen and Griffeth (1997), counter to their hypothesis, found that women did not experience information under load as compared to their male coworkers in a study of 666 workers at a Midwestern telephone company. In the study, roughly 40% were female and about half the workers were hourly employees. Gefen and Straub (1997) found that women perceived electronic mail differently, but in practice, did not use it differently in a study of 392 respondents with three different airlines in three countries. The Gefen and Straub (1997) study showed that the women respondents perceived e-mail to be of higher social presence and more useful than men; however, these same women did not find e-mail easier to use than men and did not, in fact, make greater use of e-mail when measured through self report. Research is needed to determine if gender differences exist in wireless media use.

Certainly gender, culture, and age differences may influence acceptance of wireless media. Examination of these factors, in terms of the expanded TAM model, is needed. Is the greater acceptance of wireless media in Europe and Asia due to technological or cultural factors? Looking at the applications that drive usage of these wireless media, applications are needed that not only simplify work transactions, but are fun to use and not labor intensive in terms of data entry. A new paradigm for wireless applications may be instrumental in promoting flow. A paradigm that recognizes the need for work, play, and control by the user, which in turn, can change the culture of work and play, which through the interconnectedness of the phatria, leads to new uses in terms of work, play, and control for these wireless devices.

REFERENCES

Allen, D. W., & Griffeth, R. W. (1997). Vertical and lateral information processing: The effects of gender, employee classification level, and media richness on communication and work outcomes. *Human Relations, 50* (1), 1239-1260.

Carlson, J. R., & Zmud, R. W. ((1992). Channel expansion theory and the experiential nature of media richness perceptions. *Academy of Management Journal, 42*(2), 152-170.

Crane, D. (1972). *Invisible colleges: Diffusion of knowledge in scientific communities.* Chicago: The University of Chicago Press.

Csikszentmihalyi, M. (1975). *Beyond boredom and anxiety.* San Francisco: Jossey-Bass.

Csikszentmihalyi, M. (1997a). *Creativity: Flow and the psychology of discovery and invention.* New York: Harpers-Collins.

Csikszentmihalyi, M. (1997b). *Finding flow: The psychology of engagement with everyday life.* New York: Basic Books.

Csikszentmihalyi, M. (1990). *Flow: The psychology of optimal experience.* New York: Harper & Row.

Daft, R. L., & Lengel, R. H. (1984). Information richness: A new approach to managerial behavior and organization design. In L. L. Cummings and B. M. Staw (Ed.), *Research in organizational behavior.* Greenwich, CT: JAI, 6, 191-233.

Daft, R. L., & Macintosh, V. B. (1981). A tentative exploration into the amount and equivocality of information processing in organizational work units. *Administrative Science Quarterly, 26,* 207-224.

Daft, R. L., and Weick, K. E. (1984). Toward a model of organizations as interpretation systems. *Academy of Management Review, 9,* 284-295.

Davis, F.D. (1989). Perceived usefulness, perceived ease of use, and user acceptance of information technology. *MIS Quarterly,* September, 319-340.

El-Shinnawy, M., & Markus, M. L. (1997). The poverty of media richness theory: Explaining people's choice of electronic mail vs. voice mail. *International Journal of Human-Computer Studies, 46*(4), 443-467.

Fishman, P. (1983). Interaction: The work women do. In B. Thorne, C. Kramarae, & N. Henley (Eds.), *Language, gender and society* (pp. 89-101). Cambridge, MA: Newbury House.

Fulk, J., Schmitz, J. A., & Steinfield, C. W. (1990). A social influence model of technology use. In J. Fulk and C. Steinfield (Eds.), *Organizations and communication technology* (pp. 117-140). J. Newbury Park, CA: Sage.

Gaver, B. (2001, October). Designing for ludic aspects of everyday life. *ERCIM News,* 47. Retrieved from http://www.ercim.org/publication/Ercim_News/enw47/gaver.html.

Gefen, D., and Straub, D. (1997). Gender differences in the perception and use of e-mail: An extension to the technology acceptance model. *MIS Quarterly, 21*(4), 389-401.

Ghani, J. A. (1991). Flow in human-computer interactions: Test of a model. In J. Carey (Ed.), *Human factors: Management information systems: An organizational perspective.* 229-237. Norwood, NJ: Ablex.

Ghani, J. A., and Deshpande, S. P. (1994). Task characteristics and the experience of optimal flow in human-computer interaction. *The Journal of Psychology, 128*(4), 381-391.

Habermas, J. (1984). *The theory of communicative action, Vol. 1, Reason and the rationalization of society.* Boston: The Beacon Press.

Huizinga, J. (1950). *Homo ludens.* Boston: The Beacon Press.

Lind, M. R., & Zmud, R. W. (1991). The influence of a convergence in understanding between technology providers and users on information technology innovativeness. *Organization Science, 2*(2), 195-217.

Maehr, M. L. (1989). Thoughts about motivation. In C. Ames & R. Ames (Eds.), *Research on motivation in education: Goals and cognition* (pp. 299-315). San Diego, CA: Academic Press.

Malone, T. W., & Lepper, M. R. (1987). Making learning fun: A taxonomy of intrinsic motivations for learning. In R. E. Snow & M. J. Farr (Eds.), *Aptitude, learning, and instruction* (pp. 223-253). Hillsdale, NJ: Erlbaum.

Mandigo, J. L., & Thompson, L. P. (1998). Go with their flow: How flow theory can help practitioners to intrinsically motivate children. *Physical Education, 55*(3), 145-160.

Meyers, R. A., Brashers, D. E., Winston, L., & Grob, L. (1997). Sex differences and group argument: A theoretical framework and empirical investigation. *Communication Studies, 48,* 19-41.

Miller, S. (1973). Ends, means, and galumphing: Some leitmotifs of play. *American Anthropologist*, 75, 87-98.

Ngwenyama, O. K., & Lee, A. S. (1997). Communication richness in electronic mail: Critical social theory and the contextuality of meaning. *MIS Quarterly*, 21(2), 145-168.

Parr, G. D., & Montgomery, M. (1998). Flow theory as a model for enhancing student resilience. *Professional School Counseling*, 1(5), 26-32.

Rudy, A. (1996). A critical review of research on electronic mail. *European Journal of Information Systems*, 4(4), 198-213.

Senn, J. A. (1998). *Information in business: Principles, practices and opportunities*. Englewood Cliffs, NJ: Prentice-Hall.

Shiller, H. I. (1979). Transnational media and national development. In K. Nordenstreng & H. I. Shiller (Eds.), *National sovereignty and international communication* (pp.21-29). Norwood, NJ: Ablex.

Swanson, E. B. (1988). *Information system implementation: Bridging the gap between design and utilization.*, Homewood, IL: Irwin.

Te'eni, D., Sagie, A., Schwartz, D. G., Zaidman, N. & Amichai-Hamburger, Y. (2001). The process of organizational communication: A model and field study. *IEEE Transactions on Professional Communication*, 44(1), 6-20.

Tomlinson, J. (1991). *Cultural imperialism*. Baltimore, MD: The Johns Hopkins University Press.

Trevino, L. K., & Webster, J. (1992). Flow in computer-mediated communication. *Communication Research*, 19(5), 539-574.

Turkle, S. (1984).*The second self: Computers and the human spirit*. New York: Simon and Schuster.

Yager, T. (2003). More than a cell phone. *Infoworld*, 25(5), 30.

Weick, K. E. (1969). *The social psychology of organizing.* Reading, MA: Addison-Wesley.

Weiner, B. (1990). History of motivational research in education. *Journal of Educational Psychology*, 82, 616-622.

Zmud, R., Lind, M., & Young, F. (1991). An attribute space for organizational communication channels. *Information Systems Research*, 1(4), 440-457.

This work was previously published in International Journal of Technology and Human Interaction, Vol. 3, Issue 2 , edited by B. Stahl, pp. 34-44, copyright 2007 by IGI Publishing, formerly known as Idea Group Publishing (an imprint of IGI Global).

Chapter XIII
Modeling Sociotechnical Change in IS with a Quantitative Longitudinal Approach:
The PPR Method

François-Xavier de Vaujany
Jean Monnet Université, France

ABSTRACT

The following chapter suggests a critical realistic framework, which aims at modeling sociotechnical change linked to end-users' IT appropriation: the "archetypal approach." The basic situations it includes (the "sociotechnical archetypes"), and the possible appropriative trajectories that combine them, together with three propositions linked to the model, are developed. They are illustrated by means of a case study describing the implementation of an e-learning system within a French university. Then, the article presents an instrumentation of the theoretical framework, based on a quantitative longitudinal approach: the Process Patterns Recognition (PPR) method. This one draws mainly on Doty, Glick and Huber (1993, 1994), who propose to evaluate the distance between organizational archetypes and empirical configurations by means of Euclidean distance calculus. The adaptation consists of evaluating the distance between appropriative trajectories (embodied by series of theoretically specified vectors) and empirical processes linked to the implementation of computerized tools in organizations. The PPR method is then applied to the same organizational setting as the one related to the case study. It validates the relevance of this type of a research strategy, which makes it possible to model sociotechnical dynamics related to end-users' IT appropriations.

INTRODUCTION: TOWARDS QUANTITATIVE PROCESSUAL APPROACHES?

The study of the organization-technology relationship is hardly a new topic in the social sciences. From the first research forays into the sociotechnical school by Trist and Bamforth (1951) to Orlikowski's structurational model (1992, 2000), Lin and Conford's contribution (2000), Callon and Latour's Actor Network Theory (1990, 1992), and Alter's (1985, 1995) innovation sociology in the French-speaking community, many theoretical frameworks have been developed in this perspective. With regard to information system research, they draw either on static quantitative approaches, or on more longitudinal qualitative techniques (Choudrie & Dwivedi, 2005; Pinsonneault & Kraemer, 1993). But in spite of Giddens' (1984) invitation not to "wield a methodological scalpel" towards quantitative approaches, Archer's (1995) open view on methodology or a broader discourse in most methodological research about the use of innovative quantitative techniques (assumed to be compatible with a more emergentist perspective, see for instance Thietart, 2001) and quantitative processual research is extremely rare in IS (Kaplan & Duchon, 1988; Choudrie & Dwivedi, 2005). "Process measures" (Kaplan and Duchon, 1988) are thus lacking in most IS research. This has led us to a very challenging research question:

How Could One Make Sense Quantitatively of Sociotechnical Dynamics from a Processual Perspective?

The current IS literature is not very helpful on this. Among the few longitudinal strategies[1] in IS, techniques based on surveys have been used for more than fifteen years. Most common implemented techniques with a longitudinal orientation are multivariate techniques such as log-linear models, probit and logit models, Markovian approaches, along with other linear formulations (Venkatesh and Vitalari, 1991, p. 126) or other simpler descriptive techniques. Numerous works have taken an interest in a technology acceptance evolution (like Hu, Clark, & Ma, 2003) or in the evolution of computer tools' diffusion (like Mustonen-Ollila & Lyytinen, 2003, 2004), by means of more or less complex statistical models. Beyond a classic paradigm that could be labeled "assimilationnist" (based on Roger's (1995) theory of the diffusion of innovation), several frameworks have been applied quantitatively to specific forms of organization-technology interactions. If some of these works used the same kind of techniques as those previously mentioned (like Chaomei & Roy, 1996), others, less frequently, opened the way to other longitudinal techniques linked to recurrent cross-sectional studies (often focused on a single variable, e.g., beliefs, adoption, acceptance, and so forth) or structural analysis. From a structural perspective, Burkhardt and Brass (1990) or Barley (1986, 1990) can be mentioned. Barley, notably in his study of CAT scanners as "occasions for structuring," (p. 79) used longitudinal data collection centered on direct observation of interaction scripts between technicians and radiologists. Nonetheless, the complete set seems to put aside the interpretive aspects of a critical realistic approach and of many other processual approaches (structuration, Actor-Network theory, innovation sociology, and so forth). Moreover, it is hard to see how to apply this research strategy to the case of network technologies (for which direct observation of interactions is somewhat difficult). Adopting a recurrent cross-sectional perspective, some researchers have also tried to develop specific quantitative approaches (see Karahanna, Straub, & Chervany, 1999 or Hu, Clark, and Ma, 2003). Nonetheless, most research in this case focuses on single variables (adoption, beliefs, acceptance, and so forth) and do not instrument a broader processual framework.

With regard to longitudinal content analysis like Desanctis and Poole's (1994) application of Adaptative Structuration Theory, quantitative techniques have been used for the coding of interactions and their evolutions. However, if they made it possible to follow actors' interactions, these methods had two limitations. They were weak on behavioral aspects, and made it hard to generalize any trend for a whole social system (Desanctis and Poole's techniques were applied to experimental groups).

Following the previous criticisms, the quantitative longitudinal approach that has been chosen for this research corresponds to a different research strategy, which is labeled here a processual patterns recognition (PPR) method.

The model linked to PPR is based on an "integrative approach" in the broadest sense, for example, research aiming at overcoming some classic dichotomies (actor-structure, holism-methodological individualism, structuralism-hermeneutics, IT use-IT structure, and so forth). Integrative approaches are based on several sociological theories, in particular that of Giddens (1979, 1984), but also of Bhaskar (1989), Archer (1982, 1995, 2003), or the works of Bourdieu (1972). All of these perspectives have some common points: they kindle our interest in reconsidering IT as an interpretatively and instrumentally flexible object. They also re-visit actor's status (neither a determined element nor a totally autonomous agent) and demand that researchers look at technology-organization interactions as a vast structuration process. More precisely, they emphasize "practice" (and thus IT use) as the driver of the reinforcement or transformation of social structures. Since the early eighties, several works in organization theory and information systems have applied integrative frameworks. Among the very first studies implementing an integrative perspective (mainly structurational) are the works of Barley (1986), Desanctis and Poole (1992, 1994), Orlikowski and Robey (1991), Orlikowski (1992, 2000), Walsham (1993) or even

Bouchikhi (1990), in the French-speaking world, can be included. More specifically, from a critical realistic perspective, Barley (1990), Dobson (1999, 2002, 2003), and Carlsson (2003) can also be mentioned. Here, the analysis will be focused on a critical realistic perspective: the archetypal approach.

First, the archetypal approach is introduced. It is illustrated by means of a case study about the implementation of an e-learning technology in a French economics and management faculty. Then, a specific quantitative processual device (the PPR method) is worked out and applied to the same organizational setting as that of the case study. Lastly, some contributions, limitations, and perspectives are suggested for this research.

A THEORETICAL BASE: THE ARCHETYPAL APPROACH

First, the integrative model is introduced. It will serve as a theoretical framework for the quantitative longitudinal method developed in the first part. The two fundamental elements of the archetypal approach will thus be presented: sociotechnical archetypes, and the appropriative trajectories that put them together. Then, three proposals about the deployment of trajectories will be put forward.

Archetypes and Trajectories: Some Elements for Sociotechnical Modeling

The archetypal approach is a synthesis of various works built on an integrative perspective, especially on Archer's (1995) critical realistic approach and Giddens' (1984) structuration theory. A sociotechnical archetype is the long-lasting state of a sociotechnical system, more precisely a long-lasting action-structure configuration, described by concepts and dimensions of the integrative perspective previously introduced. Sociotechnical

Table 1. The three sociotechnical archetypes

	General action-structure configuration	Status of uses	Roles and resource system	Examples
Regenerated (R)	Actions change structures	Transform the role system	Unstable, questioned	The implementation of a CAT scanner can result in significant changes in physician-technician interactions. Radiologists can add their own comments and advice through the diagnosis (Barley, 1986).
Neutral (N)	Actions reproduce and reinforce structures	Either: Do not exist (innovation is not used); Reproduce and indirectly reinforce the role system (with or without improving the efficiency of the sociotechnical system); Aim explicitly at maintaining the role system	Stable. Existence of a *status quo*	Intranets' uses can reproduce the very boundaries they are supposed to overcome. People may go only on the Web sites devoted to their departments. They can also make private jokes and use local jargon on their forums (de Vaujany, 2003).
Disrupted (D)	Actions and structures are in tension	Reproduce, transform, or interrupt the functioning of the role system by creating political or psychological tensions. In the case of an interruption, the disrupted situation is an archetype *per se*	Unstable	The implementation of an ERP can result in various political tensions within the organization, in particular, between consultants, managers, IT staff, and employees. Besides, the acceptance of the new processes included in the software may be extremely stressful for employees (Lemaire, 2003).
Catalyzed (C)	Actions related to ICT accelerate or impede other actions	Uses accelerate or inhibit trends related to non-technological fields	Unstable	Some employees may use an Intranet in a transversal way (whereas others do not). Nonetheless, people may have already started adopting decompartementalized behaviors before. The Intranet then only accelerates an exogenous trend (de Vaujany, 2003).

archetypes are stylized descriptions of what can happen when a new technology is implemented. It is suggested distinguishing four kinds: regenerated, neutral, and disrupted archetypes. All four correspond to social dynamics linked to IT use and represent a specific state of the role system and its interactional scripts (cf. Barley, 1986, 1990). The four archetypes are presented in Table 1.

In the case of a regenerated (R) situation, the role system of the organization experiences a gradual transformation, which has a certain durability. Normal interactional scripts are modified by the use of the new tools. Each one's role, resources, and beliefs are changed by the implementation of the new technology.

In the neutral situation (N), the same phenomenon can be observed (reinforcement of social structures), but associated with two different dynamics. In the first, reinforcement of those social structures supported by the role system is linked to the routine reproduction of the same interactional scripts. Reproduced actions become more and more legitimate and more and more integrated under different reflexes. This is what Orlikowski and Yates (2002) explicitly considered as a possibility with regard to temporal structures. Therefore, the reinforcement of social structures is an "unintended consequence of action" in Giddens' (1984) sense of the term[2]. In the second (where a more extended or open role system can be assumed, e.g., one which is in competition with other sub-systems), the reinforcement of social structures results from more intentional strategies, for example, ritual-based maintenance of social structures (see Giddens, 1984; Bourdieu, 1972; Archer, 1995). Bourdieu (1972) thus remarks that in the case of Kabil tribes,

Each group of agents tends to affirm its existence by continuous maintenance of a privileged network of common relationships, which integrate not only the set of genealogical relations maintained in a working state (called here usual relatives), but also the set of non-genealogical relationships that can be mobilized for more (material and commercial?) needs (called here usual relations). (p. 116)

This can also be found in some uses of e-mail systems, such as when a manager regularly sends messages to colleagues in order to maintain a certain "warmth" in his or her professional network.

In the third situation, the disrupted archetype (D), tension can be either psychological or political (de Vaujany, 2003). Thus, disruption can be linked to actors' performance anxieties regarding new tools. Technology is here a disruptive object in actors' routines. In Giddens' (1984) terminology, it can be said that the "ontological security," the

actors' feeling of continuity, is broken. In other cases, tension is more political and inscribed in the properties of the role system. Incompatibilities can emerge in the course of interactions (Archer, 1995). Resources are allocated in a disruptive manner. Interactions evolve within sub-groups in a discordant way as compared to usual interaction modalities. The system is in tension. This situation can be superimposed on the two previous archetypes (R and N). It can also be an archetypal situation per se. This situation corresponds to an interruption of processes related to the role system. The role system is neither transformed nor reproduced. It is partially or globally suspended.

Lastly, in the fourth situation, for example, the catalyzed archetype, technology appears less structuring. ICT uses are a category of actions among many others that will accelerate or impede changes related to non-technological fields. From this perspective, technology use will not be a factor of change. A broader, exogenous, change takes place within organization, and ICT-related practice will be a potential catalyzer. Recent works (see de Vaujany, 2003) have shed light on these configurations, such as in the case of Intranet or e-mail systems that sometimes accelerate a decompartmentalization of the organization that began before the implementation of the technology.

To expand on our system, some "appropriative trajectories" can be considered at this stage. They are possible combinations of archetypes. "Integrativist" literature suggests two kinds, which may be supplemented by a third one. The starting point of this exploration is an article published by Orlikowski in 2000. In this paper, she suggests that, in many situations, the appropriation process of IT does not stop with a definite sociotechnical routine, but on the contrary, takes the form of continuous "improvisations" and "reinventions" of the technology. She thus aligns her model with other works, like those carried out by Ciborra (1997, 1999, 2000, 2001), which insist on the recurrent muddling through of actors, who regularly rebuild the technology, whether inter-

Table 2. Comparison of three appropriative trajectories

	Balancing-point dynamic	Improvisational dynamic	Catalytic dynamic
Archetypal sequence	N-D-R(-N)	R1-R2-R3	C1-C2-C3
Archetypal coherence	High	Low	High
Nature of change	Alternative and quick	Continuous and slow	Continuous and slow

pretatively or instrumentally. In order to compare Orlikowski's and Ciborra's improvisational vision and the classic model to which they aim at reacting to, it is suggested that archetypes be used before a third trajectory ("catalytic") is put forward. It is more processual than the previous ones, and corresponds to those situations where technology continuously either inhibits or catalyzes change or reinforcement processes, which are exogenous to the technological field. Thus, it combines a row of catalyzed situations in a continuous way.

Finally, the three possible trajectories (applied to an overall sociotechnical system or one of its sub-units) can be described by means of Table 2.

The balancing-point dynamic deserves some explanations. Ultimately, it describes a type of a "creative destruction" process well-known by economists (see Schumpeter, 1942, 1975, p. 82). Innovation implies a process of destruction of former routines before new ones emerge. Other sub-trajectories can also be put forward. They imply a more harmonious social innovation in use, without any single stage corresponding to a disrupted situation (de Vaujany, 2003).

Moreover, the balancing-point dynamic encompasses two symbolic thresholds particularly difficult to cross before the emergence of a practicable innovation. The first corresponds to the move from routine to change. It embodies the inertia of the sociotechnical system as regards to innovation[3]. The second epitomizes the difficulties to move from apprehension to acceptance of innovation in use. The implementation of a new tool may initially be greeted by wary ten-

sion, which must be overcome in order to reach a harmonious regeneration. Therefore, the two thresholds embody symbolic gates that, if not crossed, will lead the sociotechnical system back to its initial state.

Some Broad Complementary Propositions Linked to the Archetypal Approach

Beyond the appropriative trajectories described, some propositions concerning the deployment of sociotechnical process and end-users' IT appropriation can be put forward. In the literature, three main propositions come to the forefront. First, in accordance with Barley (1990), who was inspired by Nadel's work (1957), the transformation of social structures will first involve a change in "nonrelational" aspects of the role system. "Relational" roles imply an "alter ego," another person who has a complementary position in the social order (Barley, 1990): a mother and her child, a creditor and his/her debtor, a professor and his/her student, and so forth. Conversely, non-relational roles imply a more local and less institutional construction. Barley notices: "When introduced into a work setting, new technologies initially modify tasks, skills, and other nonrelational aspects of roles." Besides, it seems that contexts where technology displays a high degree of "procedural" (e.g., technical) or "rule-setting" (e.g., social, related to norms of use), restrictiveness[4] will be more likely to lead to a quick and coherent change in the role system than those where technology is less restrictive (de

Vaujany, 2003). Thus, appropriations will produce or reproduce social structures according to the level of rigidity (e.g., restrictiveness) of initial sociotechnical structures (Poole & Desanctis, 1994). It can thus be reasonably assumed that the computerization of some French abbeys is less likely to induce relational changes than the adoption of new IS systems in SMEs with a more recent history and role system. Lastly, it seems also that appropriation drivers will be explicit in a phase of transformation of an organization's social structures. Users will be more reflexive than in routine stages. Hence, Barley and Tolbert (1997) suggest that the modification of an institution is likely to involve a more conscious choice than its subsequent reproduction.

To illustrate this archetypal approach, a case study will be suggested. It is based on the implementation of an e-learning system within a French university.

AN ILLUSTRATION OF THE ARCHETYPAL APPROACH: THE CASE OF AN E-LEARNING SYSTEM IMPLEMENTATION

First, the general history of the e-learning system implementation in a French university will be presented. Then, relevant appropriative trajectories will be put forward.

The Case Study as a Set of Archetypal Situations

The following case corresponds to the implementation of an e-learning system within a French university of management and economics. Called a "Virtual Office," ("bureau virtuel" in French), the software was intended to supplement real-time education. The principle of this system, an open-source software, is simple: each student, when he or she logs on to the system (by means of a Web browser), sees on the screen the very courses he or she is attending. Interestingly, the appearance of the virtual office is likely to be different from one student to another. The registration of a given course site depends on the teacher, the administrator, or super-administrator of the system. In order to simplify the registration procedures, each student is included in a "step code" ("code étape") with five numbers, which makes it possible to register a whole group into the system at once. The functions of the system are: "Documents," "Forums," "Agenda," "Announcements," "Groups," "Tests," "Discussion," "Course Introduction," "Hyperlinks," and "Assignments." Each of these tools can be activated or deactivated by the teacher in light of his or her needs and interests. He or she can add links to self-developed sites or html pages.

The implementation of the software was conducted by a specific commission at the university in charge of ICT devoted to teaching and gathering different "Virtual Office delegates" for each faculty. It is as one of these delegates and member of the ICT commission that I followed the overall project (and all its management components). Retrospectively, it is suggested that the history of the virtual office at the university can be divided into four main stages.

Stage 1: Initial installation of the system within the university (2002-2003)

The experiment truly began within the medicine and IUT[5] faculties of the university. Instigated by two teachers of the university, a first version of the system was implemented in 2002. The support of the Dean of the Faculty of Medicine was as strong as it was official. In a few months, the sheer number of platforms was remarkable. Most teachers of the medicine faculty, sometimes under the pressure of students, used what they named "the virtual office." In June 2003, more than 300 sites were developed, most of which used many of the advanced functions of the software.

Stage 2: Launch of a first basic version in the management and economics faculty: A "confidential" software (June-October 2003)

The first attempt at introducing the system to the management and economics faculty dates back to early 2003. After a presentation of the software, a lecturer in charge of a master's program elected to use the system for his degree. After a general presentation to faculty members in May 2003, the dean decided to offer a version of the software to his students. After an initial period of work during the summer and the first two weeks of September, a dozen sites[6] were launched in a sub-component of the faculty (IUP, graduate vocational training in business studies). Then, several problems arose. The list of students included in the step-codes was not always accurate. Besides, several errors had been made by teachers in the registration process, resulting in erroneous enrollments. Many students did not find their login and password on their student card (the same used for their university e-mail account), required for authentication on the site. Finally, and primarily because of poor communication about the tool, some teachers chose not to use the new tool. Consequently, the software initially remained little known and used. The number of business students using the software was very low (less than 50%); connections were limited as well (between three and five a day in October) for the administrative portal.

Basically, the training and communication concerning the new software were insufficient, mainly because of a lack of resources. I managed to train only 10 permanent staff lecturers and three administrative agents in the use of the virtual office. Communication was also unsatisfactory. It was limited to a public notice, presenting the tool in late September. Therefore, I decided in late October to distribute an instructional guide for the software to the faculty of management.

At this stage, a neutral situation seems to dominate: either the system is not generally used or it is appropriated in an extremely reproductive

manner. Teachers use it as a continuation of their courses. According to these perceptions, it is also rather marginal, not yet related to the core of their department's communication tools.

Stage 3: The initial and increasing use of the software by permanent lecturers of the IUP (November 2003-January 2004)

It was actually in late November and December that the Virtual Office began to take off within the faculty. The bulk of the installation problems with the step-codes (due to unpaid fees) were solved. More than 15 sites were set up within a month by permanent lecturers of the IUP. Three community sites were also put at the students' disposal: a "general culture space," a "foreign students' space," and a "research portal" devoted to academics. The problem of the reluctant faculty members was also resolved. I began to notice the students turning instinctively to the Virtual Office for administrative information. The first part-time lecturers' sites were also set up after I got in touch with them and organized individual presentations of the tool (in total, a dozen).

The number of connections skyrocketed. In the case of the administrative portal of the IUP alone, connections moved from 3-5 a day to 30-40 a day on average. This portal alone accounted for half of the online activity at the faculty of management. The administrative portal of other components of the faculty (for those with one) experienced more difficulties (notably the one linked to the department of finance). Except for its master's program, the economics department had no portal and courses on the Virtual Office were still marginal.

In the IUP, however, lecturers (especially those heavily involved in the department) promoted the virtual office during their courses. Concrete uses were nonetheless limited to the most basic functions of the software (documents, hyperlinks, course presentation, assignments). The tool gradually gained adherents among the teachers. In our own courses, I did my utmost by mentioning interesting exchanges on the various forums, in order to foster student interest.

As for the students, feedback was generally positive. Indeed, it could be noticed that the number of registered people was not representative of the actual number of users. Several students frequently shared the same password and login. Thus, a student wrote on one of our questionnaires: "Most of the time, I do not connect with my own login password." On the whole, users appreciated having much of the information they had previously had to request from the secretaries online (scheduling, grades, addresses, internal rules, and so forth).

Forums received their first contributions and soon many students had signed on. On the whole, the virtual office has been a means for students to achieve a fundamental goal of the IUP: autonomy. Accordingly, some students began using the tool to exchange ideas about a case study or a report. In the case of certain decentralized departments (60 km away from the main site), the development of an administrative portal relieved a part of the loneliness they had felt before.

At this stage, administrative agents were also relatively satisfied with the new tool, which simplified some of their tasks. Students called less to ask for information concerning schedule changes or course information.

Finally, multiple re-invention processes, for example "innovation in use," could be noticed for this third period. The tool, initially conceived as an educational resource, became an administrative tool, a research support network, and a device devoted to a specific course of the IUP (in this last case, strongly modular and frequently improvised by teachers ["cours de methode"] devoted to the management of trainees). Nonetheless, the broader sociotechnical dynamics clearly relates to a catalyzed situation. The "Virtual Office" is more a way to accelerate a pre-existing trend: the growing autonomy of most students, particularly in the case of the IUP. It is a way to find information autonomously, to get in touch directly with the professor they want to discuss with, or to get some professional information related to jobs in the continuation of the course.

Stage 4: Growth of a community of practice and first steps toward institutionalization in the faculty (February to June 2004)

During the fourth and last period of the study, the Virtual Office experienced a progressive "institutionalization." Several appraisals of the software's distribution were made during the regular meetings of the "steering committee" every two weeks. Significant information concerning the IUP department was regularly relayed online with the "Announcement tool." The first official participations took place. The dean of the IUP committed himself more strongly, and even participated in forums dealing with course features. A procedure to systematize feedback about courses was implemented by an administrative agent of the decentralized department. This was accomplished in the form of a book free to students, in which they could make their remarks, which were then relayed by the secretary. The first official meeting between the whole faculty and the computer analysts responsible for the software was held. A general evaluation of the Virtual Office was also made for the annual meeting of the IUP department (in early June 2004) along with the management committee of the institute. A "permanent working group" in charge of the virtual office and e-leaning technology within the faculty was established.

During this period, it could also be noticed that more advanced functions had been appropriated by teachers (such as the group tool and various types of online exercises). The last permanent teachers not involved in the project finally established sites. Nevertheless, some departments in the faculty (such as economics and finance) still displayed very low usage of the technology.

From late March (perhaps because of the positive reports distributed), the level of daily connections to the portal exploded to approximately 50 a day. Students automatically turned to the virtual office for newer and newer types of information. The number of contributions to forums was so high that I was compelled to delete some old topics in order to better organize the site. I also began to notice the first tensions in discussions concerning education and faculty organization. Nonetheless, it was decided not to interfere in the discussion between students and to give the exchanges complete freedom.

On the whole, the situation was far from ideal. Several students of the IUP, from then on regular users of the tool and increasingly more demanding, voiced their criticisms. They regretted that too many lecturers used their site as a sort of "PowerPoint garage" and wished that they had more sites at their disposal, notably with regard to resource management, and more up-to-date information (especially with regards to classroom assignments). Moreover, some regretted the lack of involvement of several lecturers of the institution. For the other departments in the faculty (in particular economics), this fourth period initially grew rather slowly. Several sites were set up. In the management area, I also developed an administrative portal for the final course of study still not online (the "CAAE").

At the end of this fourth stage, the faculty seems to clearly be experiencing a catalyzed situation. In spite of some "bricolages" (more related to a better efficiency than new modus operandi), the system's uses are mainly catalyzers of exogenous trends related to non-technological fields (in particular, in the case of the management department).

Overall Appropriative Trajectories Related to the Case

Finally, the same sociotechnical dynamic can be found in this case study as the one suggested by Lin and Cornford (2000, p. 9) for the implementation of a groupware technology within their university: "We see an almost casual deployment of technology attracting increasing attention, and slowly developing a profile within the university. The debate around the system moves from the individual to the informal (team), and then into the main management structures." Gradually, the virtual office became institutionalized within the different departments (especially for the IUP) thanks to the middle-management of the faculty (particularly the directors of various BA or MS courses and permanent lecturers). The increase in use of the tool has been progressive (10 sites in December 2003 for the IUP and 65 in late June 2004) and the structure of the system has been both modified and redirected, indeed more towards student-administration interactions (which is a somewhat astonishing result for a system initially designed for educational purposes).

From the archetypal approach perspective, the catalytic trajectory clearly makes sense of the situation. It seems that most e-learning-related practice either reproduces (sometimes more efficiently) usual teaching or administrative habits. On the other hand, some other actions (related to administrative portals and some teaching sites) more clearly accelerate exogenous trends (towards more autonomy).

Now, the archetypal approach has been illustrated through the classic case study research strategy; it is suggested to apply and test the model in a different way. In the continuation of the research question suggested in the introductory part, a quantitative processual approach (PPR) will be worked out. It will then be applied to the same organizational setting as that of the French university. Will it lead to the same conclusion? Will it be a way to specify some statements related to the case study?

FROM THE CASE STUDY TO THE PPR METHOD: A NEW WAY FOR SOCIOTECHNICAL MODELING?

The Starting-Point: The Works of Doty, Glick and Huber

The idea of evaluating the Euclidean distance between the appropriative trajectories of our model and empirical processes came through the reading of Doty and Glick (1994) and Doty, Glick, and Huber (1993). These authors wanted to evaluate the relevance of frameworks and hypotheses drawn from Mintzberg (1979, 1983) and Miles and Snow (1978). Dissatisfied with the usual appraisal techniques, Doty, Glick, and Huber took those specific to the field of psychology (see Cronbach & Gleser, 1953), thus enabling them to assess the degree of proximity between an individual's or group's real profile (in the form of scales integrated in a vector) and their theoretical profile (also represented by a vector representing a set of psychological features, (see Cronbach and Gleser,1953).

The strategy suggested by the authors for testing the theories of Mintzberg or Miles and Snow corresponds to a three-step methodology:

1. **Theoretical specification,** for example, the building of vectors, which are supposed to represent the ideal types and will be the benchmark for the study (for instance, the configurations originally put forward by Mintzberg). Doty and Glick (1993) suggest that three techniques can be adopted by the researcher: the author's specification itself, the specification by an expert or a panel of experts on the theory, and the placement of archetypes on a continuum[7], or the use of empirically specified ideal-types. Doty, Glick, and Huber clearly preferred the first possibility. Indeed, the second technique applies to rare cases where the typology can be inscribed in a continuum. The third, implying the use of real organizations corresponding to the ideal-types, will sometimes erase the initial richness and relevance of ideal-types.

2. **Working out of empirical vectors** from surveys returned from a vast number of organizations.

3. **Testing of the hypotheses linked to the contingency model.** For instance, in order to appraise the Mintzberg model, Doty, Glick, and Huber tested three propositions. First, the more an organization looks like an archetype, the more coherent it will be and thus, the more effective. Second, the more an organization looks like the archetype implied by the level of complexity and stability of its environment, the more effective it will be. And last, the more an organization looks like the hybrid form implied by its environment, the more effective it will be.

Explanation of the Longitudinal Technique of Euclidean Distance Calculus

After reading Doty and Glick, it was decided to take their research technique and adapt it to the archetypal approach, which supposed a more longitudinal tool than the one used previously. This work of adaptation resulted in three separate theoretical sequences (corresponding to appropriative trajectories), divided into three sets of vectors integrating scales (ranging from 1 to 5).

Table 3. The balanced trajectory

	T1	T2	T3
N	5	1 or 5	1
D	1	5	1
R	1	1 or 5	5
C	1	1	1

Table 4. The improvisational trajectory

	T1	T2	T3
N	1	1	1
D	1	1	1
R	5	5	5
C	1	1	1

The balancing-point trajectory (sequence N-D-R, see Table 3). In this case, T1 (the first coherent archetypal phase) is dominated by neutrality. The second stage (T2) can be related to various possibilities. Either disruption alone can dominate the system, or it can be mixed with neutral or regenerated situations. Then, at T3, regeneration occurs before new forms of routines are related to the sociotechnical system.

The improvisational trajectory (sequence R1-R2-R3, i.e. R at T1, R at T2 and R at T3, see Table 4).

The catalytic trajectory (sequence C1-C2-C3, see Table 5).

It can also be suggested that this dynamic can be specific to an organization's sub-components. Stakeholder 1 may experience a catalyzed situation while Stakeholder 2 may be more involved in an improvisation dynamic. Factorial analysis and standard deviation calculus may be useful to appraise the general coherence of the sociotechni-

Table 5. The catalytic trajectory

	T1	T2	T3
N	1	1	1
D	1	1	1
R	1	1	1
C	5	5	5

Table 6. Main techniques to appraise similarities between profiles.

Symbol and proponent	Procedure	Type of comparison	Remarks
D (Osgood-Suci, 1952; Cronbach and Gleser, 1952)	Distance measure	k (also k-1, k-2)	A general formula
CRL (Pearson, 1928)	Distance measure for standardized variates	k	
rp (Catell, 1949)	Transformed distance measure for standardized variates	k (also k-1)	Convert D to a scale from 1 to -1
Q (Stephenson, 1950)	Product moment correlation across variates	k-2	Symbol Q used here instead of r for clarity
Rho (Spearman)	Correlation across scores ranked within a profile	k-2	
Tau (Kendall, 1948)	Based on rank arrangements	k-2	Highly correlated with rho
r pa	Based on tally of similarity of slope along profiles	k-2	Estimate of tau based on partial data

cal trajectory under study.

Usually, distance appraisal is based on Euclidean distance calculus. Cronbach and Gleser (1953, p. 462) have suggested the following techniques to appraise similarities between profiles (see Table 6).

In order to adapt the method proposed by Doty, Glick, and Huber (based on a classic distance approach D) to the processual perspective of the archetypal approach, the following indicators can be worked out: a Total Effective Vectorial Distance (TEVD), a Total Potential Vectorial Distance (TPVD), and four Appropriative Proximity Indices (API). On the three periods, the Total Effective Vectorial Distance can be calculated as follows:

$$TEVD = \sqrt{\sum_{i=1}^{3}\sum_{l=1}^{3}(X_{ilj} - X_{ilk})^2}$$

With X_{ilj}: value at Ti on the line l of vector j, which corresponds to real appropriative states for Ti, and X_{ilk}: value at Ti on the line l of the vector k, vector treating the theoretical appropriative states for Ti.

For the TPVD calculus, the method is the same except, in the place of X_{ilj}: X_{ilr}: value at Ti on line l of vector r, the vector condensing the appropriative states is opposite those of the theoretical vector X_{ilk}.

In the continuation with Doty and Glick's method, an API can be worked out using the following formula:

API=1–*EVET/EVPT* with 0≤ *API* ≤1.

Lastly, an important problem remains: the division of the different phases, which will compose unitary vectors. How will the various stages that constitute the mean vectors be distinguished and then archetypal change isolated? The following rule will be followed: a significant change between two parameters (for instance R2 compared to R1)

validated by a mean comparison test (see Lesard Monga, 1993; Mbengue, 1999) will characterize an archetypal change (see Appendix A.5).

Modeling Suggested for the Sociotechnical System Under Study

It has been decided to follow a cautious two-step operationalization strategy. First, and in continuation with a critical, realistic perspective as proposed by Archer (1995), agents' categories have been distinguished within the role system under study (a university of management and economics): students, teachers, and administrative agents. Then, the research was centered on three axes of interaction: students-teachers, students-students and students-administrative agents. Finally, three dimensions helped us to generate our first set of items: interactions in the classroom and interactions outside the classroom, interactions within and outside the institution, and interaction with the teaching process (e.g., preparation and assessment of courses). In the end, four sub-constructs have been worked out for R:

- Student-teacher interactions in the classroom (R S-T-C), which deal mainly with relational and intra-institutional aspects;
- Student-teacher interactions outside the classroom (R S-T-OC), dealing with less relational aspects, either intra or extra institutional;
- Student-student interactions in or outside the classroom (R S-S), treating non-relational aspects, whether intra or extra-institutional;
- Student-administrative agent interactions (R S-A), dealing with nonrelational aspects, intra or extra-institution.

For the first three axes, a set of items was developed. They treated the various stages of the teaching process. The idea was the following: if the set made a concrete system (good factorial validation and internal consistency), then the theoretical trajectories proposed as referential in our first part would be maintained. However, should the set not be maintained, it will be necessary to come back to the theoretical specification work.

At the end of this first logico-deductive work, the research resulted in an initial list of items associated with a scale ranging from 1 to 5, which corresponded to respondents' level of agreement: "Strongly agree" for 1 and "Strongly disagree" for 5 (see appendix A.1).

As a conclusion to this preliminary phase of the empirical work, it is possible to expand on some quantitative techniques made for this study. The goal of this research was not to adopt a positivist stance; this would have been incoherent with the theoretical positioning of our model. In view of the fact that our theoretical framework shed light on the possibility of a co-existence of different archetypes or trajectories within the same socio-technical system, more importance was given to internal consistency and convergent factorial validation (relative to the discriminatory one). Besides, the scales and the items they include stressed the sub-dimensions (multiples) of the archetypes, instead of the usual reformulations

of questions. Lastly, the whole methodological device was used with a more comprehensive than explanatory objective.

First Results of the PPR at T1: Refinement of Scales and Some Initial Trends

Parallel to the participatory-research mentioned in the case study section, the implementation of the e-learning system in the French university has been an opportunity to apply the PPR method suggested in the first part.

The sampling was made of approximately 40 users[8], representative of the 400 students in all departments of the economics and management faculty:

- An "Institut Universitaire Professionnel de management" (IUP), ten years old. It has approximately 320 students pursuing BA and MA degrees and 80 teachers (permanent and part-time);
- An "Institut de comptabilité et de finance" ("Institute of Accountancy and Finance"), more recent, with 80 students.

Table 7. Measures (ranging from 1 to 5) of archetypal situations within the economics and management faculty

	Phase 1	Phase 2	Phase 3
Actual measures linked to vector V1, V2 and V3	R=2,64, N=2,83, P=1,53, and C=3,17	R=2,6, N=2,89, P=1,48, and C=3,14	R=2,59, N=2,39, P=1,37, and C=3,34
Theoretical measures for a balanced trajectory 1	R=0, N=5, P=0, and C=0	R=0, N=0, P=5, and C=0	R=5, N=0, P=0, and C=0
Theoretical measures for a balanced trajectory 2	R=0, N=5, P=5, and C=0	R=5, N=0, P=5, and C=0	R=0, N=5, P=0, and C=0
Theoretical measures for a balanced trajectory 3	R=0, N=5, P=0, and C=5	R=5, N=0, P=0, and C=5	R=0, N=5, P=0, and C=0
Theoretical measures for an improvisational trajectory	R=5, N=0, P=0, and C=5	R=5, N=0, P=0, and C=5	R=5, N=0, P=0, and C=5
Theoretical measures for a catalytic trajectory	R=0, N=0, P=0, and C=5	R=0, N=0, P=0, and C=5	R=0, N=0, P=0, and C=5

Table 8. Appropriative proximity Indices from T1 to T3

	Calculus	Results	Classification by descending order
API BP 1	EVET= 9,37 EVPT= 17,3	45.8%	4
API BP 2	EVET= 9,42 EVPT= 17,3	45.5	5
API BP 3	EVET= 8,87 EVPT= 17,3	48.7%	3
API C	EVET= 7,68 EVPT= 17,3	56.1 %	1
API I	EVET= 8,83 EVPT= 17,3	49%	2

For the first observation period T1 (in December 2003), convergent and discriminatory factorial analysis along with Cronbach Alpha (see Appendix A.1, A.2 and A.3) incontrovertibly confirmed the relevance of our four sociotechnical archetypes R, N, D, and C. For T1, the situation was largely dominated by a catalytic phenomenon (see Table 7).

The tool had a very moderate structuring effect. Regeneration (see Appendix A 4.1) **mainly involved student-administration interactions** (which is broadly convergent with the case study). From the students' perspective, the Virtual Office is not very disruptive, either from a psychological or from a socio-political point of view (P=1,53).

From T1 to T5 (January[9] to May 2004): Implementation of the PPR Method

As shown in Table 8, the Appropriative Proximity Indices demonstrated that the three trajectories of the archetypal approach (catalytic, balanced, and improvisational) co-exist in this case.

Nevertheless, the catalytic trajectory seems to be more present than the other two (API for the catalytic trajectory was 56.1%, whereas it was 49% for the improvisational dynamic and 45% for the balanced one, as seen in A.6.2). The

survey broadly confirms the trends advanced in the case study. The Virtual Office is a tool that primarily changes the flow of academic and administrative information about the IUP (classroom assignments, due dates, regulations for exams and reports, grades, and so forth). Eventually, **it can be noticed that the software had not really resulted in a significant decrease in administrative workload** (as suggested first at T2 by R S-A scores). Only one out of three administrative agents confirmed that the technology makes it easier for them (they receive fewer queries about IUP's administrative documents on file, less direct or phone questions about IUP's current events, and so forth). For the other two, the situation is more or less unchanged.

In the educational area (R S-T), the situation is rather neutral. Intra and extra-classroom interactions are scarcely modified by the technology (perhaps because the model was insufficiently centered on the tool's potential added values: tests used for self-evaluation, groups, forums concerned with the preparation of case-studies, and so forth). In accordance with the fact that the catalytic trajectory is most pronounced, the tool mainly served as a catalyst for the IUP project started long before the arrival of the virtual office: namely, the development of student autonomy. Through project groups, the open-mindedness of teachers, and the specific nature of the interactive and modular education, students are incited to be individually responsible as soon as they enter the IUP.

Lastly, this research clearly confirms the first two propositions raised in the first part. Over this one year and a half period, the system has led mainly to changes related to non-relational aspects of roles. Thus, R S-A interactions are more structured than R S-T ones. Moreover, this system, corresponding to a low-level of restrictiveness, is not appropriated in a very coherent way. Various sub-trajectories and archetypal situations co-exist (see A.4). With regard to the third proposition, the case and the PPR method do not make it possible to confirm or refute the statement.

DISCUSSION: CONTRIBUTION, LIMITATIONS, AND PERSPECTIVES

At this point, some implications, limitations, and extrapolations of this work can be raised. It seems that several contributions can be related to this research. First, from a methodological perspective, **the fieldwork confirms the feasibility of the PPR approach**, and its complementarity with more qualitative techniques (such as participatory research). Then, from a theoretical standpoint, the creation of new models has expanded the archetypal approach. Some obscure points concerning N and R have been defined precisely. Neutrality truly seems to be more than the simple opposite of a regenerated sociotechnical state (see A.2, A.3, and A.4 appendices). Moreover, disruption, from a psychological point of view, seems inherent to a system with disruption from a political point of view (particularly, for the case studied). In the field of education, this work enabled the expansion and refinement of models specific to graduate studies. Factorial analysis made it possible to consider that there are logically four dimensions in the interactional system under study: student-administration, teacher-student in the classroom, teacher-student

outside the classroom and student-student. The student-teacher interactions outside the classroom are the most problematic to study.

As for **the potential limitations, it seems that the overall strategy, along with the archetypal approach on which it is based, targets more** "weakly project-embedded" technologies than technologies strongly embedded in this stage. Thus, the case of Enterprise Resource Planning seems different from that of e-mail systems, Intranets, groupware, e-learning tools (at least the majority), and even CAT scanners. ERP are tools whose project phase may be extremely long: between one year and two and a half years for four complete modules (Lemaire, 2003). Conceptualization and local development of the tool are followed as well, by steps that can have strong structuring power. Key-users, intermediary managers, local computer developers, editor consultants, and setting consultants are all involved in lengthy negotiations around the processes that make ERP a highly project-embedded technology. On the other hand, projects like intranets or groupware systems, with more emerging contents, shorter duration, and smaller conception perimeter, would certainly be more relevant to the trajectories of the archetypal approach and the research strategy (from implantation to t+n) that we followed. If this were to constitute a future research agenda, the archetypal approach should be adapted to apply to restrictive and strongly "project-embedded technologies." For the time being, the way it is formulated is close to end-users' behaviors.

Another limitation lies in the sequential logic of this work, which sticks to a monthly program. The data collection schedule may have missed an important step in the structuring process of the sociotechnical system. Here, the difficulty seems to boil down to the periodicity chosen for the study. The researcher must, nonetheless, take into account the potential reactions of respondents to excessive reminders regarding the return of completed questionnaires. Besides, because of the multiplicity of methodologies used for this study, it was possible to keep an eye on changes in between the different data collection phases.

The third and last limitation is in the starting point of data collection for the survey. The immediate implementation of the questionnaire in October (e.g., the first month of the technology) would have undoubtedly valorized more of an initial neutrality. This would have contributed to increasing the Apppropriative Proximity Index for the balanced trajectory. The lack of time explains this error.

Research perspectives akin to or benefiting from this empirical study are numerous. The following represent a far from exhaustive list:

1. In accordance with the first remark, to use the method in the project stage in order to observe a restrictive tool (like an ERP) in a virtual state. This could be a structuring object for organization. Further, it implies the dissection of two types of questionnaires: one focused on N, D, R, and C in the project phase (with specific scales), and another one centered on the post-project phase (with other items and scales for N, D, R, and C);

2. Obviously, to move from the academic world to the business world. Nonetheless, this first study seems to have been an interesting preparatory phase for more company-centered research;

3. To couple user-focused questionnaires with others centered on communities in charge of IS management in order to work out and test propositions about IT appropriation and its associated effectiveness;

4. To integrate Archer's most recent work (2003), notably her propositions about the "internal conversation" of actors (interacting with a technology), which would make it possible to move from a descriptive to a more comprehensive stance;

5. To continue using the archetypal approach and to prolong its assimilation-accommo-

dation process, for instance, to discover potential new trajectories or any possible refinements of the archetypes.

ACKNOWLEDGMENT

We wish to thank Claude Pellegrin, Frantz Rowe, and Matthew Jones, as well as the associate editor (Rob Harris) and two anonymous reviewers for their detailed feedback on the manuscript. We would also like to acknowledge the great help of Kirsten Albertsen in the proofreading of this chapter.

REFERENCES

Alter, N. (1985). *La Bureautique dans l'Entreprise.* Paris: Les éditions ouvrières.

Alter, N. (1995). Peut-on programmer l'innovation. *Revue Française de gestion. 10,* 78-86.

Archer, M. (1982). Morphogenesis versus structuration: On combining structure and action. *The British Journal of Sociology, 33*(4), 455-483.

Archer, M. (1995). *Realistic social theory: The morphogenetic approach.* Cambridge, MA: Cambridge University press.

Archer, M. (2003). *Structure, agency and the internal conversation,* Cambridge, MA: Cambridge University press.

Barley, S. R. (1986). Technology as an occasion for structuring: Evidence from observations of CT scanners and the social order of radiology departments. *Administrative Science Quarterly, 31*(1), 78-108.

Barley, S. R. (1990). The alignment of technology and structure through roles and networks. *Administrative Science Quarterly, 35* (2), 61-103.

Barley, S.R., & Tolbert, P.S. (1997). Institutionalization and structuration: Studying the link between action and institution. *Organization Studies,* 93-117.

Bhaskar, R. (1989). *The possibility of naturalism* (2nd ed.). Hemel Hempstead: Harvester Wheatsheaf.

Bouchikhi, A. (1990). *Structuration des organisation.* Paris: Economica.

Bourdieu, P. (1972). *Esquisse d'un théorie de la pratique.* Paris: Edition du Seuil.

Burkhardt, M. E., & Brass, D. J. (1990). Changing patterns or patterns of change: The effects of a change in technology on social network structure and power. *Administrative science quaterly, 35*(1), 104-127.

Callon, M., & Latour, B. (1990). *La Science telle qu'elle se fait.* Paris: Editions La Découverte.

Callon, M., & Latour, B. (1992). *Aramis, ou l'amour des techniques.* Paris: Editions La Découverte.

Carlsson, S. A. (2003). Advancing information systems evaluation (research): A critical realist approach. *Electronic Journal of Information System Evalution, 6*(2).

Cattell, R. B. (1949). RP and other coefficients of pattern similarity. *Psychometrika, 14,* 279-298.

Chaomei, C., & Roy, R. (1996). Modeling situated actions in collaborative hypertext databases. *Journal of Computer Mediated Communication, 2* (3).

Choudrie, J., & Dwivedi, Y. K. (2005). Investigating the research approaches for examining technology adoption issues. *Journal of Research Practice, 1*(1).

Ciborra, C. U. (1997). De profundis? Deconstructing the concept of strategic alignment. *IRIS,* (20).

Ciborra, C. U. (1999). A theory of information systems based on improvisation. In W. L.

Currie & B. Galliers, *Rethinking management information systems* (pp.136-55).Oxford: Oxford University press.

Ciborra, C. U. (2000). A critical review of the literature on the management of corporate information infrastructure. In C. U. Ciborra, (Ed.), *From control to drift* (pp.15-41). Oxford: Oxford university press.

Ciborra, C. U. (2001). Moods, situated action and time: A new study of improvisation. *IRIS,* 24.

Cronbach, L. J., & Gleser, G. C. (1952). Similarity between persons and related problems of profile analysis. *Urbana: University of Illinois, Bureau of Research and Serviec, College of Education.*

Cronbach, L. J., & Gleser, G. C. (1953). Assessing similarity between profiles. *The Psychological Bulletin,* 50(6), 456-473.

de Vaujany, F. X. (2003). Les figures de la gestion du changement sociotechnique. *Sociologie du travail,* 45(4), 515-536.

Dobson, P. J. (1999, December). *Approaches to theory use in interpretive case studies.* Paper presented at 10th Australian Conference on Information Systems, Wellington, New Zealand.

Dobson, P. J. (2002). Critical realism and information systems research: Why bother with philosophy? [Electronic version]. *Information Research, 7*(2).

Dobson, P. J. (2003). The SoSM revisited---A critical realist perspective. In J. J. Cano (Ed.), *Critical reflections on information systems: A systemic approach* (pp. 122-135). Hershey, PA: Idea Group Publishing.

Doty, D. H., & Glick, W. H. (1994). Typologies as a unique form of theory building: Toward improved understanding and modeling. *Academy of Management Review, 19*(2), 230-251.

Doty, D. H., Glick, W. H., & Huber, G. P. (1994). Fit, equifinality, and organizational effectiveness:

A test of two configurational theories. *Academy of Management Journal, 36*(6), 1196-1250.

Giddens, A. (1979). *Central problems in social theory.* Los Angeles: University of California press.

Giddens, A. (1984). *The constitution of society: Outline of a theory of structuration.* Los Angeles: University of California press.

Hu, P. J., Clark, T. H., & Ma, W. W. (2003). Examining technology acceptance by school teachers: A longitudinal study. *Information and Management, 41*(2), 227-241.

Kaplan, B., & Duchon, D. (1988). Combining qualitative and quantitative methods in information systems research: A case study. *MIS Quarterly, 12*(4), 571-586.

Karahanna, E., Straub, D., & Chervany, N. (1999). Information technology adoption across time: A cross-sectional comparison of pre-adoption and post-adoption beliefs. *Management Information Systems Quarterly, 13*(2), 183-213.

Kendall, M. G. (1948). *Rank correlation methods.* Griffin.

Kimberly, J. (1976). Issues in the design of longitudinal research: The temporal dimension. *Sociological Methods and Research, 4*(3), 21-47.

Kimberly, J. (1980). Data aggregation in organizational research: The temporal dimension. *Organization Studies, 1*(4), 367-377.

Lemaire, L. (2003). *Systèmes de gestion integers: Des technologies à risque?* Paris: Editions Liaison.

Lesard Monga, S. (1993). *Statistique, concepts and methods.* Presses Universitaires de Montréal.

Lin, A., & Conford, T. (2000). Sociotechnical perspectives on emergence phenomena. In E. Coakes, D. Willis, & R. Lloyd-Jones (Eds.), *The New SocioTech* (pp. 51-59). London: Springer.

Mbengue, A. (1999). Tests de comparaison. In R. A. Thiétart (Ed.), *Méthodes de recherche en management* (pp. 291-334). Dunod.

Miles, R., & Snow, C. (1978). *Organizational strategy, structure and process.* McGraw-Hill.

Miller, D. T., & Friesen, P. H. (1982). The longitudinal analysis of organizations: A methodological perspective. *Management Science, 29*(9), 113-134.

Mintzberg, H. (1979). *The structuring of organizations.* Englewoods Cliffs, NJ: Prentice-Hall.

Mintzberg, H. (1983). *Structures in fives: Designing effective organizations.* Englewood Cliffs, NJ: Prentice Hall.

Mustonen-Ollila, E., & Lyytinen, K. (2003). Why organizations adopt information system process innovations: A longitudinal study using diffusion of innovation theory. *Information Systems Journal, 13*, 275-297.

Mustonen-Ollila, A., & Lyytinen, K. (2004). How organizations adopt information system process innovations: A longitudinal analysis. *European Journal of Information Systems, 13*, 35-51.

Nadel, S. F. (1957). *The theory of social structure.* London: Cohen and West.

Orlikowski, W. J. (1992). The duality of technology: Rethinking the concept of technology in organizations. *Organization Science, 3*(3), 398-427.

Orlikowski, W. J. (2000). Using technology as a practice lens for studying technology in organizations. *Organization Science, 11*, 404-428.

Orlikowski, W. J., & Robey, D. (1991). Information technology and the structuring of organizations. *Information Systems Research, 12*(2), 143-169.

Orlikowski, W. J., & Yates, J. (2002). It's about time: Temporal structuring in organizations. *Organization Science, 13*(6), 684-700.

Osgood, C. E., & Suci, G. (1952). A measure of relation determined by both mean difference and profile information. *Psychological Bulletin, 49*, 251-262.

Pearson, K. (1928). On the coefficient of racial likeness. *Biometrika, 18*, 105-117.

Pinsonneault, A., & Kramer, K. L. (1993). Survey research methodology in management information systems: An assessment. *Journal of Management Information Systems, 10*(2), 75-106.

Poole, M.S., & Desanctis, G. (1992). Microlevel structuration in computer-supported group decision-making. *Human Communication Research, 19*, 5-49.

Rogers, E. (1995). *The diffusion of innovation.* New York: Free Press, first edition 1962.

Schumpeter, Joesph A. (1942). Capitalism, socialism, and Democracy. New York: Harper and Brothers.

Schumpeter, J. A. (1975). *Capitalism, socialism and democracy.* New York: Harper (Original work published 1942).

Silver, M. S. (1988). User perceptions of decision support system restrictiveness: An experiment. *Journal of Management Information Systems, 5*(1), 51-65.

Stephenson, W. (1950). A statistical approach to typology: The study of trait-universes. *Journal of Clinical Psychology, 6*, 26-38.

Thietart, R. A. (2001). *Doing management research: A comprehensive guide.* Sage.

Trist, E., & Bamforth, K. (1951). Some social and psychological consequences of Longwall method of coalgetting. *Human Relations, 4*, 3–38.

Tyre, M. J., & Orlikowski, W. J. (1994). Windows of opportunity: Temporal patterns of technological adaption in organizations. *Organization Science, 5*(1), 98-118.

Venkatesh, A., & Vitalari, N. P. (1991). Longitudinal surveys in information systems research: An examination of issues, methods and applications. In K. Kramer (Ed.), *The information systems challenge: Survey research methods.* Harvard, MA: Harvard University press, 115-144.

Walsham, G. (1993). *Interpreting information systems in organisations.* Wiley.

ENDNOTES

[1] In a broad manner, Kimberly (1980, p. 329) defines longitudinal research method as: "Longitudinal organizational research consists of those techniques, methodologies, and activities, which permit the observation, description, and/or classification of organizational phenomena, in such a way, that processes can be identified and empirically documented." Miller and Friesen (1982) propose defining five types of longitudinal methods: "type 1," concerning non quantitative researches centred on a single organization, "type 2" studies focused on a quantitative multivariate analysis of a single organization, "type 3" quantitative studies, with a limited scope, centered on multiple organizations, "type 4" non-quantitative multivariate analysis of multiple organizations, and "type 5," quantitative multivariate analysis of multiple organizations.

[2] Orlikowski (2000) proposes two sub-situations: inertia (technology is used as a means to maintain the status quo) and application (technology is used to significantly change the status quo).

[3] See Tyre and Orlikowski (1994) on the "windows of opportunity" that sometimes occur in ICT appropriation.

[4] Silver (1988, p.52), restrictiveness is the "degree to which and the manner in which a [structure] restricts its users' decision-

making processes to a particular subset of all possible outcomes." Thus, the more restrictive the technology, the more limited is the set of unintended (non-prescribed) actions the user can take; the less restrictive the technology, the more open is the set of possible actions during the use process (Desanctis & Poole, 1994, p.126).

[5] "Institut Universitaire Technologique," for example, brief post A-level vocational training.

[6] One administrative portal (including administrative information such as internal rules, conditional scheduling of reports, daily time schedules, notes, forums, and so forth) and eleven sites devoted to teaching.

[7] "An alternative theoretical approach is possible when two of the ideal-types define the endpoints of a continuum. In this special case, one ideal-type is scored as the maximum value on each relevant construct and a second ideal type is scored as the minimum value on each construct," (Doty & Glick, 1994, p. 237).

[8] $n1=54$, $n2=48$, $n3=37$, $n4=35$ and $n5=31$.

[9] Each evaluation was carried out at the beginning of the month following the period in question. The December 2003 evaluation was thus made during the first week of January 2004.

[10] Beyond the items set out in the table, the survey also included questions about respondents' profiles, frequency, and forms of technology use.

[11] At the end of T1, two different scales were built for OC: OC1 including R 7, 12 and 15, and OC2 including R 6, 23 and 24. The next phase lead us to give up the OC 2 construct.

APPENDIX

A.1. Table of items[10]

Codes	Questions	Status
R1	My use of the virtual office has changed my participation in the course.	R S-T-C: M
R2	I think I am in a better position to understand the course since the implementation of the virtual office.	R S-T-C: M
R3	The virtual office has changed the overall management of the course as achieved by the teacher.	R S-T-C: M
R4	The use of the virtual office has not devolved into pre-existing pedagogical routines.	R S-T-C: E in T1
R5	The virtual office enables the teacher to re-center his work on essential aspects of the course.	R S-T-C: E in T2
R6	The virtual office has increased the number of interactions between the teacher and his students, notably by means of announcements, agenda, and forums.	R S-T-OC: M
R7	The virtual office makes it possible to extend the course beyond the scheduled time limit, and favors interactions that would not have taken place without the tool.	R S-T-OC: M
R8	The virtual office modifies the way the teacher manages his case studies.	R S-T-C: E in T2
R9	The virtual office modifies the way teachers present aspects of their course, especially theories, concepts, and methods.	R S-T-C: E in T1
R10	The role of teachers has been modified by the use of the virtual office	R S-T-C: E en T1
R11	The use of the virtual office leads me to ask questions I would not have raised otherwise.	R S-T-C: E en T3
R12	Since using the virtual office, I get in touch with teachers I would not have tried to meet otherwise.	R S-T-OC: M
R13	Since using the virtual office at the university, I got in touch with students I wouldn't have met otherwise.	R S-S-OC: M
R14	Since using the virtual office, I feel more involved in the course.	R S-S-OC : M
R15	With the virtual office, I guess it would be easier to cover a course I missed.	R S-T-OC: E in T3
R16	With the virtual office, I know more things about my administrative environment at the faculty.	R S-A: M
R17	With the virtual office, I work more continuously and more intensively with the members of my group for collective reports (strategic analysis, information systems reports, and so forth).	R S-S-OC: E in T1
R18	With the virtual office, I prepare case studies jointly with my colleagues.	R S-S-OC: M
R19	With the virtual office, I ask the administration for less information.	R S-A: M
R20	With the virtual office, I succeed more easily in evaluating my work (for example, via the "test" functionality).	R S-S-EI: M
R21	The virtual office helps me to stay in touch with my colleagues during the period I have to spend with my company (I must spend out of class?) .	R S-S-EI: E in T1
R22	The virtual office helps me to stay in touch with my faculty during periods of alternation or during holidays.	R S-A-EI: M

* Key to the table: S: students; T: teachers; A: administrative agents; I: institution; EI: extra-institution; C: in the classroom; OC: out of the classroom; M: maintained; E: eliminated.

continued on following page

A.1. continued

R23	The virtual office has changed the way I prepare the assignments given by my teacher.	R S-T-OC: M
R24	The virtual office has changed the way I prepare for my exams.	R S-T-OC: M
N1	The virtual office has not devolved into pre-existing routines.	N S-T: M
N2	The use of the virtual office consolidates the relationships between teachers and students that existed beforehand.	N S-T: M
N3	The use of the virtual office makes the role and status of the teacher even more legitimate.	N S-T: M
N4	With the virtual office, the usual way to do a course is finally strengthened.	N S-T: M
P1-1	I do not feel I am good enough to use this tool that looks too complicated.	P S-T-OC: M
P1-2	When I use the virtual office, I feel out of my depth with its functions and contents.	P S-T-OC: M
P1-3	I find my colleagues more at ease, which makes me nervous.	P S-S: M
P1-4	Since the virtual office has been put at our disposal, I feel more out of my depth with the course.	P S-T-C: M
P2-1	Since we have been using the virtual office, there are more tensions between teachers and students.	P S-T-OC: M
P2-2	Since we have been using the virtual office, there are more tensions between students and the administration.	P S-T-OC: M
P2-3	Since we have been using the virtual office, there are more tensions between students.	P S-S-OC: M
C1	The virtual office has only accelerated some changes initiated before the use of the tool.	C S-T-I: E in T1
C2	The virtual office has only helped me reinforce habits I had developed before my first use of the tool.	C S-T-OC: E in T2
C3	The virtual office is one factor among many others that contributes to the evolution of teachers and education.	C S-T-C: M
C4	The virtual office is parallel in importance to the course given by teachers.	C S-T-C: M
C5	The virtual office plays a very marginal role in my understanding of the course.	C S-T-C: M
C6	The virtual office plays a very marginal role in the management of the course as achieved by the teacher.	C S-T-C: M
C7	I was already used to asking my teachers questions before the virtual office was implemented, but this tool has helped me do this more.	C S-T-C: M

A.2 Cronbach Alpha from T1 to T5 (on final scales)

	Alpha T1	Alpha T2	Alpha T3
R	0,713	0,84	0,849
N	0,54	0,567	0,55
P	0,667	0,745	0,86
C	0,589	0,525	0,633
R E-P-C	0,657	0,625	0,7
R E-P-HC1	**0,45**	0,657	0,58
R E-P-HC2	0,76	**0,38**	**0,33**
R E-E	0,5	0,683	0,683
R E-A	0,83	**0,43**	0,75

NB: R E-P-HC2 has been given up.

A.3 Factorial analyses (extract).

Variables	Components			
	1 (R)	**2 (C)**	**4 (P)**	**7 (N)**
R1	**0,163**	0,79	0	0
R2	**0,250**	0,65	0	0,11
R3	**0,02**	0	0	0
R6	**0,793**	0	0,21	0,23
R7	**0,538**	0,31	0	-0,19
R12	**0,62**	0,31	-0,19	0
R13	**0,610**	0	-0,11	0
R14	**0,358**	0,125	0,16	0
R16	**0,68**	0	0	0
R18	**0,588**	0,34	0,23	0,19
R19	**0,02**	0,15	-0,3	0,26
R20	**0,05**	0,65	0	0,31
R22	**0,003**	0	0	0,325
R23	**0,433**	0,27	0	0,13
R24	**0,607**	0,51	0,13	0
N1	0	0,125	0	**0,732**
N2	0,3	0,179	0,35	**0,369**
N3	0,15	0	0,45	**0,299**
N4	0	0,256	0	**0,699**

Overall factorial analysis at T2 (without eliminated items, with Varimax rotation and eighenvalues higher than 1)

continued on following page

A.3 continued

P2	0,2	0,29	**0,786**	-0,14
P3	0	0	**0,655**	-0,11
P4	-0,21	0,15	**0,273**	0
P5	0	0	**0,04**	-0,1
P6	-0,18	0	**0,257**	0
P7	0,15	0	**0,2**	0,11
C3	0,1	**-0,09**	-0,16	-0,16
C4	0	**0**	0	0
C5	0	**-0,424**	-0,15	0
C6	-0,13	**-0,639**	0	-0,2
C7	0	**-0,2**	-0,11	-0,1

A.4 Results for each scale

A.4.1 Presentation of values corresponding to sociotechnical archetypes (with the use of final scales for the five periods)

	Mean value at T1	Mean value at T2	Mean value at T3	Mean value at T4	Mean value at T5	Items in the scale
R	2,69	2,64	2,52	2,64	2,59	R 2, 3, 6, 7, 12, 13, 14, 16, 17, 18, 19, 20, 22, 23, 24
N	2,83	2,87	2,89	2,91	2,39	N 1, 2, 3, 4
P	1,53	1,48	1,56	1,4	1,37	P 1, 2, 3, 4, 5, 6, 7
C	3,42	3,17	3,11	3,15	3,34	C 3, 4, 5, 6, 7

A.4.2 Presentation of the values for T1 and T5 for all sub-constructs (on definite scales)

	Mean value at T1	Mean value at T5	Items in the scales
R E-P-C	2,467	2,32	R 1, 2, 3
R E-P-HC1[11]	2,76	2,42	R 7, 12
R E-E	2,395	2,35	R 13, 14, 18, 20
R E-A	3,14	3,19	R 16, 19, 22
P1-i	1,58	1,25	P 1, 2, 3, 4
P 2-i	1,48	1,52	P 5, 6, 7

A.5 Results of mean comparison tests

A.5.1 General formula

Here, n is higher than 30, which makes it possible to consider samples as big and to use the following formula:

$$Tij = \frac{(Y_i - Y_j)}{(\frac{S_i^2}{n_i} + \frac{S_j^2}{n_j})}$$

With: S_i^2: variance, Y_i: mean, n_i: number of observations. Then, in order to approximate T with T N(0,1) for α=0,05, T=1,96

A.5.2 Results

Comparison	T1-T2	T2-T3	T3-T4	T4-T5
For R	0,45	1,07	1,05	0,43
For P	0,5	0,66	1,34	4,5
For N	0,2	0,14	0,19	0,26
For C	2,21	0,56	0,35	1,57

Thus, phase 1 corresponds to a unique vector (V1); phases 2, 3, 4 will have to be included in the same mean vector (V2), and phase 5 corresponds to a third vector (V3).

Chapter XIV
The U.S. Video Game Industry:
Analyzing Representation of Gender and Race

Janet C. Dunlop
Oklahoma State University, USA

ABSTRACT

Today's media are vast in both form and influence; however, few cultural studies scholars address the video gaming industry's role in domestic maintenance and global imposition of U.S. hegemonic ideologies. In this study, video games are analyzed by cover art, content, and origin of production. Whether it is earning more "powers" in games such as Star Wars, or earning points to purchase more powerful artillery in Grand Theft Auto, capitalist ideology is reinforced in a subtle, entertaining fashion. This study shows that oppressive hegemonic representations of gender and race are not only present, but permeate the majority of top-selling video games. Finally, the study traces the origins of best-selling games, to reveal a virtual U.S. monopoly in the content of this formative medium.

INTRODUCTION

Recently, the Chinese government banned 50 U.S. video games, top sellers worldwide, claiming that they are a negative influence on Chinese youth. This was seen by many as an attempt to maintain hegemonic codes in China (China Daily News Online, Sept. 28, 2005). However, throughout discussions of the role of media in establishing and perpetuating hegemonic codes in society, (Cortes, 2000; Fiske, 1992, 1994,; Gross, 2001; Hall, 2000; Hooks, 1990), few scholars address the video gaming industry's role in domestic maintenance and global imposition of U.S. hegemonic ideologies.

By and large, the most popular video games in the U.S. are also the best-selling games worldwide (Appendix B). The U.S. monopoly on the gaming software industry, as it applies to sociological effects on children, is paramount. This discussion is not to claim that all video games are bad. In contrast, games, such as *Star Wars: Knights of the Old Republic*, invite players to question ethical issues such as responsibility for one's actions. *Freedom Fighters* inverts the ideologies surrounding the U.S.-Iraq war, allowing players to question the difference between a terrorist and a freedom fighter. It points to the possibility that the labels lie only in what one believes is right and just. In *Tak and the Power of Ju Ju*, young players enjoy the role of an unlikely hero, a small, awkward tribesman who rescues the Pupununu people from the evil sorcerer, Tlalock. This game illustrates that heroism can be found in the most unlikely persons. This said, in the majority of these best-sellers, ideologies of capitalism, white male-dominance, and violence is blatant. Gamers gain prestige by earning points, which enable them to "buy" better equipment in the game. For example, in *ATV OffRoad Fury*, ATV riders can "purchase" better engines, better riders, and better equipment each time they win a race. This purchasing of gadgets is of unquestioned value, thus, capitalist ideologies are imbedded deep within the premise of the game. In this way, production or performance is constant and only consumption can be varied. Whether it is earning more "powers" in games such as *The Elder Scrolls II: Morrowind*, or earning points to purchase artillery in *Grand Theft Auto*, capitalist ideology is reinforced in subtle, engaging fashion. This study shows that the U.S. hegemonic codes of capitalism, gender, and race are not only present, but prevalent in the majority of video games. In addition, it indicates that the reason behind the monopoly of video game ideology is due to the U.S.'s domination of the gaming software industry production and sales.

THEORETICAL FRAMEWORK

In the same way that under-representation or negative stereotypical images have the ability to affect children's attitudes, values, and roles of themselves and others in society, the implications of racial diversity and stereotypes in video games have yet to be researched. A fair examination of the quality of any message that children receive also requires a close look at how people of color are depicted in video games. These images influence perceptions of societal roles, not only for youth of color, but also for white youth—boys and girls alike. In order to present a clear picture of the message that youth of all colors are receiving in video games, a racial analysis must be part of video game analysis.

Post-structuralist Jaques Lacan theorizes that in the pre-Oedipal stage, before babies develop language, they inhabit an imaginary speechless world between mother, child, and world. The acquisition of language results in the loss of the imaginary world identity with the mother, and thus, the child enters a (masculine) world that is structured by language (Crotty, 1998). Applying Lacanian symbolic theory, the individual forms identity of self and identity of others through the images one views. As the individual views images that resemble or do not resemble the self, she or he develops a perception of one's position in society (Crotty, 1998). Assuming this is true, the presence of symbolic annihilation in the video gaming industry for females and minorities is alarming. It is logical to apply Gross's (2001) ideas of symbolic annihilation to the video gaming industry where those who are at the bottom of the various power hierarchies will be kept in their places in part through relative invisibility (p.409). By focusing on the negligible representation of women and minorities, the following analysis of current popular video game selections suggests that representational issues may be at the core of the influence of gender and ethnicity on the adoption and use of gaming technology. Furthermore, it suggests that the global hegemonic effects of the U.S. monopoly of the gaming industry are an area for further research.

This chapter is intended to expand the work of cultural theorists Stuart Hall (2000), Bell Hooks (1991), Larry Gross (2001), and Herman Gray (2001), who critically question the connection between popular culture and the representation of social groups. Although video game sales are a multi-billion dollar global industry, cultural scholars are markedly mute about the effects of video games. Leonard (2004) claims, "There is a marked failure to recognize video games as sophisticated vehicles inhabiting and disseminating ideologies of hegemony," (p. 3). Video games are part of a capitalist economy—but at what cost to the social development of youth? What about ethics? In this discussion, a sample of twenty top-selling video games is analyzed to determine messages about capitalism, race, and gender. While quantification of female and minority characters in a large sample of video games is equally important in achieving an analysis of representations in video games, this study is intended to elucidate and to understand the ideological terrain of popular video games. It is through this phenomenological observation of the games, the characters, the imbedded rules, and value systems, and through "thick description" that social meanings emerge (Geertz, 1983). This task is fundamentally important in reflecting on current video games and theories of identity development in youth.

THEORETICAL PERSPECTIVE

The effect of gaming on social development of youth is the issue that moved me to examine gender and racial representation in video games. While playing *Splash Down*, a jet-ski racing game with my six-year old son, he told me that he never wanted to be the girl riders (the game allows players to choose racers from a field of two men and two women) because, "they are

slow and not as tough as the boys." Although his comment was inaccurate, the women racers in the game, maybe not as fast as the men, are more agile, and thus equally successful. It did cause me to take a step back and look at this game and others with a critical researcher's eye. Up to this point, I had never noticed the scarcity of playable female characters in my son's games. This recognition led to a critical examination of not only the games we play, but those that many other gamers play. In order to examine games in this way, it is necessary to place groups who are most often marginalized, women and minorities, at the center of the researcher's gaze; this focus suggests a critical theory perspective.

Critical theory rejects any semblance of objectivity and instead examines an issue in hopes of creating social change. Rooted in Marxism and updated in the U.S. by the radical societal struggles of the 1960's, critical theory "provides a framework—both philosophy and methods—for approaching research and evaluation as a fundamentally and explicitly political, and as change-oriented forms of engagement (Patton, 2002, p.131). Harvey (1990) describes this as the process of creating an alternative body of knowledge that is internalized through ideas, but also externalized through our conscious manipulation of objects. Harvey (1990) concludes that

Knowledge changes not simply as a result of reflection but as a result of activity too. Knowledge changes as a result of praxis. Similarly, what we know informs praxis. Knowledge is dynamic, not because we uncover more grains of sand for the bucket, but because of a process of fundamental reconceptualisation, which is only possible as a result of direct engagement with the processes and structures which generate knowledge. (p. 23)

Also present in critical social research is the argument that race is a social construction rather than a biological category, which denies that "racism is just skin-deep" (Harvey, 1990, p.

157). Race is not an empirical social category; it is an ideological construct, signifying a socially constructed set of characteristics that define race (Cohen, 1988). The critical social perspective denies the notion that racism originates from biological differentiation but instead, sees racism as an "ideological code that seizes, opportunistically, on various ideological signifiers that work most effectively at any point in time to naturalize difference and legitimize domination," (Harvey, 1990, p.157). It is this active, political process, in which ideologies about knowledge and social identity are defined, that informs inquiry into the rapidly changing and adapting world of media. The question is how video game consumers perceive negative representation of race and gender. Horkheimer and Adorno (2001) have stated,

All amusement suffers from this incurable malady. Pleasure hardens into boredom because, if it is to remain pleasure, it must not demand any effort and therefore moves rigorously in the worn grooves of association. No independent thinking must be expected from the audience: the product prescribes every reaction: not by its natural structure (which collapses under reflection), but by signals. Any logical connection calling for mental effort is painstakingly avoided. (P. 82)

The images in video games are comfortable for young U. S. consumers, for they are both familiar and entertaining in their simplicity. Worrisome, however, is whether comfort leads to complicity in the messages some video games send.

VIDEO GAME STUDIES

Wilder, Mackie, and Cooper (1985) note issues of gender roles in video games. For example, there are few playable female characters and most female characters are seen in submissive, hyper-sexualized or victim roles. Gee (2003) recognizes the seductive power of the gaming format and the

value of this format as a teaching tool. However, it was Provenzo's (1991) study of video game cover art that addressed games as "cultural texts that provide insight to ideas and values we hold as a culture" (p.99). Video games are participants in what Foucault (1980) describes as:

Dominant ways of knowing the world—making it meaningful—produced by those in power to make their ways of knowing circulate discursively around the world, generate 'regimes of truth' which come to assume an authority over the ways in which we think and act. (p. 230)

A perfect example of Foucault's (1980) notion of "regimes of truth" as expressions of hegemonic authority is in the thematic makeup of the most popular video games. In the same way Giroux argues that the U.S. cinema depicts a representation of "reality" as inner-city black-on-black youth violence, popular video games utilize gender and ethnic stereotypes in order to provide a familiar message for an over-entertained culture.

Video Game Violence Studies

Unlike the effects of racial and gender representation in video games on the identity development of youth, the psychological effects of video game violence has been well researched and well documented. Recent studies have shown the correlation between playing violent video games and decreased sensitivity to violent behavior, less trust, increased fearfulness, and decreased apathy (Griffiths, 1999). A number of recent studies have shown a relationship between playing violent video games and subsequent aggression (Anderson & Dill, 2000; Bartholow, Delamere & Waterloo, 2005; Schneider, Lang, Shin, & Bradley, 2004; Sestir, & Davis, 2005). Sakamoto (2005) reviewed Japanese literature to find maladaptive behavior in children who play violent video games. The findings in these studies establishes that video games do, in fact, affect the way some gamers think and act; therefore, it is imperative that studies likewise examine the effects of gender and racial representation. It is logical to presuppose that ethnic and gender roles in video games would likewise have an effect on gamers' thoughts and behaviors. However, there is a gap in the research, which correlates ethnic and gender roles in games to players' perceptions and subsequent behavior. Likewise, there are few qualitative analyses of racial and gender representation in games from a critical perspective (Dietz, 1998; Heintz-Knowles & Henderson, 2001).

Gender Roles

Study of gender roles in video gaming is essential because of the impact these games have on the formation of gender role expectations for both males and females. Although it can be argued that children who do not play video games are not influenced by the roles the games portray, this is not true. Every boy and girl exposed to video games takes in images and definitions of gender. In the same way any group forms ideas and behavioral expectations, through interaction with other boys and girls, these images and definitions become shared social experiences. Therefore, even children who do not play video games are indirectly affected by the images of gender that they portray (Dietz, 1998).

As Alloway and Gilbert (1997) suggest, such practices as surfing the Internet and reading video screens directly sustain and reinforce dominant discourses of hegemonic masculinity, by teaching skills that are potentially very powerful and useful in the communication technologies of the future. The vast selection of video games that attract male players, while alienating female players, may play a role in sustaining the glass ceiling of male hegemony in the lucrative, high-tech work force (Alloway & Gilbert, 1997; Heintz-Knowles & Henderson, 2001). Provenzo's (1991) research shows that through cover art, product description, and thematic images, current video game trends do exactly this.

From a critical theorist perspective, it seems that the video game industry may play into the power structure that sustains socioeconomic hegemony in two ways. First, video games are an important introduction to the world of computer technology. Becoming familiar with, comfortable with, and enjoying video games and computers may help girls develop an interest in careers in technology—a field in which women are significantly under-represented. According to U.S. Department of Labor figures, the percentage of women in the Information Technology (IT) industry declined by 18% in the last eight years, with females now representing only one quarter of IT workers. A recent study indicated that there is a correlation of computer and video games usage to gender differences in spatial ability—a desirable skill in IT professions (Terlecki & Newcombe, 2005). Although the number of female gamers is growing, they tend not to show interest in shooter games (games in which the player earns points by shooting targets or enemies) and fantasy games such as *Morrowind*, *Halo*, or *Eternal Darkness* (Hayes, 2006). In most fantasy games, playable characters are non-human and live in fantasy worlds in which these characters battle otherworld creatures in hopes of achieving domination. Girls and women more often choose casual games such as *Tetris*, relationship-centered games such as *The Sims*, or storied games, those in which playable characters are involved in a narrative and indirect competition (Angelo, 2004). According to Heintz-Knowles and Henderson (2001), there are powerful implications resulting from this trend. The scarcity of girl-friendly video games may send the wrong message to girls: using computers and video games are activities for boys and are not acceptable for girls. In addition, playing video games helps improve computer literacy by enhancing players' abilities to understand images in a three-dimensional space and to track multiple images simultaneously (p.22).

Marketing of games also plays a part and, perhaps, perpetuates the cycle of discrepancy between the numbers of boy and girl players. Tough competition in the video game industry means that only the topselling games survive. In order to reduce the chance of failure, producers and marketers of video games choose formulas that have proven successful in the past and attract predominately male players. Because "male games" are the majority produced, they are the most lucrative and the cycle continues. If, as Heintz-Knowles and Henderson (2001) propose, the lack of girl-friendly video games results in under-representation of women in technology professions (a highly lucrative and highly esteemed career path), then gender representation in video games is an important issue in gender equality.

These issues elucidate the bigger picture of how the video game industry, among other media, perpetuates hegemony by manufacturing stereotypical and, perhaps, sociologically damaging sexist and racist images of females and minorities. Moreover, the possible effects of misogynistic images and racist ideologies on any country currently struggling with women's rights or civil rights could be disastrous. Many of these images are so ingrained in dominant U.S. cultural expectations of women, ethic minorities, and their roles in society that they are perceived as normal. Thus, Gramsci's (2001) notions of social order being won and reproduced by ideological dominance emerge. Gramsci (2001) explains, in the most simplistic terms, that hegemony is the concept of a dominant way of seeing the world. It is different from ideology in that it depends on the expression of the interests of the ruling class and also on its acceptance of "commonsense" by those subordinated by it (Williams, 1983). One feature of hegemony is that in order for the powerful to maintain position, the weak must participate and agree. This is carried out in a delicate balance, whereby the dominant ideology includes bits of opposing views to appease the "mass society" (Horkheimer & Adorno, 2001). Hebdige (2001) describes Gramsci's notion of a "moving equilibrium," through which dominant

ideology is, "winning and shaping consent so that the power of the dominant classes appears both legitimate and natural," (p.204-205). In this way, subordinate groups are limited within an ideology that does not seem imposed, but instead, natural (Hebdidge, 2001).

Video Games and Gender Identity

Applying the framework of symbolic interactionism, it is known that individuals make meaning of their environment by using images and meanings that the members of that society share (Crotty, 1998). Individuals, therefore, assume roles according to society's norms or expectations. However, while there are societal norms surrounding each role, individuals also develop rules or identities that define what a particular role means to them. These meanings are often individualized and emotive in that our emotional and attitudinal responses are based on each individual's exposure to symbolic images (Angeles, 1992). Given that these societal roles are one facet used to define self, they also become a classification system by which we define the world, and ultimately, a basis for action (Mead, 1964). As Dietz (1998) states,

...they [individuals] are able to manipulate the way they "play" a specific role. Children, too manipulate and learn roles through childhood play. Play during childhood becomes an important component of socialization. (p. 426)

Mead (1964) suggests that individuals use the definitions of both themselves and others to interpret the action that surrounds them. Therefore, boys and girls depend upon images and societal expectations about both masculinity and femininity to interpret interaction and to form expectations of themselves and others. Thereby, it is known that a child's gender role expectations are affected by the messages and images of the various socialization agents to which she or he is exposed.

Mead (1964) describes how children "play" at something, pretending to be a mother, a father, a fireman, or a nurse, and in doing so, they develop gender identity through occurrences that they witness. Dietz (1998) argues that, in this process of defining gender, children will not only base gender identities upon interactions with others, but also on gender symbols (such as popular toys including Barbie dolls and G.I. Joe). Thus, feminine and masculine symbols, with which children interact, play an important role in the development of individualized gender expectations. Wilder, Mackie, and Cooper (1985) note that although video games have been seen as predominantly a masculine domain, as in other forms of technology, females have begun to play these games more. Therefore, the video game images of male and female characters inevitably affect the development of gender roles in boys and girls.

Scholars agree that the world of video games allows for subtle expression of consensual reality held by a culture (Espejo, 2003; Heintz-Knowles & Henderson, 2001; Poole, 2000; Provenzo, 1991). Video games provide insight into ideas and values we hold as a culture. Moreover, as Provenzo (1991) states,

[They]... represent cultural "texts" that can be read and interpreted on a number of different levels. In the case of women, the way in which they are portrayed, the roles they assume in game scenarios, and the extent to which they are included as part of the action of the games provide important insights into the role and status assigned to women in our culture. (p. 99)

By examining games from a gender perspective, we can see the games as socializing agents that teach both girls and boys about their roles in our society (Dietz, 1998; Espejo, 2003; Provenzo, 1991; Wilder, Mackie & Cooper, 1985). Of particular importance are the lessons that these "texts" are teaching girls and boys about body image, sexuality, dominance and submission (Provenzo,1991; Heitz-Knowles & Henderson, 2001). Cahill (1994) argues that children rarely challenge the authority of examples of gender roles in media. While women do appear in video games, their roles most frequently are as victims or sex objects (Dietz, 1998; Heintz-Knowles & Henderson, 2001; Provenzo, 1991).

One particular concern, when examining video games as gender socialization agents, is the hyper-sexualized image of women, or what Poole (2000) describes as "a ...deformed female character with massively enhanced breasts, eyes, and legs," (p.141). Even the characters regarded as most life-like, such as Lara Croft of Tomb Raider, who is touted by Poole (2000) as "a beautiful abstraction" boast scantily clad firm bodies with impossibly small waists and digitally enhanced breasts. Poole (2000) further states that this is all part of the allure:

... designers of the next generation of Tomb Raider games on Playstation 2 will surely be careful never to let Lara become too individuated. If she were to look photo realistic, too much like an actual woman, what seductiveness she possesses would thereby be destroyed. (p. 152-3)

This plays into society's love for the illusion of the "perfectly" built woman (Dietz, 1998; Poole, 2000). Examples are seen in digitally altered fashion model photos, prime time television stars, and in Barbie dolls. Poole (2000) explains this illusion further in the example of Lara Croft:

But surely she'll never be thoroughly realistic. For Lara Croft is an abstraction, an animated conglomeration of sexual and attitudinal signs (breasts, hot-pants, shades, thigh holsters) whose very blankness encourages the (male or female) player's psychological projection and is exactly why she has enjoyed such remarkable success as a cultural icon. (p. 153)

The video game female image is a warped mutation, seemingly formed from the battle between women's liberation and women's oppression. Female characters, such as Lara Croft, send a clear message to male and female players that it is okay for a woman to be tough and stand up for herself, as long as she looks sexy doing it. As Jhally (1999) explains, in media, masculinity is a performance in hyper-masculinity, and femininity is a performance in hyper-femininity.

METHODOLOGY

This study examined twenty top-selling games in the U.S created for Playstation 2 and Xbox. A sample of top-selling games from June 2002 was obtained from the industry's leader in sales rankings, gamemarketwatch.com (Appendix A), at the recommendation of an owner of four video game stores in my state (S.A. Bailey, personal communication, February 19, March 6, & April 17, 2004). The sample is intentionally nonrandom, for it was determined that a purposive sample of the most popular games would best resemble what young gamers are actually playing. Initially, Provenzo's (1991) format for analysis was used, in which he first analyzed the games selected in terms of the content of their cover, noting that these images provide visual text describing male and female status roles in American society. Secondly, utilizing Deitz's (1998) a priori codes, two coders played the games using the following categories: no female characters, female characters as hyper-sexualized objects or trophies (based on physical appearance, such as revealing clothing or unrealistic breast enhancement, or women awarded as prizes to male victors), females as the victim (women are kidnapped or assaulted), and females as the hero (action character who could possibly win the game). In addition, two more codes—games with no characters (such as automobile racing games) and characters presented as animals with no human characteristics—were added to the coding sheet.

Next, coders determined the race of each playable character according to the product description, which identified race, or by determining skin color or clothing (such as Native American headdress or Middle Eastern djellebas). Using a coding sheet with these categories, each game was evaluated. In addition, detailed descriptions of the roles of female and minority characters were obtained. Finally, using symbolic interactionism, a list of the most lucrative gaming software companies according to global sales revenue was obtained (Appendix B), to determine the origin of the company headquarters and founding date, thus forming a link between the common set of capitalist themes in the games, the origin of those themes, and the "understanding which has emerged to give meaning to people's interactions" with these texts (Patton, 2002, p.133).

FINDINGS

Cover Art

Games were analyzed using a tally system that identified males and females by their dress and physique, which was categorized as body image. In addition, male and female characters were categorized according to whether or not they were initiating action in the visual frame—for example, striking out with a weapon or as part of a military charge. Those initiating action were identified as dominant males or dominant females. Submissive characters, male or female, were identified as either being dependent upon or under the control of another figure. A final category included only graphic art or included a monster, animal, mythological or non-human figure, such as an automobile.

The results were that nine of the 20 included dominant males; none included dominant females, and half included graphic art with a non-human subject. *Medal of Honor: Frontline*, depicted only male soldiers in the cover, misrepresenting the growing number of female soldiers in service. More concerning perhaps is *WWE Wrestlemania*, which shows three massively muscular males on the cover; however, in playing the game, there are female characters that mark the division between wrestling periods by circling the wrestling ring in bikinis. In addition, female wrestlers are depicted with hyper-sexualized bodies. One buxom blond in a victory celebration over her opponent, tears off her blouse to reveal her lacy bra and swings her blouse over her head. The remaining games' cover art either depicted male characters or non-human subjects, such as automobiles (*Gran Turismo 3, Test Drive, ATV Off Road Fury*).

Only two games included a female on the cover, *Sonic Advance's* Amy, a female cutesy animal in a submissive pose, chin tucked down and smiling in demure fashion. *Grand Theft Auto 3* depicted one female character, Misty, a dancer at Sex Club Seven, a nude female dancing club, in the top right corner with her chin tucked down and gazing from heavily made up eyes. This illustrates the possibility that manufacturers choose advertising images that might attract young male players, while inadvertently alienating female players.

Product Description and Premise

Heintz-Knowles and Henderson (2001) showed findings in which a key factor in attracting female video game players was the game's premise. Those games that contained a story line were much more attractive and engaging to female players than sport or shooter games. Using the manufacturer's product description posted on Amazon.com, game premises were categorized. The following a priori categories based loosely on Provenzo's (1991) study were used:

1. A quest, including a female victim and male hero;
2. A quest, including a male victim and male hero;
3. A quest with a male victim and female hero;
4. A quest with male villain as protagonist;
5. A sport or shooter game without a story line;
6. Non human protagonists and antagonists.

Of the 20 game premises examined, a clear majority had male heroes and female victims or male victims and male heroes, while none had female heroes. Two games had themes involving the protagonist as a criminal (*Grand Theft Auto* and *Midnight Club*), and a great majority were racing, combat, or shooter games (*Medal of Honor Frontline, Grand Theft Auto, Gran Turismo 3, Dragonball Z, The Elder Scrolls III: Morrowind, Halo, Eternal Darkness, Yu Gi Oh Forbidden, Midnight Club: Street, Star Wars Episode 2, ATV Off Road Fury*). This data mirrors Dietz's (1998) findings that many of the current games are, in fact, combat, racing, and shooter games. In those with a story line, "…females are severely under-represented; they are generally cast in either insignificant props or stereotyped roles. Even when the female characters break out of the role of the helpless victim, their powers and strengths can be overshadowed by their hyper-sexualized bodies and attire" (p.30). Just as Dietz (1998), Heintz-Knowles and Henderson (2001), and Provenzo (1991) concluded in similar studies, these findings show that females are, in fact, under-represented and hyper-sexualized, perpetuating hegemonic ideas about gender roles for young players.

Body Image

In addition to game premise and cover art, the body images portrayed were analyzed. These were categorized as normal male, normal female (arms, legs, waists, and chests proportionate to those found in an average person) or as mesomorphic male (extremely muscular with arms, legs, waists, and chests disproportionate to those found in an average person) or hyper-sexualized female (disproportionate breast versus waist ratio). Of the male characters represented in the games, a significant majority was mesomorphic. Likewise, of the female characters, a clear majority was hyper-sexualized, and much fewer had normal body types, supporting an initial impression that the most purchased video games perpetuate amplified, unrealistic, and potentially damaging ideas about body image for young players.

Game Content

In this sample, games that had a story line revealed an overwhelmingly male gaze. For example, in playing *Grand Theft Auto 3*, two out of three female characters are employed at Sex Club Seven—a nude female dance club. The sign in front of the building reads, "Sex Club Seven—Where gentlemen go pop! 24 Hour a Day Fun for the Whole Family." In addition, Luigi, a male "gangster" owner touts, "You wanna have fun; you come to Luigi's. Luigi's girls are the best in town. Clean. Spic and span!" *Midnight Club: Street*, is a watered-down version of this game, with players racing through urban streets of New York and London. The game intro states that illegal street racing is the "new underground sport" for "speed freaks, car nuts, and *boy* racers." [Italics added]

Playable Characters and Race

Provenzo (1991), Dietz (1998), and Heintz-Knowles and Henderson (2001) assert that visibility is power in video gaming, and inclusion or exclusion of playable (characters that can be controlled in contrast to bystanders or props) characters, based on race or gender, sends important messages about power structure in our society. Using this premise as a guide, the playable characters in the games were analyzed. Every game in which race was identifiable included white characters, while only a few included playable black characters (*WWE Wrestlemania*, *Star Wars Episode II*) , and there was only a small number of Hispanic, Asian, Native American, Middle

Eastern, East Indian, or Islanders combined, but none of these were playable characters. Also significant is the point that all of the black characters are represented as either athletes or criminals in games such as *WWE Wrestlemania*, *Grand Theft Auto*, or *Midnight Club: Street*, perpetuating deep-seeded and damaging stereotypes. Gray (2001) describes this as production of blackness (and other minorities as well) through the "white eye," in which dominant media representations are *assimilationist* (invisibility) or *pluralist* (separate but equal) (p.450). It is logical to apply Gray's notions of assimilationist representations of blacks on television in the 1950's and throughout the 1960's as those that "…attempted to make blacks acceptable to whites by containing them or rendering them, if not culturally white, invisible." In addition, there is the "…threat of civilization being over-run or undermined by the recurrence of savagery…lurking below the surface" (Hall, p. 277). A recent trend in the U.S. video gaming industry is sport games such as *NFL Madden Football*, where African American athletes dominate the playable characters. Since 1989, 19 million units of *John Madden Football* have sold. However, Adam Clayton Powell III, son of Adam Clayton Powell Jr., the first African American Congressman, referred to this representation as "high-tech black face" in which "participants [are allowed] to try on the other, the taboo, the dangerous, the forbidden, and the otherwise unacceptable" (Leonard, 2005, p. 1). The minstrel show, or minstrelsy, was an indigenous form of American entertainment consisting of stereotypical comic skits, variety acts, dancing, and music, usually performed by white people in black face. Historian Eric Lott (1993) describes this trying on the other as a way to "facilitate safely an exchange of energies between otherwise rigidly bounded and policed cultures (p.18). While some may argue that players of color participate in the same ritual of "trying on the other," the difference is in the range of roles for white characters as compared to characters of color.

The under-representation and misrepresentation of people of color is a cultural text that may influence young players' perceptions about self and other, regardless of their own ethnic background. Perhaps, most destructive for any oppressed group is invisibility, for, as Jhally (1999) states in *Tough Guise*, "... in media, visibility is power." It seems that this is just one example of many of how media plays a role in perpetuating the socialization structures that promote hegemony in a society. Assuming the power of this medium to influence young players' views about themselves and those around them, it seems imperative to point out the origin of top-selling games. As illustrated in the introduction, video games are a global phenomenon, and thereby a global socialization agent.

DISCUSSION

The most lucrative gaming software (Appendix B) reveals that, while the leading gaming hardware companies, Sony and Playstation, suggest global influences, the software companies that produce the top-selling games are predominately U.S. companies. In the gaming industry, 95% of video games lose money and stop production, while only the top 5% are lucrative (Wikipedia, "Video Games," 2005). This results in an elite group of predominately U.S. software companies designing the games that send messages about gender, race, economics, and competition to a global audience. In addition, as discussed earlier, the most lucrative games become the "norm" in video games.

This study illustrates that the portrayal of women and minorities in top-selling U.S. video games is predominantly stereotypical, often hyper-sexualized, or worse yet, non-existent. While some sports games, such as *ATV Off Road Fury*, make an attempt to include female riders as playable characters, others such as *Gran-Turismo 3: A SPEC*, *Medal of Honor Frontline*, *Test Drive*,

Wrestlemania, and *Stuntman* ignore women altogether as participants. Games such as *WWE Wrestlemania*, *Grand Theft Auto*, and *Midnight Club: Street* depict women as mindless subordinate sex objects, while seemingly harmless games such as *Star Wars* and *Spiderman* place females in subordinate roles that are either props or much less important than men. These depictions of women are detrimental to girls and boys in that both may internalize these gender roles, playing a prominent role in the socialization of boys especially, who play these games more frequently.

Non-whites are very rarely represented, if at all. Some of the sporting games, such as *WWE Wrestlemania*, do include black and Hispanic male characters, but this is the only game in the top 20 list that includes non-whites in a positive representation. Lack of representation for both women and non-whites is perhaps the most damaging aspect of video game representation, for this amounts to symbolic annihilation, whereas those who are at the bottom of the various power hierarchies will be kept in their places, in part by their relative invisibility (Gross, 2001, p. 414). In sum, gamers are immersed in a white-washed, patriarchal view of the world.

CONCLUSION

Applying Mead's (1964) framework, showing that gender roles in both boys and girls are formed, in part, by visual examples they are exposed to during play, the purpose of this study was to analyze video games for their presentation of both gender and ethnicity. Most scholars agree that gender roles and ideas about ethnicity may be negatively impacted by visual and textual messages that some of these games illustrate (Provenzo, 1991; Dietz, 1998; Heintz-Knowles & Henderson, 2001; Poole, 2000). This study illustrates that the portrayal of women and people of color continues to be overwhelmingly stereotypical when they are represented at all. In addition, a vast majority of the games include violence in some form, ranging from violent and sometimes sexually explicit attacks on women, followed by subsequent violence by the heroes, to animated characters carrying automatic weapons and annihilating victims. These visual and thematic texts create a false reality that violence and victimization are normal components of society and that this is often amusing and fun.

In addition, thematic texts are built upon the ideologies of capitalism and consumption, thus presenting these ideas in a format that is a catalyst to the "process of normalization," or the process of hegemony (Marx & Engels, 2001). Further more, as Dietz (1998) states, in that video games are much more interactive than other media forms such as television or magazines, researchers should be cautious in minimalizing the effects of exposure to video games "based upon generalizations from research of other media forms" (p.440). Finally, because research has focused only upon the short-term effects of video game exposure, it is unclear what long-term effects and what effects from long-term exposure will occur. This discussion suggests that there is a need for more research to assess the effect of racial and gender representation in video games. Therefore, given the current trend of imbedded U.S. hegemonic ideologies of capitalism, and gender and racial misrepresentation or annihilation, it is important that continuing research be conducted to interpret what, if any, short-term and long-term effects emerge from this global socialization agent.

REFERENCES

Alloway, N. & Gilbert, P. (1997). Boys and literacy: Lessons from Australia. *Gender & Education, 9*(1), 49-62.

Angeles, P. (1992). *The Harper Collins dictionary of philosophy.* (2nd ed.). New York: Harper Collins.

Angelo, J. (2004, May 14). *New study reveals that women over 40 who play online games spend far more time playing than male or teenage gamers.* Retrieved June 3, 2006, from http://media.aoltimewarner.com/media/cb_press_view.cfm?release_num=55253774

Bartholow, B., & Sestir, M. (2005). Correlates and consequences of exposure to video game violence: Hostile personality, empathy, and aggressive behavior. *Personality and Social Psycholgy Bulletin, 11,* 1573-1586. Retrieved June 27, 2006, from PubMed database.

Cohen, P. (1988). The perversions of inheritance: Studies in the making of multi-racist Britain. In P. Cohen & Bains (Eds.), *Multi-racist Britain.* London: Pluto Press.

Cortes, C. E. (2000). *The children are watching: How the media teach about diversity.* New York: Teachers College Press.

Crotty, M. (1998). *The foundations of social research.* Thousand Oaks, California: Sage.

Delamere, F. M. (2005). 'It's just really fun to play!' A constructionist perpective on violence and gender representations in violent video games. *Dissertation Abstracts International, 65*(10-A), 3986.

Dietz, T. (1998). An examination of violence and gender role portrayals in video games:

Implications for gender socialization and aggressive behavior. *Sex Roles, 38*(516), p.425-442.

Espejo, R. (Ed.). (2003). *Video games.* San Diego: Greenhaven Press.

Fiske, J. (1992). British cultural studies and television. In R. C. Allen (Ed.), *Channels of discourse, reassembled: Television and contemporary criticism* (pp.284-326). (2nd ed.) Chapel Hill: University of North Carolina Press.

Fiske, J. (1994). Moments of television: Neither the text nor the audience. In E. Seiter, H. Brochers,

G. Kreutzner, & E. M. Warth (Eds.), *Remote control: Television audiences and cultural power* (pp. 56-78). New York: Routledge.

Foucault, M. (1980). *Power/knowledge: Selected interviews and other writings, 1972-1977.* New York: Pantheon.

Gee, J. (2003). *What video games have to teach us about learning and literacy.* New York: Palgrave/St. Martin's.

Geertz, C. (1983). Thick description: Toward an interpretive theory of culture. In R. M. Emerson (Ed.), *Contemporary field research: A collection of readings.* Prospect Heights, Illinois: Waveland Press.

Gramsci, A. (2001). The concept of ideology. In M.D. Durham & D. M. Kellner (Eds.), *Media and cultural studies* (pp.43-48). Malden, MA: Blackwell.

Gray, H. (2001). The politics of representation in network television. In M. Durham & D. Kellner (Eds.), *Media and cultural studies: Keyworks* (pp.439-461). Malden, MA: Blackwell.

Griffiths, M. (1999). Violent video games and aggression: Review of the literature. *Journal of Aggression and Violent Behavior, 4*(2), 203-212. Retrieved June 2, 2006, from Ebsco host database.

Gross, L. (2001). Out of the mainstream: Sexual minorities and mass media. In M. D. Durham & D. M. Kellner (Eds.), *Media and cultural studies* (pp.405-423). Malden, MA: Blackwell.

Grossman, D. Lt. Col., & DeGaetano, G. (1999). *Stop teaching our kids to kill: A call to action against TV, movie & video game violence.* New York: Random House.

Hall, S. (2000). Racist ideologies and the media. In P. Marris & S. Thornham (Eds.), *Media studies: A reader* (2nd ed.; pp.271-282). New York: New York University Press.

Harvey, L. (1990). *Critical social research.* London: Unwin Hyman.

Hayes, E. (2006). Women, video gaming and learning: Beyond stereotypes. *Tech Trends, 49*(5), 23-28.

Hebdige, D. (2001). From culture to hegemony; subculture; the unnatural break. In M. Durham & D. Kellner (Eds.), *Media and cultural studies: Keyworks* (pp.198-216). Malden, Massachusetts: Blackwell.

Herz, J. C. (1997). *Joystick nation: How video games ate our quarters, won our hearts, and rewired our minds.* New York: Little, Brown and Company.

Heintz-Knowles, K., & Henderson, J. (2001). *Fair play? Violence, gender and race in video games.* Oakland, CA: Children NOW. Retrieved February 18, 2004, from ERIC database.

Hooks, B. (1990). *Yearning: Race, gender and cultural politics.* Toronto: Between the Lines.

Horkheimer, M., & Adorno, T. (2001). The culture industry. In M. D. Durham & D. M. Kellner (Eds.), *Media and cultural studies* (pp.71-101). Malden, MA: Blackwell.

Jhally, S. (Director). (1999) *Tough guise: Violence, media & the crisis in masculinity* [Motion Picture]. United States: Media Education Foundation

Lee, H. (1990). *Critical social research.* London: Unwin Hyman.

Leonard, D. (2004). Unsettling the military entertainment complex: Video games and a pedagogy of peace. *Studies in Media & Information Literacy Education, 4*(4), 17-32. Retrieved May 27, 2006, from www.utpjournals.com

Leonard, D. (2005). High tech blackface—Race, sports video games and becoming the other. *Intelligent Agent, 4*(4), Retrieved June 18, 2006, from http://www.intelligentagent.com/archive/Vol4_No4_gaming_leonard.htm

Lott, E. (1993). *Love & theft: Blackface minstrelsy and the American working class.* New York: Oxford University Press.

Marx, K., & Engels, F. (1976). Ruling class and the ruling ideas. In M. D. Durham & D. M. Kellner (Eds.), *Media and cultural studies* (pp. 39-47). Malden, MA: Blackwell.

Mead, G. (1934, 1964). *Mind, self and society.* Chicago: University of Chicago Press.

Newkirk, T. (2002). *Misreading masculinity: Boys, literacy and popular culture.* Portsmouth, New Hampshire: Heinemann.

Patton, M. (2002). *Qualitative research and evaluation methods* (3rd ed.). Thousand Oaks, CA: Sage.

Poole, S. (2000). *Trigger happy: Video games and the entertainment revolution.* New York: Arcade Publishing.

Provenzo, E. F. Jr. (1991). *Video kids: Making sense out of Nintendo.* Cambridge, MA: Harvard University Press.

Sakamoto, A. (2005). Video games and the psychological development of Japanese children. In D. W. Schwalb, J. Nakazawa, & B. J. Schwalb (Eds.), *Applied developmental psychology: Theory, practice and reform from Japan* (pp. 3-21). Greenwich, CT: Information Age Publishing. Retrieved May 27, 2005, from Ebsco host database.

Schneider, E., Lang, A., Shin, M., & Bradley, S. (2004). Death with a story: How story impacts emotional, motivational and physiological responses to first-person shooter video games. *Human Communication Research, 30*(3), 361-375. Retrieved May 27, 2006, from Ebsco host database.

Terlecki, M., & Newcombe, N. (2005). How important is the digital divide? The relationship of computer videogame usage to gender differences in mental rotation ability. *Sex Roles, 53*(5-6), 433-441. Retrieved June 3, 2006, from Ebsco host database.

Wilder, G., Mackie, D., & Cooper, J. (1985). Gender and computers: Two surveys of computer-related attitudes. *Sex roles, 13*(13), 215-228. Retrieved February 18, 2004, from ERIC database.

Williams, R. (2001). Base and superstructure in Marxist cultural theory. In M. Durham & D. Kellner (Eds.), *Media and cultural studies: Keyworks* (pp. 152-165). Malden, Massachusetts: Blackwell.

APPENDIX A

Top 20 Best Selling Video Games (Gamemarketwatch.com Internet magazine—June 2002)

Game Title	Gaming Software Company
1. Medal of Honor Frontline	Electronic Arts
2. Grand Theft Auto 3	Rockstar Games
3. Gran Turismo 3: A-SPEC	Sony
4. Dragonball Z: Goku	Infogames
5. Spiderman: The Movie (PS2)	Activision
6. The Elder Scrolls III: Morrowind	Bethesda Softworls
7. WWE Wrestlemania X8	THQ
8. Test Drive	Infogames
9. Super Mario Advance 4	GBA
10. Halo	Microsoft
11. Eternal Darkness	Nintendo
12. Yu Gi Oh Forbidden	Konami
13. Midnight Club: Street	Rockstar Games
14. Star Wars Episode 2	THQ
15. Stuntman	Infogames
16. ATV Off Road Fury	Sony
17. Super Smash Brothers Melee	Nintendo
18. Sonic Advance	Sega

APPENDIX B

Video Game Software Industry Leaders (Wikipedia Online Encyclopedia—Retrieved November, 2005)

Company name	Headquarters	Founded
Gimple Software	U.S.—Pennsylvania	1984
Digi Design	U.S.—California	1985
Powersoft	U.S.—California	1985
Borland	U.S.—California, Georgia	1985
RAD Game Tools	U.S.—Washington	1988
Nu Mega	U.S.— Michigan	1973
Kinetix	U.S.—California	1983
Electric Arts	U.S.—California	1982
Equilibrium	U.S.—California	1989
Sonic Foundry	U.S.—Wisconsin, Pennsylvania	1991
Syntrillium Software	U.S.—California	1982

Cakewalk	U.S.—Massachusetts	1987
Creative Labs	Singapore	1981
Addison Wesley	U.S.—California	1996

This work was previously published in International Journal of Technology and Human Interaction, Vol. 3, Issue 2, edited by B. Stahl, pp. 96-109, copyright 2007 by IGI Publishing, formerly known as Idea Group Publishing (an imprint of IGI Global).

Chapter XV
Global Information Ethics:
The Importance of Being Environmentally Earnest

Luciano Floridi
Università degli Studi di Bari, Italy and Oxford University, UK

ABSTRACT

The article argues that Information Ethics (IE) can provide a successful approach for coping with the challenges posed by our increasingly globalized reality. After a brief review of some of the most fundamental transformations brought about by the phenomenon of globalization, the article distinguishes between two ways of understanding Global Information Ethics, as an ethics of global communication or as a global-information ethics. It is then argued that cross-cultural, successful interactions among micro and macro agents call for a high level of successful communication, that the latter requires a shared ontology friendly towards the implementation of moral actions, and that this is provided by IE. There follows a brief account of IE and of the ontic trust, the hypothetical pact between all agents and patients presupposed by IE.

INTRODUCTION: FROM GLOBALIZATION TO INFORMATION ETHICS

Globalization is a phenomenon too complex even to sketch in this brief introduction.[1] So I hope that I shall be forgiven if I am rather casual about many features that would deserve full attention in another context. Here, I wish to highlight just six key transformations characterising the processes of globalization. I shall label them *contraction, expansion, porosity, hybridization, synchroniza-*

tion, and *correlation.* They provide the essential background for making sense of the thesis developed in the rest of the chapter, which is that Information Ethics (IE) can provide a successful approach for coping with the challenges posed by our increasingly globalized reality.

Contraction

The world has gone through alternating stages of globalization, growing and shrinking, for as long as humanity can remember. Here is a reminder:

In some respects the world economy was more integrated in the late 19th century than it is today. ... Capital markets, too, were well integrated. Only in the past few years, indeed, have international capital flows, relative to the size of the world economy, recovered to the levels of the few decades before the first world war. (The Economist, 1997)

The truth is that, after each "globalization backlash" (think of the end of the Roman or British Empires), the world never really went back to its previous state. Rather, by moving two steps forward and one step back, sometime towards the end of the last century the process of globalization reached a point of no return. Today, revolutions or the collapse of empires can never shrink the world again, short of the complete unravelling of human life as we know it. Globalization is here to stay.

Globalization has become irreversible mainly thanks to radical changes in worldwide transport and communications (Brandt & Henning, 2002). Atoms and bytes have been moving increasingly rapidly, frequently, cheaply, reliably, and widely for the past 50 years or so. This dramatic acceleration has shortened the time required for any interactions: economic exchanges, financial transactions, social relations, information flows, movements of people, and so forth (Hodel, Holderegger & Lüthi, 1998). And this acceleration has

meant a more condensed life and a contracted physical space. Ours is a smaller world, in which one may multitask fast enough to give and have the impression of leading parallel lives. We may regain a nineteenth-century sense of distance (space) and duration (time) only if one day we travel to Mars.

Expansion

Human space in the twenty-first century has not merely shrunk, though. ICTs have also created a new digital environment, which is constantly expanding and becoming progressively more diverse. Again, the origins of this global, transnational common space are old. They are to be found in the invention of recording and communication technologies that range from the alphabet to printing, from photography to television. But it is only in the last few decades that we have witnessed a vast and steady migration of human life to the other side of the screen. When you ask, "Where were you?," it is now normal and common to receive the answer "Online". More than 6 million people throughout the world play *World of Warcraft,* currently the leading subscription-based MMORPG (massively multiplayer online role-playing game, http://www.blizzard.com/press/060119.shtml). Globalization also means the emergence of this sort of single virtual space, sharable in principle by anyone, any time, anywhere.

Porosity

An important relation between our contracting physical space and our expanding, virtual environment is that of *porosity.* Imagine living as a flat figure on the surface of an endless cylinder. You could travel on the surface of the cylinder as a two-dimensional space, but not through it. So in order to reach any other point on the cylinder, the best you could do would be to follow the shortest path (geodesic) on the cylindrical surface. The empty space inside the cylinder would be inconceivable, as a third dimension would. Imagine now that the surface became porous and hence that a third dimension were added. The geodesics would be revolutionized, for you could travel through the vacuum encircled by the cylinder and reach the other side, thus significantly shortening your journeys. To use the rather apt vocabulary of surfing, you would be *tubing*: space would be curling over you, forming a "tube", with you inside the cylindrical space. From a 2D perspective, you would literally come in and out of space. This sort of porosity characterizes the relation now between physical and virtual space. It is difficult to say where one is when one is "tubing", but we know that we can travel through cyberspace to interact with other physical places in a way that would have been inconceivable only a few decades ago. Telepresence (Floridi, 2005) in our porous environment is an ordinary experience and this is also what globalization means.

Hybridization

During the last decade or so, we have become accustomed to conceptualize our life online as a mixture between an evolutionary adaptation of analogue/carbon-based agents to a digital/silicon-based environment, and a form of postmodern, neocolonization of the latter by the former. This is probably a mistake. The threshold between *analogue-carbon-offline-here* and *digital-silicon-online-there* is fast becoming blurred, but this is as much to the advantage of the latter as it is of the former. Adapting Horace's famous phrase[2], "captive cyberspace is conquering its victor". ICTs are as much re-ontologising (that is, modifying the essential nature of) our world as they are creating new realities. The digital is spilling over into the analogue and merging with it. This recent phenomenon is variously known as "ubiquitous computing", "ambient intelligence", or "the Internet of things" (ITU report, November 2005, http://www.itu.int/internetofthings), and it is, or will soon be, the next stage in the digital

revolution. In the (fast approaching) future, objects will be *ITentities* able to learn, advise, and communicate with each other. "RoboticCookware" is already available (http://www.vitacraft.com. nyud.net:8090/rfiq/home.html); MP3 players will soon be able to recommend new music to their users by learning from the tunes they (the users, we had better be clear) enjoyed (http://www. semanticaudio.com/). Your next fridge (http:// www.lginternetfamily.co.uk/homenetwork.asp) will inherit from the previous one your tastes and wishes, just as your new laptop can import your favourite settings from the old one; and it will interact with your new way of cooking and with the supermarket Web site, just as your laptop can talk to a printer or to another computer. We have all known this in theory for some time; the difference is that it is now actually happening in our kitchen.

Globalization also means the emergence of this common, fully interactive, and responsive environment of wireless, pervasive, distributed, *a2a* (anything to anything) information processes, that works *a4a* (anywhere for any time), in real time. We are probably the last generation to experience a clear difference between *onlife* and *online*.

Synchronization

In a world in which information and material flows are becoming so tightly integrated and enmeshed, it is not surprising to see global patterns emerging not only from well-orchestrated operations (consider the tedious experience of any launch of a major blockbuster, with interviews in magazines, discussions on TV programs, advertisements of merchandise, and by-products throughout the world, special food products in supermarkets and fast-food, etc.), but also inadvertedly, as the result of the accidental synchronization of otherwise chaotic trends.

All of a sudden, the world reads the same novel, or wears the same kind of trousers, or listens to the same music, or eats the same sort of food, or is concerned about the same problems, or cherishes the same news, or is convinced that it has the same disease. Some of this need not be the effect of any plan by some Big Brother, a secret agency, a powerful multinational or any other *deus ex machina* that is scheming behind the curtains. After all, worldwide attention span is very limited and flimsy, and it is very hard to compete for it. The truth is that at least some global trends may merely arise from the constructive interference of waves of information that accidentally come into phase, and hence reinforce each other to the point of becoming global, through the casual and entirely contingent interaction of chaotic forces. It may happen with the stock markets or the fashion industry or dietary trends. The recurrent emergence of temporarily synchronized patterns of human behaviour, both transculturally and transnationally, is a clear sign of globalization, but not necessarily of masterminded organization. There is no intelligent plan, evil intention, autonomy, or purposeful organization in the billion snow flakes that become an avalanche. Social group behaviour is acquiring a global meaning. The distributed power that generates Wikipedia is the other side of the dark, mindless stupidity of millions of slaves of fashions and trends.

Correlation

Imagine a safety net, like the one used in a circus. If it is sufficiently tight and robust, the heavier the object that falls into it, the larger the area of the net that will be stretched, sending waves of vibration throughout the net. Globalization also refers to the emergence of a comparable net of correlations among agents all over the world, which is becoming so tight and sensitive that the time lag in the transmission of the effects of an event "dropping" on it is fast shortening, to the point that sometimes there is almost no distinction between what counts as local or remote. Global often means not everywhere but actually delocalized, and in a delocalized environment

social friction is inevitable, as there is no more room for agents that allows for absorption of the effects of their decisions and actions. If anyone moves, the global boat rocks.

Globalising Ethics

If we consider now the profound transformations just sketched, it would be rather surprising if they did not have serious implications for our moral lives (see Ess, 2002; Weckert, 2001). In a reality that is more and more physically contracted, virtually expanded, porous, hybridized, synchronized, and correlated, the very nature of moral interactions, and hence of their ethical analysis, is significantly altered. Innovative forms of agenthood are becoming possible; new values are developing and old ones are being reshaped; cultural and moral assumptions are ever more likely to come into contact when not into conflict; the very concepts of what constitutes our "natural" environment and our enhanced features as a biological species are changing; and unprecedented ethical challenges have arisen (a reference to the notorious problem of privacy is *de rigueur* here), just to mention some macroscopic transformations in which globalization factors, as sketched above, play an important role.

What sort of ethical reflection can help us to cope successfully with a world that is undergoing such dramatic changes? Local approaches are as satisfactory as burying one's head in home values and traditions. The ethical discourse appears to be in need of an upgrade to cope with a globalized world. Each ethical theory is called upon to justify its worldwide and cross-cultural suitability. This seems even more so if the theory in question seeks to address explicitly the new moral issues that arise from the digital revolution, as it is the case with IE.

I shall say more about IE in the next two sections. The specific question that I wish to address is whether, in a world that is fast becoming more and more globalized, information ethics can provide a successful approach for dealing with its new challenges. I shall argue in favour of a positive answer. But to make my case, let me first clarify what *global information ethics* may mean.

Global-Communication Ethics vs. Global-Information Ethics

There are at least two ways of understanding Global Information Ethics: as an *ethics of global communication* (Smith, 2002) or as a *global-information ethics* (Bynum & Rogerson, 1996). Since I shall concentrate only on the latter, let me briefly comment on the former first.

Global-information ethics, understood as an ethics of worldwide communication, may be seen as a commendable effort to foster all those informational conditions that facilitate participation, dialogue, negotiation, and consensus-building practices among people, across cultures and through generations. It is an approach concerned with new and old problems, caused or exacerbated by global communications or affecting the flow of information. Global-communication ethics is therefore a continuation of policy by other means, and it does not have to be reduced to a mere gesture towards the importance of mutual respect and understanding (meeting people and talking to each other can hardly do any harm and often helps). It is, however, faced by the serious problem of providing its own justification. What sort of ethical principles of communication and information are to be privileged and why? Is there any macroethics (e.g., some form of consequentialism or deontologism or contractualism) that can rationally buttress a global-communication ethics? And is not any attempt at providing such a macroethics just another instance of "globalization" of some values and principles to the disadvantage of others? Without decent theorization, the risk is that we will reduce goodness to goodiness and transform the ethical discourse into some generic, well-meant sermon. At the same time, a robust foundation for a global-communication

ethics may easily incur the problem of failing to respect and appreciate a plurality of diverse positions. The dilemma often seems to be left untouched, even when it is not overlooked. The good news is that it may be possible to overcome it by grounding a global-communication ethics on a global-information ethics.

Global-Information Ethics and the Problem of the Lion

If we look at the roots of the problem, it seems that:

1. In an increasingly globalized world, successful interactions among micro and macro agents belonging to different cultures call for a high level of successful communication; but
2. Successful, cross-cultural communications among agents require, in their turn, not only the classic three "e"s—*embodiment, embeddedness* and hence *experience* (a sense of "us-here-now")—but also a shared *ontology* (more on this presently); and yet
3. Imposing a uniform ontology on all agents only seems to aggravate the problem, globalization becoming synonymous with ontological imperialism.

By "ontology" I do not mean to refer here to any metaphysical theory of being, of what there is or there is not, of why there is what there is, or of the ultimate nature of reality in itself. All this would require a form of epistemological realism (some confidence in some privileged access to the essential nature of things) that I do not hold, and that, fortunately, is not necessary to make my case. Rather, I am using "ontology" to cover the outcome of a variety of processes that allow an agent to appropriate (be successfully embedded in), semanticize (give meaning to and make sense of), and conceptualize (order, understand, and explain) the agent's environment. In simplified terms, one's ontology is one's world; that is, the world as it appears to, is experienced and interacted with, by the agent in question.[3]

Agents can talk to each others only if they can partake to some degree in a shared ontology anchored to a common reality to which they can all refer.[4]

Imagine two solipsistic minds, α and β, disembodied, unembedded, and devoid of any experience. Suppose them living in two entirely different universes. Even if α and β could telepathically exchange their data, they could still not *communicate* with each other, for there would be absolutely nothing that would allow the receiver to interpret the sender. In fact, it would not even be clear whether any message was being exchanged at all.

The impossibility of communication between α and β is what Wittgenstein (2001) had in mind, I take it, when he wrote that "if a lion could talk, we could not understand him." The statement is obviously false (because we share with lions a similar form of embeddedness and embodiment, and hence experiences like hunger or pain) if one fails to realize that the lion is only a placeholder to indicate an agent utterly and radically different from us, like our α and β. The lion is a Martian, someone you simply cannot talk to because it is "from another ontology".[5]

From this perspective, the famous phrase *hic sunt leones* (here there are lions) acquires a new meaning. The phrase occurred on Roman maps to indicate unknown and unexplored regions beyond the southern African borders of the empire.[6] In a Wittgensteinian sense, the Romans were mapping the threshold beyond which no further communication was possible at all. They were drawing the limits of their ontology. What was beyond the border, the *locus* inhabited by the lions, was nothing, a nonplace. Globalization has often meant that what is not inglobate simply is not, that is, fails to exist.

We can now formulate the difficulty confronting a global-information ethics as *the problem of the lion*: cross-cultural communication, which is the necessary condition for any further moral

interaction, is possible only if the interlocutors partake in a common ontology. When Crusoe and Friday meet, after 25 years of Crusoe's solitude, they can begin to communicate with each other only because they share the most basic ontology of life and death, food and shelter, fear and safety. Agents may be strangers to each other ("stranger" being an indexical qualification[7]). They do not have to speak the same language, empathize, or sympathize. But they do need to share at least some basic appropriation, semanticization, and conceptualization of their common environment, as a minimal condition for the possibility of any further moral interaction.

Can information ethics provide a solution to the problem of the lion? The short answer is yes; the long one is more complicated and requires a brief diversion, since it is now necessary to be more explicit about what I mean by information ethics.

Global Information-Ethics and Its Advantages

Information ethics[8] is an *ontocentric, patient-oriented, ecological* macroethics. An intuitive way to unpack this definition is by comparing IE to other environmental approaches.

Biocentric ethics usually grounds its analysis of the moral standing of bio-entities and eco-systems on the intrinsic worthiness of *life* and the intrinsically negative value of *suffering*. It seeks to develop a patient-oriented ethics in which the "patient" may be not only a human being, but also any form of life. Indeed, land ethics extends the concept of patient to any component of the environment, thus coming close to the approach defended by information ethics. Any form of life is deemed to enjoy some essential proprieties or moral interests that deserve and demand to be respected, at least minimally if not absolutely, that is, in a possibly overridable sense, when contrasted to other interests. So biocentric ethics argues that the nature and well-being of the patient of any action constitute (at least partly) its moral standing and that the latter makes important claims on the interacting agent, claims that in principle ought to contribute to guiding the agent's ethical decisions and constraining the agent's moral behaviour. The "receiver" of the action is placed at the core of the ethical discourse, as a centre of moral concern, while the "transmitter" of any moral action is moved to its periphery.

Now substitute "existence" for "life" and it should become clear what IE amounts to. IE is an ecological ethics that replaces *biocentrism* with *ontocentrism*. It suggests that there is something even more elemental than life, namely *being*—that is, the existence and flourishing of all entities and their global environment—and something more fundamental than suffering, namely *entropy*. The latter is most emphatically *not* the physicists' concept of thermodynamic entropy. Entropy here refers to any kind of *destruction* or *corruption* of entities understood as informational objects (not as semantic information, take note), that is, any form of impoverishment of *being*, including *nothingness*, to phrase it more metaphysically.[9]

We are now ready to appreciate some of the main advantages offered by information ethics when it comes to the new challenges posed by globalization.

1. Embracing the New Informational Ontology

Not only do we live in a world that is moving towards a common informational ontology, we also experience our environment and talk and make sense of our experiences in increasingly informational ways. *Information is the medium.* This calls for an ethics, like IE, that, by prioritising an informational ontology, may provide a valuable approach to decoding current moral phenomena and orienting our choices.

2. Sharing a Minimal, Horizontal, Lite Ontology

There is a risk, by adopting an ontocentric perspective, as IE suggests, that one may be merely exchanging one form of "centrism" (American, Athenian, Bio, European, Greek, Male, Western, you-name-it) with just another, perhaps inadvertently, thus failing to acknowledge the ultimate complexity, diversity, and fragility of the multicultural, ethical landscape with which one is interacting. We saw how the problem of the lion may become a dilemma. This justified concern, however, does not apply here because IE advocates a *minimal* informational ontology, which is not only timely, as we have just seen, but also tolerant of, and interfaceable with, other local ontologies. Thick cultures with robust, vertical ontologies—that is, deeply-seated, often irreconcilable, fundamental conceptions about human nature, the value and meaning of life, the nature of the universe and our place in it, society and its fair organization, religious beliefs, and so forth—can more easily interact with each other if they can share a lite, horizontal ontology as little committed to any particular *Weltanshaung* as possible. The identification of an absolute, ultimate, monistic ontology, capable of making all other ontologies merge, is just a myth, and a violent one at that. There is no such thing as a commitment-free position with respect to the way in which a variety of continuously changing agents appropriate, conceptualize, and semanticize their environment. Yet the alternative cannot be some form of relativism. This is no longer sustainable in a globalized world in which choices, actions, and events are delocalized. There simply is not enough room for "minding one's own business" in a network in which the behaviour of each node may affect the behaviour of all nodes. The approach to be pursued seems rather to be along the lines of what IE proposes: respect for and tolerance towards diversity and pluralism and identification of a minimal common ontology, which does not try to be platform independent (i.e., absolute), but cross-platform (i.e., portable).

As in Queneau's *Exercises in Style*, we need to be able to appreciate both the ninety-nine variations of the same story[10] and the fact that it is after all the same story that is being recounted again and again. This plurality of narratives need not turn into a Babel of fragmented voices. It may well be a source of pluralism that enriches one's ontology. More eyes simply see better and appreciate more angles, and a thousand languages can express semantic nuances that no global Esperanto may ever hope to grasp.

3. Informational Environmentalism

The ontocentrism supported by IE means that at least some of the weight of the ethical interpretations may be carried by (outsourced to) the informational ontology shared by the agents, not only by the different cultural or intellectual traditions (vertical ontologies) to which they may belong. Two further advantages are that all agents, whether human, artificial, social or hybrid, may be able to share the same minimal ontology and conceptual vocabulary; and then that any agent may take into account ecological concerns that are not limited to the biosphere.

4. Identifying the Sources and Targets of Moral Interactions

One of the serious obstacles in sharing an ontology is often how the sources and targets of moral interactions (including communication) are identified. The concept of person or human individual, and the corresponding features that are considered essential to his or her definition, might be central in some ontologies, marginal in others, and different in most. IE may help foster communication and fruitful interactions among different, thick,

vertical ontologies by approaching the problem with conceptual tools that are less precommitted. For when IE speaks of agents and patients, these are neutral elements in the ethical analysis that different cultures or macro-ethics may be able to appropriate, enrich, and make more complex, depending on their conceptual requirements and orientations. It is like having an ontology of agency that is open source, and that anyone can adapt to its own proprietary *Weltanshaung*.

The Cost of a Global-Information Ethics: Postulating the Ontic Trust

It would be silly to conclude at this point that a global-information ethics may provide an answer to any challenge posed by the various phenomena of globalization. This would be impossible. Of course, there will be many issues and difficulties that will require substantial extensions and adaptations of IE, of its methodology and of its principles. All I have tried to do is to convince the reader that such a great effort to apply IE as a global ethics would be fruitful and hence worth making.

It would be equally wrong to assume that the adoption of IE as a fruitful approach to global challenges may come at no conceptual cost. Every ethical approach requires some concession on the part of those who decide to share it and IE is no exception.

The cost imposed by IE is summarizable in terms of the postulation of what I shall define as the *ontic trust* binding agents and patients. A straightforward way of clarifying the concept of ontic trust is by drawing an analogy with the concept of "social contract".

Various forms of contractualism (in ethics) and contractarianism (in political philosophy) argue that moral obligation, the duty of political obedience, or the justice of social institutions, have their roots in, and gain their support from a so-called "social contract". This may be a real, implicit, or *merely hypothetical* agreement between the parties constituting a society (e.g., the people and the sovereign, the members of a community, or the individual and the state). The parties accept to agree to the terms of the contract and thus obtain some rights in exchange for some freedoms that, allegedly, they would enjoy in a hypothetical state of nature. The rights and responsibilities of the parties subscribing to the agreement are the terms of the social contract, whereas the society, state, group, an so forth, are the entity created for the purpose of enforcing the agreement. Both rights and freedoms are not fixed and may vary, depending on the interpretation of the social contract.

Interpretations of the theory of the social contract tend to be highly (and often unknowingly) anthropocentric (the focus is only on human rational agents) and stress the coercive nature of the agreement. These two aspects are not characteristic of the concept of ontic trust, but the basic idea of a fundamental agreement between parties as a foundation of moral interactions is sensible. In the case of the ontic trust, it is transformed into a primeval, entirely hypothetical *pact*, logically predating the social contract, which all agents cannot but sign when they come into existence, and that is constantly renewed in successive generations.[11] The sort of pact in question can be understood more precisely in terms of an actual trust.

Generally speaking, a trust in the English legal system is an entity in which someone (the trustee) holds and manages the former assets of a person (the trustor, or donor) for the benefit of certain persons or entities (the beneficiaries). Strictly speaking, nobody owns the assets. Since the trustor has donated them, the trustee has only legal ownership and the beneficiary has only equitable ownership. Now, the logical form of this sort of agreement can be used to model the ontic trust, in the following way:

- The assets or "corpus" is represented by the world, including all existing agents and patients;
- The donors are all past and current *generations* of agents;
- The trustees are all current *individual* agents;
- The beneficiaries are all current and future *individual* agents and patients.

By coming into being, an agent is made possible thanks to the existence of other entities. It *is* therefore bound to all that already is both *unwillingly* and *inescapably*. It *should be* so also *caringly*. Unwillingly, because no agent wills itself into existence, though every agent can, in theory, will itself out of it. Inescapably, because the ontic bond may be broken by an agent only at the cost of ceasing to exist as an agent. Moral life does not begin with an act of freedom but it may end with one. *Caringly* because participation in reality by any entity, including an agent—that is, the fact that any entity is an expression of what exists—provides a right to existence and an invitation (not a duty) to respect and take care of other entities. The pact then involves no coercion, but a mutual relation of appreciation, gratitude, and care, which is fostered by the recognition of the dependence of all entities on each other. A simple example may help to clarify further the meaning of the ontic trust.

Existence begins with a gift, even if possibly an unwanted one. A foetus will be initially only a beneficiary of the world. Once it is born and has become a full moral agent, it will be, as an individual, both a beneficiary and a trustee of the world. It will be in charge of taking care of the world, and, insofar as it is a member of the generation of living agents, it will also be a donor of the world. Once dead, it will leave the world to other agents after it and thus becomes a member of the generation of donors. In short, the life of an agent becomes a journey from being only a beneficiary to being only a donor, passing through the stage of being a responsible trustee of the world. We begin our career of moral agents as strangers to the world; we should end it as friends of the world.

The obligations and responsibilities imposed by the ontic trust will vary depending on circumstances but, fundamentally, the expectation is that actions will be taken or avoided in view of the welfare of the whole world.

The ontic trust is what is postulated by the approach supported by IE. According to IE, the ethical discourse concerns any entity, understood informationally, that is, not only all persons, their cultivation, well-being, and social interactions, not only animals, plants, and their proper natural life, but also anything that exists, from buildings and other artefacts to rivers and sand. Indeed, according to IE, nothing is too humble to deserve no respect at all. In this way, IE brings to ultimate completion the process of enlargement of the concept of what may count as a centre of a (no matter how minimal) moral claim, which now includes every instance of *being* understood informationally, no matter whether physically implemented or not. IE holds that every entity, as an expression of *being*, has a dignity, constituted by its mode of existence and essence (the collection of all the elementary proprieties that constitute it for what it is), which deserve to be respected (at least in a minimal and overridable sense) and hence place moral claims on the interacting agent and ought to contribute to guiding and constraining the agent's ethical decisions and behaviour. The ontic trust (and the corresponding ontological equality principle among entities) means that any form of reality (any instance of information/*being*), simply by the fact of *being* what it is, enjoys a minimal, initial, overridable, equal right to exist and develop in a way which is appropriate to its nature.[12]

The acceptance of the ontic trust requires a disinterested judgement of the moral situation from an objective perspective, that is, a perspective which is as non-anthropocentric as possible. Moral behaviour is less likely without this epistemic virtue. The ontic trust is respected whenever actions are impartial, universal and "caring" towards the world.

CONCLUSION

One of the objections that is sometimes made against IE is that of being too abstract or theoretical to be of much use when human agents are confronted by very concrete and applied challenges (Siponen, 2004). Unfortunately, this is an obvious misunderstanding. Imagine someone who, being presented with the declaration of human rights, were to complain that it is too general and inapplicable to solve the ethical problems the person is facing in a specific situation, say in dealing with a particular case of cyberstalking in the company that employs the person. This would be rather out of place. The suspicion is that some impatience with conceptual explorations may betray a lack of understanding of how profound the revolution we are undergoing is, and hence how radical the rethinking of our ethical approaches and principles may need to be in order to cope with it. IE is certainly not the declaration of human rights, but it seeks to obtain a level of generality purporting to provide a foundation for more applied and case-oriented analyses. So the question is not whether IE is too abstract—good foundations for the structure one may wish to see being built inevitably lie well below the surface—but whether it will succeed in providing the robust framework within which practical issues of moral concern may be more easily identified, clarified, and solved. I agree that it is in its actual applications that IE, as a global ethics for our information society, will or will not qualify as a useful approach; yet the need to build on the foundation provided by IE is an opportunity, not an objection.

REFERENCES

Brandt, D., & Henning, K. (2002). Information and communication technologies: Perspectives and their impact on society. *AI & Society, 16*(3), 210-223.

Bynum, T. W., & Rogerson, S. (1996). Global information ethics: Introduction and overview. *Science and Engineering Ethics, 2*(2), 131-136.

The Economist. (1997, December 18). 1897 and 1997: The century the earth stood still.

Ess, C. (2002). Computer-mediated colonization, the renaissance, and educational imperatives for an intercultural global village. *Ethics and Information Technology, 4*(1), 11-22.

Floridi, L. (2005). Presence: From epistemic failure to successful observability. *Presence: Teleoperators and virtual environments, 14*(6), 656-667.

Floridi, L. (in press). Information ethics. In J. van den Hoven & J. Weckert (Eds.), *Moral philosophy and information technology.* Cambridge: Cambridge University Press.

Floridi, L., & Sanders, J. W. (2004). The method of abstraction. In M. Negrotti (Ed.), *Yearbook of the artificial. Nature, culture and technology. Models in contemporary sciences* (pp. 177-220). Bern: Peter Lang.

Floridi, L., & Sanders, J. W. (in press). *Levelism and the method of abstraction.* Manuscript submitted for publication.

Held, D., & McGrew, A. (2001). Globalization. In J. Krieger (Ed.), *Oxford companion to politics of the world.* Oxford/New York: Oxford University Press. Retrieved January 25, 2007, from http://www.polity.co.uk/global/globocp.htm

Held, D., McGrew, A., Goldblatt, D., & Perraton, J. (1999). *Global transformations: Politics, economics and culture.* Cambridge: Polity Press.

Hodel, T. B., Holderegger, A., & Lüthi, A. (1998). Ethical guidelines for a networked world under construction. *Journal of Business Ethics, 17*(9-10), 1057-1071.

Siponen, M. (2004). A pragmatic evaluation of the theory of information ethics. *Ethics and Information Technology, 6*(4), 279-290.

Smith, M. M. (2002). Global information ethics: A mandate for professional education. In *Proceedings of the 68th IFLA Council and General Conference*, Glasgow. Retrieved January 25, 2007, from http://www.ifla.org/IV/ifla68/papers/056-093e.pdf.

Weckert, J. (2001). Computer ethics: Future directions. *Ethics and Information Technology, 3*(2), 93-96.

Wittgenstein, L. (2001). *Philosophical investigations: The German text with a revised English translation* (3rd ed.). Oxford: Blackwell.

ENDNOTES

[1] For a very synthetic but well-balanced and informed overview, I would recommend Held and McGrew (2001). In their terminology, I am a subscriber to the transformationalist approach, according to which "globalization does not simply denote a shift in the extensity or scale of social relations and activity. Much more significantly, argue the transformationalists, it also involves the spatial re-organization and re-articulation of economic, political, military and cultural power" (see Held et al., 1999).

[2] Graecia capta ferum victorem cepit- Epistles.

[3] How an ontology is achieved and what sort of philosophical analysis is required to make sense of its formation is not a relevant matter in this context, but the interested reader may wish to see Floridi and Sanders (in press).

[4] More technically, this means that two agents can communicate only if they share at least some possible level of abstraction.

On the method of abstraction see Floridi and Sanders (2004) and Floridi and Sanders (in press).

[5] If it took endless time and efforts to decipher the hieroglyphics, imagine what sense an extraterrestrial being could make of a message in a bottle like the plaque carried by the Pioneer spacecraft (http://spaceprojects.arc. nasa.gov/Space_Projects/pioneer/PN10&11. html)

[6] Unfortunately, we do not have African maps drawn from the "lions' perspective". The Da Ming Hun Yi Tu, or Amalgamated Map of the Great Ming Empire, the oldest map of Africa known so far, dates back "only" to 1389.

[7] Indexical expressions, such as "here", "yesterday", or "I", acquire their meaning or reference depending on who utters them and in which circumstances. Thus, "stranger" is indexical (people are strangers to each others), whereas the original meaning of "barbarian" is not, if we believe its Greek etymology to be "to babble confusedly", that is, someone who is unable to speak Greek properly.

[8] The IEG, a research group in Oxford, has developed a general interpretation of Information Ethics in a series of papers. Here I provide a summary based on Floridi [in press]. The interested reader is invited to check the Web site of the group at http://web. comlab.ox.ac.uk/oucl/research/areas/ieg/.

[9] Destruction is to be understood as the complete annihilation of the object in question, which ceases to exist; compare this to the process of "erasing" an entity irrevocably.

Corruption is to be understood as a form of pollution or depletion of some of the properties of the object, which ceases to exist as that object and begins to exist as a different object minus the properties that have been corrupted or eliminated. This may be compared to a process degrading the integrity of the object in question.

[10] On a crowded bus, a narrator observes a young man with a long neck in a strange hat yell at another man whom he claims is deliberately jostling him whenever anyone gets on or off the bus. The young man then sits down in a vacant seat. Two hours later the same narrator sees that same young man with another friend, who is suggesting that the young man have another button put on his overcoat.

[11] There are important and profound ways of understanding this Ur-pact religiously, especially but not only in the Judeo-Christian tradition, where the parties involved are God and Israel or humanity, and their old or new covenant (διαθήκη) makes it easier to include environmental concerns and values otherwise overlooked from the strongly anthropocentric perspective prima facie endorsed by contemporary contractualism. However, it is not my intention to endorse or even draw on such sources. I am mentioning the point here in order to shed some light both on the origins of contractualism and on a possible way of understanding the onto-centric approach advocated by IE.

[12] In the history of philosophy, a similar view can be found advocated by Stoic and Neoplatonic philosophers, and by Spinoza.

This work was previously published in International Journal of Technology and Human Interaction, Vol. 3, Issue 3, edited by B. Stahl, pp. 1-11, copyright 2007 by IGI Publishing, formerly known as Idea Group Publishing (an imprint of IGI Global).

Chapter XVI
Is Information Ethics Culture–Relative?

Philip Brey
University of Twente, The Netherlands

ABSTRACT

In this chapter, I examine whether information ethics is culture relative. If it is, different approaches to information ethics are required in different cultures and societies. This would have major implications for the current, predominantly Western approach to information ethics. If it is not, there must be concepts and principles of information ethics that have universal validity. What would they be? The descriptive evidence is for the cultural relativity of information ethics will be studied by examining cultural differences between ethical attitudes towards privacy, freedom of information, and intellectual property rights in Western and non-Western cultures. I then analyze what the implications of these findings are for the metaethical question of whether moral claims must be justified differently in different cultures. Finally, I evaluate what the implications are for the practice of information ethics in a cross-cultural context.

INTRODUCTION

Information ethics[1] has so far mainly been a topic of research and debate in Western countries, and has mainly been studied by Western scholars. There is, however, increasing interest in information ethics in non-Western countries like Japan, China, and India, and there have been recent attempts to raise cross-cultural issues in information ethics (e.g., Ess, 2002; Gorniak-Ko-cikowska, 1996; Mizutani, Dorsey & Moor, 2004). Interactions between scholars of Western and non-Western countries have brought significant differences to light between the way in which they approach issues in information ethics. This raises the question whether different cultures require a different information ethics and whether concepts and approaches in Western information ethics can be validly applied to the moral dilemmas of non-Western cultures. In other words, is information ethics culturally relative or are there concepts and principles of information ethics that have universal validity? The aim of this essay is to arrive at preliminary answers to this question.

MORAL RELATIVISM AND INFORMATION ETHICS

In discussions of moral relativism, a distinction is commonly made between descriptive and metaethical moral relativism. *Descriptive moral relativism* is the position that as a matter of empirical fact, there is extensive diversity between the values and moral principles of societies, groups, cultures, historical periods, or individuals. Existing differences in moral values, it is claimed, are not superficial but profound, and extend to core moral values and principles. Descriptive moral relativism is an empirical thesis that can in principle be supported or refuted through psychological, sociological, and anthropological investigations. The opposite of descriptive moral relativism is *descriptive moral absolutism*, the thesis that there are no profound moral disagreements exist between societies, groups, cultures, or individuals. At issue in this essay will be a specific version of descriptive moral relativism, *descriptive cultural relativism*, according to which there are major differences between the moral principles of different cultures.

Much more controversial than the thesis of descriptive moral relativism is the thesis of metaethical moral relativism, according to which the truth or justification of moral judgments is not absolute or objective, but relative to societies, groups, cultures, historical periods, or individuals.[2] Whereas a descriptive relativist could make the empirical observation that one society, polygamy, is considered moral whereas in another it is considered immoral, a metaethical relativist could make the more far-reaching claim that the statement "polygamy is morally wrong" is true or justified in some societies while false

or unjustified in others. Descriptive relativism therefore makes claims about the values that different people or societies actually have, whereas metaethical relativism makes claims about the values that they are justified in having. Metaethical moral relativism is antithetical to *metaethical moral absolutism*, the thesis that regardless of any existing differences between moral values in different cultures, societies, or individuals, there are moral principles that are absolute or objective, and that are universally true across cultures, societies, or individuals. Metaethical moral absolutism would therefore hold that the statement "polygamy is morally wrong" is either universally true or universally false; it cannot be true for some cultures or societies but false for others. If the statement is true, then societies that hold that polygamy is moral are in error, and if it is false, then the mistake lies with societies that condemn it.

The question being investigated in this essay is whether information ethics is culturally relative. In answering this question, it has to be kept in mind that the principal aims of information ethics are not descriptive, but normative and evaluative. That is, its principal aim is not to describe existing morality regarding information but rather to morally evaluate information practices and to prescribe and justify moral standards and principles for practices involving the production, consumption, or processing of information. A claim that information ethics is culturally relative therefore a claim that metaethical moral relativism is true for information ethics. It is to claim that the ethical values, principles, and judgments of information ethics are valid only relative to a particular culture, presumably the culture in which they have been developed. Since information ethics is largely a product of the West, an affirmation of the cultural relativity of information ethics means that its values and principles do not straightforwardly apply to non-Western cultures.

But if the cultural relativity of information ethics depends on the truth of metaethical relativism, does any consideration need to be given to descriptive relativism for information ethics? This question should be answered affirmatively. Defenses of metaethical relativism usually depend on previous observations that descriptive relativism is true. If descriptive relativism is false, it follows that people across the world share a moral framework of basic values and principles. But if this is the case, then it seems pointless to argue for metaethical moral relativism: why claim that the truth of moral judgments is different for different groups if these groups already agree on basic moral values? On the other hand, if descriptive relativism is true, then attempts to declare particular moral principles of judgments to be universally valid come under scrutiny. Extensive justification would be required for any attempt to adopt a particular moral framework (say, Western information ethics) as one that is universally valid. In the next section, I will therefore focus on the question whether there are good reasons to believe that there are deep and widespread moral disagreements about central values and principles in information ethics across cultures, and whether therefore descriptive cultural relativism is true for information ethics.

THE DESCRIPTIVE CULTURAL RELATIVITY OF INFORMATION-RELATED VALUES

In this section, I will investigate the descriptive cultural relativity of three values that are the topic of many studies in information ethics: privacy, intellectual property, and freedom of information. Arguments have been made that these values are distinctly Western, and are not universally accepted across different cultures. In what follows I will investigate whether these claims seem warranted by empirical evidence. I will also relate the outcome of my investigations to discussions of more general differences between Western and non-Western systems of morality.

How can it be determined that cultures have fundamentally different value systems regarding notions like privacy and intellectual property? I propose that three kinds of evidence are relevant:

1. **Conceptual:** The extent to which there are moral concepts across cultures with similar meanings. For example, does Chinese culture have a concept of privacy that is similar to the American concept of privacy?

2. **Institutional:** The extent to which there is similarity between codified rules that express moral principles and codified statements that express moral judgments about particular (types of) situations. For example, are the moral principles exhibited in the laws and written rules employed in Latin cultures on the topic of privacy sufficiently similar to American laws and rules that it can be claimed that they embody similar moral principles?

3. **Behavioral:** The similarity between customs and behaviors that appear to be guided by moral principles. This would include tendencies to avoid behaviors that are immoral regarding a moral principle, tendencies to show disapproval to those who engage in such behaviors, and to show disapproval to those who do not, and tendencies to show remorse or guilt when engaging in such behaviors. For instance, if a culture has a shared privacy principle that states that peeking inside someone's purse is wrong, then it can be expected that most people try not to do this, disapprove of those who do, and feel ashamed or remorseful when they are caught doing it.

It is conceivable that in a particular culture a value or moral principle is widely upheld at the behavioral level, but has not (yet) been codified at the institutional and conceptual level. But this is perhaps unlikely in cultures with institutions that include extensive systems of codified rules, which would include any culture with a modern legal system. It is also conceivable that a moral value or principle is embodied in both behavioral customs and codified rules, but no good match can be found at the conceptual level. In that case, it seems reasonable to assume that the value or principle at issue is embodied in the culture, but different concepts are used to express it, making it difficult to find direct translations.

A full consideration of the evidence for descriptive moral relativism along these three lines is beyond the scope of this chapter. I only intend to consider enough evidence to arrive at a preliminary assessment of the cultural relativity of values in contemporary information ethics.

Privacy

It has been claimed that in Asian cultures like China and Japan, no genuine concept or value of privacy exists. These cultures have been held to value the collective over the individual. Privacy is an individual right, and such a right may not be recognized in a culture where collective interest tend to take priority over individual interests. Using the three criteria outline above, and drawing from studies of privacy in Japan, China and Thailand, I will now consider whether this conclusion is warranted.

At the conceptual level, there are words in Japanese, Chinese, and Thai that refer to a private sphere, but these words seem to have substantially different meanings than the English word for privacy. Mizutani et al. (2004) have argued that there is no word for "privacy" in traditional Japanese. Modern Japanese, they claim, sometimes adopt a Japanese translation for the Western word for privacy, which sounds like "puraibashii", and written in katakana. Katakana is the Japanese phonetic syllabary that is mostly used for words of foreign origin. According to Nakada and Tamura (2005), Japanese does include a word for "private", "Watakusi", which means "partial, secret and

selfish". It is opposed to "Ohyake", which means "public". Things that are Watakusi are considered less worthy than things that are Ohyake. Mizutani et al. (2004) point out, in addition, that there are certainly behavioral customs in Japan that amount to a respect for privacy. There are conventions that restrict access to information, places, or objects. For example, one is not supposed to look under clothes on public streets.

In China, the word closest to the English "privacy" is "Yinsi", which means "shameful secret" and is usually associated with negative, shameful things. Lü (2005) claims that only recently that "Yinsi" has also come to take broader meanings to include personal information, shameful or not, that people do not want others to know (see also Jingchun, 2005; McDougall & Hansson, 2002). This shift in meaning has occurred under Western influences. As for institutional encoding of privacy principles, Lü maintains that there currently are no laws in China that protect an individual right to privacy, and the legal protection of privacy has been weak and is still limited, though there have been improvements in privacy protection since the 1980s.

Kitiyadisai (2005), finally, holds that the concept of privacy does not exist in Thailand. She claims that the Western word privacy was adopted in the late nineteenth or early twentieth century in Thailand, being transliterated as "privade," but this word gained a distinctly Thai meaning, being understood as a collectivist rather than an individual notion. It referred to a private sphere in which casual dress could be worn, as opposed to a public sphere in which respectable dress had to be worn. In the Thai legal system, Kitiyadisai claims there has not been any right to privacy since the introduction of privacy legislation in 1997 and a Thai constitution, also in 1997, that for the first time guarantees basic human rights. Kitiyadisai argues, however, that Thai privacy laws are hardly enacted in practice, and many Thais remain unaware of the notion of privacy.

It can be tentatively concluded that the introduction of a concept of privacy similar to the Western notion has only taken place recently in Japan, China, and Thailand, and that privacy legislation has only taken place recently. In traditional Japanese, Chinese, and Thai culture, which still has a strong presence today, distinctions are made that resemble the Western distinction between public and private, and customs exist that may be interpreted as respective of privacy, but there is no recognized individual right to privacy.

Intellectual Property Rights

In discussing the cultural relativity of intellectual property rights (IPR), I will limit myself to one example: China. China is known for not having a developed notion of private or individual property. Under communist rule, the dominant notion of property was collective. All means of production, such as farms and factories, were to be collectively owned and operated. Moreover, the state exercised strict control over the means of production and over both the public and private sphere. A modern notion of private property was only introduced since the late 1980s. Milestones were a 1988 constitutional revision that allowed for private ownership of means of production and a 2004 constitutional amendment that protects citizens from encroachment of private property.

The notion of intellectual property has only recently been introduced in China, in the wake of China's recent economic reforms and increased economic interaction with the West. China is currently passing IPR laws and cracking down on violations of IPR in order to harmonize the Chinese economic system with the rest of the world. But as journalist Ben Worthen observes, "the average citizen in China has no need and little regard for intellectual property. IPR is not something that people grew up with ... and the percent of citizens who learn about it by engaging in international commerce is tiny." Worthen also points out that Chinese companies "have no

incentive to respect IPR unless they are doing work for Western companies that demand it" and that "since most of the intellectual property royalties are headed out of China there isn't a lot of incentive for the government to crack down on companies that choose to ignore IPR."[3] All in all, it can be concluded that China's value system traditionally has not included a recognition of intellectual property rights, and it is currently struggling with this concept.

Freedom of Information

Freedom of information is often held to comprise two principles: freedom of speech (the freedom to express one's opinions or ideas, in speech or in writing) and freedom of access to information. Sometimes, freedom of the press (the freedom to express oneself through publication and dissemination) is distinguished as a third principle. In Western countries, freedom of information is often defined as a constitutional and inalienable right. Laws protective of freedom of information are often especially designed to ensure that individuals can exercise this freedom without governmental interference or constraint. Government censorship or interference is only permitted in extreme situations, pertaining to such things as hate speech, libel, copyright violations, and information that could undermine national security.

In many non-Western countries, freedom of information is not a guiding principle. There are few institutionalized protections of freedom of information; there are many practices that interfere with freedom of information, and a concept of freedom of information is not part of the established discourse in society. In such societies, the national interest takes precedence, and an independent right to freedom information either is not recognized or is made so subordinate to national interests that it hardly resembles the Western right to freedom of information. These are countries in which practices of state censorship are widespread; mass media are largely or wholly government-controlled, the Internet, databases, and libraries are censored, and messages that do not conform to the party line are cracked down upon.

Let us, as an example, consider the extent to which freedom of information can be said to be a value in Chinese society. Until the 1980s, the idea of individual rights or civil rights was not a well-known concept in China. Government was thought to exist to ensure a stable society and a prosperous economy. It was not believed to have a function to protect individual rights against collective and state interests. As a consequence of this general orientation, the idea of an individual right to freedom of information was virtually unknown. Only recently has China introduced comprehensive civil rights legislation. In its 1982 constitution, China introduced constitutional principles of freedom of speech and of the press. And in 1997, it signed the International Convention on Economic, Social, and Cultural Rights, and in 1998 the International Convention on Civil and Political Rights (the latter of which it has not yet ratified).

Even though the Chinese government has recently come to recognize a right to freedom of information, as well as individual human rights in general, and has introduced legislation to this effect, state censorship is still rampant, and the principle of upholding state interest still tends to dominate the principle of protecting individual human rights. Internet censorship presents a good example of this. Internet traffic in China is controlled through what the Chinese call the Golden Shield, and what is known outside mainland China as the Great Firewall of China. This is a system of control in which Internet content is blocked by routers, as well as at the backbone and ISP level, through the "filtering" of undesirable URLs and keywords. A long list of such "forbidden" URLs and keywords has been composed by the Chinese State Council Information Office, in collaboration with the Communist Party's Propaganda Department. This system is especially geared towards censorship of content coming from outside mainland China (Human Rights Watch, 2006).

Rights-Centered and Virtue-Centered Morality

A recurring theme in the above three discussions has been the absence of a strong tradition of individual rights in the cultures that were discussed – those of China, Japan, and Thailand -—and the priority that is given to collective and state interests. Only very recently have China, Japan, and Thailand introduced comprehensive human rights legislation, which has occurred mainly through Western influence, and there is still considerable tension in these societies, especially in China and Thailand, between values that prioritize the collective and the state and values that prioritize the individual.

Various authors have attempted to explain the worldview that underlies the value system of these countries. In Japan and Thailand, and to a lesser extent China, Buddhism is key to an understanding of attitudes towards individual rights. Buddhism holds a conception of the self that is antithetical to the Western conception of an autonomous self which aspires to self-realization. Buddhism holds that the self does not exist and that human desires are delusional. The highest state that humans can reach is Nirvana, a state of peace and contentment in which all suffering has ended. To reach Nirvana, humans have to become detached from their desires, and realize that the notion of an integrated and permanent self is an illusion. In Buddhism, the self is defined as fluid, situation-dependent, and ever-changing. As Mizutani et al. and Kitiyadisai have noted, such a notion of the self is at odds with a Western notion of privacy and of human rights in general, notions which presuppose a situation-independent, autonomous self which pursues its own self-interests and which has inalienable rights that have to be defended against external threats.

In part through Buddhism, but also through the influence of other systems of belief such as Confucianism, Taoism, and Maoism, societies like those of China and Thailand have developed a value system in which the rights or interests of the individual are subordinate to those of the collective and the state. To do good is to further the interests of the collective. Such furtherances of collective interests will generally also benefit the individual. The task of government, then, is to ensure that society as a whole functions well, in a harmonious and orderly way, and that social ills are cured, rather than the ills of single individuals. In other words, government works for the common good, and not for the individual good.

Only recently have countries like China and Thailand come to recognize individual human rights and individual interests next to collective interests. But according to Lü (2005), the collectivist ethic still prevails:

Adapting to the demands of social diversity, the predominant ethics now express a new viewpoint that argues against the simple denial of individual interests and emphasizes instead the dialectical unification of collective interests and individual interests: in doing so, however, this ethics points out that this kind of unification must take collective interests as the foundation. That is to say, in the light of the collectivism principle of the prevailing ethics, collective interests and individual interests are both important, but comparatively speaking, the collective interests are more important than individual interests. (Lü, 2005, p. 12)

If this observation is correct, then the introduction of human rights legislation and property rights in countries like China is perhaps not motivated by a genuine recognition of inalienable individual human rights, but rather a recognition that in the current international climate, it is better to introduce human rights and property rights, because such principles will lead to greater economic prosperity, which is ultimately to the benefit of the collective.

The dominant value systems prevalent in China, Thailand, and Japan are examples of what philosopher David Wong (1984) has called virtue-centered moralities. According to Wong, at least two different approaches to morality can be found in the world: a *virtue-centered morality* that emphasizes the good of the community, and a *rights-centered morality* that stresses the value of individual freedom. Rights-centered morality is the province of the modern West, although it is also establishing footholds in other parts of the world. Virtue-centered morality can be found in traditional cultures such as can be found in southern and eastern Asia and in Africa. Wong's distinction corresponds with the frequently made distinction between individualist and collectivist culture, that is found, amongst others, in Geert Hofstede's (1991) well-known five-dimensional model of cultural difference. However, this latter distinction focuses on social systems and cultural practices, whereas Wong makes a distinction based in differences in moral systems.

In Wong's conception of virtue-centered moralities, individuals have duties and responsibilities that stem from the central value of a common good. The common good is conceived of in terms of an ideal conception of community life, which is based on a well-balanced social order in which every member of the community has different duties and different virtues to promote the common good. Some duties and virtues may be shared by all members. The idea that human beings have individual rights is difficult to maintain in this kind of value system, because recognition of such rights would have to find its basis in the higher ideal of the common good. But it seems clear that attributing rights to individuals is not always to the benefit of the common good. The recognition of individual property rights, for example, could result in individual property owners not sharing valuable resources that would benefit the whole community. In virtue-centered moralities, the ideal is for individuals to be virtuous, and virtuous individuals are those individuals whose individual good coincides with their contribution to the common good. Individual goods may be recognized in such communities, but they are always subordinate to the common good. Individuals deserve respect only because of their perceived contribution to the common good, not because they possess inalienable individual rights.

Conclusion

The discussion of privacy, intellectual property rights, and freedom of information has shown that a good case can be made for the descriptive cultural relativity of these values. These values are central in information ethics, as it has been developed in the West. Moreover, it was argued that the uncovered cultural differences in the appraisal of these values can be placed in the context of a dichotomy between two fundamentally different kinds of value systems that exist in different societies: rights-centered and virtue-centered systems of value. Information ethics, as it has developed in the West, has a strong emphasis on rights, and little attention is paid to the kinds of moral concerns that may exist in virtue-centered systems of morality. In sum, it seems that the values that are of central concern in Western information ethics are not the values that are central in many non-Western systems of morality. The conclusion therefore seems warranted that descriptive moral relativism is true for information ethics.

METAETHICAL MORAL RELATIVISM AND INFORMATION ETHICS

In the first section, it was argued that descriptive moral relativism is a necessary condition for metaethical moral relativism, but is not sufficient to prove this doctrine. However, several moral arguments exist that use the truth of descriptive relativism, together with additional premises, to argue for metaethical relativism. I will start with a consideration of two standard arguments of this

form, which are found wanting, after which I will consider a more sophisticated argument.

Two Standard Arguments for Metaethical Relativism

There are two traditional arguments for metaethical moral relativism that rely on the truth of descriptive moral relativism (Wong, 1993). The one most frequently alluded to is the *argument from diversity*. This argument starts with the observation that different cultures employ widely different moral standards. Without introducing additional premises, the argument goes on to conclude that therefore, there are no universal moral standards. This argument rests on what is known in philosophy as a naturalistic fallacy, an attempt to derive a norm from a fact, or an "ought" from an "is". The premise of the argument is descriptive: there are different moral standards. The conclusion is normative: no moral standard has universal validity. No evidence has been presented that the truth of the premise has any bearing on the truth of the conclusion.

A second, stronger argument for moral relativism is the *argument from functional necessity*, according to which certain ethical beliefs in a society may be so central to its functioning that they cannot be given up without destroying the society. Consequently, the argument runs, these ethical beliefs are true for that society, but not necessarily in another. However, this argument is also problematic because it grounds the truth of ethical statements in their practical value for maintaining social order in a particular society. Such a standard of justification for ethical statements is clearly too narrow, as it could be used to justify the moral beliefs of societies whose beliefs and practices are clearly unethical, for instance, fascist societies. If a society operates in a fundamentally unethical way, then the transformation of some of its social structures and cultural forms would seem acceptable if more ethical practices are the result.

Wong's and Harman's Argument for Metaethical Relativism

More convincing arguments for moral relativism have been presented by David Wong (1984, 2006) and Gilbert Harman (1996, 2000). Their argument runs, in broad outline, as follows. There are deep-seated differences in moral belief between different cultures. Careful consideration of the reasons for these moral beliefs they have shows that they are *elements of different strategies to realize related but different conceptions of the Good.* No good arguments can be given why one of these conceptions of the Good is significantly better than all the others. Therefore, these moral beliefs are best explained as different but (roughly) equally valid strategies for attaining the Good.

This is a much better argument than the previous two, since it puts the ball in the metaethical absolutist's court: he will have to come up with proof that it is possible to provide good arguments for the superiority of one particular conception of the Good over all other conceptions. Metaethical absolutists can respond to this challenge in two ways. First, they may choose to bite the bullet and claim that a rational comparison of different conceptions of the Good is indeed possible. Different conceptions of the Good, they may argue, rely on factual or logical presuppositions that may be shown to be false. Alternatively, they may argue that there are universally shared moral intuitions about what is good, and these intuitions can be appealed to in defending or discrediting particular conceptions of the Good. For instance an individual who believes that physical pleasure is the highest good could conceivably be persuaded to abandon this belief through exposure to arguments that purport to demonstrate that there are other goods overlooked by this individual that are at least as valuable. Such an argument could conceivably rely on someone's moral intuitions about the Good that could be shown to deviate from someone's explicit concept of the Good.

Second, a mixed position could be proposed, according to which it is conceded that individuals or cultures may hold different conceptions of the Good that cannot be rationally criticized (*pace* metaethical relativism) but that rational criticism of individual moral beliefs is nevertheless possible (*pace* metaethical absolutism) because these beliefs can be evaluated for their effectiveness in realizing the Good in which service they stand. After all, if moral beliefs are strategies to realize a particular conception of the Good, as Wong and Harman have argued, then they can be suboptimal in doing so. A belief that Internet censorship is justified because it contributes to a more stable and orderly society can be wrong because it may not in fact contribute to a more stable and orderly society. Empirical arguments may be made that Internet censorship is not necessary for the maintenance of social order, or even that Internet censorship may ultimately work to undermine social order, for example, because it creates discontentment and resistance.

In the existing dialogue between proponents of rights-centered and virtue-centered systems of morality, it appears that both these approaches are already being taken. Western scholars have criticized the organicist conception of society that underlies conceptions of the Good in many Asian cultures, while Western definitions of the Good in terms of individual well-being have been criticized for their atomistic conception of individuals. Rights-based systems of morality have been criticized for undervaluing the common good, whereas virtue-based systems have been criticized for overlooking the importance of the individual good. In addition, both rights-centered and virtue-centered systems of morality have been criticized for not being successful by their own standards. Western individualism has been claimed to promote selfishness and strife, which results in many unhappy individuals plagued by avarice, proverty, depression, and loneliness. Western societies have therefore been claimed to be unsuccessful in attaining their own notion of the Good, defined in terms of individual well-being. Virtue-centered cultures have been claimed to be have difficulty in developing strong economies that serve the common good, because good economies have been argued to require private enterprise and a more individualist culture. In addition, strong state control, which is a feature of many virtue-centered cultures, has been argued to lead to corruption and totalitarianism, which also do not serve the common good.

In light of the preceding observations, it seems warranted to conclude, *pace* metaethical absolutism, that rational criticism between different moral systems is possible. It does not follow, however, that conclusive arguments for universal moral truths or the superiority of one particular moral system over others are going to be possible. Critics of a particular moral system may succeed in convincing its adherents that the system has its flaws and needs to be modified, but it could well be that no amount of criticism ever succeeds in convincing its adherents to abandon core moral beliefs within that system, however rational and open-minded these adherents are in listening to such criticism.

Conclusion

I have argued, *pace* metaethical relativism, that it is difficult if not impossible to provide compelling arguments for the superiority of different notions of the Good that are central in different moral systems, and by implication, that it is difficult to present conclusive arguments for the universal truth of particular moral principles and beliefs. I have also argued, *pace* metaethical absolutism, that is nevertheless possible to develop rational arguments for and against particular moral values and overarching conceptions of the Good across moral systems, even if such arguments do not result in proofs of the superiority of one particular moral system or moral principle over another.

From these two metaethical claims, a normative position can be derived concerning the

way in which cross-cultural ethics ought to take place. It follows, first of all, that it is only justified for proponents of a particular moral value or principle to claim that it ought to be accepted in another culture if they make this claim on the basis of a thorough understanding of the moral system operative in this other culture. The proponent would have to understand how this moral system functions and what notion of the Good it services, and would have to have strong arguments that either the exogenous value would be a good addition to the moral system in helping to bring about the Good serviced in that moral system, or that the notion of the Good serviced in that culture is flawed and requires revisions. In the next section, I will consider implications of this position for the practice of information ethics in cross-cultural settings.

INFORMATION ETHICS IN A CROSS-CULTURAL CONTEXT

It is an outcome of the preceding sections that significant differences exist between moral systems of different cultures, that these differences have important implications for moral attitudes towards uses of information and information technology, and that there are good reasons to take such differences seriously in normative studies in information ethics. In this section, I will argue, following Rafael Capurro, that we need an intercultural information ethics that studies and evaluates cultural differences in moral attitudes towards information and information technology. I will also critically evaluate the claim that the Internet will enable a new global ethic that provides a unified moral framework for all cultures.

Intercultural Information Ethics

The notion of an *intercultural information ethics* (IIE) was first introduced by Rafael Capurro (2005, in press), who defined it as a field of research in which moral questions regarding information technology and the use of information are reflected on in a comparative manner on the basis of different cultural traditions. I will adopt Capurro's definition, but differ with him on what the central tasks of an IIE should be. Capurro defines the tasks of IIE very broadly. For him, they not only the comparative study of value systems in different cultures in relation to their use of information and information technology, but also studies of the effect of information technology on customs, languages, and everyday problems, the changes produced by the Internet on traditional media, and the economic impact of the Internet to the extent that it can become an instrument of cultural oppression and colonialism.

I hold, in contrast, that studies of the effects of information technology in non-Western cultures are more appropriately delegated to the social sciences (including communication studies, cultural studies, anthropology and science, and technology studies). An intercultural information ethics should primarily focus on the comparative study of moral systems. Its overall aim would be to interpret, compare, and critically evaluate moral systems in different cultures regarding their moral attitudes towards and behavior towards information and information technology.

This task for IIE can be broken down into four subtasks, the first two of which are exercises in descriptive ethics and the latter two of which belong to normative ethics. First, IIE should engage in *interpretive studies* of moral systems in particular cultures, including the systems of value contained in the religious and political ideologies that are dominant in these cultures. The primary focus in such interpretive studies within the context of IIE should be on resulting moral attitudes towards the use and implications of information technology and on the moral problems generated by uses of information technology within the context of the prevailing moral system. Second, IIE should engage in *comparative studies* of moral systems from different cultures, and arrive at

analyses of both similarities and differences in the way that these moral systems are organized and operate, with a specific focus on the way in which they have different moral attitudes towards implications of information technology and on differences in moral problems generated by the use of information technology.

Third, IIE should engage in *critical studies* in which the moral systems of particular cultures are criticized based on the insights gained through the interpretive and comparative studies alluded to above, particularly in their dealings with information technology. Critical studies may be directed towards critizing moral values and beliefs in cultures other than one's own, and proposing modifications in the culture's moral system and ways in which it should solve moral problems, but may also involve self-criticism, in which one's own moral values and the moral system of one's own culture is criticized based on insights gained from the study of alternative moral systems. Fourth, IIE should engage in *interrelational studies* that focus on the construction of normative models for interaction between cultures in their dealings with information and information technology that respect their different moral systems. Interrelational studies hence investigate what moral compromises cultures can make and ought to make in their interactions and what shared moral principles can be constructed to govern their interactions.

Global Ethics and the Information Revolution

Some authors have argued that globalization and the emergence of the Internet have created a global community, and that this community requires its own moral system that transcends and unifies the moral systems of all cultures and nations that participate in this global community. The ethics needed for the construction of such a moral system has been called *global ethics*. The idea of a global ethics or ethic was first introduced by

German theologian Hans Küng in 1990 and later elaborated by him in a book (Küng, 2001). His aim was to work towards a shared moral framework for humanity that would contain a minimal consensus concerning binding values and moral principles that could be invoked by members of a global community in order to overcome differences and avoid conflict.

Krystyna Górniak-Kocikowska (1996) has argued that the computer revolution that has taken place has made it clear that a future global ethic will have to be a computer ethic or information ethic. As she explains, actions in cyberspace are not local, and therefore the ethical rules governing such actions cannot be rooted in a particular local culture. Therefore, unifying ethical rules have to be constructed in cyberspace that can serve as a new global ethic. Similar arguments have been presented by Bao and Xiang (2006) and De George (2006).

No one would deny that a global ethic, as proposed by Küng, would be desirable. The construction of an explicit, shared moral framework that would bind all nations and cultures would evidently be immensely valuable. It should be obvious, however, that such a framework could only develop as an addition to existing local moral systems, not as a replacement of them. It would be a framework designed to help solve global problems, and would exist next to the local moral systems that people use to solve their local problems. In addition, it remains to be seen if cross-cultural interactions over the Internet yield more than a mere set of rules for conduct online, a global netiquette, and will result in a global ethic that can serve as a common moral framework for intercultural dialogue and joint action. Hongladarom (2001) has concluded, based on empirical studies, that the Internet does not create a worldwide monolithic culture but rather reduplicates existing cultural boundaries. It does create an umbrella cosmopolitan culture to some extent, but only for those Internet users who engage in cross-cultural dialogue, which is a minority, and this umbrella culture is rather superficial. Claims that the Internet will enable a new global ethic may therefore be somewhat premature. In any case, such intercultural dialogue online will have to be supplemented with serious academic work in intercultural information ethics, as well as intercultural ethics at large.

CONCLUSION

It was found in this essay that very different moral attitudes exist in Western and non-Western countries regarding three key issues in information ethics: privacy, intellectual property, and freedom of information. In non-Western countries like China, Japan, and Thailand, there is no strong recognition of individual rights in relation to these three issues. These differences were analyzed in the context of a difference, proposed by philosopher David Wong, between rights-centered moralities that dominate in the West and virtue-centered moralities that prevail in traditional cultures, including those in South and East Asia. It was then argued that cross-cultural normative ethics cannot be practiced without a thorough understanding of the prevailing moral system in the culture that is being addressed. When such an understanding has been attained, scholars can proceed to engage in moral criticism of practices in the culture and propose standards and solutions to moral problems. It was argued, following Rafael Capurro, that we need an intercultural information ethics that engages in interpretive, comparative, and normative studies of moral problems and issues in information ethics in different cultures. It is to be hoped that researchers in both Western and non-Western countries will take up this challenge and engage in collaborative studies and dialogue on an issue that may be of key importance to future international relations.

REFERENCES

Bao, X., & Xiang, Y. (2006). Digitalization and global ethics. *Ethics and Information Technology, 8*, 41-47.

Capurro, R. (2005). Privacy: An intercultural perspective. Ethics and Information Technology, 7(1), 37-47.

Capurro, R. (in press). Intercultural information ethics. In R. Capurro, J. Frühbaure, & T. Hausmanningers (Eds.), *Localizing the Internet. Ethical issues in intercultural perspective.* Munich: Fink Verlag. Retrieved January 25, 2007, from http://www.capurro.de/iie.html

De George, R. (2006). Information technology, globalization and ethics. *Ethics and Information Technology, 8*, 29–40.

Ess, C. (2002). Computer-mediated colonization, the renaissance, and educational imperatives for an intercultural global village. *Ethics and Information Technology, 4*(1), 11-22.

Gorniak-Kocikowska, K. (1996). The computer revolution and the problem of global ethics. *Science and Engineering Ethics, 2*, 177–190.

Harman, G. (1996). Moral relativism. In G. Harman & J. J. Thompson (Eds.), *Moral relativism and moral objectivity (pp. 3-64).* Cambridge, MA: Blackwell Publishers.

Harman, G. (2000). Is there a single true morality? In G. Harman (Ed.), *Explaining value: And other essays in moral philosophy* (pp. 77-99). Oxford: Clarendon Press.

Hofstede, G. (2001). *Culture's consequences.* Thousand Oaks, CA: Sage.

Hongladarom, S. (2001). Global culture, local cultures and the Internet: The Thai example. In C. Ess (Ed.), *Culture, technology, communication: Towards an intercultural global village* (pp.

307-324). Albany, NY: State University of New York Press.

Human Rights Watch. (2006). Race to the bottom. Corporate complicity in Chinese Internet censorship. *Human Rights Watch Report, 18*(8C). Retrieved January 25, 2007, from http://www.hrw.org

Johnson, D. (2000). *Computer ethics* (3rd ed.). Upper Saddle River, NJ: Prentice Hall.

Jingchun, C. (2005). Protecting the right to privacy in China. *Victoria University of Wellington Law Review, 38*(3). Retrieved January 25, 2007, from http://www.austlii.edu.au/nz/journals/VUWL-Rev/2005/25.html

Kitiyadisai, K. (2005). Privacy rights and protection: Foreign values in modern Thai context. *Ethics and Information Technology, 7*, 17-26.

Küng, H. (2001). *A global ethic for global politics and economics.* Hong Kong: Logos and Pneuma Press.

Lü, Y.-H. (2005). Privacy and data privacy issues in contemporary China. *Ethics and Information Technology, 7*, 7-15.

McDougall, B., & Hansson, A. (Eds.). (2002). *Chinese concepts of privacy.* Brill Academic Publishers.

Mizutani, M., Dorsey, J., & Moor, J. (2004). The Internet and Japanese conception of privacy. *Ethics and Information Technology, 6*(2), 121-128.

Nakada, M., & Tamura, T. (2005). Japanese conceptions of privacy: An intercultural perspective. *Ethics and Information Technology, 7*, 27-36.

Wong, D. (1984). *Moral relativity.* Berkeley, CA: University of California Press.

Wong, D. (1993). Relativism. In P. Singer (Ed.), *A companion to ethics* (pp. 442-450). Blackwell.

Wong, D. (2006). *Natural moralities: A defense of pluralistic relativism.* Oxford: Oxford University Press.

ENDNOTES

[1] By information ethics I mean the study of ethical issues in the use of information and information technology. Contemporary information ethics is a result of the digital revolution (or information revolution) and focuses mainly on ethical issues in the production, use, and dissemination of digital information and information technologies. It encloses the field of computer ethics (Johnson, 2000) as well as concerns that belong to classical information ethics (which was a branch of library and information science), media ethics, and journalism ethics.

[2] This doctrine is called metaethical rather than normative because it does not make any normative claims, but rather makes claims about the nature of moral judgments. *Normative moral relativism* would be the thesis that it is morally wrong to judge or interfere with the moral practices of societies, groups, cultures, or individuals who have moral values different from one's own. This is a normative thesis because it makes prescriptions for behavior.

[3] Worthen, B. (2006). Intellectual property: China's three realities. *CIO Blogs.* Online at http://blogs.cio.com/intellectual_property_chinas_three_realities. Accessed October 2006.

This work was previously published in International Journal of Technology and Human Interaction, Vol. 3, Issue 3, edited by B. Stahl , pp. 12-24, copyright 200t by IGI Publishing, formerly known as Idea Group Publishing (an imprint of IGI Global).

Chapter XVII
Giving and Taking Offence in a Global Context[1]

John Weckert
Centre for Applied Philosophy and Public Ethics, Charles Sturt University, Australia

ABSTRACT

This chapter examines the concept of offence, both its giving and taking, and argues that such an examination can shed some light on global ethical issues. It examines the nature of offence, what, if anything, is wrong in giving offence, the obligations on the offended, whether or not offence is objective, and offence in a global setting. It argues for the view that choice and context provide some way of distinguishing between offence which is a serious moral issue and that which is not. It is morally worse to offend those who have no choice in the area of the offence, for example race, than in areas where there is choice. Intermediate cases such as religious belief, choice depends largely on education and exposure to alternatives. Context is important in that offending the vulnerable is morally worse than offending those in more powerful, or privileged groups.

INTRODUCTION: WHY BOTHER WITH OFFENCE?

A study of the concept of offence can shed some light on global ethical issues. While offence is frequently not taken very seriously, the contention here is that it should be. A better understanding of why offence is taken and why some instances of giving offence are reprehensible and others are not can assist our understanding of what is necessary in a global ethics. The argument here focuses on the morality of giving offence rather than on what kinds of offence, if any, should be subject to legal restrictions. The recent case of the Danish cartoons illustrates the importance of the notion of offence. Unless offence is taken seriously, that case has no interesting moral dimension. It is simply an instance of someone exercising their legitimate right to freedom of expression and others unjustifiably objecting. The Danish publisher was right to do what he did and the offended Muslims were wrong to object. If, however, offence is taken seriously, then the question of who was right and who was wrong becomes more problematic, and the issue can be seen as a real clash of values. In liberal democratic states, freedom of expression is highly valued, but this is not universal. Perhaps it should be, but when considering ethics in a global context, we are not starting with a clean slate. The realities of the world are where we start. In some parts of the world the general the notion of freedom of expression is not even entertained. It simply is not an issue to be taken into account. Social cohesion and religious beliefs are all important. The society rather than the individual comes first. Once that is realised, the offence that was taken is more comprehensible. From the perspective of the offended, there is a good reason for taking offence; there has been a violation of an important religious value for no apparent reason other than denigration of the Muslim faith. While the situation was undoubtedly more complicated and some took advantage of the cartoons for their own ends, the fact is that it was relatively easy for them to do this, partly because of a lack of understanding of the importance of freedom of speech in most Western countries and the feeling that their religion was not being respected.

It is impossible to limit offence to national or cultural borders given the current state of the electronic media, particularly the Internet. Some action, acceptable in one country or culture, can be extremely offensive in another. As noted above, cartoons have played a prominent role in recent times in causing offence in countries other than those in which they were published, particularly those published in Denmark. Those cartoons depicted the prophet Mohammad in ways that much of the Muslim world considered blasphemous. Earlier a cartoon in Australia depicted a scene in which certain Israeli actions were compared with Nazi actions at Auswitch. This cartoon was severely criticised because of its offensiveness to Jews and was withdrawn. More recently an Indonesian newspaper published a cartoon showing the Australian Prime Minister and Minister for Foreign Affairs as copulating dogs. This was in response to Australia granting temporary visas to a group of illegal immigrants from the Indonesian province of Papua. In retaliation, an Australian newspaper published a cartoon of the Indonesian President and a Papuan as dogs copulating, with the President in the dominant position. Each of these cartoons was condemned in the other country as being offensive. These cases highlight various cultural differences, for example, different views on freedom of speech and expression, and on blasphemy. Where there are incompatible positions on fundamental issues, some way must be sought to solve or avoid conflict. In the Danish case mentioned, the offence caused by the cartoons led to a tragic loss of life as well as to tension between various countries. The offensiveness of the cartoons of the copulating dogs too led to an increase in tensions, in this case between Indonesia and Australia. Given the importance of the concept of offence in the global arena, it warrants examination in that context.

WHAT IS OFFENCE?

Offence is some sort of hurt or pain, displeasure, disgust, mental distress or mental suffering of some variety (see Feinberg, 1985, p. 1). Something is offensive if some people do not like it in a certain way; it hurts their feelings, it disgusts them, or something of that ilk. Strictly speaking, things do not give offence; people do through their actions. An outcrop of rock shaped like some part of the human anatomy is not offensive although a sculpture of the same shape might be. While it is common to talk of pictures, cartoons, and language as offensive, what is really offensive is that someone has acted in some way, by photographing, painting, drawing, talking, writing, or some similar activity. Giving offence involves intention. It need not be the case that the action is intended to offend (although it might be) but the action must be intentional (to emphasis the point, I am ignoring the fact that actions are often defined as intentional). An intentional action can give offence in a way that an unintentional one will not. Public nudity is often considered offensive but if on some occasion, it is a result of someone escaping a burning house, it is not likely to be seen as such. Many things done intentionally cause offence unintentionally. Often we do not know that something that we do will be offensive to some. Much offence too is a result of carelessness. Some people may not bother perhaps too much about the feelings of others. It is not that they want to cause offence, it is rather that they do not care enough to avoid causing offence or perhaps are just not perceptive enough.

Many things are described as offensive, ranging from public nudity and copulating to racist and religious actions and blasphemy, from snubs from acquaintances to insults about one's appearance. These offences are what Tasioulas (2006) calls *norm-governed*. In these cases certain norms have been violated, or at least the offended party believes so. Tasioulas distinguishes these offences from what he calls *primitive* offences. Offensive smells, for example, dihydrogen sulfide (rotten egg gas), are an example. Norm-governed offences are the ones of interest here.

Discussions of giving offence are commonly conducted in the context of freedom of speech and possible restrictions that might be justified by offensive material, or in the context of criminalisation of certain actions (Feinberg, 1973; Tasioulas, 2006). Much everyday offence is of course more personal. I am offended when I alone am not invited to the party, or when someone implies that I am incompetent or poorly dressed. Most of this kind of offensive behaviour is not seen as the proper concern of the law, except perhaps in the workplace where it can be related to harass-

ment or bullying. The most important instances of offence however, at least in the public arena, concern things like racist language, blasphemy, and indecency (although personal offence to a prominent figure can cause widespread public offence).

Taking offence might be said to involve three elements: the hurt, the judgement that the action was wrong, and some action, for example, demanding an apology or recompense. The argument here will be that, contra Barrow (2005), action is not properly part of taking offence but that, contra Tasioulas, some judgement is.

First, Barrow suggests that offence involves a demand of an apology or compensation and on this he builds his case for there being a duty not to take offence, an argument to which we will return later. The position taken here, however, is that any demand for an apology or compensation is a consequence of taking offence but not part of taking offence itself. If I am offended I might or might not demand that anything be done about it. It depends on the severity of the offence, my timidity, and other factors.

Taking offensive, however, does involve a judgement that the offending action is wrong, something that should not be done. Tasioulas (2006, p. 152-153), argues that this, while perhaps commonly the case, is not necessary. His counter-example is of a middle-aged man who has overcome his strict upbringing but still takes offence at a same-sex couple holding hands in public, even though he does not believe it wrong. He simply cannot overcome his feelings. It seems to me that a better way of describing this situation is that he does not take offence at all but merely feels uncomfortable. Having been raised a fundamentalist Lutheran, I feel uncomfortable, sometimes extremely, with certain blasphemous language even though I no longer believe it to be wrong in itself (even though I almost expect a bolt of lightening to strike the blasphemer), but to describe my feelings as offence would be inaccurate. I might judge it wrong, however, in certain contexts because it offends others.

WRONGNESS AND OFFENSIVENESS

Taking offence is clearly associated with our beliefs, in that taking offence at any particular action can only occur in certain contexts where certain beliefs are held. If I say or do something potentially offensive but nobody takes offence, it is not at all obvious that I have given offence. Perhaps it will be objected that what is important is not *giving* offence but *offence*, pure and simple. However, unless there is an *objective* norm-governed offence, something that will be contested, it is not clear that there is anything interesting in offence apart from its giving and taking. When offence is discussed as a reason for criminalising or banning certain behaviour, it is because it is offensive, that is, it gives offence and some people take offence. The behaviour might still be wrong in the absence of giving or taking offence but that is another matter that has nothing to do with offence. Feinberg divides offensive actions into two categories, those that are offensive because they are wrong and those that are wrong because they are offensive. Racist language is offensive because such language is wrong while not being invited to a party is wrong, if wrong at all, simply because it is offensive. I prefer to say that racist language is both wrong *and* offensive. It is wrong because, at least, it is disrespectful to a race and it is offensive when members of that race are subjected to it and take offence. When those racial members are subjected to it, it is doubly wrong; wrong because of the lack of respect and because it gives offensive. If there is nobody around to take offence, it is still wrong but hardly offensive.

The focus of this article is on behaviour that is, in Feinberg's terminology, wrong because it is offensive, that is, *offensive nuisances*. This of course includes, for the purposes here, behaviour that is both wrong in itself and wrong because it is offensive if offence is taken, but the focus here is on the latter.

Is giving offence really wrong? We are talking here, it must be emphasized, of things that are wrong (if they are wrong as all) *because* they are offensive, not things that are wrong in themselves and are offensive on that account alone. Nor are we talking about everything that the offended parties judge to be wrong on the grounds that they are offended. Essentially what we are talking about are those cases of offence where the offended justifiably judge that they have been wronged. One may be inclined to say that there are no such cases; that is, that there is nothing really wrong with giving offence where the only wrong is the offence itself. After all, if people are so sensitive that they become offended at something heard or seen, so much the worse for them. While this contains an element of truth, it is not the whole story. It is probably true that any offence taken at not being invited to a dinner might not matter much, but the mocking of a physical disability or a tragedy, for example, might be extremely hurtful and offensive even for those not overly sensitive. However, most offence discussed in the contest of freedom of expression or criminalization is not of these kinds. Rather it involves blasphemy, sexually explicit language, racial vilification, ridicule of culture, public nudity, or sexual activity, and a host of other things.

In order to understand more about what is wrong with giving offence, if anything is, we will consider why people take offence. Obviously, offence is taken for different reasons by different people and over a wide range of areas. Three areas will be considered. The first of these concerns things which are not necessarily directed at any person or group, such as sexually explicit language and public nudity. Some people are offended by certain language and pictures. Part of the explanation for the offence taken clearly has to do with upbringing and socialization. This, however, is not a complete explanation. Taking offence is more than merely not liking. There are many things that I do not like that do not offend me, for example, certain types of music and art.

If I find something offensive, I take it personally in some way. I am *hurt*. A reasonable explanation of why I am hurt is that I identify closely with beliefs that this sort of behavior or material is wrong, and in a way I feel violated. If you expose me to these things that you know I do not like, then you are not showing me the respect that I deserve as a person. Even if it was not directed at me in particular, I may feel that people like me, those who hold the beliefs that I hold, are not respected enough. In both cases, that is, where it is directed at us in particular and where it is not, we may feel devalued as persons

The second, and related, area is the ridiculing, mocking or even just criticizing of beliefs, commitments, and customs, particularly those based on religion and culture. We tend to identify with a set of beliefs or with a group in a way that makes those beliefs or that group part of our self-image. So when ridicule is directed at those beliefs or that group, we feel that we are being mocked or ridiculed, and again can feel that we are not being respected as persons. Those who are mocking or criticizing portray themselves as being superior to us.

The third and final area is the offence taken at language or conduct which is racist or sexist. What these share is that there is no choice involved in being a member of either of these groups. There is a real sense here in which our identity and self-image is inextricably linked with groups of these types of which we find ourselves members. Here there seems to be a particularly close link between offence and self-respect.

These three examples all show that there is a close connection between the taking of offence and respect, both respect for others and self-respect or esteem. When someone makes a remark or exhibits conduct that we find offensive, we may feel that we are not being respected as persons in the way that we ought to be. Our self-respect may be lessened to some extent. Too much of this conduct may cause us to see ourselves as people of little worth. If something which is an integral part

of me is mocked – say, my height, race, gender, or intelligence – this is evidence that others do not value me as a person to the extent that they ought. They are not showing me the respect that I deserve as a person. If I identify very closely with a political party or with a religion and if that party or religion is mocked, I may feel the same (although it will be argued later that there are relevant differences in these cases). So perhaps we can say that what is wrong with giving offence in general is that it is showing a lack of respect for others and that it may cause them to lose some of their self-respect.

It is not being argued here that showing disrespect to someone will always lead to a loss of self-respect by that person, nor does it imply that all that is wrong with showing a lack of respect is this link with self-respect. However, it is claimed that there is an important link. Not everyone has enough self-confidence to disregard all instances of perceived disrespect.

This account that links offence with respect fits our intuitions in at least two ways. First, it explains why offence connected with race, gender, and physical disability, for example, seems to be much more serious than offence related to football or political allegiances, musical taste or sensitivity to pictures of naked humans or to not being invited to the party. If we make a commitment to something, or admit that we do not like something, we should be prepared, to some extent anyway, to accept the consequences of making that commitment or admission. At any rate, there is an important difference between areas in which we have some choice, like football team allegiance, and those in which we do not, for example, race.

There are, of course, some cases which are anything but clear-cut, for example, religious belief. We will return to that in a later section.

The second way that this account of offence fits in with common feelings is that it also helps to explain why it seems more objectionable to mock or ridicule the disadvantaged than the advantaged. If someone takes offence at some mockery of an advantaged group, that person must first identify him or herself with that group; that is, they must see themselves as privileged in some way. If they can only take offence to the extent that they identify with some favored section of society, their self-respect is unlikely to suffer much. Barrow (2005, pp. 272-273) discusses this kind of case and comes to a conclusion not so different from that espoused here. He argues that he, as an Englishman and clearly in a privileged position in English society, can be offended by certain anti-English remarks, but that he has no grounds for taking any action; he has not been morally wronged.

THE DUTY NOT TO TAKE OFFENCE

Barrow argues that there is a duty not to take offence. He cannot, and does not, mean that there is a duty not to have the hurt feeling. We have little choice about that, at least in the short term. We may over time no longer feel the hurt over certain comments or actions that we once did, but it is not something that we can just turn on and off like a tap. His view is more plausible if taking offence involves judging to be wrong. We might not be able to stop the hurt but we might have some control over whether or not we judge something to be wrong. But again, while over time we change our minds regarding what we judge to be wrong in some cases, it is not something that can be done just on cue. What he really means is that there is an obligation not to demand an apology or compensation or something of that ilk when one takes offence, and this is certainly plausible. In essence, this is a plea for tolerance. I might be offended by some action; that is, I feel the hurt and I judge the action to be wrong, but it does not follow that I have a right to demand anything in return. This is of particular importance in the global context created by the electronic media. Given the

variety in cultures, customs, and religions that now come into regular contact at many different levels of society, there is bound to be much that is said and done that many find offensive. If there is to be any hope of living together more or less peacefully, not only must there be an effort not to give offence but also, and equally important, tolerance of the views and actions of others even when we find them, perhaps, extremely offensive. It has been argued here that the actions to which Barrow objects are not part of taking offence itself, so it is more accurate to say that there is a duty not to demand compensation or retribution when offended. While there is no duty not to take offence, there is a duty not to demand action as a result of the offence taken.

ARE SOME OFFENCES OBJECTIVE?

Tasioulas argues so (2006, pp. 157ff). We are talking here just of norm-governed offences, those that violate some norm. Objective offences are, or are supposed to be, actions that are offensive in themselves regardless of whether anyone takes offence at them. They violate some moral norm and moral norms can be objective and therefore so can offence. Objective offences have properties that constitute a reason for being offended. Tasioulas gives two examples of such offences: racist language and public copulation. The former has more plausibility than the latter. Racist language reveals lack of respect and lack of respect is always wrong. If I am shown lack of respect, then I have a reason for being offended. Public copulation is more problematic. While it *in fact* violates norms in, for example, Australia, it is not at all clear that it necessarily does. A society could presumably function perfectly well if public copulation were the norm. In such a society it would not be showing any lack of respect and nobody would be harmed in anyway, and it would be difficult to make a case that it was objectively morally wrong. If public copulation were the norm and was not showing any lack of respect for those who might witness the event, it is difficult to see how it could have properties that would constitute a reason for taking offence. In countries where it does violate a norm, as in Australia, it can still be considered wrong on the grounds that it is offensive (and not merely because it is against the law), but that implies nothing about it being objectively wrong in any sense.

Is racist language objectively offensive? Suppose that in some homogenous society, racist language is common. No one takes offence because there is nobody of the despised race around and none of the locals care. A good case can be made that the behaviour is wrong regardless of whether anyone takes offence because, if for no other reason, it reinforces the view that one race is inferior to another. But that seems quite different from saying that it is offensive. Things are offensive in a context. Jokes ridiculing particular Australian traits are not offensive if told by an Australian in a room full of Australians, but might be in another context. In any case, not everything that is wrong is offensive, except in a trivial sense in which our moral sensibilities are offended by all wrong actions, but then the offence taken at those actions is not worth discussing. We can get what we want just by considering the wrongness of the actions. It might be argued that the fact that it is happening at all is offensive to people of that race simply because they know that it is occurring even though none is exposed to it. We will return to this issue later.

It could still be argued of course that the mere fact that nobody is in fact offended by racist language does not show that it is not inherently offensive. Consider offensive smells. Certain smells just are offensive to humans. That is just a fact of the way that we are, and presumably is a result of our evolution. There was survival advantage in avoiding things with particular smells. So in this sense some smells are objectively offensive. Why then resist the view that some actions are

also objectively offensive? Offensive smells, as we know, frequently become less offensive once we have been continually exposed to them for some time. By analogy certain actions are offensive in themselves, and the fact that some people do not see them as such is no argument that they are not. Some people and some cultures simply have become desensitised or have not yet developed the sensitivities to recognise them as such. It is well-known that we can develop our sense of smell (and other senses) by practice. We can learn to notice smells that we had not before and learn to make distinctions that previously we had missed. The point of this is not that offensive smells are subtle and require learning to be noticed. Rather it is that the fact that some smell is not noticed or recognised does not show that it is not there in an objective sense. Similarly, actions might be offensive but not recognised as such simply as a result of undeveloped sensitivities.

It is odd though to say that some smell that we no longer find offensive is really offensive. If the smell, in the sense of a physical event, does not cause an offensive olfactory sensation, then surely it is not an offensive smell, and in the same way, if racist language does not cause offence it is not offensive, even if wrong. Something about the smell is objective, its physical properties, but its offensiveness is not objective. The utterance of the racist language is objective, but the offensiveness is not.

It might be objected that the analogy is not a good one because the offensiveness of smells does not rely on beliefs in the way that norm-governed offences do. But the situation is not so simple. The information that we receive through our senses is mediated to some extent by our beliefs and concepts; it is to some extent "theory-laden", so the difference between primitive and norm-governed offences is one of degree rather than one of kind, at least with respect to beliefs. What is different is that in the second case, but not the first, we make a judgement about the moral wrongness of an action, but that is irrelevant here where we are only concerned with the supposed objectivity of some offensiveness.

OFFENCE IN A GLOBAL CONTEXT

We will now focus on offence in a global setting. The previous sections have discussed or raised various aspects of offence that will be used to highlight its importance in discussions of global ethics. In particular we will consider the subjectivity of offences, the role of choice, that is, the difference between offences related to what we choose and those related to what we are, the context in which the offensive actions were performed, and finally indirect offence, that is, offensive actions that those offended only hear about or otherwise know about but do not directly experience.

Subjectivity

It is plausible to argue that some things are just wrong regardless of any cultural beliefs or practices. For example, murder, human sacrifice, female genital mutilation, and slavery are surely wrong even if they are an accepted part of some culture. Bernard Gert (1999) argues that there are morals that all impartial, rational persons would support and lists 10:

- Do not kill
- Do not cause pain
- Do not disable
- Do not deprive of freedom
- Do not deprive of pleasure
- Do not deceive
- Keep your promises
- Do not cheat
- Obey the law
- Do your duty

While these are not absolute and can be overridden, they are objective in the sense that they would be agreed to by impartial, rational persons.

If this is correct, then there is an obvious starting point for a global ethics. If it were the case that some offences were wrong in themselves, that is, objectively, then another rule could be added to Gert's 10, something like "Do not perform any actions that are objectively offensive". If some actions were offensive in an objective sense, then those actions, even if only wrong because offensive, would be wrong irrespective of culture. Suppose, for example, that blasphemy is objectively offensive. Publishing the Danish cartoons then was wrong regardless of the attitudes toward them in Denmark and other Western countries. We have argued however that offence is not objective, so if it is to play any role in a global ethics, that role must lie elsewhere. The offensiveness rule could of course be modified to "Do not perform any actions that are offensive" but this is much too broad and could prohibit almost anything. What is required is some way of distinguishing between different offences that does not rely on some being objective. It will be argued that choice and context give some indication of how to delineate those instances of giving offence that are serious and those that are not.

Choice

The question of choice was raised in an earlier section where it was noted that there is, or seems to be, a difference between mocking one for wearing outlandish clothes and mocking one's race. It could be argued, as it has been by Barrow, that saying something that could be taken as offensive, for example, ridiculing religious beliefs, could be a sign of respect. That person is considered an autonomous human being who is mature enough and secure enough in his or her beliefs not to take offence when those beliefs are criticised or held up to ridicule. There is something in this. Treating people as mature adults is showing more respect than treating them as people who must have their feelings protected. This argument, if it holds at all, only holds in those areas where there is genuine choice. I have no control over my race, so ridiculing that can hardly be a sign of respecting my maturity regarding my beliefs. Ridiculing my outlandish clothes, at the other extreme, does not seem so important. I choose to wear them and could wear others, in a way that I cannot become a member of another race. Culture and religion, often closely interwoven, present an intermediate and more difficult case. Religion and culture are a bit like race in that they help define who we are. I identify with them as I do with my race. On the other hand, I do have some choice in a way that I do not with my race. I can choose to be a Christian but cannot choose to be Caucasian. The situation clearly is not so straightforward. While I can chose to become a Christian or choose to leave the faith if I were one, it is not quite like choosing a new brand of breakfast cereal. The choice will usually be a culmination of belief changes over time. But choose to join or leave religions we do. There is however a difference between those with a moderately good education and those without. An educated person who knows about other religions, about scientific explanations of the world and so on, can make an informed choice in a way that someone lacking those advantages cannot. They have a greater ability to weigh up evidence and to then make their choices based on that process. An illiterate peasant farmer has probably never entertained the possibility that his religious beliefs might be, or even could be, false. Given upbringing and culture, there is little choice but to believe.

What does this have to do with giving offence? We are talking here of actions that are wrong because they are offensive. The suggestion is that there is a relationship between the degree of wrongness and the amount of choice that someone has. Mocking of race is worse than mocking of the wearing of outlandish clothes because (at least partly) one has no choice in the former while one does in the latter. Mocking the religious beliefs of an uneducated peasant, who has no real choice, is worse than mocking the religious beliefs of a

well-educated person who has the ability to weight up the evidence and make a informed choice. In the latter case, the mocking could be a sign of recognising that person's autonomy and affording him or her the opportunity to defend his or her beliefs. In the former case, this is not so. It can only be interpreted as showing disrespect.

This issue of choice clearly has relevance for offence in the global arena, even apart from offence related to race. A large proportion of the world's population is poor and relatively uneducated and without easy access to sources of information, including the Internet, that would increase their range of options regarding lifestyle and belief. If the argument of this article is correct, it is more important to try to avoid actions that would be offensive to these people than to those who are more privileged. Mocking those without choice is not respecting them as they deserve to be respected as persons.

Context

The context in which offensive actions are performed is important in assessing their wrongness. What are essentially the same actions can be very different with regard to their offensiveness. It is instructive to consider Barrow's examples (2005, pp. 267, 272-273). He suggests, though does not say explicitly, that saying offensive things about the English, Pakistanis, and Nazis is more-or-less the same; one is no worse than the others. However, being English or Pakistani is racial, in the sense that the terms are being used here. In this sense, those called Pakistanis, even if born in England, are not considered English, because of their race. On the other hand, being a Nazi is a result of choice. On the argument of the preceding section, offending Pakistanis because that is what they are is worse than offending Nazis. One is born a Pakistani but one is not born a Nazi.

The main point of this section however is highlighted by comparing offending the English and offending the Pakistanis, in England. The kind of offensive actions in mind are ones such as mocking of race, culture, or religion. Is it worse to offend Pakistanis in England than it is to offend the English in England? Barrow, as we saw, suggests not, but there are reasons for thinking otherwise. Consider again the case of the cartoons published in Denmark that seriously offended many Muslims around the world, sparking riots and a considerable number of deaths. The context in which these cartoons were published is clearly relevant to assessing the morality of the action. Many Muslims, if the press is to be believed, feel under threat. The powerful Western nations are perceived as having exploited Muslim nations for decades, and this perception has been given impetus by recent invasions and talk of invasions. Regardless of the rightness or wrongness of the wars in Afghanistan and Iraq, they are clear signs of who has the military and economy power and who has not. In this situation, it is not surprising that the cartoons caused offence. It could be easily seen as just another sign of Western lack of respect for the Muslim religion. In a different context the action might not have been wrong. Suppose that a Muslim newspaper published cartoons ridiculing Christ. In countries where Christians were dominated by Muslims, it may well cause extreme offence if the Christians felt under threat, but in the Christian world at large, it probably would not, at least in the affluent West. The difference in the situations reflects how many Christian and Muslim groups see themselves relative to the other in the current world.

We will return for a moment to the copulating dogs cartoons published in both Indonesia and Australia. If the press is to be believed, there seems to have been more offence in Indonesia over the Australian cartoon that in Australia over the Indonesian one. If this is so, context provides one reason. In recent times, the relationship between Australia and Indonesia has been uneasy at best, particularly from the time that Australia took an active part in East Timor's fight for independence from Indonesia. The granting of visas, albeit temporary ones, to a group of illegal immigrants from the Indonesian province of Papua, where there is also an independence movement, was seen by the Indonesians as a sign that Australia was supporting that movement. It was also seen as evidence that Australia believed the Papuans claims that they were being persecuted by the Indonesian authorities. Additionally, the Australian government had been taking a very hard line against illegal immigrants and the approach to the Papuans appeared to be much more lenient. In this context, the retaliatory cartoon published in Australia could be seen as just another sign of contempt and lack of respect for the Indonesians. In Australia, while some politicians claimed that the Indonesian cartoon was offensive, the reaction has been more muted. In Australia there are no independence movements and nothing that could be interpreted as an attack on its sovereignty by Indonesia. The context is quite different.

Indirect Offence

According to Tasioulas, at least regarding criminalization, the only offences that should be taken into account are direct offences, that is, those that are directly experienced. Seeing a copulating couple in a public park is offensive in a way that merely knowing that it is happening is not. Feinberg's position regarding pornography is similar:

When printed words hide decorously behind covers of books sitting passively on bookstore shelves, their offensiveness is easily avoided. ... There is nothing like the evil smell of rancid garbage oozing right out through the covers of a book. When an "obscene" book sits on the shelf, who is there to be offended? Those who want to read it for the sake of erotic stimulation presumably will not be offended (or else they wouldn't read it), and those who choose not to read it will have no experience by which to be offended. (1973, p. 45)

The example given by Feinberg makes his argument look plausible, and it is commonly used in relation to television programmes containing explicit sex and violence. It you do not like it, do not watch it. However, those who find something offensive commonly do not need to directly experience it to be offended. That it is happening at all is offensive. Wolgast makes this point in relation to pornography:

The felt insult and indignity that women protest is not like a noise or bad odor, for these are group-neutral and may offend anyone, while pornography is felt to single women out as objects of insulting attention. ... With pornography there is a felt hostile discrimination. (1987, p. 112)

A similar point can be made with regard to the Danish cartoon case. Most of those who took offence would not have seen the cartoons, certainly those in regions where the Internet is not widespread. But this lack of direct experience was largely irrelevant. The *fact* that they were published was offensive.

If offence is related to respect for others and to self-respect, as was argued earlier, the issue of reasonable avoidability does not arise. If women or some race or any particular group is singled out for treatment which shows lack of respect and which is of the type to lower self-respect, it is not an issue whether or not someone can easily avoid some instance of that type of offensive action. Some members of the racial group might avoid hearing some racially offensive language, some religious members might avoid seeing offensive cartoons, and some woman might avoid seeing pornography, but these individuals are still being shown less respect than they deserve, simply because they are members of these targeted groups.

It must be noted of course that neither Tasioulas nor Feinberg are claiming that actions or material are only offensive when directly experienced. Their argument is rather that in those cases where it is not, it is not a serious contender for criminalisation. The suggestion here is that even in at least some of those cases, indirect offence needs to be taken seriously. This is particularly so in the global case. Most of those offended by some action will be aware that it has occurred but will not have directly experienced it, but that is largely irrelevant. *That* it occurred is what is important.

CONCLUSION

The purpose of the article was to examine the concept of offence and on the basis of that examination to show its importance in considerations of a global ethic. The argument has been that offence, even actions that are thought wrong merely because they are offensive but not wrong in themselves, should not be overlooked. Careful thought should be given to actions that could be deemed offensive to certain groups, even if we think that those actions are protected by freedom of speech or expression, or by some other right or principle. It was argued that actions that offend because of attributes over which people have no choice are of more concern than those which offend because of attributes over which there is choice, and context is important. Giving offence in some contexts, for example, where the offended already feel vulnerable, is worse than giving offence in contexts where they do not. In murky areas such as religious belief, the amount of choice is related to the options available, and this in turn is related to the level of education and the information readily accessible. This suggests that one way of alleviating some problems of offence is to make a greater effort to make more information readily available to a greater number of people. On the other hand there is a duty not to take action against those who have offended. Tolerance of the views of others is always important and is especially so in a global community where there is no common legal framework and disputes are frequently settled by violence.

ACKNOWLEDGMENT

I would like to thank the participants of a seminar at the Centre for Applied Philosophy and Public Ethics (Charles Sturt University and Australian National University) for many useful comments on a draft of this article. I also wish to acknowledge the informative discussions that I have had over recent years with my colleague Yeslam Al-Saggaf.

REFERENCES

Barrow, R. (2005). On the duty of not taking offence. *Journal of Moral education, 34*(3), 265-275.

Feinberg, J. (1973). *Social philosophy.* Englewood Cliffs, NJ: Prentice Hall.

Feinberg. J. (1985). *The moral limits of the criminal law. Vol. 2: Offense to others.* Oxford: Oxford University Press.

Gert, B. (1999). Common morality and computing. *Ethics and Information Technology, 1,* 57-64.

Tasioulas, J. (2006). Crimes of offence. In A. Simester & A. von Hirsh (Eds.), *Incivilities: Regulating offensive behaviour.* Oxford: Hart.

Wolgast, E. H. (19 8 7). *The grammar of justice.* Ithaca, NY: Cornell University Press.

ENDNOTE

[1] Parts of this article are based on earlier work published in Weckert, J. (2003). Giving offense on the Internet. In S. Rogerson & T. W. Bynum (Eds.), Computer ethics and professional responsibility (pp. 327-339). Basil Blackwell Publishers, and in G. Collste (Ed.), Ethics and information technology (pp. 104-118). New Academic Publishers.

Chapter XVIII
GSM–Based SMS Time Reservation System for Dental Care

Reima Suomi
Turku School of Economics, Finland

Ari Serkkola
University of Technology, Finland

Markku Mikkonen
Social and Health Affairs - City of Lahti, Finland

ABSTRACT

In this chapter we focus on the application of a mobile time reservation system for dental care. The specific application allocates cancelled dentist times to new customers and new customers are searched from a waiting list with Global System for Mobile Communication (GSM) Short Message System (SMS) messages. This chapter shows how standard, widely used technology—when used innovatively—can bring many benefits to many stakeholders with reasonable costs and changes in business processes. We present and analyze the function of an SMS message-based dental service appointment reservation system that has been implemented in Lahti, Finland. The analysis contains a description of the system's function, as well as some assessment of the success from the service provider and customer point of view.

INTRODUCTION

Internet technology is penetrating every aspect of modern life. We speak of e-commerce, e-learning, e-health, e-everything. Health care is one of the industries in current societies where information technology is being adopted very quickly. However, the industry was late in starting. So far, the development of information systems in health care has been several years behind the general development in most other industries (Ragupathi, 1997).

Finland has been one of the pioneers in the development of mobile communication solutions (Aarnio, Enkenberg, Heikkilä & Hirvola, 2002). The environment in Finland is that of GSM (Global System for Mobile Communications). The GSM Association (2006) defines Short Messages Service (SMS), which are a core technology in our chapter, as follows: "Short Message Service; a text message service which enables users to send short messages (160 characters) to other users. A very popular service, particularly amongst young people, with 400 billion SMS messages sent worldwide in 2002". The user interface of an SMS is usually a mobile phone, but other solutions may also exist. SMS is a central application platform in the GSM system.

Several solutions have been tested, even in the health care sector. Mobile messages should improve the organization and delivery of care for the elderly in their homes (Epstar, 2003), and possibilities of getting drug information and prescribing drugs through a mobile interface have been studied (Han, Harkke, Mustonen, Seppänen & Kallio, 2004). In general, it is widely accepted that mobile solutions are increasingly being accepted, even in health care (Hameed, 2002; Porn & Kelly, 2002; Turisco, 2000).

Electronic communication in the health care sector in general has many advantages over traditional face-to-face meetings. Electronic communication is usually characterized as (MacDonald, Case & Mertzger, 2001):

- Informal
- Thoughtful
- Asynchronous
- Self-documenting
- Relationship enhancing
- Inexpensive

When it comes to SMS messages, they are usually very informal in the daily use by private people. The SMS messages in the system to be presented here are highly structured. They are always extremely thoughtful, and allow for asynchronous communication. They are relatively inexpensive and self-documenting. The aspect of relationship enhancing remains most open, especially if compared with face-to-face discussions.

Mobile communication made possible by the GSM and future UMTS technology is just one area of development. Big advances are being made alongside the Internet (Bakker, 2002; Klecun-Dabrowska & Cornford, 2000; Suomi, 2001). The application of mobile devices in health care is by no means new in health care settings, but so far we have not found any research reporting on how to perform interactions with customers via mobile phones in the dentist applications. In this way this study is of pioneering value.

Our research question in this chapter is:

How can SMS technology lower transaction costs in health care appointment scheduling?

The chapter is heavily oriented towards empirical research on the actual appointment reservation system implemented in Lahti. For that part of our research, the research question is:

Is the SMS-based system for dental care appointment reservation in Lahti effective and is it eliminating transaction costs for the parties involved?

Methodologically, our study is one of evaluation of a system. The approach contains both hermeneutical (Boland, 1991; Westrup, 1994) and grounded action research (Avison, Lau, Myers & Nielsen, 1999; Baskerville & Pries-Heje, 1999) elements.

Our chapter unfolds as follows. In the second section we discuss how the transaction cost approach can be used to structure and understand transactions and their associated costs. In the third section we introduce the actual system implemented in Lahti, and provide some results that have been gained from the evaluation of that system. Finally, in section four we draw conclusions.

THE TRANSACTION COST VIEW OF APPOINTMENT SCHEDULING INTERACTIONS

The literature is rich in articles about patient scheduling, mostly from a queue-theoretical point of view (Klassen, 2004; Rohleder & Klassen, 2000). However, other points of view have also emerged, such as catering for customer satisfaction when waiting (Katz, Larson, & R.C., 1991).

Since the classics in the field (Bailey, 1952, 1954), the key problems in patient scheduling have been:

1. Appointment time to the customer as soon as possible (minimizing the lead time to start the service)
2. Elimination of idle time for resources
3. Minimizing waiting time for customers waiting to be served

The literature has paid very little or no attention to the operating costs of the scheduling system.

Fortunately, not all health care transactions are as complicated as the "Real Life" model presents.

Our focus here is on the appointment scheduling activities that happen before the actual patient contacts, and even there in a situation when unplanned free time emerges to the service providers, usually because of customer cancellations of reserved time. The process we are discussing is presented in Figure 1.

We now briefly discuss the transaction costs in this setting. The concept of transaction cost is

Figure 1. The total process of dental service appointment scheduling with the new SMS-based system

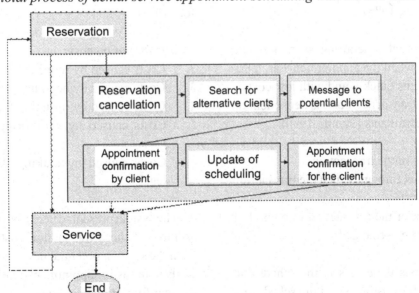

central to the transaction cost theory. Transaction costs are costs arising from business transactions. They are *the costs of running the economic system* (Arrow, 1969). As with all kinds of costs, they inhibit economic activities. In our discussion the "economic system" is that of allocating appointments to dental services.

According to the theory, a firm is established because markets fail to perform the exchange transactions. Within the firm, transactions can be performed more efficiently than in the market setting. The transaction cost theory also sees the archetypes of markets and hierarchies as platforms for performing transactions. In our case the market we speak of is one of exchanging dental services. The system to be presented will lower the transaction costs of the exchange.

Transaction costs can be compared to friction, a term used in the engineering sciences:

A transaction occurs when a good or service is transferred across a technologically separable interface. With a well-working interface, as with a well-working machine, these transfers occur smoothly. In mechanical systems we look for frictions: Do the gears mesh, are the parts lubricated, is there needless slippage or loss of energy? The economic counterpart of friction is transaction cost. (Williamson, 1985)

An appointment scheduling system would work smoothly when the appointments are allocated to the clients quickly and with low costs.

The level of transaction costs is dependent on three main determinants (Suomi, 1990):

1. The actors in the transaction
2. The channel through which the transaction takes place
3. The object of the transaction (the good or service to be exchanged)

In our analysis the actors in the scheduling transaction are the customer and the scheduling

agent working on behalf of the service provider, the dentist. The big change happens in the channel of the transaction. The old channel for the transactions was that of voice telephony and sending letters. The new channel is that of SMS messages, which are partly generated automatically without the activities of the scheduling agent. The object of the transaction, the appointment, is not changing because of the new system.

When introducing new technology, we should perform business process redesign. Business process redesign should be separated from the daily operational development of organizational routines. It should concentrate on value-adding processes, making them shorter and faster, and bring radical benefits (Davenport & Beers, 1995). It is typical to perform business process redesign in connection with introduction of new technology, such as the Internet (Broadbent, Weill & St. Clair, 1999). In our case of appointment scheduling some business process redesign took place in the way in which free time slots are allocated. This was a difficult political decision, as many thought that no customers should get any benefits because of the technical system they are using, and that people agreeing to use the SMS reservation system should have no advantage over other customers.

There are six types of transaction costs (Casson, 1982):

1. Information costs
2. Costs caused by requirement analysis
3. Costs caused by negotiating
4. Costs caused by initiating the transaction
5. Costs caused by monitoring the transaction
6. Costs caused by making the transaction legal

The system presented here has a positive effect on most of these transaction cost components. With the system, potential new customers can be easily found as an appointment time becomes free, so the information costs caused by searching for customers are reduced. The SMS message calling for a reservation and the answer to that message by the potential clients redesign the negotiation and initiation phases and, accordingly, their costs. As all the messages are automatically taken to the system's log data, monitoring of the appointment reservation becomes automatic and loaded with lower transaction costs.

Thomas Malone et al. also introduce facts to support this assessment. Several developments based on the use of information technology contribute to the balance shifting towards the markets, and eventually electronic ones (Malone, Yates & Benjamin, 1987):

1. Electronic Communication Effect
   • More information can be communicated in same amount of time or the same amount of information in less time.
2. Electronic Brokerage Effect
   • The number of alternatives that can be considered increases;
   • The quality of the alternative eventually selected increases;
   • The costs of the entire selection process decrease.
3. Electronic Integration Effect
   • Changing and tighter coupling of processes that create and use information.

In our case all these effects materialize very easily. The reservation appointment agent can contact many potential clients with less effort than in the case of the old manual system. The whole activity is about brokering, and bringing together service providers and customers. The number of alternatives grows from one (telephone call) to four (SMS message to four potential clients). As all the transaction parts are automatically recorded in electronic media, the electronic integration effect is very strong.

THE LAHTI PILOT PROJECT WITH SMS-BASED RESERVATIONS

Introduction to the Environment

The City of Lahti, with 98,500 residents, offers its inhabitants the possibility to obtain oral health care services at public dental clinics. The oral health care is provided by 28 dentists, 11 oral hygiene specialists, and 46 dental assistants and receptionists. Specialist dental care is offered in clinical dental care, correction of irregularities of the teeth, and oral surgery. In 2003 visits by clients numbered around 84,000, and half of these were by clients under the age of 18. In addition, about 60 full- or part-time private dentists work in the city. There are 18 dental clinics for clients in different parts of the city. Of these, three are larger in size and the other 15 operate near to schools for the most part. Also, mobile staff makes visits to the wards of care institutions and hospitals, and to homes.

All Finnish citizens have been entitled to public oral health care since 2002. Citizens could thus seek either municipal oral health care, or private care subsidized by health insurance; customers have selection possibilities. There is evidence that the availability of different communication channels with health care professionals and efficient scheduling solutions are key selection factors when customers select their health care providers (Gopalakrishna & Mummaleni, 1993).

Even the public health care is not free for the adult population in Finland. The customers typically pay some 10-50% of the real cost in direct payments (and the rest through taxes of course). In the private sector, the customers, after state subsidies, pay some 50-95% of the real costs. The established way of operating throughout the whole country is that dentist appointments that are cancelled at least 24 hours before the appointment are free; in later cases an office fee (usually 10-30 euro) is charged. However, this charge is not applied to schoolchildren, who do not face any penalties for not using their dentist times. Anyway, the schoolchildren cater for the most of the unused times.

In 2003 the calculated costs to the City of Lahti arising from unused oral health care appointments amounted to around 170,000 euro (at a calculated cost of 50 euro/unused appointment). The costs arising from appointments left unused by 7- to 17-year-olds were about 132,700 euro. Some of these costs are covered by inviting another patient in place of the one that has cancelled, and by a charge of 27 euro per noncancelled, unused appointment for clients over 16 years of age. Nevertheless, considerable costs are incurred due to unused appointments.

Before the introduction of the new system, clients were put on a waiting list at a dental clinic, which also manually managed queues for all the other dental clinics. Maintaining the waiting list manually was rather laborious. Clients were invited to the clinics either by telephone or by letter. Appointments that were cancelled the same day often remained unfilled, which remained a big problem.

Methods and Data Collection

A pilot project for SMS appointment reservation was launched in May 2003, and its evaluation was begun at the beginning of 2004. The aim of the evaluation was to obtain immediate feedback in order to improve the application and adopt it for regular use. We examined mobile phone appointment reservation from the perspectives of its effect on work procedure development, client satisfaction and waiting list management. As to development of work procedures, the point in question is what effect the new wireless service has on the workload and working methods of reception staff in particular. Customer satisfaction indicates how usable and functional the service is, as well as reflecting the clients' conceptions of the quality of the reception services. Waiting list management relates the study to the "treat-

ment guarantee" (implemented as changes to the Finnish "Kansanterveyslaki" (Kansanterveyslaki [Law on public health], 1972) and "Erikoissairaan-hoitolaki" (Erikoissairaanhoitolaki [Law on special health care], 1998) and in detail specified in a special act (Valtioneuvoston asetus hoitoon pääsyn toteuttamisesta ja alueellisesta yhteistyöstä [Act on delivering health service and regional co-operation], 2004)), which specifies the maximum waiting times for access to treatment. In addition, we looked at the economic effects of the service. Taken together, these perspectives of the study create a foundation for evaluating how necessary, functional, and useful the SMS service is.

As regards the development and study of working methods, we launched a new invitation procedure for appointments in which we invited clients to the clinic by means of text messages. The staff, together with the designers of the SMS solution, took an active part in developing the working procedures for appointments. The task of the study was to compare the developing work method with the original operational model. We interviewed eight receptionists, eight dental assistants, and six dentists. We asked the interviewees what effect SMS appointments had had on procedures for appointment making and reception of clients. We asked the respondents to specify the change factors from the standpoint of the traditional and the SMS appointments. Finally, we cross-checked the validity of the change factors with different people. The staff confirmed the identified changes in reception work.

Our study of customer satisfaction is based on the customer relationship management approach (Campbell, 2003), in which attention is drawn to the handling of the client relationship and to organizational learning. In our examination the client relationship is maintained by the appointment method using GSM technology. We requested feedback from dental clinic clients concerning the usability of SMS appointment reservation and the quality and characteristics of the reservation service. We looked at the different modes of the

SMS appointment reservation service, that is, filling cancelled appointments and informing waiting clients of the precise times for emergency appointments. We investigated each service by means of a semistructured questionnaire involving both structured questions and open responses. The customer satisfaction survey covered a total of 212 customers aged 15 to 80 years. In addition, we supplemented the questionnaire through open interviews with 10 people.

In the evaluation of waiting list management we used the city's statistics on kept appointments and cancelled appointments in oral health care, as well as the log data on the SMS service for 2004-2006. We followed the numbers of kept and cancelled dental clinic appointments through the statistics, and also the degree to which the SMS service was used. The aim of this examination was to identify changes that had taken place in the length and duration of the waiting list.

Operational Model for Mobile-Based Appointment Reservation

Next we discuss making appointment reservations by mobile phone in order to reallocate cancelled dental appointments and invite urgent emergency clients. The studied activities cover mobile-based appointment reservations and waiting list management in the oral health care services in the City of Lahti.

When managing the reservations by mobile phone, the dental clinic informs clients on the waiting list about the cancelled appointment time by SMS. The mobile-based reservation in this application concerns cancelled appointment times that are reallocated within the same day

(2-8 hours). For the mobile phone reservation, appointments manually recorded on paper are transferred to a database, that is, a waiting list file. In the database the clients may be grouped into either one waiting list or several, depending on the grouping principle. The basis for the grouping may be, for example, the treatment unit, the medical priority, the waiting time, or the local area. Clients can be added to or removed from the waiting list according to need. The opportunity for SMS reservation is presented to clients who wish to accept cancelled appointment times by mobile phone.

In the first service a receptionist or dental assistant sends the cancelled, available appointment time to five clients simultaneously by one press of a button. He/she only enters the free appointment time on the computer screen. The first of the five clients to reply to the text message can reserve the free appointment time. The other four clients are informed that the appointment has been filled, and they return to the top of the list to wait for the next time that becomes available. This electronic invitation, which may be either free to the client or subject to a charge, costs the service provider the price of one text message.

The content of the invitation for reallocation of cancelled times corresponds to the pattern found in Figure 2.

It is important that the text message looks like an official message and comes from a trustworthy source—a service number that is unavailable to individuals (service numbers in Finland have just five figures—individuals have phone numbers of operator pre-suffix and seven numbers thereafter). Needless to say, when in wider use, such messages could become a playground for jokers, especially

Figure 2. Example of an SMS message informing of a free appointment

> Cancelled appointment time at Laune Dental Clinic, Laune Street 74, 31 March at 12.00.
> Please reply immediately: write HA and
> send to the number 18444.
> Wait for confirmation!

Figure 3. Example of an SMS message confirming an appointment

> Your emergency dental appointment is approaching.
> Your estimated appointment time is 13:15.
> Welcome to the City Hospital emergency dental clinic!

for schoolchildren. Eliminating this possibility from the very beginning was very important in the message design.

In the second service, an urgent case, the client is given a precise time at an emergency clinic. Previously, clients reported to the emergency reception desk in person. In the pilot project – in addition to personal visits – enrollment by phone was introduced. In phone enrollment the receptionist puts questions to the client and, on the basis of these, assesses the treatment needed and its urgency. In an urgent case the client is sent a text message with the precise time of the approaching treatment, one hour before the desired arrival time. The message goes automatically as soon as a client coming from treatment is checked out. In that way the emergency client can move around freely and need not wait in the waiting room. The client's GSM number is recorded in the database. The SMS invitation system is intended for emergency clinics where waiting times can extend to several hours.

The content of the invitation to urgent emergency clients corresponds to the pattern found in Figure 3.

The whole problem of waiting list management actually concerns those on the non-urgent list. A screening method is being planned for non-urgent cases. The non-urgent waiting list is formed by order of contacts made. The SMS list, taken from this, is visible online at all the dental clinics.

Changes in Appointment Reservation and Working Methods

The mobile phone appointment reservation system has resulted in some changes in reservation procedures. The changes have concerned client service, the reception process, and, to a greater degree, forms of waiting list management. As a new tool in client service, reallocation of cancelled times and invitations to urgent emergency clients makes the everyday routines of the receptionists easier to some extent. However, bigger changes are possible when they all combine and centralize their appointment reservations. Appointment reservation by phone is therefore concentrated on one contact centre, from which the appointment times, including cancelled appointments handled by SMS, and are filled for all the dental clinics. The organizational learning procedures are presented in Table 1, where the traditional operating model is compared with the SMS service.

SMS appointment reservation is based on maintenance of the waiting list database. The waiting list is visible at each of the dental clinics in real time, and each clinic can make additions to and deletions from it. In this way the clients' positions in the waiting list can also be monitored in real time. In the pilot experiment, besides the person's name, his/her GSM phone number has become a key data item for identification. The waiting list database, however, is separate from the electronic client history and the clients' data privacy can be ensured. According to the staff, the waiting list database has made it easier to distribute the appointments and monitor the waiting list.

The job of waiting list manager has been created as another consequence of the waiting list database. Previously, the receptionist at each dental clinic used to issue appointment times from the waiting list of the particular clinic concerned. Nowadays, the waiting list manager centrally arranges appointments and offers cancelled appointment times. With the reorganization, the need for reception staff has decreased from nine receptionists to two.

During the course of the pilot experiment, there has been a move from telephone calls to text messages for making contacts to reallocate cancelled appointments. The receptionists use text messages in the first place, and telephone calls second. According to the interviewees, the ready-structured text messages are easy to send in between other tasks. The SMS appointment reservation increases the receptionists' and dental assistants' mobility in their work to some extent, as well as its ease of management. The reallocating of cancelled appointments also succeeds at the small dental clinics staffed by just a dental assistant and a dentist.

Different selection criteria can be taken into account in SMS appointment reservation. It is possible to select from the waiting list database those clients who, from the dental point of view, have the most urgent need for treatment. Invitations for the reallocation of cancelled appointments can be directed to clients in order of priority.

Earlier, clients were served on the premise that cancellation of appointments was neither a desirable nor a responsible way of using the services. Appointment cancellation has been made easier in the new system. The aim is to minimize unused appointments. Because SMS reservation makes it easier to reallocate cancelled appointments, clients can also be encouraged to actively cancel their dental appointments if they are unavoidably prevented from keeping them.

The SMS urgent emergency client system is suitable for larger emergency clinics where waiting times may extend to several hours. The invitation system operates in an emergency client situation where there are at least 10 people on the waiting list and the duration of the treatment sessions, varying from a few minutes to an hour, cannot be

Table 1. Comparison of traditional and SMS appointment reservation

	Traditional reservation	SMS reservation
Waiting list processing	Manual recording and assignment to a dental clinic	Recording in the database and online monitoring of the waiting list
Waiting list management	Separate waiting list for each dental clinic, so several persons work in reception	Joint waiting list for all the dental clinics, so one waiting list manager arranges all times
Reservation channels	Telephone most used in reallocating cancelled appointments; others are supporting procedures	Text message most used in reallocating cancelled appointments; others are supporting procedures
Contact information	Checking of clients' phone numbers afterwards	Recording of clients' phone numbers immediately on contact
Emergency duty	Continual emergency duty tied to a particular clinic	Continual, mobile emergency duty and management of own work
Size of dental clinic	Reallocating of cancelled appointments difficult when working in pairs	Reallocating of cancelled appointments possible when working in pairs
Selection from waiting list	Selection difficult from the same waiting list and using the same criteria, at many dental clinics	Selection possible from the same waiting list and using the same criteria, at many dental clinics
Cancellation	Cancellation previously haphazard, by phone or on the spot	Cancellation now active, via many channels (text message, phone, answering service)
Clients' arrival at the clinic	Clients wait in the waiting room at the clinic	Clients mostly wait somewhere other than the clinic, so the waiting room is more peaceful

predicted in advance. If the waiting list is shorter, the person working in reception can estimate the approximate treatment time. Furthermore, if the treatment time is constant, the person in reception is similarly able to inform a client of the predicted time.

The urgent emergency client system has made clinic waiting rooms more enjoyable and peaceful. Previously, the clients concerned had to wait their turn in the waiting room, sometimes even for hours. Nowadays, they can move around freely and, having received an invitation, they have an hour in which to arrive at the emergency clinic. For the staff, this has eased clientele management at the clinic.

Client Feedback on SMS-Based Appointment Reservation

Clients of the dental clinics were asked for feedback on the use of the SMS appointment reservation and urgent emergencies. This was collected through a form they could fill in when waiting for their dentist time.

In the new enrollment procedure a client can communicate the need for treatment both on the phone and on the spot at the clinic. In fact, we asked clients to express their views as to whether they would rather report directly to the emergency clinic or enroll by phone. According to the results, clients do consider phone enrollment a desirable way to report for emergency dental care. However, the responses can be divided into two groups: those who have used the SMS invitation service and those who have not. As a general rule, those who have used the SMS invitation system think phone enrollment for dental treatment is more flexible than reporting directly to the emergency clinic (80% agree, 20% disagree, 0% cannot say). Among the non-users, there are a lot that enroll by phone and also a considerable proportion that would rather report in person (69% agree, 28% disagree, 3% cannot say).

One objective of the urgent emergency client system is to free clients from having to wait in the clinic waiting room. The time within which the SMS invitation is sent can vary from 1-1.5 hours and depends on local distances and traffic conditions. According to the results, 93% of the clients mostly waited for a treatment time somewhere other than the dental clinic, and only 7% stayed to wait all the time in the waiting room. Of the clients who waited somewhere other than the clinic, 48% waited at home, 21% in the city, 16% at work, and 7% elsewhere. The results show how the mobile phone invitation gives clients the opportunity to wait for their treatment time in a place of their choosing.

SMS appointment reservation was found to be easy to use, and clients of all ages succeeded in making an appointment with no trouble. One of the respondents expressed it as follows: "The reservation succeeded easily." The replies highlighted the fact that SMS appointment reservation was trouble-free, the system functioned rapidly, and its use was easy; 89% of the respondents considered the SMS reservation system easy to use.

All age groups were of the opinion that the quality of the client service was improved by SMS reservation. Users were in agreement that the utilization of SMS made the service more efficient (89%). Those clients using the SMS service experienced that it speeded up access to treatment. One interviewee replied: "I received the message in the morning, and at midday I got in." The SMS reservation alone, however, does not have a substantial effect on shortening the waiting lists.

On the whole, the text message invitations—as a component of multichannel communication—are a necessary part of client service in present-day society. Clients who have used the service are unanimous on the subject (100% agree, 0% disagree). Non-users similarly consider the service necessary (73%), but among them are people who consider it unnecessary (14%) and those who expressed no view on the matter (13%).

According to the results, there are problems connected with SMS appointment reservation if it is only implemented as a text message service. The short messages do not give all clients sufficient information on how the appointment is to be reallocated in practice. During the pilot experiment it was possible for two or three clients to come to the clinic at the same time. They were in too much of a hurry to wait for confirmation of the appointment. The short messages do not tell the client enough about the operating principle of the reservation system as a whole, neither can they give the client sufficient guidance on how to proceed. For this reason, clients also need written instructions concerning the procedure for SMS appointment reservations. It is necessary for the SMS service to be supported by information provided at the dental clinics, in the local papers and on the Internet.

Results of SMS-Based Appointment Reservation

The efficiency of the SMS service depends on the number of clients on the waiting list, how many cancelled appointments there are, and the number of unused appointment times due to drop-out.

The SMS service will produce calculated savings for the City Corporation when at least 50 cancelled appointments are reallocated through the service per month. This result is based on a calculation whereby the costs of cancelled appointment times (at 50 euro) are compared with the costs of maintaining the service and using the services of the teleoperator.

It is shown that the system currently saves the work of two dentist—dental-assistant pairs. This easily amounts to around 200,000 euro per year.

For the service provider, SMS reservation saves about 15-20 minutes of receptionists' working time per appointment reallocated. For the customer, the service itself is very easy and fast, and considerably shortens the often painful and irritating waiting time for dental services.

SMS reservation has enabled almost all appointments cancelled by adult clients to be reallocated within the same day, at 2-8 hours' notice. On the other hand, SMS reservation cannot do anything about unused appointment times where the client does not inform the staff of cancellation. Indeed, in order to improve cost efficiency in oral health care services particular attention should be given to unused appointment times and to ensuring that clients feel some responsibility for appointment times allocated by the public dental service.

A search of the databases of the dental clinic management of Lahti showed a significant difference in the proportion of dental appointments that were cancelled and those that were left unused, by adults (aged 18-80 years) and by school-age children and young people (aged 7-17 years). In the case of cancelled appointments, those for children and young people constituted 48% of the total. As to unused appointments, however, 78% of the total was for the younger age group. The results clearly showed that young people left appointments unused much more often than adults did.

When taking a transaction cost analysis view of the system, the major benefits of the system realize themselves in the category of "initiating the transaction" in the list by Casson. The system delivers no services to the last two phases of the list of post-transaction character. The phases of information cost, requirement analysis, and negotiating are in a marginal role. When customers get to the public health care, they know they get the standard service at the lowest possible price, and that there is little room for negotiation. The care requirements are usually of a very standard nature, but, on the other hand, the customer can be sure that if something more special is needed, the dentist will give the best service possible; only in some special, pricey services (say more of a cosmetic nature) are the customers forced to turn to private services. In short, using the public dentist health care service has low transaction costs, the main costs just realizing in the scheduling. This system focuses on lowering transaction costs in this category.

The electronic communication effect by Malone et al. is very visible in our service. A lot more communication, leading to more efficiency, can be performed through automation. Efficiency is gained in two ways. First, the receptionist communication is made more efficient, saving his/her working time. The second, bigger efficiency benefit comes when the dentist working time can be used more efficiently. As we speak of the standard service with clearly the lowest prices, electronic brokerage effect is in a marginal role in this service. In the same way, the electronic integration effect is marginal in a private customer application.

Redesign of Waiting Lists Because of the New System

Appointment reservation for dental clinics in Lahti, and in other Finnish municipalities, is governed by the national recommendations for access to treatment (Finnish Ministry of Social Welfare and Health, 2003). Assessment of access to treatment is based on the need for it and how urgent it is, according to the following categories: those in urgent need of oral health care, those awaiting treatment assessment and measures within three months, and those coming for basic examination and care of the mouth within six months.

The recommendations have resulted in a four-phase waiting list procedure:

1. In the City of Lahti, urgent treatment is carried out in accordance with the recommendations. All urgent cases gain access to treatment the same day. The number of urgent treatment sessions in 2003 was 7,100, and in 2005 it had risen to 8,900.

2. The waiting list proper begins when a client reserves a non-urgent appointment time. At the end of 2003 there were 4,690 clients on the non-urgent waiting list in Lahti; at the end of 2005 there were 2,400. In this case, according to the recommendations, a treatment assessment ought to be made within three months.

3. The third list comprises those clients who visit a dentist or a dental assistant for a check-up and for whom the need for treatment or further treatment is confirmed. In Lahti, some of the assessments of treatment need are made by an oral hygiene specialist or by dental assistants. In 2005 there were a total of 79,900 dental clinic sessions. Of these, 54,700 were visits to a dentist, 18,500 to an oral hygiene specialist, and 6,600 to a dental assistant. The treatment sessions provided by oral hygiene specialists and dental assistants have substantially reduced the number of clients on the waiting list.

4. The fourth phase of waiting list management concerns those clients who have to wait for their treatment on dental grounds and/or whose treatment has been phased into several visits. According to the recommendations, the treatment ought to be started within six months at the latest. In Lahti, the longest waiting time was 16 months in 2003. By the end of 2005 the waiting time had shortened to seven months, and by mid-2006 to less than six months.

CONCLUSION

The providers of health care services are beginning to take advantage of the opportunities provided by modern communication technologies. The most promising technologies are those of the Internet and mobile computing, within which SMS messages provide an interesting niche. The literature documents that in general the acceptance of these new means of communication is good.

Scheduling for dental appointments is a typical transaction and can be analyzed in transaction cost economizing terms. As we turn communication into SMS messages, we change the means of communication. This new media brings many savings in transaction costs as such and partly through the business process redesign it makes possible.

Our empirical part shows that most of the positive effects to be expected from electronic communication really materialize in practice. This is also confirmed by the positive feedback from users and customers.

Issues related to our research questions have been tackled all through the chapter, but here we briefly return to them and summarize our findings in light of the research questions.

How can SMS technology lower transaction costs in health care appointment scheduling?

SMS technology lowered transaction costs in our case, especially those transaction costs related to information search, negotiation, and initiating the transaction. The electronic platform also provides an excellent basis for monitoring the appointment scheduling transaction.

Is the SMS-based system for dental care appointment reservation in Lahti effective and is it eliminating transaction costs for the parties involved?

The SMS-based reservation system has enabled almost all appointments cancelled by adult clients to be reallocated within the same day, at 2-8 hours' notice. The replies highlighted the fact that SMS appointment reservation was trouble-free, the system functioned rapidly, and its use was easy; 89% of the respondents considered that SMS reservation was easy to use. All age groups were of the opinion that the quality of service was improved by SMS reservation. For the staff members and the organization, the benefits in saved working time are even bigger: now a cancelled time can usually be filled with

just a few keystrokes, whereas before, each arrangement took at least 15 minutes with phone calls and manual data input.

In our case the SMS system has also brought many benefits. Its potential is still far from being exhausted. Further work on implementing the system more effectively in this environment is needed, as well as efforts to take similar systems into use in different application areas. Actually, that process is already happening in Lahti In November 2004 the system presented here received a national prize for best practices in the information society, in the area of health care applications, presented by the Finnish Prime Minister Matti Vanhanen.

The big issue for the whole system, and even for the whole of the Finnish health care system, is whether systems like this can be taken into use in different health care services. Based on the system platform, new applications are already in the development pipeline, some already in test use. It remains a task both for the practice as well as for academic research to show whether or not the concept can be adapted to new areas.

Until now, our research in the system has been in a secondary role in the work around the system. The main issue has been getting the system up and running, and, just on some critical points, some background viewpoints and recommendations from academic discussion and theory have been collected and used in the project. The system deserves a thorough study, in which, for example, more insight should be gained from the financial and customer service viewpoints. In addition, how the system has been developed under tight political decision maker control should be a source of much insight.

REFERENCES

Aarnio, A., Enkenberg, A., Heikkilä, J., & Hirvola, S. (2002). *Adoption and use of mobile services: Empirical evidence from a Finnish survey.* Paper presented at the 35th Hawaii International Conference on System Sciences, Hawaii.

Anton, J. (2000). The past, present and future of customer access centers. *International Journal of Service Industry Management, 11*(2), 120-130.

Arrow, K. (1969). *The organization of economic activity: Issues pertinent to the choice of market versus nonmarket allocation. On the analysis and evaluation of public expenditure.* Washington, DC.

Avison, D., Lau, F., Myers, M., & Nielsen, P. A. (1999). Action research. *Communication of the ACM, 42*(1), 94-97.

Bailey, N. T. (1952). A study of queues and appointment systems in hospital outpatient departments, with special reference to waiting times. *Journal of the Royal Statistical Society, 14*(2), 185-199.

Bailey, N. T. (1954). Queuing for medical care. *Applied Statistics, 3,* 137-145.

Bakker, A. R. (2002). Health care and ICT: Partnership is a must. *International Journal of Medical Informatics, 66*(2), 51-57.

Baskerville, R., & Pries-Heje, J. (1999). Grounded action research: A method for understanding IT in practice. *Accounting, Management and Information Technologies, 9*(1).

Boland, R. J. (1991). Information systems use as a hermeneutic process. In H. E. Nissen, H. K. Klein & R. A. Hirschheim (Eds.), *Information systems research: Contemporary approaches and emergent traditions* (pp. 439-464). Amsterdam: North-Holland.

Broadbent, M., Weill, P., & St. Clair, D. (1999). The implications of information technology infrastructure for business process redesign. *MIS Quarterly, 23*(2), 159-182.

Campbell, A. (2003). Creating customer knowledge: Managing customer relationship management programs strategically. *Industrial Marketing Management, 32*(5), 375–383.

Casson, M. (1982). *The entrepreneur. An economic theory.* Oxford.

Davenport, T. H., & Beers, M. C. (1995). Managing information about processes. *Journal of Management Information Systems, 12*(1), 57-81.

Epstar. (2003). *Mobiilitoiminto kotihoidon ja apteekin palveluissa* [Mobile functions in home care and pharmacy services]. Helsinki: Epstar Oy.

Erikoissairaanhoitolaki [Law on special health care]. (1998).

Finnish Ministry of Social Welfare and Health. (2003). *Kansallinen projekti terveydenhuollon tulevaisuuden turvaamiseksi. Hoidon saatavuus ja jonojen hallinta* [A national project to guarantee the future of health care. Availability of care and management of queues] (Working Group Memo 2003:33). Ministry of Social Welfare and Health.

Gopalakrishna, P., & Mummaleni, V. (1993). Influencing satisfaction for dental services. *Journal of Health Care Marketing, 13*(1), 16-22.

GSM Association. (2006). GSM World: SMS definition. Retrieved January 24, 2007, from http://www.gsmworld.com/technology/glossary.shtml

Hameed, K. (2002). The application of mobile computing and technology of health care services. *Telematics and Informatics, 20*(2), 99-106.

Han, S., Harkke, V., Mustonen, P., Seppänen, M., & Kallio, M. (2004). *Physicians' perceptions and intentions regarding a mobile medical information system: Some basic findings.* Paper presented at the 15th IRMA International Conference.

Kansanterveyslaki [Law on public health]. (1972).

Katz, K. L., Larson, B. M., & R.C., L. (1991). Prescription for the waiting-in-line blues: Entertain, enlighten, engage. *Sloan Management Review, 32*(2), 44-53.

Klassen, K. J. (2004). Outpatient appointments scheduling in a dynamic, multi-user environment. *International Journal of Service Industry Management, 15*(2), 167-186.

Klecun-Dabrowska, E., & Cornford, T. (2000). Telehealth acquires meanings: Information and communication technologies within health policy. *Information Systems Journal, 10*(1), 41-63.

Lagendijk, P. J. B., Schuring, R. W., & Spil, T. A. M. (2001). Telecommunications as a medicine for general practitioners. In R. Stegwee & T. A. M. Spil (Eds.), *Strategies for healthcare information systems* (pp. 114-125). Hershey, PA: Idea Group Publishing.

MacDonald, K., Case, J., & Mertzger, J. (2001). *E-encounters.* Oakland, CA: California Healthcare Foundation.

Malone, T. W., Yates, J., & Benjamin, R. I. (1987). Electronic markets and electronic hierarchies: Effects of information technology on market structure and corporate strategies. *Communications of the ACM, 30*(6), 484-497.

Porn, L. M., & Kelly, P. (2002). Mobile computing acceptance grows as applications evolve. *Healthcare Financial Management, 56*(1), 66-70.

Ragupathi, W. (1997). Health care information systems. *Communications of the ACM, 40*(8), 81-82.

Rohleder, T. R., & Klassen, K. J. (2000). Using client-variance information to improve dynamic appointment scheduling performance. *Omega, 28*(3), 293-305.

Suomi, R. (1990). *Assessing the feasibility of an inter-organizational information system on the basis of the transaction cost approach.* Doctoral thesis, Turku School of Economics and Business Administration, Department of Management.

Suomi, R. (2001). Streamlining operations in health care with ICT. In T. A. Spil & R. A. Stegwee (Eds.), *Strategies for healthcare information systems* (pp. 31-44). Hershey, PA: Idea Group Publishing.

Turisco, F. (2000). Mobile computing is next technology frontier for healthcare providers. *Healthcare Financial Management, 54*(11), 78-81.

Valtioneuvoston asetus hoitoon pääsyn toteuttamisesta ja alueellisesta yhteistyöstä [Act on delivering health service and regional co-operation]. (2004).

Westrup, C. (1994). Practical understanding: Hermeneutics and teaching the management of information systems development using a case study. *Accounting, Management and Information Technologies, 4*(1).

Williamson, O. E. (1985). *The economic institutions of capitalism. Firms, markets, relational constructing.* New York: The Free Press.

This work was previously published in International Journal of Technology and Human Interaction, Vol. 3, Issue 3, edited by B. Stahl, pp. 34-68, copyright 2007 by IGI Publishing, formerly known as Idea Group Publishing (an imprint of IGI Global).

Chapter XIX
An Ethnographic Study of IS Investment Appraisal

Debra Howcroft
University of Manchester, UK

Robert McDonald
University of Salford, UK

ABSTRACT

Both academics and practitioners have invested considerably in the information systems evaluation arena, yet rewards remain elusive. The aim of this chapter is to provide rich insights into some particular political and social aspects of evaluation processes. An ethnographic study of a large international financial institution is used to compare the experience of observed practice with the rhetoric of company policy, and also to contrast these observations with the process of IS evaluation as portrayed within the literature. Our study shows that despite increasing acknowledgement within the IS evaluation literature of the limitations and flaws of the positivist approach, typified by quantitative, 'objective' assessments, this shift in focus towards understanding social and organisational issues has had little impact on organisational practice. In addition, our observations within the research site reveal that the veneer of rationality offered by formalised evaluation processes merely obscures issues of power and politics that are enmeshed within these processes.

INTRODUCTION

A considerable amount of research has already been conducted in the information systems (IS) evaluation arena yet rewards remain elusive. This has been variously explained and in this chapter we aim to contribute to the evaluation literature by our examination of some of the particular political and social aspects of evaluation processes in organisations. The intention of the research is to study at close quarters the process of IS investment appraisal and ex ante evaluation as undertaken by a large international financial institution, and to assess this within the context of the established research tradition in the area. The focus of the study is on evaluations of IS project proposals; assessments which occur pre-implementation. Our objective is to compare the experience of observed practice in the studied organisation with the rhetoric of company policy, and also to contrast these observations with the process of IS evaluation as portrayed within the literature.

The structure of this chapter is as follows. We begin by providing an overview of the IS evaluation literature by highlighting the difficulties entailed. The next section discusses the ethnographic research methodology before proceeding to the analysis and findings of the study. Our intention is to highlight that despite increasing acknowledgement within the IS evaluation literature of the limitations and flaws of the positivist approach (typified by over-reliance on quantitative techniques and tools), this has had little impact on organisational practice. In addition, our observations of organisational practice reveal that the assumed rationality of formalised evaluation processes merely obscures issues of power and politics that are enmeshed within these processes. Finally, we conclude with a summary of the points made in the research study and a review of the argument presented.

The Difficulties of IS Evaluation

In considering the evaluation question (and by implication the issue of 'value' for money of information systems), the first observation to be made is the amount of attention that the subject has demanded, both in terms of the academic literature and the level of practitioner interest (Galliers, Merali & Spearing, 1994; Niederman, Branchaeu & Wetherbe, 1991). Yet in spite of this abundance of academic study and an increase in the organisational practice of evaluation, it appears we are nowhere nearer to finding a solution to the problems surrounding it (Ballantine, Galliers &

Stray, 1999) and there is little indication that the 'hard academic, foundational questions are being widely addressed, let alone answered' (Farbey, Land & Targget, 1998, p. 156).

With an increased level of investment in IS, organisations are becoming increasingly concerned to find appropriate mechanisms to measure performance and decision-makers are being pressured to better justify their IS investments. Whilst there has always been a degree of scepticism over the 'real' benefits of IS initiatives (Earl, 1996), there is now a widespread and growing concern that IS investment does not deliver value. Yet, evaluation is seen as important to business operations, being variously described as an indispensable tool for managers, a vital organisational function, and an essential part of the management process (Hirschheim & Smithson, 1988; Love, 1991; Walsham, 1993). It is closely associated with decision-making (Farbey, Land & Targett, 1995) and with management desire to improve organisational economic productivity (Picciotto, 1999). So, if careful management is seen as necessary to achieve IS benefits realisation (Earl, 1996), the obvious question that arises is why so many investments appear to evolve without undergoing any formal assessment (Wilson, 1991). This absence of formal evaluation practices does not necessarily indicate a lack of endeavour within the academic or practitioner community to devise appropriate methods: 'Many a scholar, consultant and practitioner has tried to devise a reliable approach to measuring the business value of IT at the level of the firm, none has succeeded' (Keen, 1991). IS evaluation, then, appears to be characterised by a level of complexity that renders it very difficult both conceptually and practically (Hirschheim & Smithson, 1988; Willcocks & Lester, 1999; Zuboff, 1988).

Reflecting on the growing number of roles that information systems play within organisations, assessment of the costs and benefits depends not only on the hard technical data but also the human, social, political, and cultural aspects.

The technical specialists implementing the information systems are relatively well equipped to estimate the hard costs of implementation,[1] rather the main problem appears to be the indirect, hidden, and soft costs (Hinton & Kaye, 1994) of organisational effort. The difficulties associated with this increase as information systems embrace a more prominent position within organisations and management becomes keen to demonstrate the worth of such investments.

Given this context, much attention has been paid to methodological developments in evaluation. Indeed estimates suggest that over 60 methods have been developed within the last 30 years (Renkema & Berghout, 1997). Many of these were initially based on functional and economic approaches (Hirschheim & Smithson, 1988; Symons, 1993), but the changing role and nature of IS has rendered these techniques inappropriate given the elements of intangibility and uncertainty (Remenyi, Sherwood-Smith & White, 1996). Various taxonomies have been proposed for classification of evaluation methodologies (e.g., Irani, Ezingeard & Grieve, 1997), with suggestions that the type of information systems might influence the choice of evaluation method. Of these different theoretical and methodological approaches to IS evaluation aside from a couple of notable exceptions (vis: Smithson & Hirschheim, 1998; Walsham, 1999), the social and political issues that are inherent to this process have been consistently neglected. We concur with Smithson and Hirschheim (1998) that the concentration on the means of evaluation (better tools) has detracted attention from to its end (what to measure and why).

The attitude to evaluation within the IS literature itself mirrors the evolution of the IS field and various paradigmatic developments (Orlikowski & Baroudi, 1991). Accordingly the early reliance on functional and economic approaches, with their underlying rationalist paradigm, has more recently been discredited, with critics identifying a number of flaws (e.g., Symons, 1993; Willcocks & Lester, 1999). Researchers have increasingly contrasted

the limitations of evaluation approaches imposed by the positivist tradition with the potential richness achievable using evaluation practices based upon an interpretive paradigm (e.g., Walsham, 1993). The close interdependence of evaluation process and content demands a much more profound consideration of the organisational context for IS evaluation (Serafeimidis & Smithson, 2000) and a consideration of how the evaluation approach complements organisational culture (Pouloudi & Serafeimidis, 1999). However, this human and organisational focus is largely ignored by traditional methods (Serafeimidis & Smithson, 2000).

Although the tradition of IS evaluation dictates a positivist approach 'where the decision maker allows the methodology to make the decision' (Remenyi, 1999), decisions are themselves based not only on so-called objective data but are influenced by cultural, political, personal, and other factors (Irani, 2002; Jones & Hughes, 2001; Serafeimidis & Smithson, 2003). How these influences are manifested and their effect on the decision is usually the most difficult part of the evaluation process to understand. After the data have been assessed, a judgement still has to be made, and, in the absence of complete knowledge of all the alternatives and the consequences, this is an essentially political activity. Despite this observation, which reflects the nature of the intervention as necessarily a subjective process, recent research confirms previous observations (Ballantine, Galliers & Stray, 1994) that practitioners show little sign of moving away from quantitative, financially-based data as a basis for IS investment appraisal (Ballantine & Stray, 1998; Lycett & Giaglis, 2000). Financial reviews of costs and benefits still represent the most common aspect of evaluation procedures and financial techniques such as NPV (Net Present Value) and IRR (Internal Rate of Return) predominate (Farbey et al., 1995). Despite the growth in the legitimacy of the interpretive paradigm in IS evaluation, little has changed in the hearts and minds of the decisionmakers, who continue to rely on hard financial calculations (Farbey et al., 1995).

The tendency to pursue IS evaluation as an overly rationalistic approach is understandable given that historically, the process of IS development is characterised by rationality whereby actions are justified on rational grounds and the appropriate organisational rituals are adhered to (Boland & Pondy, 1983). Such a perspective is epitomised by the assumption that information systems are designed to contribute to specific ends, ends that can be articulated, are shared, and are objective. Once built and installed, the system, itself an 'icon of rationality' (Franz & Robey, 1984), will improve the efficiency or effectiveness of decision-making processes and thus represent a sound investment. The tools and methodologies associated with the IS evaluation process also possess an aura of rationality, often based on mathematical and logical processing techniques as opposed to reliance on human intuition, judgement, and politics. This rational myth assumes a 'foreground' position, enabling organisational actors to behave in accordance with certain cultural expectations. Yet despite the predominance of the rational myth, the 'background myth' of political behaviour is of equal importance (Boland & Pondy, 1983). In fact, for some 20 years the political elements of IS development within organisations have been commented on, for example:

Political interests are of basic importance to the actors in the organization. Political actions are not isolated episodes to be interpreted within the context of rational problem-solving efforts. It is the other way round. The rational elements are tools used by participants to gain new ground or to protect ground already won. They also serve as 'facades' to mask political motives and legitimise self-interest. (Franz & Robey, 1984, p. 1209)

The focus on the rational aspects of evaluation fails to recognise the possibility that the outcome of such processes can be decided ahead and devised to support other managerial decision-making – a

phenomena known as *'de facto* decision-making' (Vroom & Yetton, 1973). One conclusion in this respect is that evaluation is a highly politicised process that is employed to justify investment and decisions already made – no matter what rhetorical disclaimers such as objectivity, rationality, or quantitative measurement are proffered. The implication for IS researchers and practitioners is that, when employed to carry out evaluations, we are engaged in a political game that is skewed from the outset, often in favour of the sponsors. In this chapter we aim to shed some light on this 'thorny problem' by focusing on the dissonance between espoused rationality and the lived experience of organisational practices, which are more typically characterised by power, politics, and conflict.

In order to provide some 'theoretical scaffolding' (Walsham, 2001) and to help make sense of our empirical study, we will draw on the work of Hardy (1985), who provides a model for understanding the different ways in which power is used. Her work integrates Lukes' (1974) three-dimensional view of power into a model which addresses how power is exercised to defeat opponents, pre-empt conflict, and prevent resistance. Many writers concern themselves with overt power, described as 'the ability to secure preferred outcomes in the face of competition and conflict among declared opponents' (p. 388). Hardy's work is of interest since she also considers *unobtrusive power*, which is centred on attempts to create legitimacy and justification for certain arrangements, so that the outcomes are never questioned.

Hardy draws upon Pfeffer's (1981) work to argue that symbolic power (language, symbols, and rituals) can be used to legitimise desired outcomes in advance in such a way that the use of overt power (such as the wielding of authority) may be unnecessary since the outcome is regarded as legitimate, acceptable, or inevitable. She outlines a number of mechanisms and sources of unobtrusive power and considers how these mechanisms are operationalised. These symbolic aspects of power include: the use of *language* to mobilise support or quieten opposition; the use of *myths* or fictional narratives to stress the importance of tradition and thereby legitimise the status quo or emphasise change and modernisation; and finally, rituals, ceremonies, and settings, which can be used to convey certain messages and meanings. These issues will be discussed in the empirical setting; this follows the details of the research approach that was employed for the fieldwork, which follows next.

RESEARCH APPROACH

The purpose of this research project is to explore the underlying political and social aspects of evaluation processes and procedures despite the emphasis on the rational, objectified measurable aspects of assessment. The research being reported here is based on an interpretivist perspective which views reality as a social construction (Walsham, 1993) and makes sense of this by focusing primarily on human interpretations and meanings (Walsham, 1995a) with each interpretation having no absolute or universal status. Given the nature of the subject under consideration and the need to understand the evaluation processes *in situ*, ethnography offers an appropriate research approach. Ethnographic research provides valuable techniques for studying the social, political, and organisational contexts of IS phenomena (Myers, 1999) whilst also attempting to 'bridge the gap' between the different concerns of academics and practitioners (Harvey & Myers, 1995). Given that one of our objectives is to consider how the shift in focus in the IS evaluation literature has impacted the conduct of evaluations within institutional contexts, ethnography enables the generation of knowledge that is appropriate to both academics and practitioners (Harvey & Myers, 1995).

One of the most valuable aspects of this research technique is its depth since the ethnographer 'lives' the situation under research and

experiences this for a considerable period of time. This provides insights into what people are *doing* and not simply what they are saying (as reported, say, in interview data). Given the longevity of an ethnographic study, the researcher can build up a richer understanding of the actors, the attitudes, culture, and artefacts of an organisation, and the broader context within which they have significance. One problem researchers are often faced with in interview situations is the 'Hawthorne effect' whereby participants respond in 'sanitised' ways in which they think the researcher wants them to respond. By contrast, intensive ethnographic observation at close quarters over a considerable period of time enables other elements to come to light, such as hidden agendas, power centres, contradictions, and behaviour that might be perceived as against the 'orthodoxy.'

However, despite the obvious strengths of an ethnographic approach, it is not without its practical difficulties, which are often perceived in terms of time demands and access to in-depth field observation (Fetterman, 1998; Yin, 1989). This issue was addressed as one of the authors was based within the organisation at the start of the study, thus allowing him to 'go native' whilst providing access to the research data over a significant time period. The research was planned to coincide with a period of paid employment within the firm and informants were made aware of the researcher's intent and the research project. The author held a pivotal position with the IS evaluation process, enabling him to observe and participate in the various stages of the process.

The role of the author as both researcher and active participant can be problematic in itself. In particular the researcher was concerned with how he might influence the practicalities of the process. Accordingly, this presented a unique contextual example of the reflexive concern that is significant to any ethnographic study. The responsibility of the ethnographer, however, did not extend beyond facilitating the workings of the IS evaluation process. He was not an *active* stakeholder with a vested interest in the outcome of any particular investment proposal, but a facilitator of the activity required to reach an investment appraisal decision.

The research itself lasted for a period of six months and was carried out largely in synchrony with the appraisal and evaluation cycles, which took place on a monthly basis. Initially a period of organisational 'induction' was undertaken, which assisted the ethnographer's understanding of the organisational history and the context of the IS evaluation process. The induction included largely unstructured interviewing of a wide variety of stakeholders who were selected because of their role in the evaluation process and because they represented differing levels of seniority within the organisation. Based on some early negative responses to tape recording and in order to encourage disclosure, handwritten notes were taken during the interviews. These interviews were useful for establishing some initial background context and were also an appropriate 'way in' to the research so that relationships could be formed with informants. It has been argued that if we are to improve our understanding of IT production and use, then an engagement in an ongoing dialogue with multiple voices can provide an enhanced

understanding of the values of the relevant actors and their framing of problems and potential solutions (Suchman, 1994). The initial interviews were carried out with representatives from the following key organisational sub-units:

- The IT group (from each distinct technology area or discipline, amounting to 12 interviews)
- The different major business areas (at senior and middle management level, amounting to 6 business units and 14 interviews)
- The Finance division at senior, middle, and junior management level (a single interview/meeting)

Generally, interviews were undertaken on a one-to-one basis and followed a semistructured approach, although for operational reasons the finance interview was undertaken as a single meeting between the researcher and three finance representatives at different organisational levels. These early interviews initiated review of further background materials, often sent to the researcher via e-mail. These documents were scanned in detail and led to the emergence of some common themes that were identified as potential areas of

Table 1. Observation background material

Observation Background material	• Company meetings, conferences, etc. • Departmental meetings • One-to-one meetings with business stakeholders • Informal discussions with employees across a range of subjects at a range of different events, both formal and informal
Observation Material in support of the evaluation process	• Attendance at all forums and meetings associated with the evaluation process (including sign-off sessions with U.K. Finance, U.K. COQ, and participation in the executive committees) • Discussion with stakeholders about the effectiveness of and potential improvements for the evaluation process • Participation in and observation of all relevant discussions and communications within the process flow, end-to-end. • Attendance at occasional projects reviews with heads of business areas • Telephone and conference call communications with the stakeholders in support of the evaluation process

interest, as they showed signs of either converging or diverging from the assumptions of practice as presented within the IS evaluation literature.

Participatory observation took the form of sitting with people and observing and taking notes of their working practices. In addition, the researcher was present at formal meetings, thus allowing him to observe the evaluation processes and procedures as they were negotiated and took shape. A period of six months of appraisal cycles was observed in this way, giving the researcher a pivotal observational role with access to all documentary evidence and stakeholders. Being permanently based on-site also meant that the researcher was able to take advantage of informal 'opportunistic' meetings (such as in the office kitchen and during ad-hoc project meetings) where it was possible to watch and listen to people's interpretations as the situation unfolded. A summary of the observation material is presented in Table 1.

In addition to the observational material, a continuous review of other material was conducted including e-mails, documents, forms, databases and spreadsheets, organisation charts, flowcharts as well as Web-based material (see Table 2). Qualitative techniques were used to analyse the data. Although the observational data and other data artefacts were collected on a daily basis, any active development of themes was not undertaken until the end of each monthly cycle, though often impressions and hunches were formed and collected during the ongoing IS investment appraisal cycle. A variety of analytical techniques were used to assess this, including content analysis, in order to develop themes to feed into the ongoing research. Simultaneous literature review and the identification of specific themes were allowed to influence the ethnography in so far as was practical by providing continuous input to the process in support of the reflexive and self-analytical

Table 2. Documentary background materials

1. **Documentary** organisational contextual information	1.	Company history presented on corporate public Web site and internal intranet
	2.	Information pack provided to new starters as part of the orientation process
	3.	Policy documents - Information Systems Development Policy (current)
	4.	Systems Development Initiation Procedure (current)
	5.	Education materials for the new process
	6.	Enhanced Project Initiation Reference Guide v.1.0
	7.	Guideline documentation for performance management, budgetary control
	8.	Employee Goals Template (current)
	9.	Employee Appraisal Template (current)
	10.	Actual performance management documentation, personnel records
	11.	Specific instances of templates referenced in 9, 10 above
	12.	BSS Systems Development Evaluation Process Instruction Manual
	13.	U.K. BSS New Starter presentation
2. **Documentary** Material in support of the evaluation process	1.	All paperwork and supporting material for all investment proposals submitted for consideration within a six-month period
	2.	Project Initiation Request form (current) - (initiation request form for information systems developments)
	3.	The minutes of business review, U.K. TAR, ITWG (weekly)
	4.	The financial cost/benefit analysis (spreadsheets and supporting documentation) for every proposed investment (one for each Project Initiation Request form)
	5.	E-mail exchanges, including the U.K. BSS to Corporate Resource Allocation exchanges
	6.	CPG/CPWG minutes (monthly)
	7.	Reports of active projects with prioritisation guidance (monthly)

nature of the ethnography itself. In this way, multilevel assessment, check pointing, reviewing and development of the research approach provided an emergent research strategy. This iterative approach of data collection, analysis, and refinement of approach or confirmation of emerging themes, characterised the ethnography throughout its lifetime. In this way the research can be said to have *evolved* as it proceeded.

The process may figuratively be characterised as bottom-up, top down, and inside-out in nature. The data collection was supported 'interactively,' that is, concurrently by analysis and creative interpretation, which fed into and influenced the subsequent approach. When analysing the data, our aim was not to uncover the consensus or majority view, but to understand the processes and themes within these multiple interpretations with a view to presenting a plausible theoretical explanation. We began with reading through all of the interview transcripts, observation notes, and documentary evidence to identify issues and topics and arrive at a common set of themes; the data were then re-examined in the light of this. Initial findings were shared with various participants within the organisation and their helpful comments confirmed and elaborated these themes. The reaction of practitioners in the field is seen to offer a crucial validation of the interpretation (Klein & Myers, 1999).

As noted elsewhere (Harvey & Myers, 1995; Myers, 1999), the write-up of ethnographic studies does not easily lend itself to conference and journal length output. Consequently, the section that follows is of necessity, segmented, and can only offer a microcosm of the larger picture.

FINDINGS AND ANALYSIS

As stated above, this ethnographic study is a slice from the organisational life of a large European bureaucratic company. The study is not intended to draw conclusions or even make recommendations, but simply open up channels for further discussion on the nature of IS evaluation. The organisation of concern was selected for this study because it provides a typical example of institutionalised IS evaluation processes. The reader will also note the existence of a number of contradictions between what is claimed on behalf of company policy regarding the 'official' evaluation process and observed practice.

Background and Setting

The organisation under review is a U.K.-based subsidiary of an international bank with its headquarters outside the U.K. The history of the organisation (as it presented itself) is that of a successful financial services company with a significant and growing market share.

The tale that follows includes a number of different stakeholder groups, often with differing interests. Details are provided of these groups who featured as *dramatis personae* in the story (Table 3).

In terms of working practices, all of the interviewees portrayed the company in positive terminology (with comments such as 'good', 'great', 'dynamic', 'interesting'). Indeed during the period of this study the company was highly rated in a U.K. survey of the best places to work (Great Place to Work Survey (U.K.) - *The Times*, 2002). However, most employees also used the term 'challenging' or spoke of 'challenges' in their daily experiences and this seemed to be part of the corporate vocabulary.

Although surface impressions were generally positive, on closer inspection it seemed that tension and conflict simmered beneath the surface. The phrase 'blame culture' was used by U.K. IT staff and business unit staff in the interviews to characterise a prevailing feature of the organisation. U.K. IT staff expressed suspicion of their business unit colleagues and questioned their motivation. One interviewee spoke of being 'shafted' in the past by information that they perceived had been

Table 3. IS evaluation stakeholders

IT group	•	the technologists based in the U.K. organisation responsible for application development, infrastructure development, and operational support.
IT Assessment Group (ITAG)	•	a subset of the IT group that is responsible for assessing proposed developments and creating initial estimates for costs, complexity, and development timescales.
Business & IT Consulting Services (BICS)	•	a team of business consultants responsible for the initiation of business system developments. Initiation includes working with the business areas in identifying business opportunity or requirement, proposing a development to the ITAG, using the defined evaluation process to the point of decision whether to make the investment, and providing business prioritisation input for the project management team for approved systems development investments.
Business Areas	•	the operational business units within the U.K. business.
Finance	•	core financial organisation within U.K. with traditional financial responsibilities. In the IS evaluation process, responsible for validating the financial cost/benefit analysis for proposed information systems investments, for confirming funding for investments and for tracking the realisation of financial benefits of information systems investments post-implementation.
Chief of Operations	•	senior executive responsible for reviewing all proposed information systems investments before submission to corporate headquarters for review.
Corporate Resources Department (CRD)	•	responsible for assessing, challenging, and validating all proposed information systems investments prior to review by senior executive committees and for approval of low-value investment requests.

deliberately misinterpreted and for which they had later been blamed. Indeed, so widespread was the perception of blame culture that it was tabled as a specific subject for discussion at the annual U.K. management conference. Its existence was vehemently denied by senior management, but this denial was later ridiculed in a number of informal conversations observed by the researcher.

Although on the surface the attitude to the U.K. organisation was positive, the relationship with the corporate parent was much more ambiguous. Much was made of the fact that the U.K. management seemed to require ratification of management decisions by the corporate parent and there was resentment expressed about what was described as interference in the affairs of the U.K. subsidiary. Indeed there were several sarcastic remarks made about the extent of this intervention which was embodied in the chief executive. One interviewee described him as having been 'parachuted in' by the corporate parent to run the U.K. on a short-term contract before being replaced by another

'big brother'. This 'interference' was coupled with what was perceived to be a lack of trust and confidence in the U.K. staff to manage their own affairs. This theme resonated on numerous occasions: some expressed it in candid and somewhat barbed terms whilst others made jokes, but what came out clearly was the way in which the parent exercised control over its subsidiary, and indeed the importance of control to the organisational culture. This control ethic was further exemplified in the performance management system, which insisted on control and compliance with company policy as a goal to be achieved by every member of the organisation.

As is typical of large bureaucratic organisations, the evaluation process consisted of approximately 12 stages (with subdivisions) and involved eight or more organisational functions. Each of these stages was observed in detail, but for simplicity the key aspects that illustrate the dissonance between organisational rhetoric and organisational practice will be reported here. Historically, the organisation has been involved in the routine conduct of IS evaluations, but the evaluation process reported here is one that has been recently introduced within the organisation.

Initial Stages: Scan Business Environment

In order to generate potential ideas for IS development, it was the responsibility of the various business areas to scan the business environment and identify any new opportunities. Business & IT Consulting Services (BICS) liaised between the business areas and the IT department in order to ensure sufficient cooperation had taken place and that the two groups were in agreement that the investment proposals were both technically feasible and practical from a business perspective. However, one of the drawbacks was that BICS offered incomplete and patchy representation of business areas as a number of business units' resisted participation in this process. Consequently, BICS did not have a full picture of the U.K. business environment and so the process of business facilitation was referred to (by a BICS consultant) as 'the blind leading the blind'.

Investment Request Submission

The next stage is the Technology Project Investment Request, which involved the completion of high-level business requirements as well as business costs and financial benefits. This request included an option for 'fast-track' IS developments which included, for example, initiatives to meet contractual commitments or legal requirements, which could be expedited for approval.

It soon became clear that the Technology Project Investment Request was treated mainly as a way to get a potential investment into the process and was regarded of little value apart from being a vehicle for collecting the required signatures. It was later seen to have little relevance as BICS management was informed by the corporate re-

sources department that the key decision-makers did not refer specifically to the details but rather summarised the request into a presentation format that relied upon verbal explanation of the project in order to elicit an executive decision. Given this disclosure, BICS relaxed their requirement of accurate and high-quality information.

Surprisingly, there was no difference in approach when assessing proposals. Thus low value investments queued patiently alongside the more substantial investments. Furthermore, despite the ability to provide support for 'fast-track' projects, during the study every 'fast-track' justification (23 in number) was ignored and proceeded in a manner that was identical to 'normal' investment proposals.

Business System Services Review

The BICS review was a weekly forum at which all new proposed submissions were presented and discussed. One of the stated objectives was to leverage a cross-divisional position, to add value in technology decisions and implementations. Accordingly each request was reviewed with the intention of identifying any synergies and potential efficiencies by expanding the scope of or altering the request in some way. Yet, in practice there were only four occasions where a material change was made to the request arising from this meeting. The practicalities of holding a meeting consisting of all the relevant stakeholders, in itself proved to be a significant challenge which was exacerbated by the fact that BICS failed to represent certain powerful departments that elected not to participate. As the evaluation cycles progressed, it became clear to BICS that the process was rigorous, demanding, and intensive. The number of initial submissions that proceeded to final approval was approximately 1 in 5. One BICS representatives made the observation that this meeting, even if fully attended, would be 'wasting its time, 80% of the time'.

IT Review

A group made up of representatives from the IT department then assessed each request based on an estimate comprising: costs to deliver, timescales, and levels of complexity. The IT assessment group (ITAG) was expected to provide such estimates within the context of a single meeting and they struggled to do so. Many expressed their concern regarding their ability to provide cost estimates based on such limited conceptual requirements. Allied to this discomfort was the demand for an immediate estimate and on numerous occasions the ITAG preferred to defer an estimate until the next meeting. This delaying tactic can also be seen as an indication of their resistance to working practices that they felt had been imposed upon them. This dislike of the process allowed delayed estimates to become established practice, so that the ITAG stated that it was their objective to provide estimates at the meeting 'only where appropriate'. The number of IS development requests that received estimates at these meetings was less than 50%.

At this stage in the process, the information required by corporate headquarters from ITAG included: project name, business sponsor, BICS relationship manager, complexity assessment, financial assessment (the cost estimate), interim funding requirements, timing, and whether or not the project was a fast-track request. However, it became clear during discussions with BICS that subsequent reviews that considered the investment proposals referred only to the financial assessment and all the other information was disregarded. Over time, the practice of accurately trying to supply the required information became completely undermined.

Because of the lengthy approval process, ITAG and BICS expressed their frustration that every type of development request was treated in the same manner. Whilst there was an acceptance that significant projects should be closely scrutinised, there was a feeling that smaller projects were

stifled because of a lack of willingness to invest in the process required for approval. As a result, a number of tactics were employed to facilitate development without having to go through the full rigours of the evaluation process. Thus, many potential projects were submitted as 'work requests' via IT helpdesk trouble tickets, thus bypassing the formal evaluation process. As IT developers and BICS representatives agreed on their local priorities, some developments were undertaken without ever entering the formal process. In addition, a number of 'deals' were made at ITAG, whereby IT staff proposed to categorise costs in a particular way such that the bill for a development would be minuted as zero. Technically even these zero-costed 'projects' should have been steered through the process but they also bypassed the formal evaluation.

Creating a 'Business Case'

The output of the ITAG review was sent to BICS so that they could construct a 'business case' to be presented to the finance department for validation. The 'business case' was used almost exclusively to describe what was essentially a cost/benefit analysis (CBA) detailing only hard costs and benefits and consisted of little more than an Excel spreadsheet. Large investments required completion of a corporate CBA spreadsheet with five-year projections and calculations of the usual capital investment financial measures (such as Net Present Value, Internal Rate of Return, and Payback Period).

The finance department, who were later required to ratify these 'business cases', introduced templates outlining 'allowable' financial models to be used by BICS which were predominantly based on financial details over any other considerations. The only benefits categories that could be shown on the investment appraisal request form were: increase in corporate revenues; reduction or avoidance of corporate costs; and reduction in corporate losses due to bad debt/fraud. Projects with large benefits in the increase in corporate revenues category received the most prompt attention as compared with other proposals. Many of these projects had the endorsement of senior management. This was even to the extent that on more than one occasion significant projects were started by the IT department before the project had even entered the formal evaluation process because it was assumed that senior executives would subsequently approve of this sort of development and so 'nod through' the project.

Every project received some financial assessment, which often amounted to reviewing costs so that these might be tracked and reviewed as the project progressed. However, for many projects, even those that were required in order to comply with legal requirements or directives, there was a pragmatic assessment made on the basis of risk exposure and the cost of potential penalties as against the cost of the investment and the timing of the spend.

One interesting development that emerged during the study was the growing awareness by the relevant stakeholders of the overwhelming importance of the financial case, expressed in hard numbers. Initial investment proposals, which included business benefit details, were soon amended as business benefits were simply no longer detailed. The reasons stated were twofold. First, the effort to produce a benefits statement was too much of an overhead given the possibility that prohibitive costs may be supplied by ITAG. As one BICS representative commented: 'We're not going to spend time working out the benefits before we know it's worth it'. Second, it was admitted that once the costs were known, a benefits assessment that would prove attractive could be 'manufactured' to provide the best chance of approval. BICS managers working within the business areas colluded in this process. As it became clear which kinds of investments were being approved, this intelligence was shared, as one business manager commented: 'If it's got a payback longer than two years, forget it!'

Finance and Funding Review

Verification from the finance department was needed before a project could be further progressed. Costs identification and assessment were based purely on hard technology and business costs with no attempt to capture softer costs of implementation. Although these benefits might be used as supporting verbal evidence, this was only ever referred to in support of financial benefits identified and modeled using financial tools. For each investment – Irrespective of value – Net Present Value (5-year), Payback Period, and Internal Rate of Return were necessary. The financial review was regarded by BICS as a 'black and white' process, and as long as the calculations had been completed in a manner that finance would find acceptable, there was little room for discussion. In this sense the evaluation was little more than a case of presentation.

Despite the so-called rigour of the evaluation process, several projects, which had been previously rejected at some stage, later re-emerged with the 'unacceptable' details changed or removed. Thus, one project, which had a supporting business case that was deemed to be financially unattractive and was rejected, simply repackaged the business case with differently stated benefits. For powerful business managers who wanted the project to be implemented, they would sidestep the process by making the presentation of the benefits more appealing. The finance department was put under pressure to validate the new case and instructed to defend the new figures vigorously. When questioned about this practice, a finance representative conceded that the business cases were often artificial and the decision as what to do had already been made and could not be influenced. The power of the finance group was such that it was seen in purely administrative terms, with one senior finance manager confiding: "I'm the highest paid administrative assistant in this company".

Chief of Operations Review

The final U.K. review was an assessment by the chief of operations to ratify the investment proposals before submission to corporate headquarters for further review. Although the final U.K.-based review was expected to be a rubber-stamping exercise, in practice more active participation was demanded by the chief of operations. Since stakeholders at corporate HQ dominated the executive decision-making process, there was sensitivity about the scrutiny that would be applied to requests. For this reason there were occasions where a project would be stopped at this stage as the visibility of the project was deemed to be unnecessary. This would result in the investment being 'approved' outside of the official process and work commencing without corporate ratification. Here, the researcher observed a number of occasions when the chief of operations decided that a particular project did not need to proceed through the approval process, he approved immediate commencement of the project and the investment proposal was then withdrawn.

Corporate Resources Department Review

Once investment proposals had been reviewed within the U.K. they were submitted to the corporate resources department (CRD) for further review. Before CRD would even consider the merits of the IS proposal, proof of adherence to the evaluation process was needed in the shape of signatures and form completion. As the study progressed, the amount of validation material required increased or changed to such an extent that the process was inconsistent from one cycle to the next. It appeared that there was a deliberate policy to challenge the resolve of the sponsoring divisions. The policy of putting practical hurdles in front of investment proposals was openly compared (by a key actor from the CRD) to the theory of evolution, with only the fittest of the investment proposals surviving.

The CRD team admitted that their intention was to test the willingness of BICS to jump over the hurdles that they invented along the way, as one CRD member noted: 'if a business area doesn't come banging on my door, I'm guessing they're not really serious about it. If they really believe in the numbers, they'll make it happen'. This was seen as a way of 'separating the wheat from the chaff'. The exchanges between CRD and BICS were often light-hearted in nature and seen on both sides as something of an intellectual game. One member of CRD admitted that their hold over the IS development process was 'theoretical rather than practical'. Typical of this was an e-mail auto signature on CRD e-mails:

My usual disclaimer: What could be perceived as petty bureaucracy is intended to ensure we make business decisions based on the best information available from the proper authorities.

The light-hearted nature of much of these communications between BICS and CRD allowed both organisations to discuss openly their feelings towards the process. The 'pointlessness' and 'futility' of the reality of the job was acknowledged by one member of the CRD department:

We all know that statistics are crap and can be used to support any bias we choose to promote.

On one occasion a very small investment proposal was discussed over a period of four months before CRD was satisfied to approve the proposal. Both BICS and CRD agreed that the cost of putting the investment through the approval was probably 20 times greater than the value of the investment, yet this overhead was never factored into the costs of an investment.

CRD and Senior Executive Review

For low value investment proposals CRD could provide approval. For higher value investments CRD was required to present the investment proposal at the executive committees. Given the scrutiny by the CRD function, it was unlikely that anything that was taken to the executive committees would be rejected. This was something of a point of honour for CRD and on the occasion that investment proposals were not approved, this was taken as a personal slight. In fact during the six-month study the committee declined only two items outright. One significant investment was deferred and the reason for this was that a member had attended the committee for the first time and appeared to have 'got out of bed with a sore head' and had been trying to 'make a noise'. BICS were assured that there would be no problem next time and were not required to answer any further supplementary questions about the proposal. When the proposal was approved at the subsequent committee meeting, CRD commented that the proposal had gone through unopposed with very little comment. 'I just jiggled the presentation up a bit—sometimes it just depends on their mood.'

Observations Outside of the Process

The processes and practices described above refer to activities that took place within the evaluation process. However, throughout the study it became clear that in practice there were many examples of investment proposals, which managed to avoid going through the prescribed evaluation process. This is in spite of the stated mission of the corporate resource allocation group, which described 'an inclusive approach to allocation of corporate financial resources'.

High-Value Corporate Investments

High value investments often did not go through any formal evaluation process as decisions were taken directly by executive management within corporate headquarters. This entailed consider-

able risk since these decisions were less likely to have been based on a full understanding of costs. Indeed, in one example IS/IT costs (which were substantial) were underestimated by a factor of approximately four. The reasons given for this avoidance of official procedure were based on the need for a quick response, although the factor of error was the subject of enormous political sensitivity. This investment 'proposal' was later put through the official evaluation process as a purely academic exercise in order to act as post mortem review by executive management. On this occasion CRD was required to dissect the business case in extreme detail.

Very Small Investments

Because of the time required to pass through the bureaucratic process, there was sometimes collusion between business areas, BICS and ITAG to find ways of initiating the development work outside of the process, for example, by exploiting other existing work structures or practices.

Contractual Commitments

Often, the marketing department would enter into contractual agreements with third parties, which required some type of IS development effort in order to fulfil contractual obligations. As many of these obligations were usually under tight time constraints, the IT department was pressured into carrying out the development without prior approval. On each occasion, BICS attempted to take the IS development request through the approval process even though work had already commenced. This represented a considerable gamble by BICS and on two occasions this risk was exposed when CRD were unconvinced of the validity of the financial case and considered rejecting the investment request. BICS were then forced to admit that the work had already begun and that any decision to proceed was illusory.

Projects with Informal Backing from Senior Executives

Whenever senior executives were convinced that an IS development was worthwhile, work was often initiated outside of the process. Here again there was no formal authority to proceed except for so-called executive intuition. Again, these proposals were formally escorted through the evaluation process to legitimise the decision, which had already taken place outside of the process. As a point of interest, these were the same executives who made the decisions at the senior executive committees to which investment proposals were submitted.

SUMMARY AND CONCLUSION

Our overview of the landscape of the IS evaluation literature reveals a trend that is mirrored in the IS field more generally; that is, the move towards the increasing concern with the social and organisational aspects of IS and, correspondingly, an increase in the use of interpretivist research as a lens to make sense of these processes. Therefore, we ask the question, how is this trend reflected in the organisational practices of IS evaluation? Are attempts being made to understand the 'softer' elements of evaluation that consider the human and organisational aspects of IS development and use? Is there an increasing recognition of the political process of evaluation and a move away from hard quantitative measures? In order to address these issues an ethnographic study of a large financial organisation with institutionalised evaluation processes was conducted. Ethnography was felt to be particularly appropriate since it enabled the researcher to become deeply immersed in the organisation to study the social and cultural context of the phenomena of interest and thus move beyond surface explanations.

In keeping with the well-founded tradition that views IS development as a process of political and social contention (Franz & Robey, 1984; Knights & Murray, 1994; Markus & Bjorn-Andersen, 1987), the results of this research reveals similar tendencies by illuminating the political context to the development and implementation activities that frame the evaluation process. The implications for those of us involved in evaluations are recognition of the social, economic, and political conditions that constitute the context within which evaluations take place.

For example, the study reveals instances of the exercise of overt power, whereby differential access to material and structural resources enables some organisational members to mobilise their power in such a way as to skew the decision-making process to suit their own interests. This is most clearly evident in the ways in which senior executives deliberately bypassed the process so that they could push through their own sponsored projects, particularly regarding high value corporate investments or projects which had a senior executive as a sponsor. Interestingly, these project proposals were later formally escorted through the evaluation process in order to legitimise and justify the decision, which had already taken place outside of the official evaluation process.

The study also illustrates the use of unobtrusive power as certain stakeholders engineered the situation in such a way as to endow their actions with legitimacy, thereby removing any opposition and achieving their objectives. In this respect, the evaluation process operated for the benefit of some and at the expense of others as legitimate alternative means ('loopholes' or workarounds) were sought to achieve their own ends or simply in order to avoid the lengthy, drawn-out process before securing project approval. For example, IT staff proposed 'zero-costed' projects as a means of bypassing the formal procedures. These various stakeholders were not unaware of the political manoeuvrings that took place and often there was acknowledgement of the futility of the process and its role in the 'rubber-stamping' of projects that may have already been started.

This was to the extent that some projects began before they had even entered the formal process since it was assumed that senior execs would 'nod them through'. They simply 'played the game' by following official procedures on most occasions, whilst cleverly avoiding them when it suited them. The legitimising devices of language, ceremony, and rituals are all evident in the way in which organisational members – more often than not – followed official procedures for project approval, even though many acknowledged that this process was little more than a façade. For example, BICS were aware that business cases were used almost exclusively as a cost benefits analysis and so they were constructed accordingly. Relevant stakeholders realised the overwhelming importance of the financial case and therefore benefits assessments were 'manufactured' in order to give them a stronger chance of success. Some projects that had previously been rejected later re-emerged with the 'unacceptable' aspects edited out.

Whilst these examples illustrate the more covert aspects of power, they also highlight the role of agency as some actors (such as BICS) deliberately undermined the IS evaluation process as a form of resistance by avoiding participation, rather than merely comply as expected. Similarly, the IT assessment group were uncomfortable about the expectation that they would to provide cost estimates and therefore used delaying tactics, to the extent that it became a common assumption that only 50% of the proposals would contain estimates. The study shows how various organisational members adopted different tactics to sidestep formalised organisational procedures, whilst simultaneously employing quantitative, 'objective' criteria to suit their own purposes.

The research study illustrates the predominance of the formal-rational management paradigm with heavy reliance on quantitative analysis to support decision-making. However, this quantitative data provided input to decision-making in complex ways. The ostensible rationality within the organisation suggests that the quantitative evaluation data provided input to a decision-making process mechanism which itself generated a decision on behalf of the organisation. However, observations suggest that the data were often treated in a less 'objective' manner and those outcomes from the decision-making process owed much to the political positioning and manoeuvring of the various stakeholders, with the 'official' rationality of the evaluation process being used to justify decisions taken in a far less rational or scientific manner. These findings are consistent with Ballantine et al.'s observation (1994) that there is a reluctance to move away from the comfort of traditional 'hard' evaluation techniques towards the more interpretive paradigm suggested increasingly in the literature. Within a large bureaucratic financial organisation, this is perhaps unsurprising. However, this positivist machinery in fact masks the less comfortable reality that significant business decisions are being taken outside of the organisation's management orthodoxy. Furthermore it seems that the formal-rational process of approval also influences the type of information system proposed, such that efficiency-based applications predominate. Whilst these may be worthy in themselves, there is a risk of diminishing returns when pursuing this type of limited application portfolio and the process of innovation may be constrained or even stagnate. This is itself reflected in the rather limited strategic intention within the organisation, which emphasises growth of market share by acquisition over more imaginative forays into new product sets or diversifications. In this respect, the shackles of the IS evaluation process risk stifling innovative development.

REFERENCES

Ballantine, J., Galliers, R., & Stray, S. (1994). Information system/technology investment decisions: The use of capital investment appraisal techniques in organisations. In *Proceedings of the 1st European Conference on IT Investment Evaluation* (pp. 148-166), Henley, United Kingdom.

Ballantine, J., Galliers, R. D., & Stray, S. J. (1999). Information systems/technology evaluation practices: Evidence from UK organizations. In S. Lester (Ed.), *Beyond the IT productivity paradox* (pp. 123-150). Chichester: John Wiley & Sons.

Ballantine, J., & Stray, S. (1998). Financial appraisal and the IS/IT investment decision making process. *Journal of Information Technology, 13*(1), 3-14.

Boland, R. J., & Pondy, L. R. (1983). Accounting in organizations: A union of natural and rational perspectives. *Accounting, Organanizations and Society, 8*, 223-234.

Earl, M. (1996). Putting information technology in its place: A polemic for the nineties. *Journal of Information Technology, 7*, 100-108.

Farbey, B., Land, F. F., & Targett, T. (1995). A taxonomy of information systems applications: The benefits' evaluation ladder. *European Journal of Information Systems, 4*, 41-50.

Farbey, B., Land, F., & Targget, D. (1998). Editorial. *European Journal of Information Systems, 7*, 155-157.

Fetterman, D. (1998). *Ethnography*. Thousand Oaks, CA: Sage Publications.

Franz, C. R., & Robey, D. (1984). An investigation of user-led systems design: Rational and political perspectives. *Communications of the ACM, 27*(12), 1202-1209.

Galliers, R. D., Merali, Y., & Spearing, L. (1994). Coping with information technology? How british executives perceive the key information systems management issues in the mid-1990s. *Journal of Information Technology, 9*(4), 223-238.

Hardy, C. (1985). The nature of unobtrusive power. *Journal of Management Studies, 22*(4), 384-399.

Harvey, L., & Myers, M. (1995). Scholarship and practice: The contribution of ethnographic research methods to bridging the gap. *Information Technology & People, 8*(3), 13-27.

Hinton, C., & Kaye, G. (1994). The hidden investments in information technology: The role of organisational context and system dependency. *International Journal of Information Management, 16*(6), 413-427.

Hirschheim, R., & Smithson, S. (1988). A critical analysis of IS evaluation. In G. B. Davis (Ed.), *Information systems assessment: Issues and challenges* (pp. 17-37). Amsterdam: North-Holland.

Irani, Z. (2002). Information systems evaluation: Navigating through the problem domain. *Information & Management, 40*, 11-24.

Irani, Z., Ezingeard, J., & Grieve, R. (1997). Integrating the costs of a manufacturing IT/IS infrastructure into the investment decision-making process. *Technovation, 17*(11/12), 695-706.

Jones, S., & Hughes, J. (2001). Understanding IS evaluation as a complex social process: A case study of a UK local authority. *European Journal of Information Systems, 10*, 189-203.

Keen, P. (1991). *Shaping the future: Business design through information technology*. Boston: Harvard Business School Press.

Love, A. (1991). *Internal evaluation: Building organizations from within*. Newbury Park, CA: Sage Publications.

Lukes, S. (1974). *Power: A radical view*. London: MacMillan.

Lycett, M., & Giaglis, G. (2000). Component-based information systems: Towards a framework for evaluation. In *Proceedings of the 33rd Hawaii*

International Conference on Systems Sciences (pp. 1-10).

Markus, M. L. (1983). Power, politics, and MIS implementation. *Communications of the Association for Computing Machinery, 26*(6), 430-444.

Myers, M. D. (1999). Investigating information systems with ethnographic research. *Communication of the AIS, 2,* 1-20.

Niederman, F., Branchaeu, J. C., & Wetherbe, J. C. (1991). Information systems management issues for the 1990s. *MIS Quarterly, 15*(4), 475-499.

Orlikowski, W. J., & Baroudi, J. J. (1991). Studying IT in organizations: Research approaches and assumptions. *Information Systems Research, 2*(1), 1-28.

Pfeffer, J. F. (1981). *Power in organizations.* Cambridge, MA: Ballinger.

Picciotto, S. (1999). Introduction: What rules for the world economy? In R. Mayne (Ed.), *Regulating international business: Beyond liberalization.* London: Macmillan.

Pouloudi, A., & Serafeimidis, V. (1999). Stakeholders of information systems evaluation: Experience from a case study. In *Proceedings of the Sixth European Conference on IT Investment Evaluation* (pp. 91-98), Brunel University, Uxbridge.

Remenyi, D. (1999). *Stop IT project failures through risk management.* Oxford: Butterworth Heinemann.

Remenyi, D., Sherwood-Smith, M., & White, T. (1996). Outcomes and benefit modelling for information systems investment. In *Proceedings of the 3rd European Conference on Information Technology Investment Evaluation* (pp. 101-119).

Renkema, T., & Berghout, E. (1997). Methodologies for information systems investment evaluation at the proposal stage: A comparative review. *Information and Software Technology, 39,* 1-13.

Serafeimidis, V., & Smithson, S. (2000). Information systems evaluation in practice: A case study of organizational change. *Journal of Information Technology, 15,* 93-105.

Serafeimidis, V., & Smithson, S. (2003). Information systems evaluation as an organizational institution: Experience from a case study. *Information Systems Journal, 13,* 251-274.

Silverman, D. (1985). *Qualitative methodology and sociology.* Aldershot: Gower.

Silverman, D. (2000). *Doing qualitative research: A practical handbook.* London: Sage.

Smithson, S., & Hirschheim, R. (1998). Analysing information systems evaluation: Another look at an old problem. *European Journal of Information Systems, 7,* 158-174.

Symons, V. (1993). Evaluation and the failure of control: Information systems development in the processing company. *Accounting, Management and Information Technology, 3*(1), 51-76.

Vroom, V. H., & Yetton, P. W. (1973). *Leadership and decision-making.* Pittsburgh: University of Pittsburgh Press.

Walsham, G. (1993). *Interpreting information systems in organizations.* Chichester: John Wiley & Sons.

Walsham, G. (1999). Interpretive evaluation design for information systems. In S. Lester (Ed.), *Beyond the IT productivity paradox* (pp. 363-380). Chichester: John Wiley & Sons.

Willcocks, L., & Lester, S. (1999). In search of information technology productivity: Assessment issues. In S. Lester (Ed.), *Beyond the IT productivity paradox* (pp. 69-98). Chichester: John Wiley & Sons.

Wilson, T. (1991) Overcoming the barriers to the implementation of information system strategies. *Journal of Information Technology, 6,* 39-44.

Yin, R. K. (1989). *Case study research: Design and methods*. London: Sage.

Zuboff, S. (1988). *In the age of the smart machine: The future of work and power*. New York: Basic Books.

ENDNOTE

[1]   Although even this is contentious.

This work was previously published in International Journal of Technology and Human Interaction, Vol. 3, Issue 3, edited by B. Stahl , pp. 69-102, copyright 2004 by IGI Publishing, formerly known as Idea Group Publishing (an imprint of IGI Global).

Chapter XX
Reframing Information System Design as Learning Across Communities of Practice

Kevin Gallagher
Northern Kentucky University, USA

Robert M. Mason
University of Washington, USA

ABSTRACT

This chapter frames the requirements definition phase of systems design as a problem of knowledge transfer and learning between two communities of practice: IS designers and system users. The theoretical basis for the proposed approach is Wenger's (1998) framework for social learning, which involves three dimensions: alignment, imagination, and engagement. The chapter treats the requirements definition task in systems design as a set of activities involving mutual learning and knowledge transfer between two communities of practice (CoP) along these three dimensions. In taking this approach, the chapter maps the results of past research on the systems design process onto this CoP framework and illustrates that the proposed framework encompasses the same activities used by traditional methods of requirements definition. However, this approach focuses attention on the learning that must take place between the two CoPs and thereby helps resolve some of the inherent shortcomings of prior efforts and approaches. The framework provides both a more encompassing conceptual lens for research on improving the requirements definition task and practical guidance for managers who are charged with a systems design project.

INTRODUCTION

Requirements definition is a critical step in systems development that requires the identification of information needs and knowledge of a system's processes (Nelson & Cooprider, 1996; Vessey, 1994). Historically, researchers examined the requirements-definition stage of system design as a process of inquiry (Boland, 1978; Salaway, 1987). Problems with identification, articulation, and communication of information needs have long been identified with the challenges of information system design (Boland, 1987). There have been different approaches in attempting to meet these challenges, but none has completely resolved the issues.

Land (1998) notes that because systems are so different, a contingency approach—using different methods for different types of systems—is appropriate. Others have suggested more structured analyses of the design process itself, establishing metrics for requirements engineering (Costello & Liu, 1995) and developing tools for each aspect of the problem (Nature_Team, 1996). Some researchers have suggested that the process of design must remain flexible and that a management structure that encourages an evolutionary design process is associated with greater effectiveness (Ravichandran & Rai, 2000). In considering software project risk and software quality, organizational issues as well as technical issues are important (Wallace, Keil & Rai, 2004). Others also emphasize the critical nature of human-intensive dimensions of the process (Tamai, 1993). It also has been noted that evolutionary designs are necessary as complexity increases (Mens & Eden, 2005). Larman (2004) argues that an "agile" and iterative design process is key to software development success.

The approach that we want to explore in this chapter emphasizes these human-intensive dimensions of the design process. Although the design process involves many actors (Lamb, 2003), we want to focus on two roles: the designer (who has technical knowledge) and the user (who has knowledge of the application and context of use). The conceptual approach is one that considers requirements definition as an instance of knowledge acquisition (Byrd, Cossick & Zmud, 1992).

Recently, organizations and researchers have begun investigating the potential of knowledge transfer (Alavi & Leidner, 2001) to make organizations more effective when engaging in information intensive work. Such knowledge transfer is necessary because clients are not sure what is possible and are unclear about their needs, and IT designers thus are unable to work toward an outcome that meets clear specifications (as in designing a product for production) (Larman, 2004).

To date, however, conceptualizations of knowledge transfer in software development do not completely capture the complexity and richness of this process by which clients and designers work together. As Polyani (1966, p. 4) says, "We know more than we can tell." Regardless of how well we articulate knowledge, it always contains a tacit dimension. Hence, simple inquiry is insufficient for the requirements definition process because it is able to access only explicit, leaky knowledge (Von Hipple, 1994). The information transferred through traditional elicitation approaches is only part of what someone knows, and it rarely includes *how* or *why* they know it (Lanzara & Mathiassen, 1985).

Because of the tacit dimension of knowledge involved in most tasks and processes, it is difficult, if not impossible, for people to articulate exactly what it is that they need prior to design. Even if they can articulate what they need, the system development effort is hampered if the system developers do not understand why and how users need what they need. With an understanding of the why's and how's of information, developers can be more innovative in their delivery of requirements. For example, unless developers understand which information is used together and how it is connected, they will be unlikely to find ways to combine and simplify tasks.

If we keep the traditional concept of inquiry as the basis for eliciting requirements, the effort must always be incomplete. The language or metaphor of "inquiry" or "capturing requirements" is part of the problem. The choice of metaphor can inhibit the range of approaches to information systems (Mason, 1991), and recently the metaphor of "engineering" has been questioned as the basis for approaching software development (Bryant, 2000).

What is needed is an approach that engages users in such a way that they can elucidate not only what they know, but also how and why they know it. In addition, users must learn about how systems in general, and this system in particular, will be developed. An improvement over current approaches is to engage designers so that they really understand what the users are telling them, and to ensure that they effectively share their knowledge of both the systems and the processes for which they are developing technology (Boland, 1978). To accomplish this, both users and developers must share their knowledge and learn from each other (Boland, 1978; Churchman & Schainblatt, 1966). In short, what is needed is a process of mutual learning in which designers and users engage in a process of learning from each other.

In order to work toward such a process, we turn to the concept of a community of practice (Lave & Wenger, 1991). The concept, first used to help understand situated learning, refers to a group of people defined by an interest in a specific subject or problem who collaborate to share ideas and resolve issues common to the group. In this chapter, we posit that information system (IS) designers and IS users belong to two distinct communities of practice (CoPs) as they work together in a systems development context. The system designers comprise one community and the users for which the system is being designed comprise the other (Churchman & Schainblatt, 1965). The term "users" may cover many roles, including managerial, and in the following we may use "managers" to provide a specific context for the discussion or simply say "users" for the generic situation. The requirements definition phase of IS design requires that these two groups engage in mutual learning both to share knowledge and to develop new mutual understandings of the possibilities as a system design emerges. The knowing of managers (or other users) is formed by a very different practice than the knowing of IT professionals (Brown & Duguid, 2001), resulting in different ways of knowing (Boland & Tenkasi, 1995). Knowing is not easily shared across these two groups because of their different histories and perspectives.

The chapter extends Wenger's (1998) design for social learning within a CoP (p. 236) to learning across two communities of practice. Wenger's model comprises three dimensions: alignment, engagement, and imagination. We apply this framework of social learning across the two CoPs (i.e., managers and designers) and show that the framework not only is consistent with prior research on the information system design (ISD) process but also is suggestive of how the design process can become more effective.

The remainder of the chapter comprises three sections. The next section, Social Learning, reviews the concept of social learning and distinguishes it from simple knowledge transfer. This section further illustrates why the characteristics of social learning are the characteristics required for an effective requirements definition process.

The subsequent section presents an architecture for social learning. It reviews the three dimensions of Wenger's model for social learning in a community of practice and notes that factors considered essential to the requirements definition phase of the system development process can be mapped onto these dimensions.

The final section summarizes the application of the model for information system design, outlines issues in implementing the architecture, and discusses the implications for research and practice.

SOCIAL LEARNING

Knowledge and Knowing

Viewed from a social learning perspective, knowledge is social, not individual (Brown, 2002), and is a matter of our competence with respect to some valued enterprise (Wenger, 1998). Knowledge encompasses aspects of experience, action, and the accomplishment of some activity. In this perspective, knowledge is more than stored information, even more than codified and structured information.

It is helpful to distinguish "knowing" from "knowledge." In common usage, "knowledge" brings with it the context of an accumulation of facts and "know what." On the other hand, use of the term "knowing" conveys more of a sense of engagement in a process of learning and becoming. Knowing is not only an accumulation of facts, but an accumulation and assimilation of experiences and learning that alter who we are as well as what we know. As we learn *about*, we also learn *to be* (Brown & Duguid, 2001). Levels of participation or nonparticipation reveal a sense of relation, familiarity, and belonging to the situation. These aspects of identity development affect one's modes of involvement and willingness to engage in activities. The attributes of identity are developed, and reciprocally supported, through the process of learning.

We are constantly engaged in accomplishing activities and we typically become more proficient with experience. Our knowing, therefore, resides in our practice (Cook & Brown, 1999), which is how we accumulate experience and situated ways of knowing. Participation is our "knowing in action," so a design processes can benefit from participation by those who know the existing process.

Apprenticeship and Communities of Practice

Communities of practice provide a theoretical framework for understanding how the dynamics of social structures influence learning and practice. The origins of communities of practice are grounded in apprenticeship and their ability to support situated learning through social coparticipation (Hanks, 1991; Wenger, 1998). Understanding how apprenticeship promotes learning within a community can help in understanding how learning can occur across communities. Learning through practice is exemplified in apprenticeship, whereby a community regenerates itself through a process of participation and training. When the transfer of explicit knowledge is supported by sharing the practices in which it makes sense, it is possible to *understand* its meaning in a way that makes it most useful, actionable, and purposeful.

Participation is the key to developing and sustaining communities of practice, but observation also plays a critical role by allowing one to participate on the periphery of a community. While the master remains engaged in the craft, the apprentice learns by means of "legitimate peripheral participation" (Lave & Wenger, 1991), observing the practices and developing the tacit dimension of knowing. By engaging in practice, the master is able to communicate more than what can be said and the apprentice is able to learn more than what can be heard.

The roles of a community's members are not rigidly defined; however, a key to apprenticeship is that members can engage in varying roles simultaneously. Legitimate peripheral participation supports learning without requiring members to acquire all of the necessary knowledge for full membership in that community. In this way, a member can span the boundary of a community and still be able to observe, understand, and learn.

Participation and observation (nonparticipation) together define our levels of engagement as we employ these modes of engagement in attaining knowledge of our own communities and other communities from which we may learn.

To participate on the periphery allows one access to a community through passive modes of observation and similar activities that do not overly dominate or eliminate participation altogether. This is exemplified by active listening. Conversely, marginality is a mode of nonparticipation that stifles participation, as exemplified by listening in on a conversation in which the terminology is foreign. In both cases, there is exposure to a community of new information. The first situation offers a mode of nonparticipation that facilitates learning. In the second, the learning becomes stifled.

Apprenticeship is offered here as the starting point of a model to use when designing a way for two communities to come together, share knowledge, and learn. In the case of requirements definition, it may be enlightening to consider the IT professionals to be apprentices to the user community (Beyer & Goltzblatt, 1995) and the users to be apprentices to the IT community. Through apprenticeship, the participants learn about practice. To make "know that" useful requires appropriate "know how" that we can only gain through practice in both senses of the word: to do and to improve (Brown & Duguid, 2001). The need to involve users in system design has been a long held belief for requirements definition; however, involving IT in the practices of the users is less established, but has the potential to be quite revealing.

Knowing as a Challenge for IS Design

The challenge for IS design is to enable participation by both users and designers in a process that both conveys knowledge and enables knowing. In any social process, our experience informs our knowing, but the structure of the relevant social arrangement orients and guides our experiences. We develop personal histories from experience, and, through practice, we negotiate and form the meanings we give to things. Identity is how we see our role in the process that then influences our level of engagement.

Both users and designers must be engaged in the process of knowing about the other's needs and the opportunities afforded by alternative designs. Engagement is a social process, one not naturally emerging nor easily brought about by fiat.

Prior researchers have acknowledged the social aspects of information system design. For example, political arrangements in organizations and dynamics of relative power among design participants can influence the degree to which they feel safe participating in activities (Hayes & Walsham, 2001). Others have noted the importance of the relationship between users and designers in the design process (Beath & Orlikowski, 1994; Hirschheim & Klein ,1994; Ives & Olsen, 1984). Mutual learning can only take place when users and designers are able to engage in effective modes of participation when they are involved in requirements definition activities. Through appropriate modes of participation, requirements are informed both by what the participants know and by how and why they know it

What we want to accomplish in the IS design process is to enable both designers and users to engage in a learning process that enables safe but effective participation in the design activities. The apprenticeship model of social learning in a community of practice, coupled with Wenger's (1998) architecture for social learning (p. 237), provides a model for such a process.

AN ARCHITECTURE FOR SOCIAL LEARNING

Processes of social engagement differ in their ability to support learning. Figure 1 illustrates

Figure 1. Wenger's architecture for social learning

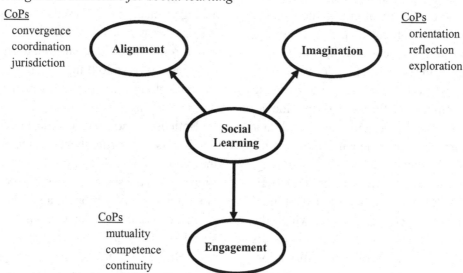

CoPs
convergence
coordination
jurisdiction

CoPs
orientation
reflection
exploration

CoPs
mutuality
competence
continuity

Wenger's (1998) architecture for social learning in a community of practice, showing arrangements for alignment, imagination, and engagement. When engaged in practices across communities, the support of such social arrangements can facilitate a sense of belonging for members that helps to ensure participation and learning. Collectively, the three dimensions enable members of the community to learn with each other. The architecture provides a framework for considering the requirements of the process of IS design, particularly the requirements definition phase of this process.

The three dimensions are interdependent and, in fact, have inherent tensions among them. For example, a structure that assures close coordination for alignment can inhibit imagination and engagement. Conversely, imagination without alignment can result in activities that do not contribute to the overall learning process.

Alignment ensures coordination of the community's activities and resources toward achieving an objective. In the case of system design, this means achieving a fit between the local needs of a business unit and the new design. Learning is important to such a practice, as working through

the development of a design raises new questions from which participants can learn about the existing system (Kyng & Morten, 1995). However, there are many ways to establish a fit during design, some of which may inhibit future flexibility (Allen & Boynton, 1991) and lead to rapid obsolescence or an inability to adapt. Alignment alone is not enough to support learning. A community of practice, and perhaps more importantly, the interaction between two communities, must also support what Wenger labels *imagination*.

In Wenger's terms, imagination provides the opportunity to create new possibilities. The benefits of creativity and innovation in the development of systems are well established in the field of information systems (Cougar, 1996). However, creativity without the appropriate information as to the possibilities and constraints of a design or an appropriate vision of the future may lead to poor implementation (Zmud & Apple, 1992). Therefore, a process of mutual adaptation is necessary to achieve an improved design and a successful implementation (Leonard-Barton, 1993). Mutual adaptation can be viewed as an accommodation of both alignment and imagination that can be accomplished through learning.

The third dimension of Wenger's design, the concept of *engagement*, represents active involvement in the negotiation of meaning during the learning process. Engagement requires appropriate modes of participation. Appropriate modes of engagement by participants can ensure a balance between alignment and imagination. By supporting participants' engagement in a social process, it becomes far more difficult for any one set of perspectives or goals to dominate the process. However, engagement is difficult to ensure. Psychologically, individuals must feel it is safe for them to engage in an activity, that it will be a meaningful investment, and that the personal and professional resources that are necessary for participation are available to them (Kahn, 1990).

In the apprenticeship model of learning, engagement in practice by the bearers of knowledge will assist in their grasping, articulating, and transferring knowledge to others. Furthermore, peripheral participation by those who are in apprenticeship roles facilitates their ability to appropriate the meanings conveyed in specifications by those engaging in the design process. In sum, engaging in the practice of design can help us to understand and transfer what we know.

The challenge in employing Wenger's design for learning in the IS design process is balancing the tensions inherent in each of the three dimensions (See Figure 2 below.). Traditionally, IT departments have been concerned with alignment. They feel a need to align themselves with business strategy, with user functions, with business processes, and with organizational objectives (Chan, Huff, Barclay & Copeland, 1997; Reich & Benbasat, 1996). They have perceived standardization of systems and control over the design process as the key to alignment (Kirsch, 1996). However, with excessive alignment, imagination is curtailed and success becomes elusive (Baskerville & Stage, 1996). Excessive imagination and creativity, on the other hand, can lead to idiosyncratic designs and unworkable heterogeneity, reducing the abil-

ity to share, diffuse innovations, and efficiently develop new systems.

The quest for alignment makes its necessary for IT and users to work together. Yet, mutual engagement in these activities is in direct tension with the development of functional expertise within the organization. It also raises organizational tensions around leadership and decision making, between working together and understanding who has jurisdiction. As many IT scholars have claimed, partnership is key to IS success (Henderson, 1990). Partnership addresses the tension between conflicting power bases in the organization, but a successful design environment must also address the tension between imagination and alignment. Wenger's design for learning recognizes the need to balance these tensions in the design of a learning environment that will support the appropriate modes of engagement and thereby facilitate and balance the tension between alignment and imagination.

The information system design (ISD) literature is consistent with this three-dimensional framework of learning in a community of practice. The literature on use of methods and controls is consistent with Wenger's dimension of alignment. The need for imagination during system design is supported by the ISD research on learning by doing, performed though modeling and prototyping. Research on user participation and involvement supports the need for engagement.

The next section discusses the commonalities between Wenger's framework and the ISD literature, explains further the facilities used to implement the model, and highlights the challenges of applying the principles and balancing the tensions in the ISD setting.

Alignment

In Wenger's model (Figure 1), alignment is comprised of three facilities: *convergence* provides a common focus; *coordination* provides methods and procedure; and *jurisdiction* provides policies

Figure 2. Wenger's architecture for social learning adapted for requirements determination

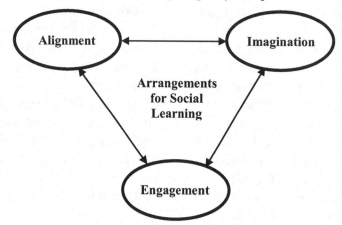

and procedures. Similar themes are found in the IS literature, which describes the need to pursue objectives, employ standard methods, and control the design process.

Objectives are defined based on user needs and the possibilities the system affords, negotiated through a social process of mutual adaptation (Leonard-Barton, 1993). Through methods, activities are organized to achieve these objectives. Yet, methods often give primacy to designers over users (Beath & Orlikowski, 1994) or to problem solving over alternative rationalities (Boland, 1979). Thus, formalizing methods serves to structure activities, thereby imposing controls that promote and suppress certain behaviors.

The IS design process requires more than obedience to method, it must also be a reflective activity (Iivari, 1987). System design requires iterative and adaptive planning as the acquired experience and learning from each sub phase informs the ongoing effort (Iivari, 1987). Thus, development efforts must recognize the need to balance iterative development with complimentary methods of control.

Control is complicated by the fact that coordination and communication necessary to complete the tasks spans organizational departments (Kirsch, 1997). A complex relationship

exists between efficiency and quality. Different strategies of control lend themselves to different situations. Informal methods of control are used when understanding of the process and outcome measures are inexact (Ouchi, 1979) and depend on social strategies (Eisenhardt, 1985). Self-control relies on the motivation of individuals, and in IS it is strongest among personnel who take part in defining work procedures (Kirsch & Cummings, 1996).

Clan is another informal control characterizing a group that is dependent on one another to achieve a common objective (Ouchi, 1980). Boland (1979) distinguishes "control over" from "control with" in order to distinguish bureaucratic processes from those where shared values and beliefs serve as the basis for coordinated action. Through appropriate selection of members and use of appropriate training and socialization processes, individuals in a group can develop a stronger sense of identity and commitment (Kirsch, 1996). Appropriate activities serve as rituals to reinforce acceptable behaviors. The development of identity and commitment are equally vital components in apprenticeship, where methods of training and socialization are employed to facilitate learning directed toward achieving objectives. In the end, certain modes of control, especially in excess, can have a negative impact on both engagement and imagination.

Imagination

Imagination is comprised of three facilities (Wenger, 1998): *orientation* provides a location relative to the organization; *reflection* provides facilities for comparison and evaluation; and *exploration* provides opportunities for envisioning, creating and testing new ideas. Again, similar themes are found in the IS literature that emphasize a need to understand situational context and explore possibilities through processes that support discovery and innovation.

Systems requirements are the first step in defining possibilities for new information technologies. As previously noted, the development of system requirements is often conducted through inquiry and other elicitation methods, intended to identify user needs. Yet, this step is highly prone to unintended influence through bias and error (Salaway, 1987). In addition, interviewing can close down inquiry, if motivated to solve problems rather than explore the appropriateness of different possibilities for an organizational situation (Boland, 1979).

Another method of elicitation is the use of design tools, such as computer assisted software engineering (CASE) or use cases, which help users describe the organizational situations in which they are involved and convey what they know (Lanzara & Mathiassen, 1985). Such tools help users move from the current situation to the enactment of a new one (Lanzara & Mathiassen, 1985). For instance, redirecting the attention away from the existing system and refocusing on a new realm of possibilities (Wastell, 1999) is one such example. To reframe a situation leads to a discovery of possibilities.

Drawing on theories of action, Lanzara and Mathiassen (1985) are critical of most existing tools. They suggest that better tools are needed to bring the "background into the foreground" by offering ways to make procedure more explicit, thereby relating descriptions to the actual settings. This advances a user's opportunity to question the appropriateness of existing solutions, challenge their adequacy, and take more responsibility for initiating a more positive action.

Similarly, prototyping enables a common reference point for users and developer, which helps to develop a mutual understanding and draw out and refine user requirements (Alavi, 1984). Reifying what is known helps to reveal what is not fully understood and offers alternative active techniques for articulating and defining existing situations that allow the designs and users to engage in a social process of simultaneous definition, design, and discovery.

To summarize, there is great support in the IS literature for imagination in the design process. There also is great concern regarding the mutual understanding of context among users and designers, which is necessary to define the present situation and to inform an effective process of discovering new possibilities. Furthermore, the tools we have available are limited in their ability to support and encourage these activities. Tools alone are not sufficient without the social and human elements that can encourage and inform their use; engagement provides these elements.

Engagement

Engagement is facilitated by *mutuality* though: reciprocity and interdependence, which provides opportunities to form and share perspectives; *competence,* which supports the occasion for applying knowledge and exercising judgment; and *continuity,* which supports mechanisms of memory, which work as repositories for information created through social encounters. Similarly, IS research has found that the design process and subsequent adoption of a technology benefit from user involvement, which enhances confidence and acceptance of the technology (Hartwick & Barki, 1994; Ives & Olsen, 1984).

Including users in the design process involves more than their presence, however; it also requires overcoming conflicts of interest and effects of authority (Mumford, 1983, p. 31). Often users are given relatively passive roles, despite being required to sign off on requirements (Beath & Orlikowski, 1994). As a result, patterns of user participation vary according to who controls the selection of features and the coordination of activities (Kirsch & Beath, 1996). Participation, therefore, is often token or compliant, rather than shared.

The participative design (PD) movement highlights empowerment of users as important in their ability to influence the overall design process (Hirschheim & Klien, 1994). Joint application design (JAD) is designed to actively engage users and designers in activities, often away from their usual work settings and organizational roles, recognizing the importance that altering structures has on the dynamics of a design process.

One way that JAD involves users is through modeling and prototyping. Models support the development of shared understanding between users and developers, thereby building confidence in what is established as knowledge during inquiry. Prototypes serve to cultivate user participation and help build credibility and establish good working relations.

As with alignment and imagination, there is great support in the IS literature for engagement as a key component of RD success, but there is concern about our ability to successfully nurture it. The following section discusses the results from several researchers who have provided insight into approaches and tools that may help to overcome some of the most frequently encountered impediments to successful alignment, imagination, and engagement in the RD and ISD processes.

Summary: Designing an ISD Process for Social Learning

Table 1 illustrates the parallels between Wenger's model of social learning, an apprenticeship model,

and the factors judged important to successful design from the ISD literature. What remains is the construction of social learning processes that enable a project to implement and balance these factors.

Designing Structures for Social Learning

The social process of ISD, whereby users and developers collectively define requirements, is complicated in that participants may differ in their backgrounds, cognitive styles, personality, job characteristics, organizational circumstances, affiliations, or location (Robey & Markus, 1984). As one might expect, this leads to differing interpretation, confrontation, and misunderstanding.

A major concern, therefore, is that the discourse required for an effective process of inquiry is distorted in traditional organizational structures. Altering the structure of a design process through choices regarding the number of participants, the activities conducted, and the role of users and designers can offer greater opportunity for users to raise issues, question the appropriateness of choices, make and demand commitments, and express attitudes and concerns (Hirschheim & Klien, 1994).

Nonaka and Takeuchi (1995) show that through organizational design actions enacted through structured mechanisms, knowledge creation is facilitated. Churchman and Schainblatt (1965) note that researchers and managers viewed problem-solving differently and propose a dialectic approach to manager-researcher communication. Boland (1979) found that structuring problem-solving processes in ways that are enabled by differing rationales encouraged participants to share their knowledge and arrive at different types of solutions. Different processes for understanding and applying knowledge are influenced by the controls placed over the process of user-designer interaction.

Altering the structures of user-designer interaction may provide benefits beyond improved

Table 1. Correspondence between Wenger's model and information system design literature

Dimension	Community of Practice	ISD Literature
Alignment	• convergence • coordination • jurisdiction	• objectives • methodology • control
Imagination	• orientation • reflection • exploration	• context • possibilities • discovery
Engagement	• mutuality • competence • continuity	• participation • self efficacy • joint tasks

specifications or overcoming user resistance. Bringing users into close interaction with designers promotes social sense making (Boland, 1984) and shared understanding (Nelson & Cooprider, 1996). Information analysis, extended to include the context within which data are interpreted, also provides design mechanisms that can support self-reflection (Boland, 1979).

In summary, the IS literature shows support for the notions resident in Wenger's design for social learning. However, it does not explicitly address the tension inherent in alignment, imagination, and engagement. By exploring structures that balance these tensions, the process of system design may benefit, as we demonstrate in the next section.

Resolving and Managing Tensions as a way of Explaining Successes and Failures

In this section, we revisit three previously published studies to illustrate the value that the social learning model adds to the literature in information system design. The studies we examine used three different methods: controlled experiments, field research, and comparative analysis of previously collected case studies. The authors of each study include in their data and their analysis consideration to all three of the dimensions in our

model: alignment, engagement, or imagination. However, in each study, one of the dimensions is used as the primary focus of investigation and therefore becomes a primary explanation for the results and the authors' understanding of what distinguishes effective from ineffective design processes.

For each study, we offer an alternative explanation that encompasses the original differentiating characteristics but offers additional insights into how to manage the process of information systems development. With these insights, the tensions among all three dimensions are included in the management framework rather than emphasizing one dimension of the model over the others. Consequently, this research contributes to the research literature by emphasizing the need to balance the dimensions in the model, and the result is a broader perspective on the practice of managing the system development process.

Boland (1978)

In the first study we examined, Boland (1978) addressed the question of how a user is involved in system design. Employing an experimental research design, "two radically different processes of interaction between a systems designer and a manager were compared in an information system design exercise." The author refers to the first as traditional and the later as an alternative. The first process was conducted by having the designer interview the manager. Afterward, the designer made suggestions for the design. In the second process, there was an initial sharing of information followed by a period of mutual suggestion and critique by each participant.

In the study, the structure (methodology and control) influences the interaction between the user and the manager. Based on how this protocol or interaction takes place, the problem solution is derived. The author states "the alternative interaction approach produced higher quality designs with important implementation advantages." From these results, Boland suggests that the protocols "may help to define different problems, and thereby produce different, but equally rational, solutions." As stated in the chapter, "the structure of their interaction is defined as the protocols or accepted patterns they follow in punctuating their exchange of messages." Using the model proposed in this research, the causal direction between the dimensions inferred in this statement is quite clear. Alignment, which includes methodology and control, sets the stage for how users and designers will engage in the process. The author also states, "the structure of their interactions serves as the context for the generation, interaction, and interpretation of ideas between them. The protocols they followed are seen as a source of rationality in the design process, as they guide in bounding the problem space, drawing inferences, and defining an 'appropriate' information space." From the social learning model perspective, the protocol influences design activities, or, in other words, the causal direction inferred is (the words of our model) "alignment affects imagination."

A richer explanation, employing the proposed social learning model, is that the alternative process resolved tensions in the process and, compared with the traditional process, struck a better balance in what was emphasized as important. Protocols, as a part of a prescribed methodology, served to organize the process or inquiry, but as exhibited in the study, they may not engage users in ways that promote knowledge transfer or afford the ability to imagine the design of an innovative system. The alternative process certainly undertook a different rationality, as the author went on to discuss, but it also undertook a more balanced approach across the three dimensions of the proposed model. By having participants first share information, then describe solutions and discuss pros and cons, both engagement and imagination were enhanced.

Wastell (1999)

In the second study we analyzed, Wastell (1999) also viewed social structure as a vehicle for learning and as a critical element in information system design. The study involved field research and employed an action research approach. Opportunities for design to influence the structure of interactions between participants or the development environment and the way it is managed and controlled are surfaced in the study. Three case studies are described. In each case, the author suggests approaches, and then describes how these changes improved performance. Using a theoretical perspective from psychology, the author proposed that antilearning defenses create difficulties for information systems design.

Stress and anxiety, arising from the group defenses of those involved in the system development effort are at the center of this approach. For example, following traditional protocols allows participants to adhere to prescribed behavior rather than engaging the participants from other groups in a common set of tasks. The approach to improving method and involvement are to reduce stress and defense avoidance behaviors. As prescribed by the author, modeling and other activities of design provide the design process with transitional objects, which facilitate involvement by designers and managers. As a result, the use of these objects promotes a learning environment, or transitional space. Thus, use of transitional objects "can facilitate the change process by providing a source of support through the transition, redirecting the anxieties that could otherwise lead to erection of defenses."

In this framework, one role of the project manager is to maintain, rather than create, this learning environment. Thus, Wastell places the focus of his investigation, and prescriptions for improvements, on the process of modeling and designing. These concepts are incorporated in the imagination dimension of the proposed model.

For example, in one of three cases the author uses in the chapter, the company, Acme, is described as exhibiting "overly fastidious attention to notational detail and the aesthetics of diagrams . . . and users complained that they would be presented with large sets of diagrams which they found difficult to understand; one commented that 'we did not know what we were doing or why we were doing it'." The author's diagnosis of the problem was that these methods of design "provided IS professionals with an illusion of control." Users "drew back from the real job of analysis, of engaging with users in an open and frank debate about IS requirements."

Using the author's proposed framework, the causal direction of this theoretical approach is that imagination influences both the engagement of users and designers and the alignment or management of the process by which design is conducted. The prescription offered by the author is that design activities should be used as transitional objects. The use of these objects facilitates the creation of a transitional space. This space is a structure that promotes learning, allowing designer and mangers to safely engage in activities. Once created, management must try to support the existing environment, which is quite different from the idea that methods and controls are needed to ensure the effectiveness of a process.

The author sums up the problem in this case as a situation in which "a highly prescriptive methodology is imposed by fiat" compared with an alternative that works better. The alternative, described in a similar case study, is a process in which practitioners create their "own methodological ideas before consolidating these experiences into new working practices."

Using the social learning framework model, we might explain the findings as one in which there was a shift in emphasis from a strong adherence to an ineffective method toward greater emphasis on both modeling and engagement of users and designers. The emphasis has moved toward greater engagement of users and what is described as a more "experimental" approach to development, and created a transitional space for those involved in the project. In this social learning explanation, the shift is toward a greater balance between the engagement and imagination dimensions of the model.

Kirsch and Beath (1996)

In this third study, the researchers again analyzed participation in system development projects. Kirsch and Beath (1996) analyzed data from eight case studies as a way to understand the relationships between different modes of involvement, the processes of coordination between designers and manager, and the product of the design effort. The process of user involvement is examined in terms of how involvement is actually enacted, as apposed to how methodologies may be prescribed in the literature. The authors examine this relationship from several directions in discussions at the end of the chapter, but their initial focus in terms of theoretical direction of causation is that participants will enact a methodology, rather than just following it blindly. The product of design is also examined by looking at who makes the selection of system features.

These authors focus on the effect of involvement, or engagement as defined in the social learning model. The study identified three different patterns of user participation: token, shared, and compliant. Each is shown to have different implications for a set of outcomes: task-system fit of the resulting system and management of conflict among these outcomes.

The authors propose that these patterns (token, shared, and compliant user involvement) vary in terms of who contributes technical and domain knowledge to the project and who controls feature selection. Involvement by users also influences the coordination mechanisms employed, the level of conflict, and how these conflicts are resolved. The data are examined in a number of ways, but the emphasis is placed on understanding how engagement influences the process by which the project is coordinated (alignment) and by which the system is designed (imagination).

To the first point, the authors state that the "enactment [of user involvement] is as much the choice of the client as it is the choice of systems developers." This leads the authors to suggest that methods might focus less on the way that designers should try to engage users but more on developing mechanisms to elicit user knowledge. To the second point, regarding the influence of user involvement on the modeling and design process or the effect of engagement on imagination, the authors conclude that high user involvement is not always necessary for task-system fit. The findings show, however, that when the system design features were derived by a process of negotiation between users and designers, the process yielded two of the three highest quality designs in terms of task-system fit.

Using our social learning model, an alternative explanation is that the processes that engaged users and designers took into account what participants do (imagination) and how the learning process is managed (alignment). As a consequence, the engagement process struck a better balance among the three dimensions in the proposed model. Engaging in a complex and often ambiguous process can be troublesome, especially if there is a great deal of conflict. In this study of eight cases, the three cases that had the highest rating overall had the least conflict. And while selection of features plays an important role in determining fit, as pointed out by the authors, feature selection does not have to be controlled by users. But their engagement and participation in negotiating the design process yielded the two cases with the highest ranking overall.

Summary: Additional Insights Using the Social Learning Model

As noted, each of these studies discussed the interaction of the three dimensions in the pro-

posed social learning model. In each study, causal inference was not the primary object of their investigation, as each study undertook a process perspective in their research approach, which we acknowledge and appreciate. These studies collected and reported rich sets of data and offered thoughtful and insightful analysis, enabling us to revisit them from the perspective of the tensions inherent in the social learning model.

By using these particular studies as a baseline, we are able to explore alternative explanations for the results of each. That is, we can offer different, richer explanations for how the studies unfolded, and more importantly, how the results came about. The studies started with different foci: Boland with control and method, Wastell with modeling and design, and Kirsch and Beath with user involvement. As a result, the three studies examined their data using different theoretical perspectives and thereby derived very different causal explanations of what occurred.

The social learning model does not resolve the conflicting direction of causation implied by these earlier studies. Instead, the learning model provides a "both/and" rather than an "either/or" explanation. Our model shows the relationships between the dimensions in the model as interrelated, with tensions that need to be resolved, rather than the need to optimize any one of the dimensions.

Finally, we note that all three studies demonstrate the need to balance engagement and imagination. While Boland found that more engagement was related to more and better designs, and Wastell found that the activities of design helped to engage the two communities in a more effective social process, Kirsch and Beath found that varying combinations of user and designer involvement has differing effects, dependent on many other factors. As a consequence, simply trying to increase involvement of users does not necessarily lead to better designs. Alternatively, the availability of an innovative or a structured design processes will not insure users' participation, nor can the design process insure that those users will acquire a sense of involvement.

DISCUSSION AND CONCLUSION

This chapter has posited that the necessary exchange of knowledge between the designers and the users of information systems during the design process may be viewed as exchanges between two communities of practice. The chapter further suggests that the apprenticeship model of learning is an appropriate model for this knowledge exchange in which there is mutual learning. In this model, the user is the apprentice to the designer (when learning of technical capabilities) and the designer is the apprentice to the user (when learning of the system requirements and use). Apprenticeship conceptualizes knowledge as constituted in action, so separating the tacit from the explicit is not possible. Our knowledge exists in our competencies to perform or engage in action, and these competencies are formed in our learning through the negotiation of meaning. It is through this mutual apprenticeship process that we can grasp and articulate the meanings of the information we need to transfer. Mutual apprenticeship is a means by which both communities can learn, enabling the sharing of both the tacit and explicit dimensions of each knowledge domain.

Apprenticeship is the most accessible example of the benefits of both participation and nonparticipation and how the evolution of shared histories and development of the roles played by the apprentice and the master bring about the transfer of knowledge. If a master is asked to merely explain certain knowledge to the apprentice, the conversation would be flawed by the misunderstanding arising from the differing interpretations of the words that were used. However, through a process of engagement in a situated practice, development of competencies, and the evolution of identities, knowledge is transferred across communities

via the apprenticeship model. The architecture for learning provides focus for balancing the tensions among alignment, imagination, and engagement.

Changes in structure can allow a community to move beyond just transferring "know what" to sharing greater degrees of "know how" and "know why." By engaging in common practices, communities can understand greater degrees of the tacit dimension that exists in all knowledge (Brown & Duguid, 2001). However, even communities who work at the same practices can have differing ways of knowing. These differences result in knowledge being sticky and difficult to transfer, and they demonstrate the social dimensions of knowledge arising from the situated ways in which practices may develop.

By altering modes of participation in line with an apprenticeship model of learning and by supporting alignment and imagination through each community's engagement in practice, managers can reduce the difficulties of sharing knowledge across the communities of users and designers. Perhaps of greater value, the knowledge shared across these communities, through altering modes of participation and balancing dimensions of the learning process as defined in Wenger's model, can result in greater degrees of "know how" as well as "know what." Furthermore, communication of related practice associated with the knowledge transferred and communication of the historical reasons for the practices used and the meaning appropriated in activities express aspects of a "know why" dimension embedded in the community's way of knowing. Each of these changes should yield more creative designs and systems that have a greater degree of alignment with the organization's goals.

We examined several cases of success and failure from the perspective of the causal explanations put forth by the investigators and using the model proposed here. In particular, we found it enlightening to compare the balance among the three dimensions of the model in successful and unsuccessful projects, which showed how the former had exercised a better balance than the latter. Ultimately, alignment, imagination, and engagement must all be supported, but focusing too heavily on one dimension may disrupt the balance among them. Similarly, the various modes of participation in the apprenticeship model have the potential to benefit a learning process, but their implementation as changes to an overall process may have very subtle influences based on the number of participants and their role in the organization.

The model provides important insights into how apprenticeship and knowing across communities can contribute to the theory and practice of information system design. Through the development of learning environments that span communities and support engagement of practice and appropriate modes of participation, organizations can create, focus, and transfer system knowledge through an apprenticeship model of learning. For information systems researchers, the model provides new opportunities for examining and evaluating requirements definition approaches. All of the issues raised in this chapter require further investigation. Many opportunities exist for future research to further understand, validate, and extend this work.

For practitioners, the model provides insights into the importance of context in understanding what is known in organizations and the importance of practice in forming the way that we know it. For project managers and executives, creating an environment in which both designers and users are encouraged to be both masters and apprentices may well prove to be a critical factor for project success.

REFERENCES

Alavi, M. (1984). An assessment of the prototyping approach to information systems development. *Communications of the ACM, 27*(6), 556-563.

Alavi, M., & Leidner, D. E. (2001). Review. Knowledge management and knowledge management systems: Conceptual foundations and research issues. *MIS Quarterly, 25*(1), 107-136.

Allen, B. R., & Boynton, A. C. (1991). Information architecture: In search of efficient flexibility. *MIS Quarterly*.

Baskerville, R. L., & Stage, J. (1996, December). Controlling prototype development through risk analysis. *MIS Quarterly*, 481-503.

Beath, C. M., & Orlikowski, W. J. (1994). The contradictory structures of systems development methodologies: Deconstructing the IS-user relationship in information engineering. *Information Systems Research, 5*(4), 350-377.

Beyer, H. R., & Goltzblatt, K. (1995). Apprenticing with the customer. *Communications of the ACM, 38*(5), 45-54.

Boland, R. J. (1978). The process and product of systems design. *Management Science, 24*(9).

Boland, R. J. (1979). Control, causality and information system requirements. *Accounting, Organization and Society, 4*(4), 259-272.

Boland, R. J. (1984). Sense-making of accounting data as a technique of organizational diagnosis. *Management Science, 30*(7), 868-882.

Boland, R. J. (1987). In-formation in information system design. In R.L. Boland & R.A. Hirschheim (Eds.), *Critical issues in information systems research*. New York: Wiley.

Brown, J. S., & Duguid, P. (2001). Knowledge and organization: A social-practice perspective. *Organization Science, 12*(2), 198-213.

Brown, J. S., & Duguid, P. (2002). *The social life of information*. Boston: Harvard Business School Press.

Boland, R. J., & Tenkasi, R.V. (1995). Perspective making and perspective taking in communities of knowing. *Organization Science, 6*(4), 350-372.

Bryant, A. (2000). It's engineering Jim … but not as we know it. Software engineering: Solution to the software crisis, or part of the problem? In *Proceedings of the 22nd International Conference on Software Engineering* (pp. 78 – 87), Limerick, Ireland.

Byrd, T. A., Cossick, K. L., & Zmud, R. W. (1992). A synthesis of research on requirements analysis and knowledge acquisition techniques. *MIS Quarterly, 16*(1), 117-138.

Carmel, E., Whitaker, R. D., & George, J. F. (1993). PD and joint application design: A transatlantic comparison. *Communications of the ACM, 36*(4), 40-48.

Chan, Y. E., Huff, S. L., Barclay, D. W., & Copeland, D. G. (1997). Business strategic orientation, information systems strategic orientation, and strategic alignment. *Information Systems Research, 8*(2), 125-51.

Churchman, C. W., & Schainblatt, A. H. (1965). The researcher and the manager: A dialectic of implementation. *Management Science, 11*(4), 69-87.

Cook, S. D. N., & Brown, J. S. (1999). Bridging epistemologies: The generative dance between organizational knowledge and organizational knowing. *Organization Science, 10*(4).

Costello, R. J., & Liu, D.-B. (1995). Metrics for requirements engineering. *Journal of Systems and Software, 29*(1), 39-63.

Cougar, J. D. (1996). Creativity *& innovation in information systems organizations*. Danvers: Boyd & Fraser.

Eisenhardt, K. M. (1985). Control: Organizational and economic approaches. *Management Science, 31*(2), 134-149.

Hanks, W. F. (1991). Forward in situated learning: Legitimate peripheral participation, by Lave, J. and E. Wenger, Cambridge, UK: Cambridge University Press.

Hartwick, J., & Barki, H. (1994). Explaining the role of user participation in information system use. *Management Science, 40*(4), 440-465.

Hayes, N., & Walsham, G. (2001). Participation in groupware-mediated communities of practice: A socio-political analysis of knowledge working. *Information and Organization, 11*, 263-288.

Henderson, J. (1990, Spring). Plugging into strategic partnerships: The critical IS connection. *Sloan Management Review*, 7-18.

Hirschheim, R., & Klein, H. K. (1994, March). Realizing emancipatory principles in information systems development: The case for ETHICS. *MIS Quarterly*, 83-109.

Iivari, J. (1987, September). The PIOCO model for information systems design. *MIS Quarterly*, 401-419.

Ives, B., & Olsen, M. (1984). User involvement and MIS success: A review of research. *Management Science, 30*(5), 586-603.

Kahn, W. A. (1990). Psychological conditions of personal engagement and disengagement at work. *Academy of Management Journal, 33*(4), 692-724.

Kirsch, L. J. (1996). The management of complex tasks in organizations: Controlling the systems development process. *Organization Science, 7*(1), 1-21.

Kirsch, L. J. (1997). Portfolios of control modes and IS project management. *Information Systems Research, 8*(3), 215-239.

Kirsch, L. J., & Beath, C. M. (1996). The enactments and consequences of token, shared and compliant participation in information systems development. *Accounting, Management and Information Technology, 6*(4), 2221-154.

Kirsch, L. J., & Cummings, L. L. (1996). Contextual influences on self-control of IS professionals engaged in systems development. *Accounting,*

Management and Information Technologies, 6(3), 191-219.

Kyng, M., & Morten (1995). Representations of work: Making representations work. *Communications of the ACM, 38*(9).

Lamb, R., & Kling, R. (2003). Reconceptualizing users as social actors in information systems research. *Management Information Systems Quarterly, 27*(2), 197-235.

Larman, C. (2004). *Agile and iterative development: A manager's guide/Craig Larman.* Boston: Addison-Wesley.

Larzara, G. F., & Mathiassen, L. (1985). Mapping situations within a system development project. *Information and Management, 8*, 3-20.

Lave, J., & Wenger, E. (1991). *Situated learning: Legitimate peripheral participation.* Cambridge University Press.

Leonard-Barton, D., & Sinha, D. K. (1993). Developer-user interaction and user satisfaction in internal technology transfer. *Academy of Management Journal, 36*(5).

MIS Quarterly, 25(1): 107-136

Markus, M. L., & Robey, D. (1988). Information technology and organizational change: Causal structure in theory and research. *Management Science, 34*(5), 583-598.

Mason, R. M. (1991, Fall). The role of metaphors in strategic information systems planning. *Journal of Management Information Systems, 8*(2), 11-30.

Mens, T., & Eden, A. H. (2005). On the evolution complexity of design patterns. *Electronic Notes in Theoretical Computer Science, 127*(3), 147-163.

Mumford, E., & Olive, B. (1967). *The computer and the clerk.* London: Routledge & K. Paul.

Nature_Team. (1996). Defining visions in context: Models, processes and tools for requirements engineering. *Information Systems, 21*(6), 515-547.

Nelson, K. M., & Cooprider, J. G. (1996, December). The contribution of shared knowledge to IS group performance. *MIS Quarterly*, 409-432.

Nonaka, I., & Takeuchi, H. (1995). *The knowledge-creating company: How Japanese companies create the dynamics of innovation.* New York: Oxford University Press.

Ouchi, W. G. (1979). A conceptual framework for the design of organizational control mechanisms. *Management Science, 25*(9), 833-848.

Polyani, M. (1966). *The tacit dimension.* Garden City, NY: Doubleday and Co.

Reich, B. H., & Banbasat, I. (1996). Measuring the linkage between business and information technology objectives. *MIS Quarterly, 20*(1), 55-82.

Robey, D., & Markus, M. L. (1984, March). Rituals in information system design. *MIS Quarterly*, 5-15.

Salaway, G. (1987). An organizational learning approach to information systems development. *MIS Quarterly, 11*(2), 245-264.

Tamai, T. (1993). Current practices in software processes for system planning and requirements analysis. *Information and Software Technology, 35*(6-7), 339-344.

Vessey, I., & Conger, S. A. (1994). Requirements specification: Learning object, process and data methodologies. *Communications of the ACM, 37*(5), 102-113.

Von Hippel, E. (1994). Sticky information and the locus of problem-solving-implications for innovation. *Management Science, 40*(4), 429-439.

Wallace, L., Keil, M., & Rai, A. (2004). How software project risk affects project performance: An investigation of the dimensions of risk and an exploratory model. *Decision Sciences, 35*(2), 289-321.

Wastell, D. G. (1999). Learning dysfunctions in information systems development: Overcoming the social defenses with transitional objects. *MIS Quarterly, 23*(4), 581-600.

Wenger, E. (1998). *Communities of practice: Learning, meaning and identity*. Cambridge University Press.

Zmud, R. W., & Apple, L. E. (1992). Measuring technology incorporation/infusion. *Journal of Product Innovation Management, 9*(2), 148-155.

This work was previously published in International Journal of Technology and Human Interaction, Vol. 3, Issue 4 , edited by B. Stahl, pp. 13-32, copyright 2007 by IGI Publishing, formerly known as Idea Group Publishing (an imprint of IGI Global).

Chapter XXI
Successes and Failures of SAP Implementation:
A Learning Perspective

Tanya Bondarouk
University of Twente, The Netherlands

Maarten van Riemsdijk
University of Twente, The Netherlands

ABSTRACT

In this chapter, we conceptualize the implementation process associated with SAP_HR as an experiential learning one (Kolb, 1984), and analyze qualitative data collected using discourse analysis during a six-month case study. We saw that a lack of communication plus misunderstandings between the different parties involved in the project led to mistakes in working with the system. However, with encouragement from the "top" to improve learning, working with the system became easier for the whole group involved and for the individual users. Although Kolb's theory is widely acknowledged by academics as a fundamental concept that contributes towards our understanding of human behavior, we propose another use: to consider this theory in association with an IT implementation strategy to identify the mechanism of IT adoption in an organization.

INTRODUCTION

This chapter is about the implementation of information technology (IT). Although this topic has been debated for several decades, the practical arena is still confronted with the so-called "go-live" problems with IT projects being less successful than predicted.

It is widely recognized that "go-live" IT use often develops in a different way to that in the plans made, and that the degree to which the use of a technology corresponds to the anticipated rules and norms can vary considerably, depending on the organizational context, the type of IT, and the end users' awareness of the system. (Arkich, 1992; Bardram, 1998; Bikson & Eveland,

1996; Ciborra, 1996; DeSanctis & Poole, 1994; Orlikowski, 1996).

There has been much research with consequent recommendations on how to introduce a new IT to employees in order to minimize or avoid troubles during IT projects. However, IT introductions are still known to be time consuming, indirect, and sometimes impulsive developments, leading to a mismatch between the initial ideas behind the information technology, and its real use seen through the employees' perceptions and experiences.

So, why have we apparently learned so little from IT failures? There are two popular reasons. It is argued that traditional IT research, focused as it is on IT implementation factors, has failed to identify the true causes of failure (Sauer, 1999). Perhaps, the traditional factors and processes considered are symptoms of, rather than the reasons for, the failure and, if so, attacking the symptoms will not cure the disease. The other popular possible reason is that even if the identified failure factors *are* the causes of the IT failure, they are not easy to avoid (Kling, 1987). Arguably there is a third possibility: that the traditional studies do not mirror the interactive, complex reality of the IT implementation process in which users are involved.

Given this situation, this chapter proposes to look at IT implementation from an interactive prospective, focusing on the collaborations among users while working with the newly introduced technology. Almost all modern technologies have networked, or collaborative, fragments, and users are engaged in common tasks through these "fragments." With the rise of wireless, mobile, and Internet technologies on the one hand, and with integrated office environments on the other, organizations are increasing their demands for cooperative working. Cooperative "fragments" can often be recognized in various work situations ranging from document sharing, cross-functional and cross-departmental projects, to incidental correspondence between employees linked by a given task. Stand-alone computers nowadays are generally used only for trials and experiments in organizations, the most common situation sees workstations hooked up to an organizational network.

Fundamentally, users communicate with *one another* when using IT. The communications during an IT implementation project reflect a situation in which groups of users are developing a common understanding of the technology they are forced to (or want to) use through learning processes amongst themselves.

The importance of several aspects of learning within collaborative settings has been seen in various IT studies:

- Changes in technology may lead to changes in various aspects of professional competency such as knowledge, skills, and attitudes. These, in turn, can influence the ongoing use of the system. Hence, in theory, there is an ongoing process of professional and technological development which is referred to as a learning process by Neilson (1997).

- User groups have to adapt to a novel way of working when a new technology is introduced. Adaptive structuration theory has shown that not all groups do this in the same manner, and the adoption process, referred to as "appropriation," depends on the group processes and the way in which people interact with one another (DeSanctis & Poole, 1994; Hettinga, 2002; Ruel, 2001).

- In the "extended version" of the structurational perspective, Orlikowski (2000) proposes looking at "communication, mutual coordination, and storytelling" as important determining sources for engagement with the system (p.411).

Although some "feeling" for the topic now exists, and recent research has emphasized the importance of certain elements of learning for IT implementation, systematic insights are still lacking. In this chapter, we propose a new view on IT implementation; one that considers the learning processes as the key factor in "getting used" to a new system. To the end, we strive to answer the question as to the role of group learning in the IT implementation process, and to illustrate our answer with findings from a longitudinal case study.

In the following sections, we first briefly present the basics of learning, and especially of experiential learning, in IT implementation. We then discuss the research methodology, followed by the empirical results from a longitudinal case study in a Dutch university.

LEARNING AND IT IMPLEMENTATION

An examination of existing studies has revealed that there is little theoretical or empirical research with a particular focus on the role of learning in explaining and resolving the problems of implementing and using information technologies in organizations. The emerging studies that do attempt to address both organizational learning and information technology consider learning as an alternative antidote to the organizational struggles associated with IT (Robey, Boudreau & Rose, 2000).

The current view of the link between "learning" and "IT implementation" in the literature can be seen as two-fold: as formal training as a way to overcome knowledge barriers, and through the role of experience in IT implementation.

Literature on formal training in IT implementation usually focuses on the individual level and deals directly or indirectly with overcoming barriers to acquiring new knowledge in IT use.

The second, and the major, literature stream on learning and IT implementation results from research on experience-based organizational learning. There is strong evidence suggesting that an organization's own experiences provide

a knowledge base which guides future actions. Case study literature provides greater detail on the role of experience in IT implementation: some offer evidence of the benefits of experience in achieving a successful implementation (Caron, Jarvenpaa & Stoddard, 1994; Yetton, Johnston & Craig, 1994); while others illustrate the difficulties of learning from experience (Ang, Thong & Yap, 1997; Robey & Newman, 1996).

However, the reported studies do not discuss instances where organizations fail to learn from their own experiences. Another limitation is that the authors do not discuss the "competition" between recent and earlier events as sources of experience. How can an organization adapt an old experience to a new situation? Clearly, learning from experience is more complex than simply adjusting current actions based on previous outcomes. What are the common key issues and processes in experience-based organizational learning? How can one transfer conclusions from an IT experience in one company to another, and is this even necessary? Finally, when and where are the lessons applied and really learned? Such questions remain unanswered in the existing studies.

Organizational Learning

Before introducing our concept, we briefly discuss the main issues associated with organizational learning. This is presented in the literature as a combination of two different approaches: learning as an outcome or "intended product," and learning as a process. For example, Agyris and Schön (1978) define learning as a process of detecting and correcting error. Kolb (1984) stresses the importance of the transformation of human experience (the process) that leads to new knowledge (the result). It is also recognized that an outcome of the learning process could be a more experienced person, one who might have a changed self-concept (Jarvis, 1987). Marsick (1987) focuses on learning as acquisition, interpretation, or assimilation of information, skills, and feelings. The learning-as-object approach is still influential. However, of late, there has been an increasing emphasis on learning-as-process (Gourlay, 2006; Tsoukas & Vladimirou, 2001; Walsham, 2005). Learning is increasingly being seen as a process of drawing "distinctions within a collective domain of action, based on appreciation of context or theory" (Tsoukas and Vladimirou, 2001, p. 979). Leaning is further considered to take place only within communities, where human performance is articulated through social interaction (Walsham, 2005, p. 10).

This chapter focuses on the dynamic acting-interpreting learning that is "deeply involved in human processes of communication, and which cannot be divorced from the context" (Walsham, 2005, p. 7).

In this study, in an attempt to bring learning into IT implementation, we define learning as all the interactional processes through which users develop **their understanding of** a newly introduced technology and that helps them to implement it.

Experience-Based Learning

Within learning-as-process concepts, a further refinement is made in the direction of experiential learning (Kolb, 1984) in which the concept of "experience" is central. This provides an opportunity to "begin" the learning process *only after* the employees get a new technology and start working with it; that is when they gain "experience."

Learning involves the interplay between two interdependent dimensions of knowledge: acquisition and transformation. Knowledge acquisition requires an individual to resolve the tension between apprehension (concrete experience) and comprehension (abstract conceptualization). Apprehension requires an individual to accept new knowledge through direct experience with the world (feelings and emotions). In contrast, comprehension occurs when an individual obtains

knowledge through abstract concepts; in other words, when a person breaks down experience into meaningful events.

Transformation is another dimension of knowledge with a dialectical tension: between intention (reflective observation) and extension (active experimentation). During knowledge intention, a person learns by reflecting upon previously acquired knowledge. In contrast, learning by extension requires an individual to interact with an external environment.

In responding to the dialectical tensions of knowledge, individuals orchestrate their way around the cycle in a continuous process of interactions between personal and environmental demands (Kayes, 2002).

The learning cycle begins when one experiences the world through one's actions of "doing" (Dixon, 1994). This immediate, concrete experience is the basis for the next stage of "reflecting," which allows us to learn from our experiences. Observations are assimilated into a theory that makes sense of what we have experienced. The third step is abstract conceptualization, or "thinking." The final phase is "deciding," and actively testing the concepts that have been created from a real world experience. Following the fourth step, new implications leading to concrete action can be developed. Thus, one continually cycles through a process of collecting experiences, or a set of conceptualizations (Swieringa & Wierdsma, 1994).

Although there are other models of experiential learning, Kolb's theory continues to attract attention because of its completeness and generalizability. Since 1971, over 1,500 studies, refereed articles, dissertations, and papers have reflected the work of Kolb, and provided insights into a broad range of learning processes (Kayes, 2002). The basic "wheel" has appeared in a variety of guises. Argyris and Schön (1978) refer to a *discovery-invention-production-generalization* cycle of learning. Deming (1993) depicts a *do-check-act-plan* wheel. Kim (1993), basing his model on Kofman's version, sees an *observe–assess–design–implement* cycle. Senge, Kleiner, Roberts, Ross, and Smith (1994) build the wheel as *a doin- reflecting-connecting-deciding* process. Swieringa and Wierdsma (1994) refer to a *doing-reflecting-thinking-deciding* wheel. Crossan, Lane, and White (1999) describe the "4I" model as *intuiting-interpreting-integrating-institutionalizing*. As Schippers (2003) argues, "all proposed learning cycles state that it is important to experience or observe, reflect on the experience or observation, and decide or act accordingly" (p.16).

Kayes (2002) noted that Kolb had outlined the relationship between individual and social knowledge:

Apprehension of experience is a personal subjective process that cannot be known by others except by the communication to them of the comprehensions that we use to describe our immediate experience... From this it follows that there are two kinds of knowledge: personal knowledge, the combination of my direct apprehensions of experience and comprehensions I use to explain this experience; and social knowledge, the independent, socially and culturally transmitted network of words, symbols and images that is based solely on comprehension. (Kolb, 1984, p.105)

If we understand learning as changing knowledge and behavior through actions with IT, then we should acknowledge the importance of social experience and context in learning (Barrett, Cappleman, Shoib & Walsham, 2004; Thompson & Walsham, 2004; Tsoukas & Vladimirou, 2001), and therefore also the importance of interactions among individuals.

IT Implementation as Experiential Learning

Although Kolb's theory is widely acknowledged by academics as a fundamental concept that

contributes toward our understanding of human behavior, we propose another view: to see Kolb's theory as reflecting a kind of IT implementation strategy and suggesting a mechanism for IT adoption in organizations.

Learning begins with the experiences and actions of the targeted employees when a new IT is introduced. It is likely they will have to start operating with the system in order to execute their tasks. This process can develop from operating with the basic system modules in performing their everyday tasks through to searching for new techniques and possibilities present in the system (West, 2000).

The next activity in the learning cycle is *reflection* and this can occur at various points: after carrying out a few operations with the system, later during implementation, but also even before the system's introduction as future users discuss technology design issues. Discussions, open dialogue, focus groups, and meetings with a project team might well focus on speaking out about difficulties or perceived difficulties in using the system. Users might express doubts and suspicions, or trust and belief in the existing ways of solving IT-related difficulties, consider the possible reasons for, and the outcomes of, mistakes made when operating the system, or discuss errors that occur in working with various IT functionalities (Schippers, 2003; Stahl, 2000; Tucker, Edmondson & Spear, 2001).

The *conceptualization* process may also take on a great variety of forms, but will always lead to a shared interpretation of the system among the users (Mulder, Swaak & Kessels, 2002). They will share their understandings of the role of IT in the company and its intentions towards every member of the group, as well as the design intentions of the system's developers (Nelson & Cooprider, 1996; Hendriks, 1999).

Planning, when initiated by the users, aims to establish agreements on improving the use of the system. Employees may take the initiative to arrange additional training sessions, develop further instructions or manuals, or carry out other related activities. Developing policies in order to improve the use of a technology can become a crucial issue, especially if the users have never worked as a group before. For example, this might involve establishing responsibilities for making inputs and schedules for producing outputs. Decisions may also be made about the sorts of documents that should be submitted to the system, or about data traffic and classification (Hettinga, 2002).

We would emphasize that we do not see these steps as necessarily taking place in this order. However, the breakdown of the process into these steps is a logical one, and helps to understand the learning processes.

RESEARCH METHODOLOGY

Having conceptualized IT implementation as experiential learning, we should next justify the choice for interpretive research methods in this study. Firstly, an interpretive view corresponds fully with the theory of learning that we applied to IT implementation. It represents the idea that learners—the users of the technology—do not accept "the truth" about the IT as offered by the managers and project leaders, but actively construct their own views of it through their own experiences. Secondly, when talking about users' interpretations of a technology, these are seen as reflecting the nonstatic and repeated developments in their communications towards understanding and using a system.

A case study was conducted in order to provide examples to support (or contradict) the theoretical discussion on the implementation of IT as learning, and to clarify the contents of the learning processes. We did not set strict criteria for the company to be involved in this project, but it was important that it had a recently introduced information technology. In terms of the unit of analysis, the investigation focused on the end users within an IT project. The case study techniques,

that is, the research instruments, strived to build a platform for interpretive analysis and included document analysis, interviews, and participatory observations.

Collecting Empirical Data

We carried out a six-month case study in a Dutch university that was in the process of introducing SAP_HR. Data was collected using qualitative methods: semi-structured interviews, observations, and document analysis. The 24 interviews each lasted from one to 1 ½ hours. Five university HRM units were investigated in the research: the Service Centre HRM (SC_HRM), the Faculty of Social Sciences HRM (SS_HRM), the Faculty of Arts HRM (A_HRM), the Faculty of Geographical Sciences HRM (GS_HRM), and the Veterinary Laboratory HRM (AL_HRM).

Representatives of three groups of SAP_HR users were interviewed:

- Five employees involved in steering the project in the university, referred to here as project team members. They provided support for end users, carried out help-desk duties, maintained the functional and technical administration of the system, and analyzed on-going use of the system.
- Four leaders from the various faculties' HRM departments who were responsible for the personnel policy and administration. These were not active end users of the system themselves, but SAP implementation did bring changes to their departments.
- Fifteen end users: four salary administrators from the central Salary Department and eleven HR specialists from five HRM departments, including five key users who were seen as advanced users of the SAP_HR system. In this way we interviewed HRM specialists whose daily tasks had to be performed through the system.

The questions put during the interviews were in line with the operationalization shown in Table 1.

Transcripts of the interviews were checked and corrected by the respondents involved. Additional information was obtained during informal conversations and through participating in key-user meetings. We also studied relevant documents, namely, the Development Plan of the University "Perspectief 2010," the Project Plan and the Fit/Gap Analysis for the SAP_HR implementation, the plan for the SAP_HR pilot implementation, reports and notes from key-user meetings (04.02.2003, 18.02.2003, 04.03.2003), a special issue of the university newspaper (N26, 2001/02), plus the main manual and 36 sub-manuals covering the use of SAP_HR for the University.

Data Analysis

The collected data were analyzed using discourse analysis. Our primary concern was the social context of the technology use and the discourse that supported it. We distinguished four steps in our interpretation of the data (Van Dijk, 1997; Oevermann, 1996; Titscher, Meyer, Wodak & Vetter, 2000).

The first step involved gaining an overall impression of the views presented in the interviews and linking this to the context that was derived from the documents and observations. Knowledge of the context was crucial in order to understand and *feel* the implementation of SAP_HR. The second step aimed to describe the learning processes on the basis of text units from the interview transcripts. To achieve this, we had to distinguish and codify the text units from all the interview transcripts on the basis of our operationalization scheme. We used a qualitative approach along the lines indicated in the operationalization scheme ("strong – weak," "high – low," etc.).

Next, the third step involved identifying the significance and linguistic representation of each text unit. We wanted to reveal a range of semantic features such as vagueness of opinions, doubts, clarity, and hidden meanings, but also the factual representation of the text units for each component. Finally, the fourth step involved refining our conclusions.

FINDINGS: CONTEXT OF SAP_HR IMPLEMENTATION

Background of the SAP_HR Project

The university had a long history as a knowledge center in the fields of scientific research and higher education. Today, it is one of the largest institutions in the Netherlands, with more than 23,000 students, and 7,000 employees. It has 18 schools and 15 support and administrative units.

Table 1. Operationalization of IT implementation as a learning process

Learning Dimensions / Range	Components
1. Learning as acting: task-related operations undertaken with the system by users/ *Active - Passive*	• Operating with basic modules in performing everyday tasks • Searching for new techniques in the system
2. Learning as reflecting: communicating upon the extent to which the system supports task performance/ *Strong - Weak*	• Discussing difficulties in using the system • Comparing with other software experiences • Declaring individual problems in using the system
3. Learning as conceptualizing: the level of common meaning of the system regarding its role and functionality/ *High - Low*	• Clarity about the purpose of the system • Understanding the operation of the modules in the system • Attitudes towards system functionality
4. Learning as planning: activities that aim to reach agreements on on-going use of the system / *Strong - Weak*	• Arranging additional learning activities to improve use of the system • Developing policies • Evaluating intermediate results

By 1994, most of the faculties in the university were using a COMI-P personnel information system that was becoming outdated. The supplier no longer guaranteed updates or further development of COMI-P, and therefore there was felt a need to look for a new personnel IT system. In 1998, the directors of the faculties and other services determined the functional demands for the new system, which had to meet the following basic requirements:

- To have the ability to be integrated with the existing financial and salary administration software packages;
- To have clear and well-designed functionalities in the standard version; and
- To be easily adopted and implemented in the university environment.

On the basis of these specifications, the University Board made the decision in November 2000 to purchase the SAP_HR personnel management system. At that point, the university was already using SAP_Financial, the financial module from SAP®. In choosing SAP_HR, the organization hoped for a painless implementation trajectory based on their existing experience with SAP_Financial, and expected to achieve an easy match between their HR and financial administrations.

The SAP_HR Introduction in the University

In the annual university report on IT (2002), under the heading "Administration and IT" one can read the following statement:

The implementation of the personnel module within the SAP system reveals more outset problems than was expected, especially in management information reports and matching with the salary administration system.

Problems in matching with the salary administration system" in fact meant delays, mistakes, and other difficulties in the payment of salaries. The university's weekly newspaper published a small article that highlighted such problems (dated 14 March 2002, # 26):

Tens of employees have got less salary than they should have... Especially those who had any changes in their contracts since 1 January 2002 and those who had multiple short-term contracts. On the other hand, those employees whose contracts expired on the 1st of January 2002 continued to be paid... According to the project team, the origins of the problems are too complex.

A historical account of the SAP_HR implementation project is given below.

In December 2000, the university started searching for a consultancy firm to help with the implementation. In April 2001, a consultancy firm was chosen on the basis of its experience with both SAP® and IPA technologies.

The period April through December 2001 was expected to see a "fast implementation" of SAP_HR. The steering group looked for discrepancies between SAP_HR and the existing systems. Six project groups worked on different aspects of the implementation: realization, salary/IPA, acceptance, technique, conversion, and training. One unforeseen event which interfered with the project was that the expert from the consultancy firm who specialized in developing an interface with the IPA external salary system left the project. In October 2001, pilots took place in four units: the faculties of biology, pharmacy, and chemistry, and the P&O Service Centre. During November and December 2001, all the future users of the system took training courses. Preparation was carried out on technical issues such as conversion and transportation.

On January 1st 2002, SAP_HR was introduced in 12 faculties and in all the support and administrative services in the university. Two faculties refused SAP_HR, and kept their old personnel systems. In the opinions of the users, the introduction date for the new system was not ideal since it coincided with the introduction of a new Collective Agreement for the Dutch Universities (which had to be processed through personnel administration). Further, some units were restructured requiring further new paperwork.

Documents show that an evaluation of the implementation was already scheduled for March through April 2002, that is, three to four months after the SAP_HR introduction. However, shortly after the introduction, and continuing through to the summer of 2002, unexpected difficulties arose related to inputs and outputs to SAP_HR, and with sending data to the external IPA salary system.

The extent of the drama during the first 7 to 8 months was expressed in various ways. For example, we heard of about 3,000 mistakes being registered in the database with only a third being resolved, 450 e-mails in 6 months from the users reporting problems, 75 "crucial" problems that had to be resolved, 10-20 technical changes/improvements *per day*, and finally about 300-400 university employees who experienced problems in getting their salaries.

The first months were really terrible. We made inputs in accordance with our experiences and the knowledge we got from the course, but most of the time there were mistakes, and IPA rejected the data. As a result, employees did not get their salary. Sometimes this went on for some months. Mistakes could be very simple and unexpected, but they took a long time to identify. (Roy, A_P&O)

Now I am sure—if they want to do something like this again in the same way—I am leaving. I really mean that! It was just one big disaster from the beginning. People did not get any income for three months. It was terrible and unclear who was responsible for what. Many HRM specialists became sick....(Erik, SS_P&O)

We did not observe a "happy ending" to the SAP_HR implementation phase during our 6 months of involvement. However, at least the number of employees experiencing problems with their salaries had decreased from 300-400 in spring 2002 to 60-100 by March 2003.

Tasks and Responsibilities of the SAP_HR Users

After SAP_HR was introduced on January 1st 2002, the various HRM specialists were compelled to collaborate with each other. In total, there were about 50 users who worked in six different university units: four HRM departments from the faculties, the Service Centre's HRM, and the central Salary Department. They were located in various places: two in the administrative building on the university campus, three in other buildings on the same campus, and one in the historical center of the city. All the users had their own managers, either in their own HRM units or in the salary department as appropriate.

In terms of the SAP_HR implementation, each unit had two types of users: "regular" users and "key" users. Key users were responsible for correspondence with the project team, helping "regular" users, searching for new possibilities in the system, and attending special meetings.

At the time of our research, the personnel administrators were busy processing changes in the personnel files of the university employees. These files were either paper-based or based on SAP_HR. We found about 40 tasks performed using SAP_HR that could be grouped into ten categories: (1) appointment of an employee (subtasks concerning the appointment of a new employee or an external worker, stagier, and those with nil-contracts); (2) modification of basic information, payment information, working time registration and other data; (3) relocation processing; (4) promotion; (5) work time registration; (6) administration of leave (sabbatical, sick, parental, and pregnancy); (7) processing an optional model for employment conditions which is only in part executed through SAP_HR; (8) administration of declarations; (9) vacations; and (10) producing HR statistical reports and information management reports (sick leave reports, HR financial reports, etc.).

We observed some variations among the five units in terms of:

- The number of employees working in the HRM units: SC_HRM (11 employees), SS_HRM (9 employees), A_HRM (9 employees), GS_HRM (5 employees), AL_HRM (1 employee);

- The number of employees making inputs to SAP_HR: SC_HRM (all 11 employees), SS_HRM (3), A_HRM (2), GS_HRM (3), AL_HRM (1);

- In some of the HRM units, all the employees would perform all the HR administration-related tasks, while in others some were only responsible for communicating with the employees of the faculty while others performed key user tasks with SAP_HR; and

- The functions of key users were assigned differently. For example, in SC_HRM, all employees could represent the unit as its key user, while in others there were strict divisions.

Each faculty had its own special characteristics that influenced the use of SAP_HR in its HR administration. For example, the Service Centre was a special structure within the university that provided HRM services to more than 400 employees including those in three smaller faculties and more than 20 administrative and support services such as the university library, museum, and communication department. Another example is from the "GS" faculty where there were many short-term workers who did not work fixed hours and did not receive a regular salary. Student assistants generally fell within this category (flex workers)

in this faculty as they were usually appointed to execute specific tasks within projects. Of about 320 employees, 1/4 were classed as flex-workers.

These examples indicate how the task needs and divisions differed per unit based upon the "idiosyncrasies" of the faculties. As a result, the ways used to process HR information also varied, and these differences needed to be acknowledged in SAP_HR.

Changes Brought by SAP_HR for the Users

The interviews with the SAP_HR users showed that an apparently straightforward technical intention had brought with it many social changes. We have clustered these into three groups:

1. HRM administrators had increased responsibilities for the transactions they completed; as one of them noted:

With SAP we gained extra control, but also more responsibilities. We have to be very careful with all inputs. Earlier everything was on paper, but now we have to concentrate more intensively in order to avoid faults. (Roy, A_HRM)

2. Task interdependence had changed radically. Instead of being concerned only with internal paperwork within the faculties, all the inputs made by personnel administrators now became interdependent with the inputs of salary administrators, and over time with the IPA Salary Information System that was located outside the organization.

3. Unlike the old situation, online working with personnel and salary documents demanded standardization in the operationalization of the personnel and salary tasks and processes by the entire group of users. Whereas, as we have already discussed, the HRM units all had their own traditions and rules in the pre-SAP situation, the new circumstances

required clear definitions of all the terms and processes used. This reinforced inter-dependency between all the units.

LEARNING IN SAP_HR IMPLEMENTATION

We were able to distinguish two distinct periods in the implementation of SAP_HR: the first 6 to 8 months which were described as a "disaster" (time-1), and later when the situation had improved (time-2).

Learning as Acting

When they began to work with the system, the users strived to handle basic tasks such as input-ting personnel data, sick leave administration, time registration, and applying the right types of contracts through SAP_HR. They expressed the view that they were initially afraid to work with the system because they could not predict whether many of the transactions would be correct or not. In such cases, they preferred to contact a salary specialist or a key user and ask them to execute the task.

The users had to operate the system because it was necessary in order to perform their primary tasks. However, the intensity of use did differ from unit to unit. For example, based upon the interviewees' estimates, the Salary Department processed about 250 transactions per week and the A_HRM unit about 250 transactions per month, whereas the user in AL_HRM worked for no more than two hours per week with SAP_HR.

Initially, the users sensed a lack of time or motivation to search for new possibilities within SAP_HR but, after 6 months, the situation changed: they could now work with the system without asking for help every time, and they could begin to search for new possibilities in SAP_HR. For example, there was a special application called "Query" through which a user could generate a range of HR reports. The interviewees emphasized that they found it interesting to combine HR and financial data. All the key users had test versions of SAP_HR, with which they could experiment and search out new possibilities and produce reports. However, it was commented that these versions did not indicate any link to IPA, something that was essential for much of the work.

Learning as Reflecting

The interviewees expressed the view that, initially, there were no fruitful communications across the entire group of users. Opinions were expressed that no one wanted to admit their own mistakes and so always blamed others, for example:

Sometimes it was not only technical difficulties that caused the problematic situation. Correct and timely communication is very important. Even within those groups closely related to the salary administration groups we cannot always find consensus: when anything goes wrong, everybody is sure that they did their own job well, and the problem must be elsewhere. Such communications do not help to improve the situation, and we might face similar difficulties in the future. (Daniel, SAP technical administrator)

Lack of time was considered as the main reason for the lack of cross-communication, for example:

We did not communicate with the HRM units about the use of the system. We did not even think about that—there were so many mistakes that had to be corrected; it was easier to do this ourselves instead of talking with the HRMs. It was terrible that we had to correct all the inputs. (Karen, Salary Administration).

However, within the units, there were active discussions about the problems with the SAP_HR administration system. In the A_HRM unit, meetings took place every two weeks, and in SS_HRM every week. The personnel administrator from GS_HRM described the situation as follows:

We [the Personnel Department] worked together very well. We discussed difficulties and helped each other with this system. We made reports about mistakes ourselves, and the key-user took these to the regular meetings. In our faculty, we are lucky to have such a strong team. With all these SAP problems we became even closer to each other. (Tom, GS_HRM)

Gradually, after some months of working with SAP_HR, the users from the various units became more open in the discussions. They expressed enthusiasm for communicating across the entire group in this later phase of SAP_HR use:

Also we communicate with other HR managers to ask questions and share difficulties. In this way, people from the Service Centre helped us a lot at the beginning. We also found it useful to discuss SAP with the HRMs from the Social Sciences faculty. (Roy, A_HRM)

Key-user meetings became an important event for information exchange. The key users took the latest news to and from the meetings; and users started sending e-mails across the group with their questions. The meetings of key users became a strong group device; even non-key users attended in order to participate in the communication process. During the interviews, all the respondents acknowledged the importance of these meetings:

I like communicating with other users. During the key-user meetings we raise a range of questions and exchange our ideas. It is very helpful. Actually I am not a key-user, but I like to attend those meetings (together with the 'real' key-user from our unit) to gather all the news and to communicate with others. There, I always meet the

Salary Administration people and talk with them. I also visit them after each meeting—to chat face-to-face—otherwise we would communicate only by telephone. (Marijke, A_HRM).

Learning as Conceptualizing

All the interviewees were well-informed and understood the goals behind introducing SAP_HR. They gave two main objectives as being behind SAP_HR's introduction: replacing an outdated system, and matching the SAP modules already being used in the university. Those involved in the working project groups were all of the opinion that, by January 2006, the IPA system would be replaced by SAP_Payroll, and thought that SAP functionality would then become even more valuable.

The comment below from one of the interviewees shows the clarity of his awareness of the goals behind SAP_HR:

The system was introduced in January 2002 because of two reasons. Firstly, there was already SAP_Financial, and the financial department had worked with SAP for some time. I think the management desired to have the university's ICT from a single supplier. Another reason for the introduction of SAP_HR was that the contract with COMI-P had expired by January 1st 2002. (Roy, A_HRM).

None of the users however expressed a need for a new system and none of them felt an urgent need to replace the "old" technology. On the contrary, they stressed that the previous technology was reliable enough, simple, and worked correctly. An interviewee from the AL_HRM department gave several reasons why she did not need SAP_HR:

I think SAP_HR is a good system. You can do many things with it, but I don't need many things. For example, we have our own system for sick leave administration. The same applies to time registration - there is our internal ATREA system. This contains various special items such as overtime, working during the weekends or holidays, and evening work. It has existed for ten years already. Maybe it can be incorporated into SAP, I don't know. Therefore, I don't use the sick leave administration and time registration components in SAP_HR. I don't use the 'arrangements' application either. They do this task in the performance appraisal files and keep them on paper. With SAP, this would be extra work for me. Other examples of useless applications are the 'previous employer' field, and the 'children' and 'subscriptions' fields - I don't need them. (Monique, AL_HRM)

During the first 6 months, the users felt that they did not really understand how to operate SAP_HR. All the 24 interviewees commented that they lacked an understanding of the logic of the system. For example, a salary administrator said:

It was terrible that we had to correct inputs, and that we did not have enough knowledge about the system and how to work with it. We did not even have an image of a good input, and how a correct input should look. It was very confusing for us because one month an input 'A' was good and accepted by the IPA system, but the next month the same input 'A' was certified as bad and rejected by the same IPA. It was not clear what went on behind the screen. (Karen, Salary Administration)

The main complaints were about the lack of understanding of what was "behind the screen." It was not difficult to click the buttons, but they needed to foresee the outputs of the transactions and the connection with IPA which, at the beginning, seemed to be a big black box.

Based on many of the opinions expressed, the situation at the beginning could be characterized as one of high uncertainty. Most problems and their

understanding would only come from experience; they could not be predicted in advance:

The situation at the beginning could, in general, be characterized as one of high uncertainty – COMI-P was very rapidly replaced with SAP_HR. We got a new system, but we did not know sufficiently what to do. The biggest problem, and the highest priority, was to keep to the transaction deadlines. (Sandra, SS_HRM)

In fact, none of the project leaders realized that we – the HRM specialists – did not know about IPA. We had never worked with it. The end-users in their day-to-day work only see SAP screens. We were often confused because sometimes SAP_HR would allow us to input a number (as a code), but then it was then forbidden by IPA, etc. (Lucie, GS_HRM).

In assessing the users' attitudes towards the functionality of the system, we note that most opinions were negative. Criticisms concerned both technical and contextual aspects of SAP_HR. We have produced the following summary of criticisms that arose during the interviews:

- Making mistakes was "blind": a user could not understand why an input was wrong;
- Some problems were too difficult to solve;
- Employee classification in the system was too complex;
- Searching for new possibilities was limited as the system was very standardized;
- Producing historical overviews was impossible;
- The codes in SAP_HR were different from the codes in IPA, and therefore there was a need to memorize them;
- Useless functionalities (such as inputting educational data on the employees and data on their children which was not processed in calculating salary); and

- Some issues that are common in a university environment were not incorporated in SAP_HR (conference leave, sabbatical leave, and CAO à la carte).

One of the personnel administrators described her attitudes towards SAP_HR as follows:

In April 2002 I started to hate both the system and working with it. I had a feeling that everything I did went wrong, and that it was all about salaries and bonuses. (Monique, AL_HRM)

At the same time, the functional and technical administrators of the system were of the opinion that SAP_HR was very logical, technically reliable, and easy to use.

Learning as Planning

Arranging activities to improve system use became an observable occurrence after several months of practical experience. In the beginning, activities, if any, were initiated by the project team and not by the users. However, since spring 2002, as the interviewees themselves noted, the users have tried to initiate actions in addition to the key-user meetings. Thus, "informal discussions over a cup of tea" were arranged between the SS_HRM unit and the Salary Department. Discussions about certain transactions were also initiated outside of official meetings (e.g., the development of a report for the Executive Board).

We also discovered differences in the policies developed by the users in the various units:

- Control over transactions was organized in various ways, from triple control involving the head of the HRM unit, to double checking by the same user in AL_HRM;
- In GS_HRM, there was an agreement that the key user would decide whether to inform regular users about e-mails from the project team or not, in order not to "overload" them;

- Each HRM unit had its own time schedule within its faculty for making changes to personnel files, and they agreed a schedule with the Salary Department for providing them with the data that would guarantee timely salary payments; and
- In January/February 2003 (a year after the system was introduced), the Salary Department introduced "report forms" for those HRMs who had questions/problems in order to initiate discussions rather than just correcting the mistakes themselves.

All the interviewees noted that there were no evaluation rounds throughout the project.

DISCUSSION

Success of SAP_HR Implementation and the Role of Learning Processes

When we started the case study we knew that the SAP_HR implementation had developed many problems at the university. The users had struggled with problems associated with SAP_HR for 6 to 8 months before working with the technology became easier although still not fully enjoyable. After this initial period, the employees became more willing to cooperate with each other in order to develop their work with the technology. How did this develop?

After 8 months of preparation, the technology was introduced to the users on January 1st 2002. Although the users received instructions and participated in workshops about setting up and converting to SAP_HR prior to its introduction, they found that they were not ready to operate the system but lacked the option of rejecting it.

The introduction of SAP_HR was initiated and promoted by the top management in the university, and this choice of technology was never fully supported by the future users. SAP_HR use became obligatory with the objective of replacing what was seen in some quarters as the outdated COMI-P system and so standardizing HRM and salary administration in the organization.

What did the users experience and feel once SAP_HR had been introduced to them? Personnel administrators saw significant changes in their daily tasks: greater responsibilities for making online inputs, and more control over those inputs, the need to become interdependent with the salary administrators, and a need to collaborate with other personnel administrators whom they did not previously know. Salary administrators also gained new tasks: to control the inputs from the HRM departments, to collaborate with them, and to learn how to operate SAP_HR. One additional issue that complicated working with SAP_HR was that the interface with the external IPA salary system often obscured the SAP_HR inputs.

Stress, greater responsibilities, and uncertainty in making inputs, all brought about by SAP_HR, stimulated negative interpretive schemes about the technology among the users. They were unwilling to invest a lot of effort and were disappointed by the technology. Right from the beginning, the users perceived the system as not worth learning about, and in fact, worse than the previous technology. The negative opinions about SAP_HR strengthened daily as the users collected and accumulated disappointments, including seemingly small details and misunderstandings with the project team.

Neither did we see strong user participation in the project. Only the key users actively took part in the preparation and conversion of the system. A pilot for introducing the system took place in four units in the university. Although the users did not agree with the official, positive evaluation of this, their opinions were largely ignored.

Although a negative opinion about SAP_HR grew within the user group, use of the provided technology remained obligatory for the staff. Slowly, after 6 to 8 months, the interpretations of SAP_HR began to move in a positive direction.

The employees started to find ways of avoiding or overcoming the major problems they had found with SAP_HR.

The question is how does a group learning perspective help us to explain the developments in the SAP_HR implementation? We saw how group learning among the SAP_HR users developed from an initially low level to moderate after 8 months of using the system. This development was slow and this created difficulties for the users. The qualitative analysis of the transcribed interviews and documents has enabled us to distinguish and grade all the learning processes twice, at the beginning of the SAP_HR implementation and after 6 to 8 months (see Table 2).

The four learning processes all progressed in a positive direction over time although mutual adjustment processes progressed only slowly.

In terms of acting, the users progressed from being afraid to click the buttons at the beginning to attempting to generate a range of HR reports. The key users remained the most active, but the rest of the group also became more active. Everybody found routine administrative tasks easier to execute over time. Reflection among the targeted employees also developed progressively. Initially, discussions about SAP_HR implementation took place only at the microlevel, that is, within the units, and there were no fruitful interunit communications, not even between Salary Administration and the HRM departments. However, later, this developed with e-mail, telephone, and other informal ways of corresponding and discussing SAP_HR taking place across the units. The key-user meetings became especially popular.

The general understanding of the purpose of the system coincided with the reality. All the users were informed about the goals of SAP_HR and could express them correctly. However, they perceived it as useless, and they did not feel there had been any immediate need for a technological change in their tasks. We did not find users expressing needs in terms of SAP_HR, even during the later stages of working with it. Users'

Table 2. Development of the learning processes in SAP_HR implementation

	SAP_HR users – Learning January 2002	*SAP_HR users – Learning* August 2002
Learning as acting	Moderate	High
Learning as reflecting	Low	Moderately high
Learning as conceptualizing	Low	Moderate
Learning as planning	Low	Generally low

attitudes towards the functionality did not improve during the observed period and remained negative. Only key users appreciated the possibilities of generating reports. We did not discover any activities arranged by the ordinary users in order to improve their work with SAP_HR, in fact there were only two informal meetings and these were initiated by the SS_HRM department. Most policies were developed at the microlevel in the units (such as rules to control the inputs or processing CAO à la carte). There were no evaluation rounds established to assess the system, the project, or cooperation.

We found that, at the beginning of the project, the learning processes had mainly occurred at the microlevel within the units. Further, the interaction processes across the entire group of users were at a very low level during the first months following implementation. We attribute this to the initial lack of shared structural and nonstructural group features.

CONCLUSION

Our case study concerned the implementation of a personnel administration system in a university environment. A six-month investigation period allowed insights to be gained into the processes involved in adopting the system by the user group.

Learning among the SAP_HR users emerged as soon as the system was introduced. We ob-

served the slow but steady development of all the learning processes over time. Initially, the extent of the learning was not sufficient to handle the system, with interactions mostly taking place at the level of the units. The lack of communication and the misunderstandings across the entire group of users led to mistakes in working with the system when it was first introduced. The system triggered learning by calling for a redirection of all processes towards a new and larger community. After 8 months, learning moved towards stronger cross-unit cooperation and the exchange of users' experiences.

We began the theoretical discussion with an understanding of IT implementation as a user-centered process in which employees together develop interpretive schemes about a newly introduced technology. In this study, we based the concept of learning on the model of experiential learning by Kolb (1984) in which learning is considered as: (1) a process rather than simply outcomes; (2) a problem-solving process that is always practice-oriented; and (3) a mechanism for everyday activities, occurring both consciously and unconsciously. It is argued that learning within a group of users is more than simply the summation of individual learning processes. The character of group processes becomes more complex as they acquire a social context.

In answering the central research question – What is the role of experiential learning in IT implementation? – we would stress four issues: (a) learning is a process-based activity; (b) it rests on the interaction processes between members of a user group; (c) these processes begin when a new technology is introduced,; and (d) these processes lead to changes in knowledge about the IT and in users' behaviors (ways of operating the system).

The main role/function of learning processes in IT implementation is that they become a "hidden" mechanism in the IT implementation. Several theoretical components can be added here to articulate the strategic potential of experiential learning in IT implementation. First, there are two learning processes – acting and reflecting – that concern individual behavior. Observations have shown that these occur immediately after a technology is introduced to the targeted employees. Once users are "thrown to chaos" (Weick, Sutcliffe & Obstfeld, 2005), they have to (or choose to) experience it, and their next implicit step will be to judge it. The other two processes—conceptualizing and planning—bridge individual and group learning. These two steps concern "talking a situation into existence" (Taylor & Emery, 2000) and articulating and integrating labels.

We observed that verbally expressing concerns developed more extensively when groups of users established such characteristics as trust, knowing each other, and openness in risk-taking conversations (known as psychological safety) (Edmondson, 1999). These characteristics were seen to develop during the IT project.

Findings elsewhere have shown that group learning processes do not follow a linear sequence, but develop as cycles. Within a group, discussions occur both before and after actions and so it is difficult to distinguish a "point of departure" in an experiential group learning cycle.

Finally, we argue that learning can be considered as a "hidden" mechanism for speeding up or slowing implementation. As Weick et al. (2005) remarked, it is a micromechanism that can bring macro-changes. If a group of users appreciate the technological help provided for their tasks, share positive attitudes, help each other, and attribute

growth in performance to the system, they will learn the relevant issues concerning a technology. In so doing, the system will be discovered, "studied," and better understood, and through this the technology will become more relevant for the job tasks and easier to work with. This can lead to a better and quicker acceptance by the users. The opposite scenario was initially observed in our case study when the users only complained about the system, perceived it negatively, and convinced each other of its uselessness. Even small details that would be ignored in other situations received the attention of the group. In such a scenario, employees learn of issues that reinforce earlier negative attitudes. Their views became increasingly negative about the relevance of the system to their tasks, and they saw the technology as too complex to operate. Thus, the technology became "even less relevant" for their work in the opinions of the users, and they learned of issues that discouraged them from accepting the system.

Further research could greatly contribute to the understanding of the origins and differences in learning by taking into account differences in work environments. Insights could be gained by exploring IT implementation in various types of work and work environments (such as process-based, product-based, logistics-based, and administrative work). Determining whether there is a link between the type of work environment or the type of organization, group learning in IT implementation would add to the current findings.

Practical Implications

Our findings suggest that the main thrust of managerial support during the implementation of information technologies should be in promoting interaction processes geared towards adopting the system. We observed a number of good practices in the case study that did stimulate constructive learning. These were:

- Having a help desk or front/back office services on system functionality available for the users at any time;
- Creating and distributing a list of experts on the system's functionality within the group (generally these were the advanced users among the targeted employees) whose experience could be very helpful to others;
- Introducing an e-mailing list including all the users (setting up a hot-line chat room would be an alternative);
- Scheduling informal meetings (such as during coffee breaks) for the group of users;
- Agreeing how to involve new employees in using the system (what to explain to them, who is responsible, etc.);
- Distributing special notebooks amongst the users for ideas, proposals, and complaints; and
- Accepting proposals that come from the users and reacting to them (negotiating).

This list is far from exhaustive since it includes only those practices that we observed in the implementation of the SAP_HR system at the university. However, we did observe how all the above practices advanced learning in the "right" direction.

REFERENCES

Ang, K.-T., Thong, J.Y.L., & Yap, C.-S. (1997). IT implementation through the lens of organizational learning: A case study of INSUROR. In K. Kumar & J.I. DeGross (Ed.), *Proceedings of the 18th international conference on information systems (ICIS'97)* (December, 15–17) (pp. 331– 48). Atlanta.

Argyris, C, & Schön, D. (1978). *Organisational learning: A theory of action perspective.* Massachusetts: Addison-Wesley.

Arkich, M. (1992). The de-scription of technical artifacts. In W.E. Bijker & J. Law (Eds.), *Shaping technology/building society: Studies in sociotechnical change* (pp. 205–224). Cambridge, MA: MIT Press.

Bardram, J. (1998). Designing for the dynamics of cooperative work activities. In *Proceedings of the ACM 1998 Conference on Computer Supported Cooperative Work* (pp. 89–98), New York City, New York. ACM Press.

Barrett, M., Cappleman, S., Shoib, G., & Walsham, G. (2004). Learning in knowledge communities: Managing technology and context. *European Management Journal, 22*(1), 1–11.

Bikson, T.K., & Eveland, J.D. (1996). Groupware implementation: Reinvention in the sociotechnical frame. In M. Ackerman (Ed.), *Proceedings of the ACM 1996 conference on computer-supported cooperative work* (pp. 428–437). New York: ACM Press.

Caron, R.J., Jarvenpaa, S.L., & Stoddard, D.B. (1994). Business reengineering at CIGNA Corporation: Experiences and lessons learned from the first five years. *MIS Quarterly, 18*(3), 233–250.

Ciborra, C.U. (1996). Introduction. In C.U. Ciborra (Ed.), *Groupware & teamwork: Invisible aid or technical hindrance?* Chichester, U.K.: Wiley.

Crossan, M.M., Lane, H.W., & White, R.E. (1999). An organisational learning framework: From intuition to institution. *Academy of Management Review, 24*(3), 522–537.

Deming, W.E. (1993). *The new economists of industry, government, education.* Cambridge, MA: MIT Centre for Advanced Engineering Study.

DeSanctis, G., & Poole, M. (1994). Capturing the complexity in advanced technology use: Adaptive structuration theory. *Organization Science, 5,* 121–147.

Dixon, N. (1994). *The organisational learning cycle*. London: McGraw-Hill.

Edmondson, A. (1999). Psychological safety and learning behavior in work teams. *Administrative Science Quarterly, 44*(2), 350–383.

Gourlay, S. (2006). Conceptualizing knowledge creation: A critique of Nonaka's theory. *Journal of Management Studies, 43*(7), 1415–1436.

Hendriks, P. (1999). Why share knowledge? The influence of ICT on the motivation for knowledge sharing. *Knowledge and Process Management, 6*, 91–100.

Hettinga, M. (2002).*Understanding evolutionary use of groupware*. Telematica Instituut Fundamental Research Series (Report No. 007, TI/FRS/007). Enschede, The Netherlands: Telematica Instituut.

Jarvis, P. (1987). *Adult learning in the social context*. London: Croom Helm.

Kayes, D.C. (2002). Experiential learning and its critics: preserving the role of experience in management learning and education. *Academy of Management, Learning & Education, 1*(2), 137–150.

Kim, D.H. (1993). The link between individual and organizational learning. *Sloan Management Review, 35*(1), 37-50.

Kling, R. (1987). Defining the boundaries of computing across complex organizations. In R. Boland & R.A. Hirscheim (Eds.), *Critical issues in information systems research*. Chichester: Wiley.

Kolb, D.A. (1984). *Experiential learning. Experience as the source of learning and development*. Englewood Cliffs, NJ: Prentice-Hall.

Marsick, V. (1987). *Learning in the workplace*. London: Croom Helm.

Mulder, I., Swaak, J., & Kessels, J. (2002). Assessing group learning and shared understanding in technology-mediated interaction. *Educational Technology and Society, 5*(1), 35-47.

Neilson, R.E. (1997). *Collaborative technologies and organisational learning*. Hershey, PA: Idea Group Publishing.

Nelson, K.M., & Cooprider, J.C. (1996). The contribution of shared knowledge to IS group performance. *MIS Quarterly, 20*, 409–429.

Oevermann, U. (1996). Becketts 'Endspiel' als Prüfstein hermeneutischer methodologie. Eine interpretation mit den verfahren der objektiven hermeneutik. In. H.-D. König (Ed.), *Neue Versuche,Becketts Endspiel zu Verstehen* (pp.93 – 249). Frankfurt: Suhrkamp.

Orlikowski, W.J. (1996). Improvising organizational transformation over time: A situated change perspective. *Information Systems Research, 7*, 63–92.

Orlikowski, W. (2000). Using technology and constituting structures: A practice lens for studying technology in organizations. *Organization Science, 11*(4), 404–428.

Robey, D., Boudreau, M.-C., & Rose, G.M. (2000). Information technology and organisational learning: A review and assessment of research. *Accounting Management and Information Technologies, 10*, 125–155.

Robey, D., & Newman, M. (1996). Sequential patterns in information systems development: An application of a social process model. *ACM Transactions on Information Systems, 14*(1), 30–63.

Ruël, H.J.M. (2001). *The non-technical side of office technology; managing the clarity of the spirit and the appropriation of office technology*. The Netherlands: Twente University Press.

Sauer, C. (1999). Deciding the future for IS failures not the choice you might think. In W.

Currie & R. Galliers (Eds.), *Rethinking management information systems* (pp. 279–309). Oxford University Press.

Schippers, M. (2003). *Reflexivity in teams.* Unpublished doctoral thesis, University of Amsterdam.

Senge, P.M., Kleiner, A., Roberts, C., Ross, R.B., & Smith, B.J. (1994). *The fifth discipline field book: Strategies and tools for building a learning organisation.* New York: Currency Doubleday.

Stahl, G. (2000). A model of collaborative knowledge building. In *Proceedings of the Fourth International Conference of the Learning Sciences* (pp. 70–77), Ann Arbor, Michigan.

Swieringa, J., & Wierdsma, A. (1994). *Becoming a learning organisation.* Addison-Wesley Publishing.

Taylor, J., Emery, J, van (2000). *The emergent organization: Communication as its site and surface.* Mahwah, NJ: Erlbaum.

Thompson, M.P.A., & Walsham, G. (2004). Placing knowledge management in context. *Journal of Management Studies, 41*(5), 724–747.

Titscher, S., Meyer, M., Wodak, R., & Vetter, E. (2000). *Methods of text and discourse analysis.* London: Sage Publications.

Tsoukas, H., & Vladimirou, E. (2001). What is organizational knowledge? *Journal of Management Studies, 38*(7), 973–993.

Tucker, A.L., Edmondson, A.C., & Spear, S. (2001). When problem solving prevents organizational learning (Working Paper No. 01-073). Harvard Business School.

Van Dijk, T.A. (1997). *Discourse as structure and process* (Vol. 1, 2). London: Sage.

Walsham, G. (2005). Knowledge management systems: Representation and communication in context. *Systems, Signs & Actions, 1*(1), 6–8.

Weick, K., Sutcliffe, K.M., & Obstfeld (2005). Organizing and process of sensemaking. *Organization Science, 16*(4), 409–421.

West, M.A. (2000). Reflexivity, revolution and innovation in work teams. In M.M. Beyerlein & D.A. Johnson (Eds.), *Product development teams* (Vol. 5, pp. 1–29). Stamford, CT: JAI Press.

Yetton, P.W., Johnston, K.D., & Craig, J.F. (1994, Summer). Computer-aided architects: A case study of IT and strategic change. *Sloan Management Review,* 57–67.

This work was previously published in International Journal of Technology and Human Interaction, Vol. 3, Issue 4, edited by B. Stahl, pp. 33-51, copyright 2007 by IGI Publishing, formerly known as Idea Group Publishing (an imprint of IGI Global).

Chapter XXII
Anthropomorphic Feedback in User Interfaces:
The Effect of Personality Traits, Context and Grice's Maxims on Effectiveness and Preferences[1]

Pietro Murano
University of Salford, UK

Patrik O'Brian Holt
The Robert Gordon University, Scotland

ABSTRACT

Experimental work on anthropomorphic feedback in user interfaces has shown inconsistent results and researchers offer differing opinions as to the potential usefulness of this style of user interaction. A review of the literature shows that experimental work can be improved and enhanced by taking into account issues that characterise human-human communications. Results from three experiments are reported that exhibit the previously observed inconsistencies but this is arguably a function of task context. An alternative explanation is that the results are a reflection of the cognitive nature of tasks. Overall, the results point the way to further and future results in terms of refining procedures but also in terms of theoretical focus.

INTRODUCTION

Human-computer interaction (HCI) focuses on the dialogue between users and computers through the user interface (UI). The past 20 years have seen UI developments that range from command line interfaces through to modern graphical user interfaces (GUIs) based on the now familiar desktop metaphor. Regardless of the type of UI, the feedback provided to users is an important area of concern and remains an active area of research. Feedback to users as part of human computer dialogue can take a number of forms such as text, graphics, animation, speech, and so forth. Anthropomorphic interfaces are a way of delivering feedback that in some way takes on the characteristics or role of a human. Typically, anthropomorphism involves a nonhuman entity, usually some element of the user interface, taking on some human quality (De Angeli, Johnson & Coventry, 2001), for example a talking dog or a cube with a face that can talk. A well known example is the Microsoft Office Paper Clip. It could also be the actual manifestation of a real human, such as a video of a human (Bengtsson, Burgoon, Cederberg, Bonito & Lundeberg, 1999).

It can be argued that from a common sense point of view anthropomorphic interfaces ought to be of some benefit to users as these in some way or form mimic 'natural human communication or characteristics.' However, the usefulness (however defined) and desirability of anthropomorphic interfaces remains a moot issue. While some researchers provide evidence and argument in favour of using anthropomorphic interfaces (e.g., Agarwal, 1999; Cole, Massaro, Rundle, Shobaki, Wouters, Cohen, et al., 1999; Dertouzos, 1999; Guttag, 1999; Koda & Maes, 1996a, 1996b; Maes, 1994; Zue, 1999), others have cast doubt on this style of interaction (e.g., Shneiderman 1997; Shneiderman & Plaisant, 2005).

The work reported and discussed in this chapter aims to review previous work showing that results have been inconsistent and there is not agreement as to the potentially positive or negative influences of anthropomorphic UIs. It will be argued that experiments need to take into account context and Grice's maxims as outlined by Reeves and Nass (1996). Results from experiments will be presented that cast some light on effectiveness of anthropomorphic interfaces in relation to context and the potential role of Grice's maxims.

As part of developing user support and increased usability, Microsoft has experimented with anthropomorphic feedback using work by Nass, Steuer, and Tauber (1994) as a foundation. This work formed part of the Persona Project where an anthropomorphic character, a parrot called Peedy, is used to help a user find and play music tracks. A user can interact with the system using automatic speech recognition (ASR) (e.g., Bradshaw, 1997).

Support for the effectiveness of anthropomorphic feedback can, for example, be found in the work of Maes (1994) and coworkers who use the term 'personification' to characterise this type of feedback.

Maes (1994) has developed an agent for e-mail handling that is described in the context of agents as 'learning' in the sense of becoming an effective personal assistant. This agent takes the form of a drawn face where various facial expressions are used to convey a particular state of the agent, for example 'working' and so forth. This 'facial agent' can be applied in various other contexts (e.g., scheduling meetings). Experimentation with this type of agent showed that users produced positive comments and seemed to indicate that users judged the input of the agent to be helpful. This can be taken as an indication of positive approval of anthropomorphic feedback.

Further support for anthropomorphic feedback is provided by Koda and Maes (1996a, 1996b) who conducted experiments in which users played poker using the Web. The aims were to understand:

1. The effect of having a face and facial expressions in an interface, such as required attention, engagement, and distraction.
2. What kind of facial features (gender, humanity, and realism) make the agent look intelligent, likeable, and comfortable to work with.
3. Whether people's impression of an agent is determined by its representation, by its performance, or both.

4.   Whether people's impression of the faces differs by their gender or opinion about personification.

The experimental results from this poker playing context showed that a face at the user interface is judged to be more likeable, engaging, and comfortable as compared to other feedback styles. It was also concluded that the impression individuals had of a face differed if the face was on its own or if the person interacted with the face to accomplish some task. It should be noted that the results are based on measures that relate to aesthetic issues but not on user approval concerning what helped them most. No results are provided as regards effectiveness.

While the results from the work presented above relates to specific contexts and tasks, then the results and their implications can be generalised to be relevant to issues of judging usefulness and preferences (or liking) for anthropomorphic feedback. Overall, the work of Maes can be regarded as providing support for anthropomorphic feedback, but other reported work provides less support.

Quintanar, Crowell, Pryor, and Adamopolous (1982) compared anthropomorphic textual feedback and non-anthropomorphic textual feedback in a quiz setting. The quiz involved questions about 'psychology' to undergraduate students. The aim was to determine the user's thoughts about the system and the effectiveness of the two types of feedback. Some of the findings relevant to this research include the fact that they found users perceived the anthropomorphic feedback to be 'more human, less honest and slightly less courteous' compared with the non-anthropomorphic feedback. Quintanar et al. also found the anthropomorphic textual feedback to be more effective, that is, the quiz scores were higher and the amount of time spent thinking about the questions presented and the system's responses was higher. While the study only focused on textual feedback (e.g., as opposed to video or synthetic

characters) it does imply that anthropomorphic feedback is effective.

However, the opposite could be concluded from a study by Brennan and Ohaeri (1994) based on latencies. This was a study involving 33 subjects in between users design involving six travel situations and the booking of airline tickets. Each subject was randomly allocated to 1 of 3 types of textual feedback (anthropomorphic, fluent [e.g., 'where are you departing from?'] and telegraphic [e.g., needed: point of departure]). The following hypotheses were tested:

1.   'People will model the kind of language used by a computer agent,
2.   Systems that present complete-sentence responses and error messages will take more effort to deal with than those that present more concise messages,
3.   People will (mis)attribute more intelligence to systems that use complete sentence responses, and
4.   People will (mis)attribute more intelligence to natural language (NL) systems that present themselves as anthropomorphic by using the first person pronouns in messages.' The main results and conclusions obtained were that users of the anthropomorphic feedback seemed to 'treat the computer more like a social partner.

The anthropomorphic feedback 'led to more indirect requests and conventional politeness.' Based on the ratings given by users in each group, users did not rate one type of feedback as being more intelligent than another.

The facts to consider about this study are that it does not give any conclusive results regarding effectiveness or user approval. It could be considered a negative point that the anthropomorphic messages led to longer inputs. This however may not be a problem within certain contexts and if the user was to accomplish a task more effectively. This is in the sense of being able to achieve the task compared to perhaps not being able to complete the task without errors. Further, the anthropomorphism was in the form of text, and hence the whole area of video or synthetic characters was not explored or considered. More recent work has not been supportive of anthropomorphic feedback.

Rickenberg and Reeves (2000) have shown empirically that experimental participants felt more anxious when an animated character appeared to be monitoring their 'online' activities. This was particularly the case with participants who felt that 'others' could affect the outcome of 'tasks' they may have been doing. However, the role of anxiety is not clear as the authors suggest that it may be both negative and positive depending on the context. These results however do not clarify issues relating to effectiveness and judged preferences.

Shneiderman and Plaisant (2005) have argued that some users may feel deceived and maltreated with anthropomorphic interfaces and that not using anthropomorphism helps to 'clarify the differences between people and computers.' It is also argued that anthropomorphic feedback can be effective for educational software or agents like Avatar guides. However, this argument lacks clarity as the differences between people and computers are usually clear, as it is obvious if one is interacting with a hardware component such as a computer or another person, regardless of anthropomorphism or not. Where the difference may be less clear is in the case of a program attempting to deceive a user, perhaps in some form of Turing test. They also give some examples of failed attempts in the area of anthropomorphic interfaces, such as 'Tillie,' a bank teller, and the 'Postal Buddy,' which had been designed to provide postal services. Further, systems such as Ananova ™ are also cited as a failure. To date, when one accesses the Ananova ™ Web site (www. ananova.com), the anthropomorphic character is not visible, suggesting a reflection of failure.

The work reviewed above is not exhaustive but give examples that are typical of the current state of research; that is, that results are not consistent in showing the potential value of anthropomorphic feedback, either in terms of effectiveness or user preference. It would seem that results are dependent upon type and style of anthropomorphic feedback, the nature of tasks, and measures used. However, it is contended that a number of inconsistencies can potentially be explained by taking cognisance of evidence produced by Reeves and Nass (1996). This evidence can be used to provide a theoretical framework that has not been present in previous work.

Refinements to Thinking about Anthropomorphic Feedback

The selective literature review presented above represents typical experiments and corresponding results that are not altogether consistent in providing support or otherwise for the effectiveness and preferences for anthropomorphic feedback. As with any area of study, research on anthropomorphic interfaces may well benefit from a detailed analysis of experimental tasks, procedures, and context, which may include more refined definitions and taxonomic analysis. While this is outwith the scope of the work reported and discussed, the literature reviewed in the section above suggests several areas of focus. Additionally, in 1996 Reeves and Nass published a book titled *The Media Equation: How People Treat Computers, Television, and New Media Like Real People and Places* in which they argue that people react to and interact with various modern media as if they were engaging in human dialogue or interpersonal interactions (Reeves & Nass, 1996). Four specific areas of concern and improvement emerge:

1.   In human-to-human communication matching modalities is an important norm and part of effective exchange of information. For

example, more effective communication is achieved if an e-mail message is responded to with another e-mail as opposed to using another modality such as a telephone. This should also apply to human computer dialogue. For example, if an electronic voice provides feedback to the user it would be better to have the system accept input verbally from the user.

2.   In anthropomorphic user interfaces using photographs of people, users show similar reactions and responses as when interacting with other people. Here, there are clear implications for the design of anthropomorphic user interfaces as well as research in the area.

3.   Activity in anthropomorphic user interfaces needs to be controlled carefully. In particular, this relates to activity in the periphery that may cause attention switching or distraction that would contribute confounding variance.

4.   Subjective judgments or ratings provided by users should be collected independently of the computer that delivered the experimental trials. This is arguably more natural and avoids problems with social rules.

At a more general level Reeves and Nass (1996) argue that in natural interpersonal communications between two or more people there is inherent politeness that is acquired and developed from an early age. In a loose way politeness can be defined as a set of rules that govern how humans communicate with each other face-to-face. It would therefore seem reasonable to attempt to take into account rules of politeness when designing anthropomorphic feedback as this would provide a more natural form of communication and increased ecological validity (Neisser, 1976) in studies.

Reeves and Nass (1996) discuss and recommend that four maxims put forward by Grice (1967) should be taken into account in the design

of anthropomorphic user interfaces and feedback. In any experimental work the guidelines that arise from the maxims would apply equally to anthropomorphic feedback as well as other forms of feedback used as controls. These can be summarised as seen in Box 1.

The refinements and clarifications suggested by Reeves and Nass (1996) do not appear to have been taken into account in anthropomorphic feedback studies.

EXPERIMENTAL STUDIES

The preceding review has shown that research on anthropomorphic feedback has yielded results that are ambiguous and therefore resulting discussions are not in agreement as to the potential usefulness or efficiency of this style of human computer dialogue. It was also argued that experimental work can be improved and enhanced in a number of aspects.

This section presents three experiments[2] that attempt to investigate the efficiency and reactions to anthropomorphic user interfaces within different task contexts. The work reported also takes into account the work of Reeves and Nass (1996) that indicates

1.   The use of matching modalities.
2.   The separation of user evaluation from the experimental computer.
3.   The avoidance of peripheral motion in stimuli.

Additionally, the experiments were designed to take account of Grice's Maxims (Grice, 1967) of interpersonal communication by presenting unambiguously truthful information that is clear and relevant to the experimental tasks.

Given the ambiguous nature of research on anthropomorphic feedback and user interfaces it is not realistic to attempt to formally state hypotheses. However, a hypothetico-inductive approach (Popper, 1959) was adopted which is in line with current thinking for example in research in psychological sciences (Hayes, 2000). This allows for a more exploratory approach to collect data in a systematic way to address more general questions.

Experiment One

The context of the first experiment is software support for in-depth understanding. This was specifically English as a foreign language (EFL) pronunciation. The language group used was Italian native speakers who did not have 'perfect' English pronunciation. Participants with imperfect pronunciation were recruited so that the learning (or correctional) features of the software could be applied. Experimental software was specifically designed to automatically handle user speech via an automatic speech recognition (ASR) engine (IBM, 1998). Furthermore, in line with EFL literature (Kenworthy, 1992; Ur, 1996) exercises were designed and incorporated as part of the software to test problem areas that Italian speakers have when pronouncing English.

Experimental Design and Variables

In this experiment two feedback conditions (independent variable) were used: video (anthropomorphic) and two-dimensional images with guiding text (non-anthropomorphic). All participants were subjected to both experimental feedback conditions (within subjects design) while carrying out a number of exercises. The feedback was randomly allocated, that is, a particular exercise phrase was not linked to the same feedback.

The anthropomorphic feedback condition took the form of a video of a real EFL tutor giving feedback. This was specifically designed and recorded for this experiment. This in effect was a set of dynamically loaded video clips which were activated based on the software's decision concerning the potential error a user had done (if no errors were made no pronunciation corrections were made by the software). This type of feedback was compared against a non-anthropomorphic equivalent. In this case two-dimensional diagrams with guiding text were used. The diagrams were facial cross-sections aiming to assist a user in the positioning of their mouth and tongue and so forth for the relevant pronunciation of a given exercise. This type of feedback was based on EFL principles explored by Baker (1981, 1998). No feedback type was ever tied to the same exercise, that is, feedback was randomly assigned to an exercise.

The dependent variables were effectiveness and user satisfaction. Effectiveness was measured by the number of times a participant self-corrected themselves once an error was flagged by the system. Specifically, three points were allocated

Box 1.

Quality	The information provided to users should be truthful in the sense of being believable and unambiguous	
Quantity	This can be regarded as falling within the boundaries of general HCI guidelines of the right amount of feedback at the right speed. As regards anthropomorphic feedback a key issue would be to emulate natural communications in terms of amount and speed	
Relevance	Feedback should not contain any data that is not relevant to the message and the aims of the communication	

if the participant corrected themselves properly on the first attempt. Two points were allocated if the participant corrected themselves on the second attempt and one point was allocated if the self-correction took three attempts. No points were given if the participant failed to self-correct themselves on the third attempt.

User satisfaction of the specific feedbacks was elicited from the participants by a questionnaire using Likert type scales (Likert, 1932), where a low score (e.g., 1) was a negative response and a high score (e.g., 9) was a positive response. Participants were asked subjective questions relating to the general user interface and the actual feedback they had encountered.

Users

The participants were all Italian. All the participants spoke English with an Italian accent. They did not have 'perfect' English skills. They were all adult males and females with different backgrounds. In all 18 participants were recruited from a university population.

Procedure

Each participant was treated in the same manner and each session was conducted in the same laboratory with constant environmental conditions. For each participant the experiment lasted approximately one hour. The first stage consisted of the participant being briefed regarding the purpose of the experiment. The second stage involved each participant being asked to read a short paragraph of material so that it could be informally ascertained if their standard of read English was approximately equivalent to the other participants. It was found that no one had perfect English and each participant was judged to have a similar level of English. The third stage involved the participants being shown a brief demonstration of the system (without revealing any of the exercises). The fourth stage involved the participants trying out the exer-

cises and randomised feedback if an error was made. If an error was flagged by the system, the participant would take the feedback and then attempt the same exercise again. This was done a maximum of three times.

Results

A summary of the results for the 18 Italian participants is shown in Table 1 below.

The summary shows that anthropomorphic feedback (video) appears to be more effective than non-anthropomorphic feedback. Table 2 shows the results from a t-test for related samples and this confirms a statistically significant difference at the 0.05 level.

Overall, participants tended to prefer anthropomorphic feedback as shown in Table 3. However, this observed difference is not significantly different, as shown in the t-test presented in Table 4.

Overall the results suggest that the anthropomorphic feedback is more effective than the non-anthropomorphic feedback, in this specific context. However, for user satisfaction, the results were less clear as no significance was found, despite the overall means showing a preference for the anthropomorphic feedback.

Table 1. EFL experiment (effectiveness scores)

N = 18	Mean	Standard Deviation
Video	1.69	1.06
Diagrams and Text	0.94	1.15

Table 2. Comparison of video vs. diagrams and text

DF = 17	Comparison of Video Vs. Diagrams and Text
t-Observed	2.14
t-Critical (5%)	1.74

Table 3. Overall user preferences

	Overall User Preferences	
	Mean	Standard Deviation
Video	8.06	1.39
Diagrams and Text	7.22	2.05

Table 4. Comparison of video vs. diagrams and text (subjective preferences)

DF = 17	Comparison of Video Vs. Diagrams and Text (subjective preferences)
t-Observed	1.55
t-Critical (5%)	1.74

Experiment Two

The context for the second experiment was feedback for online systems usage. This was specifically concerned with the use of UNIX commands by novices. This was an interesting area as typically novice users of UNIX commands can find it difficult to master the concepts of the command structure and to remember relevant commands in the first place (Herrera & Ward, 2005). Software was designed to emulate a small session at the UNIX shell covering a subset of UNIX commands. An ASR engine was used which allowed the users to 'query' the system verbally. The 55 users for the experiment were recruited from the university 'student population' and were complete novices to UNIX commands.

Experimental Design and Variables

As in Experiment 1, anthropomorphic and non-anthropomorphic conditions (independent variable) were compared, in this instance video vs. textual feedback. Participants did both conditions

(within subjects design). The anthropomorphic feedback consisted of dynamically loaded video clips of a person giving the command verbally for the current context the user was in. The feedback was prompted by the user requesting the feedback from the system (through the ASR engine). The non-anthropomorphic feedback was a textual equivalent (based on the structure used in Gilly [1994]) appearing in a supplementary window next to the main X-Window. A small set of typical tasks a beginner might engage in, involving UNIX commands, were designed. Four tasks were designed, where each involved file management issues. Specifically these were to do with displaying files in a certain manner and compressing and deleting files. Since the users had no knowledge of UNIX commands, they were obliged to make use of the feedback if they wished to complete the tasks. The two types of feedback were randomly assigned to the tasks so that one task was not tied to one type of feedback. For example, if the first task invoked the anthropomorphic feedback, the second task would invoke the non-anthropomorphic feedback or vice versa.

The dependent variables for this experiment were the aspects measured for attempting to discover effectiveness and user satisfaction. Effectiveness was measured by the number of attempts a participant had to carry out in order to complete a task, number of visible signs of frustration on the part of the user (e.g., frowning and expletives etc.), and if the actual tasks were completed as specified. A points system was used for obtaining one score for each user. For each task each participant (unknown to them) was started on 10 points. Each incorrect attempt meant that one point would be subtracted. Each hesitation observed, meant that 0.5 points were subtracted. A completed task resulted in the score remaining as described. An incomplete task resulted in a further 1.5 points being subtracted from the score. The points system was used to represent fairly a participant's overall results (e.g., hesitations observed ought to have less weight than an actual error). Further, the various elements of the points system were considered to be related. For example, a participant not completing a task may have been due to hesitations. The scores were plotted on a normal distribution plot diagram, which showed the data to be approximately normally distributed. This increased confidence in the points system. User satisfaction of the specific feedbacks was elicited from the participants as in Experiment 1.

Users

All the participants taking part in the study were adults. Males and females took part. In all, 53 participants were recruited from a university population.

Procedure

Each participant was treated in the same manner and each session was conducted in the same laboratory with constant environmental conditions. For each participant the experiment lasted approximately 30 minutes. The first stage consisted of the participant being briefed regarding the purpose of the experiment. The second stage involved the participant being given a brief overview of the system. The third stage involved the participant being given a list of tasks to accomplish. The fourth stage involved the participant in actually invoking the feedback (randomised) and then attempting to carry out the task based on the feedback received. When a task was completed, the participant was able to proceed to the next task, until all tasks were completed. During this time the experimenter recorded the attempts, hesitations and task completions of the participant.

Results

A summary of the results for efficiency are shown in Table 5 below and these do seem to show a trend that favours anthropomorphic feedback.

A related sample t-test was carried out (see Table 6 below) and showed a significant differ-

ence between the two conditions at a level below 0.01.

Table 7 shows the participant subjective opinions gathered through the postexperiment questionnaire which indicated a preference for anthropomorphic feedback.

A related samples t-test showed that this indication of preference is statistically significant at the 0.05 level.

Hence it is concluded that anthropomorphic feedback is more effective and preferred by users in the context of online feedback for systems usage.

Experiment Three

The task context of Experiment 3 was online factual delivery in the form of direction finding. Software was developed to give directions to two different but equivalent locations (equivalence was concerned with approximately equal

Table 5. UNIX commands experiment (effectiveness scores)

N = 55	Mean	Standard Deviation
Video	18.73	2.09
Text	14.56	3.26

Table 6. Comparison of video vs. text

DF = 54	Comparison of Video Vs Text
t-Observed	10.21
t-Critical (5%)	1.67

Table 7. Overall user preferences

	Overall User Preferences	
	Mean	Standard Deviation
Video	7.53	1.40
Text	6.35	1.84

Table 8. Overall user preferences significance test

DF = 54	Overall User Preferences Significance Test
t-Observed	3.83
t-Critical (5%)	1.67

distances and difficulty), where the aim was for participants to physically find their way to the given locations. The participants were to use the directions given to them by the system. Hence it was a prerequisite that the participants should not know where the locations were before taking part in the experiment. Therefore 53 participants were recruited from a university student population. A pretest questionnaire was used to determine that those recruited to take part in the experiment did not know the locations being used for the experiment.

Experimental Design and Variables

Two conditions were used: anthropomorphic feedback and a non-anthropomorphic equivalent with participants doing both (within subjects design). Anthropomorphic feedback consisted of dynamically loaded video clips of a person giving directions to a location. This was compared with an equivalent non-anthropomorphic feedback consisting of a map with guiding text based on the principles found in Southworth and Southworth (1982). One type of feedback was not tied to one particular location in the experiment. The feedback was rotated so that each location had either type of feedback at some point in the experiment. The two locations were balanced in terms of distances covered and complexity of turns required to reach the location.

The dependent variables for this experiment were effectiveness and subjective satisfaction. Effectiveness was measured by observing and recording the number of incorrect turns taken by the participant (i.e., turns deviating from the prescribed route), number of visible hesitations (e.g., participant asking the participant where to go next), and if the final destination was found. Subsequently the same scoring formula was applied to the collected data as described in Experiment 1 above (incorrect attempt was replaced with wrong turning). User satisfaction ratings were collected as in Experiments 1 and 2 above.

Users

All 55 participants taking part in the study were adults and were recruited from a university population.

Procedure

Each participant was treated in the same manner and no major variations in the external environment were observed. For each participant the experiment lasted approximately 30 minutes. The first stage consisted of the participant being briefed regarding the purpose of the experiment. The second stage involved the participant being given a brief overview of the system. The third stage involved the participant being given a list of the two tasks to accomplish. The fourth stage resulted in the system running and giving the participant the directions to the first location. Then the participant had to physically leave the laboratory and walk to the location. As this happened the experimenter followed the participant (i.e., walked behind the participant at a distance of a few meters) and noted any wrong turns taken, any visible hesitations, and finally if the location was actually found. When this task was completed, the participant and experimenter returned together to the laboratory where the second task with the different feedback mode was undertaken in a similar manner.

Results

A summary of results for the main experimental conditions are presented in Table 9 below and indicate that anthropomorphic feedback is less efficient as compared to non-anthropomorphic feedback. Table 10 shows the results of a comparison using an F-test (one way ANOVA).

The F-test shows a significant difference at the 0.05 level in favour of non-anthropomorphic feedback.

Preferences were less clear and a summary gathered from the postexperiment questionnaire is shown in Table 11.

A t-test for related groups (see Table 12) did not show a significant difference between the two feedback conditions.

Overall, the results for effectiveness suggested that the map with guiding text feedback was more effective. However there was no difference for subjective preferences. As debriefing took place at the end of the experiment it was revealed that many of the users liked very much the idea of having 'someone' giving them directions rather than using the map.

Table 9. Direction finding experiment (effectiveness scores)

N = 53	Mean	Standard Deviation
Video	8.09	1.90
Map	8.58	1.4

Table 10. F-test results - diagram vs. video

DF = 52	Comparison of Diagram(Map) Vs Video
F-Observed	1.85
F-Critical (5%)	1.60

Table 11. Overall user preferences

	Overall User Preferences	
	Mean	Standard Deviation
Video	6.42	1.68
Diagram (Map)	6.74	1.62

Table 12. Overall user preferences significance test

DF = 52	Overall User Preferences Significance Test
t-Observed	0.99
t-Critical (5%)	1.67

CONCLUSION AND DISCUSSION

The experimental work reported shows that anthropomorphic feedback does result in greater efficiency but these results are not consistent across the three experiments. As discussed in the first section, this type of inconsistency is something that characterises work in anthropomorphic user interfaces. Taking account of work such as that by Reeves and Nass (1996) and Grice (1967) has not yielded unambiguous results.

However, the effectiveness of such feedback is dependent on the domain of concern or context. Hence certain domains appear to not be suited to anthropomorphic feedback, such as the domain for online factual delivery, particularly the direction finding context. This is also confirmed by the suggestion based on other research discussed by Dehn and van Mulken (2000). However as the third experiment showed, users still like seeing and interacting with anthropomorphic feedback even if it is not the best mode of feedback for them to achieve their tasks. Context dependency has been observed in other work, for example, learning and anthropomorphic feedback (Moreno, Mayer & Lester, 2000; Moundridou & Virvou, 2002).

The results for the user satisfaction aspect are less clear. The mean scores generally show that the anthropomorphic feedback was well received. However, the statistical test did not show an acceptable level of significance for the English as a foreign language pronunciation (although the observed difference is close to being significant) and direction finding contexts. There was significance found for the UNIX commands context, in favour of the anthropomorphic feedback.

These results suggest the conclusion that it would be better for designers of feedback to include anthropomorphic feedback in the domains shown to be better suited to such a style. For the domains not suited to anthropomorphism, it clearly needs stating that a suitable non-anthropomorphic feedback should be used instead. Since the results for user satisfaction are less clear, it may be suitable to combine non-anthropomorphic feedback with some form of anthropomorphic feedback with the option of removing a particular feedback should users find it unsatisfying. This would allow the users to have the best of both kinds of feedback with the easy option of tailoring their user interface to their own preferences.

An alternative explanation for the observed results can be suggested and is more oriented towards the cognitive nature of the tasks used in the three experiments reported. While the context differed in Experiments 1 and 2, it can be argued that both shared a cognitive dimension of verbal processing. In both experiments participants were asked to follow verbal instructions but in different contexts. The verbal instructions were delivered through text or diagram (non-anthropomorphic) or by a video of a person (anthropomorphic). In both experiments anthropomorphic feedback was shown to result in greater efficiency. In both experiments participants expressed a preference for anthropomorphic feedback although this observation just fails to reach significance in Experiment 1.

In Experiment 3 participants also followed instructions in the context of direction finding.

As in the other experiments the anthropomorphic condition involved a video of a person giving instructions while the non-anthropomorphic condition used a map and text. In this context anthropomorphic feedback was less efficient. Here, it can be argued that the cognitive dimension is spatial processing. This argument sets Experiment 3 apart from the first two experiments and may indicate why efficiency was poorer for anthropomorphic feedback. Spatial information is arguably better conveyed through visual information such as maps with some verbal information or delivering spatial information through human speech may result in some form of interference.

This alternative explanation does not replace the potential importance of context but rather adds another dimension for further and future study.

The issues discussed above provide a reasonable explanation based on empirical findings concerning the reasons for the anthropomorphic feedback being more effective (in two of the three contexts tested). However the user satisfaction ratings are much less clear. Although the mean scores regarding user satisfaction are positive towards the anthropomorphic feedback, only one of the three contexts revealed significance in the results.

Despite the fact that humans tend to apply social rules whilst interacting with a computer, as Reeves and Nass (1996) found, when more realistic tasks and domains are used the implication is that effectiveness and user satisfaction cannot be assumed with the use of anthropomorphic feedback. If the results for effectiveness and user satisfaction had been significant for all domains, then it could be tentatively argued that they are applicable to most other domains. Therefore, this means that much more work is required to determine which domains and specific contexts benefit from using anthropomorphic feedback. Additionally, attention needs to be paid to the cognitive nature of tasks in relation to domains as these two variables may interact. It is tempting to suggest that context and cognitive dimensions may, at least in part, account for the inconsistent results observed in anthropomorphic feedback studies but only further work will clarify these issues. Human communication is a complex phenomenon and applying it in human-computer interaction should not be anything but a complex activity.

Ultimately, a taxonomy of possible domains and suitable types of feedback could be devised over time. If this was available and based on empirical findings, user interface designers could be helped when they are faced with the many decisions they have to take when designing user interfaces.

A further area that would need investigating is feedback in a virtual reality setting and investigating feedback for pilots under various working conditions. Such investigations could lead to some interesting findings and perhaps a more comprehensive taxonomy of the kind suggested in the previous paragraph.

Concerning interface designers it is suggested that they should not automatically assume that one kind of feedback is categorically better than another. Ideally if various types of interface or feedback are being considered, the best approach would be to test and evaluate relevant options. The aim of interface designers should be to develop user interfaces that are easy to use, intuitive, easy to come back to, and easy to learn. Designers should avoid obliging users to adapt their ways of working and communicating for the sake of the software they are using.

ACKNOWLEDGMENT

The authors would like to acknowledge the support of Professor Tim Ritchings, The School of Computing, Science and Engineering, University of Salford; School of Computing, The Robert Gordon University, Aberdeen; Department of Computer Science Heriot-Watt University, Edinburgh. Farid Meziane for his advice in preparing the initial working draft of the journal version of this chapter.

REFERENCES

Agarwal, A. (1999). Raw computation. *Scientific American, 281*, 44-47.

Baker, A. (1981). *Ship or sheep? An intermediate pronunciation course.* Cambridge University Press.

Baker, A. (1998). *Tree or three? An elementary pronunciation course.* Cambridge University Press.

Bengtsson, B., Burgoon, J.K., Cederberg, C., Bonito, J., & Lundeberg, M. (1999). The impact of anthropomorphic interfaces on influence, understanding and credibility. In *Proceedings of the 32nd Hawaii International Conference on System Sciences*, IEEE.

Bradshaw, J.M. (1997). *Software agents.* Menlo Park, CA: AAAI Press/MIT Press.

Brennan, S.E., & Ohaeri, J.O. (1994). *Effects of message style on users' attributions toward agents.* Paper presented at the CHI '94 Human Factors in Computing System.

Cole, R., Massaro, D.W., Rundle, B., Shobaki, K., Wouters, J., Cohen, M., et al. (1999). *New tools for interactive speech and language training: Using animated conversational agents in the classrooms of profoundly deaf children.* Paper presented at the ESCA/SOCRATES Workshop on Method and Tool Innovations for Speech Science Education.

De Angeli, A., Johnson, G.I., & Coventry, L. (2001). The unfriendly user: Exploring social reactions to chatterbots. In *Proceedings of the International Conference on Affective Human Factors Design,* London. Asean Academic Press.

Dehn, D.M., & van Mulken, S. (2000). The impact of animated interface agents: A review of empirical research. *International Journal of Human-Computer Studies, 52,* 1-22.

Dertouzos, M.L. (1999). The future of computing. *Scientific American, 281,* 36-39.

Gilly, D. (1994). *UNIX in a nutshell.* Cambridge, MA: O'Reilly and Associates.

Grice, H.P. (1967). Logic and conversation. In P. Cole & J. Morgan (Eds.), *Syntax and sematics 3: Speech acts* (pp. 41-58).

Guttag, J.V. (1999). Communications chameleons. *Scientific American, 281,* 42-43.

Hayes, N. (2000). *Doing psychological research.* Milton Keynes: Open University Press.

Herrera, D., & Ward, N. (2005). Training wheels for the command line. In *Proceedings of the 11th International Conference on Human-Computer Interaction (HCI International),* New Jersey. Lawrence Erlbaum Associates.

IBM (1998). IBM *ViaVoice 98 user guide.* IBM

Kenworthy, J. (1992). *Teaching English pronunciation.* Harlow: Longman.

Koda, T., & Maes, P. (1996a). Agents with faces: The effect of personification. In *Proceedings of the 5th IEEE International Workshop on Robot and Human Communication, IEEE.*

Koda, T., & Maes, P. (1996b). Agents with faces: The effects of personification of agents. In *Proceedings of the HCI '96, British HCI Group,* London. British Computer Society.

Likert, R. (1932). A technique for the measurement of attitudes. *Archives of Psychology, 140,* 55.

Maes, P. (1994). Agents that reduce work and information overload. *Communications of the ACM, 37*(7), 31-40.

Moreno, R., Mayer, R. E., & Lester, J. C. (2000). Life-like pedagogical agents in constructivist multimedia environments: Cognitive conse-

quences of their interaction. *In Proceedings of the ED-MEDIA 200* (pp. 741-746), Chesapeake, Virginia. AACE Press.

Moundridou, M., & Virvou, M. (2002). Evaluating the persona effect of an interface agent in a tutoring system. *Journal of Computer Assisted Learning, 18,* 253-261.

Murano, P. (2001a). *A new software agent 'learning' algorithm people in control. Paper presented at the International Conference on Human Interfaces in* Control Rooms, Cockpits and Command Centres. UMIST, UK: IEE.

Murano, P. (2001b). *Mapping human-oriented information to software agents for online systems usage people in control.* Paper presented at the International Conference on Human Interfaces in Control Rooms, Cockpits and Command Centres. UMIST, UK: IEE.

Murano, P. (2002a). *Anthropomorphic vs. non-anthropomorphic software interface feedback for online systems usage universal access theoretical perspectives, practice and experience* [Lecture Notes in Computer Science (C)]. Springer.

Murano, P. (2002b). Effectiveness of mapping human-oriented information to feedback from a software interface. In *Proceedings of the 24th International Conference on Information Technology Interfaces* (pp. 24-27). Cavtat, Croatia.

Murano, P. (2003, July). *Anthropomorphic vs. non-anthropomorphic software interface feedback for online factual delivery.* Paper presented at 7th International Conference on Information Visualisation (IV 2003) An International Conference on Computer Visualisation and Graphics Applications (pp. 16-18), London, England.

Nass, C., Steuer, J., & Tauber, E.R. (1994). *Computers are social actors.* Paper presented at the CHI '94 Human Factors in Computing Systems – 'Celebrating Interdependence,' Boston, Massachusetts. ACM.

Neisser, U. (1976). *Cognition and reality.* San Francisco: W. H. Freeman and Co.

Popper, K. (1959). *The Logic of scientific discovery.* London: Hutchinson.

Quintanar, L.R., Crowell, C.R., Pryor, J.B., & Adamopoulos, J. (1982). Human computer interaction: A preliminary social psychological analysis. *Behaviour Research Methods and Instrumentation, 14*(2), 210-220.

Reeves, B., Lombard, M., & Melwani, G. (1992). Faces on the screen: Pictures or natural experience. *International Communication Association.*

Reeves, B., & Nass, C. (1996). *The media equation: How people treat computers, television and new media like real people and places.* Cambridge University Press.

Rickenberg, R., & Reeves, B. (2000). The effects of animated characters on anxiety, task performance, and evaluations of user interfaces. In *Proceedings of the CHI 2000* (pp. 329-336).

Shneiderman, B. (1997) Direct manipulation vs. agents: Paths to predictable, controllable, and comprehensible interfaces In J. Bradshaw (Ed.), *Software agents* (pp. 97-106). Menlo Park, CA: AAAI Press.

Shneiderman, B., & Plaisant, C. (2005). *Designing the user interface: Strategies for effective human computer interaction.* Boston: Addison-Wesley.

Southworth, M., & Southworth, S. (1982). *Maps a visual survey and design guide.* Boston: Little, Brown and Co.

Ur, P. (1996). *A Course in language teaching: Practice and theory.* Cambridge University Press.

Weiss, N.A. (1999). *Introductory statistics.* Boston: Addison Wesley.

Zue, V. (1999, August). Talking with your computer. *Scientific American, 281,* 40.

ENDNOTES

[1] A shorter version of this chapter was presented at the Seventh International Conference on Enterprise Information Systems, Miami, USA, 24-28 May 2005.

[2] Summaries of certain aspects of the experiments have been presented prior to analysis in Murano (2001a, 2001b, 2002a, 2002b, 2003)

This work was previously published in International Journal of Technology and Human Interaction, Vol. 3, Issue 4, edited by B. Stahl, pp. 52-63, copyright 2007 by IGI Publishing, formerly known as Idea Group Publishing (an imprint of IGI Global).

Chapter XXIII
Several Simple Shared Stable Decision Premises for Technochange

Richard Diamond
University of East Anglia, UK

ABSTRACT

This study explores decision premises that were used to manage and stabilise a complex technochange programme in a financial institution. Decision premises were extracted from business maxims, principles and rules using linguistic techniques. In the paper, the premises are juxtaposed with their consequences. The evidence of documents, observable practices and software configurations supports the analysis. It is found that decision premises form a hierarchical, self-causal as well as self-contradictory system of reasoning that was applied over any individual situation, particularly a conflict. By virtue of being several but not many, decision premises reinforce the 80-20 rule of many consequences stemming a few causes. In the case firm, decision premises were used in order to make technochange efficient as well as institute cost-saving and business ownership of software development. But there were drawbacks of intensified politics, software development delays, short-sighted capability decisions and work fragmentation for the front-line employees.

INTRODUCTION: DECISION PREMISES AND IT MANAGEMENT

In organisations, many decisions and processes are based upon premises that go without question.

Everyone is familiar with decisions, which appear irrelevant or inefficient at the moment, but turn out to be wise. The wisdom, in part, is about the benefit of continuity. Good decisions are typically made within a system of premises, be it an explicit corporate strategy or not-so-obvious top managers' beliefs about how to run a business. A list of beliefs can be short and simple, but they usually comprise a densely connected system with certain hierarchical relations between beliefs.

Having the benefit of hindside, after the exploration of top managers' decision premises, I propose that their disregard of circumstances and workplace issues is an outcome of dynamics rather than intention. Critical management researchers observed that organisational growth does not provide opportunities to improve the contemporary workplace that is characterised as tense and fragmented (Marchington, Grimshaw, Rubery & Willmott, 2005). Organisation behaviour researchers observed the self-contradictory expression and double-bind of middle management's position, as managers needed to demonstrate sympathy and make necessary changes at the same time (Huy, 2002).

What makes it harder to make good decisions is a degree of lock-in that occurs in complex projects of technology implementation, because 'small' decisions mount up and make future changes expensive. Also, organisation-wide implementation of information systems or any other high technology is inseparable from change in business processes, culture, and strategy. In order to conceptualise this, Lynne Marcus (2004) introduced the idea of *technochange*. Central to technochange are the ideas of interdependence and diversity of initiatives and outcomes. In highly interdependent circumstances of technochange, it is difficult to either forecast the results of individual decisions or follow a logical and elaborate strategy. It is also difficult to forecast how much of resources will be spent, committed, or gained. Scientific and operational research methods provide only limited assistance in such forecasting. Therefore, a study of 'primitive' but practical ways of complexity managements of operations would be a contribution. This chapter makes an initial step towards the objective. It utilises understandings of applied linguistics and coaching practice in order to identify a system of decision premises as 'a map of the world,' within which managers make decisions in technochange projects.

DEFINITION AND DYNAMICS

The term 'decision premises' was introduced by March and Simon (1958). Other names were 'business maxims,' interpretative schemes, and cognitive maps. I consider three dimensions to a definition of decision premises that shed light on how decision premises operate. The dimensions are presuppositions, frames, and beliefs.

Presupposition is an implication of a statement that remains logically true, whether or not the statement itself is true (Bandler & Grinder, 1975). For example, a business process might or might not have an owner, but it is presupposed that there is ownership. For another example, a decision might be made to fix a flaw in software because it will save future costs, or the same flaw can be left based on the same premise of the necessity of making the most economical decisions about costly IT.

An epistemologist would say that every activity or communication is made within a frame that defines its meaning (Bateson, 1972). Alternatively, meaning of a communication can derive from its context and surrounding communications. Frames are a construct of a higher logical order. For example, the frame of a strategy-away day is different from the frame of a board meeting. The term 'technochange' is a frame itself as it regulates broader consequences than the term 'software update' would.

Term 'decision premises' presupposes, literally, that decision premises do not exist in isolation. Typically, there are several, but not many, decision premises and they form a system with its own self-developing (sometimes self-referential) logic. Therefore, personal development literature talks about 'belief systems' and 'value systems.' In this study, beliefs are treated as something that is either described by managers or observed in behaviour, documents, or decisions. Therefore, a clear boundary is set in order to prevent psychodynamic and psychoanalytical interpretations. With these brief definitions at hand, we only highlight the linkages between decision premises and the dynamics of human values.

Operation Out of Stable Decision Premises

Decision premises about 'how to manage' are generalised from rich experience and ongoing evidence. But when such a generalisation is formed, it is applied *over* any individual situation. Thus, decision premises are oriented towards process and structure, rather than content.

Decision making occurs within 'a model of the world' that is only a model. In order to raise awareness about this, Gregory Bateson (1972) points out that 'the map is not the territory.' Hence, the value of a belief system is not in being true but in providing guidance. It is *useful* to operate out of certain beliefs in order to get things done, even and especially if actual circumstances are not favourable. Under complexity and uncertainty, humans naturally and gainfully adhere to their familiar beliefs (Weick & Sutcliffe, 2001). This strategy also helps to economise on information processing and avoid information overload.

In the world of business, talented, highly paid and irreplaceable consultants and CEOs are those who internalised a good system of decision premises that, in turn, facilitates core competencies (Miles, 1982; Prahalad & Hamel, 1990). Such value systems are hard to imitate and replicate. The mental habits of holding a vision and treating decision premises as always-true presuppositions make their impact on reality strong, enduring, and observable. Thus, for talented managers 'territory is the map;' they utilise technology, people, and organisational resources in their attempts and achievements of change of reality.

RESEARCH METHODOLOGY

Search for Decision Premises

The chapter is based on a longitudinal empirical case study of a retail bank, referred to as *Alpha*. A breadth of data was collected about Alpha's IT and business operations. Generic data was collected about the company's strategy formation (e.g., balanced scorecard, structure of top management, and steering committees). Some decision premises are simply repeated with high frequency in such data. To check the actual consequences of decision premises, interviews with top managers were juxtaposed with documents and observations made at banking branches. Detailed data about computer systems was collected including printouts of screens, software specifications and instructions, and drawings of the corporate IT infrastructure. However, technical information told relatively little about decision premises of technology management, which characterises value-based dynamics of decision premises, rather than circumstance-based.

It was interesting to explore implementation and distortion of decision premises in practice, in other words, to compare 'what they say' to 'what it means' in terms of observable consequences. Gathering data about 'what they say' included interviews with top managers and application of linguistic and behavioural techniques. Gathering data about 'what it means' included documentary analysis and interviews with people at the lower organisational levels, specifically, professional contractors and workers at the front-line of customer services and software development.

Along with typical research methods of qualitative enquiry described above, three specific techniques were used in order to identify and confirm decision premises. (1) Linguistic search for presuppositions was based on reverse scenario questions (e.g., what if the situation is precisely the reverse) (Bandler & Grinder, 1975). (2) Literalism of the definition of 'several simple shared stable decision premises' directed the search towards simple language forms and phrases that were shared by the most people. (3) Behavioural signals of value activation and personal significance were observed (Andreas, 2002).

The interviews, especially ones with executive and top IT managers, provided the most input to the study of decision premises. 27 semistructured interviews were conducted; an average interview continued for one-and-a-half hour. Interview schedule is presented in Table 1. The people from all business functions were interviewed. Particularly interesting exchanges happened with the Alpha's Associate Director of Risk & Compliance and Associate Director of IT Support & Infrastructure. Overall, the selection of interviewees was defined by the *network traversal* of task and other interdependencies that were explored well beyond the formal authority hierarchy. The

network traversal method involves exhaustive and sometime repetitive exploration of all task relations named by an interviewee. In order to keep track of interdependencies, Protégé software was used. The dataset allowed dynamic interaction; that is, the researcher interacted with the dataset on his laptop and asked questions about presence and details of interdependence in question. The visual representation plug-ins of the software allowed quick identification of the individuals who were in key positions in relation to a particular issue or business process, thus making network traversal intelligent.

Social encounters also provided a valuable opportunity for data interrogation (e.g., with unprepared replies). Under a condition of limited access to financial and operational plans, social encounters were particularly helpful in gaining information that was not recorded formally, but

Table 1. Alpha case: Interviews

Role	Amount
Operations and IT Director, Technochange Project Co-Director	3
Business Change Director, Technochange Project Co-Director	4 (1 in Jan, 1 in March, 2 in May)
Project Manager (long-term professional contractor)	1
Project Analyst (Project Office)	1
Associate Director for IT Infrastructure	1
Design Authority Team Leader (systems specification)	1
Assistant to Operations and IT Director	1
Business Operations Support Function Leader and liaison between branch (sales) and centralised customer services (operations)	3 (1 in April and 2 in May along with time spent in branch visits)
Training and Communications Team Leader (consultant)	3 (1 in April, 1 in May and 1 in June)
ACE Team Leader	1
Associate Director for IS Development	1
IT professional (SOS Division)	1
Delivery and Acceptance Team Leader	1
Associate Director for Compliance and Operational Risk	1
Financial Officer (liaising AlphaCoreIS project)	1
Various branch staff	3 plus one-off questions, observation and hearing to situations at work (day) 2 (Branch Manager, Branch Associate)
Total:	27

one would expect it to be so. Such information concerns long-lasting IT issues, prioritisation of IT tasks, and real options of the technochange.

Case Study Vignette

Alpha is a top U.K. building society. After three acquisitions in early 2000s, Alpha now operates a network of more than three hundred branches. With its developed brand, Alpha pursues 'a branch-led blended distribution strategy' and focuses on mortgages and savings. In the summer of 2000, Alpha completed its IT strategy review and a five-year corporate strategic plan. The main result was a decision to purchase the new banking systems as an integrated package. The International Com-

prehensive Banking Systems (ICBS) software was purchased for £17 million. The strategic change concerned IT infrastructure, customer services, back office, risk management, and regulatory compliance. The project was publicised and given a clear priority against other projects.

ANALYSIS AND EXAMPLES OF DECISION PREMISES IN IT MANAGEMENT

The result of the analysis of the decision premises are presented in Table 2. They formed clusters or shared themes of technochange management, economising on IT-operations, and complexity

Table 2. Several stable shared simple decision premises for technochange

'What they say': surface language structure	'What it means': political uses and observable implications
Technochange Management (business processes and software development)	
(1) 'Business change first'	Considerable business change is necessary in order to succeed in technochange, but IT professionals exploit the idea in order to pursue technological solutions that are easier to maintain
(2) 'It is easier to change business processes rather than software.' 'Adjust business processes to IT solutions'	Organising and structuring *around* information systems. Decisions about IS made difficult and institutionalised (e.g., checked against 'how is it done elsewhere?')
(3) 'It is OK for business process to have caveats.' This was used in sign-off procedures	Commitment is necessary in order to make operations managers to sign up to work with new software and processes
(4) 'Each business process should have an owner' (5) 'Business ownership of software development'	A personalised owner is assigned to each business process and can resign only if another owner is found Business functions are responsible for their software development But the IT function retains control over releasing software in 'the production mode'
(6) 'Brokerage of acceptable business solutions, and quality of the relationships with vendors' are responsibilities of top managers	Practices of championship and sponsorship were expected from top management for mustering political support and securing necessary commitment. Assignment of certain tasks to top-managers directly creates 'ambidexterity' and benefits IT professionals
Technochange Economics	
(7) 'Change in practices is cheaper than change in IT solutions.'	Implications for work organisation were increased workload, disturbance, and stress for the front-line workers
(8) 'IT department is committed to providing an efficient and cost effective service.'	As economic beliefs begin to govern IS strategy and delivery, the politics of IT support thrives on economics
(9) Institutional criteria for software selection, for example, 'Where else is the software installed?'	Purposefully simple and institutionalised criteria for selection of software and complex IT solutions
Complexity Management (rules for interdependence and trade-offs)	

continued on following page

Table 2. continued

(10) 'Process orientation' (11) 'No key-man dependence'	Interdependence within the overall organisation increases
(12) 'Processing of operations that require expert knowledge should be centralised.' The sorting of knowledge-intensive and labour-intensive operations	Risk-averse decision of avoiding investment into the high-turnover branch workforce. Removal of capability (e.g., knowledge and know-how of software use) from end-users in banking branches. New professional groups and ambidextrous organisational forms (e.g., Business Operations Support and software rules team)
(13) 'Queue management'	Acceptable queue levels were defined as policy and constitute main efficiency criteria around which work was organised in retail branches and the call centre both
(14) 'Cultural change from service to sales'	Cultural management of complexity perceptions, which resulted in appraisal schemes, tension and 25% turnover

management. The first two set priorities and the third set process rules. Technochange management resembled commonplace ideas about business process re-engineering. Complexity management was not articulated but regulated quite specific parameters (e.g., team size, difference between) using intuitive rules, such as 'no key-man dependence.'

Decision premises had a systemic organisation. There were at least three kinds of connection, specifically, *repetition-embeddedness, cause-effect,* and *contradiction.* Let us provide some illustrations. The premises (2) and (7) are repetitive about the core idea of adjustment of business processes and work practices to IT solutions. The premises (2) and (7) altogether causally support the premise (9); that is, application of simplistic institutional criteria. The premise (5) about the separation of work on software development and IT infrastructure is a specific version of a general complexity management rule (12) about separation of knowledge-intense and labour-intense operations. In other words, the premise (5) is embedded in (12). The contradiction is also a necessary element of a system of values. For example, the premise (1) 'business change first' contracts the premises (2), (7), and (8) that advise of the most economic IT solutions and adjustment of business to those solutions.

Now, we will provide several quotes from documents and interviews that illustrate the actual implications of decision premises.

Cost-Saving

Cost-saving was constantly emphasised in IT policy documents and interviews of IT top managers. As a consequence of sharp categorisation, more than two thirds of IT task requests were rejected or put on hold with resolutions 'good, will wait' or 'we will return when resources are in place' (Associate Director IT Support).

'The IT department is committed to providing an efficient and cost effective service to its customers' (IT Service Level Objectives Agreement).

[Category of IT Task Request] B – Highly desirable (i.e., the work has a demonstrable short term payback). (Project Methodology: IT Task Request)

Business Ownership of Software Development

Decision premises prescribed that a manager of a suitable business function should take responsibility for adjustment of software functionality as necessary. This led to the separation of IT support and software development work as described in Table 3. 'Business ownership' shifted responsibility from IT professionals to business managers, but the need of an active involvement of IT specialists did not disappear. In the onion-like IT infrastructure, a 'small' change in software might require further changes on the various levels of database design, client-server middleware, operation systems, and network configuration that, in turn, might require changes in hardware and telecommunications. These technical changes were not facilitated by the fact that IT professionals prioritised technology and business-as-usual over software development and technochange.

Priorities are clear: telecommunications, banking branches, new software project.(Associate Director IT Support)

As a result, the second-order effect of cost-saving decision premises was not as cost-saving.

The practice of business ownership satisfied the decision premises of IT economising but caused considerable delays of the in-house software development—that is, delays of delivery of much needed business functionality.

Things take a lot longer...2-5 months delays in in-house software development became normal. (Team Leader of Systems Development).

How much does it take for IT people to deliver computer environments? Is it a tricky question? In practice to prepare some small database on customers, it took a week to communicate and prepare. Such work is supposed to be one-off. Communication back and forth on computer configuration [with SOS Division] is generally an issue for struggle. (Team Leader for developing marketing campaigns functionality).

Logic of Systems

Even if business functioning was aligned by decision premises, every software had its own 'built-in' logic. Workarounds and the sheer complexity of such logic can override decision premises. The logic manifested itself in about 30,000 specialised and interlinked parameters of the International Comprehensive Banking Systems software that was used by Alpha.

There are experts in certain business areas, but even they tend to forget the meaning of parameters they use... effects could be unpredictable, difficult

Table 3. Practice of 'business ownership for software development'

Tasks charged to business functions	Tasks cannot be done without IT teams
Specification of business needs into software requirements, a job of business analyst.	Most operations with software development required assistance by the specialised teams of Systems Operation Support (SOS) Division.
In-house programming and adjustment of third-party software. Provision of management information and customised documentation (e.g., letters to customers).	The typical of such operations area bout helping with software development tools, dataset preparation in a corporate DB/2 database and computer environment preparation.
Configuration of International Comprehensive Banking Systems (e.g., branch information and product information).	SOS Division retained the right of release of software into 'production mode' in which the software is expected to run at the agreed level of stability.
Support of software-in-use, such as preparation of instructions and ongoing in-house training.	

and timely to resolve and ramify. ...There are 29 products and large number of parameterised rules for each one. There is a clear issue to maintain rules, we do not understand all the rules' meaning and consequences. To discover the right setting of one parameter for product maturity took 7 days.(Business Change Director)

DISCUSSION. IMPACT OF DECISION PREMISES

Irregularities of IT Management

People do hide issues.(IT and Operations Director).

This was perhaps the major reason for having decision premises in the first place. The Directors of Alpha acknowledged 'managerial problems' of the large federalised IT-operations function. IT professionals arranged their work organisation with hidden, amorphous, and ambidextrous structures, all underlined by high interdependence. Prioritisation of tasks by IT professionals was far from clear. IT professionals were also exploiting 'the strategic use of information' (Pfeffer, 1992), such as interpretation from an advantageous viewpoint, selective presentation, and creating an appearance of rationality and success with regular presentations to end-users that were held in executive suits. In their dealing with end-users, IT managers relied upon *frequent communication* and *enforcement of policy* in order to stabilise technology usages and secure operations within certain boundaries of reliability. The decision premises of economising guided the preference of enforcement of policy rather than configuration of complicated software—the first one is deemed as quicker and cheaper. Alpha's policies were framed in the language that *limited IT service delivery levels, provided rules to refuse or postpone task requests, formalised and limited definitions of faults,* as well as *outlined responsibilities of end-users.*

The decision premises overall and particularly (9) and (5) served the interest of IT professionals who limited their own responsibility but retained control. They also made IT support less accessible. Getting new functionality or new form of reporting delivered or getting an issue to the top management's agenda became burdensome and political activities.

The dynamics of decision premises also questions the productivity of *hybrid managers,* an approach that suggests a transfer of business managers to IT projects (Earl, 1989). The transferred managers in Alpha ended up being constrained by budgets, scarcity of qualified IT human resources, and project schedules even more than IT managers, because they were lacking background, professional affiliation, and support from the core IT staff who retained control over infrastructure and databases.

Change of Work

The following decision premises particularly affected the work organisation and day-to-day running of banking branches in Alpha.

- *(2) It is easier to change business processes rather than software. (7) Change in (workplace) practices is cheaper than change in IT solutions.*
- *(12) Removal of complex, knowledge-intensive operations from branches.* (This was deemed good for branch personnel because it lessens their workload and helps to maintain low queues.)
- *(13) Delivering of only acceptable levels of service (e.g., as measured by queue size) whilst maintaining operational efficiency.*
- *(14) Service-to-sales cultural change.* (Every employee was expected to look for sale opportunity and refer customers to a specialised advisor.)

The consequences of these simple decision premises were far-reaching. The new software and 'service to sales' cultural change threatened the autonomy of the Alpha's operational workforce. Such autonomy was built upon knowing and having a relationship with their local customers. Also, pressure was put on branch staffs in order to input customer relationship information into the system in a real-time mode. Branch staffs used to organise their work with a paper diary.

The [paper] diary is an advance warning of what is going to have to be done on the system, although you're right that some pieces of work like following up on a lead or calling a customer—the procedure is that they should record that on the contact log on the system, but in a busy branch like that, I doubt they do both steps, I suspect that they rely on a paper version. (Branch Associate).

The removal of complex operations from branches did not relieve staffs' responsibilities to customers but did leave them without knowledge of rather proprietary systems. It became harder for them to maintain a relationship with customers and explain all sorts of delays, loss of original paperwork, and other issues of centralised processing.

Sometimes [the centralised] branch support is really good, you can get things done. Financial Accounts—you have to e-mail, Taxation—you have to e-mail... that's fine and that's usually done within 2-3 days. They don't respond back and say 'it has been done.' We do have problems, when things get lost, especially if we're sending up to head office, power of attorney, if it's going on account, we take all documents and it goes to head office. I am sure you can work out how to do it [within the software locally], but I won't do it. (Branch Associate)

We did a pilot in a different branch, when all of the calls for that branch went to the head office. But we found that 70-80% of those calls were still for the branch, so they ended up being put through, so they would then were double-handled. There were things that could only be answered at that branch. (Business Change Manager)

As we can observe, top management applied the decision premises *over* the existent context of work organisation in branches purposefully and consistently. Reduction of the staff's knowledge about software led to a reduced need of IT support. Overall, the decision premises, the quick roll-out of new systems (6 months), and the pressure to sell, all led to a high staff turnover of 25% annually. Nonetheless, the dynamics of decision premises helped to achieve the standardised levels of customer service with relatively low-qualified staffs.

CONCLUSION

The usage of the decision premises was a prerogative of Alpha's top management who were applying them in routine situations as well as critical decision making. The dynamics of decision premises can be summarised as follows:

- Applied with limited attention to the context of circumstances and people; sometime, applied 'ahead of the game.'
- Activated in order to manage 'no win' situations and trade-offs (e.g., sales vs. service); and
- Upheld in conflict situations.

The system of decision premises was multilevel (e.g., specific premises were embedded into general ones), self-causal, as well as self-contradictory. It embraced both continuity and discontinuity. The system also produced *durable and multiple outcomes*. By virtue of being several but not many, the decision premises reinforced the dynamics of many outcomes stemming from a few causes, known as 'the 80-20 rule.'

One interesting and specific outcome of the decision premises operating as a system was *irreversibility*. Software can be reconfigured, and locked-in computer platforms might be changed. However, decision premises define the usage and social order around any technology. Thought operations with technology have an immediate effect – they are easily reversible. On the other hand, policy choices might go unnoticed but, being enforced, they have enduring effects and 'maximize the power of the guy at the top to influence action' (Quinn 1998, p. 4).

The *system* of decision premises was also a tool of operational efficiency. It is well known that coordination is effectively (and most cheaply) facilitated by shared norms. The decision premises helped to limit the number of ways of usage of software, thereby, ensuing stable operations. In Alpha, the dynamics of decision premises led to the situation of *triple economising* on technology, coordination, and adoption.

The IT efficiency outcomes of the system of decision premises had two problems. First, the stable IT-operations should be juxtaposed with severe delays and overload of in-house software development. Second, decision premises stimulated fragmentation of work for the front-line workers in banking branches and processing centres (Frenkel, 1999). It was observed and confirmed with interviews that banking branch workforce ended up with more demanding and fragmented work, yet the same pay and fewer incentives for learning.

In our case study, the decisions that defined the course of technochange were not made by IT professionals. Still, the dynamics led to the focusing on efficiency of technology and compromising on business processes, products, and quality of working life.

This is only an introductory study of decision premises. Further connections are possible to the body of knowledge about human values. For the purpose of being practical, relevant, and inductive, the chapter was limited from interpretations and elaborates frameworks of psychological theories and decision-making theories of economic sort.

ACKNOWLEDGMENT

I would like to thank my good colleagues Anita Greenhill and Bernd Stahl with who we convened a stream of work on post-modern elements in technology management and related organisational change, and an earlier special issue of this journal.

REFERENCES

Andreas, S. (2002). *Transforming your self: Becoming who you want to be*. Moab, Utah: Real People Press.

Bandler, R., & Grinder, J. (1975). *The structure of magic I. A book about language and therapy* (Vol. I). Palo Alto, CA: Science and Behavior Books, Inc.

Bateson, G. (1972). *Steps to an ecology of mind*. New York: Ballantine Books.

Earl, M. J. (1989). *Management strategies for information technology*. Cambridge University Press/Prentice Hall International.

Frenkel, S., Korczynski, M., Shire, K., & Tam, M. (1999). *On the front line. Organisation of work in the information economy*. Ithaca: Cornell University Press.

Huy, Q. N. (2002). Emotional balancing of organizational continuity and radical change: The contribution of middle managers. *Administrative Science Quarterly, 47*, 31-69.

Lund, V. T., Raposo, J., & Watson, (2003). *From banks to banking: The on demand journey*. New York: IBM Institute for Business Value.

March, J. G., & Simon, H. A. (1958). *Organizations*. New York: Wiley.

Marchington, M., Grimshaw, D., Rubery, J., & Willmott, H. (Eds.). (2005). *Fragmenting work: Blurring organizational boundaries and disordering hierarchies*. Oxford University Press.

Marcus, M. L. (2004). Technochange management: Using IT to drive organizational change. *Journal of Information Technology, 19*, 3-19.

Miles, R. H. (1982). *Coffin nails and corporate strategies*. Englewood Cliffs, NJ: Prentice Hall.

Pfeffer, J. (1992). *Managing with power: Politics and influence in organizations*. Boston: Harvard Business School Press.

Prahalad, C. K., & Hamel, G. (1990). The core competence of the corporation. *Harvard Business Review, 68*(3), 79-91.

Quinn, J. B. (1998). Organizing around intellect [Interview]. *Harvard Management Update*.

Weick, K. E., & Sutcliffe, K. M. (2001). *Managing the unexpected: Assuring high performance in an age of complexity*. San Francisco: Jossey-Bass.

This work was previously published in International Journal of Technology and Human Interaction, Vol. 3, Issue 4 , edited by B. Stahl, pp. 66-75, copyright 2007 by IGI Publishing, formerly known as Idea Group Publishing (an imprint of IGI Global).

Chapter XXIV
Trusting Computers Through Trusting Humans:
Software Verification in a Safety–Critical Information System

Alison Adam
University of Salford, UK

Paul Spedding
University of Salford, UK

ABSTRACT

This chapter considers the question of how we may trust automatically generated program code. The code walkthroughs and inspections of software engineering mimic the ways that mathematicians go about assuring themselves that a mathematical proof is true. Mathematicians have difficulty accepting a computer generated proof because they cannot go through the social processes of trusting its construction. Similarly, those involved in accepting a proof of a computer system or computer generated code cannot go through their traditional processes of trust. The process of software verification is bound up in software quality assurance procedures, which are themselves subject to commercial pressures. Quality standards, including military standards, have procedures for human trust designed into them. An action research case study of an avionics system within a military aircraft company illustrates these points, where the software quality assurance (SQA) procedures were incommensurable with the use of automatically generated code.

INTRODUCTION

They have computers, and they may have other weapons of mass destruction. Janet Reno, former US Attorney General

In this chapter our aim is to develop a theoretical framework with which to analyse a case study where one of the authors was involved, acting as an action researcher in the quality assurance procedures of a safety-critical system. This involved the production of software for aeroplane flight systems. An interesting tension arose between the automatically generated code of the software system (i.e., 'auto-code'—produced automatically by a computer, using CASE [Computer Aided Software Engineering] tools from a high level design) and the requirement of the quality assurance process which had built into it the requirement for human understanding and trust of the code produced.

The developers of the system in the case study designed it around auto-code—computer generated software, free from 'human' error, although not proved correct in the mathematical sense, and cheaper and quicker to produce than traditional program code. They looked to means of verifying the correctness of their system through standard software quality assurance (SQA) procedures. However, ultimately, they were unable to bring themselves to reconcile their verification procedures with automatically generated code. Some of the reason for this was that trust in human verification was built into (or inscribed into [Akrich, 1992]) the standards and quality assurance procedures which they were obliged to follow in building the system. Despite their formally couched descriptions, the standards and verification procedures were completely reliant on human verification at every step. However these 'human trust' procedures were incompatible with the automated production of software in ways we show below. The end result was not failure in the traditional sense but a failure to resolve incom-

mensurable procedures; one set relying on human trust, one set on computer trust.

Our research question is therefore: How may we understand what happens when software designers are asked to trust the design of a system, based on automatically generated program code, when the SQA procedures and military standards to which they must adhere demand walkthroughs and code inspections which are impossible to achieve with auto-code?

The theoretical framework we use to form our analysis of the case study is drawn from the links we make between the social nature of mathematical proof, the need to achieve trust in system verification, the ways in which we achieve trust in the online world, the methods of software engineering, and within that, the software quality movement and the related highly influential domain of military standards.

In the following section we briefly outline the social nature of mathematical proof. The next section discusses the debate over system verification which encapsulates many of the ideas of mathematical proof and how such proofs can be trusted by other mathematicians. The chapter proceeds to consider 'computer mediated' trust, briefly detailing how trust has been reified and represented in computer systems to date, mainly in relation to the commercial interests of e-commerce and information security. Trust is particularly pertinent in the world of safety-critical systems, where failure is not just inconvenient and financially damaging, although commercial pressures are still evident here, but where lives can be lost. The model of trust criticised by e-commerce critics is more similar to the type of trust we describe in relation to safety-critical systems, than one might, at first, expect. Understandably, we would like to put faith in a system which has been mathematically proved to be correct. However computer generated proofs, proofs about correctness of computer software, and automatically generated code are not necessarily understandable or amenable to inspection by people, even by experts. The question then arises of whether we can bring ourselves to trust computer generated proofs or code, when even a competent mathematician, logician, or expert programmer cannot readily understand them.

Following this, we describe the evolution of software development standards and the SQA movement. We argue that the development of quality assurance discourse involves processes of designing human ways of trusting mathematical evidence into standardisation and SQA. Military standards are an important part of the SQA story, having consequences far beyond the military arena. Standards are political devices with particular views of work processes inscribed (Akrich, 1992) in their design. We note the way that military standards, historically, moved towards formal verification procedures only to move back to rely more on 'human' forms of verification such as code walkthroughs and inspections in the later 1990s. The story is shot through with a tension between finding ways to trust the production of information systems and finding ways to control them. Formal methods, based on mathematical proof offer the promise of control, but only if we can bring ourselves to trust a proof generated by a machine rather than a proof constructed by another person. We present the background to the case study in terms of a description of the complex 'post cold war' military and commercial environment. This is followed by a description of the action research methodology employed in the project, an outline of the case study and an analysis of the case study findings in terms of our theoretical framework. In the conclusion we briefly note that mathematicians and others are gradually finding ways of trusting computers.

THE SOCIAL NATURE OF MATHEMATICAL PROOF

At first sight, the concept of mathematical proof appears to be relatively simple. The idea of a logical and rigorous series of steps, leading from one or more starting positions (previous theorems or axioms) to the final conclusion of the theorem seems to be the basis of mathematics. The concept of mathematical proof leading inexorably to true and incontrovertible truths about the world is very compelling. It is not surprising that we would like to apply the apparent certainty and exactness of mathematical approaches to computer programming. However if we consider briefly how agreement on mathematical proof and scientific truth is achieved by communities of mathematicians, then the social and cultural dimension of proof, as an agreement amongst trusted expert witnesses, reveals itself.

With the epistemological and professional success of mathematical proof, many of the cultural processes which go into making a proof true sink from consciousness and are only rendered visible in times of dispute; for example as in claims to the proof of Kepler's conjecture or Fermat's last theorem (Davies, 2006; Kuhn, 1962; Singh, 1997). Only on the margins then do we call into question our ability to trust these people when a mathematical proof cannot be agreed to be true by an expert community of mathematicians, as sometimes happens.

The apparently pure and abstract nature of mathematical proof fairly quickly breaks down when we inspect it more closely. In particular, when there is disagreement about a proof, the nature of proof is revealed as a social and cultural phenomenon; the matter of persuading and convincing colleagues. DeMillo, Lipton, and Perlis (1977, p. 208) wrote

Mathematicians talk to each other. They give symposium and colloquium talks which attempt to convince doubting (sometimes hostile) audiences of their arguments, they burst into each others' offices with news of insights for current research, and they scribble on napkins in university cafeterias and expensive restaurants. All for the sake of convincing other mathematicians. The key is that other mathematicians are inclined to listen!

This traditional approach towards mathematical proof, which could be described as one of *persuasive rigorous argument between mathematicians leading to trust,* is not the only way to address the idea of proof. A quite different approach appeared in the 1950s and was based on the work on logic developed by Bertrand Russell and others in the 1930s and used the newly invented electronic computer. This new logic-based approach was not dependent on the computer, but the computer's speed and accuracy had a major impact on its application to the proof of theorems in replacing the persuasive rational argument of competent mathematicians with a *formal* approach which sees any mathematical proof as a number of steps from initial axioms (using predicate logic), to the final proof statement (based purely on logical inference) without the requirement of a human being.

Many proofs can be completed by either method. For instance, many persuasive rigorous argument proofs can be converted to formal proofs (MacKenzie, 2004). It should be emphasised, however, that there is a real difference between the two types of proof. We are not simply talking about a machine taking on the role of a competent mathematician. Some proofs which are readily accepted by mathematicians rely on arguments of symmetry and equivalence, analogies, and leaps of imagination, which humans are very good at understanding but which a formal logic approach cannot replicate. Symmetry and analogy arguments of this type cannot be established by formal methods based on logical progression because symmetry relies on understanding semantics and cannot be gleaned from the syntax of a proof.

Whereas the persuasive rigorous argument, the 'human' approach, has been used for thousands of years, the formal or 'computer generated' approach has been in use for only about half a century. Clearly, the two methods are not treated in the same way by the expert community of mathematicians. With a rigorous argument type of proof, although one may expend much energy convincing one's colleagues of the validity of the proof, the *potential* for coming to agreement or trust of the proof is there. Essentially, in trusting that a mathematical proof is correct, mathematicians are demonstrating their trust in other competent mathematicians. However, expert mathematicians clearly have trouble bringing themselves to trust computer proofs, for good reason, as a computer cannot explain the steps in its reasoning (Chang, 2004).

COMPUTER SYSTEM VERIFICATION: TRUST AND THE SOCIAL

The preceding section contrasted the *use* of computer technology in a claimed proof: the formal method and the human 'rigorous argument' approach to proof. Although this is not the same thing as the proof or verification of a computer system *itself,* in other words the formal, computer generated proof that the computer system matches the specification, the question of whether we can trust the computer is exactly the same.

The idea of *proof* or *verification* of a program is quite different from simply testing the program. Typically, a large suite of programs might have thousands or millions of possible inputs, and so could be in many millions or even billions of states. Exhaustive testing cannot be possible. If a computer system is to be used in the well-funded and high-profile military field to control a space craft, aeroplane, or a nuclear power station, it is highly desirable if the system can be actually *proved* to be correct, secure, and reliable. Since testing, although vital, can never prove the system's correctness, more mathematical methods involving the notion of proof became of great interest in the late 1960s and have remained so ever since.

In fact the history of the verification of computer systems echoes that of mathematical proof, with basically the same two approaches: those who support the rigour of formal methods and those who believe that the purely formal, mechanised proof lacks the crucial element of human understanding (Tierney, 1993). In a paper to an ACM Symposium, DeMillo et al. (1977) argued that the two types of proof were completely different in nature, and that only the persuasive rigorous argument proof with its strong social aspect will ultimately be believable and capable of earning *trust*

COMPUTER-MEDIATED TRUST

In ethical terms, trust is a complex phenomenon and is essentially a human relationship (Nissenbaum, 1999; Stahl, 2006). We think of trust in terms of a trustor who does the trusting and a trustee who is trusted. The trustee does not of course have to be human, but Nissenbaum (1999) suggests that the trustee should be a being to whom we ascribe human qualities such as intentions and reasons, what might be termed an 'agent.' Trust allows meaningful relationships and a vast range of intuitions to work. Nissenbaum (1999) argues that when we are guaranteed safety trust is not needed: 'What we have is certainty, security, safety – not trust. The evidence, the signs, the cues and clues that ground the formation of trust must always fall short of certainty; trust is an attitude without guarantees, without a complete warrant.' Intrusive regulation and surveillance are attempts at control and bad for building trust.

This generalised definition of trust clearly maps onto our description of mathematicians trusting proofs. They may not have complete certainty over the correctness of a mathematical proof, but they have good reason to trust a competent member of the community of expert mathematicians. Therefore they can trust the proof supplied by such a person.

Understandably, there has been much interest in trust in the online world, both in terms of online security and trust in e-commerce transactions. Nissenbaum (1999) suggests that excessive safety

controls, say in e-commerce, may encourage participation but they limit experience: 'Through security we may create a safer world, inhospitable to trust not because there is distrust, but because trust cannot be nourished in environments where risk and vulnerability are, for practical purposes, eradicated.'

Stahl's (2006) take on trust in e-commerce shows another example of the intangible human nature of trust, which has become reified and commodified, so that it can be measured and exchanged in machine transactions. Like Nissenbaum (1999), Stahl points to the way that a trustor does not have complete control over a trustee; vulnerability and uncertainty must be accepted in a trusting relationship. This of course includes business transactions, and is especially important in e-commerce as many of the traditional ways of developing trust are absent from online transactions. Trust becomes a way of generating profit; small wonder that trust, including technological ways of creating trust and maintaining it, has been of so much interest in e-commerce. In the world of e-commerce research, trusts lose its relational aspects and becomes a form of social control. 'If trust is limited to calculations of utility maximisation in commercial exchange, then most of the moral underpinnings of the mechanisms of trust become redundant. Trust changes its nature and loses the binding moral quality that it has in face-to-face interaction.' (Stahl, 2006, p. 31)

Although, on the face of it, Nissenbaum's and Stahl's arguments on the problems of online trust in e-commerce are not the same as the issue of trust described in the body of this chapter, there are important congruencies which are very directly applicable to our characterisation of trust. Whether it is a human trusting another human or an expert mathematician trusting another expert mathematician to supply an accurate proof, the same relationship between trustor and trustee obtains.

For Nissenbaum and Stahl, the issue is what happens to trust when it is commodified within an online relationship. In other words, what happens when the human-trusting-human relationship is mediated by technology? In this chapter we also consider what happens when the human-trusting-human relationship—in terms of a human trusting another human's mathematical proof, or computer program—is replaced by a human having to trust a machine. Of course, in this trustor-trustee relationship, the trustee, that is, the machine, cannot be understood in the way that another person can be.

The pressure to create computer-mediated trust is completely bound up with commercial pressures. The maximisation of profit drives the reification of trust in e-commerce. Similarly in the world of military avionics we describe, it is the commercial pressure of building systems more cheaply and faster which provides the impetus to turn over proofs, testing of programs, and automatic generation of code to a machine. A third aspect of similarity between Stahl's and Nissenbaum's view of computer-mediated trust and ours relates to the tension between trust and control. This is clearly present in the debate over trust in e-commerce. But it is also present in software quality discourse as we discuss below.

In the following section we briefly discuss some of the ways in which human trust has traditionally been built into procedures designed to verify program correctness, and how this can be seen to mirror an ideal group of mathematicians agreeing upon a mathematical proof.

BUILDING TRUST INTO A COMPUTER SYSTEM

We argue that, historically, much of the development of the software engineering discipline can be understood in terms of the development of procedures, through which we can convince ourselves to trust, and control, the development of information systems and the production of software. For instance, Myers' (1979) classic book on software testing explores the topic of human testing in detail, justifying methods such as formal *code inspections* and *code walkthroughs*. The differences between the two methods depend on different usages of the terms 'inspection' and 'walkthrough,' but the important point is that both involve a small group of professionals carefully reading through code together. We argue that this can be viewed as an imitation of the social (persuasive rigorous argument) form of proof described earlier where 'mathematicians talk to each other' in symposia and colloquia and so on (DeMillo et al., 1977). The original programmer should be in the group, analogous to the mathematician demonstrating a proof or principle to expert colleagues. The aim (as originally suggested by Weinberg [1971]—an 'egoless' approach) is to discover as many errors as possible rather than to try to demonstrate that there are none. So the team is to act as an idealised group of 'Popperian' scientists looking for 'refutations' (Popper, 1963). Under such an approach, one can never be entirely sure that the code is correct. But, as the walkthrough proceeds, the original programmer and the code inspection team can gradually come to trust the code as bugs are weeded out and fixed.

Myers claims positive advantages of code inspections and walkthroughs, including the value of the original programmer talking through the design (and thus spotting the errors). He also notes the ability of human testers to see the causes and likely importance of errors (where a machine might simply identify symptoms) and also the likelihood that a batch of errors will be identified simultaneously. Also the team is able to empathise with and understand the thought processes of the original programmer in a way which a machine arguably cannot. Importantly, the team can be *creative* in its approach. In working together they also, inevitably, form something of a sharing and trusting community (even if it is disbanded after a day or two).

The lesson gleaned from human verification techniques, such as walkthroughs and code inspections, is that these have been regarded, for some time, as reliable, if not exhaustive, ways of ensuring reliability of software.

SOFTWARE QUALITY ASSURANCE AND MILITARY STANDARDS FOR SOFTWARE

The software verification techniques of code walkthroughs and inspections are important parts of the armoury SQA. Effectively, we argue that SQA is a branch of software engineering which formalises and standardises the very human methods of trust, and ultimately control outlined above, which we need to build into software engineering procedures. The SQA movement is an important part of the story of the growth of software engineering because of its quest for rigour and control of potentially unruly programs and programmers.

First of all, SQA offers a promise of rational control over software, the software development process, and those who produce software. Software quality criteria include features for directing, controlling, and importantly, measuring the quality of software (Gillies, 1997). 'Qualification' is achieved when a piece of software can be demonstrated to meet the criteria specified in these quality procedures. An important aspect of SQA involves demonstrating that software meets certain defined independent standards.

The development and adherence to software standards is a very important part of the story of SQA. Generic industry standards are available, but also of much interest—particularly for the case study set out later in the chapter—are military standards. Indeed, the defence industry is so influential that Tierney (1993) argues that military standards influence software engineering far beyond applications in defence. Hence military standards are a very important part of SQA, and ultimately are important in formalising ways in which designers of computer systems can

come to trust the systems and the production of correct software.

A number of military standards have been developed to regulate and control the use of software in defence applications. For instance, US standards DOD-STD-2167A (1988), MIL-STD-498 (1994), and ISO/IEC 12207 (1995) respectively established the requirements for software development and documentation in all equipment to be used by the US military (and effectively that of all Western armed forces), introduced object oriented development (OOD) and rapid application development (RAD), then broadened the scope of international standards to include acquisition and maintenance. (DSDM Consortium, 2006).

The relevant UK standard 00-55, (MoD, 1997) *Requirements for Safety Related Software in Defence Equipment,* was published in 1997 and echoes much of MIL-STD-498, but moves the discussion on provably correct software in a particular direction. At first sight, this seems highly significant to the current argument, because it clearly expressed a preference for *formal* methods, in other words mathematical procedures whereby the software is proved to be correct by a machine (MacKenzie, 2001).

Tierney (1993) argues that the release of UK Defence Standard 00-55 in draft in 1989 had the effect of intensifying the debate over formal methods in the UK software engineering community. It devoted as much space to regulating and managing software development labour processes as the techniques and practices to be used for formal designs. This reinforces our argument that SQA is concerned with control of work processes and those who perform them, the software developers. On the one hand, many argued that mathematical techniques for software development and verification could only ever be used sparingly, as there simply was not enough suitable mathematical expertise in most organisations and it increased software quality at the expense of programmer productivity. On the other side, those from a more mathematical camp argued that there was commercial advantage in proving software correctness as errors could be trapped earlier in the software development cycle (Tierney, 1993, p. 116).

Designed into the MoD (UK Ministry of Defence) standard was a view of safety-critical software as an important area of regulation and control. Some of the reason for this was a change in its own organisation from the 1980s. The UK government sought to open up work traditionally done in-house by the MoD in its own research establishments to private contractors (Tierney, 1993, p. 118). Given that it had to offer its software development to the private sector, it built in ways of controlling it within its defence standards (Tierney, 1993, p. 118). Further political impetus was offered by the introduction of consumer protection legislation in the UK in the late 1980s which required software developers to demonstrate that their software had not contributed, in the event of an accident enquiry, and that they had demonstrably attended to safety. Thus we can see that in Def Stan 00-55, politics, in the shape of the MoD's need to open up software development to the private sector and also to avoid being held responsible for inadequate software in the event of an accident, played an important role.

However, more significantly, this document has itself been superseded in 2004 by (draft) standard 00-56 (MoD, 2004). Def Stan 00-55 has now become obsolete. The changes involved in Def Stan 00-56 are of great interest, in that the preference for formal method is lessened. In the new standard, it is accepted that provably correct software is not possible in most cases and that we are inevitably involved in a human operation when we attempt to show that code is reliable in a safety-critical environment. Without a more detailed consideration of the history of formal methods in the UK over the last decade, which is beyond the scope of the present chapter, a strong claim that the move back to more human methods of verification might be difficult to sustain.

Nevertheless it is interesting to note the way that Def Stan 00-5, with its emphasis on formal approaches and attendant onerous work practices, has been consigned to the history books with a clear move back to human verification.

CASE STUDY CONTEXT

The case study relates to a large European military aircraft company (MAC) with which one of the authors was engaged as a researcher in a joint research project, lasting around three years, during the mid to late 1990s. A high proportion of the senior management were men and its culture was masculine in style, particularly emphasising an interest in engineering and technical mastery (Faulkner, 2000). Indeed there was much interest, pleasure, and admiration for elegant products of engineering (Hacker, 1991). When one of their fighter planes flew over (an event difficult to ignore on account of the engine noise), offices would clear as employees went outside to admire the display of a beautiful machine. A certain amount of military terminology was used, sometimes ironically, in day-to-day work. A number of employees had links with the armed forces. MAC was exclusively involved in the defence industry, with the UK's MoD being its largest customer and other approved governments buying its products.

As a manufacturing company in an economy where manufacturing was in steep decline and with its ties to the defence industry, if a major defence contract went elsewhere, jobs would be on the line. Despite the 'hi-tech' nature of its work, MAC had a traditional feel to it. The company had existed, under one name or another, right from the beginning of the avionics industry. The defence industry, and within that the defence aerospace industry, faced uncertain times as the UK government was redefining its expectations of the defence industry in post-Cold War times. It quickly came to expect much clearer demonstrations of value for money (Trim, 2001).

Therefore, the 'peace dividend' brought about by the end of the Cold War meant uncertain times for the defence aerospace industry as military spending was reduced significantly (Sillers & Kleiner, 1997). Yet, as an industry contributing huge amounts to the UK economy (around £5 billion per annum in export earnings Trim (2001, p. 227)), the defence industry is hugely important in terms of revenue and employment. Defence industries have civil wings (which was the case with MAC) and it was seen as important that the defence side of the business did not interfere with civil businesses. For instance, BAE Systems is a partner in a European consortium and was pledged £530 million as a government loan to develop the A3XXX aircraft to rival the USA's Boeing 747 (Trim, 2001, p. 228).

Although not strictly a public sector organisation itself, its location in the defence industry put MAC's business in the public sector. However, in the UK, views of public sector management were undergoing rapid change in the mid 1990s and it was seen as no longer acceptable that the taxpayer should underwrite investment (Trim, 2001). Such firms were required to be more competitive and to be held more accountable financially. Hence, quality management and value for money were becoming key concepts in the management repertoire of the UK defence industry from the mid 1990s onwards. As we discuss in the preceding section, this was at the height of the UK MoD's interest in formal approaches to the production of software. In a climate where post-Cold War defence projects were likely to demand a shorter lead time, there was considerable interest in speeding up the software development process.

Computer technology and related activity clearly played a central role in MAC. One division of MAC, the Technical Directorate (TD), developed most of the airborne software (much of it real-time). This software clearly has a central role in ensuring aircraft performance and safety. Around 100 people were involved in developing systems computing software. It was in this divi-

sion that Software Development System (SDS), a safety-critical airborne software system for flying military aircraft, was developed.

Research Methodology

The methodological approach of the research was based on action research (Myers & Avison, 2002). As several successful participant observation studies in technology based organisations have been reported in the literature (Forsythe, 2001; Low & Woolgar, 1993; Latour & Woolgar, 1979), an ethnographic approach holds much appeal. However, a strict ethnographic approach was neither feasible nor desirable in this study. As someone with technical expertise, the researcher could not claim to be the sociologist or anthropologist, more typical of reported ethnographic studies of technological systems (Low & Woolgar, 1993; Forsythe, 2001). This also meant that he was not 'fobbed off' by being directed into areas that the participants thought he wanted to look at or where they thought he should be interested in as happened in the Low and Woolgar (1993) case study. Based in the Quality Assurance Division (QAD) in the SQA team, early in his research, the researcher proved his technical credentials by helping run a workshop on software metrics and this helped to gain him full inclusion in the technical work. Although as a technical researcher, rather than a social researcher, it was arguably difficult for him to maintain the 'anthropological strangeness' which ethnographers look for in explaining the common sense and every day logistics of working life. In any case, he had been invited, through this research, to make a contribution to the improvement of SQA procedures. Therefore the research can be characterised as a form of action research (Baskerville & Wood-Harper, 1996), where potential improvements to SQA were to be seen as the learning part of the action research cycle.

Although action research receives a mixed press from the IS research community (Baskerville & Wood-Harper, 1996; Lau, 1999), it is nevertheless seen as a way of coming to grips with complex social settings where interactions with information technologies must be understood within the context of the whole organisation. Baskerville (1999) notes the growing interest in action research methods in information systems research. Two key assumptions are that complex social settings cannot be reduced for meaningful study and that action brings understanding (Baskerville, 1999). The culture of MAC was extremely complex, as we characterise above and discuss again in what follows. Arguably, key elements would be lost were the researcher to have adopted a more distant role, relying on interviews and questionnaires rather than becoming fully immersed and contributing to the detail of the project. The researcher adopted an interpretivist approach, looking to the interpretations of the other participants of the research. But by allowing for social intervention he became part of the study, producing shared subjective meanings between researcher and subjects as coparticipants in the research (Baskerville, 1999).

For a period of over one year out of the three that the whole project lasted, the researcher spent, on average, one day per week working with MAC staff with access to a variety of staff across the organisation, and was therefore able to participate in a range of meetings and workshops and to gain a familiarity with the individuals concerned. This could not easily have been gained from interviews or surveys. These events included meetings where software quality staff considered quality policy, such as the implication of international standards, to broader meetings where technical staff were considering development methods in detail. Free access was allowed to relevant policy and development documents. This permitted an overview of the detailed practices and culture of this large and complex organisation.

Analysis of Case Study Findings

The initial remit of the researcher was to work with staff to optimise the use of software quality assurance within the organisation. The use of cost benefit analysis was originally suggested by senior management. Given our characterisation of the UK defence industry's particular focus on management of quality and value for money, as described above, it is entirely in keeping with the industry's changing needs that the researcher was initially directed into these areas. The researcher viewed it as problematic to assign monetary cost to SQA activities, and even harder to assign monetary benefits. However, these concerns were never addressed directly in the project as it soon emerged that there was greater interest in a new approach to software development being pioneered by MAC.

Ince (1994, p. 2-3) tells the story of a junior programmer's first day in a new job. A senior programmer shows him around, advising him where to buy the best sandwiches at lunchtime, where to find the best beer after work, and other similarly important matters. Then the senior colleague points to a door. 'Whatever you do don't go through that door, the people there have been given the job of stifling our creativity.' The door, of course, led to the quality assurance department.

The staff of MAC's Quality Assurance Division expressed some similar feelings, albeit less dramatically. They wanted to act as consultants, offering a measure of creativity to the technical development process, although safely wrapped in appropriate quality assurance processes, but all too often they felt like the police. The strong awareness of the safety-critical nature of software development, and the related fairly advanced organisation of quality assurance in MAC, thanks in no small measure to the necessity to adhere to MoD standards, meant that SQA was never going to get quite the negative press that it attracted in Ince's (1994) anecdote. Nevertheless, there was still some feeling that the Quality Assurance Division could be brought on board in a project some time after the Technical Division had time to do the creative part.

Hence, TD had been prototyping the new SDS system for about a year when they decided to bring in Quality Assurance Division. As we explain below, the newness of the style of development in SDS made it unclear how it was to be quality assured. Unsure of how to proceed, the SQA manager turned to the researcher for suggestions. The researcher now became involved in investigating the use of the new software development approach, which would involve the inclusion of computer generated program code ('auto-code') in safety-critical airborne software systems, leading to the approval of the new approach and its incorporation into MAC's software quality assurance systems.

Although there has been a long tradition of using computers to aid the process of software engineering itself, such CASE tools (Pressman, 2005) have not generally been used to generate safety-critical code (this was always written by human programmers). The new MAC SDS was an ambitious system whose targets were principally to reduce avionics systems development time by 40% and the cost by 30%, whilst maintaining the very high quality standards necessary for computer-based system which fly—and therefore can crash—military aircraft.

A key aspect of SDS was process integration using an integrated modeling environment. There was consequentially a heavy reliance on automated methods. A specification was developed in a formal modeling language and this generated programming code automatically. In particular, automatic code generation was eventually to lead to aircraft flying 'auto-code' in safety-critical systems. Two aspects of SDS stand out in the climate of defence spending of the mid 1990s. First, there was pressure to reduce costs and show value for money. Second, the use of formal methods in computer programming received a huge boost in the mid-1990s through the Defence standard DEF Stan 00-55 which mandated the use of formal methods base approaches in safety-critical software. It is not surprising that there was

considerable interest in a system which offered the promise of considerably reduced software production times.

MAC invested a great deal of money and time in SDS in the hope that the improved time-scales which SDS promised, together with reduced costs, could keep major current aircraft developments on course. This was particularly important in an environment of political intervention and considerable public interest and concern over escalating costs and delivery times in the public sector, including the defence industry. These benefits could only accrue to MAC if the quality, that is, correctness of the software, could be assured.

SDS was heavily dependent on software (CASE) tools. MAC had used these for many years, and had procedures in place for their qualification (i.e., acceptance) in certain circumstances. However, these applied to mission-critical rather than safety-critical systems. Furthermore, the movement towards auto-generated code led to a different environment than one where tools improved and speeded up the design process, but where failure would show up and be merely time-wasting. There was seen to be a need for a major improvement/update of these procedures, a quantum change, before they would be acceptable for safety-critical applications.

Some tools being used had major world-wide user communities, associated academic conferences, and came from supposedly secure and reliable suppliers. Others might not be so well supported, both intellectually and commercially. (For instance, it might be no use having an ideal tool if the supplier was small and unlikely to survive for many years.) Methods already existed for supplier qualification. These methods were undertaken by software quality staff. However, the qualification of these suppliers could be a crucial issue in the qualification of the tool and ultimately the integrity of the avionics system. The issue was not merely one of qualification, it was also one of *demonstration* of qualification to customers. Ultimately, the need in some sense to *prove* the new methods became paramount. Hence we can see that quality procedures did not just involve procedures, such as code walkthroughs through which software teams could persuade themselves to trust program code, they also applied to the question of choosing and trusting suppliers.

A number of meetings took place with members of the SDS team. This discussion was very useful for an understanding of SDS and gave the researcher a richer understanding of the SQA needs. It soon became apparent that the necessary fundamental problems with SQA in SDS were going to be difficult to answer.

The difficulties were centred around two conflicting ideas. The first of these was that for the *persuasive rational argument* approach to be successful there would be a need for a group of professionals to participate in code walkthroughs, with consequent discussion and persuasion. On the face of it, this was simply not possible, since the computer which wrote the auto-code could not take part in such a discussion. Alternative approaches were considered. Clearly there would be a stage before the auto-code (at the requirements specification level) where human agents were involved, but this was found to be too high level to meet the relevant military standards (the US MIL-STD-498 [1994] and the UK standard 00-55 [MoD, 1997]). Both standards are very specific about the exact conduct of the necessary walkthrough. It had to be a *code* walkthrough.

On the other hand, for the *formal proof* approach method to work, there would first need to be such a formal proof. This did not seem within the capability of the QAD itself, despite the division being quite well resourced. MAC referred back to the auto-code tools suppliers, but once again there was no such proof and no realistic possibility of achieving such a proof. Although MAC was an important customer for the auto-code tool suppliers, they were not prepared to expend the necessary resources. Furthermore, a 'weakest link' argument demonstrates a fundamental flaw with the formal approach in computer systems. If

the auto-code tool itself could be formally verified, it would then become necessary also to consider the operating system on which the tool would run and the hardware systems involved. Potentially this could involve a seemingly infinite regression of hardware and software systems having to be proved correct, where the system is only as good as its weakest link. Frustration grew as no solution was forthcoming and ultimately SDS was shelved indefinitely.

We have argued that mathematical proof is essentially a human achievement between members of the expert mathematical community who are persuaded of the correctness of mathematical proofs because they trust each other. These processes of trust are replicated in the procedures that have been developed in software engineering, and within that, software quality assurance. As part of the defence industry, developing safety-critical systems, MAC had highly developed SQA procedures which were obliged to follow international military standards. Their code walkthroughs, which are analogous to the ways mathematicians achieve trust in a proof, were an important part of such quality procedures. Formal methods offer the promise of an attractive certainty and control over software production and hence control over the work processes of human programmers. They also offer the promise of automatic verification of software systems which, potentially, could be much cheaper than traditional human based approaches to the verification of software through traditional SQA procedures.

SDS achieved very little despite the huge efforts put into it by the many people working for MAC. Although it was not, at the time, formulated in such stark terms, success was elusive because an attempt was being made to achieve the impossible: namely using auto-code whilst being held to quality assurance procedures which demanded code walkthroughs which could not possibly be achieved in an auto-code system. Attempts were made to consider formally proving the correctness of the auto-code. In addition to supplier reluctance, this raised the spectre of the infinite regress. If one looks to proving the auto-code correct, then the operating system must be proved correct, the hardware platform and so on.

This was at the height of interest in formal methods for safety-critical systems for defence, a view embodied in Def Stan 00-55. The rise of formal methods is crucially linked to the defence industry. The interest in formal methods and automated approaches arrived as pressure mounted on Western governments to prove cost effectiveness due to the changing nature of defence developments after the end of the Cold War and the need to avoid litigation for software that might be implicated in an accident. Yet the difficulties of applying formal methods in systems of any level of complexity and the need to trust the program code acted as a spur to maintain complex human centred software quality assurance procedures.

CONCLUSION: TRUSTING COMPUTERS

There is much evidence that we already *do* trust computers in many walks of life without formal proof or other formal demonstration, even to the extent of trusting safety-critical systems such as the 'fly by wire' software in the Boeing 777 airliner, two million lines of code which have not been fully proved (Lytz, 1995). Expert mathematicians have begun to accept computer generated proofs, albeit in qualified ways (Chang, 2004). As MacKenzie (2001, p. 301) argues, 'moral entrepreneurs' of computerised risk ensure that warnings about computerised risk are heeded so that safety-critical software is avoided and, where it is unavoidable, much care is taken over its development. Military standards, so detailed about the use of formal methods in software design and attendant work processes in the 1990s, have moved a decade later to be much less prescriptive about the work methods of ensuring software quality, thereby allowing for the crucial element

of human inspection in order that the software may be trusted. As Collins (1990) notes, we are remarkably accommodating to computers, making sense of them and involving them in our social networks, and will continue to find imaginative ways of doing so. This echoes Nissenbaum's (1999) view that we may trust computers if we can treat them as 'agents.' We may meaningfully ascribe intentions and reasons to them.

In this chapter we have sought to tell a story of trust, in particular how software may be trusted when it is not produced by a human programmer. This involves consideration of a complex set of discourses including the question of mathematical proof and how proof is achieved within mathematical communities. We see a similar need to replicate such human processes of trust in trusting computer systems. We have argued that the making of standards to be applied within software quality assurance procedures shows ways in which mechanisms of trust are inscribed in software standards. Our case study, an action research project in a military aircraft company, demonstrates the difficulties which occur when quality assurance procedures involving code walkthroughs—procedures with built-in human trust mechanisms—are incommensurable with a system which relies on auto-code. The climate of defence research and spending was a major influence, both on our case study and the wider development of standards. There is a continued tension between needing to trust and trying to control: trusting the software and controlling its production. The story which we tell here is one of continuing human ingenuity in finding ways of trusting computer software.

REFERENCES

Akrich, M. (1992). The de-scription of technical objects. In W. E. Bijker & J. Law (Eds.), *Shaping technology/building society: Studies in sociotechnical change* (pp. 205-224). Cambridge, MA/London: MIT Press.

Baskerville, R. Investigating information systems with action research. *Communications of the Association for Information Systems, 19*(2). Retrieved October 5, 2006, from http://www.cis.gsu.edu/~rbaskerv/CAIS_2_19/CAIS_2_19.htm

Baskerville, R., & Wood-Harper, A.T. (1999). A critical perspective on action research as a method for information systems research. *Journal of Information Technology, 11*, 235-246.

Chang, K. (2004, April 6). In math, computers don't lie. Or do they? *New York Times.* Retrieved October 5, 2006, from http://www.math.binghamton.edu/zaslav/Nytimes/+Science/+Math/sphere-packing.20040406.html

Collins, H.M. (1990). *Artificial experts: Social knowledge and intelligent machines.* Cambridge, MA: MIT Press.

Davies, B. (2006, October 3). Full proof? Let's trust it to the black box. *Times higher education supplement.*

De Millo, R.A., Lipton, R.J., & Perlis, A.J. (1977). Social processes and proofs of theorems and programs. In *Proceedings of the 4th ACM Symposium on Principles of Programming Language* (pp. 206-214).

DSDM Consortium. (2006). White papers. Retrieved October 5, 2006, from *http://www.dsdm.org/products/white_papers.asp*

Faulkner, W. (2000). The power and the pleasure? A research agenda for 'making gender stick.' *Science, Technology & Human Values, 25*(1), 87-119.

Forsythe, D.E. (2001). *Studying those who study as: An anthropologist in the world of artificial intelligence.* Stanford University Press.

Gillies, A.C. (1997). *Software quality: Theory and management* (2nd ed.). London/Boston: International Thomson Computer Press.

Hacker, S. (1989). *Pleasure, power and technology: Some tales of gender, engineering, and the co-operative workplace.* Boston: Unwin Hyman.

Ince, D. (1994). *An introduction to software quality assurance and its implementation.* London: McGraw-Hill.

Kuhn, T.S. (1962). *The structure of scientific revolutions.* University of Chicago Press.

Latour, B., & Woolgar, S. (1979). *Laboratory life: The social construction of scientific facts.* Princeton University Press.

Lau, F. (1999). Toward a framework for action research in information systems studies. *Information Technology & People, 12*(2), 148-175.

Low, J., & Woolgar, S. (1993). Managing the sociotechnical divide: Some aspects of the discursive structure of information systems development. In P. Quintas (Ed.), *Social dimensions of systems engineering: People, processes and software development* (pp. 34-59). New York/London: Ellis Horwood.

Lytz, R. (1995). Software metrics for the Boeing 777: A case study. *Software Quality Journal, 4*(1), 1-13.

MacKenzie, D.A. (2001). *Mechanizing proof: Computing, risk, and trust.* Cambridge, MA/London: MIT Press.

MacKenzie, D.A. (2004). *Computers and the cultures of proving.* Paper presented at the Royal Society Discussion Meeting, London.

Ministry of Defence (MoD). (1997). Requirements for safety related software in defence equipment Retrieved October 5, 2006, from http://www.dstan.mod.uk/data/00/055/01000200.pdf

Ministry of Defence (MoD). (2004). Interim defence standard 00-56. Retrieved October 5, 2006, from http://www.dstan.mod.uk/data/00/056/01000300.pdf

Myers, G.J. (1979). *The art of software testing.* New York: Wiley.

Myers, M.D., & Avison, D.E. (Eds). (2002). *Qualitative research in information systems: A reader.* London: Sage Publications.

Nissenbaum, H. (1999). Can trust be secured online? A theoretical perspective. *Etica e Politica, 2.* Retrieved October 5, 2006, from http://www.units.it/~etica/1999_2/nissenbaum.html

Popper, K.R. (1963). *Conjectures and refutations.* New York: Harper.

Pressman, R. (2005*). Software engineering: A practitioner's approach* (6ᵗʰ ed.). London/New York: McGraw Hill.

Sillers, T.S., & Kleiner, B.H. (1997). Defence conversion: Surviving (and prospering) in the 1990s. *Work Study, 46*(2), 45-48.

Singh, S. (1997). *Fermat's last theorem.* London: Fourth Estate.

Stahl, B.C. (2006). *Trust as fetish: A Critical theory perspective on research on trust in e-commerce.* Paper presented at the Information Communications and Society Symposium, University of York, UK.

Tierney, M. (1993). The evolution of Def Stan 00-55: A socio-history of a design standard for safety-critical software. In P. Quintas (Ed.), *Social dimensions of systems engineering: People, processes and software development* (pp. 111-143). New York/London: Ellis Horwood.

Trim, P. (2001). Public-private partnerships and the defence industry. *European Business Review, 13*(4), 227-234.

Weinberg, G. (1971). *The psychology of computer programming.* New York: Van Nostrand Reinhold.

Compilation of References

Aarnio, A., Enkenberg, A., Heikkilä, J., & Hirvola, S. (2002). *Adoption and use of mobile services: Empirical evidence from a Finnish survey.* Paper presented at the 35th Hawaii International Conference on System Sciences, Hawaii.

Abdinnour-Helm, S. F., Chaparro, B. S., & Farmer, S. A. (2005). Using the End-User Computing Satisfaction (EUCS) Instrument to Measure Satisfaction with a Web Site. *Decision Sciences, 26*(2), 349-364.

Abramson, M. A., & Means, G. E. (2001). E-Government 2001. *IBM Center for the Business of Government Series*, Rowman and Littlefield, Lanham.

Achterberg, J., van Es, G., & Heng, M. (1991). Information systems research in the postmodern period. In H. Nissen, H. Klein, & R. Hirschheim (Eds.), *Information systems research: Contemporary approaches and emergent traditions* (pp. 281-292). Amsterdam: Elsevier Science.

Ackerman, M., & Haverton, C. (2004). Sharing expertise: The next step for knowledge management. In M. Huysman & V. Wulf (Eds.) *Social capital and information technology* (Chapter 11). Cambridge, USA and London, England: The MIT Press.

Adams, D. A., Nelson, R. R., & Todd, P. A. (1992). Perceived usefulness, ease of use, and usage of information technology: A replication. *MIS Quarterly, 16*(2), 227-247.

Agar, J. (2003). *Constant Touch: A Global History of the Mobile Phone.* UK: Icon Books

Agarwal, A. (1999). Raw computation. *Scientific American, 281*, 44-47.

Agres, C., Edberg, D., & Igbaria, M. (1998). Transformation to virtual societies: Forces and issues. *The Information Society, 14*(2), 71-82.

Ahire, S. L., Golhar D. Y., &. Waller, M. A. (1996). Development and Validation of TQM Implementation Constructs. *Decision Sciences, 27*(1), 23-56.

Akrich, M. (1992). The de-scription of technical objects. In W. E. Bijker & J. Law (Eds.), *Shaping technology/ building society: Studies in sociotechnical change* (pp. 205-224). Cambridge, MA/London: MIT Press.

Aladwani, A. M. (2002). Organizational actions, computer attitudes, and end-user satisfaction in public organizations: an empirical study. *Journal of End User Computing, 14*(1), 42-49.

Alavi, M. (1984). An assessment of the prototyping approach to information systems development. *Communications of the ACM, 27*(6), 556-563.

Alavi, M., & Leidner, D. E. (2001). Review. Knowledge management and knowledge management systems: Conceptual foundations and research issues. *MIS Quarterly, 25*(1), 107-136.

Albert, S. (2005). Smart community networks: Self-directed team effectiveness in action. *Team Performance Management, 1*(5), 144-156.

Albrecht, H. (1993). Technik – Gesellschaft – Zukunft. In: H. Albrecht & C. Schönbeck (Eds.), *Technik und Gesellschaft* (=Technik und Kultur, Bd. 10) (pp.451-474) Düsseldorf; Germany: VDI-Verlag.

Albright, D. (2003, Winter). Tales of the city: Applying situationist social practice to the analysis of the urban drama. *Criticism*.

Al-Gahtani, S. S., & King, M. (1999). Attitudes, satisfaction and usage: factors contributing to each in the acceptance of information technology. *Behaviour & Information Technology, 18*(4), 77-297.

Al-Jabri, I. M., & Al-Khaldi, M. A. (1997). Effects of user characteristics on computer attitudes among undergraduate business students. *Journal of End User Computing, 9*(2), 16-22.

Allen, B. R., & Boynton, A. C. (1991). Information architecture: In search of efficient flexibility. *MIS Quarterly*.

Allen, D. W., & Griffeth, R. W. (1997). Vertical and lateral information processing: The effects of gender, employee classification level, and media richness on communication and work outcomes. *Human Relations, 50* (1), 1239-1260.

Allen, J. P. (2000). Information systems as technological innovation. *Information Technology and People, 13*(3), 210-221.

Alloway, N. & Gilbert, P. (1997). Boys and literacy: Lessons from Australia. *Gender & Education, 9*(1), 49-62.

Alter, N. (1985). *La Bureautique dans l'Entreprise*. Paris: Les éditions ouvrières.

Alter, N. (1995). Peut-on programmer l'innovation. *Revue Française de gestion. 10*, 78-86.

Alter, S. (1996). *Information systems: A management perspective*. Menlo Park, CA: The Benjamin/Cummings Publishing Company.

Alvarez, R. (2002). Confessions of an information worker: a critical analysis of information requirements discourse. *Information and Organization, 12*(2), 85-107.

Andersen, K. (1998). A virtual derive. Retrieved September 17, 2006, from http://www.aac.bartlett.ucl. ac.uk/ve/Work9798/kristina/derive.html

Anderson, J. C., & Gerbing, D. W. (1988). Structural Equation Modeling in Practice: A Review and Recommended two-step Approach. *Psychological Bulletin, 103*, 411-423.

Anderson, W. L., & Crocca, W. T. (1993). Engineering practice and codevelopment of product prototypes. *Communications of the ACM, 36*(4), 49-56.

Andreas, S. (2002). *Transforming your self: Becoming who you want to be*. Moab, Utah: Real People Press.

Andreasen, M., Nielsen, H., Schrøder, S., & Stage, J. (2006). Usability in Open Source Software Development: Opinions and Practice. *Information Technology and Control 25*(3A), 303-312.

Ang, K.-T., Thong, J.Y.L., & Yap, C.-S. (1997). IT implementation through the lens of organizational learning: A case study of INSUROR. In K. Kumar & J.I. DeGross (Ed.), *Proceedings of the 18th international conference on information systems (ICIS'97)* (December, 15–17) (pp. 331– 48). Atlanta.

Angeles, P. (1992). *The Harper Collins dictionary of philosophy*. (2nd ed.). New York: Harper Collins.

Angelo, J. (2004, May 14). *New study reveals that women over 40 who play online games spend far more time playing than male or teenage gamers*. Retrieved June 3, 2006, from http://media.aoltimewarner.com/media/ cb_press_view.cfm?release_num=55253774

Anton, J. (2000). The past, present and future of customer access centers. *International Journal of Service Industry Management, 11*(2), 120-130.

Aquarelle (1999). *Sharing Cultural Heritage through Multimedia Telematics*. DGIII, ESPRIT Project 01/01/1996 - 31/12/1998.

Archer, M. (1982). Morphogenesis versus structuration: On combining structure and action. *The British Journal of Sociology, 33*(4), 455-483.

Archer, M. (1995). *Realistic social theory: The morphogenetic approach*. Cambridge, MA: Cambridge University press.

Archer, M. (2003). *Structure, agency and the internal conversation,* Cambridge, MA: Cambridge University press.

Ardichvili, A., & Cardozo, R. N. (2000). A model of the entrepreneurial opportunity recognition process. *Journal of Entreprising Culture, 8*(2), 103-119.

Argyris, C, & Schön, D. (1978). *Organisational learning: A theory of action perspective.* Massachusetts: Addison-Wesley.

Arino, A., & de la Torre, J. (1998). Learning from failure: Towards an evolutionary model of collaborative ventures. *Organizational Science, 9*(3), 306-325.

Arkich, M. (1992). The de-scription of technical artifacts. In W.E. Bijker & J. Law (Eds.), *Shaping technology/building society: Studies in sociotechnical change* (pp. 205–224). Cambridge, MA: MIT Press.

Arnott, S. (2003). NHS reform makes IT a political issue, *Computing.* Retrieved January 4, 2004 from http://www.computing.co.uk/Analysis/1137926

Arrow, K. (1969). *The organization of economic activity: Issues pertinent to the choice of market versus nonmarket allocation. On the analysis and evaluation of public expenditure.* Washington, DC.

Asaro, P. M. (2000). Transforming Society by Transforming Technology: the science and politics of participatory design. *Accounting, Management and Information Technologies, 10,* 257-290.

Atkitson, M. A., & Kydd, C. (1997). Individual characteristics associated with Wold Wide Web use: an empirical study of playfulness and motivation. *The DATA BASE for Advances in Information Systems, 28*(2), 53-62.

Aucella, A. (1997). *Ensuring Success with Usability Engineering.* Interactions May + June.

Avison, D., Lau, F., Myers, M., & Nielsen, P. A. (1999). Action research. *Communication of the ACM, 42*(1), 94-97.

Avison, D.E., & Fitzgerald, G. (1994). Information systems development. In W. Currie & R. Galliers (Eds.), *Rethinking management information systems: An interdisciplinary perspective* (pp. 250-278). Oxford: Oxford University Press.

Bailey, Darlyne, & McNally-Koney, K. (1996). Interorganizational community-based collaboratives: A strategic response to shape the social work agenda. *Social Work, 41*(6), 602-610.

Bailey, N. T. (1952). A study of queues and appointment systems in hospital outpatient departments, with special reference to waiting times. *Journal of the Royal Statistical Society, 14*(2), 185-199.

Bailey, N. T. (1954). Queuing for medical care. *Applied Statistics, 3,* 137-145.

Baker, A. (1981). *Ship or sheep? An intermediate pronunciation course.* Cambridge University Press.

Baker, A. (1998). *Tree or three? An elementary pronunciation course.* Cambridge University Press.

Bakker, A. R. (2002). Health care and ICT: Partnership is a must. *International Journal of Medical Informatics, 66*(2), 51-57.

Ballantine, J., & Stray, S. (1998). Financial appraisal and the IS/IT investment decision making process. *Journal of Information Technology, 13*(1), 3-14.

Ballantine, J., Galliers, R. D., & Stray, S. J. (1999). Information systems/technology evaluation practices: Evidence from UK organizations. In S. Lester (Ed.), *Beyond the IT productivity paradox* (pp. 123-150). Chichester: John Wiley & Sons.

Ballantine, J., Galliers, R., & Stray, S. (1994). Information system/technology investment decisions: The use of capital investment appraisal techniques in organisations. In *Proceedings of the 1st European Conference on IT Investment Evaluation* (pp. 148-166), Henley, United Kingdom.

Bandler, R., & Grinder, J. (1975). *The structure of magic I. A book about language and therapy* (Vol. I). Palo Alto, CA: Science and Behavior Books, Inc.

Bansler, J. (1989). Systems development research in Scandinavia: Three theoretical schools. *Scandinavian Journal of Information Systems, 1,* 3-20.

Bansler, J. P., & Bødker, K. (1993). A Reappraisal of Structured Analysis. *ACM Transactions on Information Systems, 11*(2),165-193.

Bansler, J. P., & Kraft, P. (1994). Privilege and invisibility in the new work order: A reply to Kyng. *Scandinavian Journal of Information Systems, 6*(1), 97-106.

Bao, X., & Xiang, Y. (2006). Digitalization and global ethics. *Ethics and Information Technology, 8,* 41-47.

Bardram, J. (1998). Designing for the dynamics of co-operative work activities. In *Proceedings of the ACM 1998 Conference on Computer Supported Cooperative Work* (pp. 89–98), New York City, New York. ACM Press.

Barki, H., & Hartwick, J. (1989). Measuring User Participation, User Involvement, and User Attitude. MIS Quarterly. (pp. 59-81).

Barley, S. R. (1990). The alignment of technology and structure through roles and networks. *Administrative Science Quarterly, 35* (2), 61-103.

Barley, S. R. (1986). Technology as an occasion for structuring: Evidence from observations of CT scanners and the social order of radiology departments. *Administrative Science Quarterly, 31*(1), 78-108.

Barley, S.R., & Tolbert, P.S. (1997). Institutionalization and structuration: Studying the link between action and institution. *Organization Studies, 93-117.*

Barrett, M., Cappleman, S., Shoib, G., & Walsham, G. (2004). Learning in knowledge communities: Managing technology and context. *European Management Journal, 22*(1), 1–11.

Barrow, R. (2005). On the duty of not taking offence. *Journal of Moral education, 34*(3), 265-275.

Bartholow, B., & Sestir, M. (2005). Correlates and consequences of exposure to video game violence: Hostile personality, empathy, and aggressive behavior. *Personality and Social Psycholgy Bulletin, 11,* 1573-1586. Retrieved June 27, 2006, from PubMed database.

Basden, A. (2005). The lifeworld: Dooyeweerd's approach to everyday experience. Retrieved September 17, 2006, from http://www.isi.salford.ac.uk/dooy/everyday.html#chcs

Baskerville, R. Investigating information systems with action research. *Communications of the Association for Information Systems, 19*(2). Retrieved October 5, 2006, from http://www.cis.gsu.edu/~rbaskerv/CAIS_2_19/CAIS_2_19.htm

Baskerville, R. L., & Stage, J. (1996, December). Controlling prototype development through risk analysis. *MIS Quarterly,* 481-503.

Baskerville, R., & Pries-Heje, J. (1999). Grounded action research: A method for understanding IT in practice. *Accounting, Management and Information Technologies, 9*(1).

Baskerville, R., & Pries-Heje, J. (1998). Information technology diffusion: Building positive barriers. *European Journal of Information Systems, 7,* 17-28.

Baskerville, R., & Pries-Heje, J. (2004). Short cycle time systems development. *Information Systems Journal, 14*(3), 237-265.

Baskerville, R., Travis, J., & Truex, D. (1992). Systems without method: The impact of new technologies on information systems development projects. In K. Kendall, K. Lyytinen, & J. DeGross. (Eds.), *The impact of computer supported technologies on information systems development* (pp. A-8). Amsterdam: Elsevier Science.

Baskerville, R., & Wood-Harper, A.T. (1999). A critical perspective on action research as a method for information systems research. *Journal of Information Technology, 11,* 235-246.

Bateson, G. (1972). *Steps to an ecology of mind.* New York: Ballantine Books.

Baudrillard, J. (1988). The year 2000 has already happened. In A. Kroker & M. Kroker (Eds.), *Body invaders:*

Sexuality and the postmodern condition. Basingstroke: Macmillian Press.

Baudrillard, J. (1998). *The transparency of evil* (J. Benedict, Trans.). London: Verso.

Bauman, Z. (1992). *Moderne und Ambivalenz. Das Ende der Eindeutigkeit.* Hamburg, Germany: Junius Verlag GmbH.

Bauman, Z. (1999). *Unbehagen in der Postmoderne.* Hamburger Edition, Hamburg, Germany.

Baumol, W. (2002). *The free-market innovation machine.* Princeton, NJ: Princeton University Press.

BBC News (2004). Africans rush for mobile phones. BBC News. Published May 5, 2004. http://news.bbc.co.uk/1/hi/world/africa/3686463.stm

Bearden, W. O., Sharma, S., & Teel, J. E. (1982). Sample Size Effects of Chi-Square and Other Statistics Used in Evaluating Causal Models. *Journal of Marketing Research, 19,* 425-430.

Beath, C. M., & Orlikowski, W. J. (1994). The contradictory structures of systems development methodologies: Deconstructing the IS-user relationship in information engineering. *Information Systems Research, 5*(4), 350-377.

Beath, C.M., & Orlikowski, W. (1994). The contradictory structure of systems development methodologies: Deconstructing the IS-user relationship in information engineering. *Information Systems Research, 5*(4), 350-377.

Beck, E. E. (2002). P for Political. Participation is not enough. *Scandinavian Journal of Information Systems 14*(1), 77-92.

Bell, R. (2001). *Benchmarking the intelligent community—a comparison study of regional communities.* The Intelligent Community Forum of World Teleport Association.

Bellman, S., Lohse, G.L., & Jordan, E.J. (1999). Predictors of online buying behavior. *Communications of the ACM, 42*(12), 32-38.

Bengtsson, B., Burgoon, J.K., Cederberg, C., Bonito, J., & Lundeberg, M. (1999). The impact of anthropomorphic interfaces on influence, understanding and credibility. In *Proceedings of the 32nd Hawaii International Conference on System Sciences,* IEEE.

Benson, C., Müller-Prove, M., & Mzourek, J. (2004). Professional usability in open source projects: GNOME, OpenOffice.org, NetBeans. *Extended Abstracts of the Conference on Human Factors in Computer Systems (CHI2004).* New York, ACM Press, 1083-1084.

Bergson, H. (1910). *Time and free will: An essay on the immediate data of consciousness* (F. Pogson, Trans.). London: George Allen and Unwin.

Bernier, C., & Laflamme, S. (2005). Uses of the Internet according to type and age: A double differentiation. [Usages d'Internet selon le genre et l'age: Une double differenciation] *The Canadian Review of Sociology and Anthropology/La Revue Canadienne De Sociologie Et d'Anthropologie, 42*(3), 301-323.

Beyer, H. R., & Goltzblatt, K. (1995). Apprenticing with the customer. *Communications of the ACM, 38*(5), 45-54.

Beyer, H., & Holtzblatt, K. (1998). *Contextual Design: Defining Customer-Centered Systems.* San Francisco: Morgan Kaufmann Publishers.

Beynon-Davies, P., Carne, C., Mackay, H., & Tudhope, D. (1999). Rapid application development (RAD): An empirical review. *European Journal of Information Systems, 8,* 211-223.

Bhabha, H. (Ed.) (1990). *Nation and Narration.* London: Routledge, an imprint of Taylor & Francis Books.

Bhabha, H. (Ed.) (2000). *Die Verortung der Kultur.* Tübingen, Germany: Stauffenburg Verlag.

Bhagwati, J. (1984, June). Splintering and disembodiment of services and developing nations. In J. Bhagwati (Ed.), *The world economy.* (Reprinted from *Writings on International Economics,* pp. 433-446, Oxford: Oxford University Press. (& Delhi 1998: Oxford University Press).

Bhaskar, R. (1989). *The possibility of naturalism* (2nd ed.). Hemel Hempstead: Harvester Wheatsheaf.

Bias, R., & Reitmeyer, P. (1995). Usability Support Inside and Out. *Interactions,* April, 29-32.

Biggs, J. (2003). *Teaching for Quality Learning at University: What the Student Does* (2nd ed.). Philadelphia, Pa: Society for Research into Higher Education & Open University Press.

Bikson, T.K., & Eveland, J.D. (1996). Groupware implementation: Reinvention in the sociotechnical frame. In M. Ackerman (Ed.), *Proceedings of the ACM 1996 conference on computer-supported cooperative work* (pp. 428–437). New York: ACM Press.

Billingsley, P. (1995). Starting from Scratch: Building a Usability Program at Union Pacific Railroad. *Interactions,* October, 27-30.

Bjerknes, G., & Bratteteig, T. (1995). User Participation and Democracy. A Discussion of Scandinavian Research on System Development. *Scandinavian Journal of Information Systems, 7*(1), 73-98.

Block, P. (1993). *Stewardship—Choosing service over self-interest.* San Francisco: Berrett-Koehler Publishers.

Blois, K. (1990). Research notes and communications—transaction costs and networks. *Strategic Management Journal, 11,* 493-496.

Blomberg, J., & Henderson, A. (1990). Reflections on Participatory Design: Lessons from the Trillium Experience. In *proceedings of CHI90.* New York: ACM Press. (pp. 353-359).

Bloomer, S., & Croft, R. (1997). Pitching Usability to Your Organization. *Interactions* November & December, 18-26.

Bloomfield, B., & Vurdubakis, T. (1997). Visions of Organization and Organizations of Vision: The Representational Practices of Information Systems Development. *Accounting, Organizations and Society, 22*(7), 639-668.

Bluedorn, A. C., Kaufman, C. J., & Lane, P. M. (1992). How Many Things Do You Like to Do at Once? An Introduction to Monochronic and Polychronic Time. *The Academy of Management Executive,* 17-26.

Bødker, M., Nielsen, L., & Orngreen, R. (2007). Enabling User-Centered Design Processes in Open Source Communities. In N. Aykin (ed.), Proc. Human Computer Interaction International, Part I: Usability and Internationalization. *LNCS* 4559, pp. 10-18.

Bødker, S., & Buur, J. (2002). The Design Collaboratorium – a Place for Usability Design. *ACM Transactions on Computer-Human Interaction, 9*(2), 152-169.

Bødker, S., & Iversen, O. (2002). Staging a Professional Participatory Design Practice. Moving PD Beyond the Initial Fascination of User Involvement. In Proc. 2nd Nordic conference on Human-computer interaction. New York: ACM Press. Pp. 11 – 18.

Bødker, S., Nielsen, C., & Petersen, M. G. (2000). Creativity, cooperation and interactive design. In *Proc. of DIS 2000,* 252-261.

Boisot, M. (1998). *Knowledge assets.* Oxford: Oxford University Press.

Boivie, I., Åborg, C., Persson, J., & Löfberg, M. (2003). Why usability gets lost or usability in in-house software development. *Interacting with Computers, 15,* 623-639.

Boland, R. J. (1979). Control, causality and information system requirements. *Accounting, Organization and Society, 4*(4), 259-272.

Boland, R. J. (1987). In-formation in information system design. In R.L. Boland & R.A. Hirschheim (Eds.), *Critical issues in information systems research.* New York: Wiley.

Boland, R. J. (1991). Information systems use as a hermeneutic process. In H. E. Nissen, H. K. Klein & R. A. Hirschheim (Eds.), *Information systems research: Contemporary approaches and emergent traditions* (pp. 439-464). Amsterdam: North-Holland.

Boland, R. J. (1978). The process and product of systems design. *Management Science, 24*(9).

Boland, R. J. (1984). Sense-making of accounting data as a technique of organizational diagnosis. *Management Science, 30*(7), 868-882.

Boland, R. J., & Pondy, L. R. (1983). Accounting in organizations: A union of natural and rational perspectives. *Accounting, Organanizations and Society, 8*, 223-234.

Boland, R. J., & Tenkasi, R.V. (1995). Perspective making and perspective taking in communities of knowing. *Organization Science, 6*(4), 350-372.

Boland, R.J., & Tenkasi, R.V. (1995). Perspective making and perspective taking in communities of knowing. *Organization Science, 6*(4), 350-372.

Booth, N. (2002). *Making the right choices- using computer consultation.* Retrieved January 4, 2004 from http://www.ncl.ac.uk

Bostrom, R.P., & Heinen, J.S. (1977). MIS problems and failures: A socio-technical perspective. Part I: The causes. *MIS Quarterly, 1*(3), 17-32.

Bouchikhi, A. (1990). *Structuration des organisation.* Paris: Economica.

Boudreau, M., Gefen, D., & Straub, D.W. (2001). Validation in Information Systems Research: A State-of-the-Art Assessment. *MIS Quarterly, 25*(1), 1-16.

Bourdieu, P. (1972). *Esquisse d'un théorie de la pratique.* Paris: Edition du Seuil.

Bouwen, R., & Taillieu, T. (2004). Multi-party collaboration as social learning for interdependence: Developing relational knowing for sustainable natural resource management. *Journal of Community & Applied Social Psychology, 14*, 137-153.

Bradford, R. (2003). Public-private partnerships? Shifting paradigms of economic governance in Ontario. *Canadian Journal of Political Sciences, 36*(5), 1005-1033.

Bradshaw, J.M. (1997). *Software agents.* Menlo Park, CA: AAAI Press/MIT Press.

Brandt, D., & Henning, K. (2002). Information and communication technologies: Perspectives and their impact on society. *AI & Society, 16*(3), 210-223.

Bray, J. (2005) *International companies and post-conflict reconstruction* (Social Development Papers No.79). Washington DC: The World Bank

Brennan, S.E., & Ohaeri, J.O. (1994). *Effects of message style on users' attributions toward agents.* Paper presented at the CHI '94 Human Factors in Computing System.

Broadbent, M., Weill, P., & St. Clair, D. (1999). The implications of information technology infrastructure for business process redesign. *MIS Quarterly, 23*(2), 159-182.

Brosnan, M. (1998). The impact of computer anxiety and self-efficacy upon performance. *Journal of Computer Assisted Learning, 14*, 223-234.

Brosnan, M. (1998). *Technophobia. The psychological impact of information technology.* London: Routledge.

Brown, J. S., & Duguid, P. (2001). Knowledge and organization: A social-practice perspective. *Organization Science, 12*(2), 198-213.

Brown, J. S., & Duguid, P. (2002). *The social life of information.* Boston: Harvard Business School Press.

Brown, M., O'Toole, L., & Brudney, J. (1998). Implementing information technology in government: An empirical assessment of the role of local partnerships. *Journal of Public Administration Research and Theory, 8*(4), 499-525.

Brown, R. (1990). Rhetoric, textuality and the postmodern turn in sociological theory. *Sociological Theory, 8*(2), 188-197.

Browne, M. W., & Cudeck, R. (1993). Alternate Ways of Assessing Model Fit. In K.A. Bollen & J.S. Long (Ed.) *Testing Structural Equation Models* (pp. 139-154). Newbury Park, CA: Sage Publications,

Bryant, A. (2000). It's engineering Jim ... but not as we know it. Software engineering: Solution to the software crisis, or part of the problem? In *Proceedings of the 22nd International Conference on Software Engineering* (pp. 78 – 87), Limerick, Ireland.

Buber, M. (1993). *Sinä ja minä* [I and Thou]. Juva: WSOY.

Burke, J. (1978). *Connections*. London: Macmillian Press.

Burkhardt, M. E., & Brass, D. J. (1990). Changing patterns or patterns of change: The effects of a change in technology on social network structure and power. *Administrative science quaterly, 35*(1), 104-127.

Burns, T. (1992), *Erving Goffman*. London: Routledge

Buur, J., & Bagger, K. (1999). Replacing Usability Testing with User Dialogue. *Communications of the ACM, 42*(5), 63-66.

Bynum, T. W., & Rogerson, S. (1996). Global information ethics: Introduction and overview. *Science and Engineering Ethics, 2*(2), 131-136.

Byrd, T. A., Cossick, K. L., & Zmud, R. W. (1992). A synthesis of research on requirements analysis and knowledge acquisition techniques. *MIS Quarterly, 16*(1), 117-138.

Byrne, B. M. (1998). *Structural Equation Modeling with LISREL, PRELIS, and SIMPLIS: Basic Concepts, Applications, and Programming*. Mahwa, NJ: Lawrence Erlbaum Associates.

Callon, M., & Latour, B. (1990). *La Science telle qu'elle se fait*. Paris: Editions La Découverte.

Callon, M., & Latour, B. (1992). *Aramis, ou l'amour des techniques*. Paris: Editions La Découverte.

Campbell, A. (2003). Creating customer knowledge: Managing customer relationship management programs strategically. *Industrial Marketing Management, 32*(5), 375–383.

Canadian National Broadband Taskforce. (2001). *Report of the national broadband taskforce: The new national dream: Networking the nation for broadband access*. Ottawa, Canada: Industry Canada.

Canadian Rural Partnership. (2004, October). *Report of the advisory committee on rural issues*. Paper presented at the Third National Rural Conference, Red Deer, Canada.

Capurro, R. (in press). Intercultural information ethics. In R. Capurro, J. Frühbaure, & T. Hausmanningers (Eds.), *Localizing the Internet. Ethical issues in intercultural perspective*. Munich: Fink Verlag. Retrieved January 25, 2007, from http://www.capurro.de/iie.html

Capurro, R. (2005). Privacy: An intercultural perspective. Ethics and Information Technology, 7(1), 37-47.

Carlson, J. R., & Zmud, R. W. ((1992). Channel expansion theory and the experiential nature of media richness perceptions. *Academy of Management Journal, 42*(2), 152-170.

Carlsson, S. A. (2003). Advancing information systems evaluation (research): A critical realist approach. *Electronic Journal of Information System Evalution, 6*(2).

Carmel, E., Whitaker, R. D., & George, J. F. (1993). PD and joint application design: A transatlantic comparison. *Communications of the ACM, 36*(4), 40-48.

Caron, R.J., Jarvenpaa, S.L., & Stoddard, D.B. (1994). Business reengineering at CIGNA Corporation: Experiences and lessons learned from the first five years. *MIS Quarterly, 18*(3), 233–250.

Carroll, J. M. (2001). Community computing as human – Computer interaction. *Behaviour & Information Technology, 20*(5), 307-314.

Carroll, J. M., & Rosson, M. (2001). Better home shopping or new democracy? Evaluating community network outcomes. *3*(1), 372-377.

Castells, M. (1998). *End of millennium, vol. 3 of the information age: Economy, society and culture*. Oxford: Blackwell.

Casson, M. (1982). *The entrepreneur. An economic theory*. Oxford.

Castells, M. (1996-1998). *The information age: Economy, society and culture*. 3 volumes. Oxford: Blackwell.

Castells, M. (2001). *The Internet galaxy*. Oxford: Blackwell.

Castells, M. (1997). *The power of identity, vol. 2 of the information age: Economy, society and culture*. Oxford: Blackwell.

Castells, M. (1996). *The rise of network society, vol. 1 of the information age: Economy, society and culture*. Oxford: Blackwell.

Catarci, T., Matarazzo, G., & Raiss, G. (2002). Driving usability into the public administration: the Italian experience. *International Journal of Human-Computer Studies, 57*, 121-138.

Cattell, R. B. (1949). RP and other coefficients of pattern similarity. *Psychometrika, 14*, 279-298.

Caves, R. (2001). E-commerce and information technology: Information technologies, economic development, and smart communities: Is there a relationship? *Economic Development Review, 17*(3), 6-13.

CDER. (2004). *FDA/Centre for Drug Evaluation and Research, medication errors*. Retrieved November 11, 2004 from http://www.fda.gov/cder/drug/MedErrors/default.htm

Cetin, G., Verzulli, D., & Frings, S. (2007). An Analysis of Involvement of HCI Experts in Distributed Software Development: Practical Issues. In D. Schuler (ed.). Proc. Human Computer Interaction International: Online Communities and Social Computing. *LNCS, 4564*, 32-40.

Chan, Y. E., Huff, S. L., Barclay, D. W., & Copeland, D. G. (1997). Business strategic orientation, information systems strategic orientation, and strategic alignment. *Information Systems Research, 8*(2), 125-51.

Chang, K. (2004, April 6). In math, computers don't lie. Or do they? *New York Times*. Retrieved October 5, 2006, from http://www.math.binghamton.edu/zaslav/Nytimes/+Science/+Math/sphere-packing.20040406.html

Chaomei, C., & Roy, R. (1996). Modeling situated actions in collaborative hypertext databases. *Journal of Computer Mediated Communication, 2* (3).

Chau, P. Y. K. (2001). Influence of computer attitude and self-efficacy on IT usage behavior. *Journal of End User Computing, 13*(1), 26-33.

Checkland, P. (1981). *Systems thinking, systems practice*. Chichester: Wiley.

Checkland, P., & Howell, S. (1998). *Information, systems and information systems: Making sense of the field*. Chichester: Wiley.

Chen, L., Gillenson, M., & Sherrell, D. (2002). Enticing online consumers: An extended technology acceptance perspective. *Information & Management, 39*(1), 705-719.

Childers, T., Carr, C., Peck, J., & Carson, S. (2001). Hedonic and Utilitarian motivations for online retail shopping behaviour. *Journal of Retailing, 77*(4), 35-48.

Chin, W. W., &. Newsted, R. N. (1995). The Importance of Specification in Causal Modeling: The Case of End-User Computing Satisfaction. *Information Systems Research, 6*(1), 73-81.

Choi, B., Lee, I., Kim, J., & Jeon, Y. (2005). A Qualitative Cross-National Study of Cultural Influences on Mobile Data Service Design. In *Proceedings of CHI 2005*, (Portland, Oregon, USA), pp.. 661-670.

Choudrie, J., & Dwivedi, Y. K. (2005). Investigating the research approaches for examining technology adoption issues. *Journal of Research Practice, 1*(1).

Churchill, E. (2001). *Getting About a Bit: Mobile Technologies & Mobile Conversations in the UK*. FXPL. International Technical report, FXPAL.TR.01-009.

Churchman, C. W., & Schainblatt, A. H. (1965). The researcher and the manager: A dialectic of implementation. *Management Science, 11*(4), 69-87.

Ciborowski, T. J. (1979). Cross-Cultural aspects of Cognitive Functioning: Culture and Knowledge. In A. J. Marsella, R. G. Tharp, and T. J. Ciborowski (Eds), *Perspectives on Cross-Cultural Psychology*. New York, NY: Academic Press Inc.

Ciborra, C. (2002). *The labyrinths of information*. Oxford: Oxford University Press.

Ciborra, C. (Ed.). (1996). Introduction. *Groupware and teamwork, invisible aid or technical hindrance?* (pp. 1-19). Chichester: Wiley.

Ciborra, C., & Failla, A. (2000). Infrastructure as a process: The case of CRM in IBM. In C. Ciborra, & Associates, *From control to drift* (pp. 105-124). Oxford: Oxford University Press.

Ciborra, C., & Hanseth, O. (1998). From tool to gestell. *Information Technology and* People, *11*(4), 305-327. (Reprinted as Ch. 4, pp. 56-82, by C. Ciborra, 2002).

Ciborra, C., & Hanseth, O. (2000). Introduction. In Ciborra & Associates, *From control to drift* (pp. 1-15) Oxford: Oxford University Press.

Ciborra, C. U. (2000). A critical review of the literature on the management of corporate information infrastructure. In C. U. Ciborra, (Ed.), *From control to drift* (pp.15-41). Oxford: Oxford university press.

Ciborra, C. U. (1997). De profundis? Deconstructing the concept of strategic alignment. *IRIS, (20)*.

Ciborra, C.U. (1996). Introduction. In C.U. Ciborra (Ed.), *Groupware & teamwork: Invisible aid or technical hindrance?* Chichester, U.K.: Wiley.

Ciborra, C. U. (2001). Moods, situated action and time: A new study of improvisation. *IRIS*, 24.

Ciborra, C. U. (1999). A theory of information systems based on improvisation. In W. L. Currie & B. Galliers, *Rethinking management information systems* (pp.136-55).Oxford: Oxford University press.

Clement, A. (1994). Computing at Work: Empowering Action By 'Low-level Users'. *Communications of the ACM, 37*(1), 52-63.

Clement, A., & Van den Besselaar, P. (1993). A Retrospective Look at PD Projects. *Communications of the ACM, 36*(4), 29-37.

Clifford, J., & Marcus, G. (1986). *Writing culture: the poetics and politics of ethnography.* Berkeley: University of California Press.

Cohen, P. (1988). The perversions of inheritance: Studies in the making of multi-racist Britain. In P. Cohen & Bains (Eds.), *Multi-racist Britain.* London: Pluto Press.

Cole, R., Massaro, D.W., Rundle, B., Shobaki, K., Wouters, J., Cohen, M., et al. (1999). *New tools for interactive speech and language training: Using animated conversational agents in the classrooms of profoundly deaf children.* Paper presented at the ESCA/SOCRATES Workshop on Method and Tool Innovations for Speech Science Education.

Collins, H.M. (1990). *Artificial experts: Social knowledge and intelligent machines.* Cambridge, MA: MIT Press.

Compeau, D. R., & Higgins, C. A. (1995). Computer self-efficacy: Development of a measure and initial test. *MIS Quarterly, 19*(2), 189-211.

Considine, M., & Lewis, J. (2003). Networks and interactivity: Making sense of front-line governance in the United Kingdom, the Netherlands and Australia. *Journal of European Public Policy, 10*(1), 46-58.

Cook, S. D. N., & Brown, J. S. (1999). Bridging epistemologies: The generative dance between organizational knowledge and organizational knowing. *Organization Science, 10*(4).

Cooper, A. (1999). *The inmates are running the asylum: Why high-tech products drive us crazy and how to restore the sanity.* Indianapolis: Sams.

Cooper, C., & Bowers, J. (1995). Representing the users: Notes on the disciplinary rhetoric of human-computer interaction. In Peter J. Thomas (Ed.), *The Social and Interactional Dimensions of Human-Computer Interfaces.* Cambridge: Cambridge University Press. Pp. 48-66.

Cooper, G. (2000). *The Mutable Mobile: Social Theory in the Wireless World.* Paper presented at the 'Wireless World' workshop, University of Surrey, April 7th.

Corbett, A. (2002). Recognizing high-tech opportunities: A learning and cognitive approach. *Frontiers of Entrepreneurship Research* (pp. 49-60).Wellesley, MA: Babson College.

Cortes, C. E. (2000). *The children are watching: How the media teach about diversity.* New York: Teachers College Press.

Costello, R. J., & Liu, D.-B. (1995). Metrics for requirements engineering. *Journal of Systems and Software, 29*(1), 39-63.

Cotterman, W.W., & Kumar, K. (1989). User cube: A taxonomy of end users. *Communications of the ACM, 32*(11), 1313-1320.

Cougar, J. D. (1996). Creativity & *innovation in information systems organizations.* Danvers: Boyd & Fraser.

Coursey, D., & Killingsworth, J. (2000). Managing Government Web Services in Florida: Issues and Lessons. In D. Garson (Ed.), *Handbook of Public Information Systems.* New York: Marcel Dekker.

Crane, D. (1972). *Invisible colleges: Diffusion of knowledge in scientific communities.* Chicago: The University of Chicago Press.

Cronbach, L. J., & Gleser, G. C. (1952). Similarity between persons and related problems of profile analysis. *Urbana: University of Illinois, Bureau of Research and Serviec, College of Education.*

Cronbach, L. J., & Gleser, G. C. (1953). Assessing similarity between profiles. *The Psychological Bulletin,* 50(6), 456-473.

Crossan, M.M., Lane, H.W., & White, R.E. (1999). An organisational learning framework: From intuition to institution. *Academy of Management Review, 24*(3), 522–537.

Crossan, M.M., Lane, H.W., & White, R.E. (1999). An organizational learning framework: From intuition to institution. *Academy of Management Review, 24*(3), 522-537.

Crotty, M. (1998). *The foundations of social research.* Thousand Oaks, California: Sage.

Crowley, D. (2002). Where are we now? Contours of the internet in Canada. *Canadian Journal of Communication, 27*(4), 469-508.

Csikszentmihalyi, M. (1975). *Beyond boredom and anxiety.* San Francisco: Jossey-Bass.

Csikszentmihalyi, M. (1997b). *Finding flow: The psychology of engagement with everyday life.* New York: Basic Books.

Csikszentmihalyi, M. (1997). *Creativity: Flow and the psychology of discovery and invention.* New York: Harpers-Collins.

Csikszentmihalyi, M. (1990). *Flow: The psychology of optimal experience.* New York: Harper & Row.

Daft, R. L., & Lengel, R. H. (1984). Information richness: A new approach to managerial behavior and organization design. In L. L. Cummings and B. M. Staw (Ed.), *Research in organizational behavior.* Greenwich, CT: JAI, 6, 191-233.

Daft, R. L., & Macintosh, V. B. (1981). A tentative exploration into the amount and equivocality of information processing in organizational work units. *Administrative Science Quarterly, 26*, 207-224.

Daft, R. L., and Weick, K. E. (1984). Toward a model of organizations as interpretation systems. *Academy of Management Review, 9*, 284-295.

Dagwell, R., & Weber, R. (1983). System designers' user models: A comparative study and methodological critique. *Communications of the ACM, 26*(11), 987-997.

Davenport, T. H., & Beers, M. C. (1995). Managing information about processes. *Journal of Management Information Systems, 12*(1), 57-81.

Davies, B. (2006, October 3). Full proof? Let's trust it to the black box. *Times higher education supplement.*

Davis, F. D. (1989). Perceived usefulness, perceived ease of use, and user acceptance of information technology. *MIS Quarterly, 13*(3), 319-340.

Davis, F. D. (1993). User acceptance of information technology: System characteristics, user perceptions and behavioral impacts. *International Journal of Man Machine Studies, 38*, 475-487.

Davis, F. D., Bagozzi, R. P., & Warshaw, P. R. (1989). User acceptance of information technology: A comparison of two theoretical models. *Management Science, 35*(8), 982-1003.

Davis, F. D., Bagozzi, R. P., & Warshaw, P., R. (1989). User acceptance of computer technology: A comparison of two theoretical models. *Management Science, 35*(8), 982-1003.

Davis, F. W. (1989). Perceived usefulness, perceived ease of use, and user acceptance of information technology. *MIS Quarterly, 13*(3), 319-340.

Day, C. (2002). *The information society—a sceptical view.* Malden, MA: Blackwell Publishers.

De Angeli, A., Johnson, G.I., & Coventry, L. (2001). The unfriendly user: Exploring social reactions to chatterbots. In *Proceedings of the International Conference on Affective Human Factors Design,* London. Asean Academic Press.

De Certeau. (1988). *The practice of everyday life.* Berkeley.

De George, R. (2006). Information technology, globalization and ethics. *Ethics and Information Technology, 8,* 29–40.

De la Mothe, J. (2004). The institutional governance of technology, society, and innovation. *Technology in Society, 26,* 523-536.

De Millo, R.A., Lipton, R.J., & Perlis, A.J. (1977). Social processes and proofs of theorems and programs. In *Proceedings of the 4th ACM Symposium on Principles of Programming Language* (pp. 206-214).

de Vaujany, F. X. (2003). Les figures de la gestion du changement sociotechnique. *Sociologie du travail, 45*(4), 515-536.

Debord, G. (1994). *Society of the spectacle.* (D. Nicholson-Smith, Trans.). New York: Zone Books.

Debord, G. (2002). Editorial notes: Priority communication. In T. McDonough (Ed.), *Guy Debord and the situationist international: Text and documents.* Cambridge, MA: The MIT Press.

Debord, G., & Wolman, G. (1956, May). A user's guide to détournement. *Les Lèvres Nues, 8.* Retrieved September 17, 2006, from http://www.bopsecrets.org/SI/detourn.htm

Deetz, S. (1996). Describing differences in approaches to organization science: Rethinking Burrell and Morgan and their legacy. *Organization Science, 7*(2), 191-207.

Dehn, D.M., & van Mulken, S. (2000). The impact of animated interface agents: A review of empirical research. *International Journal of Human-Computer Studies, 52,* 1-22.

Delamere, F. M. (2005). 'It's just really fun to play!' A constructionist perpective on violence and gender representations in violent video games. *Dissertation Abstracts International, 65*(10-A), 3986.

Delone, W. H., & McLean, E. R. (1992). Information Success: The Quest for the Dependent Variable. *Information Systems Research, 3*(1), 60-95.

DeLone, W. H., & McLean, E. R. (1992). Information systems success: The quest for the dependent variable. *Information Systems Research, 3*(1), 60-95.

Deming, W.E. (1993). *The new economists of industry, government, education.* Cambridge, MA: MIT Centre for Advanced Engineering Study.

Deng, X., Doll, W. J., Al-Gahtani, S. S., Larsen, T. J., Pearson, J. M., & Raghunathan, T. S. (2008). A cross-cultural analysis of the End-User Computing Satisfaction instrument: A multi-group invariance analysis. *Information & Management, 45*(4), 211-220.

Derrida, J. (1972). *Die Schrift und die Differenz.* Frankfurt/Main, Germany: Suhrkamp Verlag.

Derrida, J. (1978). *Writing and difference.* (A. Bass, Trans.). London: Routledge & Kegan Paul.

Dertouzos, M.L. (1999). The future of computing. *Scientific American, 281,* 36-39.

DeSanctis, G. (1983). Expectancy theory as an explanation of voluntary use of a decision support system. *Psychological Reports, 52*(247-260).

DeSanctis, G., & Poole, M. (1994). Capturing the complexity in advanced technology use: Adaptive structuration theory. *Organization Science, 5*, 121–147.

Dietz, T. (1998). An examination of violence and gender role portrayals in video games:

Dishaw, M. T., & Strong, D. M. (1999). Extending the technology acceptance model with task-technology fit constructs. *Information & Management, 36*(1), 9-21.

Dixon, N. (1994). *The organisational learning cycle.* London: McGraw-Hill.

Dobson, P. J. (1999, December). *Approaches to theory use in interpretive case studies.* Paper presented at 10th Australian Conference on Information Systems, Wellington, New Zealand.

Dobson, P. J. (2002). Critical realism and information systems research: Why bother with philosophy? [Electronic version]. *Information Research, 7*(2).

Dobson, P. J. (2003). The SoSM revisited---A critical realist perspective. In J. J. Cano (Ed.), *Critical reflections on information systems: A systemic approach* (pp. 122-135). Hershey, PA: Idea Group Publishing.

Doll, W. J., & Torkzadeh, G. (1988). The Measurement of End-User Computing Satisfaction. *MIS Quarterly, 12*(2), 259-274.

Doll, W. J., Deng, X., Raghunathan, T. S., Torkzadeh, G., & Xia, W. (2004). The Meaning and Measurement of User Satisfaction: A Multigroup Invariance Analysis of the End-User Computing Satisfaction Instrument. *Journal of Management Information Systems, 21*(1), 228-262.

Doll, W. J., Xia, W., & Torkzadeh, G. (1994). A Confirmatory Factor Analysis of the End-User Computing Satisfaction Instrument. *MIS Quarterly, 18*(4), 453-461.

Donner, J. (2005c). *The Rules of Beeping: Exchanging Messages using Missed Calls on Mobile Phones in Sub-Saharan Africa.* Paper presented at the 55th Annual Conference of the International Communication Association: Questioning the Dialogue, New York.

Doolin, B. (1999). Information Systems, Power, and Organizational Relations: A Case Study. In Prabuddha

De, Janice I. DeGross (Eds.), *Proc. 20th International Conference on Information Systems*, December 13-15, 1999 Charlotte, USA. (pp. 286-290).

Dosi, G., Teece, D., & Chytry, J. (Eds.) (1997). *Technology, organization, and competitiveness.* Oxford: Oxford University Press.

Doty, D. H., & Glick, W. H. (1994). Typologies as a unique form of theory building: Toward improved understanding and modeling. *Academy of Management Review, 19*(2), 230-251.

Doty, D. H., Glick, W. H., & Huber, G. P. (1994). Fit, equifinality, and organizational effectiveness: A test of two configurational theories. *Academy of Management Journal, 36*(6), 1196-1250.

Dowing, C. E. (1999). System usage behaviour as a proxy for user satisfaction: An empirical investigation. *Information & Management, 35*, 203-216.

Doz, Y. (1996). The evolution of cooperation in strategic alliances: Initial conditions or learning processes? *Strategic Management Journal, 17*, 55-83.

DSDM Consortium. (2006). White papers. Retrieved October 5, 2006, from *http://www.dsdm.org/products/white_papers.asp*

Du Gay, P., Hall, S., Janes, L., Mackay, H., & Negus, K. (1997). *Doing cultural studies: The story of the Sony, Walkman,* London and New Delhi: Sage.

Earl, M. (1996). Putting information technology in its place: A polemic for the nineties. *Journal of Information Technology, 7*, 100-108.

Earl, M. J. (1989). *Management strategies for information technology.* Cambridge University Press/Prentice Hall International.

Ebers, M. (2002). *The formation of inter-organizational networks.* Oxford: Oxford University Press.

Eco, U. (1986). *Nachschrift zum Namen der Rose.* München, Germany: dtv.

Edmondson, A. (1999). Psychological safety and learning behavior in work teams. *Administrative Science Quarterly, 44*(2), 350–383.

Eger, J. (2001, November). *The world foundation for smart communities.* Retrieved January 28, 2003 from www.smartcommunities.org

Eisenhardt, K. M. (1985). Control: Organizational and economic approaches. *Management Science, 31*(2), 134-149.

Elliot, S. & Loebbecke, C. (2000). Interactive, inter-organisational innovations in electronic commerce. *Information Technology and People, 13*(1), 46-66.

El-Shinnawy, M., & Markus, M. L. (1997). The poverty of media richness theory: Explaining people's choice of electronic mail vs. voice mail. *International Journal of Human-Computer Studies, 46*(4), 443-467.

Epstar. (2003). *Mobiilitoiminto kotihoidon ja apteekin palveluissa* [Mobile functions in home care and pharmacy services]. Helsinki: Epstar Oy.

Erikoissairaanhoitolaki [Law on special health care]. (1998).

ESHA (2004, July). *Strategic health authority internal NPfit staff bulletin.* (2).

Espejo, R. (Ed.). (2003). *Video games.* San Diego: Greenhaven Press.

Ess, C. (2002). Computer-mediated colonization, the renaissance, and educational imperatives for an intercultural global village. *Ethics and Information Technology, 4*(1), 11-22.

Ess, C. (2002). Computer-mediated colonization, the renaissance, and educational imperatives for an intercultural global village. *Ethics and Information Technology, 4*(1), 11-22.

EU Report (2008). *Preparing Europe's digital future i2010 Mid-Term ReviewCOM,* 199, SEC(2008) 470 Volumes 1, 2, 3, April, ISBN 978-92-823-2434-9, European Communities.

Evans, J., & Brooks, L. (2005). Understanding collaboration using new technologies: A structural perspective. *Information Society, 21*(3), 215-220.

Evers, V., & Day, D. (1997). The Role of Culture in Interface Acceptance. In Mende S. Howard, J. Hammond

and G.Lindgaard, *Proceedings of the Human Computer Interaction INTERACT'97 Conference* (pp. 260 – 267). Sydney: Chapman and Hall.

Failla, A. (1996). Technologies for co-ordination in a software factory. In C. Ciborra (Ed.), *Groupware and teamwork, invisible aid or technical hindrance?* (pp. 61-88). Chichester: Wiley.

Failla, A., & Mazzotti, S. (2004). *Competent. Project Validation phase of Scenario 1 Human Resources Developer: Valorising the Company Asset Base.* Fondazione IBM Italia Milano.

Fairclough, N., & Wodak, R. (1997). Critical Discourse Analysis. In Teun A. van Dijk (ed.): Discourse as Social Interaction. *Discourse Studies: A Multidisciplinary Introduction, 2,* 258-284London: SAGE Publications.

Fairey, M. (2003). Barriers to the success of delivering 21st century IT support for the NHS. *British Journal of Healthcare Computing & Information Management, 20*(2), 28-31.

Farbey, B., Land, F. F., & Targett, T. (1995). A taxonomy of information systems applications: The benefits' evaluation ladder. *European Journal of Information Systems, 4,* 41-50.

Farbey, B., Land, F., & Targget, D. (1998). Editorial. *European Journal of Information Systems, 7,* 155-157.

Faulkner, W. (2000). The power and the pleasure? A research agenda for 'making gender stick.' *Science, Technology & Human Values, 25*(1), 87-119.

Feinberg. J. (1985). *The moral limits of the criminal law. Vol. 2: Offense to others.* Oxford: Oxford University Press.

Feinberg, J. (1973). *Social philosophy.* Englewood Cliffs, NJ: Prentice Hall.

Feldman, M., & March, J. (1981). Information in organizations as signal and symbol. *Administrative Science Quarterly, 26,* 171-186.

Fellenz, C. B. (1997). Introducing Usability into Smaller Organizations. *Interactions* September/October, 29-33.

Feller, J., & Fitzgerald, B. (2000). A Framework Analysis of the Open Source Development Paradigm. In *Proc. 21ˢᵗ International Conference on Information Systems*, December 10-13, 2000, Brisbane, Australia, pp. 58-69.

Fenech, T. (1998). Using perceived ease of use and perceived usefulness to predict acceptance of the world wide web. *Computer Networks and ISDN Systems, 30*, 629-630.

Fetterman, D. (1998). *Ethnography.* Thousand Oaks, CA: Sage Publications.

Finken, S. (2003). Discursive conditions of knowledge production within cooperative design. *Scandinavian Journal of Information Systems, 15*, 57-72.

Finnish Ministry of Social Welfare and Health. (2003). *Kansallinen projekti terveydenhuollon tulevaisuuden turvaamiseksi. Hoidon saatavuus ja jonojen hallinta* [A national project to guarantee the future of health care. Availability of care and management of queues] (Working Group Memo 2003:33). Ministry of Social Welfare and Health.

Firth, P. (2003). Preparing for healthcare and social care integration: Some current barriers to ICT based sharing of information. *The British Journal of Healthcare Computing & Management, 20*(5), 21-24.

Fischer, G., Scharff, E., & Ye, Y. (2004). In M. Huysman & V. Wulf (Eds.). *Social capital and information technology* (Chapter 14). Cambridge, MA and London: The MIT Press.

Fishbein, M., & Ajzen, I. (1975). *Belief, Attitude, Intention, and Behavior: An introduction to theory and research.* Reading, Massachusetts: Addison-Wesley Publishing Company.

Fishman, P. (1983). Interaction: The work women do. In B. Thorne, C. Kramarae, & N. Henley (Eds.), *Language, gender and society* (pp. 89-101). Cambridge, MA: Newbury House.

Fiske, J. (1992). British cultural studies and television. In R. C. Allen (Ed.), *Channels of discourse, reassembled: Television and contemporary criticism* (pp.284-326). (2ⁿᵈ ed.) Chapel Hill: University of North Carolina Press.

Fiske, J. (1994). Moments of television: Neither the text nor the audience. In E. Seiter, H. Brochers, G. Kreutzner, & E. M. Warth (Eds.), *Remote control: Television audiences and cultural power* (pp. 56-78). New York: Routledge.

Fitzgerald, B. (2006). The Transformation of Open Source Software. *MIS Quarterly*, (3), 587-598.

Floridi, L. (in press). Information ethics. In J. van den Hoven & J. Weckert (Eds.), *Moral philosophy and information technology.* Cambridge: Cambridge University Press.

Floridi, L. (2005). Presence: From epistemic failure to successful observability. *Presence: Teleoperators and virtual environments, 14*(6), 656-667.

Floridi, L., & Sanders, J. W. (2004). The method of abstraction. In M. Negrotti (Ed.), *Yearbook of the artificial. Nature, culture and technology. Models in contemporary sciences* (pp. 177-220). Bern: Peter Lang.

Floridi, L., & Sanders, J. W. (in press). *Levelism and the method of abstraction.* Manuscript submitted for publication.

Flusser, V. (1993). *Digitaler Schein.* In: Ders. *Lob der Oberflächlichkeit. Für eine Phänomenologie der Medien.* (= Schriften Bd.1) p.272-285.Mannheim, Germany: Bollmann.

Folkman, S., & Moskowitz, J.T. (2000). Positive affect and the other side of coping. *American Psychologist, 55*(6), 647-654.

Fornell, C., & Larker, D. F. (1981). Evaluating Structural Equation Models with Unobserved Variables and Measurement Error. *Journal of Marketing Research, 18*, 39-51.

Forsythe, D.E. (2001). *Studying those who study as: An anthropologist in the world of artificial intelligence.* Stanford University Press.

Fortunati, L. (2000). *The Mobile Phone: New Social Categories and Relations.* Paper presented at the seminar 'Sosiale Konsekvenser av Mobiltelefoni', organised by Telenor, 16ᵗʰ June, 2000, Oslo.

Foster, H. (1983). Postmodernism: A preface. In H. Foster (Ed.), *Postmodern culture*. London: Pluto Press.

Foucault, M. (1972). *The Archaeology of Knowledge and the Discourse on Language*. New York: Pantheon Books.

Foucault, M. (1980). *The History of Sexuality. Volume 1: An Introduction*. Translated by Robert Hurley. New York: Vintage Books.

Foucault, M. (1980). *Power/knowledge: Selected interviews and other writings, 1972-1977*. New York: Pantheon.

Fountain, J. (2001). *Building the Virtual State: Information Technology and Institutional Change*. Brookings Institution, Washington.

Fountain, J. (2003). Electronic Government and Electronic Civics. In B. Wellman(Ed.), *Encyclopedia of Community*. Great Barrington, Berkshire, 436– 441.

Francis, H. (1993). Advancing phenomenography: Questions of method. *Nordisk Pedagogik, 13*, 68-75.

Franke, N., & von Hippel, E. (2003). Satisfying heterogeneous user needs via innovation toolkits: the case of Apache security software. *Research Policy, 32*, 1199-1215.

Franklin, U. (1999). *The real world of technology*. Toronto: House of Anansi Press.

Franz, C. R., & Robey, D. (1984). An investigation of user-led systems design: Rational and political perspectives. *Communications of the ACM, 27*(12), 1202-1209.

Fredrickson, B.L., & Branigan, C. (2001). Positive emotions. In T. Mayne & G. Bonanno (Eds.), *Emotions: Current issues and future directions* (pp. 123-151). New York: Guilford Press.

Frenkel, S., Korczynski, M., Shire, K., & Tam, M. (1999). *On the front line. Organisation of work in the information economy*. Ithaca: Cornell University Press.

Frishberg, N., Dirks, A. M., Benson, C., Nickel, S., & Smith, S. (2002). Getting to know you: Open source development meets usability. *Extended Abstracts of the Conference on Human Factors in Computer Systems (CHI 2002)*. New York, ACM Press, pp. 932-933.

Fulk, J., Schmitz, J. A., & Steinfield, C. W. (1990). A social influence model of technology use. In J. Fulk and C. Steinfield (Eds.), *Organizations and communication technology* (pp. 117-140). J. Newbury Park, CA: Sage.

Funke-Kloesters, B. (2004). *Autostadt GmbH: Marketing und Kultur*. unveröffentlichter Text, Wolfsburg, Germany.

Galliers, R. D., Merali, Y., & Spearing, L. (1994). Coping with information technology? How british executives perceive the key information systems management issues in the mid-1990s. *Journal of Information Technology, 9*(4), 223-238.

Game, A. (1996). *Passionate sociology*. London: Sage Publications.

Gardner, C., & Amoroso, D. L. (2004). *Development of an instrument to measure the acceptance of Internet technology by consumers*. Paper presented at the Proceedings of the 37th Hawaii International Conference on System Sciences.

Gärtner, J., & Wagner, I. (1996). Mapping Actors and Agendas: Political Frameworks of Systems Design and Participation. *Human-Computer Interaction, 11*, 187-214.

Gaver, B. (2001, October). Designing for ludic aspects of everyday life. *ERCIM News*, 47. Retrieved from http://www.ercim.org/publication/Ercim_News/enw47/gaver.html.

Gee, J. (2003). *What video games have to teach us about learning and literacy*. New York: Palgrave/St. Martin's.

Geertz, C. (1983). Thick description: Toward an interpretive theory of culture. In R. M. Emerson (Ed.), *Contemporary field research: A collection of readings*. Prospect Heights, Illinois: Waveland Press.

Gefen, D., and Straub, D. (1997). Gender differences in the perception and use of e-mail: An extension to the technology acceptance model. *MIS Quarterly, 21*(4), 389-401.

Gellerson, H., & Gaedke, M. (1999). Object orientated web application development. *IEEE Internet Computing, 3*(1), 60-68.

Gergen, K., & Thatchenkery, T. (2004, June). Organization science as social construction: Postmodern potentials. *The Journal of Applied Behaviorial Science, 40*(2), 228-249.

Gert, B. (1999). Common morality and computing. *Ethics and Information Technology, 1,* 57-64.

Geser, H. (2005). Towards a Sociological Theory of the Mobile Phone. In Zerdick, A., Picot, A, Scrape. K., Burgleman, J-C, Silverstone, R., Feldmann, V., Wernick, C. and Wolff, C. (Eds.). *E-Merging Media: Communication and the Media Economy of the Future.* Springer, Berling. (pp.235-60). Also available at http://socio.ch/mobile/t_geser1.pdf

Ghani, J. A. (1991). Flow in human-computer interactions: Test of a model. In J. Carey (Ed.), *Human factors: Management information systems: An organizational perspective.* 229-237. Norwood, NJ: Ablex.

Ghani, J. A., and Deshpande, S. P. (1994). Task characteristics and the experience of optimal flow in human-computer interaction. *The Journal of Psychology, 128*(4), 381-391.

Giddens, A. (1979). *Central problems in social theory.* Los Angeles: University of California press.

Giddens, A. (1984). *The constitution of society: Outline of a theory of structuration.* Los Angeles: University of California press.

Giddens, A. (1995 &1990). *Konsequenzen der Moderne.* Frankfurt/Main, Oxford: Suhrkamp.

Gigerenzer, G. (2000). *Adaptive thinking.* Oxford: Oxford University Press.

Gigerenzer, G., Todd, P., & the ABC Research Group (1999). *Simple heuristics that make us smart.* Oxford: Oxford University Press.

Gillies, A.C. (1997). *Software quality: Theory and management* (2nd ed.). London/Boston: International Thomson Computer Press.

Gilly, D. (1994). *UNIX in a nutshell.* Cambridge, MA: O'Reilly and Associates.

Gilovich, T., Griffin, D., & Kahnemann, D. (2002). *Heuristics and biases.* Cambridge, MA: Cambridge University Press.

Ginsburg, M. (2001, November). *Realizing a framework to create, support, and understand virtual communities.* Maastricht, Holland: Infonomics.

Glaser, B.G., & Strauss, A.L. (1967). *The discovery of grounded theory. Strategies for qualitative research.* London: Weidenfeld and Nicolson.

Glaser, H. (1994). *Industriekultur und Alltagsleben. Vom Biedermeier zur Postmoderne.* Frankfurt/Main, Germany: S.-Fischer-Verlag.

Glatter, R. (2004). Collaboration, collaboration, collaboration: The origins and implications of a policy. *MiE, 17*(5), 16-20.

Goffman E. (1963). *Behaviour in Public Places. Notes on the Social Organization of Gatherings.* New York: Free Press.

Gopalakrishna, P., & Mummaleni, V. (1993). Influencing satisfaction for dental services. *Journal of Health Care Marketing, 13*(1), 16-22.

Gorniak-Kocikowska, K. (1996). The computer revolution and the problem of global ethics. *Science and Engineering Ethics, 2,* 177–190.

Goupil, D. (2000). End-user application development: Relief for IT. *Computing Channels*(June), 2-4.

Gourlay, S. (2006). Conceptualizing knowledge creation: A critique of Nonaka's theory. *Journal of Management Studies, 43*(7), 1415–1436.

Gramsci, A. (2001). The concept of ideology. In M.D. Durham & D. M. Kellner (Eds.), *Media and cultural studies* (pp.43-48). Malden, MA: Blackwell.

Gray, B. (1985). Conditions facilitating interorganizational collaboration. *Human Relations, 38*(10), 911-936.

Gray, B., & Hay, T. (1986). Political limits to interorganizational consensus and change. *The Journal of Applied Behavioral Science, 22*(2), 95-112.

Gray, H. (2001). The politics of representation in network television. In M. Durham & D. Kellner (Eds.), *Media and cultural studies: Keyworks* (pp.439-461). Malden, MA: Blackwell.

Greenbaum, J., & Kyng, M. (Eds.) (1991). *Design at Work. Cooperative Design of Computer Systems*. New Jersey: Lawrence Erlbaum Associates.

Greenhill, A. (2002, August 9-11). Critiquing reality: The mind/body split in computer mediated environments. In R. Ramsower, J. Windsor, & J. DeGross (Eds.), *Proceedings of the 8th Americas Conference on Information Systems*.

Greenhill, A., & Isomäki, H. (2005). Incorporating self into Web information system design. In A. Pirhonen, H. Isomäki, C. Roast, & P. Saariluoma (Eds.), *Future interaction design* (pp. 52-66). London: Springer-Verlag.

Grice, H.P. (1967). Logic and conversation. In P. Cole & J. Morgan (Eds.), *Syntax and semantics 3: Speech acts* (pp. 41-58).

Griffiths, M. (1999). Violent video games and aggression: Review of the literature. *Journal of Aggression and Violent Behavior, 4*(2), 203-212. Retrieved June 2, 2006, from Ebsco host database.

Gross, L. (2001). Out of the mainstream: Sexual minorities and mass media. In M. D. Durham & D. M. Kellner (Eds.), *Media and cultural studies* (pp.405-423). Malden, MA: Blackwell.

Grossman, D. Lt. Col., & DeGaetano, G. (1999). *Stop teaching our kids to kill: A call to action against TV, movie & video game violence*. New York: Random House.

Grudin, J. (1991a). Interactive Systems: Bridging the Gaps Between Developers and Users. *IEEE Computer 24*(4), 59-69.

Grudin, J. (1991b). Systematic Sources of Suboptimal Interface Design in Large Product Development Organizations. *Human-Computer Interaction, 6*, 147-196.

GSM Association. (2006). GSM World: SMS definition. Retrieved January 24, 2007, from http://www.gsmworld.com/technology/glossary.shtml

Guimaraes, T., & Igbaria, M. (1997). Assessing user computing effectiveness: An integrated model. *Journal of End User Computing, 9*(2), 3-14.

Gurstein, M. (2000). *Community informatics: Enabling communities with information and communications technologies* (Introduction, pp. 1-29). Hershey, PA: Idea Group Publishing.

Guttag, J.V. (1999). Communications chameleons. *Scientific American, 281*, 42-43.

Habermas, J. (1984). *The theory of communicative action, Vol. 1, Reason and the rationalization of society*. Boston: The Beacon Press.

Hacker, S. (1989). *Pleasure, power and technology: Some tales of gender, engineering, and the cooperative workplace*. Boston: Unwin Hyman.

Haddon, L. (2000). *The Social Consequences of Mobile Telephony: Framing Questions*. Paper presented at the seminar 'Sosiale Konsekvenser av Mobiltelefoni', organised by Telenor, 16th June, 2000, Oslo.

Haefner, K. (1984). *Mensch und Computer im Jahre 2000. Ökonomie und Politik für eine humane computerisierte Gesellschaft*. Basel, Boston, Stuttgart: Birkhäuser Verlag AG.

Hair, J. F. Jr., Anderson, R. E., Tatham, R. L., & Black, W. C. (1992). *Multivariate Data Analysis with Readings, Third Edition*. New York, NY: Macmillan Publishing Company, 426-496.

Halawi, L., & McCarthy, R. (2007). Measuring faculty perceptions of Blackboard using the Technology Acceptance Model. *Issues in Information Systems, 8*(2), 160-165.

Hall, E. T. (1976). *Beyond Culture*. Garden City, NY: Anchor Doubleday Press

Hall, S. (2000). Racist ideologies and the media. In P. Marris & S. Thornham (Eds.), *Media studies: A reader*

(2nd ed.; pp.271-282). New York: New York University Press.

Hameed, K. (2002). The application of mobile computing and technology of health care services. *Telematics and Informatics, 20*(2), 99-106.

Han, S., Harkke, V., Mustonen, P., Seppänen, M., & Kallio, M. (2004). *Physicians' perceptions and intentions regarding a mobile medical information system: Some basic findings.* Paper presented at the 15th IRMA International Conference.

Han, S. H., & Hong, S. W. (2003, October). A systematic approach for coupling user satisfaction with product design. *Ergonomics, 46*(13/14), 1441-1461.

Hanks, W. F. (1991). Forward in situated learning: Legitimate peripheral participation, by Lave, J. and E. Wenger, Cambridge, UK: Cambridge University Press.

Hardy, C. (1985). The nature of unobtrusive power. *Journal of Management Studies, 22*(4), 384-399.

Hardy, C., & Phillips, N. (1998). Strategies of engagement: Lessons from the critical examination of collaboration and conflict in interorganizational domain. *Organizational Science, 2*, 217-230.

Harman, G. (1996). Moral relativism. In G. Harman & J. J. Thompson (Eds.), *Moral relativism and moral objectivity (pp. 3-64).* Cambridge, MA: Blackwell Publishers.

Harman, G. (2000). Is there a single true morality? In G. Harman (Ed.), *Explaining value: And other essays in moral philosophy* (pp. 77-99). Oxford: Clarendon Press.

Harrison, A. W., & Rainer, R. K. (1992). The influence of individual differences on skill in end-user computing. *Journal of Management Information Systems, 9*(1), 93-111.

Hartmann, M. (2003, May 19-23). Situationist roaming online. In *Proceedings of MelbourneDAC 2003, The 5th International Digital Arts and Culture Conference.*

Hartwick, J., & Barki, H. (1994). Explaining the role of user participation in information system use. *Management Science, 40*(4), 440-465.

Harvey, L. (1990). *Critical social research.* London: Unwin Hyman.

Harvey, L., & Myers, M. (1995). Scholarship and practice: The contribution of ethnographic research methods to bridging the gap. *Information Technology & People, 8*(3), 13-27.

Hawgood, L., Land, F., & Mumford, E. (1978). A participative approach to forward planning and systems change. In G. Bracchi, & P.C. Lockermann (Eds.), *Information systems methodology. Proceedings of the 2nd Conference of the European Cooperation in Informatics* (pp. 39-61), Venice, Italy. Springer-Verlag.

Hayes, E. (2006). Women, video gaming and learning: Beyond stereotypes. *Tech Trends, 49*(5), 23-28.

Hayes, N. (2000). *Doing psychological research.* Milton Keynes: Open University Press.

Hayes, N., & Walsham, G. (2001). Participation in groupware-mediated communities of practice: A sociopolitical analysis of knowledge working. *Information and Organization, 11*, 263-288.

Hebdige, D. (2001). From culture to hegemony; subculture; the unnatural break. In M. Durham & D. Kellner (Eds.), *Media and cultural studies: Keyworks* (pp.198-216). Malden, Massachusetts: Blackwell.

Hedberg, B., & Mumford, E. (1975). The design of computer systems: Man's vision of man as an integral part of the system design process. In E. Mumford, & H. Sackman (Eds.), *Human choice and computers* (pp. 31-59). Amsterdam: North Holland.

Heinrichs, J. H., Lim, K. S., & S., L. J. (2007). Determining factors of academic library Web site usage. *Journal of the American Society for Information Science and Technology, 58*(14), 2325-2334.

Heintz-Knowles, K., & Henderson, J. (2001). *Fair play? Violence, gender and race in video games.* Oakland, CA: Children NOW. Retrieved February 18, 2004, from ERIC database.

Held, D., & McGrew, A. (2001). Globalization. In J. Krieger (Ed.), *Oxford companion to politics of the world.*

Oxford/New York: Oxford University Press. Retrieved January 25, 2007, from http://www.polity.co.uk/global/globocp.htm

Held, D., McGrew, A., Goldblatt, D., & Perraton, J. (1999). *Global transformations: Politics, economics and culture.* Cambridge: Polity Press.

Henderson, J. (1990, Spring). Plugging into strategic partnerships: The critical IS connection. *Sloan Management Review,* 7-18.

Hendrickson, A. R., Glorfeld, L. W., & Cronan, T. P. (1994). On the Repeated Test-Retest Reliability of the End-User Computing Satisfaction Instrument: A Comment. *Decision Sciences, 25*(4), 665-667.

Hendriks, P. (1999). Why share knowledge? The influence of ICT on the motivation for knowledge sharing. *Knowledge and Process Management, 6,* 91–100.

Heng, M.S.H., Traut, E.M., & Fischer, S.J. (1999). Organisational champions of IT innovation. *Accounting, Management and Information Technology, 9*(3), 193-222.

Herrera, D., & Ward, N. (2005). Training wheels for the command line. In *Proceedings of the11th International Conference on Human-Computer Interaction (HCI International),* New Jersey. Lawrence Erlbaum Associates.

Herz, J. C. (1997). *Joystick nation: How video games ate our quarters, won our hearts, and rewired our minds.* New York: Little, Brown and Company.

Hettinga, M. (2002).*Understanding evolutionary use of groupware.* Telematica Instituut Fundamental Research Series (Report No. 007, TI/FRS/007). Enschede, The Netherlands: Telematica Instituut.

Heylighen, F. (1998). Basic concepts of the systems approach. *Principia Cybernetica Web.* Retrieved September 17, 2006, from http://pespmc1.vub.ac.be/SYSAPPR.html

Hinton, C., & Kaye, G. (1994). The hidden investments in information technology: The role of organisational context and system dependency. *International Journal of Information Management, 16*(6), 413-427.

Hirschheim, R., & Klein, H. (1989). Four Paradigms of Information Systems Development. *Communications of the ACM 32*(10), 1199-1216.

Hirschheim, R., & Klein, H. K. (1994, March). Realizing emancipatory principles in information systems development: The case for ETHICS. *MIS Quarterly,* 83-109.

Hirschheim, R., & Klein, H.K. (1989). Four paradigms of information systems development. *Communications of the ACM, 32*(10), 1199-1216.

Hirschheim, R., & Newman, M. (1991). Symbolism and Information Systems Development: Myth Metaphor and Magic. *Information Systems Research, 2(*1), 29-62.

Hirschheim, R., & Smithson, S. (1988). A critical analysis of IS evaluation. In G. B. Davis (Ed.), *Information systems assessment: Issues and challenges* (pp. 17-37). Amsterdam: North-Holland.

Hirschheim, R., Klein, H., & Lyytinen, K. (1995). *Information systems development and data modelling: Conceptual and philosophical foundations.* Cambridge: Cambridge University Press.

Hirschheim, R., Klein, H.K., & Lyytinen, K. (1995). *Information systems development and data modeling. Conceptual and philosophical foundations.* Cambridge University Press.

Ho, A.T.-K. (2002). Reinventing Local Governments and the E-Government Initiative. *Public Administration Review, 62*(4), 434–445.

Hock, D. (2000). Birth of the chaordic age, *Executive Excellence, 17*(6), 6-7.

Hodel, T. B., Holderegger, A., & Lüthi, A. (1998). Ethical guidelines for a networked world under construction. *Journal of Business Ethics, 17*(9-10), 1057-1071.

Hoffman, D.L., & Novak, T.P. (1996). Marketing in hypermedia computer-mediated environments: conceptual foundations. *Journal of Marketing, 60*(3), 50-68.

Hofstede, G. (1980). *Culture's Consequences: International Differences in Work-Related Values.* Beverly Hills, California: SAGE Publications.

Hofstede, G. (1980). Motivation, leadership and organization: Do American theories apply abroad. *Organizational Dynamics, 9*(1), 42-63.

Holtzblatt, K., & Beyer, H.R. (1995). Requirements gathering: The human factor. Communications of the ACM 38(5), 31-32.

Hongladarom, S. (2001). Global culture, local cultures and the Internet: The Thai example. In C. Ess (Ed.), *Culture, technology, communication: Towards an intercultural global village* (pp. 307-324). Albany, NY: State University of New York Press.

Honold, P. (1999, May). Learning How to Use a Cellular Phone: Comparison Between German and Chinese Users. *Jour Soc. Tech. Comm., 46*(2), 196-205.

Hooks, B. (1990). *Yearning: Race, gender and cultural politics.* Toronto: Between the Lines.

Hoover, M., & Stokes, L. (1998, Fall). Pop music and the limits of cultural critique: Gang of four shrinkwraps entertainment. *Popular Music and Society.*

Horkheimer, M., & Adorno, T. (2001). The culture industry. In M. D. Durham & D. M. Kellner (Eds.), *Media and cultural studies* (pp.71-101). Malden, MA: Blackwell.

Howcroft, D., & Wilson, M. (2003). Paradoxes of participatory practices: the Janus role of the systems developer. *Information and Organization, 13*, 1-24.

Hu, P. J., Clark, T. H., & Ma, W. W. (2003). Examining technology acceptance by school teachers: A longitudinal study. *Information and Management, 41*(2), 227-241.

Hubona, G. S., & Cheney, P. H. (1994). System effectiveness of knowledge-based technology: The relationship of user performance and attitudinal factors. *Proceedings of the Twenty-Seventh Hawaii International Conference on System Sciences, 4*, 532-541.

Huizinga, J. (1950). *Homo ludens.* Boston: The Beacon Press.

Human Rights Watch. (2006). Race to the bottom. Corporate complicity in Chinese Internet censorship. *Human Rights Watch Report, 18*(8C). Retrieved January 25, 2007, from http://www.hrw.org

Husserl, E. (1995). Fenomenologian idea. Viisi luentoa [The phenomenological idea. Five lectures] (Himanka, Hämäläinen & Sivenius, Trans.). Helsinki: Loki-kirjat.

Huxham, C., & Vangen, S. (2000). Ambiguity, complexity and dynamics in the membership of collaboration. *Human Relations, 53*(6), 771-805.

Huy, Q. N. (2002). Emotional balancing of organizational continuity and radical change: The contribution of middle managers. *Administrative Science Quarterly, 47*, 31-69.

Huysman, M., & Wulf, V. (2004). *Social capital and information technology.* Cambridge, MA and London: The MIT Press.

Huysman, M., & Wulf, V. (2005). The role of information technology in building and sustaining the relational base of communities. *The Information Society, 21*(2), 81-89.

Huyssen, A. (1992). Mapping the postmodern. In H. Haferkamp & N. Smelser (Eds.), *Social change and modernity.* Berkeley: University of California Press.

Hwang, H., Chen, R., & Lee, J. Measuring customer satisfaction with internet banking: an exploratory study. *International Journal of Electronic Finance, 1*(3), 321-335.

IBM (1998). IBM *ViaVoice 98 user guide.* IBM

Idowu, B., & Ogunbodede, E. (2003). Information and communication technology in Nigeria. *Journal of Information Technology Impact, 3(2),* 69-76

Igbaria, M. (1990). End-User Computing Effectiveness: A Structural Equation Model. *OMEGA International Journal of Management Science, 18*(6), 637-652.

Igbaria, M. (1993). User Acceptance of Microcomputer Technology: An Empirical Test. *OMEGA International Journal of Management Science, 21*(1), 73-90.

Igbaria, M., & Iivari, J. (1995). The effects of self-efficacy on computer usage. *OMEGA International Journal of Management Science, 23*(6), 587-605.

Igbaria, M., & Tan, M. (1997). The consequences of information technology acceptance on subsequent individual performance. *Information & Management, 35*(1), 113-121.

Igbaria, M., & Zviran, M. (1996). Comparison of end-user Computing characteristics in the U.S., Israel and Taiwan. *Information & Management, 30*(1), 1-13.

Igbaria, M., (1992). An examination of microcomputer usage in Taiwan. *Information & Management, 22*(1), 9-28.

Igbaria, M., Guimaraes, T., & Davis, G. B. (1995). Testing the determinants of microcomputer usage via a structural equation model. *Journal of Management Information Systems, 11*(4), 87-114.

Igbaria, M., Shayo, C., & Olfman, L. (1999). *On becoming virtual: The driving forces and arrangements* (pp. 27-41). New Orleans, LA: ACM.

Igbaria, M., Zinatelli, N., & Cavaye, A. L. M. (1998). Analysis of information Technology Success in Small Firms in New Zealand. *International Journal of Information Management, 18*(2), 103-119.

Iivari, J. (1987, September). The PIOCO model for information systems design. *MIS Quarterly,* 401-419.

Iivari, J., & Hirschheim, R. (1996). Analyzing Information Systems Development: a Comparison and Analysis of Eight IS Development Approaches. *Information Systems, 21*(7), 551-575.

Iivari, N. (2006). Exploring the 'Rhetoric on Representing the User' - Discourses on User Involvement in Academia and in Software Product Development Industry. *International Journal of Technology and Human Interaction, 2*(4), 53-80.

Iivari, N. (2008a). Usability in open source software development – an interpretive case study. In W. Golden, T. Acton, K. Conboy, H. van der Heijden, V. Tuunainen (Eds.), *Proc. 16th European Conference on Information Systems,* Galway, Ireland, June 9.-11.2008.

Iivari, N. (2008b). Empowering the Users? A Critical Textual Analysis of the Role of Users in Open Source Software Development. Accepted for Publication in AI & Society.

Iivari, N., Hedberg, H., & Kirves, T. (2008). Usability in Company Open Source Software Context. Initial Findings from an Empirical Case Study. In Proc. 4th International Conference on Open Source Systems (co-located with the World Computer Congress), 7.-10.9. 2008, Milan, Italy.

Implications for gender socialization and aggressive behavior. *Sex Roles, 38*(516), p.425-442.

Ince, D. (1994). *An introduction to software quality assurance and its implementation.* London: McGraw-Hill.

Industry Canada. (2002a, April 4). *Fostering innovation and use.* Retrieved July 30, 2002 from http://broadband.gc.ca/Broadband-document/english/chapter5.htm

Industry Canada. (2002b, April 4). *Smart communities broadband.* Retrieved July 12, 2002 from http://smart-communities.ic.gc.ca/index_e.asp

Internationale Situationiste (1958, June) Definitions. No. 1. Retrieved October 12, 2006, from http://www.cddc.vt.edu/sionline/si/definitions/html

Internetworldstats (2006, December). www.Internetworldstats.com/stats.htm [accessed January 2007]

Irani, Z. (2002). Information systems evaluation: Navigating through the problem domain. *Information & Management, 40,* 11-24.

Irani, Z., Ezingeard, J., & Grieve, R. (1997). Integrating the costs of a manufacturing IT/IS infrastructure into the investment decision-making process. *Technovation, 17*(11/12), 695-706.

ITU (International Telecommunications Union). (2003). *World summit on the information society* (pp. 1-9). Retrieved from www.itu.int

ITU- International Telecommunications Union (2004). Social and Mobile Communications for a more Mobile World. *Background Paper ITU/MIC Workshop on shaping the Future Mobile Information Society,* International Telecommunications Union, 2004.

Ives, B., & Olsen, M. (1984). User involvement and MIS success: A review of research. *Management Science, 30*(5), 586-603.

Ives, B., & Olson, M.H. (1984). User Involvement and MIS Success: A Review of Research. *Management Science, 30*(5). 586-603.

Jameson, F. (1983). Postmodernism and consumer society. In H. Foster (Ed.), *Postmodern culture*. London: Pluto Press.

Jarillo, C. (1988). On strategic networks. *Strategic Management Journal, 9*(1), 31-41.

Jarvis, P. (1987). *Adult learning in the social context*. London: Croom Helm.

Jencks, C. (1992). Preface: Post-modernism - the third force. In C. Jencks (Ed.), *The post-modern reader*. London: Academy Editions.

Jhally, S. (Director). (1999) *Tough guise: Violence, media & the crisis in masculinity* [Motion Picture]. United States: Media Education Foundation

Jingchun, C. (2005). Protecting the right to privacy in China. *Victoria University of Wellington Law Review, 38*(3). Retrieved January 25, 2007, from http://www.austlii.edu.au/nz/journals/VUWLRev/2005/25.html

Johnson, D. (2000). *Computer ethics* (3rd ed.). Upper Saddle River, NJ: Prentice Hall.

Jones, B., & Miller, A. (2004). *Competent. The connexions partnerships: Pilot site scenario 3: UK public employment services*. Manchester School of Management European Work & Employment Research Centre.

Jones, B., & Miller, B. (2006). *Innovation diffusion in the new economy: Tthe tacit dimension*. London: Routledge.

Jones, C., Herterly, W., & Borgatti, S. (1997). A general theory of network governance: Exchange conditions and social mechanisms. *Academy of Management Review, 22*(4), 911-945.

Jones, S., & Hughes, J. (2001). Understanding IS evaluation as a complex social process: A case study of a UK local authority. *European Journal of Information Systems, 10*, 189-203.

Jung, H., & Von Matt, J.-R. (2002). *Momentum*. Die Kraft, die Werbung heute braucht. Berlin, Germany: Lardon Verlag.

Kahn, W. A. (1990). Psychological conditions of personal engagement and disengagement at work. *Academy of Management Journal, 33*(4), 692-724.

Kahnemann, D., Slovic, P., & Tversky, A. (Eds.). (1982). *Judgement under uncertainty: Heuristics and biases*. Cambridge, MA: Cambridge University Press.

Kaplan, B., & Duchon, D. (1988). Combining qualitative and quantitative methods in information systems research: A case study. *MIS Quarterly, 12*(4), 571-586.

Karahanna, E., Straub, D., & Chervany, N. (1999). Information technology adoption across time: A cross-sectional comparison of pre-adoption and post-adoption beliefs. *Management Information Systems Quarterly, 13*(2), 183-213.

Katz, K. L., Larson, B. M., & R.C., L. (1991). Prescription for the waiting-in-line blues: Entertain, enlighten, engage. *Sloan Management Review, 32*(2), 44-53.

Kauffman, S. (1995). *At home in the universe*. New York: Oxford University Press.

Kaufmann, S. (1993). *The origins of order*. New York: Oxford University Press.

Kautz, K. and Pries-Heje, J. (1996). *Diffusion and adoption of information technolog.,* London: Chapman & Hall.

Kayes, D.C. (2002). Experiential learning and its critics: preserving the role of experience in management learning and education. *Academy of Management, Learning & Education, 1*(2), 137–150.

Keen, P. (1991). *Shaping the future: Business design through information technology*. Boston: Harvard Business School Press.

Keenan, T., & Trotter, D. (1999). The changing role of community networks in providing citizen access to the Internet. Internet Research. *Electronic Networking Applications and Policy, 9*(2), 100-108.

Kelly, T., Minges, M., & Gray, V. (2002). *World Telecommunication Development report: reinventing Telecoms, Executive summary.* Available at http://ww.itu.int

Kendall, M. G. (1948). *Rank correlation methods.* Griffin.

Kenworthy, J. (1992). *Teaching English pronunciation.* Harlow: Longman.

Kerlinger, F. N. (1986). *Foundations of Behavioral Research, Third Edition.* Fort Worth, TX: Harcourt Brace Jovanovich College Publishers.

Kickul, J., & Gundry, L. (2000). Pursuing technological innovation: The role of entrepreneurial posture and opportunity recognition among internet firms. In *Frontiers of Entrepreneurship Research,* MA: Babson College.

Kiernan, K. S. (1981). *Beowulf and the Beowulf Manuscript.* Rutgers University Press, New Brunswick.

Kim, D.H. (1993). The link between individual and organizational learning. *Sloan Management Review, 35*(1), 37-50.

Kim, S., & McHaney, R. (2000). Validation of the End-User Computing Satisfaction Instrument in Case Tool Environments. *Journal of Computer Information Systems, 41*(1), 49-55.

Kimberly, J. (1976). Issues in the design of longitudinal research: The temporal dimension. *Sociological Methods and Research, 4*(3), 21-47.

Kimberly, J. (1980). Data aggregation in organizational research: The temporal dimension. *Organization Studies, 1*(4), 367-377.

Kirs, P.J., Pflughoeft, K., & Kroeck, G. (2001). A process model cognitive biasing effects in information systems development and usage. *Information & Management, 38,* 153-165.

Kirsch, L. J. (1996). The management of complex tasks in organizations: Controlling the systems development process. *Organization Science, 7*(1), 1-21.

Kirsch, L. J. (1997). Portfolios of control modes and IS project management. *Information Systems Research, 8*(3), 215-239.

Kirsch, L. J., & Beath, C. M. (1996). The enactments and consequences of token, shared, and compliant participation in information systems development. *Accounting, Management, & Information Technologies, 6*(4), 221-254.

Kirsch, L. J., & Beath, C. M. (1996). The enactments and consequences of token, shared and compliant participation in information systems development. *Accounting, Management and Information Technology, 6*(4), 2221-154.

Kirsch, L. J., & Cummings, L. L. (1996). Contextual influences on self-control of IS professionals engaged in systems development. *Accounting, Management and Information Technologies, 6*(3), 191-219.

Kitiyadisai, K. (2005). Privacy rights and protection: Foreign values in modern Thai context. *Ethics and Information Technology, 7,* 17-26.

Klassen, K. J. (2004). Outpatient appointments scheduling in a dynamic, multi-user environment. *International Journal of Service Industry Management, 15*(2), 167-186.

Klawe, M., & Shneiderman, B. (2005). Crisis and Opportunity in Computer Science. *Communications of the ACM,* November, *48*(11), 27-28.

Klecun-Dabrowska, E., & Cornford, T. (2000). Telehealth acquires meanings: Information and communication technologies within health policy. *Information Systems Journal, 10*(1), 41-63.

Klein, H.K., & Hirschheim, R.A. (1993). The application of neo-humanist principles in information systems development. In D.E. Avison, T.E. Kendall, & J.J. DeGross (Eds.), *Human, organizational, and social dimensions of information systems development* (pp. 263-280). Amsterdam: Elsevier.

Klein, N. (2001). *No Logo!* Der Kampf der Global Players um Marktmacht. Ein Spiel mit vielen Verlierern und wenigen Gewinnern. München, Germany: Goldmann Verlag.

Kling, R. (1977). The Organizational Context of User-Centered Software Designs. MIS Quarterly 1(4), 41-52.

Kling, R. (1987). Defining the boundaries of computing across complex organizations. In R. Boland & R.A. Hirscheim (Eds.), *Critical issues in information systems research*. Chichester: Wiley.

Klopping, I. M., & McKinney, E. (2004). Extending the Technology Acceptance Model and the Task-Technology Fit model to consumer E-commerce. *Information Technology, Learning, and Performance Journal, 22*(1), 35-48.

Klotz, H. (1988). *The history of postmodern architecture*. (R. Donnell, Trans.). Cambridge, MA: The MIT Press.

Koda, T., & Maes, P. (1996a). Agents with faces: The effect of personification. In *Proceedings of the 5th IEEE International Workshop on Robot and Human Communication, IEEE*.

Kogut, B., & Zander, U. (1992). Knowledge of the firm, combinative capabilities and the replication of technology. *Organization Science, 3*(5), 383-397.

Kohn, L. T., Corrigan, J.M., & Donaldson, M.S. (Eds). (2000). *To err is human: Building a safer health system*. Chicago: Institute of Medicine.

Kolb, D.A. (1984). *Experiential learning. Experience as the source of learning and development*. Englewood Cliffs, NJ: Prentice-Hall.

Kraft, P., & Bansler, J. (1994). The Collective Resource Approach: The Scandinavian experience. *Scandinavian Journal of Information Systems, 6*(1), 71-84.

Kreuzer, H. (Ed.) (1987). *Die zwei Kulturen: Literarische und naturwissenschaftliche Intelligenz*. C.P. Snows These in der Diskussion. München, Germany: d-tv / Klett-Cotta Verlag.

Kuhn, T.S. (1962). *The structure of scientific revolutions*. University of Chicago Press.

Kumar, K., & Bjørn-Andersen, N. (1990). A cross-cultural comparison of IS designer values. *Communications of the ACM, 33*(5), 528-538.

Kumar, K., & Welke, J. (1984). Implementation failure and system developer values: Assumptions, truisms and empirical evidence. In *Proceedings of the 5th International Conference on Information Systems* (pp. 1-12), Tucson, AZ.

Küng, H. (2001). *A global ethic for global politics and economics*. Hong Kong: Logos and Pneuma Press.

Kyng, M. (1994). Scandinavian Design: Users in Product Development. In Proc. CHI 1994. New York: ACM Press. (pp. 3-9).

Kyng, M. (1998). Users and computers: A contextual approach to design of computer artifacts. *Scandinavian Journal of Information Systems, 10(*1&2), 7-44.

Kyng, M., & Morten (1995). Representations of work: Making representations work. *Communications of the ACM, 38*(9).

Lagendijk, P. J. B., Schuring, R. W., & Spil, T. A. M. (2001). Telecommunications as a medicine for general practitioners. In R. Stegwee & T. A. M. Spil (Eds.), *Strategies for healthcare information systems* (pp. 114-125). Hershey, PA: Idea Group Publishing.

Lagopoulos, A. (1993). Postmodernism, geography, and the social semiotics of space. *Environment and Planning D: Society and Space, 11*, 255-278.

Lakhani, K., & von Hippel, E. (2003). How Open Source Software Works: "Free" User-to-User Assistance. *Research Policy, 32*(6), 923-943.

Lakoff, G. (1987). *Women, fire and dangerous things*. University of Chicago Press.

Lamb, R., & Kling, R. (2003). Reconceptualizing users as social actors in information systems research. *Management Information Systems Quarterly, 27*(2), 197-235.

Larman, C. (2004). *Agile and iterative development: A manager's guide/Craig Larman*. Boston: Addison-Wesley.

Larzara, G. F., & Mathiassen, L. (1985). Mapping situations within a system development project. *Information and Management, 8*, 3-20.

Lasen, A. (2002b). *A comparative Study of Mobile Phone Use in London, Madrid and Paris.*

Latour, B., & Woolgar, S. (1979*). Laboratory life: The social construction of scientific facts.* Princeton University Press.

Lau, F. (1999). Toward a framework for action research in information systems studies. *Information Technology & People, 12*(2), 148-175.

Lave, J. (1988). *Cognition in practice.* Cambridge, MA: Cambridge University Press.

Lave, J., & Wenger, E. (1991). *Situated learning: Legitimate peripheral participation.* Cambridge University Press.

Lawrence, T., Phillips, N., & Hardy, C. (1999). Watching whale watching. *The Journal of Applied Behavioral Science, 35*(4), 479-502.

LeBrasseur, R., Whissell, R., & Ojha, A. (2002). Organizational learning, transformational leadership and implementation of continuous quality improvement in Canadian hospitals. *Australian Journal of Management, 27*(2), 141-162.

Lederer, A. L., Maupin, D. J., Sena, M. P., & Zhuang, Y. (2000). The technology acceptance model and the world wide web. *Decision Support Systems, 29*, 269-282.

Lee, A. S. (1999). Rigor and relevance in MIS research: beyond the approach of positivism alone. *MIS Quarterly, 23*(1).

Lee, H. (1990). *Critical social research.* London: Unwin Hyman.

Lefebvre, H. (1992). *The production of space.* Oxford: Blackwell.

Lemaire, L. (2003). *Systèmes de gestion integers: Des technologies à risque?* Paris: Editions Liaison.

Leonard, D. (2004). Unsettling the military entertainment complex: Video games and a pedagogy of peace. *Studies in Media & Information Literacy Education, 4*(4), 17-32. Retrieved May 27, 2006, from www.utpjournals.com

Leonard, D. (2005). High tech blackface—Race, sports video games and becoming the other. *Intelligent Agent, 4*(4), Retrieved June 18, 2006, from http://www.intelligentagent.com/archive/Vol4_No4_gaming_leonard.htm

Leonard-Barton, D., & Sinha, D. K. (1993). Developer-user interaction and user satisfaction in internal technology transfer. *Academy of Management Journal, 36*(5).

Lesard Monga, S. (1993). *Statistique, concepts and methods.* Presses Universitaires de Montréal.

Liaw, S.-S. (2002). An Internet survey for perceptions of computers and the world wide web: Relationship, prediction, and difference. *Computers in Human Behavior, 18*, 17-35.

Licoppe, C., & Heurtin, J-P, (2002). France: Preserving the Image. In J. Katz and R. Aakhus (eds) *Perpetual Contact: Mobile Communication, Private Talk, Public Performance.* Cambridge: Cambridge University Press. (pp. 99-108).

Likert, R. (1932). A technique for the measurement of attitudes. *Archives of Psychology, 140*, 55.

Lim, K. S., Lim, J. S., & Heinrichs, J. H. (2005). Structural model comparison of the determining factors for E-purchase. *Seoul Journal of Business, 11*(2), 119-143.

Lin, A., & Conford, T. (2000). Sociotechnical perspectives on emergence phenomena. In E. Coakes, D. Willis, & R. Lloyd-Jones (Eds.), *The New SocioTech* (pp. 51-59). London: Springer.

Lincoln, J., & Ahmadjian, C. (2001). Shukko (employee transfers) and tacit knowledge exchange in Japanese supply networks. In I. Nonaka & T. Nishiguchi (Eds.), *Knowledge emergence* (pp. 247-269). Oxford: Oxford University Press.

Lind, M. R., & Zmud, R. W. (1991). The influence of a convergence in understanding between technology providers and users on information technology innovativeness. *Organization Science, 2*(2), 195-217.

Ling, R. (2004). *The mobile connection: The cell phone's impact on society.* San Francisco: Morgan Kaufmann.

Loasby, B. (1976). *Choice, complexity, and ignorance.* Cambridge, MA: Cambridge University Press.

Loebbecke, C., & Thaller, M. (2005). Preserving Europe's Cultural Heritage in the Digital World. *Proceedings of the European Conference on Information Systems (ECIS)*, Regensburg, Germany, May.

Lott, E. (1993). *Love & theft: Blackface minstrelsy and the American working class.* New York: Oxford University Press.

Love, A. (1991). *Internal evaluation: Building organizations from within.* Newbury Park, CA: Sage Publications.

Love, S. (2001). Space invaders: Do mobile phone conversations invade people's personal space? In Human factors in telecommunication. In K. Nordby (Ed.), *Bergen, Human Factors in Telecommunications.*

Love, S. (2005) Understanding Mobile Human-Computer interaction. Elesvier Blueworth Heinemann, London.

Love, S., & Perry, M. (2004). Dealing with mobile conversations in public places: some implications for the design of socially intrusive technologies. Proceedings of CHI 2004, Vienna, 24-29 April, ACM 1-58113-703-6/04/2004.

Low, J., & Woolgar, S. (1993). Managing the socio-technical divide: Some aspects of the discursive structure of information systems development. In P. Quintas (Ed.), *Social dimensions of systems engineering: People, processes and software development* (pp. 34-59). New York/London: Ellis Horwood.

Löwgren, J. (1995). Applying Design Methodology to Software Development. In *Proc. Designing Interactive Systems (DIS '95).* New York: ACM Press. (pp. 87-95).

Löwgren, J., & Stolterman, E. (1999). Design Methodology and Design Practice. *Interactions* January/February, 13-20.

Lowndes, V., & Skelcher, C. (1998). The dynamics of multi-organizational partnerships: An analysis of changing modes of governance. *Public Administration, 76*, 313-333.

Loyd, B. H., & Gressard, C. (1984). Reliability and factorial validity of computer attitude scales. *Education and Psychological Measurement, 44*, 501-505.

Lü, Y.-H. (2005). Privacy and data privacy issues in contemporary China. *Ethics and Information Technology, 7*, 7-15.

Lucas, H. C., & Spitler, V. K. (1999). Technology use and performance: A field study of broker workstations. *Decision Sciences, 30*(2), 291-311.

Lukes, S. (1974). *Power: A radical view.* London: Mac-Millan.

Lund, V. T., Raposo, J., & Watson, (2003). *From banks to banking: The on demand journey.* New York: IBM Institute for Business Value.

Lycett, M., & Giaglis, G. (2000). Component-based information systems: Towards a framework for evaluation. In *Proceedings of the 33rd Hawaii International Conference on Systems Sciences* (pp. 1-10).

Lyotard, J. (1986). *Das Postmoderne Wissen.* Wien, Östereich: Passagen Verlag.

Lyotard, J. (1989). *Der Widerstreit. München.* Germany: Fink Wilhelm Verlag.

Lytz, R. (1995). Software metrics for the Boeing 777: A case study. *Software Quality Journal, 4*(1), 1-13.

Lyytinen, K. (1999). Empirical research in information systems: on the relevance of practice in thinking of IS research. *MIS Quarterly, 23*(1), 25-28.

Lyytinen, K. J., & Damsgaard, J. (2001, April). *What's wrong with the diffusion of innovation theory.* Paper presented at the Diffusing software product and process innovations, Banff, Canada.

Ma, Q., & Liu, L. (2004). The technology acceptance model: A meta-analysis of empirical findings. *Journal of Organizational and End User Computing, 16*(1), 60-72.

Maar, C. / Burda, H. (2004). *Iconic Turn. Köln.* Germany: Dumont Literatur und Kunst Verlag.

MacDonald, K., Case, J., & Mertzger, J. (2001). *E-encounters*. Oakland, CA: California Healthcare Foundation.

MacKenzie, D.A. (2001). *Mechanizing proof: Computing, risk, and trust*. Cambridge, MA/London: MIT Press.

MacKenzie, D.A. (2004). *Computers and the cultures of proving*. Paper presented at the Royal Society Discussion Meeting, London.

Maehr, M. L. (1989).Thoughts about motivation. In C. Ames & R. Ames (Eds.), *Research on motivation in education: Goals and cognition* (pp. 299-315). San Diego, CA: Academic Press.

Maes, P. (1994). Agents that reduce work and information overload. *Communications of the ACM, 37*(7), 31-40.

Magal, S. R., & Mirchandani, D. A. (2001). *Validatiion of the technology acceptance model for Internet tools*. Paper presented at the Proceedings of the Americas Conference on Information Systems.

Malone, T. W., & Lepper, M. R. (1987). Making learning fun: A taxonomy of intrinsic motivations for learning. In R. E. Snow & M. J. Farr (Eds.), *Aptitude, learning, and instruction* (pp. 223-253). Hillsdale, NJ: Erlbaum.

Malone, T. W., Yates, J., & Benjamin, R. I. (1987). Electronic markets and electronic hierarchies: Effects of information technology on market structure and corporate strategies. *Communications of the ACM, 30*(6), 484-497.

Mandigo, J. L., & Thompson, L. P. (1998). Go with their flow: How flow theory can help practitioners to intrinsically motivate children. *Physical Education, 55*(3), 145-160.

March, J. G., & Simon, H. A. (1958). *Organizations*. New York: Wiley.

Marchington, M., Grimshaw, D., Rubery, J., & Willmott, H. (Eds.). (2005). *Fragmenting work: Blurring organizational boundaries and disordering hierarchies*. Oxford University Press.

Marcus, A., & Gould, E. W. (2000). Crosscurrents: Cultural dimensions and global Web user-interface design. *Interactions, 7*(4), 32-46.

Marcus, M. L. (2004). Technochange management: Using IT to drive organizational change. *Journal of Information Technology, 19*, 3-19.

Marion, R. (1999). *The edge of organization*. Thousand Oaks: Sage.

Markus, M. L. (1983). Power, politics, and MIS implementation. *Communications of the Association for Computing Machinery, 26*(6), 430-444.

Markus, M. L., & Robey, D. (1988). Information technology and organizational change: Causal structure in theory and research. *Management Science, 34*(5), 583-598.

Marshall, A. (1949). *Principles of economics* (8th ed). London: Macmillan. 1st ed. 1890, 8th. ed. 1920; pp. 271-272, pp. 225-226 in the 1949 reprint

Marsick, V. (1987). *Learning in the workplace*. London: Croom Helm.

Martin, L., & Matlay, H. (2003). Innovative use of the Internet in established small firms: The impact of knowledge management and organizational learning in accessing new opportunities. *Qualitative Market Research, 6*(1), 18-26.

Martins, E. & Terblanche, F. (2003). Building organisational culture that stimulates creativity and innovation. *European Journal of Innovation Management, 6*(1), 64-74.

Marton, F. (1981). Phenomenography: Describing conceptions of the world around us. *Instructional Science, 10*, 177-200.

Marton, F., & Booth, S. (1997). *Learning and awareness*. Mahwah, NJ: Lawrence Erlbaum.

Marx, K., & Engels, F.(1976). Ruling class and the ruling ideas. In M. D. Durham & D. M. Kellner (Eds.), *Media and cultural studies* (pp.39-47). Malden, MA: Blackwell.

Mason, R. M. (1991, Fall). The role of metaphors in strategic information systems planning. *Journal of Management Information Systems, 8*(2), 11-30.

Mason, R. O. (1978). Measuring information output: A communication systems approach. *Information and Management, 1*(5), 219-234.

Mathiassen, L. 1998. Reflective systems development. *Scandinavian Journal of Information Systems, 10*(1/2), 67-118.

May, C. (2002). *The information society—A sceptical view.* Cambridge, UK: Polity Press.

Mayhew, D. J. (1999). Strategic Development of Usability Engineering Function. *Interactions,* (5),27-34.

Mayhew, D. J. (1999). *The usability engineering lifecycle: A practitioner's handbook for user interface design.* San Francisco: Morgan Kaufmann Publishers, Inc.

Mbengue, A. (1999). Tests de comparaison. In R. A.Thiétart(Ed.), *Méthodes de recherche en management* (pp. 291-334). Dunod.

McDougall, B., & Hansson, A. (Eds.). (2002). *Chinese concepts of privacy.* Brill Academic Publishers.

McGill, T., Hobbs, V., & Klobas, J. (2003). User developed applications and information systems success: A test of DeLone and McLean's model. *Information Resources Management Journal, 16*(1), 24-45.

McHaney, R., & Cronan, T. P. (2001). A Comparison of Surrogate Success Measures in On-Going Representational Decision Support Systems: An Extension of Simulation Technology. *Journal of End User Computing, 13*(2), 15-25.

McHaney, R., & Cronan, T. P. (1998). Computer simulation success: on the use of the End-User Computing Satisfaction instrument. *Decision Sciences, 29*(2), 525-536.

McHaney, R., Hightower, R., & Pearson, J. (2002). A validation of the End-User Computing Satisfaction instrument in Taiwan. *Information & Management, 39*(6), 503-511.

McHaney, R., Hightower, R., & White, D. (1999). EUCS test-retest reliability in representational model decision support systems. *Information & Management, 36*(2), 109-119.

McKnight, B. & Bontis, N. (2002). E-improvisation: Collaborative groupware technology expands the reach and effectiveness of organizational improvisation. *Knowledge and Process Management, 9*(4), 219-227.

Mead, G. (1934, 1964). *Mind, self and society.* Chicago: University of Chicago Press.

Mens, T., & Eden, A. H. (2005). On the evolution complexity of design patterns. *Electronic Notes in Theoretical Computer Science, 127*(3), 147-163.

Merleau-Ponty, M. (1962). *Phenomenology of perception.* London: Routledge.

Merleau-Ponty, M. (1966). *Phänomenologie der Wahrnehmung.* Berlin, Germany: Gruyter Verlag.

Meyers, R. A., Brashers, D. E., Winston, L., & Grob, L. (1997). Sex differences and group argument: A theoretical framework and empirical investigation. *Communication Studies, 48,* 19-41.

Miles, R. H. (1982). *Coffin nails and corporate strategies.* Englewood Cliffs, NJ: Prentice Hall.

Miles, R., & Snow, C. (1978). *Organizational strategy, structure and process.* McGraw-Hill.

Miller, D. T., & Friesen, P. H. (1982). The longitudinal analysis of organizations: A methodological perspective. *Management Science, 29*(9), 113-134.

Miller, S. (1973). Ends, means, and galumphing: Some leitmotifs of play. *American Anthropologist, 75,* 87-98.

Ministry of Defence (MoD). (1997). Requirements for safety related software in defence equipment Retrieved October 5, 2006, from http://www.dstan.mod.uk/data/00/055/01000200.pdf

Ministry of Defence (MoD). (2004). Interim defence standard 00-56. Retrieved October 5, 2006, from http://www.dstan.mod.uk/data/00/056/01000300.pdf

Mintzberg, H. (1983). *Structures in fives: Designing effective organizations.* Englewood Cliffs, NJ: Prentice Hall.

Mintzberg, H. (1979). *The structuring of organizations.* Englewoods Cliffs, NJ: Prentice-Hall.

Mizutani, M., Dorsey, J., & Moor, J. (2004). The Internet and Japanese conception of privacy. *Ethics and Information Technology, 6*(2), 121-128.

Mohamed, A. (2006, January 24). Managing complexity is the main event. *Computer Weekly*, 20.

Molich, R. (1999). *Bruger-venlige edb-systemer.* (in Danish) Teknisk Forlag, Copenhagen.

Mooij, M. (2002). Convergence and divergence in consumer behavior: implications for international retailing. *Journal of Retailing, 78*, 61-69.

Mooij, M. (2003). *Consumer Behavior and Culture. Consequences for Global Marketing and Advertising.* Thousand Oaks, CA: Sage Publications Inc.*Eurobarometer 55 and The Young Europeans* (2001) Brussels: European Commission Directorate.

Moon, J.-W., & Kim, Y.-G. (2001). Extending the TAM for a world-wide-web context. *Information and Management, 38*, 217-230.

Moon, M.J. (2002). The Evolution of E-Government among Municipalities: Reality or Rhetoric? *Public Administration Review, 62*(4), 424–433.

Moreno, R., Mayer, R. E., & Lester, J. C. (2000). Life-like pedagogical agents in constructivist multimedia environments: Cognitive consequences of their interaction. *In Proceedings of the ED-MEDIA 200* (pp. 741-746), Chesapeake, Virginia. AACE Press.

Morgan, G., & Smircich, L. (1980). The case for qualitative research. *Academy of Management Review, 5*(4), 491-500.

Moundridou, M., & Virvou, M. (2002). Evaluating the persona effect of an interface agent in a tutoring system. *Journal of Computer Assisted Learning, 18*, 253-261.

Mulder, I., Swaak, J., & Kessels, J. (2002). Assessing group learning and shared understanding in technology-mediated interaction. *Educational Technology and Society, 5*(1), 35-47.

Muller, M. J., & Carey, K. (2002). Design as a Minority Discipline in a Software Company: Toward Requirements for a Community of Practice. In *Proc. CHI 2002 1*(1), 383-390. New York: ACM Press.

Mumford, E., & Olive, B. (1967). *The computer and the clerk.* London: Routledge & K. Paul.

Murano, P. (2001). *Mapping human-oriented information to software agents for online systems usage people in control.* Paper presented at the International Conference on Human Interfaces in Control Rooms, Cockpits and Command Centres. UMIST, UK: IEE.

Murano, P. (2001). *A new software agent 'learning' algorithm people in control.* Paper presented at the International Conference on Human Interfaces in Control Rooms, Cockpits and Command Centres. UMIST, UK: IEE.

Murano, P. (2002a). *Anthropomorphic vs. non-anthropomorphic software interface feedback for online systems usage universal access theoretical perspectives, practice and experience* [Lecture Notes in Computer Science (C)]. Springer.

Murano, P. (2002b). Effectiveness of mapping human-oriented information to feedback from a software interface. In *Proceedings of the 24th International Conference on Information Technology Interfaces* (pp. 24-27). Cavtat, Croatia.

Murano, P. (2003, July). *Anthropomorphic vs. non-anthropomorphic software interface feedback for online factual delivery.* Paper presented at 7th International Conference on Information Visualisation (IV 2003) An International Conference on Computer Visualisation and Graphics Applications (pp. 16-18), London, England.

Murtagh G. M. (2001). Seeing the rules preliminary observations of action, interaction and mobile phone use. In B. Brown, N. Green, & R. Harper, (Eds), *Wireless World. Social and Interactional Aspects of the Mobile Age.* London: Springer-Verlag. (pp. 81-91).

Mustonen-Ollila, A., & Lyytinen, K. (2004). How organizations adopt information system process innovations: A longitudinal analysis. *European Journal of Information Systems, 13*, 35-51.

Mustonen-Ollila, E., & Lyytinen, K. (2003). Why organizations adopt information system process innovations: A longitudinal study using diffusion of innovation theory. *Information Systems Journal, 13*, 275-297.

Myers, G.J. (1979). *The art of software testing.* New York: Wiley.

Myers, M. D. (1999). Investigating information systems with ethnographic research. *Communication of the AIS, 2*, 1-20.

Myers, M.D., & Avison, D.E. (Eds). (2002). *Qualitative research in information systems: A reader.* London: Sage Publications.

Nadel, S. F. (1957). *The theory of social structure.* London: Cohen and West.

Nakada, M., & Tamura, T. (2005). Japanese conceptions of privacy: An intercultural perspective. *Ethics and Information Technology, 7*, 27-36.

Nakazawa, M., Mukai, T., Watanuki, K., & Miyoshi, H. (2001). Anthropomorphic agent and multimodal interface for nonverbal communication. In N. Avouris, & N. Fakotakis (Eds.), *Advances in human-computer interaction I. Proceedings of the PC HCI 2001* (pp. 360-365), Athens, Greece.

Nandhakumar, J., & Jones, M. (1997). Designing in the Dark: the Changing User-Developer Relationship in Information Systems Development. In *Proc. ICIS 1997*, 75-86.

Nass, C., Steuer, J., & Tauber, E.R. (1994). *Computers are social actors.* Paper presented at the CHI '94 Human Factors in Computing Systems – 'Celebrating Interdependence,' Boston, Massachusetts. ACM.

Nature_Team. (1996). Defining visions in context: Models, processes and tools for requirements engineering. *Information Systems, 21*(6), 515-547.

Neilson, R.E. (1997). *Collaborative technologies and organisational learning.* Hershey, PA: Idea Group Publishing.

Neisser, U. (1976). *Cognition and reality.* San Francisco: W. H. Freeman and Co.

Nelson, K. M., & Cooprider, J. G. (1996, December). The contribution of shared knowledge to IS group performance. *MIS Quarterly*, 409-432.

Nelson, K.M., & Cooprider, J.C. (1996). The contribution of shared knowledge to IS group performance. *MIS Quarterly, 20*, 409–429.

Nelson, R. (1990). Capitalism as an engine of progress. *Research Policy* (pp. 193-214). (Reprinted The sources of economic growth (1996) pp.52-83, by R. Nelson, Cambridge. MA/London: Harvard University Press).

Nelson R. (1998). Computerized patient records improve practice efficiency and patient care. *Health Care Data Systems, 52*(4), 86,88.

Nelson, R. (1996). *The sources of economic growth.* Cambridge, MA/London: Harvard University Press.

Nelson, R. (1991). Why do firms differ, and how does in matter? *SMJ, 4*, 61-74. (Reprinted from pp.100-119, by R. Nelson, 1996).

Nelson, R. R., & Todd, P. (1999). Strategies for managing EUC on the web. *Journal of End User Computing, 11*(1), 24-31.

Nelson, R., & Winter, S. (1982). *An evolutionary theory of economic change.* Cambridge, MA: Harvard University Press.

New Economy Development Group Inc. (2001). *Sustainability project on sustainable communities.* Paper presented at the Canadian Rural Partnership. Rural Research and Analysis, Government of Canada.

Newkirk, T. (2002). *Misreading masculinity: Boys, literacy and popular culture.* Portsmouth, New Hampshire: Heinemann.

Newman, M., & Noble, F.(1990). User involvement as an interaction process: A case study. *Information Systems Research, 1*(1), 89-110.

Ngwenyama, O. K., & Lee, A. S. (1997). Communication richness in electronic mail: Critical social theory and the contextuality of meaning. *MIS Quarterly, 21*(2), 145-168.

NHS. (2002). *The NHS explained the NHS IM/T 21st century strategy*. Retrieved January 29, 2003 from http://www.nhs.uk/thenhsexplained/how_the_nhs_works.aspNHS

NHSIA. (1998). *An information strategy for the modern NHS 1998-2005, a national strategy for local implementation*. Retrieved January 29, 2003 from http://www.nhsia.nhs.uk/def/pages/info4health/contents.asp

Niblett, P., & Graham, S. (2005, December). Events and service-oriented architecture: The OASIS Web services notification specifications. *IBM Systems Journal, 44*(4), 869-887.

Nichols, D., & Twidale, M. (2003). The Usability of Open Source Software. *First Monday, 8*(1), 21.

Nichols, D., & Twidale, M. (2006). Usability Processes in Open Source Projects. *Software Process Improvement and Practice, 11*, 149-162.

Niederman, F., Branchaeu, J. C., & Wetherbe, J. C. (1991). Information systems management issues for the 1990s. *MIS Quarterly, 15*(4), 475-499.

Niederman, F., Davis, A., Greiner, M., Wynn, D., & York, P. (2006). A Research Agenda for Studying Open Source I: A Multilevel Framework. *Communication of the Association for Information Systems, 18*, 129-149.

Nielsen, J. (1993). *Usability engineering*. Boston: Academic Press.

Nielsen, J. (2005). B-to-b users want sites with b-to-c service, ease. *B to B, 90*(7), 48.

Nielsen, J., & Landauer, T. K. (1993). A mathematical model of the finding of usability problems. *Proceedings of ACM INTERCHI'93 Conference*, Amsterdam, The Netherlands, 24-29 April, 206-213.

Nielsen, S. (1999). Talking about Change: An Analysis of Participative Discourse Amongst IT Operations Personnel. In *Proc. 10th Australasian Conference on Information Systems*, (pp. 691-702).

Nissenbaum, H. (1999). Can trust be secured online? A theoretical perspective. *Etica e Politica, 2*. Retrieved October 5, 2006, from http://www.units.it/~etica/1999_2/nissenbaum.html

Nonaka, I., & Takeuchi, H. (1995). *The knowledge-creating company: How Japanese companies create the dynamics of innovation*. Oxford University Press.

Nonaka, I., & Takeuchi, H. (1998). *The knowledge-creating company*. New York: Oxford University Press.

Nooteboom, B. (1999). Innovation and inter-firm linkages: New implications for policy. *Research Policy, 28*(8), 793.

Norman, D.A. (1989). *Miten avata mahdottomia ovia? Tuotesuunnittelun salakarit* [The psychology of everyday things]. Jyväskylä: Gummerus.

Nunally, J. C. (1978). Psychometric Theory. New York: McGraw-Hill.

O'Connor, E. (1995). Paradoxes of Participation: textual analysis and organizational change. *Organization Studies, 16*(5),769-803.

O'Toole, L. (1997). Treating networks seriously: Practical and research-based agendas in public administration. *Public Administration Review, 57*(1), 45-52.

OECD. (1997). Organisation for economic co-operation and development. *Towards a global information society*. Paris: OECD.

OECD. (2004). Organization for economic co-operation and development. *Information and communication technologies and rural development*. Paris, France: OECD Publication Service.

Oevermann, U. (1996). Becketts 'Endspiel' als Prüfstein hermeneutischer methodologie. Eine interpretation mit den verfahren der objektiven hermeneutik. In. H.-D. König (Ed.), *Neue Versuche, Becketts Endspiel zu Verstehen* (pp.93 – 249). Frankfurt: Suhrkamp.

Oliver, A., & Ebers, M. (1998). Networking network studies: An analysis of conceptual configurations in the study of inter-organizational relationships, *Organization Studies, 19*, 549-83.

Olk, P., & Young, C. (1997). Why members stay in or leave an R&D consortium: Performance and conditions of membership as determinants of continuity. *Strategic Management Journal, 18*(11), 855-877.

Orlikowski, W. J. (1992). The duality of technology: Rethinking the concept of technology in organizations. *Organization Science, 3*(3), 398-427.

Orlikowski, W. J. (2000). Using technology as a practice lens for studying technology in organizations. *Organization Science, 11*, 404-428.

Orlikowski, W. J., & Baroudi, J. J. (1991). Studying IT in organizations: Research approaches and assumptions. *Information Systems Research, 2*(1), 1-28.

Orlikowski, W. J., & Robey, D. (1991). Information technology and the structuring of organizations. *Information Systems Research, 12*(2), 143-169.

Orlikowski, W. J., & Yates, J. (2002). It's about time: Temporal structuring in organizations. *Organization Science, 13*(6), 684-700.

Orlikowski, W., & Gash, D. (1994). Technological frames: Making sense of information technology in organizations. *Transactions on Information Systems, 12*(2), 174-207.

Orlikowski, W., & Iacano, C. (2001). Research Commentary: Desperately Seeking the "IT" in IT Research – A Call to Theorizing the IT Artifact. *Information Systems Research, 12*(2), 121-134.

Orlikowski, W.J. (1992). The duality of technology: Rethinking the concept of technology in organizations. *Organization Science, 3*(3), 398-427.

Orlikowski, W.J. (1996). Improvising organizational transformation over time: A situated change perspective. *Information Systems Research, 7*, 63–92.

Orlikowski, W.J., & Baroudi, J.J. (1991). Studying information technology in organizations: Research approaches and assumptions. *Information Systems Research, 2*(1), 1-28.

Orlikowski, W.J., & Gash, D.C. (1994). Technological frames: Making sense of information technology in organizations. *ACM Transactions on Information Systems, 12*(2), 174-207.

Orr, C., Allen, D., & Poindexter, S. (2001). The effect of individual differences on computer attitudes. *Journal of End User Computing, 13*(2), 26-39.

Osgood, C. E., & Suci, G. (1952). A measure of relation determined by both mean difference and profile information. *Psychological Bulletin, 49*, 251-262.

Ouchi, W. (1980). Markets, bureaucracies, and clans. *Administrative Science Quarterly, 1*, 129-141.

Ouchi, W. G. (1979). A conceptual framework for the design of organizational control mechanisms. *Management Science, 25*(9), 833-848.

Oyelaran-Oyeyinka, B., & Nyaki Adeya, C. (2004). Internet Access in Africa: Empirical Evidence from Kenya and Nigeria. *Telematics and Informatics, 21*(1), 67-81.

Palen, L. (2002). *Mobile Telephony in a Connected Life.* Communications of the ACM, *45*(3), 78-82.

Palen, L., Salzman, M., & Youngs, E. (2000). Going Wireless:Behaviour and Practice of New Mobile Phone Users. *Proceedings of the Conference on Computer Supported Cooperative Work (CSCW'00)*, 201-210.

Papazafeiropoulou, A. (2002). *A stakeholder approach to electronic commerce diffusion.* Unpublished doctoral dissertation, Brunel University, London.

Parish, T. S., & Necessary, J. R. (1996). An examination of cognitive dissonance and computer attitudes. *Educational Technology, Research and Development, 116*(4), 565-566.

Parr, G. D., & Montgomery, M. (1998). Flow theory as a model for enhancing student resilience. *Professional School Counseling, 1*(5), 26-32.

Patton, M. (2002). *Qualitative research and evaluation methods* (3rd ed.). Thousand Oaks, CA: Sage.

Pearson, K. (1928). On the coefficient of racial likeness. *Biometrika, 18*, 105-117.

Pedhazur, E. J., & Schmelkin, L. P. (1991). *Measurement, Design, and Analysis: An Integrated Approach.* Hillside, NJ: Lawrence Erlbaum Associates.

Penrose, E. (1995). *The theory of the growth of the firm* (3rd ed.). Oxford: Oxford University Press.

Peterson, M. (1998, January-February). Embedded organizational events: The units of process in organization science. *Organization Science, 9*(1), 16-33.

Pettigrew, A. (1992). The character and significance of strategy process research. *Strategic Management Journal, 13*, 5-16.

Pettigrew, A. (1987). Context and action in the transformation of the firm. *Journal of Management Studies, 24*(6), 649-670.

Pfeffer, J. (1992). *Managing with power: Politics and influence in organizations.* Boston: Harvard Business School Press.

Pfeffer, J. F. (1981). *Power in organizations.* Cambridge, MA: Ballinger.

Piatelli-Palmarini, M. (1994). *Inevitable illusions.* New York: Wiley.

Picciotto, S. (1999). Introduction: What rules for the world economy? In R. Mayne (Ed.), *Regulating international business: Beyond liberalization.* London: Macmillan.

Pigg, K. (2001). Applications of community informatics for building community and enhancing civic society. *Information, Communication & Society, 4*(4), 507-527.

Pikkarainen, K., Pikkarainen, T., Karjaluoto, H., & Pahnila, S. (2006). The measurement of End-User Computing Satisfaction of online-banking services: empirical evidence from Finland. *The International Journal of Bank Marketing, 24*(3), 158-172.

Pinch, T.J. and Bijker, W.E. (1984). The social construction of facts and artefacts: Or how the sociology of science and the sociology of technology might benefit each other. *Social Studies of Science, 14*(1), 399-441.

Pinsonneault, A., & Kramer, K. L. (1993). Survey research methodology in management information systems: An

assessment. *Journal of Management Information Systems, 10*(2), 75-106.

Pissarra, J., & Jesuino, J. (2005). Idea generation through computer-mediated communication: The effects of anonymity. *Journal of Management Psychology, 20*(3/4), 275-291.

Plant, S. (1997). *The most radical gesture: The situationist international in a postmodern age.* London: Routledge.

Plant, S. (2002). *On the Mobile: The Effects of Mobile Telephones on Social and Individual Life.* Motorola, London. Available at http://motorola.com/mot/doc/0/267_MotDoc.pdf

Polanyi, M. (1958). *Personal knowledge.* Chicago: University of Chicago Press/London: Routledge & Kegan Paul.

Polanyi, M. (1966). *The tacit dimension.* Chicago: University of Chicago Press.

Polanyi, M. (1969). *Knowing and being.* In M. Grene (Ed.). London: Routledge & Kegan Paul.

Polanyi, M., & Prosch, H. (1975). *Meaning.* Chicago: University of Chicago Press.

Pólya, G. (1959). Heuristic reasoning in the theory of numbers. *American Mathematical Monthly, 66*, 375-384. (Reprinted Mathematics and plausible reasoning (1968) pp. 193-202, by G. Pólya, (vol. II) Princeton : Princeton University Press).

Pólya, G. (1968, 1954). *Mathematics and plausible reasoning* (2nd ed.). 2 vol. Princeton, NJ: Princeton University Press.

Pólya, G. (1990, 1945). *How to solve it.* London: Penguin.

Polyani, M. (1966). *The tacit dimension.* Garden City, NY: Doubleday and Co.

Poole, M.S., & Desanctis, G. (1992). Microlevel structuration in computer-supported group decision-making. *Human Communication Research, 19*, 5-49.

Poole, S. (2000). *Trigger happy: Video games and the entertainment revolution.* New York: Arcade Publishing.

Popper, K. (1968, 1959). *The logic of scientific discovery* (3rd ed.). London: Hutchinson.

Popper, K.R. (1963). *Conjectures and refutations.* New York: Harper.

Porn, L. M., & Kelly, P. (2002). Mobile computing acceptance grows as applications evolve. *Healthcare Financial Management, 56*(1), 66-70.

Pouloudi, A., & Serafeimidis, V. (1999). Stakeholders of information systems evaluation: Experience from a case study. In *Proceedings of the Sixth European Conference on IT Investment Evaluation* (pp. 91-98), Brunel University, Uxbridge.

Pouloudi, A., & Whitley, E.A. (2000). Representing human and non-human stakeholders: On speaking with authority. *Organisational and Social Perspectives on Information Technology. Department of Information systems London School of Economics and Political Science Working Paper Series 88.* Retrieved January 4, 2004 from http://is.lse.ac.uk/wp/pdf/WP88.PDF

Poyhonen, A., & Smedlund, A. (2004). Assessing intellectual capital creation in regional clusters. *Journal of Intellectual Capital, 5*(3), 351-365.

Prahalad, C. K., & Hamel, G. (1990). The core competence of the corporation. *Harvard Business Review, 68*(3), 79-91.

Preece, J. (1994). *Human-computer interaction.* Harlow, UK: Addison-Wesley.

Prescott A. (1997). The Electronic Beowulf and Digital Restoration, *Literary and Linguistic Computing, 12,* 185-195.

Pressman, R. (2005*). Software engineering: A practitioner's approach* (6th ed.). London/New York: McGraw Hill.

Provenzo, E. F. Jr. (1991). *Video kids: Making sense out of Nintendo.* Cambridge, MA: Harvard University Press.

Pulkkinen, L. (1996). Female and male personality styles: A typological and developmental analysis. *Journal of Personality and Social Psychology, 70*(6), 1288-1306.

Quinn, J.B. (1992). The intelligent enterprise: A new paradigm. *Academy of Management Executive, 6*(4), 48-63.

Quinn, J. B. (1998). Organizing around intellect [Interview]. *Harvard Management Update.*

Quintanar, L.R., Crowell, C.R., Pryor, J.B., & Adamopoulos, J. (1982). Human computer interaction: A preliminary social psychological analysis. *Behaviour Research Methods and Instrumentation, 14*(2), 210-220.

Ragupathi, W. (1997). Health care information systems. *Communications of the ACM, 40*(8), 81-82.

Rauhala, L. (1983). *Ihmiskäsitys ihmistyössä* [The conception of the human being in human work]. Helsinki: Gaudeamus.

Reeves, B., Lombard, M., & Melwani, G. (1992). Faces on the screen: Pictures or natural experience. *International Communication Association.*

Reeves, B., & Nass, C. (1996). *The media equation: How people treat computers, television and new media like real people and places.* Cambridge University Press.

Reich, B. H., & Banbasat, I. (1996). Measuring the linkage between business and information technology objectives. *MIS Quarterly, 20*(1), 55-82.

Remenyi, D. (1999). *Stop IT project failures through risk management.* Oxford: Butterworth Heinemann.

Remenyi, D., Sherwood-Smith, M., & White, T. (1996). Outcomes and benefit modelling for information systems investment. In *Proceedings of the 3rd European Conference on Information Technology Investment Evaluation* (pp. 101-119).

Renkema, T., & Berghout, E. (1997). Methodologies for information systems investment evaluation at the proposal stage: A comparative review. *Information and Software Technology, 39,* 1-13.

Rickenberg, R., & Reeves, B. (2000). The effects of animated characters on anxiety, task performance, and evaluations of user interfaces. In *Proceedings of the CHI 2000* (pp. 329-336).

Ring, P. (2002). Processes facilitating reliance on trust in inter-organizational networks. In M. Ebers (Ed.), *The formation of inter-organizational networks* (pp. 113-45). Oxford, England: Oxford University Press

Ring, P., & Van de Ven, A. (1994). Developmental processes of cooperative interorganizational relationships. *Academy of Management Review, 19*, 90-118.

Riviere, C. A., & Licoppe, C. (2005). From voice to text: Continuity and change in the use of mobile phones in France and Japan (pp 103-126). In R. Harper (Eds.), *The Inside Text: Social Perspectives on SMS in the Mobile Age*. London: Springer-Verlag.

Robbins, S., & Barnwell, N. (1994). *Organisation theory in Australia*. New York: Prentice Hall.

Roberts, N., & Bradley, R. (1991). Stakeholder collaboration and innovation: A study of public policy initiation at the state level. *Journal of Applied Behavioral Science, 27*(2), 209-227.

Robey, D. (1979). User attitudes and management information system use. *Academy of Management Journal, 22*, 527-538.

Robey, D., & Markus, M. L. (1984). Rituals in Information System Design. *MIS Quarterly*, 5-15.

Robey, D., & Newman, M. (1996). Sequential patterns in information systems development: An application of a social process model. *ACM Transactions of information systems, 14*(1), 30-63.

Robey, D., Boudreau, M.-C., & Rose, G.M. (2000). Information technology and organisational learning: A review and assessment of research. *Accounting Management and Information Technologies, 10*, 125–155.

Robillard, P.N. (1999). The role of knowledge in software development. *Communications of the ACM, 42*(1), 87-92.

Rogers, E. M. (1995). *Diffusion of innovations* (4th ed.). New York: Free Press.

Rohleder, T. R., & Klassen, K. J. (2000). Using client-variance information to improve dynamic appointment scheduling performance. *Omega, 28*(3), 293-305.

Rose, G. M., Evaristo, R., & Straub, D. (2003). Culture and Consumer Responses to Web Download Time: A Four-Continent Study of Mono-and Polychronism. *IEEE Transactions on Engineering Management, 50*(1), 31-44.

Rosenbaum, S., Rohn, J. A., & Humburg, J. (2000). A Toolkit for Strategic Usability: Results from Workshops, Panels, and Surveys. In *Proc. CHI 2000. CHI Letters, 2* (1), 337-344.

Rozzell, E. J., & Gardner, W. L. I. (1999). Computer-related success and failure: A longitudinal field study of the factors influencing computer-related performance. *Computers in Human Behavior, 15*, 1-10.

Rudy, A. (1996). A critical review of research on electronic mail. *European Journal of Information Systems, 4*(4), 198-213.

Russo, N., & Graham, B. (1998). *A first step in developing a web application design methodology: Understanding the environment*. Paper presented at the Sixth International Conference on Information Systems Methodology, Salford University, Manchester, U.K.

Rust, J., & Golombok, S. (1989). *Modern pychometrics: The science of psychological assessment*. New York: Routledge.

Ruël, H.J.M. (2001). *The non-technical side of office technology; managing the clarity of the spirit and the appropriation of office technology*. The Netherlands: Twente University Press.

Rycroft, R. (2003). Technology-based globalization indicators: The creativity of innovation network data. *Technology in Society, 25*(3), 299-317.

Saade, R. G., Nebebe, F., & Tan, W. (2007). Viability of the "Technology Acceptance Model" in Multimedia Learning Environments: A comparative study. *Interdis-*

ciplinary Journal of Knowledge and Learning Objects, 3, 175-184.

Sadler, S. (1998). *The situationist city.* Cambridge, MA: The MIT Press.

Sakamoto, A. (2005). Video games and the psychological development of Japanese children. In D. W. Schwalb, J. Nakazawa, & B. J. Schwalb (Eds.), *Applied developmental psychology: Theory, practice and reform from Japan* (pp. 3-21). Greenwich, CT: Information Age Publishing. Retrieved May 27, 2005, from Ebsco host database.

Salaway, G. (1987). An organizational learning approach to information systems development. *MIS Quarterly, 11*(2), 245-264.

Säljö, R. (1994). Minding action. Conceiving the world vs. participating in cultural practices. *Nordisk Pedagogik, 14,* 71-80.

Sandberg, J., (2000). Understanding human competence at work: An interprettive approach, *Academy of Management Journal* 43(1), 9-25.

Sarkkinen, J., & Karsten, H. (2005). Verbal and visual representations in task redesign: how different viewpoints enter into information systems design discussions. *Information Systems Journal, 15*(3), 181-211.

Sauer, C. (1999). Deciding the future for IS failures not the choice you might think. In W. Currie & R. Galliers (Eds.), *Rethinking management information systems* (pp. 279–309). Oxford University Press.

Sayer, K., & Harvey, L. (1997). Empowerment in Business Process Reengineering: an Ethnographic Study of Implementation Discourse. In Kumar, K and DeGross, J I (eds.): Proc. 18th International Conference on Information Systems, Atlanta, USA. Pp 427 – 440.

Scacchi, W. (2002). Understanding the requirements for developing open source software systems. *IEE Proceedings – Software 149*(1), 24-39.

Scheel, C. (2002). Knowledge clusters of technological innovation systems. *Journal of Knowledge Management, 6*(4), 356-367.

Scheer, A.-W., Kruppke, H., Jost, W., & Kindermann, H. (2006). *Agility by ARIS Business Process Management: Yearbook Business Process Excellence 2006/2007,* X, 281 p. 125, ISBN: 978-3-540-33527-6.

Schippers, M. (2003). *Reflexivity in teams.* Unpublished doctoral thesis, University of Amsterdam.

Schneider, E., Lang, A., Shin, M., & Bradley, S. (2004). Death with a story: How story impacts emotional, motivational and physiological responses to first-person shooter video games. *Human Communication Research, 30*(3), 361-375. Retrieved May 27, 2006, from Ebsco host database.

Schuler, D., & Namioka, A. (Eds.) (1993). *Participatory Design: Principles and Practices.* New Jersey: Lawrence Erlbaum Associates. (pp. 41-78).

Schultz, R. L., & Slevin, D. P. (1975). *Implementing Operations Research/Management Science.* New York: American Elsevier.

Schumpeter, J. A. (1975). *Capitalism, socialism and democracy.* New York: Harper (Original work published 1942).

Schumpeter, Joesph A. (1942). Capitalism, socialism, and Democracy. New York: Harper and Brothers.

Schütz, A. & Luckmann, T. (1984). *Strukturen der Lebenswelt.* Bd.2, p.197. Frankfurt/Main, Germany: Utb Verlag.

Schwandt, T., (2000). Three epistemological stances for qualitative inquiry. Interpretivism, hermeneutics, and social constructionism. In Denzin, N.K. &Y.S. Lincoln (Eds.) The handbook of qualitative research (2nd ed.). Thousand Oaks, CA: Sage, 189-213.

Seffah, A., & Andreevskaia, A. (2003). Empowering Software Engineers in Human-Centered Design. In *Proc. 25th IEEE International Conference on Software Engineering,* May 3-10, 2003, Portland, Oregon, USA.

Sen, S., Padmanabhan, B., & Tuzhilin, A. (1998). The Identification and Satisfaction of Consumer Analysis-Driven Information Needs of Marketers on the WWW. *European Journal of Marketing, 32* (7/8), 688-702.

Senge, P.M., Kleiner, A., Roberts, C., Ross, R.B., & Smith, B.J. (1994). *The fifth discipline field book: Strategies and tools for building a learning organisation.* New York: Currency Doubleday.

Senn, J. A. (1998). *Information in business: Principles, practices and opportunities.* Englewood Cliffs, NJ: Prentice-Hall.

Serafeimidis, V., & Smithson, S. (2000). Information systems evaluation in practice: A case study of organizational change. *Journal of Information Technology, 15*, 93-105.

Seyal, A. H., Rahman, M. N. A., & Rahim, M. M. (2002). Determinants of academic use of the Internet: A structural equation model. *Behavior and Information Technology, 21*(1), 71-86.

Shah, D. (2002). Nonrecursive models of internet use and community engagement: Questioning whether time spent online erodes social capital. *Journalism & Mass Communication Quarterly, 79*(4), 964-987.

Sharma, S. (1996). *Applied Multivariate Techniques.* New York, NY: John Wiley and Sons.

Shayo, C., Guthrie, R., & Igbaria, M. (1999). Exploring the Measurement of End User Computing Success. *Journal of End User Computing, 11*(1), 2-26.

Shi, Y., & Scavo, C. (2000). Citizen Participation and Direct Democracy through Computer Networking. In D. Garson (Ed.), *Handbook of Public Information Systems.* New York: Marcel Dekker.

Shiba, T., & Shimotani, M. (Eds.). (1997). *Beyond the firm. Business groups in international and historical perspective.* Oxford: Oxford University Press.

Shields, R. (1992). Spaces for the subject of consumption. In R. Shields (Ed.), *Lifestyle shopping: The subject of consumption.* London: Routledge.

Shiller, H. I. (1979). Transnational media and national development. In K. Nordenstreng & H. I. Shiller (Eds.), *National sovereignty and international communication* (pp.21-29). Norwood, NJ: Ablex.

Shneiderman, B. (1997) Direct manipulation vs. agents: Paths to predictable, controllable, and comprehensible interfaces In J. Bradshaw (Ed.), *Software agents* (pp. 97-106). Menlo Park, CA: AAAI Press.

Shneiderman, B., & Plaisant, C. (2005). *Designing the user interface: Strategies for effective human computer interaction.* Boston: Addison-Wesley.

Siala, H., O'Keefe, R., & Hone, K. (2004). The Impact of Religious Affiliation on Trust in the Context of Electronic Commerce. *Interacting with Computers, 16*(2004) 7-27.

Sillers, T.S., & Kleiner, B.H. (1997). Defence conversion: Surviving (and prospering) in the 1990s. *Work Study, 46*(2), 45-48.

Silver, M. S. (1988). User perceptions of decision support system restrictiveness: An experiment. *Journal of Management Information Systems, 5*(1), 51-65.

Silverman, D. (1985). *Qualitative methodology and sociology.* Aldershot: Gower.

Silverman, D. (2000). *Doing qualitative research: A practical handbook.* London: Sage.

Simon, S. J., Grover, V., Teng, J. T. C., & Whitcomb, K. (1996). The relationship of information training methods and cognitive ability to end-user satisfaction, comprehension, and skill transfer: A longitudinal field study. *Information Systems Research, 7*(2), 466-490.

Singh, S. (1997). *Fermat's last theorem.* London: Fourth Estate.

Siponen, M. (2004). A pragmatic evaluation of the theory of information ethics. *Ethics and Information Technology, 6*(4), 279-290.

Skinner, B.F. (1991). The behavior of organisms: An experimental analysis. Acton, MA: Copley. Originally published in 1938.

Slater, D. (1997). *Consumer culture and modernity.* Malden, MA: Blackwell.

Smith A., Dunckley, L., French, T., Minocha, S., & Chang, Y. (2004). A Process Model for Developing Usable

Cross-Cultural Websites. *Interacting with Computers, 16*, 63–91.

Smith, A. (1997). *Human computer factors: A study of users and information systems*. London: McGraw-Hill.

Smith, A., French, T., Chang, Y., & McNeill, M. (2001). E-Culture: A comparative study of eFinance web site usability for Chinese and British users. Designing for global markets. Conference (6th. 2001). In D. Day & L. Duckley (Eds.), *Proceedings of the third international workshop on internationalisation of products and systems*. Buckinghamshire: The Open University. (pp. 87-100).

Smith, M. M. (2002). Global information ethics: A mandate for professional education. In *Proceedings of the 68th IFLA Council and General Conference*, Glasgow. Retrieved January 25, 2007, from http://www.ifla.org/IV/ifla68/papers/056-093e.pdf.

Smithson, S., & Hirschheim, R. (1998). Analysing information systems evaluation: Another look at an old problem. *European Journal of Information Systems, 7*, 158-174.

Snow, C. & Thomas, J. (1993). Building networks: Broker roles and behaviours. In P. Lorange, B. Chakravarthy, J. Roos, & A. Van de Ven (Eds.), *Implementing strategic processes: Change, learning and co-operation* (pp. 217-38). Oxford: Blackwell.

Snow, C. (1967). *Die zwei Kulturen: Literarische und naturwissenschaftliche Intelligenz*. Stuttgart, Germany: Klett Verlag.

Somers, T. M., Nelson, K., & Karimi, J. (2003). Confirmatory Factor Analysis of the End-User Computing Satisfaction Instrument: Replication within an ERP Domain. *Decision Sciences, 34*(3), 595-621.

Sorensen, E. (2002). Democratic theory and network governance. *Administrative Theory & Praxis, 24*(4), 693-720.

Southworth, M., & Southworth, S. (1982). *Maps a visual survey and design guide*. Boston: Little, Brown and Co.

Spinuzzi, C. (2002). A Scandinavian Challenge, a US Response: Methodological Assumptions in Scandinavian and US Prototyping Approaches. In *Proc. SIGDOC 2002*. Pp. 208-215.

Stahl, B.C. (2006). *Trust as fetish: A Critical theory perspective on research on trust in e-commerce*. Paper presented at the Information Communications and Society Symposium, University of York, UK.

Stahl, G. (2000). A model of collaborative knowledge building. In *Proceedings of the Fourth International Conference of the Learning Sciences* (pp. 70–77), Ann Arbor, Michigan.

Stallabrass, J. (2003). *Internet art: The online clash of culture and commerce*. London: Tate Publishing.

Stephanidis, C. (2001). Human-computer interaction in the age of the disappearing computer. In N. Avouris, & N. Fakotakis (Eds.), *Advances in human-computer interaction I. Proceedings of the PC HCI 2001* (pp. 15-22), Athens, Greece.

Stephenson, W. (1950). A statistical approach to typology: The study of trait-universes. *Journal of Clinical Psychology, 6*, 26-38.

Sterling, T.D. (1974). Guidelines for humanizing computerized information systems: A report from Stanley House. *Communications of the ACM, 17*(11), 609-613.

Stevenson, T. (2002). Communities of tomorrow. *Futures, 34*(8), 735-744.

Strauss, A., & Corbin, J. (1990). *Basics of qualitative research: Grounded theory procedures and techniques*. Newbury Park, CA: Sage Publications.

Subramanian, G. H. (1994). A replication of perceived usefulness and perceived ease of use measurement. *Decision Sciences, 25*(5,6), 863-874.

Suire, R. (2004). Des réseaux de l'entrepreneur aux ressorts du créatif Quelles stratégies pour les territoires? *Revue Internationale PME, 17*(2), 123-143.

Sun, H. (2003). *Exploring Cultural Usability: A Localization Study of Mobile Text Messaging Use*. Paper presented at the CHI 2003, Ft. Lauderdale, FL.

Sun, H., & Zhang, P. (2006). Causal relationships between perceived enjoyment and perceived ease of use: An alternative approach. *Journal of the Association for Information Systems, 7*(9), 618-645.

Sun, H., & Zhang, P. (2008). An exploration of affect factors and their role in user technology acceptance: Mediation and causality. *Journal of the American Society for Information Science and Technology, 59*(8), 1-12.

Sun, H., & Zhang, P. (2006). The role of moderating factors in user technology acceptance. *International Journal of Human-Computer Studies, 64*, 53-78.

Suomi, R. (1990). *Assessing the feasibility of an inter-organizational information system on the basis of the transaction cost approach.* Doctoral thesis, Turku School of Economics and Business Administration, Department of Management.

Suomi, R. (2001). Streamlining operations in health care with ICT. In T. A. Spil & R. A. Stegwee (Eds.), *Strategies for healthcare information systems* (pp. 31-44). Hershey, PA: Idea Group Publishing.

Swann, P., Prevezer, M., & Stout, D. (Eds.). (1998). *The dynamics of industrial clustering, international comparisons in computing and biotechnology.* Oxford: Oxford University Press.

Swanson, E. B. (1987). Information channel disposition and use. *Decision Sciences, 18*, 131-145.

Swanson, E. B. (1988). *Information system implementation: Bridging the gap between design and utilization.*, Homewood, IL: Irwin.

Swieringa, J., & Wierdsma, A. (1994). *Becoming a learning organisation.* Addison-Wesley Publishing.

Symon, G. (1998). The Work of IT System Developers in Context: An Organizational Case Study. *Human-Computer Interaction, 13*(1), 37-71.

Symons, V. (1993). Evaluation and the failure of control: Information systems development in the processing company. *Accounting, Management and Information Technology, 3*(1), 51-76.

Tamai, T. (1993). Current practices in software processes for system planning and requirements analysis. *Information and Software Technology, 35*(6-7), 339-344.

Tan, M. (1999). Creating the digital economy: Strategies and perspectives from Singapore. *International Journal of Electronic Commerce, 3*(3), 105-22.

Tasioulas, J. (2006). Crimes of offence. In A. Simester & A. von Hirsh (Eds.), *Incivilities: Regulating offensive behaviour.* Oxford: Hart.

Taylor, J., Emery, J, van (2000). *The emergent organization: Communication as its site and surface.* Mahwah, NJ: Erlbaum.

Taylor, M. J., McWilliam, J., Forsythe, H., & Wade, S. (2002). Methodologies and Web site development: A survey of practice. *Information and Software Technology, 44*(6), 381-391.

Te'eni, D., Sagie, A., Schwartz, D. G., Zaidman, N. & Amichai-Hamburger, Y. (2001). The process of organizational communication: A model and field study. *IEEE Transactions on Professional Communication, 44*(1), 6-20.

Tella, S., & Mononen-Aaltonen, M. (2000). *Towards Network-Based Education:*

Teo, S. H. T., Lim, V. K. G., & Lai, R. Y. C. (1999). Intrinsic and extrinsic motivation in Internet usage. *OMEGA International Journal of Management Science, 27*, 25-37.

Terlecki, M., & Newcombe, N. (2005). How important is the digital divide? The relationship of computer videogame usage to gender differences in mental rotation ability. *Sex Roles, 53*(5-6), 433-441. Retrieved June 3, 2006, from Ebsco host database.

Tesch, R. (1990). *Qualitative research: Analysis types and software tools.* New York: Falmer Press.

The Economist. (1997, December 18). 1897 and 1997: The century the earth stood still.

The New York Times (2005). *Cellphones catapult rural Africa into the 21st Century.* Accessed 25th August 2005.

Thietart, R. A. (2001). *Doing management research: A comprehensive guide*. Sage.

Thomas, J. C., & Streib, G. (2003). The New Face of Government: Citizen-Initiated Contacts in the Era of E-Government. *Journal of Public Administration Research and Theory, 13*(1), 83–101.

Thompson, M.P.A., & Walsham, G. (2004). Placing knowledge management in context. *Journal of Management Studies, 41*(5), 724–747.

Tierney, M. (1993). The evolution of Def Stan 00-55: A socio-history of a design standard for safety-critical software. In P. Quintas (Ed.), *Social dimensions of systems engineering: People, processes and software development* (pp. 111-143). New York/London: Ellis Horwood.

Titscher, S., Meyer, M., Wodak, R., & Vetter, E. (2000). *Methods of text and discourse analysis*. London: Sage Publications.

Todd, P., & Gigerenzer, G (2000). Précis of simple heuristics that make us smart. *Behavioural and Brain Sciences, 23*, 737-780.

Tomlinson, J. (1991). *Cultural imperialism*. Baltimore, MD: The Johns Hopkins University Press.

Torkzadeh, G., & Van Dyke, T. P. (2002). Effects of Training on Internet Self-Efficacy and Computer User Attitudes. *Computers in Human Behavior, 18*(5), 479-494.

Trevino, L. K., & Webster, J. (1992). Flow in computer-mediated communication. *Communication Research, 19*(5), 539-574.

Trim, P. (2001). Public-private partnerships and the defence industry. *European Business Review, 13*(4), 227-234.

Trist, E., & Bamforth, K. (1951). Some social and psychological consequences of Longwall method of coalgetting. *Human Relations, 4*, 3–38.

Truex, D. P., Baskerville, R., & Klein, H. K. (1999). Growing Systems in Emergent Organisations. *Communications of the ACM, 42*(8), 117-123.

Tsoukas, H., & Vladimirou, E. (2001). What is organizational knowledge? *Journal of Management Studies, 38*(7), 973–993.

Tucker, A.L., Edmondson, A.C., & Spear, S. (2001). When problem solving prevents organizational learning (Working Paper No. 01-073). Harvard Business School.

Tudor, L. (1998). Human Factors: Does Your Management Hear You? Interaction January + February.

Turisco, F. (2000). Mobile computing is next technology frontier for healthcare providers. *Healthcare Financial Management, 54*(11), 78-81.

Turkle, S. (1984). *The second self: Computers and the human spirit*. New York: Simon and Schuster.

Twidale, M. & Nichols, D. (2005). Exploring Usability Discussions in Open Source Development. In *Proc.38th Hawaii International Conference on System Sciences HICSS*. IEEE.

Tyre, M. J., & Orlikowski, W. J. (1994). Windows of opportunity: Temporal patterns of technological adaption in organizations. *Organization Science, 5*(1), 98-118.

Uljens, M. (1991). Phenomenography: A qualitative approach in educational research. In L. Syrjälä, & J. Merenheimo (Eds.), *Kasvatustutkimuksen laadullisia lähestymistapoja*. Oulun yliopiston kasvatustieteiden tiedekunnan opetusmonisteita ja selosteita 39 (pp. 80–107).

United Nations. (1998). *Knowledge societies: Information technology for sustainable development*. Report prepared by R. Mansell & U. Wehn. Oxford: United Nations Commission on Science and Technology for Development/Oxford University Press.

Ur, P. (1996). *A Course in language teaching: Practice and theory*. Cambridge University Press.

Urry, J. (2002). The global complexities of September 11th. *Theory, Culture & Society, 19*(4), 57-69.

Uslaner, E. M. (2004). Trust, civic engagement, and the Internet. *Political Communication, 21*(2), 223-242.

Valery, P. (1924). Eupalinos ou l'Architecte. In: Architectures, *Edité par Gallimard*, Paris.

Valtioneuvoston asetus hoitoon pääsyn toteuttamisesta ja alueellisesta yhteistyöstä [Act on delivering health service and regional co-operation]. (2004).

Van de Ven, A. & Poole, M. (1995). Explaining development and change in organizations. *Academy of Management Review, 20*(3), 510-540.

Van den Hooff, B., de Ridder, J. & Aukema, E. (2004). Exploring the eagerness to share knowledge: The role of social capital and ICT in knowledge sharing. In M. Huysman, & V. Wulf (Eds.), *Social capital and information technology* (Chapter 7). Cambridge, USA and London, England: The MIT Press.

Van der Heijden, H. (2004). User acceptance of hedonic information systems. *MIS Quarterly, 28*(4), 695-704.

Van Dijk, T.A. (1997). *Discourse as structure and process* (Vol. 1, 2). London: Sage.

Venkatesh, A., & Vitalari, N. P. (1991). Longitudinal surveys in information systems research: An examination of issues, methods and applications. In K. Kramer (Ed.), *The information systems challenge: Survey research methods*. Harvard, MA: Harvard University press, 115-144.

Venkatesh, V., & Davis, F. D. (1996). A model of the antecedents of perceived ease of use. *Decision Sciences, 27*(3), 451-481.

Venkatesh, V., & Davis, F. D. (1994). Modeling the determinants of perceived ease of use. *15th International Conference on Information Systems*, 213-227.

Vessey, I., & Conger, S. A. (1994). Requirements specification: Learning object, process and data methodologies. *Communications of the ACM, 37*(5), 102-113.

Viorres, N., Xenofon, P., Stavrakis, M., Vlanhogiannis, E., Koutsabasis, P., & Darzentas J. (2007). Major HCI Challenges for Open Source Software Adoption and Development. In D. Schuler (Ed.), Proc. Human Computer Interaction International: Online Communities and Social Computing. *LNCS 4564*, 455-464.

Von Hippel, E. (1994). Sticky information and the locus of problem-solving-implications for innovation. *Management Science, 40*(4), 429-439.

Von Oetinger, B. (2005). From idea to innovation: Making creativity real. *The Journal of Business Strategy, 25*(5), 35-41.

Vredenburg, K. (1999). Increasing Ease of Use – Emphasizing organizational transformations, process integration, and method optimisation. *Communications of the ACM, 42*(5), 67-71.

Vredenburg, K., Mao, J, Smith, P. W., & Casey, T. (2002). A survey of user-centered design practice. In D. Wixon (ed.). *Proc. Conference on Human Factors in Computing Systems: Changing our World, Changing Ourselves*, New York: ACM Press. (pp. 471-478).

Vroom, V. H., & Yetton, P. W. (1973). *Leadership and decision-making*. Pittsburgh: University of Pittsburgh Press.

Waits, M. (2000). The added value of the industry cluster approach to economic analysis, strategy development, and service delivery. *Economic Development Quarterly, 14*(1), 35-50.

Wallace, L., Keil, M., & Rai, A. (2004). How software project risk affects project performance: An investigation of the dimensions of risk and an exploratory model. *Decision Sciences, 35*(2), 289-321.

Walsh, E. (1994). Phenomenographic analysis of interview transcripts. In J.A. Bowden, & E. Walsh (Eds.), *Phenomenographic research: Variations in method* (pp. 17-30). The Warburton Symposium. Melbourne: The Royal Melbourne Institute of Technology.

Walsham, G. (1993). *Interpreting information systems in organisations*. Chichester: Wiley.

Walsham, G. (1993). *Interpreting information systems in organizations*. Chichester: John Wiley & Sons.

Walsham, G. (1995). Interpretive case studies in IS research: Nature and method. *European Journal of Information Systems, 4*(2), 74-81.

Walsham, G. (1999). Interpretive evaluation design for information systems. In S. Lester (Ed.), *Beyond the IT productivity paradox* (pp. 363-380). Chichester: John Wiley & Sons.

Walsham, G. (2005). Knowledge management systems: Representation and communication in context. *Systems, Signs & Actions, 1*(1), 6– 8.

Ward, L. (2005, February 2). Careers and guidance service may be replaced. *The Guardian.* http://education.guardian.co.uk/schools/story/0,,1403768,00.html

Warkentin, C., & Mingst, K. (2000). International institutions, the state, and global civil society in the age of the World Wide Web. *Global Governance, 6*(2), 237-257.

Wastell, D. G. (1999). Learning dysfunctions in information systems development: Overcoming the social defenses with transitional objects. *MIS Quarterly, 23*(4), 581-600.

Weckert, J. (2001). Computer ethics: Future directions. *Ethics and Information Technology, 3*(2), 93-96.

Weedon, C. (1987). *Feminist Practice and Poststructuralist Theory.* Oxford: Basil Blackwell Ltd.

Weedon, C. (2004). *Identity and Culture: Narratives of Difference and Belonging.* New York: Open University Press.

Weick, K. E. (1969). *The social psychology of organizing.* Reading, MA: Addison-Wesley.

Weick, K. E., & Sutcliffe, K. M. (2001). *Managing the unexpected: Assuring high performance in an age of complexity.* San Francisco: Jossey-Bass.

Weick, K., Sutcliffe, K.M., & Obstfeld (2005). Organizing and process of sensemaking. *Organization Science, 16*(4), 409–421.

Weinberg, G. (1971). *The psychology of computer programming.* New York: Van Nostrand Reinhold.

Weiner, B. (1990). History of motivational research in education. *Journal of Educational Psychology, 82,* 616-622.

Weiss, N.A. (1999). *Introductory statistics.* Boston: Addison Wesley.

Wellman, B., Haase, A. Q., Witte, J., & Hampton, K. (2001). Does the internet increase, decrease, or supplement social capital? Social networks, participation, and community commitment. *American Behavioral Scientist, 45*(3), 436-455.

Wenger, E. (1998). *Communities of practice: Learning, meaning and identity.* Cambridge University Press.

Wenn, A., Tatnall, A., Sellitto, C., Darbyshire, P. & Burgess, S. (2002). *A socio-technical investigation of factors affecting IT adoption by rural GPs.* Paper presented at IT in Regional Areas, ITiRA conference, Rockhampton, Australia.

West, D. M. (2004). E-Government and the Transformation of Service Delivery and Citizen Attitudes. *Public Administration Review, 64*(1), 15–27.

West, M.A. (2000). Reflexivity, revolution and innovation in work teams. In M.M. Beyerlein & D.A. Johnson (Eds.), *Product development teams* (Vol. 5, pp. 1–29). Stamford, CT: JAI Press.

Westrup, C. (1994). Practical understanding: Hermeneutics and teaching the management of information systems development using a case study. *Accounting, Management and Information Technologies, 4*(1).

Wheelan, S. (1999). *Creating effective teams: A guide for members and leaders* (p. 154). Thousand Oaks, CA: Sage Publications.

Whitfield, L. (2003). NHS staff buy-in is essential for project success. *Computing.* Retrieved January 4, 2004 from http://www.computing.co.uk/News/1143868

Wiegers, K. (1999). Software process improvement in web time. *IEEE Software, 16*(4), 78-86.

Wilder, G., Mackie, D., & Cooper, J. (1985). Gender and computers: Two surveys of computer-related attitudes. *Sex Roles, 13*(3/4), 215-228.

Wilenius, R. (1978). *Ihminen, luonto ja tekniikka* [The human being, nature and technology]. Jyväskylä: Gummerus.

Willcocks, L., & Lester, S. (1999). In search of information technology productivity: Assessment issues. In S. Lester (Ed.), *Beyond the IT productivity paradox* (pp. 69-98). Chichester: John Wiley & Sons.

Williams, R. (2001). Base and superstructure in Marxist cultural theory. In M. Durham & D. Kellner (Eds.), *Media and cultural studies: Keyworks* (pp.152-165). Malden, Massachusetts: Blackwell.

Williams, R., Stewart, J., & Slack, R. (2005). *Social learning in technological innovation—Experimenting with information communication technologies.* Cheltenham, UK and Northampton, USA: Edward Elgar.

Williamson, O. E. (1985). *The economic institutions of capitalism. Firms, markets, relational constructing.* New York: The Free Press.

Wilson, T. (1991) Overcoming the barriers to the implementation of information system strategies. *Journal of Information Technology, 6*, 39-44.

Winograd, T. (1995). From programming environments to environments for designing. *Communications of ACM, 38*(6), 65-74.

Wittgenstein, L. (2001). *Philosophical investigations: The German text with a revised English translation* (3rd ed.). Oxford: Blackwell.

Wolgast, E. H. (1987). *The grammar of justice.* Ithaca, NY: Cornell University Press.

Wong, D. (1984). *Moral relativity.* Berkeley, CA: University of California Press.

Wong, D. (2006). *Natural moralities: A defense of pluralistic relativism.* Oxford: Oxford University Press.

Wong, D. (1993). Relativism. In P. Singer (Ed.), *A companion to ethics* (pp. 442-450). Blackwell.

Wood, D., & Wood, G. (1991). Toward a comprehensive theory of collaboration. *Journal of Applied Behavioral Science, 27*(2), 139-162.

World Bank (1999). *World development report 1998/99: Knowledge for development.* New York: Oxford University Press.

Wynn, E. H., Whitley, E. A., Myers, M. D., & DeGross, J. I. (Eds.) (2002). *Global and organizational discourse about information technology.* Boston: Kluwer.

Yager, T. (2003). More than a cell phone. *Infoworld, 25*(5), 30.

Ye, Y., & Kishida, K. (2003). Toward an Understanding of the Motivation of Open Source Software Developers. In *Proc. 25th International Conference on Software Engineering (ICSE), IEEE,* pp. 419-429.

Yetton, P.W., Johnston, K.D., & Craig, J.F. (1994, Summer). Computer-aided architects: A case study of IT and strategic change. *Sloan Management Review,* 57–67.

Yin, R. K. (1989). *Case study research: Design and methods.* London: Sage.

Zhao, L. & Deek, F. (2006). *Exploratory inspection: A learning model for improving open source software usability. Extended Abstracts of the Conference on Human Factors in Computer Systems (CHI 2002),* New York, ACM Press, pp. 1589-1594.

Zhao, L., & Deek, F. (2005). *Improving Open Source Software Usability. In Proc. 11th Americas Conference on Information Systems (AMCIS2005),* Omaha, USA, August 11-14, pp. 923-928.

Zima, P. (1997),. Moderne —Postmoderne. Gesellschaft, Philosophie, Literatur. p.18.Tübungen, Germany: Utb Verlag.

Zmud, R., Lind, M., & Young, F. (1991). An attribute space for organizational communication channels. *Information Systems Research, 1*(4), 440-457.

Zmud, R.W. (1979). Individual Differences and MIS Success: A Review of the Empirical Literature. *Management Science, 25*(10), 966-979.

Zmud, R. W., & Apple, L. E. (1992). Measuring technology incorporation/infusion. *Journal of Product Innovation Management, 9*(2), 148-155.

Zollo, M., Reuer, J., & Singh, J. (2002). Interorganizational routines and performance in strategic alliances. *Organizational Science, 13*(6), 701-713.

Zuboff, S. (1988). *In the age of the smart machine: The future of work and power.* New York: Basic Books.

Zue, V. (1999, August). Talking with your computer. *Scientific American, 281,* 40.

Zviran, M., Glezer, C., & Avni, I. (2006). User Satisfaction from commercial web sites: The effect of design and use. *Information & Management, 43*(2), 157-178.

About the Contributors

Panayiotis Zaphiris, City University London Panayiotis, is a reader at the Centre for Human-Computer Interaction Design. Before joining City University, he was a researcher at the Institute of Gerontology at Wayne State University from where he also got his PhD in human-computer interaction (HCI). His research interests lie in human-computer interaction with an emphasis on inclusive design and social aspects of computing. He is especially interested in HCI issues related to the elderly and people with disabilities. He is also interested in Internet related research (web usability, mathematical modelling of browsing behaviour in hierarchical online information systems, online communities, e-learning, computer aided language learning (CALL) and social network analysis of online human-to-human interactions). Panayiotis was the principal investigator of the JISC Information Visualisation Foundation Study and a co-investigator on the DRC Formal Investigation into Web site accessibility (managing the automatic testing of 1000 websites) and the JISC Usability Studies for JISC Services and Information Environment projects.

Chee Siang Ang is a research fellow in the Centre for Human-Computer Interaction (HCI) Design. He is interested in human interactions and social tendencies in the virtual world, particularly Second Life, from a sociological, psychological and HCI perspective. His main research interests include the psychology and sociology of computer games, virtual worlds or 3D Computer-Mediated Communication (CMC), learning theories particularly in gaming, digital media such as interactive narrative and simulation.

* * *

Samantha Bax is an associate lecturer in the School of Information Technology at Murdoch University in Western Australia. She also works as an application developer. Her research interests include end user development and information systems success, as well as online learning environments.

Jorge Brusa is an associate professor at Texas A&M International University. He has an undergraduate degree from the Universidad del Litoral (Argentina), master's degree from the University of Arkansas at Little Rock, and doctoral degrees from the Universidad de Belgrano (Argentina) and the University of Arkansas. His research interests include the study of new technologies in international markets and the effect of technology in financial markets. His studies have been published in numerous finance and technology journals.

Andrea Carugati is associate professor at Århus School of Business. Andrea's research focuses on information systems development and on the use of systems theory to create business-relevant systems. Andrea Carugati has published on the *European Journal of Information Systems*, on *International Journal of Human and Technology Interaction*, at the International Conference on Information Systems, and at the European Conference on Information Systems.

Elias Hadzilias is currently professor at the Hellenic Management Association in Greece. He is also a visiting assistant professor at the IÉSEG School of Management of the Lille Catholic University and the Graduate School of Management of Brittany (ESC Brest) in France. He has a Diploma in mechanical engineering (1997) and a doctorate of business process engineering (2003) from the National Technical University of Athens in Greece. His research interests are enterprise modelling, total quality management, ARIS, virtual enterprises, strategic management, management information systems, cultural information systems and e-government. In parallel to his academic activities, he is actively involved in consulting projects especially in the public sector on the application of the common assessment framework.

George E. Heilman is an associate professor of management information systems at Winston-Salem State University. He has undergraduate degrees in computer technology from Purdue University, graduate degrees in business and public affairs from Indiana University, and a PhD in computer information systems from the University of Arkansas. His research interests include the use and impact of technology in multicultural environments, financial markets, entrepreneurial organizations, and the healthcare industry. He is also interested in pedagogical issues.

Claus-Dieter Hohmann is the chief technology officer of Autostadt in Germany. He has served as the senior executive for this communicative platform for marketing and culture demonstrating the latest automotive technology, since April 2002. Previously, Mr. Hohmann served as Autostadt's chief information officer, responsible for bringing the park to the digital age. His interest in the organizational unconscious began 6 years ago at which point he started to develop insights on management and organization practical experience and theory from a psychoanalytic perspective. His main interests are specialized in the field of networked societies, where virtual impressions do not reach the strength of real experiences, thus one looses the ability to deal with strong emotions since it is possible to always escape into virtual realities. Furthermore Mr. Hohmann currently serves as a lecturer and associated academic in seminars dealing with the psychodynamics in international organizations since April 2008 at Johann Wolfgang Goethe University in Frankfurt.

Netta Iivari has a doctoral degree in information systems and a master's degree in cultural anthropology. Currently, she works as an assistant professor in the department of information processing science in the University of Oulu, Finland. In her doctoral thesis, she critically analyzed the discourses constructing 'organizational culture' and 'usability work' in the software product development context. Her research relies on interpretive and critical research traditions. Currently, she is specifically interested in the discursive construction of 'users' and 'their role' in the open source software development context. She has published in a number of human computer interaction and information systems research conferences and journals.

Ishraga Khattab works for the Sudan Academy for Banking and Financial Science. Previously, Ishraga was a PhD student in the School of Information Systems, Computing and Mathematics at Brunel University. She obtained her PhD from the Brunel University in July 2007. The main focus of her PhD studies was on exploring the impact of cultural differences in the use of mobile phones in both public and private locations. Ishraga also has a master's degree in Internet and multimedia information systems and a first degree in economics and political science.

Steve Love works in the School of Information Systems, Computing and Mathematics at Brunel University, West London, UK. His research interests primarily focus on looking at the social impact of mobile technology on people's behaviour and its affect on their perception of the usability of mobile services and applications. He has led a number of industrially funded research projects in the area of mobile application interface design and evaluation. In addition, he is on the editorial boards of the *International Journal of Technology Human Interaction* and the *Mobile Communication Research Annual*.

Tanya McGill is a senior lecturer in the School of Information Technology at Murdoch University in Western Australia. She has a PhD from Murdoch University. Her major research interests include end user computing and information technology education. Her work has appeared in various journals including the *Journal of Research on Computing in Education, European Journal of Psychology of Education, Decision Support Systems, Information Resources Management Journal* and *Journal of Organizational and End User Computing*.

Index

)